THE UNFREE PROFESSIONS

The Unfree Professions

GERMAN LAWYERS, TEACHERS, AND ENGINEERS, 1900–1950

KONRAD H. JARAUSCH

New York Oxford
OXFORD UNIVERSITY PRESS
1990

Oxford University Press

Oxford New York Toronto
Delhi Bombay Calcutta Madras Karachi
Petaling Jaya Singapore Hong Kong Tokyo
Nairobi Dar es Salaam Cape Town
Melbourne Auckland

and associated companies in
Berlin Ibadan

Published by Oxford University Press, Inc.,
200 Madison Avenue, New York, New York 10016

Library of Congress Cataloging-in-Publication Data
Jarausch, Konrad Hugo.
The unfree professions : German lawyers, teachers,
and engineers, 1900–1950 / Konrad H. Jarausch.
p. cm.
ISBN 0–19–504482-7
1. Professional employees—Government policy—Germany—History—20th century. 2. Professions—Government policy—Germany—History—20th century. 3. Lawyers—Legal status, laws, etc.—Germany—History—20th century. 4. Teachers—Legal status, laws, etc.—Germany—History—20th century. 5. Engineers—Legal status, laws, etc.—Germany—History—20th century. 6. Germany—Politics and government—1933–1945. I. Title.
HD8038.G3J37 1990
331.7′12′09430904—dc20 89-36827 CIP

2 4 6 8 9 7 5 3 1

Printed in the United States of America
on acid-free paper

To Bruno and Konrad Jarausch

Professionals and Patriots

PREFACE

The contribution of the professions to modern life has been profoundly ambiguous. On the one hand, the improvement of the legal system, the spread of learning, and the development of machines have increased justice, enlightenment, and comfort, thereby earning for professionals public gratitude and material rewards. On the other hand, the same experts have perpetrated callous injustice, engaged in stultifying indoctrination, and created engines of death for their own gratification and benefit. Hence critical observers have begun to question the social costs of professionalization: Are such recurrent abuses merely perversions of a positive ideal or are they inherent in the very nature of the professions? An extreme example, removed in time and place from present concerns, might illuminate this paradox historically by bringing the fundamental issues into clearer focus. Perhaps the most dramatic corruption of professionalism in the twentieth century was the evolution of German professionals from internationally respected experts to accessories to Nazi crimes.

Investigating how this happened and what it might mean requires an exploration of the history of professions. Until recently expert occupations have been the domain of sociologists who (with only a few exceptions) were more interested in theorizing about their current problems than in studying their development. At important anniversaries, professionals themselves have chronicled their evolution, but such *Festschriften* tend to be self-congratulatory and amateurish. Historians rarely explored the professions, which seemed remote from the excitement of grand politics and, when they did so, their accounts were often dull and uninteresting. This neglect is a pity, because most working adults spend the majority of their waking hours at their job. When asked to identify themselves, people give their name, residence, and occupation—not their religion, political affiliation, or other characteristics that are more frequently studied. "A profession becomes a man's fate. In the course of time it shapes and penetrates his whole being," the educational philosopher Eduard Spranger reflected on the German view of *Beruf* in 1927. "Not only do we have a profession, but a profession has us. That is why the profession determines a considerable part of our *Weltanschauung;* it is the perspective from which we view the world." Especially important for male self-consciousness, professional identity links cultural attitudes and material interests to politics. By mediating between the globalism of *Gesellschaftsgeschichte* and the particularism of everyday history, professions provide a largely unexplored but fruitful framework for understanding individual lives and collective experiences in the past.

This current study is a logical outgrowth and a necessary extension of my previous work. Because earlier findings often raise fresh questions, former interests still echo in the present text. Trained as a diplomatic historian on the European response to Hitler's seizure of power, I investigated the failure of the German leadership before and during the First World War in the person of Chancellor Bethmann Hollweg. Appalled by the narrowness of choices perceived by imperial elites, I then set out to examine their structural and ideological underpinnings through the institution of the university. This exploration of the rise of academic illiberalism suggested a comparative look at the uniqueness or representativeness of the German transformation of higher learning in which I encountered the problem of professionalization. My subsequent synthesis of student social structure, subculture, and politics implied the need to follow graduates beyond university doors into their professional lives and to pursue their careers across conventional historical divides. This progression of questions led me to acquire quantitative skills and to venture methodologically into the direction of historical social science. While building upon the insights of some of my prior studies, the work at hand also attempts to learn from their shortcomings so as to answer some of the critics. No doubt, by trying to transcend previous limitations, this investigation will raise new problems in turn.

The richness but unevenness of source materials (Appendix B) suggests structuring the history of German professions through a professionalization approach. Since temporal scope and spatial breadth prohibit documentary or narrative completeness, the topic requires selective conceptual analysis. Instead of borrowing eclectically, the present study departs from a unified perspective by reshaping professionalization theory for its own purpose. Nonetheless, this book is historical in orientation, because the temporal sequence is central to its explanation. Moreover, the neglected evidence of the professions also sheds fresh light on a number of well-worn controversies of German historiography. Blending chronological exposition with systematic reflection, the presentation compares three distinctive occupations so as to avoid the pitfalls of a single profession focus by including contradictions and ambiguities. Obviously, it focuses more on collective patterns than on prominent individuals, thereby seeking to reconstruct the parameters within which single lives took place. In order to recover lost experiences, the text quotes extensively from contemporary debates while confronting the subjective voices of professionals with measurable objective indicators (Appendix A). In exploring the interaction of professional structure and mentality, the study consistently seeks to introduce a political dimension so as to situate the aspirations of practitioners within wider society, culture, and polity, and to scrutinize the broader implications of their actions.

Since scholarship is a social enterprise, the Humboldtian cliché of ''solitude and freedom'' notwithstanding, a complex study incurs numerous debts. A Deutsche Forschungsgesellschaft guest professorship at Göttingen University in 1982–1983 stimulated the inception of the project. A generous grant from the National Endowment for the Humanities funded essential research assistance and released time, while an International Research and Exchange Board fellowship facilitated archival work in the German Democratic Republic. The Netherlands Institute for Advanced Studies in Wassenaar offered congenial surroundings in the spring of 1986, the University of North Carolina supported a leave during the fall semester of that year, the Zentrum für Interdisziplinäre Forschung in Bielefeld provided intellectual stimulation during the summer of 1987, and the Swedish Collegium for Advanced Studies in Uppsala facilitated the revision of the manuscript. Archivists at the major German depositories (listed in Appendix B), Detlev K. Müller (papers of the Westphalian Philologenverein), and Walter Kempowski (manuscript autobiographies) made their collections available, while Albert Schaich of the Deutscher Anwaltverein and Wolfgang König, then of the Verein deutscher Ingenieure, dispensed helpful advice. The QUAKRI group at Göttingen headed by Hartmut Titze, the comparative professions circle organized by Arnold Heidenheimer, the professions and conflict team led by Rolf Torstendahl, the *Bildungsideale* cluster at NIAS, the *Bürgertum* project directed by Jürgen Kocka, and panels at German Studies Association (GSA) meetings—involving Geoffrey Cocks or Charles McClelland—served as sounding boards. Old friends like Gerhard Arminger, Larry E. Jones, Michael H. Kater, and Wilhelm H. Schroeder helped resolve statistical or source problems while cooperative colleagues like Gerhard Weinberg and Richard Soloway aided in maintaining enthusiasm for the project. Finally, Ingrid Richards' eye-blurring perusal of journals and Eric Yonke's indefatigable coding of membership files speeded the completion of this study by several years.

Although the temptation to moralize about the catastrophes of recent German history is overwhelming, drawing overly facile lessons ought to be resisted. The past has a dignity that begs to be understood on its own terms. Of course, it is equally misleading to approach the upheavals of the first half of the twentieth century in a machinelike "objective" fashion. Values of the historian and the reader necessarily enter into interpretation, because humans are not robots. But instead of putting the past on trial or revising it to fit one's prejudices, personal assumptions need to be called into question as well. The heated *Historikerstreit* demonstrates conclusively that neither ritualized condemnation nor revisionist apologetics fully illuminate the troubled German experience. Rather than presupposing the answer, a historian must painstakingly reconstruct the complex relationships between structures, ideologies, and actions in a particular instance. At the same time larger, present-day concerns ought to inform his research, lest it degenerate into antiquarianism. Beyond the horrifying dialectic of the perpetrators and victims, the historian must also seek to come to terms with the often subterranean experience of the overwhelming majority of people. From such a perspective of critical historicization, this study of the German professions in the first half of this century tries to wrestle with the broader question: What is the relationship between professionalism and freedom in general?

Chapel Hill, North Carolina K. H. J.
April 1990

CONTENTS

ABBREVIATIONS

Abl	*Anwaltsblatt*
AG	Amtsgericht
ADLZ	*Allgemeine Deutsche Lehrerzeitung*
AHR	*American Historical Review*
BA	Bundesarchiv (Federal Archives in Coblenz)
BDC	Berlin Document Center
BhB	Bund höherer Beamter
BNSDJ	Bund NS Deutscher Juristen
BT	*Berliner Tageblatt*
ButiB	Bund technisch-industrieller Beamter (renamed ButaB)
CEH	*Central European History*
DATSCH	Deutscher Ausschuß für technisches Schulwesen
DAV	Deutscher Anwaltverein
DBB	Deutscher Beamtenbund
DEG	Deutsche Erziehergemeinschaft
DHS	*Deutsche Höhere Schule*
DJ	*Deutsche Justiz,* formerly *Justiz-Ministerialblatt*
DLV	Deutscher Lehrerverein
DR	*Deutsches Recht*
DRZ	*Deutsche Rechts-Zeitschrift*
DT	*Deutsche Technik*
EGH	Ehrengerichtshof (professional honor court)
GEW	Gewerkschaft Erziehung und Wissenschaft
GG	*Geschichte und Gesellschaft*
GSR	*German Studies Review*
HEQ	*History of Education Quarterly*
HfL	Hochschule für Lehrerbildung
HS	*Höhere Schule*
HSR	*Historical Social Research*
HTL	Höhere Technische Lehranstalt (former middle school)
HZ	*Historische Zeitschrift*
IASL	*Internationales Archiv zur Sozialgeschichte der Literatur*
IfZG	Institut für Zeitgeschichte
IZEBF	*Inf. zur Erziehungs- und Bildungshistorischen Forschung*
JCH	*Journal of Contemporary History*
JMH	*Journal of Modern History*
JSH	*Journal of Social History*
JW	*Juristische Wochenschrift* (after 1945 *NJW*)
KA	Kempowski Archiv

KDAI	Kampfbund deutscher Architekten und Ingenieure
KLV	Kinderlandverschickung
LG	Landgericht
NSBDT	NS Bund deutscher Technik
NSLB	NS Lehrerbund
NSRB	Nationalsozialistischer Rechtswahrerbund
OLG	Oberlandesgericht
Phbl	*Philologenblatt*
PhVb	Philologenverband
PrGStA	Preußisches Geheimes Staatsarchiv (Dahlem)
PSK	Provinzial-Schulkollegium
RAO	Rechtsanwaltsordnung of Reich (R) or Fed. Rep. (B)
RAK	Rechtsanwaltskammer of Reich (R) or Fed. Rep. (B)
RDE	*Reichszeitung der deutschen Erzieher (NS Lehrerzeitung)*
RDT	Reichsbund Deutscher Technik
RhB	Reichsbund höherer Beamter
RTA	Reichsgemeinschaft der Technisch-wissenschaftlichen Arbeit
SE	*Schule und Evangelium*
TH	Technische Hochschule
VB	*Völkischer Beobachter*
VDDI	Verband deutscher Diplom-Ingenieure
VdH	Verband deutscher Hochschulen
VDI	Verein Deutscher Ingenieure
VDIN	*VDI Nachrichten*
VfZG	*Vierteljahrshefte für Zeitgeschichte*
VSWG	*Vierteljahrschrift für Sozial- und Wirtschaftsgeschichte*
VZ	*Vossische Zeitung*
WPhV	Westfälischer Philologenverein
ZfP	*Zeitschrift für Pädagogik*
ZStA	Zentrales Staatsarchiv (in Me = Merseburg or Po = Potsdam)
ZVDDI	*Zeitschrift des VDDI*
ZVDI	*Zeitschrift des VDI*

TABLES

THE UNFREE PROFESSIONS

1

Professionalization German Style

In the spring of 1933, most German professionals rushed to curry favor with the new Nazi government. On March 26, the prominent Lawyer Association (Deutscher Anwaltverein, DAV) "welcome[d] the strengthening of national thought and will which has taken place in Germany." It vowed "to concentrate its energy on serving the recovery of the nation and the empire, on making the state secure and on unifying the people across classes and occupations." Trying to balance the imperatives of power and justice, the attorneys publicly acclaimed Hitler's New Order in spite of legal transgressions in the wake of the seizure of power.[1] A week later the purged leadership of the secondary schoolteachers' Philologenverband pledged its willingness to serve. "There is no turning back. . . . We endorse the new departure and want to contribute our share to help it succeed." Quick, voluntary collaboration might carve out an important role for a profession in the Third Reich. "Our goal must be to preserve the tradition, competence and vitality of our organization and to join the valuable experiences of the past with the living forces of the present."[2] For Hitler's birthday, the prestigious engineering association, Verein deutscher Ingenieure (VDI), also proclaimed its cooperation in the national tasks of finding work, reclaiming the soil, teaching technology, supplying the country with consumer goods, and "rearmament" *(Wehrhaftmachung),* because the "national revolution" would provide many attractive opportunities for capable engineers.[3]

What is one to make of these zealous protestations of loyalty, which were repeated by hundreds of groups all over Germany? More than half a century later they have a pathetic and distasteful ring. Certainly it was legitimate for professional associations to try to work with a new government in the interest of their members. However, the Nazis did not lead just another cabinet of the ill-fated Weimar Republic and, beyond the general national revival, these declarations endorsed the specific spirit of National Socialism. "Rise out of the trenches and try to join the victorious storm-troops as long as they are still within reach," the new Nazi board member of the Anwaltverein Dr. Voß called upon his fellow advocates in April 1933 to "become soldiers of the Third Reich."[4] Whenever they do confront this blot on their record, professionals claim unconvincingly that they were caught unawares, had no other choice, or were misled by the brown hordes. However, the critical accusation, leveled by foreign observers or younger Germans, that authoritarian practitioners embraced Hitler as a kind of *Ersatzkaiser* oversimplifies their complex and contradictory responses as well.[5] Taken on its own terms, the professionals' behavior toward the Nazis poses a disturbing double question: How could competent, individually decent university graduates fall collectively for the Austrian corporal? What material and ethical price did these experts pay for their collaboration in the inhumanity of the Third Reich?

Answers to such queries about professionals and National Socialism are hard to obtain and remain less than persuasive. The extensive literature on the fall of the Weimar Republic and the rise of Hitler virtually ignores the professions.[6] The volumes commemorating the fiftieth anniversary of the seizure of power in 1933 summarize the political, diplomatic, constitutional, and military research of the previous decades, but pay less attention to the social dimension of this process.[7] Those historians who seek to explore the societal dynamics of Hitler's electoral successes[8] or of the composition of the Nazi party,[9] sometimes touch upon professionals, but have found them too small a group to have much statistical impact. Similarly, scholars investigating the collapse of bourgeois politics or interest group blocs have rarely been able to isolate the professions within their larger aggregates.[10] Historians directly concerned with the educated middle class have tended to be preoccupied with the more visible professors[11] or students[12] rather than with prosaic practitioners. The few researchers who have specifically written on the professions present a wealth of internal information, but often lack a conceptual framework and rarely integrate their findings into the broader discussion.[13] Only in the last few years has a critical, social approach to the rise of the German professions, especially medicine, begun to emerge that confronts their travails in this turbulent century.[14]

THE GERMAN CONCEPT OF PROFESSION

Thinking about Central European professions has been rendered difficult by the very absence of the term in the German language. Imported from the French in the eighteenth century as a secular concept for occupation, the notion narrowed in the usage of the nineteenth century as *Professionist* to mean artisan. Only after the Second World War was it reintroduced by Anglo-Saxon social scientists in order to provide a word for the process of *Professionalisierung,* which was otherwise lacking.[15] Instead, the central German concept is *Beruf,* a Lutheran notion of calling, which turned into an idea of inner vocation when secularized during the nineteenth century. In social and political discourse, it is usually linked with the formerly feudal idea of *Stand,* meaning estate, to form *Berufsstand.* Although this hybrid does carry some hierarchical connotation of order, it is used more narrowly to mean occupation and, when modified by the adjective "academic" to form *akademischer Berufsstand,* it indicates profession.[16] Equally important in practical rhetoric were its derivatives, such as the adjective *standesgemäß,* which was usually associated with life-style or behavior. As a central part of informal intercourse and formal honor codes, this concept indicated socially acceptable ways of conduct. Another correlate, which permeates professional journals and speeches, is the term *Standespolitik* (with or without the prefix of *Beruf*), meaning the organized pursuit of the collective interests of the members of an occupation. Concretely, this notion tends to contain such aspirations as upgrading training, increasing pay, raising social esteem, and improving ethics, which make it quite similar to the American usage of professionalism.[17] A final related term is the cluster *Freie Berufe,* denoting the "free professions." However, as in the United States, its application in the German census is not limited to college graduates, including also various artists, midwives, or river pilots and other self-employed. Though referring to doctors, lawyers, and architects, it excludes the more numerous state-employed academics as well as graduates engaged in industry. Therefore, it seems preferable to treat the Freie Berufe as one of three subspecies of the professions rather than to reserve the notion for them alone.[18]

Alternative concepts for dealing with the group of college graduates are even more problematic, because they are largely static and descriptive. Out of the hallowed Humboldtian ideal of cultivation *(Bildung),* there gradually evolved the notion of *Bildungsbürgertum* to describe the educated, noneconomic middle class. Reflecting contemporary self-consciousness, the term denotes that sociocultural milieu out of which the professions emerged during the course of the nineteenth century. Playwrights like C. Sternheim were forever making fun of *Bildung* and *Besitz,* namely education and property, as twin pillars of the bourgeoisie. However, as a diverse social stratum, the Bildungsbürgertum has no clear boundaries (is one *gebildet* [educated] when leaving middle school, with graduation from the Gymnasium, or with a university degree?) and little coherence (being merely linked through common habits, forms of communication, and sociability). Because it had few shared institutions (aside from some cultural circles such as literary clubs), it did not act collectively on the stage of history.[19] A more precise substitute might be the term *Akademiker,* which emerged in the last decades of the nineteenth century to describe university graduates and later also graduates of technical schools. Still employed in social discourse as marriage advertisements in *Die Zeit* and other newspapers frequently attest, the notion—used adjectivally—modifies the higher callings and thereby sets them apart from the less educated pursuits. However, the Akademiker rarely banded together, indicating that their collective consciousness was weaker than their identification with an individual Berufsstand. During the course of the nineteenth century, the modern professions developed out of the older *akademische Berufe,* partly by changing their role and partly by upgrading nonacademic occupations.[20] Equally problematic for Central Europe is the Marxist notion of the intellectual, because the self-selected radical intelligentsia covers only a small minority of higher education graduates.[21]

More attuned to analyzing change, professionalization theory has evolved considerably from approval to criticism in the last half century. The initial taxonomic effort of the 1930s sought to describe the positive features of professions through lists of ideal typical traits, including advanced education, certifying examinations, a code of conduct, an altruistic ethic, a special social or economic position, and professional autonomy.[22] After the Second World War, optimistic functionalists like Talcott Parsons normatively saw professionalization as unquestioned progress: "The massive emergence of the professional complex, not the special status of capitalistic or socialistic modes of organization, is the crucial structural development of twentieth century society." Similarly, Daniel Bell asserted that "the heart of the post-industrial society is a class that is primarily a professional class."[23] No wonder that during the 1970s scholars like Eliot Freidson, Magali S. Larson, and Burton Bledstein began to look more critically at the implications of the "professionalization project" of various occupations. Instead of applauding the rise of the professions as a self-evident improvement, they questioned its price and viewed market monopoly or professional ideology as instruments for achieving dominance and social advancement.[24] More recently this critique, inspired by social closure, has grown into a near-conspiratorial view of professionalism as taking away control from laypeople, eliminating competitors, and exploiting junior ranks within an occupation, thereby exploding the rhetoric of public service as crass pursuit of self-interest.[25]

Transposing this sociological discourse to Central Europe presents some difficulties, because the professionalization approach is time- and context-bound. First, the concept was initially developed in an Anglo-American setting, stressing the market, associational self-control, and autonomy, features that are likely to be less important in Germany.[26] Second, most hypotheses were derived from an analysis of a single profession, making their generalizations problematic for other occupations by insufficiently taking differences into account.[27] Third, much abstract theorizing distinguished merely between preindustrial and postindustrial professions. When addressing change directly, it was more preoccupied with the inevitable "rise of the professions" than with the implications of their existence for society and polity.[28] Fourth, in taking professional ideology at face value, many social thinkers shied away from linking questions about the self-interest of the professions and their use of power to their class position within society.[29] Finally, the laudatory tradition tended to be apolitical while the critical approach focused on internal group struggles, thereby neglecting external socioeconomic dimensions and the general politics of professionals.[30] To become useful for the analysis of functionally equivalent *akademische Berufsstände,* the professionalization perspective needs to be reshaped temporally and spatially. Even if such a rethinking is unlikely to achieve a perfect fit, the tension between Anglo-American static theory and Central European historical evidence promises to yield fresh insights for both.

A more comprehensive approach requires a wider definition of attributes and actors. Drawing on both the American and German experience, Jürgen Kocka distills a promising ideal type: " 'Professions' are non-manual full-time occupations which presuppose a long specialized and tendentially also scholarly . . . training which imparts specific, generalizable and theoretical professional knowledge, proven by examinations." Based on this competence, "professionals claim a monopoly of services," usually guaranteed by governmental regulation. Moreover, they "demand a high measure of freedom from control by laymen . . . and offer in exchange certain forms of collective self-control" such as honor codes. Finally, justified by "the central importance of their achievements for society, professionals insist on comparatively big income and high social esteem."[31] Though providing interrelated identifying traits, this broadened definition nevertheless remains incomplete, because it fails to mention the crucial aspects of self-consciousness and association. Moreover, it does not establish dimensions of the professional arena that determine the success or failure of professionalizing efforts. Beyond Anglo-American actors such as individual or organized practitioners and single clients or mass consumers, continental protagonists must also include legislating politicians or regulatory officials as well as university professors or researchers. Recognition of the role of the state as the source of licensing or social policies, and of the importance of education as fountainhead of scientific knowledge or practical skill, provides a more comprehensive understanding of the professional universe. By focusing on the interplay between material conditions and cultural perceptions, a refocused professions approach transcends academic "fields of discourse" to study the practicing carriers of knowledge wherever they are employed.[32]

Recast in this fashion, professionalization theory suggests a number of fruitful questions for historical investigation.[33] (1) By definition, all professions require some kind of higher education, which imparts general cultivation, a scientific knowledge base, and sometimes also particular applied skills. (2) Closely related in Central Europe are testing and certification, which control entry into a profession and thereby govern the number of incoming practitioners. (3) For many professionals the primary goal is economic reward, with their material circumstances affected not only by market monopoly but also by mutual competition or general economic conditions. (4) For other experts social status and prestige—often derived from the aura of science—are more important than money, thus making for much conflict among and within occupations. (5) The quality and autonomy of practice also varies over time, with job satisfaction depending on state regulation, on responses of the clientele, and on even more general contexts. (6) Equally significant is the mentality of professionals, because their elaborate self-image—justified in terms of broad cultural values—colors their perception and aspirations, while their codified ethos constrains their actions to acceptable conventions. (7) Finally, an effective organization is the instrument for collective action, elaborating or changing all the other aspects of professional life and influencing individual members, political decision makers, or the public.[34] Though slighting such interesting topics as sociability or life-style, a selective focus on training and certification, socioeconomic conditions, practice as well as self-perception, and organizational politics transforms the description of professional evolution into an analytical professionalization history.

If placed in context, this approach offers useful categories for probing the relationship between internal professional development and external social or political transformations. To begin with, professionalization theory clearly defines processes as the acquisition or loss of the traits just suggested. When pressing problems reach an intense level, they might be called a "professional crisis"; a return to a prior satisfactory state might be labeled "reprofessionalization," while the loss of professional gains could be termed "deprofessionalization." Typical interactions can also be distinguished, such as cooperation among practitioners for common professional goals, competition for markets and rewards among individuals or groups, and occupational conflicts for social closure to gain undisputed authority over a field of practice. Depending on the dominance of a particular actor, patterns of development such as state hegemony or practitioner control might be elaborated, and specific phases of evolution be discerned, which are conditioned by the prevailing form of organization such as guilds, corporations, and the like.[35] The ambiguous position of the professions in the social hierarchy can be clarified further by exploring their fit into the economic or academic middle class and their special ethos. Finally, the interaction between professional politics and the politics of professionals can be addressed by looking more closely at structural characteristics such as their relationship to the polity and its policies. Dependent on close links with parties and bureaucracies, the success or failure of the experts' collective aspirations regarding training, market control, suitable income, respected status, rewarding practice, an ethical self-image, and successful collective action is likely to be decisive for their political orientation.[36]

The risks of reading the evolution of German professions in the present century in professionalization terms might be reduced by some further specification. To avoid generalizing from one occupation, it is essential to represent the three basic employment situations in which university graduates are found. Among the free professions, lawyers are a key group, because they are connected to the central legal underpinnings of the respective governmental system.[37] Among state officials, academic high school teachers *(Studienräte)* are particularly interesting because they are public employees, but not so prone to a bureaucratic outlook that they should be better analyzed as *Beamte*.[38] Among white-collar employees in business and industry, college-trained engineers *(Diplomingenieure)* are especially important because technical experts play an increasingly important role that is often neglected. These three sample professions illustrate the dual nature of conflict within one occupational field such as technology and between callings such as jurisprudence and teaching.[39] To grasp the dynamics of the process, it is also vital to compare different stages of the professionalization sequence. Attorneys had already become professionalized in the late 1870s through the liberal Imperial Lawyer Code; high school teachers followed suit in the first decade of the twentieth century with the foundation of a comprehensive national association, while engineers were still struggling for acceptance and autonomy after 1918. Finally, in order to get at the interaction of professions and politics in a concrete and experiential way, it is imperative to follow the whole "long generation" from the relative normalcy of the late empire across the caesuras of war, revolution, inflation, stabilization, depression, Nazi seizure of power, rearmament boom, victory, and final defeat. Historians often unnecessarily break this continuity by limiting themselves to one of these periods, whereas most adult Germans lived and learned through several, if not all of them.[40]

PROFESSIONS IN IMPERIAL GERMANY

Between 1871 and 1914 the slow process of professionalization culminated for the older learned occupations. Beginning in the eighteenth century, the state extended control over corporations of practitioners through increasingly comprehensive and systematic examinations in order to ensure standardized qualifications. Moreover, with the gradual emergence of civil society, the members of the akademische Berufsstände organized themselves so as to campaign for better training, material rewards, recognition, autonomy, and ethics.[41] Although liberal imperial codes and examination regulations created unified professions such as medicine, practitioners did not obtain all their cherished desires while other occupations like primary schoolteachers remained frustrated "semiprofessionals."[42] At their national convention in 1911, attorneys vigorously debated whether "the legal profession is declining" or whether lawyers were "actually gaining, in spite of economic problems."[43] Disagreeing on the extent of improvement for practitioners or the public, historians have similarly discussed the nature, extent, and implications of German professionalization.[44] This dual argument mirrors the larger controversy on the fundamental structure of the empire between the Bielefeld school, which sees it as authoritarian background to the Third Reich, and the Anglo-American revisionists, who tend to stress its more progressive features.[45] As an essential part of the educated middle class, the professions provide important evidence about the degree to which the *Bürgertum* controlled its own destiny.[46] What therefore was the character and situation of German professionals during the last decades of imperial Germany?

The oldest and most prestigious free profession were the lawyers. Subjected to the same state examinations as other university graduates of law since 1693 and 1737, advocates had to undergo a lengthy practical training, which was extended to four years in Prussia after 1851. The rise of the administrative state had reduced the *Justizkommissare* (1793) to a precarious status between bureaucratic control and client patronage, while the distinction of *Prokuratur* (courts) and *Advokatur* (briefs) fragmented them internally and competing legal traditions (Roman, Germanic or state law, and the Code Napoleon) divided them territorially. Because an independent bar would be a bulwark of a modern, middle-class government, liberal German reformers like Rudolf Gneist tirelessly campaigned for a *freie Advokaktur,* a free legal practice, abolishing all unnecessary restrictions. Established as a complex compromise between lingering state supervision, market freedom, and corporate self-control, the astoundingly liberal Imperial Lawyer Code of July 1, 1878 created the nationally uniform *Rechtsanwalt,* thereby "founding a profession in the real sense." Resentment of political repression and favorable employment prospects made attorneys willing to run the risk of opening admission and liberating the legal market, although democratic laicization attempts of the bar failed and some procedural safeguards such as localization and a fixed-fee schedule sought to mitigate the dangers of excessive competition. According to Ernst Fuchs, "a free advocate is allowed to champion anything and anyone, regardless of reason of state, as long as he does not show himself unworthy of the respect and trust which his profession demands."[47]

The *Reichsrechtsanwaltsordnung* stipulated that attorneys were to study law at the universities and pass the same state examination as future bureaucrats. The dominant theory of legal positivism dictated that aspiring lawyers had to learn how to apply existing regulations rather than how to resort to natural law or equity. The prevalent historical approach to Roman and Germanic law made little concession to modern economic and technical questions. Moreover, the didactic tradition of mass lectures led to rote memorization and last minute cramming rather than to a scholarly understanding of legal principles. Nonetheless, a widespread reform movement remained ineffectual against official inertia, which preferred practical apprenticeship.[48] The first state examination was followed by a four-year traineeship *(Referendariat)*, two-thirds of which was spent in district and superior courts whereas the remaining year was divided between serving with a district attorney and as an intern in a law firm. The subsequent second state examination was the actual gateway to the profession, because the status of free attorney meant that anyone qualified as a judge had the right to be admitted to the bar. In this regard, German lawyers were a more thoroughly "free" profession than their Anglo-American colleagues whose bar associations could and did restrict access. During the empire, roughly one-quarter of the graduates went into private practice as attorneys, and their number increased sharply whenever government hiring was slow. The rapid growth of enrollment in law from 2864 in 1871 to 11,976 in 1906 created a pervasive sense of "over-crowding of the legal profession" (Table A.1).[49]

Though not extravagant, the average income of most attorneys was ample, because they possessed a virtual market monopoly and a fixed-fee schedule. Even if nonacademic legal consultants *(Rechtskonsulenten)* competed by dispensing advice in minor matters, only lawyers had the right to appear in court *(Anwaltzwang)*. Although the *Gebührenordnung* of 1879 limited what attorneys could charge (except for specially negotiated supplements in complicated cases), it did put a financial floor under legal practice. A 1913 bar association survey yielded net earnings of 3300 marks per annum for district court attorneys, 4400 for superior court lawyers, and 6300 for appeals court advocates, which were roughly comparable to the upper middle ranks of the judiciary (Table 1.1). In the Saxon cities of Dresden, Leipzig, and Chemnitz, 16 percent of attorneys had gross earnings of less than 3000 marks, 47 percent of less than 9000 marks, and 37 percent of more than 9000 marks. A growing minority had difficulty making ends meet, since small towns usually had less business, and lawyers had to defray office costs out of their own pocket while saving for retirement.[50]

Although it ranked somewhat lower than the esteem of prominent public officials, the status of lawyers as "the first among the free professions" was nevertheless solidly established as part of "good society." About the year 1910, law was the most exclusive and male university faculty with the most classical training, the highest number of nobles, the largest share from academic backgrounds, the wealthiest families, and the most fraternity members (Table A.2). In spite of considerable self-recruitment, the private bar attracted more politically liberal, religiously diverse (Jews and Catholics) as well as socially less elitist practitioners

Table 1.1. Lawyer Income from Civil Cases, 1913

Court	Number	Cases	Fees	Cost percentage	Hours	Case earnings	Annual income
District	127	46,202	711,304	41	6.0	9.5	3,297
Superior	242	81,262	2,106,323	49	6.5	14.7	4,398
Appellate	63	17,635	720,171	45	6.8	25.0	6,307
TOTAL/AVERAGE	432	145,099	3,537,798	46	6.4	14.3	4,187

than the other legal careers. If the 723 Celle lawyers admitted between 1881 and 1910 are any indication, attorneys hailed from educated (208) and well-to-do circles rather than the lower middle class (96), but the unknown origins of over one third also suggest considerable heterogeneity. Especially in commercial towns, lawyers frequently intermarried with members of the propertied middle class and, as local notables, were quite active in civic affairs. A few literary critics of legalism aside, the frequent bestowal of the *Justizrat* title for successful attorneys demonstrated their membership in the lower reaches of the elite: "Law is and should remain a pursuit of gentlemen, a free profession whose reputation does not depend upon external honors but upon the degree of prestige and respect which individual members achieve through their own personality."[51]

Judging by memoir accounts, the practice of law in the empire was still a fairly simple and autonomous affair. In the state where they had passed their examinations, lawyers were admitted to one specific locality and court *(Lokalisierung).* Either they practiced in a district *Amtsgericht* (AG), which was competent for minor cases, or a superior *Landgericht* (LG) which heard major cases (disputed value of more than 600 marks after 1909) as well as first appeals, or in both. A select few also worked at the *Oberlandesgericht* (OLG), the highest state appellate court or the Reichsgericht, the supreme national court. The rise in law graduates pushed an increasing number of attorneys into the lower courts so that by 1913 23.91 percent were at the AG, 36.42 percent in both, and only 28.66 percent at the LG (in contrast to 4.03 percent, 21.09 percent, and 74.87 percent respectively in 1880), thereby creating an underprivileged underclass. A lawyer usually had his office in his own house or apartment and employed a secretary or a legal assistant, although partnerships were becoming more frequent. Moreover, many lawyers (except in southern Germany) were also notary publics, which was quite a lucrative office, because any number of documents had to be drawn up and witnessed for a fee.[52] The self-image of German attorneys was self-consciously liberal, according to the precepts of Rudolf Gneist: "Freedom of advocacy is neither a slogan nor a dogma, but the most precious and inalienable possession of the legal profession." Another core value was service to "the public need for protection through academically trained legal advisors in large and complicated conflicts." These self-conceptions also guided professional ethics, which were codified in elaborate honor codes and enforced by self-governing *Ehrengerichte,* defining the mores of lawyer behavior (e.g., forbidding advertisement).[53]

To watch over professional conduct, the Imperial Lawyer Code (RAO) also created a compulsory lawyers' chamber or *Rechtsanwaltskammer* (RAK) for each superior court (OLG) district. This corporate body was in effect an elected organ of self-government that controlled access to local practice and maintained professional and personal discipline through its honor courts. However, its restricted membership of notables could not provide effective general leadership. Therefore, the older state lawyers' organizations of Prussia, Bavaria, and the like[54] merged in 1870 into a national bar association (Deutscher Anwaltverein), which represented the interests of the legal profession as a whole in order to "advance legal service and legislation of the Reich." The DAV not only edited a scholarly journal (*Juristische Wochenschrift* beginning in 1872) and a practical newsletter (*Anwaltsblätter* starting in 1914), but also sponsored biennial national congresses

(*Anwaltstage* after 1859), and submitted petitions to the justice ministries. Gradually attracting more than three-quarters of all lawyers among its members, the Anwaltverein developed into the central spokesman of the legal profession, seeking to enhance "collegiality and scholarship" as well to "pursue professional interests." In order to become more representative and vigorous, the DAV instituted board elections, hired a permanent business manager to oversee a budget of a quarter million marks and established a national office in the last decade before the First World War. In the absence of welfare legislation, it also provided a charitable *Hülfskasse,* which aided about forty destitute colleagues, widows, and orphans per year.[55]

Due to rapid expansion and growing diversity, the law profession faced increasing tensions before 1914. As a result of widespread concern about declining business, the main topic of the 1911 Würzburg congress concerned overcrowding in legal practice. The doubling of the number of lawyers since 1890 from about 5500 to more than 11,000 led to a rise in their ratio to the population from 1 : 11,057 in 1880 to 1 : 5605 in 1911. In spite of a considerable increase in litigation, the average case load dropped by one-third (Table 2.1). Although law enrollments had already begun to subside several years earlier, the examination time lag still produced a growing throng of graduates who could not find state employment and threatened to swamp attorneys in the future. In Prussia, only 350 of 3000 *Assessoren* received a government position in 1910 and there were more than 7600 *Referendare* waiting in the wings. For several decades, critics had been arguing that legal business was not expanding quickly enough to keep up with this dramatic influx so that "professional income was declining to at most 4–5,000 Mk per year," legal mores were deteriorating, and the profession as a whole was decreasing in public esteem. Because 51.3 percent of a survey of 4772 lawyers agreed, the malcontents proposed either a *numerus clausus* (a list system based on seniority) or an additional two-year training period before admission to the bar. Arguing that he who "asks for such help from the state puts himself into a certain [lower] class to which we do not want to belong," the leadership of the DAV turned a deaf ear to these vocal complaints, because "for the blessings of freedom, . . . its disadvantages have to be borne as well." After a passionate debate, the general meeting defeated barring access by 619 to 244 votes, indicating that the majority only wanted to improve the antiquated fee schedule. However, fed by another poll in which 6447 favored some restriction of access, the agitation refused to die down, because the panacea of a *numerus clausus* appealed to growing numbers of less fortunate attorneys.[56]

The internal rivalries among different levels of lawyers came to a head in the 1913 deliberations in Breslau. Organized on their own since 1909, the underprivileged district court lawyers had demanded simultaneous admission to the superior courts as a matter of prestige, but their better situated LG colleagues resisted for economic reasons. While AG attorneys argued that "localization of district court lawyers degrades the entire bar" by making them into "second-class lawyers," superior court attorneys warned that the experiment of simultaneous admission would do "grave economic harm to LG lawyers."[57] Although the DAV was sympathetic to demands for greater equality, the leadership generally endorsed the thirty-five-year-old lawyer code as fundamentally sound and needing only minor adjustment. As soon as legal training was made more uniform, lawyers ought not only be admitted to a specific state but nationwide as an "imperative of *Standes-politik.*" According to Max Friedländer, the hallowed principle of localization ought only to be modified to allow district court lawyers to handle the appeals of their own cases, if the appellate jurisdiction was in the same town. Because of vocal superior court opposition to sharing practice with lower court colleagues, the question was referred to committee, where it died in January 1914. The niches for different levels of attorneys had become so well established that they could not be overturned by common agreement. The congress also resolved to combat the "influx of unclean elements into the profession" more flexibly by such measures as "limited local disbarment." However, the supreme honor court at Leipzig was to be strengthened through appointing more lawyers, because it was none too lenient, having only lifted 41 sentences and reduced 88 punishments out of 376 appeals.[58]

After unification, German lawyers therefore became a free profession with some safeguards against client control and unrestrained competition. Residual bureaucratic influence was still visible in training and certification, which insisted on equivalence to a judge as prerequisite for admission to the bar. However, laicization of law was prevented by the principle of Anwaltzwang in all except the trade courts. Although attorneys had to compete with each other, the vagaries of the economic market were somewhat curbed by localization and a fixed-fee schedule. Finally, the price of this emancipation was a vigorous system of self-discipline by honor code, which was institutionalized in lawyer's chambers. Spurred by rapid professional growth, the reform proposals of the last prewar decade, though deeply felt, basically represented attempts to fine-tune a well-functioning system. "The modern legal profession can in every respect risk comparison with [before] 1879; in the purity of its morals and ethics it is equal and in serious work as well as scholarly or practical achievements in legal service it is superior." National Liberal party leader Ernst Bassermann, himself an attorney from Mannheim, formulated the imperial sense of success unmistakably: "I believe that the public has never been served as well, as promptly and as reliably as today, even if that is quite strenuous for us lawyers. . . . Let us keep what we have!"[59]

"The youngest academic profession," according to the educational historian Friedrich Paulsen, was high school teaching. Created by the state examination *pro facultate docendi* in 1810, Gymnasium instruction gradually became emancipated from a transition stage for theologians into a full-time secular career for graduates of the philosophical faculty. Having jettisoned utilitarian pedagogy for philological Hellenism, academically trained teachers based their claims to professionalism on the authority of neohumanist scholarship, thereby establishing *Philologen* as a collective term. In the gradually differentiating public school system, they occupied the highest institutional rung, which prepared pupils for university study through a rigorous classical curriculum and achieved the title *Oberlehrer* in Prussia after 1892. The minority of male secondary schoolteachers succeeded in being accepted as an academic profession by excluding the majority of less well-trained (and increasingly female) primary-school instructors from academic status. However, for decades secondary schoolteachers were split by the struggle over classical or modern training, which involved not only opposing educational philosophies but also competing institutional interests and career opportunities. Philologues also became increasingly divided over the legitimacy of academic secondary instruction for girls, which challenged accepted pedagogical theory and threatened the male occupational monopoly. Envious of the more established legal officials and eager to improve their social standing, high school pedagogues began to coalesce into a cohesive profession only around the turn of the present century.[60]

According to elaborate regulations, high school teachers were trained in the philosophical faculty of the universities in three subjects. During the course of the nineteenth century, the emphasis shifted from general cultivation *(Allgemeinbildung)* obtained in lectures to specialized knowledge drawn from advanced seminars, leading to the gradual emergence of a subject specialist *(Fachlehrer)* for all secondary schools. Reflecting the rapid differentiation of scholarship, this transformation was somewhat limited by the crystallization of topical clusters (such as the ancient languages, German, history, the sciences, and the arts,) for instructional purposes. As in law, studies were concluded by a state examination, divided in 1898 into a general test of Bildung and a specific exam of subject competence, one area of which had to show sufficient mastery to allow a candidate to teach the most advanced grades. Practical training was prolonged to two years in 1890 in order to supply some pedagogical grounding in a seminar attached to a leading secondary school before the *Probejahr* would begin the trial teaching apprenticeship. Extending preparation to eight semesters, a second state examination was introduced in 1917 to demonstrate theoretical and practical command of teaching before a "probationary candidate" could become an "academic assistant teacher" waiting for permanent state appointment.[61] In spite of rising standards and increasing failure rates (approaching two-fifths of the candidates), philological enrollment surged during the Empire from 2724 to 15,045 in the humanities and from 829 to 8243 in the sciences. Slowed down by the hiring freeze in the second half of the overcrowded 1880s, the Prussian philologue corps grew almost threefold from 3675 to 10,167 between 1870–1871 and 1913–1914, indicating that secondary schoolteaching was becoming a dynamic career (Table A.1).[62]

Even after some improvement in 1892 and 1897, the modest pay of secondary schoolteachers fell short of their own expectations. In Prussia, the salary of state-employed academic instructors started at 2700 marks annually and could rise to 5100 marks after 21 years of service, supplemented by a housing allowance of between 420 and 900 marks, depending on the size of the town. Not only was this remuneration more meager than the pay of legally trained higher officials, but it also seemed less than the amount considered necessary for a *standesgemäß* lifestyle of a university graduate (because it was not sufficiently compensated by the security of an eventual pension).[63] As a typical platform for lower middle-class mobility, the Oberlehrer enjoyed a lower social status than the traditional professions. By the year 1914, barely more than three-fifths of the philology students were trained at the classical Gymnasium and about ten percent were female, which was the highest proportion in any academic career! In 1911–1912, only half as many future teachers came from academic backgrounds (14.43 percent) as did prospective lawyers (29.56 percent), and their self-recruitment was considerably lower at Bonn University (37 percent) than the self-perpetuation of jurists (64 percent) (Table A.2). A sympathetic observer like Paulsen complained that "our activity, the education of the young, is not as highly valued as the vocation of lawyers, academic foresters, etc." An ample literature (such as Heinrich Mann's *Professor Unrat*) attests that philologues frequently were the butt of satire as pedantic *Pauker,* drumming knowledge into unwilling heads. Though led by a few exceptional pedagogues, the generational rebellion of the *Wandervogel* youth movement was also directed in no small measure against the teachers as representatives of parental authority. Even retired Chancellor Otto von Bismarck wondered about the "disproportion between the importance of the higher teachers for our national future and their low esteem."[64]

Teaching practice was directly controlled by the state or the city, because the high school pedagogue was "a cultural official." Whereas the Ministry of Justice also established a general framework within which attorneys could function, the Ministry of Culture dictated conditions and content of teaching more specifically through the provincial school boards *(Provinzialschulkollegien).* Somewhat modified in the direction of collegiality (through the introduction of conferences in 1910), the Prussian *Dienstanweisung* endowed the director with ultimate responsibility for all institutional decisions. Moreover, the ministry periodically issued lesson plans *(Lehrpläne),* specifying the time allotment for different subjects as well as instructional goals and methods. In 1892 the number of teaching hours was set at 24 per week (to be reduced after 12 years to 22 and eventually to 20). Maximum class size was limited to fifty pupils for the introductory grades, 40 for the middle years, and 30 for the *Oberstufe* leading to graduation, but in practice the pupil/teacher ratio was only 19 : 1.[65] In order to maintain some autonomy within the classroom, the self-image of the Gymnasium teachers centered on the role of "representing scholarly culture, and being deeply scientific," because this participation in *Wissenschaft* distinguished them from various lower orders of teaching. Although the number of publications declined from 500 per annum in 1876 to 272 in 1908 and the proportion of doctors of philosophy decreased, this aspiration was central to philologue self-consciousness. At the same time, an academic teacher was to strive for "lifting up the high school and thereby raising the cultural level of our people," especially in the small towns. This neohumanist ideal of cultivation through scholarship left little room for the practical focus of everyday teaching activity, namely "the art" of educating the young, which formed a third, more weakly developed dimension of the teacher self-image.[66]

Although high school teachers had already banded together in the middle of the nineteenth century, territorial, subject matter, school type, religious, and gender fragmentation postponed the emergence of a comprehensive professional association. Because the scholarly "Assembly of German Philologists and Teachers" had failed to address issues of pay and working conditions, provincial Prussian organizations (formed in 1872) began to cooperate on the state level beginning in 1880. However, it took until after the resolution of the school war between classicists and modernists for a national association to be founded by frustrated Hessian (50 percent), Prussian (42.4 percent), and Badensian (4.8 percent) teachers in 1903–1904. Including Gymnasium philologues (35 percent), this movement for internal reform and external respect was spearheaded by Realgymnasium and Oberrealschule pedagogues (33 percent), but also mobilized the lesser Realschule faculty (21 percent) as well as girls' school (4 percent) instructors. With about two-fifths holding a doctorate, the founders represented all ranks from directors (8 percent) through titular professors (34 percent) and Oberlehrer (46 percent) down to trainees (10 percent).[67] The new "Vereinsverband akademisch-gebildeter Lehrer Deutschlands" strove to

1. unify the entire German school system if possible,
2. create an Oberlehrer profession with uniform training, title and rank,
3. have academic teachers equal the rank and salary of the other academically trained professions. . . .

Since it also sponsored an increasingly reputable journal (known eventually as *Philologenblatt*), the PhVb grew from 14,000 to more than 20,000 members in forty associations by 1912, an impressive affiliation level approaching 90 percent, which indicates the philologues' determination to catch up. The Prussian Ministry of Culture was hardly overjoyed by the emergence of a teacher interest group and only gradually realized that there were advantages in working with rather than against it: "They want to be officials in the less positive sense of the word. Questions of title and rank made up the main part of their discussions."[68]

Because they were still professionalizing, high school teachers were quite candid about a multitude of problems that confronted their occupation. Most important symbolically and materially was the inadequacy of pay. Recurrent promises since 1845 for salary equality with judges had foundered on the rock of insufficient state finances and of legal arrogance, unwilling to concede the same remuneration to fellow academics who as philosophical graduates were not from the higher faculties. Constant public agitation against such "shoe-shiner treatment," repeated resolutions demanding that "academic teachers are to be treated as equals of regular judges," and lengthy memoranda on the "importance of the teaching profession for state and society" gradually changed the public climate. Because all parties agreed, the Prussian lower house unanimously adopted a liberal resolution calling for equal pay in 1907.[69] Pressure from the leading education official Friedrich Althoff, unequivocal support from Minister of Culture Ludwig Holle ("not the financial aspect but the question of dignity is decisive"), fear of the radicalization of the frustrated teachers through the agitation of Heinrich Schröder, a personal assurance of Chancellor Bernhard von Bülow, and the intercession of the aged imperial tutor Georg Hintzpeter with William II combined to wear down the resistance of the upper house, the Ministry of Finance, and the cities that were going to have to absorb the costs. "For the development of the high-schools it is of utmost importance that this quarrel be resolved, the sense of discrimination lifted from the Oberlehrer, and their profession honored by the state in the same way as the judges." On June 5, 1909, the Kaiser finally signed the historic law, adopting the principle of equality.[70] Whereas beginning pay remained at 2700 marks (because teachers were younger when appointed), after 9 years the scale became identical with judges and the end salary was therefore raised to 7200 marks per year, which was an impressive 20 percent increase overall.[71]

Another status issue was the absence of unified terminology applied to the occupation as a whole and to individual career stages. Because seminar-trained middle-school pedagogues were increasingly appointed to the lower grades of the high schools and functioned as Oberlehrer, academic teachers cast about for another term that would be reserved for them alone. However, in spite of heated discussions, the PhVb failed to agree because of divergent local traditions. The question was complicated in 1906 by the Prussian decision to bestow the titular "professor" upon almost one-half of the older teachers of scholarly distinction, who naturally did not want to relinquish it. Because in a bureaucratic society pay and rank depended on one's title, it seemed "a thoroughly ideal quest to wish that the unity of our profession be expressed through a uniform terminology." Eventually even science teachers accepted the word *Philologe,* so that regional associations slowly changed their names into *Philologenverbände*. Because "the issue of equal treatment with jurists is a matter of life and death for our profession," a consensus gradually emerged on adding the prefix *Studien* (meaning studies) to existing bureaucratic terminology of Referendar for trainees, Assessor for probationers, and *Rat* for tenured teachers (thereby dropping the titular professor against some protest). Although the Prussian government introduced the *geheimer Studienrat* title to honor "older directors . . . as well as deserving professors" in 1913, the debate dragged into the last war years until the problem was ultimately resolved.[72]

Because they had further to go than lawyers, academic high school teachers made considerable progress in becoming professionals in the last years of the empire. Constituted as "pedagogical community" by Wilhelm von Humboldt through academic training and examination, high school teachers slowly and painfully developed a secular career dedicated to the scholarly cultivation of the future elite. Obviously, state or city officials could never reach the same degree of autonomy as attorneys. However, the thesis of the "transformation of the liberal-democratic teacher of the people into a conformist teaching official preoccupied with self-interest" somewhat oversimplifies the process. In the organizational struggle with the patriarchical administration, teachers not only won increases in pay and status but also gained professional self-consciousness, a sense of independence, competence, and ethical obligation (calling for greater participation in disciplinary courts), which in turn improved the quality of their teaching. In the last prewar years, philologues began to establish a successful working relationship with the Prussian government so that cultural official Karl Reinhardt publicly stated that "everything which advances this profession" also helped the work of the ministry. The historian Otto Hintze observed sagaciously: "None of the higher professions has achieved so much success during the last generation as the Oberlehrer; to a large degree this is due to their powerful organization and their emphatic pursuit of collective interests *(Standesinteressen).*"[73]

Less successful in professionalizing during the empire than the high school teachers were the German engineers. In the middle of the nineteenth century, the disparate artisans, government builders, military officers, and technical teachers began to coalesce into a single career because of their shared polytechnical training at the *Technische Hochschule* (TH), which was made academic after 1879. With the rise of the large industrial firm, the work situation of the rapidly growing number of higher technicians also homogenized in a newly emerging white-collar role. However, in spite of such achievements as the formal equality of the THs with the universities and the establishment of a uniform degree, the engineering occupation was too heterogeneous to gain market control. Split between business and industry (as owners or white-collar employees), government service (professors, technical bureaucrats, soldiers), and finally even the free professions (consulting engineers), technicians were unable to unite effectively behind a set of common goals. "The technical profession in Germany has succeeded less than in other civilized countries in achieving that public position and respect which corresponds to its importance for the creation and advancement of our culture and which it needs in order to unfold its creativity for the common weal." Because many technicians emulated the uniform training, academic status, autonomous practice, and coherent consciousness of the older academic callings, their frustrating struggle seems, nevertheless, to have been directed toward professional goals.[74]

First-rate engineers were trained at the Technische Hochschule, a technical institute that achieved university status in 1899 and stressed a combination of basic research and applied technology. Students were required to have the graduation certificate *(Abitur)* of a recognized academic high school and to study for three years, preceded by a one year internship in industry. The middle layer of engineers had only incomplete secondary training *(Mittlere Reife),* followed by a three-year apprenticeship in a trade, before enrolling in a technical middle school for a two-year course that was more practically oriented. At a lower level, there were middle schools and *Werkmeister* schools to train technicians who, if exceptionally gifted, might also rise into engineering functions within a company.[75] In contrast to the elaborate state examination system that controlled entry into the public professions, there were only academic tests for engineers. Already in 1895 the TH Hanover suggested the title *diplomierter Ingenieur* for academic engineers, but the bureaucratic discussion remained inconclusive until William II in 1899 authorized a graduate diploma, creating the *Diplom-Ingenieur*. With a leaving certificate from a higher technical school, a technician was called *graduierter Ingenieur;* even if he had no formal examination at all, he might still be called engineer, if he persuaded his employer that he could do the job. For a professor or higher technical official a TH or HTL (Höhere Technische Lehranstalt) degree was essential; however, for consulting or industrial employment, there existed no formal entrance requirement, because less formally trained engineers were generally less expensive for a company.[76] Therefore, TH enrollment grew intermittently from 2242 in 1870–1871 to 12,576 in 1903–1904 before leveling off at about 11,451 in 1914. At the same time, student numbers in the various kinds of less prestigious institutes increased from about 1400 in the late 1880s to almost 11,000 by 1910, setting off a fierce rivalry between academic and nonacademic technicians.[77]

The heterogeneity and the uncertain boundaries of the engineering occupation make it difficult to characterize the income of engineers in general terms. During the first decade 12,930 Diplom-Ingenieure graduated; this number roughly doubled by 1914, and there were about another 120,000 less-trained engineers and technicians.[78] Whereas entrepreneurs and managers as well as engineering professors and technical bureaucrats were financially comfortable, the majority of technical practitioners had to struggle considerably more than free professional lawyers or government-employed teachers. According to a 1906 Berlin survey, one-half of academic engineers earned less than 2100 marks per year, with another quarter less than 3000 marks and only the last quarter making more! Interestingly enough, two-thirds of the publicly employed technicians fell into the highest income bracket while substantially more than two-fifths of industrial employees remained economically marginal. It was cold comfort for the Diplom-Ingenieure that nonacademic engineers were even worse off with more than three-fifths earning less than 2,100 marks and only one-seventh making more than 3,000 marks. Another inquiry into the salaries of technicians with middle-school training a few years later revealed a range of annual income from 2,064 marks (for industrial employees) to 3260 marks (for public officials), leading to complaints about a "thorough leveling process." The fierce rivalry between increasing numbers of TH and middle-school graduates kept starting salaries so low that some academics were reputed to be earning as little as 600–1400 marks a year. Therefore, in 1905 the THs demanded a clear separation of engineering titles to counter "the sharpest competition from the overwhelming number of technicians who depress not only the pay but also the prestige of the profession."[79]

The social status of engineers was ambivalent and contradictory. On the one hand, capitalists, directors of firms, professors, and higher public officials could claim high prestige without reference to engineering (that just happened to be their specialty). On the other hand, traditional Akademiker did not regard even TH graduates as equals, because technicians lacked general cultivation, and both looked down upon the alumni of the various kinds of technical schools. Although only about a quarter of academic engineers was classically trained, the profession was virtually male and was recruited more from academic families (above one-fifth) than were teachers (Table A.2). Like university students, about half of Badensian TH pupils came from upper middle layers of German society, drawn somewhat more from commerce and industry (36.3 versus 25.1 percent) and the new lower middle class (20.3 versus 16.7 percent) than from higher public service circles (15 versus 24.5 percent) or white-collar ranks. In contrast, nonacademic engineers clearly came from lower artisan, employee and working-class families remote from the professions, because fewer than one-twentieth had academic backgrounds. Graduates of THs resented that they "often had to work under the same conditions as middle-school technicians or under their direction. Rarely were these benevolent," delighting instead in hazing their intellectual superiors. Because of their "appalling lack of esteem" no matter how much they contributed to the rise in prosperity or in military might, engineers concentrated on school and title questions in struggling for "just recognition of the technical intelligentsia."[80]

Whereas owners of firms, professors, and consulting engineers enjoyed considerable autonomy, the growing group of white-collar engineers found its practice increasingly bureaucratized. On the one hand, the change of employment gradually shortened the workday to less than ten hours and also improved working conditions, providing protection from the weather and dangerous machinery. On the other hand, the rise of the large industrial firms made it even harder for engineers to become entrepreneurs outside the building trade, limiting them to an intermediary role between capital and labor (see Table 1.2). Their astounding youth made supervising older technicians or workers difficult. The growing importance of finances in corporate decision making also tended to shift some managerial functions to accountants. Although many machine builders still led actual production, chemical and electrical engineers were increasingly restricted to de-

Table 1.2. Prussian Engineers, 1907

	Architects/ Contractors	Machine	Electrical	Mining	Other	Middle-School Technicians
Number	19,876	17,806	5,017	4,036	10,134	121,911
Percentage independent	20.4	1.7	4.2	7.7	10.0	0.1
Percentage under age 30	61.0	56.6	58.8	55.9	51.0	18.1

signing products with less voice in whether and how to make them.[81] In contrast to this routinized practice, their self-image was inextricably intertwined with the progress of technology, which was assumed to be an unquestioned benefit for mankind. Instead of serving justice or culture, engineers were improving the lives of their fellow human beings with machines. Visible monuments to a better tomorrow such as railway stations, suspension bridges, and gigantic ocean liners demonstrated humanity's increasing mastery over nature, born of a practical kind of idealism. Professor Adolph Slaby proudly claimed in 1906: "Correctly understood, the engineering profession also has an ideal core."[82]

Already in 1856 engineers mobilized to upgrade their training institutions into Technische Hochschulen and created a vigorous national association, the Verein deutscher Ingenieure. The VDI goal "of rallying the spiritual forces of German technology for the welfare of the entire industry of the fatherland" is a clear reflection of the dominance of engineering professors ("spiritual forces"), which gradually turned into a preponderance of capitalist entrepreneurs ("the entire industry"). Typically, the formula did not even mention engineering as a Berufsstand. To the degree that support for modern secondary schooling, agitation for steam engine safety, or the foundation of a glossy technological journal *(VDI-Zeitschrift)* coincided with the needs and desires of white-collar engineers, the VDI helped them professionalize. Championing a reform of the patent law, promulgating general cultivation at the THs, breaking the legal monopoly for higher administration, or advancing engineering participation in local government promoted technology in general. However, for a long time the illusion of technical neutrality and the repeated refusal to make academic training mandatory for admission hampered the emergence of a unified and respected profession, capable of pursuing its own interests. The divergent VDI membership prevented a united professional stance because it included many capitalists such as 8 percent factory owners, 13 percent directors, and 8 percent production managers, a segment of public officials such as the 7 percent engineering professors and 8 percent bureaucrats, and more than half white collar industrial employees (Table A.10). Moreover, in contrast to other professions, the impressive number of 24,000 VDI members actually organized less than one-fifth of all practicing engineers.[83]

One response to the frustrations of incomplete professionalization was to abandon the goal altogether and to opt for a class strategy. Increasingly, white-collar engineers considered the general promotion of technology as an insufficient solution for their problems. Confronted with overcrowding, inadequate pay, decreasing chances of advancement, lessening control over the work process, the younger nonacademic technicians, particularly, joined discontented chemists in founding a "Bund technisch-industrieller Beamter" (ButiB) in 1904. "Facing the choice either of working, without prospect of advancement, for a wage which a carpenter or mechanic would refuse, or of being pushed aside by masses of annually entering graduates or technicians, [the engineer] fills the ranks of an intellectual proletariat.'' Instead of professionalization, the ButiB pushed unionization of technicians to whom appeals to a middle-class *Standesbewußtsein* by a capital-(44 percent) and government (35 percent)-dominated VDI board seemed a mockery. Appealing for a ''a systematic worker policy,'' these white-collar radicals sought to counter exploitation by employee solidarity in order to improve their ''public position,'' raise their pay, limit the length of the working day, and obtain social insurance. Directed toward equality with commercial employees, freedom to change jobs, and inventor protection, the confrontation tactic of the ButiB attracted 24,313 members by 1914, two-fifths of whom were disgruntled Diplom-Ingenieure who provided much of the leadership. Such a union approach to professionals threw a scare into the older VDI, forcing it to initiate sociopolitical initiatives in uncontested areas as well.[84]

The other alternative to partial professionalization was the determination to proceed with redoubled vigor. When their situation had not improved five years later, some TH graduates opted for the opposite remedy—making engineering completely academic. On June 28, 1909 Alexander Lang founded the Verband deutscher Diplom-Ingenieure (VDDI), seeking to organize the newly graduated academic engineers and actually enrolling some 4000 (less than 15 percent) before the outbreak of the First World War. With two-fifths of its members in public service and another quarter as independent entrepreneurs or consultants, the VDDI embraced an educational Standespolitik, emulating the older professions, by asking for:

1. the exemption of the Diplom-Ingenieur from labor law,
2. the creation of public-law corporations (chambers) like the existing lawyer and doctor *Kammern,* in which Diplom-Ingenieure themselves can regulate their professional concerns and their relations to the public and the bureaucracy,
3. [and] the protection of their title *(Standesbezeichnung).*

Supplemented by demands for ''improving technical education,'' representation in parliament or public service, and an independent technical bureaucracy, title protection quickly became the central concern of the movement, because limiting the term to TH graduates would create a market monopoly and thereby improve their pay, status, practice, and so on.[85] Industrialists especially opposed academization because they wanted to maintain a steady supply of cheap, practically trained technicians who were, incidentally, also more tractable. When the VDI could no longer dodge the issue, a curious alliance of entrepreneurs and nonacademic engineers, with the help of some reformist professors, refused to create new social barriers, because about one-half of the new VDI members in 1911 would not have qualified, thereby limiting its future growth. Although the Ministry of Culture and the military sympathized somewhat, repeated attempts at legal title protection and at creating self-governing engineering chambers failed, because resistance of the VDI board majority proved too strong.[86]

In spite of considerable gains about the turn of the century, German engineers still faced a professionalization deficit in the last years of the empire. Although their numbers were increasing rapidly, their field was expanding and their calling was becoming more important, the emerging technological occupations retained a frustrating sense of inferiority. Because they lacked uniform academic training and examination, received widely differing pay, possessed an uncertain status, lost autonomy of practice, and were still struggling for cohesive self-consciousness, technicians were unsuccessful in achieving full professional status. The organizational fragmentation of roughly 4000 Diplom-Ingenieure in the VDDI, 4800 in the ButiB, and 6012 in the VDI also hampered the achievement of professional goals. Not yet sufficiently differentiated from the related careers of architects and chemists, academic technicians compensated with verbal blustering: "Today we engineers clearly agree that the time must finally come in which technicians are not only recognized as equals of the other professions, but in which they have to join them in a leading role."[87]

NEOCORPORATE PROFESSIONALISM

While professionalism created increasing strains in the last years of the empire, most practitioners took pride in their success, confident that the remaining problems would be solved in due course. Older academic occupations such as the law which had existed for centuries, became modern professions after 1871. Because the training and examinations were already established, attorneys improved their autonomy, self-conception, organization and eventually also their income and status. These achievements gave lawyers a new sense of identity: "A free legal profession is crucial for the existence of the rule of law, it is the guarantor of justice."[88] Newer callings of university graduates like secondary schoolteaching tried to emulate the legal pattern so as to become prestigious professions as well. The systematization of state examinations created an ever more highly qualified teaching corps, which wrested increases in pay and gains in status from a reluctant government, even if it could never achieve the same autonomy as lawyers. "In the interest of the prestige of the high school and of our occupation, we must remain a cohesive profession like the other academic vocations, because only a respected pursuit can recruit the best talent which, for the sake of the thorough cultivation of our people, no one needs as we do."[89] Even newer occupations like engineering, which were still establishing themselves as separate careers, sought most of all to improve their training and examinations in order to claim the remaining accoutrements of professionalism. However, external resistance and lack of internal cohesion kept the Diplom-Ingenieure from gaining market control, which was essential to "the best development opportunities for academic technical intelligence," Academization failed, because the introduction of educational barriers "would close the path to independence for non-academic engineers."[90] Although the process originated earlier and continued beyond it, professionalization achieved its crucial breakthrough in the empire.

In international perspective, German professionalization was a distinctive variant of the continental pattern.[91] The recent comparative discussion has established three alternative ideal types: A first variety of professional dominance is characterized by the professional being in charge and the association holding collective power over decisions. For instance, in American medicine the interests of the profession (as expressed through the AMA) dominate the delivery of health care, which tends to be clinically oriented. A second variant of lay power is defined by clients' influence on professionals whom they employ. For instance, in German medicine around the turn of this century, mutual-aid insurance funds determined priorities, which usually stressed health maintenance through prevention. The third version of state control implies that government officials dominate professionals. For instance, in tsarist Russia and even more so in the Soviet Union, doctors, providing social medicine, have been at the mercy of bureaucratic decisions about what to practice. To complete the conceptual scheme, one might want to add a fourth variety of academic hegemony in which the university dominates practitioners. For instance, many scientists such as astronomers are not only predominantly employed by academe but their work agenda is also directed toward research rather than applied goals.[92] As "professionalization from above," the German development is usually assumed to fit the third mold, because in central Europe the state created and largely employed the professions, and, when threatened, the professionals turned back to the bureaucracy for help. Moreover, their limited autonomy and public service role expectations seem to reinforce this case. At the same time, the strong role of higher education in training as well as certifying also suggests elements of the fourth academic type.[93]

The evidence of individual professions, however, somewhat disagrees with the model of state control and university dominance. For lawyers, Hannes Siegrist sees "a mixture of bureaucratic model, traditional French type and a modern variant of profession." Although German attorneys had been quasi officials, after 1879 they did achieve "limited professional autonomy" of practice, associations, and honor courts, which came close to the Anglo-American pattern.[94] For teachers, "the decisive context" was, indeed, the role of state official, which hampered their self-definition as professionals. However, according to Elmar Thenorth, "the relative autonomy of educational processes" in the classroom challenged philologues to emancipate themselves from bureaucratic control and to assert pedagogical independence as a cohesive interest group, demanding concessions.[95] For the "highly fragmented and amorphous German engineering occupation," according to Cornelis Gispen, it was the "double" subordination to the "traditional bureaucratic elites" and to "the captains of industry" that made "the road toward professional autonomy and power . . . arduous and uncertain." However, in contrast to the managerial orientation of the VDI and the union leanings of the ButiB, the VDDI did develop a professionalizing program for white-collar employees.[96] The lawyers' experience indicates that there was more autonomy for free professionals than is often recognized; teachers demonstrate that even public officials can advance toward a profession through powerful organization; engineers show that one can emancipate from initial government employment, even if one fails in securing full professionalism. In spite of academic deference, the expansion of practical training and the dwindling role of professors in associations also suggest a waning of university influence over professional practice.

Although their rise was heavily influenced by the bureaucracy and academy, the German professions ultimately sought to transcend them. Except for the contested case of social medicine, there was little pressure for lay or client control in Central Europe. By forming independent interest groups, the various academic occupations strove beyond their bureaucratic base to increase their income or status and to assert their autonomy or identity. Notwithstanding professorial rhetoric, practitioners in law, teaching, or technology also set their own work agenda independent of academic concerns. Yet many professionals did not completely trust the vagaries of the free market and feared the effects of unregulated competition. Therefore, most aspired to a *berufsständische* corporatism that would use the state to secure income and social position, while at the same time rejecting its control over practice and organization. Similarly, practitioners appealed to the nimbus of Wissenschaft for legitimacy and resorted to educational entitlements to disbar competitors while refusing to follow professorial dictates. The ideal of a successful profession was therefore a chamber system of self-government for credentialed university graduates, enjoying a legal market monopoly and invested with quasi-public authority over its members, regardless of employment. A late liberal compromise, this *Kammer* strategy sought to establish autonomy from government, client, or university dominance, while protecting the experts against the dangerous consequences of "free field" competition with neotraditional state intervention, which was typical of "organized capitalism." Although it was never completely achieved, the thrust of German professionalization was therefore characterized by a mixed fifth variant of professional neocorporatism.[97]

The postliberal politics of the German professions in the late empire wavered between the illustrious legacy of liberalism and a rising tide of "academic illiberalism."[98] As an independent and public profession, attorneys clustered in the left bourgeois parties, providing more than one-tenth of all Reichstag deputies! "Many liberal leaders . . . have emerged out of the freie Advokatur before and after the founding of the Empire," the latest of which was National Liberal party Chairman Ernst Bassermann. Though sharing this liberal heritage, the less active secondary schoolteachers stressed cultural nationalism. For the Philologenverband, Dr. Mertens vowed to Chancellor Bernhard von Bülow that philologues would dedicate themselves "to the holy duty of reciprocating the state's recognition of their importance and achievements by loyally discharging their office and trying to raise and nurture a truly national spirit among their young charges in the future." Because they were still clamoring for "the respect and position which they deserve due to their incredible achievements," engineers were least overtly political, gravitating also to the liberal camp (Table 3.2).[99] As a result of their key position in the Bildungsbürgertum, professionals participated in the bourgeois shift from liberal to national attitudes in the late empire. Because professionalization was one of the great achievements of the challenging middle class, there were still many liberalizing echoes in professional rhetoric stressing bourgeois values such as competence, individualism, and responsibility. However, increasing strains of success were breaking down the self-evident nexus between professionalism and liberalism, leading to a diffusion of political allegiances. Once most professionalization battles had been won, professional elites grew protective of their material and political gains and became instinctively conservative, blunting their reform impetus. Dissatisfied with corporatist immobilism, some progressive spirits searched for a neoliberal agenda and a few frustrated individuals even flirted with socialism. Frightened by an excess of modernity, some marginal *völkisch* practitioners also began calling for a radical return to a mythical German past, ominously foreshadowing the disasters to come.[100]

I

PROFESSIONS IN CRISIS

2

Democratizing the Professions

The outbreak of the First World War rudely interrupted the evolution of the German professions. Because the fighting seemed like a heroic adventure after two generations of peace, professionals enthusiastically welcomed "the present world war, forced upon the German Reich."[1] Thousands rushed to the colors in August 1914 while their remaining colleagues waged the war on the home front. "In this fateful hour, we Diplom-Ingenieure shall not lag behind." However, the bloody reality of the trenches gradually had a sobering effect, and hunger, cold, manpower shortage, and material scarcity increasingly disrupted professional practice.[2] Most experts defined the Great War as an exceptional trial, requiring special sacrifices. But when glorious victory refused to come, the educated grew impatient with the Kaiser's civilian government and cast about for alternatives such as the Supreme Command or the socialist Left. The postponement of corrective action until after the war created rising pressures for professional reform and political reorientation.[3] Exacerbating prewar tensions, the increasingly total struggle initiated a malaise that would bedevil professionals for the better part of four decades. In popular memory, the "tranquil" progress of the empire was "disturbed" by the war's "starvation, [and] inflation," leading to "postwar unemployment, [and] partisan strife" until the increasing confusion "unleashed the evil time in 1933."[4]

The four-and-one-quarter year struggle severely impaired training and credentialing. The Prussian introduction of an emergency graduation *(Notabitur)* in 1915 lowered secondary-school standards, and the South German cancellation of the final high school year shortened university preparation in spite of supplementary courses for veterans. The military even pressed for a complete closing of the universities "as far as the irrefutable need of an individual profession (doctors) permits." However, unwilling to overthrow the entire entitlement system, educational officials only offered to keep the soldiers from being "disadvantaged" and to interpret existing regulations in "an unbureaucratic spirit."[5] Nonetheless, enrollment virtually collapsed. With around four-fifths of the males serving at the front, actual attendance dropped from 60,225 university students in 1914 to 18,208 by 1917 before slightly recovering to 22,726 in 1918.[6] In contrast to the popularity of medicine, the faculties of law and philosophy decreased below the average drop to 21.4 percent of the prewar figure, while technical training numbers sank to 19 percent. Hence the proportion of females in the student body increased, with women making absolute (to 7182) and relative (to two-fifths in 1916) gains.[7] Because about one-quarter of a cohort (16,000) died in the fighting, the supply of newcomers dried up just when it was most needed to replace the loss of about one-twelfth of practitioners (such as 800 lawyers and 2567 high school teachers), reducing the expert labor force in general. The number of lawyers decreased to 12,030, and about 10 percent of the high school teaching positions remained unfilled by 1918.[8] The postponement of study of an entire cohort penned up a need that would later break like a tidal wave over the universities and professions.

The Great War also impoverished many practitioners. ''No other occupation has been affected more severely than law,'' because lawyers in uniform received only minimal military pay, making it impossible to keep their staff and maintain their family's living standard. Attorneys who remained at home did little better, because simplification of civil and criminal procedure (*Entlastungsverordnung* of 1915) reduced business while litigation decreased precipitously. Between 1913 and 1917 legal business (combining AG and LG civil cases with AG criminal cases) dropped almost three times from 633 to 232 actions per lawyer (Table 2.1).[9] As a result of the ''extraordinary increase in living costs,'' which doubled office expenses, average income decreased to between 2400 and 3200 marks: ''Clearly, one cannot live on that and it is not enough for today's needs.'' Because wealthier lawyers were depleting their savings and poorer colleagues faced utter ruin, attorneys pleaded that ''fees must be increased considerably.'' However the Ministry of Justice only conceded a small raise in office expenditures *(Pauschsätze)* and waited until April 1918 before modestly augmenting most legal charges by 30 percent.[10] Though protected by the continuation of their regular salaries, high school teachers also saw their living standard decline with inflation. The Prussian government was slow to adjust pay to rising prices, granting only a 5 percent war aid *(Kriegsbeihilfe)* and a 13.5 percent supplement in early 1918. Enraged by the doubling of lower bureaucrats' pay, teachers complained about ''a 'proletarianization' of the higher officials, understood as the decline of their salaries below the pay of a manual worker.''[11] With construction, electrical, and mechanical technicians greatly in demand, most engineers did somewhat better because their remuneration usually increased with creeping inflation.[12]

In contrast to these material hardships, the social status of professionals changed little. Whereas civilians lost some importance in public opinion compared with glamorous soldiers, the war was too much of an exception to overturn hierarchies completely. Lawyers had to resist the attempts of judges—organized in the Deutsche Richterbund—to use the opportunity for diminishing the role of their adversaries in the courtroom.[13] Teachers were more fortunate, since in late 1917 the government suggested ''introducing the *Studienrat* title in place of the previous professor'' as a boost in prestige. According to Minister of Culture Friedrich Schmidt-Ott, this status equalization with other academic officials intended not only to stimulate ''scholarly activity'' and to improve teaching, but also to ''keep [teachers] from pursuing professional and political interests,'' thereby making them more docile. Nonetheless, philologues were grateful for their ''imperial birthday present,'' because it laid ''the basis for a unified and exclusive official designation of ranks for our profession.''[14] Though more important to the war effort, engineers received no symbolic reward. Upset by the ''misuse of the term 'engineer' '' by anyone who claimed to be one, TH graduates tried to use the ''gigantic technical problem'' of modern warfare to gain ''that respect and position which they deserve on the basis of their unforgettable achievements.'' On the one hand, the VDDI sought to establish the consulting engineer as a self-governing free profession by arguing that it would advance ''the interests of all concerned.'' On the other hand, it pursued legal title protection by restricting ''engineer'' to ''studies at a technical institute.'' But in spite of army and Ministry of Culture support, academic engineers could not overcome VDI and business resistance before November 1918.[15]

During the long years of fighting, professional practice also deteriorated noticeably. With the more thorough mobilization of manpower, more than one-half of attorneys eventually (1917) served in the military. Although the proportion of teachers drafted was somewhat smaller, it is unlikely to have been less than one-third; furthermore, a substantial number of engineers (perhaps as many as one-fourth) from nonessential industries also went to the front.[16] The most pressing practical problem was therefore the replacement of missing practitioners. Lawyers had a formal system of substitution *(Vertretung)* in which another attorney would take care of cases provisionally for a split fee, albeit without permanently alienating clients, thereby consolidating remaining business. Teachers simply had to teach longer hours in the classroom and cover for extracurricular ''voluntary'' activities without any adjustment in pay. Sometimes shifted to different industries, engineers were forced to work with reduced staffs and substitute *(Ersatz)* raw materials, resulting in much overtime and scrambling to keep things going. At the same time, professional activity was increasingly militarized and regimented, since the district commanders and not the civil authorities were in charge. Only with difficulty could university graduates secure assignment to quasi-professional duties under the Auxiliary Service Law, because many soldiers relished a bit of revenge by putting shovels into softened academic hands.[17]

To forget such problems, professionals redoubled their dedication to patriotism. Traditionally overrepresented in nationalist pressure groups, they joined professors in waging spiritual warfare for the fatherland. While lawyers denounced international law as a sham, teachers celebrated the advances of German arms on the map and instilled confidence in victory by assigning for essays such themes as ''Germany's difficult struggle'' or ''our Hindenburg.'' Preoccupied with the practical challenges of the war of attrition, engineers seem to have paid less attention to chauvinistic rhetoric.[18] Professional journals were filled with honor lists of dead colleagues, appeals for help for wounded survivors, and thundering calls to subscribe to war loans: ''We Germans are living through an incomparable time in history, we are going through a martyrdom which has never yet been imposed upon a nation,'' high school teacher A. Biese told his Frankfurt pupils in the fall of 1918: ''We are surrounded by an immense sea of hatred. . . . At our inner fibre gnaw . . . partisanship, greed, profiteering and selfishness.'' However, from the heroic images of Luther, Goethe, and Bismarck he drew the resolve: "Germany shall not perish!"[19] While most professionals joined the annexationists, clamoring for unrestricted submarine warfare and total victory, a minority supported peace moves and welcomed the beginning of domestic reform.[20] Although practical frustrations made professionals critical of the government, propaganda service nationalized their self-consciousness.

After initial dormancy, organizational life reemerged, coordinating self-help and lobbying in order to meet wartime hardships. In the first two years, journals, which were reduced in size and scope, barely survived; most local or national meetings were cancelled; professional associations had to fight hard in order not to lose too many members.[21] Aside from keeping in touch with colleagues at the front, activity focused on mutual support of wounded veterans or of survivors at home. Associations established a "war aid committee," collected funds by assessments or donations, and disbursed them to the needy. For instance, the legal aid fund had, by May 1917, distributed 1,123,000 marks to the deserving poor. Another potential measure of self-help was a voluntary fee increase by 25 percent, but the national DAV delegate meeting rejected the principle, only allowing more frequent exceptions in the future. Distressed attorneys also began discussing a "social organization of lawyers," but the Reichstag failed to enact health and accident insurance or pensions because of practitioner reluctance to join a compulsory system.[22] Frustrated by the VDI refusal "to develop into a professional association," academic technicians joined forces with Austrians in a "Mitteleuropäischer Verband akademischer Ingenieurvereine" in order to pursue professionalization with the help of those colleagues who had just secured the protection of their title.[23] However, in the long term, self-help proved inadequate, and greater state support was rarely forthcoming.

Ultimately the war broke the bond between professionals and the imperial system. Material suffering such as the "plight of the attorneys" created political resentment: "The State has not fulfilled its duty" of helping the professions. Lawyers faced rising noncompliance with the wartime emergency decrees that were perceived as unjust by the population. Although most pedagogues thought that nationalist teaching was essential, they were increasingly confronted by hollow-cheeked and unruly children. As potential "general staff . . . for the economic mobilization of the German people," engineers also chafed at military misuse of scarce resources. In June 1917, the VDI board petitioned the Ministry of War to improve the economic and technical coordination of the German war effort by giving engineers a greater role in its direction. But technocratic promises of improving "the fighting power of our army . . . while reducing the cost of warfare by using fewer men and material" did not sway the Prussian military, thereby prompting engineers to question bureaucratic control.[24] When, in spite of all patriotic efforts, defeat became inescapable, it was psychologically shattering. "The collapse of a strong people, which for years went from victory to victory and conquered by arms a territory greater than its own Reich, through the superior number of its enemies and the excessive length of the suffering which did not defeat it but wear it down" appeared to professionals as "the greatest tragedy in history."[25] The unexpected collapse *(Zusammenbruch)* shook allegiances to the inept Kaiser and made previous suffering seem pointless. How would professionals react: Would they cling, more stubbornly than ever, to the glory of the past or would they seize the political chance to forge something new?[26]

THE CHALLENGE OF REFORM

"The storm of the Revolution swept with such speed over our fatherland," high school teacher K. Link reflected in early December 1918 "that under the powerful impression of the upheaval entire occupational groups . . . did not dare join this movement in order to protect their interests."[27] Stunned by the military collapse and political upheaval, most professionals considered the November revolution real enough to be frightened rather than exhilarated. Because of their fixation on the working classes and preoccupation with the failure of a radical new beginning, historians have neglected the role of the bourgeois strata and belittled modest reform efforts in November 1918. "The greatest research deficit is for officials, teachers and technical experts." The lack of basic information on the involvement of the educated has produced contradictory interpretations, stressing either intoxicating cultural departures or an unbroken continuity of academic authoritarianism.[28] To determine how far the revolution went beyond politics toward remaking society, it is necessary to explore the interaction between reform impulses and situational or structural obstacles in specific case studies such as the professions. Sparked by the illiberal features of the imperial system and penned up during the war, pressures for change erupted with surprising force and variety during the early Weimar years.

After the paralyzing shock had worn off, professionals began to wonder what the collapse and revolution would do to their own lives. "The democratization of Germany—that is the sign of the new times. It must involve all areas of the state, last but not least the field of secondary education," pondered Oberlehrer E. Umbach. But what would democratization mean for the professions in terms of their own work, their relations to the wider society, and their involvement in an emerging republican polity? In the fluid revolutionary situation, established patterns could be challenged and new courses of action seemed suddenly possible. First, most practitioners agreed that the authoritarian military and civilian restrictions of the imperial system would have to be eliminated in order to allow the professions to develop more freely. Second, groups that had been subject to discrimination before hoped that the power of traditional elites might be overthrown so that the internal structure of professions could become more egalitarian and accessible. Third, disenfranchised clients and laypeople tried to take away control of services from the experts in order to make them more responsive to public needs. Finally, democratic activists as well as pragmatic centrists sought to move the political outlook of professionals toward support of the new republic as a basis for a working relationship. The revolutionary upheaval therefore presented both opportunities and threats, inextricably intertwining internal professional reform with general political democratization.[29]

With the exception of single individuals like the Communist attorney Karl Liebknecht, the direct involvement of professionals in the revolution was slight. In the initial struggle for survival both the professions and provisional government reluctantly came to rely on one another. "In this serious time for our fatherland, the undersigned economic and technical organizations call upon their members, each in his place, to . . . work for maintaining German economic life, because otherwise untold suffering will result for the entire population." One day after the armistice, academic engineers suggested that "practical experts" ought to lead the campaign against mounting material hardship, thereby hoping to improve the "reputation of the technicians."[30] On November 13, between 600 and 800 Berlin Anwaltverein members resolved, after a stormy discussion, "to support the present government in the pressing tasks of legal service, emergency measures and in the areas of legislation and legal care." On the following day high school teachers joined other bureaucrats in declaring: "German public officials, represented by these organizations with more than 1.5 million members, put themselves at the disposal of the current government to serve the common weal in nation, state and community." The price of such nonideological cooperation was the "guarantee of all rights, assured through law and contract" by the workers' and soldiers' council.[31] Recognizing the provisional government as key to their own survival, professional associations pledged their pragmatic support so as to restore order and forestall more drastic measures. Although radicals wanted to abolish academic prerogatives, moderates in the new cabinet, out of respect for competence, considered experts essential to overcoming the postwar crisis, as long as these followed "governmental orders . . . irrespective of their personal political attitude."[32]

Somewhat surprisingly, revolutionary councils also spread to the professions. In many cities lawyers, teachers, and engineers joined soviets of workers and soldiers, but they were a tiny and often suspect minority. Efforts to create countervailing bourgeois or bureaucratic councils *(Räte)* were rarely successful.[33] More dominated by professionals were the "councils of intellectual workers," which sprang up in Berlin, Hamburg, Munich, Königsberg, Stuttgart, Cologne, and Leipzig beginning on November 10. Striving for "cultural-political radicalism based on a Socialist republic," the Berlin group, led by literati and academics such as Kurt Hiller, Siegfried Jacobson, Rudolf Leonhard, Leo Matthias, Helene Stöcker, Frank Thieß, and Armin Wegener, supported pacifism, "just distribution of property," separation of church and state, freedom of press and assembly, and "defense of an all-German Socialist Republic." In law, they demanded "the limitation of punitive justice to protection of interests . . . thorough sexual liberation . . . [and] humanization of punishment," whereas in education they called for a "radical reform of public instruction," including a "comprehensive school . . , no authoritarian teacher–pupil relationship . . . [and] abolition of the Abitur." In contrast, the Hamburg "council of workers of the mind" more modestly insisted on "regaining for intellectual ability that place in state and economy which it deserves." Similarly, the Karlsruhe soviet, composed of doctors, lawyers, journalists, engineers, teachers, clergymen, students, actors, and artists, pursued "apparently largely professional" goals. An exciting forum for recasting cultural life, these *Räte der geistigen Arbeiter* quickly vanished, because they lost the initiative to the workers' and soldiers' councils and the revolutionary cultural ministries.[34]

Some professions with enough members in a given city also founded separate councils to work out a reform agenda. On November 12, Hamburg teachers met in a large and stormy assembly, which was dominated by "radicals," and constituted a teachers' council *(Lehrerrat)* that championed the program of creating a national school law, implementing the comprehensive school, introducing self-government, and safeguarding freedom of conscience. Although some demands might diminish their own privileges, progressive high school teachers went along "with the trend of the times" for the sake of teacher unity, hoping to establish a "teacher parliament" that might curb the bureaucracy. But this alliance between reformist secondary-school instructors and more numerous primary-school pedagogues was short-lived, since "conflicts due to differences in training, school-type, professional interests and goals, and also political affiliation" created incessant strife. Moreover, in the May 1919 Hamburg elections the Socialists obtained only 10 seats in contrast to 18 for the Democrats and 19 for nonpolitical teachers, while three still identified with the Right. Although Prussian Minister of Culture Konrad Haenisch hoped that comprehensive provincial chambers would reconcile "the manifold frictions" among different types of teachers, lower level officials were less willing to listen to advice from educators and sought to reassert their authority.[35] Overtaken by the resurgent bureaucracy, the council movement therefore left few permanent marks.

Within the professions, the revolution triggered a lively debate about future structure and ideology. A reform-minded minority demanded the immediate application of the "democratic principle." In a Berlin meeting of December 22, 1918, progressive attorneys talked of "liberation from authoritarian state supervision" by lifting localization or admission restrictions, making notary publics universal, invigorating their professional association, and creating a national lawyers' chamber in order to set a strengthened advocate profession truly free.[36] To break with "militarism and *Schulmeistertum,*" liberal philologues called for collegial administration, a voice in ministerial decisions, abolition of secret conduct lists, freedom of organization, and the creation of a comprehensive school and of parent associations. A "few socialist and democratic pedagogues" even demanded student participation, an end to chauvinist instruction, and the suspension of religious teaching.[37] Engineers who resented the "militarism [that] kept German technology from being effective" in the war insisted on greater involvement in politics as "civic duty."[38] But the moderate majority, though willing to make incremental changes, was reluctant to abandon its prior professional practice. Welcoming the "social impulse" and demanding a larger role for themselves, leading lawyers cautioned against abolishing their learned legal profession.[39] Centrist teachers, claiming to uphold the high school's "cultural mission," resisted the introduction of the *Einheitsschule,* because a unified school necessarily meant a uniform teaching career.[40] Even if some VDI chapters suggested social activism, most engineers insisted "on objectively researching questions concerning the progress of technology by carefully steering clear of any interest group policy."[41] A sizable but mute minority of traditionalists opposed all tampering with hallowed customs. Liberal lawyers abhorred socialist demands for lay justice, academic teachers rejected dangerous school experiments, and engineers retreated into a shell of sociopolitical neutrality.

Since existing organizations were slow to democratize, special activist groups emerged to champion reform more energetically. Among lawyers and judges, a "free association for law and socialism" debated the reform of the Prussian administration in May 1919 in Berlin. Because the Anwaltverein was relatively open to discussion, it took until 1921 for 800 jurists to form a "Republican Judges' League" in order to democratize the judiciary, which also included some 200 progressive attorneys.[42] Among engineers, the impulse toward stronger political engagement led to the foundation of a League of Technical Professions on November 16, 1918 in order "to obtain the participation of technology in government on the basis of the number of our members." Including all technical occupations from foreman to manager in one grand technical organization (as something of an *Ingenieurrat*), the group, renamed as the Reichsbund Deutscher Technik during 1920, endorsed "a free democratic constitution." However, the reluctance of the VDI to commit itself and the VDDI and ButaB's dislike of crossing class lines doomed it to ineffectiveness.[43]

Among teachers, the most innovative and controversial group was Paul Oestreich's Bund entschiedener Schulreformer. Founded by Berlin philologues critical of the timid Philologenverband, this League of Decided School Reformers also rejected the partisan politics of the nascent socialist teachers' union. Instead, it approached Prussian Minister of Culture Haenisch in October 1919 "so that you can see how a small but energetic circle of reformist Oberlehrer tries, without regard to pretended professional interests and only concerned with the improvement of public education *(Volksbildung),* to blaze a trail towards the new school against the resistance of its colleagues." These courageous reformers aimed at nothing less than "the moral and spiritual renewal of our instruction" in order to create a social community. Concretely, the league adopted many of the demands of the teachers' councils such as a flexible comprehensive school or collegial self-government: "In the school of the future there will be only one unified teaching profession based on achievement and not on gender or level of training." Initially, the ministry was somewhat sympathetic, but the steady stream of reform memoranda soon led Haenisch to caution "that the practical implementation of such far-reaching demands can only take place gradually." Eventually Prussian officials no longer even bothered to reply to the league's missives, because its proposals became ever more radical without concern for feasibility.[44]

When reformist pressure had little success, disadvantaged segments of the professions began to organize on their own. Among lawyers, the most downtrodden were the attorneys of the lower courts whose income was the smallest by a considerable margin. War and inflation increased their bitterness: "We *Amtsgerichtsanwälte* have lost out [and] are being deprived of our good right." Hermann Raabe of Barmen vocalized three specific gravamens: "This is apparent in our position within the lawyer code, in the remuneration of our work and finally also in the limitation of our field of endeavor." District court attorneys lacked equal representation in the chambers; they were less well paid, because fee-splitting with superior court attorneys was forbidden, furthermore, their exclusion from pleading in higher courts drastically limited their business. The organization of AG lawyers, refounded in 1920, was so persuasive in claiming equality that the Anwaltverein board endorsed the principle of "simultaneous admission at the district and superior courts." This concession incensed the LG attorneys from Prussia and Bavaria (where *Simultanzulassung* was not yet allowed) so that they founded a counterorganization in January 1921. Candidly, *Justizrat* Carstens argued that "simultaneous admission would not only be harmful for justice but also for the economic existence of the LG attorneys."[45] Split between the more prestigious superior court lawyers and the rapidly multiplying district court advocates, the legal profession failed to resolve the conflict internally. In the summer of 1922, the AG lawyers appealed to Reich Justice Minister Gustav Radbruch, who supported simultaneous admission in order to pacify the lawyers; however, the refusal of his Prussian colleague Hugo am Zehnhoff to break with the LG attorneys postponed action for several more years.[46]

The most discontented teachers were the trainees and probationers, the newly created Studienreferendare and Assessoren. The freeze for candidates who had passed their examination after April 1, 1915 reduced Prussian hiring by three-fifths (to only 200 positions annually) so that by the war's end 3224 Assessoren were waiting for a permanent job (compared to 9632 Oberlehrer), even if more than half of them were employed as auxiliary staff *(Hilfslehrer)*.[47] Under pressure from the PhVb, the Ministry of Culture, on November 28, 1918, ordered the hiring of veterans and the reduction of class size as well as of teaching loads to the prewar limits. Nonetheless, in late December a Berlin assembly of Assessoren and Referendare decided "on a closer union within the overall organization in order to represent the special interests of probationers and trainees with their official superiors."[48] Because of difficult circumstances and bleak prospects, this movement spread rapidly in the Philologenverband despite the skepticism of older colleagues. When the minister met with young teachers on February 7, 1919, Konrad Haenisch was receptive to trainee wishes for access to their evaluations, greater financial support, and pressure on the cities to fill all openings. Through the hiring of some 1009 Assessoren and other relief measures "the most pressing needs of the probationers" began to be met. Pay was being improved and the position of the probationers within the school faculty strengthened somewhat. Because it was tied to the politically sensitive need of helping veterans, which appealed to socialist sympathies and spoke through the larger Philologenverband, young teacher agitation was surprisingly successful in attenuating the sharp philologue hierarchy.[49]

Women were similarly disadvantaged, because they were either barred from the professions or treated as unequal colleagues within them. Despite a few dozen female jurisprudence students in the empire, law careers remained closed until the revolution created a new climate with the constitutional guarantee of equality. Progressive legal opinion concluded in late 1918: "It will be impossible to maintain the exclusion of women from state positions and the law profession." But male traditionalists fought a tough rearguard battle against rising pressure from women in the Reichstag (this was the one issue on which all female deputies agreed, regardless of party). Although the lawyer chamber presidents rejected their admission in 1919, the deputy assembly of the DAV discussed the issue once more in January 1922. The chief reporter, Justizrat Bieber, argued coolly that resistance was useless, but the coreporter, Dr. Ebertsheim, appealed emotionally to biological prejudice (women as the weaker sex), moral purity (exposure to criminal corruption), and overcrowding in the law profession (which would worsen with competition from women). By a vote of 45 to 20, the lawyers resolved that "women are not suited to becoming attorneys or judges" and rejected their admission as "detrimental to the legal system." However, political momentum in the Reichstag and support from the Reich Justice Minister brushed professional scruples away and on July 11, 1922, the law career was opened to women by parliamentary fiat. Because continuing prejudice made training difficult, only seventy-nine women had succeeded in becoming attorneys by January 1932.[50]

Gradually admitted to secondary school teaching from 1888 on (*pro facultate docendi* 1905), women struggled mainly for equality within their career during the Weimar Republic. By the year 1919, there were 306 female teachers and 15 principals (plus 75 probationers and 224 trainees as well as 202 auxiliary teachers) in girls' schools compared to 1111 male pedagogues and 246 directors as well as 132 members of the auxiliary staff. While women instructors were making rapid progress, men continued to predominate as administrators in Prussia![51] The constituent assembly largely accepted "woman principals and exclusively female homeroom teachers for girls schools," but the right of married women to continue teaching remained contested. Because the "goals pursued by the *Oberlehrerinnen* can be reconciled neither with the welfare of the school nor with the interests of male philologues," the Philologenverband refused to admit academically qualified women, forcing them to found their own organization. By supporting the "preservation of male influence on the faculty, direction and administration" of girls schools, the overwhelmingly male profession took a sexist stand, which was only thinly disguised by rhetoric about safeguarding the "scholarly" quality of female instruction by having at least one-half of the staff university-trained. Hoping to perpetuate the employment of men, since "female influence was a fiasco during the war," the 1922 Philologenverband principles called for complete parity in girls' schools and supported the male teachers' refusal to serve under women directors![52] However, bowing to political pressure, the Ministry of Culture kept appointing women so that they gradually began to outnumber their male colleagues in girls' schools.[53]

Democratization could also be forced upon reluctant professions from the outside. Nonacademic competitors such as legal consultants or factory technicians repeatedly appealed to public opinion to strip professionals of their privileges, challenging their market control. Because many prerogatives were based on law, the Reichstag or the appropriate state Landtag became important battlegrounds for the reshaping of the professions, especially for those internal minorities or external rival groups and laymen, who were unable to persuade professional elites. A strong current in the democratic and socialist parties wanted to popularize law by introducing lay judges, extending conciliation, and eliminating lawyers from disputes. Denouncing the incursion of laymen into the courtroom as "Bolshevik legal sabotage," legal professionals argued vigorously against the expected cost reductions (which appealed to business) and simplification of procedure (which attracted bureaucrats) in order to keep control over their own market: "Judges, attorneys and notaries need professional training like all experts" claimed a joint declaration of the Juristenbund, Anwaltverein, and Notarverein in October 1921. United resistance to "political considerations" succeeded in limiting laicization to some subordinate areas such as labor law, but populist currents were responsible for creating free legal consulting offices *(Rechtsberatungsstellen)*.[54] In the less well-established engineering field, popular pressures for solidarity with workers propelled the technicians' league (renamed ButaB) to join the proletarian free trade unions. However, an economic labor strategy could also be used for academic ends, as the hybrid creation of a "professional union," the Bund angestellter Chemiker und Ingenieure, demonstrates.[55]

Another powerful agent of reform was the Ministry—when it spoke with a united voice. Whereas engineers were relatively remote from bureaucratic control, lawyers saw the framework of their practice circumscribed by government action and teachers had even the specific content of their activity dictated. Intent on "pursuing a revolutionary policy," the Prussian minister of culture, on November 15, 1918, issued a decree against chauvinist history teaching that prohibited warmongering as well as "counter-revolutionary agitation." Although his experienced councillors predicted "great excitement . . . and strong opposition to the new government," Konrad Haenisch sent a long letter directly to the teachers, promising "full freedom of opinion and speech" but emphasizing also "the clearly defined duties of an official." Never again should the school foster nationalist hatred: "A new wind of freedom must blow through our entire education system." Still shocked by the unprecedented style and substance of the message, teachers were incensed when Haenisch addressed the pupils directly, suggesting a "school community" *(Schulgemeinde)* and student councils, based on Gustav Wynecken's Youth Movement ideas.[56] Moreover, in the name of freedom of conscience, his more radical USPD colleague, Adolf Hoffmann, cancelled school prayer, obligatory attendance at church services, and compulsory religious instruction. This well-meant attempt to foster secular democratic and socialist ideas aroused a storm of resistance not only from pedagogues, parents, and pupils, but also from churches and bourgeois parties that vitiated its intent.[57] Somewhat chastened, the new government was more cautious in reforming the internal structure of the high school piecemeal. Guided by a philologue vote for increased teacher power, the administrative instructions were rewritten in protracted negotiations to increase the importance of collegial self-government, giving faculty meetings a greater voice in school policy, class issues, and subject questions without completely overthrowing the authority of the principal.[58]

Public, legislative, and ministerial reform pressures came to a head in the national school conference of June 1920. Called in response to DLV desires for "unified organization of the training and remuneration of the entire teaching profession," the *Reichsschulkonferenz* was a gigantic hearing for the purpose of elaborating a consensus out of pedagogical reform debates, democratic and socialist promises, and bureaucratic initiatives.[59] Among the 640 representatives, primary schoolteachers (19.7 percent) and progressive forces had a clear majority, but high school teachers (8.3 percent) and other traditional interests were well enough represented to provide some counterweight. Although claiming "to take the healthy progressive ideas into account," the PhVb dug in its heels, demanding that primary schools "be limited to at most four years" and high schools ought to last nine years, "if their previous aims are to be achieved." Although Minister of Interior Erich Koch-Weser called for "calm, considered progress," opinions clashed vehemently. When philologues warned against "the decline of German education" and criticized the participation of the DLV general secretary "in questions for which he lacks the necessary training,'' Johannes Tews in turn demanded ''a six-year public school as a minimum'' as well as ''one teaching profession.'' For the Decided School Reformers, Fritz Karsen wanted ''to change the outward form completely,'' but the director of a Catholic girls school cautioned ''that our teachers are not prepared to undertake big changes'' and ''finances also do not allow it.''[60]

Beneath the clash over educational philosophy simmered a conflict about teacher professionalization. Primary pedagogues demanded university training ''in order to gain higher prestige and recognition of their equality.'' However, secondary schoolteachers insisted on academic exclusivity and sought to deflect this desire with Eduard Spranger's help into new ''teachers colleges'' *(Pädagogische Hochschulen)*. To advance their own field, teachers of German channeled mounting criticism of the irrelevance of the classical curriculum into calls for the introduction of a more modern, national, and popular high school, the *Deutsche Oberschule*. In spite of deep resentment of philological ''arrogance,'' Felix Behrend eventually worked out a compromise with professorial support in a spirit of mutual respect: a four-year common primary school would supersede various older institutions (such as special preparatory schools); the high school was to remain at nine-years but a new German type should be added (thus saving many positions for philologues); furthermore, primary schoolteachers would, in Prussia, be trained at newly founded *Pädagogische Akademien,* whereas Bavaria and Württemberg retained seminaries and Saxony, Hamburg, and some smaller states admitted them to pedagogical faculties at the university. While primary schoolteachers did raise their prestige and moved closer to professionalization, secondary school pedagogues succeeded in maintaining their own domain, superior pay, and full academic status.[61]

The dual impulse of democratization and self-defense also led to a transformation of the professional associations from loose collections of notables to tight interest groups. ''A closing of the ranks, a drawing together is the imperative of the hour,'' reflected a lawyer upon the need to speak with a united voice in the more competitive organizational politics of the Weimar Republic. For instance, attorneys debated whether to create a national lawyers' chamber with compulsory dues and welfare functions (e.g., pensions, insurance) or whether to continue the dual structure of public chambers and private associations, only strengthening voluntary initiatives. Because of the liberal tradition of the freie Advokatur, the latter won out, and the September 1919 attorneys' meeting only broadened the board to 15, with two members representing the lower courts and one the appellate and the imperial courts, respectively.[62] Another innovation was the creation of subgroups to discuss special problems such as criminal law.

The reorganization of high school teachers was more thorough. Although ''the Philologenverband cannot be a union in the strict sense'' (because it did not represent laborers), teachers could learn from them ''the closest possible coordination of all trainees, probationaries, Oberlehrer, Studienräte and directors in one powerful professional movement.'' To influence the ministry, the Landtag and the press ''with all modern agitation methods,'' Prussian pedagogues in 1919 transformed their provincial federations into one statewide ''Preußischer Philologenverein'' with local chapters and a Berlin-based executive committee. Similarly, the Vereinsverband akademisch gebildeter Lehrer Deutschlands tried to knit 38 different state and school-type associations into a tighter national philologues' association, by mediating between clashing regional demands and interest group wishes. Except for excluding women and nonacademic secondary schoolteachers, the PhVb succeeded in representing all ranks of the high school faculty, even drawing in principals, trainees, and male teachers in girls' schools through special working groups.[63] This interest group strategy paid off when Minister of Culture Haenisch tried to counter unrest about radical innovation by assuring the philologues that "in the future I shall call upon the[ir] association in the discussion of all significant high school questions, if possible." Although resenting the interference of "single persons or organizations," the ministry had to start taking the teachers' collective voice into account.[64]

Among engineers, the technical-industrial orientation of the VDI prevented structural changes and the leadership continued to be dominated by entrepreneurs and professors. Technical specialization led to a proliferation of more than forty committees, some of which grew like the *Metallausschuß* into organizations of their own. Eschewing professional neutrality, the VDDI vigorously debated the question of unionization among academic engineers in response to the technicians' ButaB, which was associated with the democratic labor movement. Because in the second largest chapter at Essen more than half of the Diplom-Ingenieure occupied "leading [industrial] positions," the board opposed the creation "of an employee section on a union basis." After heated discussions almost broke up the Verband, the winter 1919 membership meeting rejected unionization in favor of a continued professionalization strategy. Unlike the Christian "professional union" (BaCI), which combined chemists with engineers or the resurgent ButaB (with 30,143 members), the VDDI vigorously opposed the introduction of a compulsory labor exchange as detrimental to academic superiority.[65]

As a result of surprising reform pressures after November 1918, the potential for democratizing the professions was greater than is usually realized. Disappointed with the defeated empire, a sizable minority of professionals welcomed the new republic as a chance for implementing those innovations about which they had long dreamed. Stunned by the defeat, the majority of experts saw reform efforts as "grave dangers" and many traditionalists instinctively "tried to maintain the old when nothing better can be put in its place." However, the discontented and disadvantaged practitioners continued to press for changes, because the discrediting of imperial hierarchies offered a unique opportunity for remaking their profession. Moreover, the socialist and democratic forces in control of the government often represented lay or client demands and aspirations of competitors that they tried to impose by legislative fiat. Some progressive bureaucrats such as State Secretary of Culture Carl Heinrich Becker sought to abolish traditional abuses. In response to such challenges, professional elites mobilized to defend their privileges, albeit with a new language, based on service to the public and profession rather than inherited prerogative. A tough struggle within, among, and about the professions gradually ensued in the press, the parliaments, and the ministries until the reform impetus waned with the moderating political climate in succeeding years.[66]

Compared to imperial practice, the results of the reform efforts were not as negligible as is sometimes assumed. Most overt imperial restrictions such as the prohibition against women becoming lawyers and some covert authoritarian patterns such as the militarization of the schools were abolished. Internally, professions were somewhat democratized, giving disadvantaged segments such as Assessoren or AG attorneys greater representation, thus forcing the leadership to be more responsive to the needs of ordinary members. There were even a few elements of laicization such as the ban on lawyers in labor courts or the introduction of pupil and/or parent councils for schools. Yet client power never got very far, because the legal, educational, and technical consumers were not sufficiently organized. However, compared to the sanguine expectations of reformers, these partial achievements were bound to seem paltry. What were the reasons for this indifferent success?

STRUCTURAL AND IDEOLOGICAL CONSTRAINTS

Coping with labor problems as a consequence of defeat was the most immediate challenge in 1918–1919. Returning veterans needed to be reintegrated into their profession; colleagues displaced from lost territories had to be relocated; the wounded and survivors required care. Teachers had an easier time of it, because as state or local officials they could simply reclaim their old position, even if some 800 pedagogues from lost districts had to be absorbed in Prussia alone. Engineers faced transitional unemployment, but their skills were in demand for the rebuilding. In contrast, "no profession in the nation has been more affected by the war than the lawyers!" Returning attorneys "almost had to begin their practice anew," while about one thousand lawyers were likely to be displaced from former German provinces, which were now under different legal systems.[67] Professional associations tried to help by appeals in the press, mutual aid, and petitions to the government. For instance, the legal war aid committee established an employment exchange. The DAV also called upon the state to "care effectively for those lawyers or dependents that were wounded or economically harmed by the war" through public funding of poor-law cases and legal aid. Sympathetic, but hampered by precedent, the bureaucracy interpreted existing rules in favor of veterans by appointing them more quickly as notaries or by assigning them inheritance and estate cases, but opposed more far-reaching measures.[68] Eventually mutual aid, government assistance, and self-help reintegrated most veterans, but many continued resenting the lack of civilian sympathy.

Another pressing issue that hampered reform was the postwar overcrowding of universities and thereby also of the professions. In contrast to 60,225 enrolled in prewar universities, 89,312 students thronged into the lecture halls in 1919, and the flood only subsided after several years. Specifically, the number of law students more than doubled from 9896 to 23,638 in 1923, while the faculty of philosophy swelled from 27,715, to 39,439 in 1921. At the same time, attendance in the technical colleges also jumped from 11,451 to 26,224 in the winter of 1922–1923, raising the relative percentage of the 18- to 23-year-old cohort from 0.71 to 1.06 between 1910 and 1919. In retrospect, these increases seem modest, but to academics of that time they appeared dramatic, because the leap from about 30,000 actual students in the last war semester to more than 125,000 in the summer of 1923 was fourfold (Table A.1)![69] This rush into higher education was due to an upswing in long-term enrollment cycles and to short-term postwar circumstances. As the figure of 56,493 for the special 1919 interim semester indicates, more than half of the university enrollment increase came from returning veterans, who had been allowed to matriculate during the war but could not actually study. Reflected in the rise of high school graduates from 15,990 to 19,470 in 1923, there was also some growth of the student-aged cohort, which was largely filtered through the expansion of the modern secondary schools. Another cause was the continued increase in women from 6.73 percent to 10.26 percent of university students in 1923. Although the veterans could be expected to finish quickly, modern secondary-school graduates and women students would continue to crowd into the professions in years to come.[70]

With the delay of some two to three years, this enrollment boom led to a drastic rise in graduates clamoring for entry into the professions. The prewar glut of law trainees and wartime surplus of probationers quickly filled postwar government demand and reversed the "favorable prospects for the free professions" (Table A.5b). Once the hiring deficit had been eliminated, long-term structural overcrowding of attorneys resumed, because Prussian judicial positions had increased only 75 percent, whereas lawyers multiplied 2.64 times between 1872 and 1910. Growing from 12,030 in 1919 to 12,297 in 1923, the number of attorneys swelled whenever bureaucratic hiring lagged, because the practice of law was the only career alternative for students of jurisprudence aside from business. When budget problems decreased annual Prussian teacher hiring from 1009 in 1919 to 167 in 1925, the number of Assessoren more than doubled from 1909 to 4960. Though auxiliary instructors expanded from 1706 to 3837, 14.5 percent of the teaching candidates were unemployed (Table A.6b). By the year 1925, for every two tenured teachers, one aspirant was waiting in the wings, increasing the time between examination and appointment to more than eight years with new Oberlehrer averaging 35.5 years of age! While there was greater demand for academic engineers, the explosion of TH graduates also created fierce competition among them and with those less well trained.[71] Although the excess of educated men was a relative assumption rather than an absolute condition, overcrowding and consequent proletarianization became central fears of the professions during the republic.

The response of the professions to the oversupply was only partly effective. Because most practitioners associated the problem with the defeat, they could blithely assume that it would solve itself in time. Among lawyers, calls for a *numerus clausus* resurfaced: "The Prussian state must dam up the excessive flow into the careers of judge or prosecutor . . . ; at least it has to make sure that the present misery will be avoided in the future." However, the majority of attorneys still refused to abandon the free play of the market, while proponents of professional protectionism disagreed on the timing of barring access (beginning of study or career entry) and on the modalities of selection (one suggested a lottery).[72] Although an employable career, engineers faced an even greater influx of fresh graduates, they did not address the overcrowding problem directly and proposed no specific remedy. The VDI rather obliquely opposed the foundation of another

TH in Thuringia, claiming "there is no need whatsoever for such a new educational institution," because available resources did not suffice to fund the existing institutes adequately. Convinced that "somehow the influx must be halted, if hopeless conditions are to be avoided," the VDDI put its efforts instead into job placement for all academic professions.[73]

Because the labor market for teachers was virtually controlled by the state, the "poor job" prospects for candidates were more obviously amenable to collective action. Philologenverband statisticians Wilhelm Oberle and Eduard Simon wrote numerous articles "on the overcrowding of the high-school teaching career," or "the lack of prospects in philological studies," lamenting: "The flooding of our heavily chastened fatherland with an academic proletariat is one of the greatest dangers for the country as well as for the people involved." Already in the spring of 1919 the chairman of the Vereinsverband akademisch gebildeter Lehrer issued a formal *"warning against entering our profession,"* echoed a year later by the government. Admitting in the Landtag that "these alarms are little or no help," Prussian ministerial director Richard Jahnke, nonetheless, rejected general closure.[74] Whereas tenured philologues urged the conversion of cheap auxiliary positions into expensive permanent jobs, the probationers demanded a *numerus clausus* based on seniority. In order to deal with the growing numbers of candidates, the Ministry of Culture preferred meritocratic selection instead. The bureaucratic salary law of May 7, 1920 demanded that all future officials be entered into state lists with only so many admitted as would be needed five years later. Because of the outcry of the Assessoren that "the demands of the different examination offices are unequal," the Prussian government centralized the testing procedure through a new Landesprüfungsamt. After philologues had become resigned to the inevitable, the *Anwärterordnung* of 1924 finally clarified the procedure by accepting only one-half of a cohort into the official list with appointment proceeding chronologically, and within years on the basis of "aptitude." The rest were simply pushed into private teaching or into a different career.[75]

More devastating yet was the impact of the hyperinflation. This unparalleled deterioration of the exchange value—until 1 dollar was worth 4.1 trillion marks—appeared as a confusing process, creeping during the war, openly galloping in the winter 1919–1920, slowing until the summer of 1921, and then rising exponentially until November 1923. Professionals clearly realized the disastrous effects of the rapid loss of buying power, which made "consumption decline. . . . levelled pay and salaries," and shrank "rent income . . . dividend yield . . . industrial profit [or] capital." However, the causes and thereby the cures remained obscure so that many blamed "the burdens of the Treaty of Versailles" for the imbalance of German public finances.[76] Perceptive observers like the economist Franz Eulenburg analyzed the "social impact of the currency situation" with greater lucidity. Because "all creditor property, such as deposits, savings, mortgages or government bonds, has lost its entire value, as have pension funds, based on insurance premiums, retirement pay, social security or whatever," he called the hyperinflation "the greatest expropriation of history." Although most strata suffered in one way or another, "hardest hit were probably the free professions [and] higher officials plus officers. For them ownership of capital was an important part of their actual income." Eulenburg did not mince words: "They are in danger of degradation which has already occurred among some individuals.'' Even the engineers who were somewhat shielded by the postwar boom, suffered from ''the devaluation of intellectual labor.'' Therefore, the professions were the chief victims of this ''social crisis of the educated strata.''[77]

Lawyers faced particular difficulties, because the state regulated their fees but did not share their risks. When the inflation began to accelerate in the summer of 1919, even the reluctant DAV board agreed that until the Gebührenordnung was revised, ''attorneys must help themselves by negotiating their fees'' and regularly demanding a 50 percent surcharge. By the end of the year, 103 local chapters with more than 8000 members were resorting to this makeshift remedy.[78] However, when the ''situation continued to deteriorate,'' the Anwaltverein petitioned the Reichsrat for ''remuneration appropriate to the general economic situation ,'' doubling fees and paying poor-law cases out of public funds. Although Reich Justice Minister Eugen Schiffer admitted the ''noticeable plight of attorneys,'' lack of funds and public insistence on ''affordable litigation'' limited the increase of fees to between 30 percent (cases less than 60 marks) and 100 percent (more than 3400 marks) in the bill of December 12, 1919.[79] The agitation briefly died down, but the erosion of buying power renewed complaints in the spring of 1921 and made fee reform the central concern of the legal profession for the next two years. In order to regulate supplements, the Reichstag law of July 6, 1921 recognized their legality, but rejected automatic indexing, so that at ''each considerable change in the economic situation'' the chambers had to petition jointly for adjustment. Although the fear of pricing themselves out of the market made many Kammern reluctant to file for increases, eventually this cumbersome procedure was invoked more than ten times![80]

Subsequent inflation rapidly outstripped the administrative decree mechanism, threatening the very survival of the legal profession. Doubling between 1917 and 1921, the total number of litigation cases had once again declined by one-third as of 1923 (Table 2.1). A special DAV delegate meeting in Berlin in the fall of 1922 and an emergency congress *(Notanwaltstag)* in Weimar during early 1923 urgently debated the ''attorneys' plight.'' Because ''devaluation gallops or drives a car . . . while legislation runs behind on foot,'' lower court advocates especially were beginning to abandon their careers: ''Savings have been used up, people live from advances, but new cases are getting scarcer and many fresh colleagues as well as older Justizräte have to pawn or sell their valuables, jewelry and even the dresses of their wives!'' Although on February 2 a sympathetic Reichstag finally accepted state reimbursement for poor-law cases, the Reichsrat continued to reject ''appropriate remuneration,'' which would have ended fee regulation and allowed more flexible bargaining between clients and counsel.[81] Because bill collection lagged behind and legislative fee adjustments were ''always too little and too late,'' the suffering of marginal practitioners ''reached a level not matched by any other social group.'' They were simply unable to make ends meet. ''It is no exaggeration that *thousands of German attorneys and their families face hunger.''* Attorney C. Spohr warned the minister directly: ''The German legal profession stands at the brink of total collapse.'' Once again the law of August 18, 1923 was out of date before its ink was dry, leaving attorneys to look for more radical solutions such as the eight points proposed by the Berlin Anwaltverein. Finally,

Table 2.1. Evolution of Legal Business[82]

Year	Total cases	Number of lawyers	Cases per capita
1891	5,023,256	5,317	944.8
1901	5,778,495	6,800	849.8
1911	7,074,721	10,817	654.0
1913	7,786,267	12,297	633.0
1915	4,049,502	13,024	311.0
1917	2,870,535	12,393	231.6
1919	3,722,810	12,030	309.5
1921	5,774,176	12,276	470.4
1923	4,063,955	12,727	319.3
1925	10,333,974	13,537	763.4
1927	10,818,394	14,894	726.4
1929	14,522,578	15,846	916.5
1931	16,095,806	17,184	936.7
1933	8,833,125	19,208	460.9
1935	8,071,595	18,780	429.8
1937	7,333,586	17,109	428.6
1939	4,953,244	14,734	336.2

Justice Minister Radbruch conceded the indexing of fees in the twelfth emergency decree of September 27, 1923, just when the inflation was reaching its dizzying peak. Coming only when the specter was to vanish within weeks, this effective measure preserved one-third of prewar income.[83]

Although their salaries were guaranteed by the state, teachers faced a similar crisis, because pay increases inevitably failed to keep pace with rising prices. To compensate for the loss of more than half of their prewar buying power, the Philologenverband demanded in October 1919

> a thorough reform of remuneration which adequately takes into account today's inflation and galloping rise in prices, corresponds completely to the long, expensive and difficult training as well as the responsible work of higher officials and puts an end to the threatening loss of esteem and the material degradation of the intellectual professions.

Moreover, probationers insisted on "equal pay for equal work," whereas trainees demanded increases in the few marks of their token support. Worried about "the political implications" of teachers' discontent, Minister of Culture Haenisch agreed to the necessity of reform because he was under massive pressure by primary-school pedagogues "to bring their salaries close to the Oberlehrer scale."[84] Directed toward helping the more numerous and radical elementary schoolteachers, the provisional Prussian law of April 1920 "deeply disappointed" high school philologues, because the salary of their inferiors was being raised dramatically from 47 percent to 74 percent of their own! While accepting the simplification of pay grades and the softening of barriers, Prussian philologues vigorously protested against their lack of advancement possibilities *(Beförderungsstellen)* and the inadequate pay for Assessoren. However, the paper avalanche of 65 protests by local Philologenvereine was in vain. The final law of December 17, 1920 was "a great defeat'' for Prussian philologues and ''an incredible injustice,'' because lack of solidarity among bourgeois parties achieved only marginal improvements for secondary-school principals.[85]

The extent of the ''enormous decline in the living standard'' of philologues emerges from several regional surveys taken in Berlin, the Rhineland, and Hanover. After dropping from 533 to 195 marks per month, average pay no longer sufficed to maintain a *bildungsbürgerliche* living standard, which two-thirds could only keep ''at the expense of their health and family'' (Table 2.2). Many were able to afford meat merely once a week, no longer had milk for their children, and were forced to give up all extras such as coffee and alcohol. Purchasing clothes and furniture was impossible, and everything grew threadbare. There was neither enough money for proper health care nor for the education of the young who had to lower their aspirations and earn a living immediately. Participation in cultural life, concerts, and so on ''declined extraordinarily,'' and continuing scholarly self-improvement was out of the question. Between two-thirds and three-quarters of the households let their servants go, thereby ''impairing the health of the wife.'' The great majority took on additional jobs such as private lessons; if they could not find employment, they had to sell off valuables (two-fifths) or go into debt (one-third). Because ''these efforts to increase income strained the psychological, intellectual and physical powers of the individual,'' eventually they also had to have ''deleterious effects on the quality of teaching.''[86]

Impassioned protests, press releases, and lobbying of Landtag deputies in favor of ''an indexing of salaries to the value of the mark'' were of little avail. After renewed instability in 1921, special supplements were quickly overtaken by additional inflation so that by April 1922 real income had dropped to 165 marks a month. In spite of subsequent corrections, the fluctuating take-home pay deteriorated in comparison with blue-collar wages. With insufficient revenues, left-wing cabinets gave political priority to the preservation of buying power for the more numerous lower civil service grades, because these incomes were closer to the survival margin. The greater salary loss of the higher ranks narrowed pay differ-

Table 2.2. Inflation and Philologue Salaries

Year	Monthly pay	Nominal increase	Real salary
1913	533		533.0
April 1920	1,963	3.68	188.3
Jan. 1921	2,304	4.32	195.4
Aug.	2,631	4.94	197.4
Oct.	4,300	8.06	285.9
Jan. 1922	4,467	8.38	218.9
April	5,680	10.65	164.9
July	11,110	20.84	200.9
Oct.	43,321	81.28	199.0
Jan. 1923	202,020	379.02	176.4
April	530,790	995.85	181.7
July	7,657,000	14,365.85	228.8
Sept.	3,705,000,000	6,951,219.50	247.0
Dec.	274.5	0.51	274.5

entials between levels XI and III from 4 : 1 to 2 : 1 (1913–1922), so that it apparently no longer paid to be educated. By the year 1923, the philologue agitation did result in the creation of the new rank of Oberstudienrat as assistant principal in the larger schools or as head teacher for special subjects. Although it improved long-term advancement possibilities, the concession was cold comfort in the "still increasing economic plight." Only when the inflation had run its course did some semblance of order return, with the average salary pegged at 274.5 marks per month, but at one-half of their prewar earnings, as disappointed teachers were quick to point out.[87]

In the long run, reform of the professions was hindered not just by material problems but also by ideological preconceptions inherited from the past. Virtually all adults active in the first years of the Weimar Republic were trained and initiated into their professions during the empire. Though highly competent, they shared a largely illiberal imprinting as academics, combining a disdain for politics with social elitism and cultural nationalism. Their notions of what it meant to be a lawyer, high school teacher, or engineer had also been formed under more fortunate circumstances.[88] No wonder that many older professionals who had been titled by the monarchy were dismayed: "The peace which offered a modest but secure basis for our scholarly and professional activity [has been] disturbed and we stand now in midst of ruins." Because "boundless reform plans" threatened established practices, it seemed that "even intellectual values are in jeopardy." Younger university graduates with less emotional attachment to the Kaiser were more open to new departures, but they also expected enough stability to pursue their career and make some modest improvements. "In struggle and hard work we will have to forge a new future." Although the imperial legacy initially hastened reform, in the chaotic republican present it eventually assumed a nostalgic glow of *die gute alte Zeit,* which made democratization difficult. Therefore, the best the republic could hope for was a pragmatic willingness "to fulfill the justified demands" for change "without eliminating the lawyer," abolishing the academic teacher, or replacing the engineer.[89]

When confronted with Weimar realities, imperial leadership expectations led to the perception of a loss of social status. Collectively, professionals seemed to have become less important than capitalists, labor leaders, or politicians. Individually, each profession also discovered particular disappointments. Although some attorneys were politically or socially prominent, lawyers complained that "the legal profession is not at all liked by the public." The old prejudice against the "perverters of law" resurfaced in criticism of pointless legal rhetoric *(Rabulistik)* so that the Leipzig DAV chapter sued the publisher Georg Hirzel for slander.[90] Considered as "second-class academics," high school teachers felt unappreciated: "The teaching profession has never had it easy. Parents cannot forgive it for giving bad grades to untalented or lazy pupils and graduates consider school hours largely a waste of time." When the Prussian cabinet classified the Studienrat title as purely honorific and decided to abolish it along with other imperial distinctions, it required a long struggle to get it reinstated as part of the office *(Amtsbezeichnung)*![91] Engineers in turn felt frustrated by the gap between their aspirations and achievements. Graduates of THs bitterly resented the proliferation of their diploma to such unexpected occupations as "*Dipl.* cow milker." In order to counter the "disinterest of the daily press" in technology, the VDI created media committees that directed a "stream of technical information" to the papers. However, the long-standing campaign to get more engineers into local government and break the legal monopoly yielded "little success," because technicians hesitated to pursue a public career and the electorate did not consider them particularly qualified for public office.[92]

Traditional practices and self-images also hampered adaptation to postwar circumstances. Although the plight of the attorneys was a powerful incentive for specialization, the inherited conception of free advocacy effectively barred such innovation. Reformers argued rationally that "an equal and comprehensive mastery of *all* areas of law is impossible today"; legal specialization already existed in some areas like patent law, therefore the only change needed was announcing a specialty in public. However, traditionalists countered emotionally: "We ought rather to renounce the term *Fachanwälte!* We shall proudly continue to be advocates of law and want to reject all advertising in the future." Although there was some controversy over how to prove competence and how to communicate it to the public, the key dispute centered on the conception of the lawyer as a generalized professional or as a specialized expert. Barring all advertisement seemed closer to disinterested public service, because even announcing a specialty on the letterhead smacked of business. After a heated debate on the need "to change professional ethics," the lawyers' congress in Leipzig rejected specialization together with other insidious innovations like contingency fees *(Erfolgshonorar)*: "In the most dangerous of times . . . the legal profession has, with impressive unanimity, adhered to the basic tenets and to the constitutional structure to which German lawyers owe their success during prosperity and their strength in adversity."[93] The instinctive traditionalism of the majority of small-town generalists triumphed over the reformism of an innovative urban minority.

The ideal of "the academically trained high-school teacher" also inhibited major restructuring. Aware that "today a new type of pedagogue must be defined," philologues were unsure whether to become " 'cosmopolitan educators' or 'state instructors'—the right expression has yet to be coined." Although "educating" was growing more important, "the noblest task of those concerned with the welfare of the high schools is to keep alive a spirit of true scholarship among the Oberlehrer." Even if the Weimar government had less money than its imperial predecessor to support refresher courses, sabbaticals, and publications, participation in scholarly discourse was essential for philologue self-consciousness and superiority. Reform pedagogues argued that "the high-school teacher should not only do research, but also be able to teach and educate. Hence a thorough study of pedagogy is inescapable." However, students shunned education courses and succeeded in defeating their mandatory imposition in subsequent years. To maintain "the uniqueness of their profession," philologues opposed a practical apprenticeship before matriculation and rejected a common introduction in a pedagogical academy. Because a leading minority continued to publish and aspired to university posts, the PhVb insisted on "a differentiated teaching occupation," which was split along academic lines.[94] Although material motives did play a role, the opposition to pedagogical innovation chiefly derived from the traditional scholarly self-definition that rested on such central cultural values as *Wissenschaft*.

Fascinated with the infinite possibilities of technical progress, engineers cultivated a self-conception that was more open to the future. But resentment against "the slighting of technology" in military and bureaucratic circles was profound. Therefore, engineers tended to be susceptible to flattery, welcoming, for instance, Oswald Spengler's characterization of technicians as "knowing priests of the machine" and "actual lords" of modern industry. Especially Richard von Moellendorff's celebration of "efficiency" as a central principle for restructuring modern society and the economy attracted a following in the immediate postwar chaos. "Economically and politically indifferent," technical efficiency might become "a decisive weight on the scale of values, a neutral point in the mechanism of societal motives." Although such social Taylorism appeared to promise a third way between capitalism and socialism, technocratic *Gemeinwirtschaft* quickly ran aground politically when the Reichswirtschaftsrat turned out to be ineffective. In order to counteract the widespread disdain for technology, some academic engineers began to emphasize its "cultural value" as a strategy for at last achieving acceptance by the older cultivated professions: "Technology cannot be separated from culture," forming "its basis, support, handmaiden, distributor and participant."[95]

A final constraint was the inadequate organization of the professions. Instead of yielding to democratizing impulses, the restructured associations sought to develop a corporatist alternative. Because "there is actually no organ which could speak for all . . . attorneys," Max Friedländer called for the transformation of lawyers' chambers into a mandatory "representation of professional interests," culminating in a *Reichsanwaltkammer*. But since they did not want to bargain with corporate representatives of the legal profession, the justice ministries balked, and the dual structure of compulsory chambers, only loosely coordinated by their presidents, and the voluntary DAV continued.[96] Engineers also picked up the chamber idea, because it promised to articulate the "professional" interests of the white-collar employees who considered themselves to be neither managers nor workers. Promoted by the VDDI, the issue was raised by a resolution from the Lenne chapter in the VDI committee on "professional questions," which was itself a concession to the agitation. However, in his report K. Mühlmann doubted "the necessity of such a law" because it would "carry new class tensions into the technical professions" and seemed inappropriate for engineers. In June 1921, a reluctant VDI board buried the initiative because of much local opposition and only vaguely "support[ed] the creation of chambers for consulting engineers."[97] Ultimately neither lawyers nor engineers reached their corporatist goals during the Weimar Republic.

Although chambers originated among the free professions, Halle secondary schoolteachers also petitioned on May 15, 1919 for "the creation of provincial *Oberlehrerkammern* as legal representation." Using ministerial support for comprehensive provincial councils, traditionalist philologues tried to turn them into corporate self-governments, which were authorized to "discuss all important questions of higher instruction, legal and bureaucratic rules and wishes or complaints." In some cities like Berlin, progressive philologues initially cooperated with their lower level colleagues in one council; but fear of being outvoted by their more radical competitors made the majority of secondary schoolteachers quickly retreat into separate chambers.[98] In September 1919, the Philologenverband "rejected the submerging of philologues in a general council'' and called for their own chamber ''to be heard in an advisory capacity before the announcement of all important regulations and decrees and to have a right of co-determination in decisions about the administration and functioning of the school.'' When Socialists and reformists (BeS) complained about ''the terrorism of the reactionary majority,'' the ministry correctly defined the issue as ''a question of power.'' Confronted with provincial philologue chambers, the government stuck to the principle of ''having all teachers represented . . . not only those who belong to some professional organization.'' Because Minister Otto Boelitz refused to construe democracy as mandatory consultation, the war of memoranda eventually killed the philologues' ''wish for a recognized professional representation'' by postponing action. However, traditionalists could take comfort in defeating radical teachers' councils or DLV unionization impulses and plugging a source of further reform.[99]

The failure of corporatism encouraged issue-oriented coalition building with more powerful allies. Overcoming their rivalry, lawyers cooperated with other legal occupations such as judges in general questions concerning the judicial system. In economic matters, they joined the free professions in demanding an exemption from the sales tax before the Reichwirtschaftsrat.[100] Because of their intense competition, high school teachers would rarely collaborate with primary-school pedagogues in a common cause. Philologues preferred to work through the Bund höherer Beamter, founded on October 8, 1918, ''to ensure that the interests of higher officials are sufficiently taken into account . . . especially concerning pay and legal position.'' Eventually including Protestant pastors, higher administrative and technical bureaucrats as well as judges, the BhB first tried to agitate within the one-million-member Beamtenbund (which represented middle and lower level officials). However, when it became clear that their economic interests collided over pay scales and political preferences clashed over democratization, the higher level officials withdrew in March 1920 with ''sharpest protests.'' Representing only about 100,000 members by 1924, the Reichsbund höherer Beamter compensated for its numerical inferiority by greater prestige and close ties to the German People's Party (DVP).[101] Engineers in turn cooperated in various technical groupings such as the German committee for technical schools (DATSCH), which tried to improve technical training, or the Deutsche Verband technisch-wissenschaftlicher Vereine (DVtwV) that promoted the general interests of technology.[102]

Some professionals also strove to increase their influence by banding together in an academic pressure group. Emerging out of a fraternity war aid committee (called Akademischer Hilfsbund), the National Committee for the Academic Professions sought to rally professionals in one comprehensive organization. Combining university students, professors, and graduates would ''unify'' their voice and lend it ''greater force.'' Because the revolution ''tried to denigrate us academics, the leaders of the German workers of the mind, [by turning us] into tools,'' A. Pinkerneil called on professionals and their organizations to join hands in order to reclaim their endangered leadership. The Reichsausschuß akademischer Berufsstände therefore tried ''to become a power'' in order to represent the ''social and cultural interests of professionals'' as effectively as labor unions did for the proletariat. Claiming that ''the economic position of academics has never been as poor,'' the council threatened that discontent would make professionals embrace irresponsible politics. In contrast to resounding pronouncements, the actual work of the Reichsausschuß consisted of serving as a modest clearing house for advice on academic careers. Because the differences between the various professions ran too deep to be bridged, this pan-academic initiative achieved only marginal success, much to the disappointment of academic engineers. A similar attempt by Otto Everling in 1923 to create a ''protective cartel of the suffering cultural strata of Germany'' was hardly any more successful.[103]

The failure of cooperation left the professions little choice but to bring ''the plight of intellectual workers'' directly before the public. The ''proletarianization'' of the professions and ''the underestimation and undervaluation of intellectual work'' were too diffuse for concerted action until the prestigious Verein für Sozialpolitik addressed them at its annual meeting in 1922.[104] In the keynote address, the sociologist Alfred Weber defined *geistige Arbeiter* as ''those strata which we today call writers and scholars, artists, higher officials, clergymen . . . to a certain degree also doctors, lawyers and such . . . as well as perhaps technicians, engineers, leading employees and the like.'' The social cohesion of the Bildungsbürgertum was threatened by the erosion of its economic base. Put more bluntly, ''the spiritual is in danger of becoming an appendage of the material.'' In the inconclusive debate on potential remedies such as unionization, state subsidy, or self-help, Weber suggested combining work and thought in an *Arbeitsintellektualismus,* implying a radical recasting of professionalism without actually using the term.[105] The meeting did succeed in ''rousing public opinion'' sufficiently to have the Reichswirtschaftsrat create a special subcommittee on the plight of intellectual workers. Its tame recommendations for lawyers and engineers such as freedom of coalition and fee reform rejected more drastic remedies such as simultaneous admission or chambers of technology. Eventually struggling journalists, writers, artists, and musicians captured the hearings, narrowing their scope and making them irrelevant to the professions at large.[106]

In the initial years of the Weimar Republic, the obstacles to reform and democratization were therefore daunting. The external pressures are well known: Defeat, revolution, punitive peace, quasi-civil war within, undeclared war without, strikes and social strife, inflation, as well as the occupation of the Ruhr unsettled professionals. Moreover, they created specific problems of reintegrating veterans, overcrowding universities, and impoverishing academics. No wonder that survival and a return to some kind of normalcy had higher priority than a new beginning. The internal hindrances were, however, also considerable. Formed in the empire and hardened in the war, the outlook of professionals was hardly cosmopolitan, egalitarian, or progressive. Therefore, corporatist solutions, ensuring collective professional power, were more attractive than unionist alternatives of solidarity between workers of the ''fist'' and of the ''mind.'' The organized voice of practitioners was just strong enough to bar changes but too weak to impose its own vision. Only a minority viewed the revolution as an opportunity for remedying long-standing abuses within the professions.[107] Most professionals reacted defensively to the social republic, seeking to maintain and enhance their imperial gains instead of sharing them with a democratic state or a lay clientele. The blockage of reform was therefore not unalterably predetermined, but rather the result of powerful constraints, operating in and on the professions.

INTEREST GROUP PROFESSIONALISM

At the end of 1923 Julius Magnus, the editor of the *Juristische Wochenschrift,* reflected on the travails of the early Weimar Republic: "*A year of suffering!* For eight years Germany had to use this heading for each preceding year, hoping steadily that it would be the last." The democratization of the professions could hardly have been attempted under more traumatic circumstances, because "next to pensioners, the German academics have felt the great misery most strongly." But the defeat and the collapse of the old order also made reform imperative. "A new justice had to be created, while keeping the old forms and observing the old laws." In contrast to the "complete breakdown and total destruction" in Soviet Russia, Weimar reformers faced the perhaps more difficult task of "rebuilding within the existing structures."[108] Yet initially, the prospects for democratization seemed promising, because progressive professionals, discontented subgroups, and interested parts of the public pressured the government for substantial change. Although their achievements, especially in abolishing imperial restrictions, were greater than is sometimes supposed, they fell far short of expectations in overthrowing hierarchies and increasing lay influence. Structural, ideological, and organizational constraints blunted the impetus and gave the entrenched elites a chance to regroup. Becoming marginally more open, egalitarian, and responsive under pressure, the professions turned into efficient interest groups instead. Faced with sociopolitical obstacles, associations mobilized their members, nationalized their organization, created business offices, bombarded the press, and lobbied the parties more effectively.[109]

Consequently, political democratization remained incomplete. Even if few professionals were revolutionary, most were realistic enough to understand that the monarchy had failed and that they had to come to terms with the new order somehow. Recoiling from violence and expropriation, most members of the Bildungsbürgertum tried, like the well-known attorney Max Hachenburg, "to find the right middle" course of liberty coupled with order. Whereas individual responses varied considerably, the collective actions of the associations suggest that the professions were reluctant to take a stand on the principles of the new order. Although lawyers tried to work within the constitution, teachers tended only to be loyal to the state, irrespective of its current form. Typically, the League of Higher Officials (Bund höherer Beamter, BhB), and with it the philologues, refused to strike, even against the reactionary Kapp putsch! Admitting "a certain opposition to the tendencies of the new state," engineers denounced this general strike as "a night-frost on the buds of" economic recovery and opposed the eight-hour day as excessive leveling.[110] The distinctive tone of their respective journals indicates that beyond academic disdain for politics, attorneys tended to be somewhat more liberal, teachers more nationalist, and engineers more antisocialist. Because of the official neutrality of the associations, small political groups formed within some professions to defend the republic or promote socialism, leading to the creation of nationalist and völkisch counterorganizations to denounce them.[111]

In contrast to domestic reticence, the professions were all the more vociferous about foreign policy. Academics unanimously rejected the *Diktat* of the Treaty of Versailles and welcomed John M. Keynes's indictment as revisionist "proof that the peace treaty rests on falsehood and demonstration of the impossibility of fulfilling it." While the Philologenverband mobilized its members for the frontier plebiscites, the VDI protested "against Entente despotism," which demanded the technical plans of ship machinery, forbade the building of heavy diesel engines, and so on. In October 1920, the RDT also appealed "to the technicians of the world" against reparations: "The coal deliveries to the Entente threaten Germany's technical economy with complete collapse, leading to destruction of culture as well as hunger and suffering for millions."[112] The Ruhr occupation met with united condemnation. While lawyers claimed that "the law of all nations has been violated," all levels of teachers fumed about the threat to German culture, and engineers claimed: "Violence interferes roughly in your work and threatens the basis of your creativity." Calling on their members to resist passively, professional associations like the VDI created assistance funds for jailed colleagues in the "incursion area."[113] In pronouncements on general politics, the professionals shared the educated middle-class consensus, stressing order at home and nationalism abroad.

The professionals' skepticism of democracy was also based on the perceived inadequacy of government response to their particular needs. Although lawyers had a direct line to one desk in the Ministry of Justice, their wishes were often overshadowed by the desires of the judges and prosecutors who, after all, were state officials. Attorneys were incensed by what they considered an insufficient defense of their work domain *(Arbeitsgebiet)* against incursions of laymen and of mandatory arbitration.[114] Teachers were "deeply hurt and agitated" about the "unprecedented and boundless accusations" of Socialist Minister of Culture Konrad Haenisch against philologues for blocking reform. To restore confidence, they "must demand that in the future the minister consult their representatives in all important decisions . . . and, above all, cease undermining their authority in front of the pupils and diminishing the reputation of their profession." After this initial row, high school teachers had Studienrat R. Lange and then board member Felix Behrend appointed to the Prussian Ministry of Culture to represent their views. However, when the latter was disavowed by the Philologenverband due to the lack of results, "strong tension between the ministry and the association" once again blocked cooperation.[115] Having no special ministry to address (because the Ministry of Public Works only dealt with construction specialists), engineers resented political and managerial attention to the laboring masses instead of their better qualified superiors. Although professional organizations demanded a formal right of codetermination, the ministries were willing to listen only when it suited their purposes. Even when the bureaucracy intended to help, its suggestions were all too often vetoed by the finance minister or by the cabinet due to lack of funds or for general political reasons. "Some say that the monarchy perished because of its mistakes," AG attorney Hawlitzky grumbled in the summer of 1923. "The same will be true of the Republic, if the government continues to act in this way."[116]

The combination of political turmoil, professional problems, and government inaction inhibited the bonding of the professions to the Weimar Republic. Politicized somewhat against their will, professionals reacted to the new system in several characteristic ways: Impressed by the failure of the empire and frustrated by their lack of internal influence, a minority took a democratic or socialist stance. The young, urban, secular, and disadvantaged welcomed the republic—only to be somewhat disappointed by its lack of radical reform. The established majority, crushed by the defeat, was skeptical of democracy but loyal to the state as long as it provided enough law and order to carry out their work. An older minority of small-town and often bigoted practitioners hearkened nostalgically back to the empire in which it had received more respect. The youngest beginners who had been indoctrinated with pan-German rhetoric and often not fought in the war, dreamed of more radical right-wing departures in a völkisch anti-Semitic key. The Weimar Republic had difficulty in winning the crucial allegiance of the professional centrists who controlled the associations, because its initial social reform efforts were seen as antiprofessional. Moreover, the left-center cabinets responded inadequately to the first flare-up of the material, ideological, and organizational crisis of the professions. Nonetheless, the partial successes of the associations in winning some concessions created the potential for a positive working relationship between the professions and a more stable democracy in the future.

3

Regaining Professional Stability

During the mid-1920s, economic recovery began to brighten the political prospects of the Weimar Republic. The annual VDI report concluded that "the stabilization of the currency in late 1923 liberated the German people from the enervating tensions of speculation and, in spite of remaining obstacles, made it slowly possible for the productive forces of the economy to gather strength." In early 1926, the attorney Julius Magnus became hopeful that the slow improvement of the diplomatic situation would moderate "the dire consequences of the so-called 'peace treaty. . . .' Though the present is still burdened by excessive unemployment for manual and intellectual workers, business, industry and trade look with more optimism into the future." Three years later the philologue W. Bolle interpreted current "fermentation and division" as an "attempt to build and forge ahead politically, economically, socially and culturally," signaling a new beginning for high school teachers.[1] Such representative statements indicate that many practitioners shared in the "golden twenties" recovery, which has so often been celebrated in literature and film. Returning prosperity enabled some experts to strive to regain a measure of professional stability.

The somber undertone of these reflections, nonetheless, betrays a fundamental insecurity fed by resentment of the cost of stabilization. Because the pro-debtor revaluation sealed their inflation losses, attorneys protested against the "further erosion and weakening of the position of the legal profession." Their sanguine hopes of recovering their wealth were "bitterly disappointed" by the reduction of fees, the shrinking of their work sphere, and renewed overcrowding: "The swelling number of jurists bodes ill for the future."[2] High school teachers paid for the restoration of public finances by the dismissal of hundreds of their colleagues: Since "we have to economize, it is a bitter necessity that we must reduce personnel in education," Prussian Minister of Culture Boelitz justified the cuts. Even engineers, the most direct beneficiaries of the economic upturn, worried about "relapses in convalescence" that interrupted the recovery. Because the fiscally popular "rationalization" movement put nonessential personnel out of work, technicians worried: "Our productive work is dangerously restricted by external and internal politics. Need knocks at the door of many a colleague."[3] While associations habitually complained in order to hold the attention of their members, the depth and magnitude of their concerns indicate the continued existence of real problems. Although some professionals enjoyed the glitter of success, for many others the promise of Weimar stabilization was at best a half-truth.

The period of "deceptive stability" has therefore left a profoundly ambivalent image. "For one historical moment," the writer Stefan Zweig remembered, "it seemed as if our afflicted generation might know a normal life again." Whereas textbooks still perpetuate the "roaring twenties" cliché, Weimar's "cabaret" atmosphere rather suggests a delirious dance on a volcano about to erupt. In contrast to the dramatic inflation or depression crises, most scholars have neglected the "pause in the succession of catastrophes," because relative normality seems less interesting. However, some economic historians are starting to probe the political effects of devaluation for the causes of the ensuing disaster, and specialists in electoral politics are beginning to analyze the mid-1920s as a source of the later disintegration of bourgeois allegiances.[4] Due to the discrepancy between objective indications of recovery and subjective feelings of frustration, the role of the professions during the mid-1920s remains confused. Scholars mainly disagree on the extent of the improvement in the material situation and on the depth of antirepublican instincts of professionals.[5] The complex relationship between economic security and political orientation suggests the dual question: How successful was the professions' quest for stability and how sincere was their conversion to the republic?

THE PRICE OF NORMALCY

After four years of war and five years of postwar chaos, most Germans wanted, above all, to return to some kind of normalcy. For professionals, this seemingly self-evident desire for stability meant the modernization of training and the recasting of certification to bring manpower supply and demand cycles under control. It also implied the improvement of income to provide an adequate living and halt the erosion of social status. Moreover, it signified the removal of obstacles to regular practice and the resumption of normal work. At the same time, it necessitated a rethinking of professional self-images within democratic values. Finally, it required a reorganization of the collective pursuit of interests, in the hope that greater efficiency might lead to success within the framework of the republic.[6] Because the collapse of the Wilhelmian hierarchy had discredited authority, the professions had to develop a new identity within the social and democratic context of Weimar. Compared to postwar chaos, the precarious economic renewal and the political stabilization of the mid-1920s provided more propitious circumstances for the resolution of professional difficulties.

Not given to startling departures, professionals began to modernize their training by incorporating advancements of knowledge and changes in practice. Because jurisprudence was dominated by academic theory and bureaucratic experience, lawyers tried to inject a practitioner perspective into the canon of civil, criminal, and state law. Despite some concessions to the "incredible expansion of material," the importance of socioeconomic topics, and the introduction of practical instruction, major reform was prevented by entrenched professorial and official interests. From a conservative perspective, the combination of scholarly preparation and bureaucratic apprenticeship was the result of "centuries of experience in how best to train jurists."[7] When primary schoolteachers demanded academization of instruction, philologues, intent on maintaining their superiority in pay and prestige, only conceded separate and unequal pedagogical academies in Prussia. According to a British observer, the root of the conflict was the "obstinate determination to look upon the teacher in the Elementary School as a different sort of being" of inferior standing.[8] More constructive was the introduction of additional pedagogy at the university and the Rhenish creation of central district seminars to systematize practical training according to the principle, "first practice and then theory." Because these groups of about 20 Referendare flexibly combined teaching experience with pedagogical reflection and subject matter didactics, these *Bezirksseminare* became popular in reconciling philological with didactic imperatives.[9] Among engineers, the professor of mechanics, Heinrich Aumund, proposed far-reaching improvements along the lines of a "higher school for technology and economy" in order to increase practical relevance. More modestly, the Prussian reform authorized only the establishment of external TH institutes, the dissertation right for the general departments, and equality in training science teachers. However, the Ministry of Culture also combined technical sections into four faculties and revised the examination system to create more uniformity and choice, thereby further approximating university status.[10] Although fiscal constraints shelved other plans, commercial pressure led to the introduction of business engineers in Munich and Berlin while continuing education courses communicated the rapid advances of technology.[11]

Normalization also brought a temporary drop in higher education enrollment during the mid-1920s. In contrast to more than 125,000 students in 1923, there were only about 89,000 youths in academic studies by 1925. Decreasing from 87,370 (summer 1921) to 58,724 (winter 1925–1926), university attendance fell even below the last prewar figures. This one-third decline was remarkably uniform, with the faculty of law contracting from 23,638 (1923) to 16,399 and the faculty of philosophy shrinking from 39,439 (1921) to 29,094 (1925). Even enrollment in technical colleges sank from 26,224 (1922–1923) to 20,300 (1925). Veterans had finally finished their training and the declining birth cohorts decreased the number of *Abiturienten* by one-quarter between 1920 and 1924. The favorable economic climate and warnings against overcrowding also attracted high school graduates directly into business.[12] Though welcome, the relief was short-lived, because the improvement of prospects once again encouraged youths to study. By the year 1929, university enrollment surged higher than ever to 93,090, with law rising again to 22,990 and the faculty of philosophy topping its previous peak with 42,544 inscriptions. Only the TH ran counter to the trend, continuing to contract to 20,045 by 1928. The mid-1920s dip was only temporary, because the causes of long-range growth had not been reversed. The combination of stronger birth cohorts and modern secondary schools produced ever more graduates, almost doubling Prussian Abiturienten between 1924 and 1929! Women continued their progress, rising to 16 percent of university inscriptions by 1929. Moreover, underlying economic difficulties deflected many youths from business into higher education, raising the share of Prussian graduates willing to study from 59.5 percent (1923) to 78.9 percent (1928).[13]

Because the academic job market hardly had a chance to normalize, professionals began to call for some form of closure. With the government hiring more slowly than jurists graduated, "the influx grows while the outflow stops." According to the official DAV count, the number of German attorneys steadily increased from 12,276 in 1921 to 13,537 in 1925 to 15,846 in 1929 (Table A.5a). Whereas the immediate postwar graduates had compensated for wartime losses, beginning in 1924 the profession grew at the rate of 660 attorneys per year, amounting to more than a 25 percent gain overall![14] Reexamining their self-images as free professionals, lawyers grumbled about the unfair competition of part-time corporate solicitors or dismissed public officials. When in 1928 the number of Prussian trainees approached 6000, the chamber presidents "raise[d] their voice in warning against the continuing rush to legal studies." At the same time, calls for a *numerus clausus* resurfaced: "The legal profession must be closed or it shall cease to exist!" Although cooler heads cautioned that closure was "impossible today," moderates suggested "a waiting period of several years after the second examination" as well as "the limitation of the number of annual trainees" as alternatives.[15] As a result of rising pressure for action, the 1928 Frankfurt DAV delegate meeting—after passionate debate—abandoned the principle of free advocacy by 61 to 56 votes, but failed to agree on concrete measures of protection.[16] Careers in technical subjects grew increasingly overcrowded as well. With an estimated annual TH output of about 3000 plus a middle-school production of 10,000, "German industry and commerce cannot absorb the incredible number of graduates in such a manner that the costly training will pay off." Because closure was impossible for "free competitors," academic engineers agitated for career counseling and labor exchanges instead. When the business climate once again deteriorated in the late 1920s, engineers began to talk ominously about a "profession without space," an all too obvious allusion to the völkisch cliché of *Ein Volk ohne Raum.*[17]

When among teachers the excess supply reached its peak in the mid-1920s, the implementation of the *numerus clausus* law proved unavoidable. Because the lack of funds prevented the hiring of all of the 4642 probationers in 1923, the Prussian government decided to break with the tradition of entitlement and limited acceptance of Studienassessoren into an official candidate list to the projected demand five years in the future. Although those 2000 probationers who feared being left out insisted on strict seniority, the ministry, aware that "age coupled with overcrowding means the de facto closing of this career," insisted on meritocratic selection by the provincial school boards. In spite of angry protests that such "psychological pressure" would lead to "lying and *Strebertum* [pushiness]," the government prevailed with the support of liberal opinion, because a guarantee of appointing the most promising 1000 men and 200 women, such as the Protestant religion instructor Dr. Konrad Jarausch, seemed better than unemployment for everyone.[18] Coupled with resumption of hiring (880 annually 1926–1929), this draconian system cut the number of Prussian Assessoren by 1930 to 2132, only

40 percent more than the number of places on the official list (Table A.6b). Ironically, the very success in reducing overcrowding had a boomerang effect, because more students once again chose a teaching career, thereby preventing a lasting recovery of demand.[19] To counter the impression "of a great deficit of philologues," the PhVb collected reams of material as proof that "there can be no talk of a present or future lack of teachers." In spite of the hiring of about 3000 auxiliary instructors and some local shortages in modern languages or mathematics, the long-term chances of tenured state appointment remained dismal. Warning in flyers, articles, and ministerial rescripts against the study of philology, the PhVb cautioned against a false sense of security. "It is crystal clear that this crazy influx leads to hopeless overcrowding," which was bound to create a "catastrophic oversupply." Because current hiring belied such warnings, no one seems to have listened.[20]

During stabilization, the income of many professionals improved, but sizable minorities were left out with the return to prosperity. Although inflation-related cases declined, regular legal business, both civil (i.e., debt collection, contracts, etc.) and criminal (i.e., misdemeanors), almost trebled between 1923 and 1929 (Table 2.1). Lawyers were cautiously optimistic when the thirteenth decree of December 13, 1923, returned fees to the gold standard, simplified accounting, and established a sliding scale from 2 to 10 marks for cases involving values between 20 and 200 marks, as well as 5 percent to 0.5 percent for values from 500 to more than 100,000 marks. But since the balancing of public finances required drastic savings, the government rolled back full reimbursement for poor-law cases, reducing peak charges from 75 to 35 marks. Leaders of the DAV protested that the slashing of *Armengebühren* "proved how little parliament takes into account the desires of a stratum which does not represent a great mass of voters."[21] Similarly, commercial interests—represented in the Industrie- und Handelstag—pressed to reduce charges for higher value classes as part of a general lowering of costs *(Preisabbau)*. Vigorously objecting to such a "special measure against one specific profession," lawyers were "grievously disappointed" when a government draft suggested substantial reductions because the highest fees exceeded prewar rates by five times.[22] Instead, the DAV claimed that the 1923 schedule allowed "only a rather modest standard of living" and that income had declined "disturbingly" during 1926 so that office costs rose to more than 45 percent of receipts. In spite of complaints about the drastic fee reduction law of April 1, 1927, lawyers averaged 18,428 marks of gross income in 1928, providing an ample 10,135 marks after expenses (which was somewhat skewed by large earnings). However, one-third made less than 8000 marks (4400 in real terms), indicating that many young, lower court, and marginal practitioners were left behind.[23]

Teachers had to pay an even higher price for normalcy. On October 16, 1923, the Prussian cabinet decided to reduce the number of public officials by 25 percent in order to stave off financial collapse by saving personnel costs. Because the Ministry of Culture had to dismiss some of its own bureaucrats, it frantically began trying to identify potential cuts. As a result of the resentment of the cities against "the exaggerated social aspirations of most teachers," Finance Minister Hans Luther insisted on including the schools—much to the horror of the philologues, who argued that this would save at best 1 percent of all expenditures. The draft law especially targeted teachers older than 58 years of age to be pensioned prematurely, younger professionals with less than 10 years of service, and married female pedagogues. Outraged by the threatened dismissal of one-quarter of its members, the Prussian PhVb countered that "the potential savings stand in no relationship to the harm which will be inflicted on the spiritual and physical education of our youth and thereby the future of our people." Probationers feared losing the appointment rights promised by their acceptance on the *numerus clausus* list.[24] In a rare show of unanimity, philologues joined primary schoolteachers in "the struggle against this terrible decimation of the schools," while all levels of bureaucrats cooperated in protesting against this "violation of officials' rights." Spurred on by a Berlin assembly of 4000 angry educators, newspapers as diverse as the liberal *Berliner Tageblatt,* the Catholic *Neuland,* or the socialist *Vorwärts* criticized the plans to close institutions, cut weekly class hours, and raise teaching loads as "destruction of culture."[25]

To calm the waves, Minister of Culture Otto Boelitz stated to the press that he intended "to save money while serving educational goals through improvements and possible simplifications." Teachers not fired would just have to work harder and classes would have to be larger! Unable to obtain more from the ministry than a promise to proceed slowly, the Prussian Philologenverband warned the Landtag that such "measures have incredible implications," such as "endangering the school and strongly burdening the pupils." Although accepting the need for some reduction, Boelitz struggled within the cabinet to save as much of his staff as he could. In early 1924, the Prussian Ministry of State therefore revised the target downward to 15 percent.[26] As a result of continued parental resistance from the whole breadth of the political spectrum and of numerous local protests, the final Landtag bill omitted specifying a figure altogether and stipulated the first of April as the beginning date. "Everything which can be sacrificed must be cut in order to preserve the essentials," Boelitz instructed the provincial Schulkollegien on how to implement the dismissals: "Professional merit is, above all, decisive for the state administration." If weekly school hours could be reduced to thirty, then necessity might even be turned into a virtue: "The useless teachers have to be pensioned. That could be a blessing [in disguise] for the schools."[27]

Powerless to prevent the reductions, the PhVb did succeed in keeping most marginal institutions open and in saving probationers from being excluded wholesale. The final tally showed that until December 1924 about one of every ten Prussian teachers was released in contrast to 16.3 percent of all public officials in the Reich (Table 3.1). Although cuts differed regionally (8 to 14 percent) and

Table 3.1. Secondary Schoolteacher Dismissals in Prussia[28]

School type	Number of teachers	Number of dismissals	Percentage
State	3,583	505	14.09
City	11,404	1,008	8.83
Total tenured	14,987	1,513	10.09
Probationary teachers	3,511	426	12.13

between states (3.5 to 15.4 percent), all levels of teachers were involved, not even excepting principals. Among Prussian primary-school pedagogues, the firings fell more heavily on older educators (constituting two-thirds of the dismissals) than on younger males (only one-quarter) or the youngest (one-eighth). About one-tenth of those fired were married women. Although the government claimed that performance, not politics, was the criterion, teacher associations were not so sure. Having to teach one additional hour, the remainder could take comfort in their rising salaries, which improved from an average of 341.5 marks to 534.8 marks during 1924 (Table A.12). However, for the prematurely pensioned, the beginners denied entry into their chosen career, and married women, there remained nothing but bitterness about a state that had taken their work away.[29]

Although engineers fared better, they had problems of their own during stabilization. Technical experts in industry could normally count on a starting salary of 260 marks per month, rising after several years of experience to 550 marks. However, in the mid-1920s, the American gospel of "rationalization" of production and distribution replaced technical considerations with concern for profits. In countless speeches and journal articles, a "national commission for efficiency" propagated *Wirtschaftlichkeit* through more effective industrial organization, implying the primacy of accountants and, most importantly, the dismissal of inessential personnel.[30] In the name of rationality, numerous older engineers were sacked while young graduates often had difficulty landing a first job. Even during 1926, official statistics listed 8.4 percent of technicians as unemployed (Table 8.1), indicating "that there is strong unemployment among Diplom-Ingenieure." Starting in 1923, the quarterly job market surveys of the VDDI recorded about 1780 vacancies in the recovery winter of 1925, but by the following January the growth recession cut the number to 674. Demand rose again in the winter of 1927 to a peak of 1950, and fell to 1320 a year later (Table A.13). At the same time, two-thirds of the 1075 academic engineers registered with the VDDI placement service were out of work, and the absolute as well as relative number of unemployed was only cut in half right before the deluge in 1928.[31] The VDI made some efforts to help by transforming its charitable *Ingenieurhilfe*—founded in 1919—into a more vigorous *Ingenieurnothilfe* in 1926, which supported about 500 needy colleagues the following year. However, appeals to charity in order "to lessen the need of unemployed engineers" could provide no permanent solution. Although most technicians profited from the business upturn, a less fortunate minority was left out. It was no wonder that engineers were ambivalent about the message of Henry Ford.[32]

The consolidation of the economic situation helped professionals to combat the erosion of their social status. Since the constitution prohibited the use of titles in Paragraph 109, legal traditionalists pleaded for the reintroduction of the imperial Justizrat—still borne by 16 percent—in order to "increase external respect." Denied their own honor by the Reichsgericht in 1929, lawyers increasingly acquired the "doctor of jurisprudence" and criticized the use of titles by former officials as unfair competition (Table A.8).[33] To eliminate "public resentment against attorneys," they counseled using "the press [as] the primary means" to polish the image of the law career. Successful star defenders like Max Alsberg demonstrated their prestige through big limousines, expensive villas, and sumptuous dinners, hosting celebrities such as Chancellor Heinrich Brüning, minister Gustav Stresemann, artist Max Reinhardt, and musician Bruno Walter.[34] Even during the prosperous Weimar years, high school teachers continued to feel slighted: "It appears to be our tragedy to be misunderstood by the powers above." The "lack of popularity of our calling" seemed to be due to its late emergence as a profession, the conflict with influential parents, and the "duty to maintain a certain level of school performance."[35] Resenting the paucity of advancement opportunities compared to jurists, philologues agitated throughout the mid-1920s for their upgrading beyond category X of the pay scale and the expansion of the Oberstudienrat rank in level XI and above. To remedy "the discrimination of philologues compared to other higher officials," supervisory subject positions gradually increased to one-sixth of all regular appointments.[36] When the Studienrat title was diluted to include nonacademic high school teachers, the "extraordinarily upset philologues" began to demand the term *Studienprofessor.*[37]

"The low esteem of technology as cultural factor" also impelled academic engineers to continue their struggle for chambers and title protection. In the year 1926, the Association of German Architectural and Engineering Organizations presented a draft law to the Ministry of Economics, covering free professionals. Although the TH graduates demanded academic training as a membership prerequisite, the more general VDI emphatically rejected the proposal, thereby dooming it. "We do not want to create privileges and to limit the development [of technology] through prerogatives."[38] Because the continuing misuse of the title Diplom-Ingenieur eroded its value, the VDDI tried to mobilize industry, technical institutes, and the profession to take legal action. Once again, the VDI balked, stressing achievement over training, because it feared loss of its nonacademic members. Instead, the 1926 convention suggested "self-help" by tightening admissions and allowing engineers to add the abbreviation VDI as identification. Although more than half of new VDI members were TH graduates, the 1928 board meeting rejected title protection because of the tradition of technological neutrality and an unwillingness to get involved in social conflicts. Professionalization aspirations were just strong enough to keep the issue alive, but the resistance of industry, of the technical middle schools, and of social progressives was too powerful to permit its resolution.[39]

During the stable period of the Weimar Republic, professional practice improved somewhat. Among lawyers, there was fierce competition for clients and much effort to develop new areas of business. Although some law firms employed as many as sixty staff members, smaller partnerships with a couple of associates, an office manager, and several secretaries were the norm. When the budget cuts pushed erstwhile officials into the private sector, the DAV protested, only reluctantly admitting more than 600 of them in the end. Self-employed lawyers also sought to restrict the after hours activity of corporate attorneys by insisting on an independent practice—a requirement that was circumvented all too easily.[40] When about 3000 nonacademic legal consultants—organized in the Reichsbund deutscher Rechtsbeistände—tried to displace 27,000 nonorganized competitors and gain admission to the courts, the DAV vigorously defended its turf. However, lawyers failed to prevent the creation of a Prussian Councillor of Administrative Law *(Verwaltungsrechtsrat)*—a strange hybrid of bureaucrat and advocate—although they succeeded in limiting his practice to administrative matters.[41] More important was the struggle over labor courts, because unions—resentful against "class justice"—demanded the establishment of lay institutions. The DAV "consider[ed] the exclusion of lawyers from labor court procedure . . . an unwarranted insult" as well as a "grave harm to the justice-seeking parties." Nevertheless, the leftist parties and Ministry of Labor prevailed: "The battle for the labor court law has . . . generally been lost by the defenders of the German legal system." Beginning in 1926, attorneys were excluded from this rapidly developing area of litigation. However, an increasing number of advocates began to work as consultants for business firms and cartels.[42]

High school teachers who had escaped the cuts were considerably overworked: "Aside from insufficient pay which . . . stifles joyful commitment through material concerns, the gravity of the extraordinary increase in the work-load of philologues can no longer be denied." Unappreciative of the resistance from Minister of Culture Boelitz to fiscal demands for even greater work loads, pedagogues claimed that their assignments of 25 hours for beginning teachers, decreasing to 23 and 20 after each additional 12 years, were the highest in Europe. At the same time, class sizes ranged up to 55 for the beginning level of the Gymnasium (fifth grade). Course preparations and corrections, scholarly self-improvement, and involvement in extracurricular activities meant that philologues claimed they labored nine hours a day for six days a week. No wonder that such overburdening produced "an unusually high number of diseases," resulted in numerous "breakdowns in office," and "led to frequent deaths."[43] Seconded by the universities, the philologues pressed for "some relief" until Minister of Culture C. H. Becker publicly acknowledged the need for reductions, deferring them only because of lack of means. Deluged with graphic material, the Prussian Landtag requested funds for the 1927–1928 budget to return teaching loads and class sizes to pre-1924 levels, but the Ministry of Finance refused.[44] Becker was merely able to reduce the class limit for the entering secondary grade to 50 by administrative decree. Even during the best Weimar years, lack of money hampered reform and "the barbaric overburdening" of the philologues was not eliminated.[45]

The employed engineers faced the challenge of developing innovative technologies and coping with novel forms of production. Many traditional practices continued successfully, but new areas also developed quite rapidly. For instance, voluntary cooperation between "producers, consumers and scholars" in creating "German industrial norms," which had started in 1917, made further progress so that many DIN standards were accepted internationally. Similarly, engineers remained committed to improving safety. When the Prussian minister of commerce insisted on adding labor representatives to the steam boiler supervisory boards, the VDI protested against "dragging in political organizations," but to no avail.[46] According to articles and pictures in the technical journals, the traditional work areas of machine building and civil construction were gradually being supplemented by designing automobiles and airplanes, farm machinery, and household appliances. The spread of rationalized mass production transformed factory work from single-piece or series output to assembly-line methods, requiring a quantum leap in division of labor and mechanization that created new problems of planning and control. Although "pioneering technical achievements have propelled industrial advancement,'' the recent ''uncontrolled development of gigantic corporations and the preponderance of profits keeps the engineer from influencing his enterprise.'' In spite of such threats to their authority, academic engineers maintained that ''the path to leadership positions'' ran through professional merit rather than collective bargaining.[47]

During the recovery, professionals tried to reconcile traditional self-conceptions with the altered circumstances of the Weimar Republic. The fiftieth anniversary of the Imperial Lawyer Code proved the success of ''attorney monopoly and free advocacy'' in generating personal independence, ethical responsibility, ''a high scholarly standard,'' and a considerable public presence. But socioeconomic pressures created ''ferment and motion as never before,'' prompting ''discontent, a search for something new, a questioning of old institutions.''[48] An unfortunate case in point was the conflict over establishing a compulsory pension system to help ''incapacitated attorneys, widows and orphans suffering hunger.'' When a skeptical ministry considered ''the unprecedented step of creating a social insurance scheme for a free profession,'' Hamburg attorneys criticized the DAV initiative for ''making the lawyers dependent upon the state,'' providing ''useless benefits'' and not aiding the truly needy. Because the existing auxiliary fund (to which only 20 percent subscribed) failed to meet the practical need, the 1924 DAV delegate meeting approved the proposal by a vote of 62 to 11.[49] But when ''the unscrupulous propaganda of private insurance companies'' created ''many false impressions'' among the uninformed rank and file, the labor ministry called for another consultation of the membership.[50] The disputed law envisaged ''pension pay'' and widow or orphan benefits for all lawyers, based on contributions from members and the public (as surcharge on fees). Although supporters argued from self-interest and social concern, opponents rejected the move as ''endangering the freedom and independence of our profession.'' The spring 1926 delegate meeting found lawyers ''divided into two big camps,'' with the majority of the chambers and the local association leaders opposing the innovation, because the ''burden on the profession seemed unbearable.'' The brilliant rhetorical battle ended in a defeat for compulsory pensions by 48 to 38 votes, which was sweetened unconvincingly by an appeal to strengthen the existing charitable fund. In the end, lawyers failed to rally behind a beneficial reform because it required redefining their image.[51]

The self-conception of secondary schoolteachers remained defensive and was characterized by the slogan ''enemies all around us!'' Instead of looking to the future as an opportunity, many Studienräte saw themselves as guardians of endangered cultural traditions. Although funding was reduced and publication chances diminished, philologues stubbornly clung to scholarship, seeking to stay in touch with research discussions through continuing education courses and subject matter conferences. Traditionalists were more comfortable with the academic lectures of the old association of ''philologues and schoolmen'' than with the professional agitation of the PhVb. Progressive pedagogues looked rather to innovative institutions such as the ''free school–community'' of Wickersdorf.[52] Wilhelm Bolle attributed this malaise to the intellectual climate, which was marked by ''a certain inchoateness, a chaos which does not seem ripe for the creation of a purified and non-material *Weltanschauung*.'' In the year 1924, the innovative Prussian *Lehr-*

pläne—designed by Hans Richert—jettisoned neohumanism and intellectualism, opening the door to a reformed and intuitive, historical, artistic, and work-oriented instruction. Although younger teachers welcomed these curricular improvements—promoted by special courses—older instructors grumbled about such "wallowing in pedagogical phrases" and attempted to resist. According to elitist critics, such coddling of pupils would "level the differences of talent or rank and democratize and utilitarianize cultivation," thereby leading to "ruin." Many teachers appeared to "suffer from psychological and economic depression and demand . . . a great, inspiring program which . . . overcomes the apathy of the masses." Unwillingness to develop a democratic teacher ideal and pedagogical methods left numerous philologues with a dangerous spiritual void.[53]

Believing in the inevitability of technical progress, engineers tried to demonstrate the cultural creativity of their work in order to gain greater recognition by the other professions. In the "dispute over technology," cultural critics attacked the machine as dehumanizing while its technical defenders praised its civilizing benefits. Both were "separated by a chasm, a dualism of thinking which goes so far that professions do not understand each other, as if they spoke different languages." To counter antitechnological attacks, engineers claimed "technology as a cornerstone of culture." Carl Weihe, the editor of the VDDI journal *Technik und Kultur,* argued that human mastery over nature via the machine made "technology the foundation and essential supporter of all culture."[54] Engineers also celebrated "the beauty of engineering construction" and organized an unprecedented exhibition on "art and technology" at the Folkwang Museum in Essen in 1928.[55] Most ambitious was the attempt to develop a philosophy of technology by the Catholic theoretician Friedrich Dessauer. In Kantian categories, he talked about a "fourth realm" of technological solutions to be created by the engineer in a "categorical imperative of technology." Widely debated, this search for a technical world view was at least potentially directed toward "progress for mankind."[56]

During normalization, professionals struggled to transform their associations into more unified and influential interest groups. Although the DAV leaders succeeded in stalling the establishment of a politically more useful second business office in Berlin, the size of the board had to be increased to 20 as a result of the polarization between lower and appellate court lawyers.[57] By 1927, the election system for the delegate assembly was changed to allow national slates, standing for particular interests or points of view (lower court attorneys). To counteract divisiveness, the National Lawyers' Conference restructured the DAV by incorporating the local associations as the bottom layer of the overall organization.[58] However, renewed demands for the establishment of a comprehensive "national attorneys' chamber" and other reform initiatives produced little positive result.[59]

Philologues reconciled internal differences more successfully, but fretted at their presumed lack of results. After "the fundamental organizational restructuring" in 1922, every high school teacher automatically became a member of the state PhVb, which was in turn subdivided into provincial and local groups. Probationers, male teachers of girls' schools, directors, and administrators clustered in subsections, creating an inclusive "association of all philologues regardless of rank and location." The Berlin business office tirelessly lobbied the Landtag, worked up press releases, informed the members, and cooperated with the "school committee" of the universities (Verband deutscher Hochschulen, VdH) in educational questions or the reorganized Reichsbund höherer Beamter in pay issues.[60] Negotiating with the ministry was frustrating because its paternalistic attitudes and political constraints often led to disappointments. While as member Boelitz considered "the PhVb's position very important for my decisions," as minister he maintained that "I cannot allow any interest group an influence on educational policy." Whenever the leaders concluded a necessary compromise, uninformed members criticized them for not pursuing their interests vigorously enough. Caught between bureaucratic immobility and grass roots activism, the PhVb often fell into the role of "an irritating nagger or unpleasant critic," even when things were going well enough.[61]

During stabilization, engineers streamlined their organization but remained unable to overcome their fragmentation. The prestigious VDI continued to be successful and self-confident—but it was not a professional association in the strict sense. Housed in its own impressive building in Berlin, its business office employed 220 people, whereas the DAV or the PhVb had to get along on a marginal staff of fewer than a dozen. The VDI owed its prosperity to the decision to publish its own journals, which, after near bankruptcy during the inflation, began to turn ever larger profits. The secret of success was not membership size (about the same as the PhVb), but expensive industrial advertisement as well as diversification into the established *VDI Zeitschrift,* the newer *VDI Nachrichten,* and a number of specialized monthlies like *Technik und Wirtschaft.* A second leg of the organizational empire consisted of "scientific work," which was coordinated by an advisory board and divided into specific committees that sponsored exhibitions and conferences. The third dimension of VDI structure consisted of local chapters, which organized several hundred lectures and meetings each year. Finally, the association also worked like a holding company through a number of affiliates and committees like the DATSCH to influence the technical community and the public.[62] In contrast, the academic VDDI tried to become a real "professional association," but did not succeed. Because its program of separating TH graduates from the rest of the technicians ran counter to the Weimar spirit of "leveling social differences," it could only generally promote "the victorious power of technology in the struggle for culture." Although support of study reforms and job placement provided some services, its more modest membership—stagnating at about 4000—could neither keep Diplom-Ingenieure from joining the VDI nor galvanize the more than 100,000 unorganized engineers.[63]

The return of favorable economic and political conditions during the mid-1920s allowed the professions to make considerable progress toward stability. Training was reformed, fewer graduates entered careers, income improved somewhat, status stabilized, practice became more normal, self-images partly adapted, and organizations strengthened. However, the recovery was only temporary and incomplete, leaving out uncompetitive minorities such as beginning, elderly, or marginal practitioners. Moreover, normalcy came at a considerable price. Fee reduction for lawyers, civil service cuts *(Beamtenabbau)* for teachers, and rationalization unemployment for engineers were the order of the day. Professionals therefore viewed stabilization ambivalently. For debtors, some improvement was undeniable. However, for creditors, many real and imagined disappointments lingered, especially when compared to the order and prosperity of the empire. Part of this frustration was due to specific devaluation policies of the Weimar Republic. Another part was a legacy of the failures of the Second Reich, which all too few observers were willing to admit. Finally, yet another part stemmed from worldwide political and economic problems over which German governments had no control. While lawyers tenaciously clung to their self-definition of freie Advokatur, teachers tried to defend a waning cultural hierarchy, and engineers dreamed of technological leadership of society. How would such diverse professionals respond politically?

PROFESSIONS AND POLITICS

Reactions to the chaotic beginning of the Weimar Republic had revealed deep ideological cleavages within the professions. Because both proponents and opponents of democracy were in a minority, the crucial contest in the ensuing years involved the allegiance of the apolitical majority. Internally, the professions reluctantly began to rethink their rhetoric, self-images, and ethical norms, adapting them to a democratic state. Externally, professionals were necessarily drawn into the altered political process in order to achieve their aims. But beyond pragmatic concessions, the emergence of a republican professionalism implied an explicit commitment to the new constitution. How far did professionals revise the political content of their practice during stabilization? Democratic professions also needed to be integrated organizationally into parliamentary politics. What kind of links and affinities did professionals develop during normalcy? Finally, a change in attitudes required favorable government responses to basic professional desires. How successful were practitioners in achieving essential aims during the better Weimar years? The quality of their ideological, organizational, and practical interaction with the republic largely determined their subsequent allegiances. In turn, the actual political behavior of professionals also helped color the views of the parties and the nature of governmental decisions toward them.

With a new constitution and novel legislation, law became a material and ideological battleground. While some understood that "the administration of justice must be simplified and made more popular," most judges thought that "in the main *Rechtspflege* [would] remain essentially the same." Because imperial judges continued in office, their rejection of the democratic constitution soon precipitated a "crisis of confidence in the judiciary."[64] Leftist parties and the press were outraged that "political verdicts continually violate the sense of justice of large parts of the population," acting "not as guardians of legal equality, but as creators and protectors of injustice." Punishing 22 left-wing murders more harshly than 354 right-wing killings, conservative judges handed down numerous misjudgments such as in the Erzberger libel trial, the Hitler case, or the Free corps atrocities, which the lay public could only understand as *Rechtsbeugung,* or as a perversion of law. Socialists and Democrats criticized "the incredible differences in sentencing," the insufficient adherence to the constitution and the lack of equal safeguards for republican politicians.[65] After the passage of a special law to protect the republic in July 1922, the government insisted on sharper suppression of sedition against both extremes, even if a skeptical judiciary continued to view such demands as "politicization of justice."[66] Many judges felt threatened by democratic clamor for lay justice and resented their relative loss of prosperity compared to administrative officials. Instead of responding to criticism, the president of the German Judges' League therefore claimed disingenuously: "The complaints which have been raised are not generally justified."[67] It seemed a bitter irony that the very concept of "judicial independence," which had once protected liberal judges from the wrath of the emperor, was now used by monarchists to shield antirepublican verdicts from review.

Lawyers reacted ambivalently to the crisis of public confidence in the legal system. On the one hand, they collectively endorsed judicial demands for continued independence, because of an understanding of professional ethics that forbade attorneys "to impute ill will to the majority of judges or to vilify them in general." Although many legal quarrels were in essence political, the *Juristische Wochenschrift* embraced professional neutrality by claiming to "serve exclusively the administration of justice and legal scholarship, but not politics." Similarly, a special lawyers' convention on "the plight of law" in 1925 demanded "legal order and stability, now that the economy has been straightened out." To restore the authority of justice, moderate attorneys called for an end to the flood of emergency decrees and hasty simplification measures, while a small minority supported laicization and reform. However, the imperative of neutrality neither kept nationalist attorneys like Friedrich Grimm from tenaciously fighting against the diplomatic, economic, and disarmament "injustices," imposed by the victors in the Treaty of Versailles. Nor did it prevent political lawyers like the left Socialist Paul Levi from joining the radical critique of the judiciary which undermined faith in Weimar justice.[68]

On the other hand, dedicated lawyers could and did use the constitutional guarantees to defend their clients in celebrated political trials. However, the "double standard" between Right and Left that, for the same politically inspired crimes, yielded slaps on the wrist for the former and stiff sentences for the latter, made their work difficult. Only with extraordinary ingenuity could leftist star defenders like Alfred Apfel get communist (Max Hoelz), pacifist (Carl von Ossietzky), or bohemian (Georg Grosz) clients acquitted. Rightist advocates like Walter Luetgebrune had less difficulty obtaining leniency for völkisch (Erich Ludendorff), neoconservative (Organisation Consul), or militarist (Schwarze Reichswehr) terrorists or murderers. In this highly charged partisan atmosphere, attorneys became pawns in a political struggle over patriotism or internationalism that they did not fully comprehend. In the service of ideology, some lawyers were even willing to violate professional ethics. Although his judgment in emigration seems somewhat overdrawn, Apfel saw correctly:

> Whenever the advocates' societies should have worked to maintain the first principle of law, its impartiality, they failed ignominiously. Even when the freedom of defense was curtailed, they made no firm stand against it. Timid and concerned merely with the letter of the matter, they confined themselves to discussions of professional trivialities, and at their meeting uttered nothing but outworn, self-

> sufficient phrases. With few exceptions, they accepted their role in the forensic drama, not as coactors with judges and the prosecution, but as confederates of the accused.

Though they were more libertarian than judges, lawyers could not act as a judicial corrective, because they did not understand liberalism as a precondition for the freie Advokatur.[69]

The reactionary activities of some pedagogues and older pupils also turned the high school into a political battleground. When public outrage about Walther Rathenau's murder demanded action, Minister of Culture Boelitz emphasized the teachers' special responsibility for educating youths toward "living citizenship." Although nationalists warned against "violating the civil rights of pedagogues," republican officials considered it an essential "faculty duty to respect the existing constitution." Because the Law for the Protection of the Republic forbade influencing "pupils by denigrating the constitution," the Ministry of Culture debated whether to forbid extremist student groups and how to democratize the educators. Although several school boards urged "changing the teachers' attitude towards the constitution," DVP member Boelitz shied away from compulsion, striking any direct references to the republic from ministerial draft decrees! Nevertheless, the national "Guidelines for the Cooperation of Schools and Universities in the Protection of the Republic" of July 1922 stressed the necessity "of creating new history texts . . . , introducing civics," and revising teacher training: "It is not enough to avoid . . . denigrating the constitution or government of the Reich and the states, but [a teacher] has to prepare youth for participation in the people's state, educate it in responsibility for public welfare as well as awaken and nurture state consciousness." Opposed by the PhVb as political, these regulations were a modest attempt at republican self-protection, which defused the issue in the short term.[70]

Such a moderate approach to democratization eventually proved inadequate, because it left too much room for pedagogical initiative. Right-wing papers attacked Boelitz' warning against extremist student societies as "carrying partisan politics into the school." To the *Berliner Tageblatt,* the minister denied that high schools were "a playground of reaction," cautioned that one could not make youths republican by force, and stressed that teachers needed to cooperate without having their rights abridged.[71] While progressive philologues tried to produce republican teaching materials, antidemocratic incidents continued: "Constitution day—and the Republic is so strange to me," the trade schoolteacher Bruno Jarausch sighed in his diary. Accused of weapons smuggling and of using school rooms for reactionary purposes, *Oberlehrer* Fischer swore on his "service oath that I have never abused the lectern for party-political purposes." Because right-wing agitation was considered "national" and above politics, progressive complaints were difficult to substantiate and punishments usually mild, such as transfer to another institution. Administrators tended to argue that cases of Nazi student activity or anti-Semitic agitation were "in no way to be attributed to the influence of the school." To counter the image that "philologues are fundamentally reactionary," association leaders felt it necessary to stress that they were "utterly apolitical."[72]

When in 1925 "pupil partisanship began to endanger civic education and disturb school peace,'' Minister of Culture Becker forbade membership in subversive organizations or display of controversial symbols and abandoned explicit democratization: ''Working towards depoliticizing school-life through sensitive enlightenment of everyone concerned will be an important challenge.'' The Philologenverband was overjoyed, because it had long denounced the ''intrusion of politics into the school'' as well as the ''party geometry'' of political appointments. In order to resist a democratization of personnel, the PhVb demanded that ''professional and personal aptitude should alone be decisive'' in hiring or firing. In theory, the philologues' ''politically neutral professional organization'' did endorse ''the duty of civic spirit and of respect for the state and its laws.'' However, in practice this was hardly a democratic commitment, because it was a loyalty only to the state as such, as expressed by the Conservative Karl Helfferich in these words: ''We serve the state as it is.'' Not that the majority of the teachers was actively working for the overthrow of the republic; but many philologues merely tolerated the Weimar system rather than supporting it wholeheartedly. Therefore, the Socialists criticized the high school as a domain of monarchist teachers in the Prussian Landtag and Democrats demanded more civic training, but the other bourgeois parties warned against ''compulsory republicanization.'' When Minister of Culture Becker cautioned in 1927 that, as government officials, teachers had to ponder ''how far their public political statements are compatible with their duties,'' secondary schoolteachers, instead of applauding the self-evident, ''raised serious pedagogical and legal objections.''[73]

Intended to calm passions, depoliticization of the school failed to speed the democratization of teachers or pupils. When, during the 1928 constitution day at the Werner von Siemens Gymnasium in Berlin, a teacher ''clearly betrayed disregard and hostility toward the Republic,'' some students protested and demanded a republican celebration of their own. Whereas conservative philologues were aghast at such ''pedagogical impudence,'' the ministry, through supervisor Wilhelm Hartke, warmly ''welcomed'' this initiative and chided the principal. During a crowded second observance, the president of the student council exclaimed: ''We want to demonstrate for a school in which it is not shameful to confess republican loyalty and in which it is nothing more than a duty to accept all the outsiders and oppressed into a great community.''[74] Typically enough, the Philologenverband, reflecting the ''agitation'' of its members, protested against this breach of ''school rules''—without criticizing the offending teacher's lack of support for the constitution in any way! When the conservative Deutschnationale Volkspartei (DNVP) interpellated in the Prussian Landtag about ''the freedom of conscience'' as well as the ''pedagogical authority'' and an ''apolitical school,'' Becker easily refuted the charge of meddling: ''Except for a few utterly unimportant outsiders, the teachers of our secondary schools stand loyally behind the state, even in its present form.''[75] However, by the end of the 1920s, the very term republic had acquired ''a partisan flavor which is repugnant to many members of the PhVb.'' Instead, most teachers hoped that a ''healthy national feeling'' could lead to a ''positive attitude'' toward the Weimar Republic, seen as ''a synthesis of the old and new Germany, represented by Hindenburg.'' These nationalists supported a strong republic as continuation of the German state as long as it strove for ''the idea of military force, the restoration of the colonies, the promotion of spiritual and cultural salvation of the German minorities, a revision of the Eastern border, and finally the refutation of the war guilt lie.''[76]

Although engineering work was less overtly political, the development of technology also had political ramifications. During the May 1925 inauguration of the Deutsche Museum in Munich as a temple of technology, Chancellor Luther praised inventiveness: ''This spirit animates the great numbers of German engineers and other technicians, who forge practical implements out of the spiritual creations of the masters.'' Engineers had considerable responsibility, because the economical production of synthetic fuels or the achievement of agricultural autarchy through technology ''had incalculable political implications.''[77] In some areas such as the building of highways or of municipal public works, the promotion of technological progress largely served the general welfare. In other fields, such as the regaining of ''equality for German air traffic,'' military applications were not far behind.[78] Although their practice was less ideological than that of other professionals, engineers opposed socialist efforts to shorten the workday, but felt insufficiently appreciated by entrepreneurs and complained that they ''hardly ha[d] a discernible voice in public issues.'' For the VDDI, ''these questions remain unresolved because the Diplom-Ingenieure are not inspired by a healthy and justified professional consciousness, resting on pride of work and on true academic spirit.'' Although the technological modernism of the Weimar Republic attracted some engineers, many TH graduates were afraid of its attendant ''deacademization'' and ''leveling.''[79]

In struggling for their members, the professional associations were forced to establish links with other interest groups and with political parties in state or national parliaments. Lawyers were well connected, since the holding of public office was a tradition among them. Many a minister of justice or head of another department had, like Erich Koch-Weser, started out as a member of the bar. In the Weimar Republic, attorneys in the Reichstag no longer clustered in the liberal parties (down from four-fifths to two-fifths) but spanned the entire spectrum from the Socialist Left (one-fifth) to the Nationalist Right (one-fifth) (See Table 3.2). Because their representation had dropped by over half since the empire, attorneys

Table 3.2. Professionals in the Reichstag, 1867–1933[80]

		Political Party (Percentage)									
Profession	Period	KPD	SPD	Prog.	NLs	Cent.	Cons	Other	Nazi	Total	Share
Lawyers	Empire		3.5	24.1	54.7	19.6	3.2	4.5		311	11.2
	Weimar	3.2	14.0	28.0	10.8	23.2	7.5	1.1	11.8	93	5.2
Primary Pedagogues	Empire		14.0	36.0	15.1	24.4	5.8	4.7		86	3.1
	Weimar	8.9	25.9	13.4	6.1	13.4	10.7	3.6	17.9	112	6.2
Philologues	Empire		2.5	22.5	28.8	36.3	6.3	3.8		80	2.9
	Weimar	1.3	11.8	11.8	7.8	33.3	17.6	3.9	11.8	51	2.8
Engineers	Empire		7.1	7.1	42.8	28.6	14.3			14	0.5
	Weimar	3.8	7.7		11.5	15.4	11.5		50.0	26	1.4
Total		1.9	9.8	22.3	26.6	22.3	6.9	3.2	6.9	773	

complained about "suffering from lack of influence in flagrant contradiction to [their] powers and achievements" and bewailed their "indisputable setbacks in the last few years." What could explain this parliamentary decline? The Berlin advocate Wrzeszinski claimed that "no party is friendly to lawyers; all are more or less alien, that is ignorant of our calling, its ideals and economic importance." As organization spokesmen, lawyers advocated the concerns of others and had little interest in representing the demands of their occupation in the Reichstag. The transition from notables' representation to professional politics coupled with the economic malaise also made lawyers less attractive as candidates. The 1927 Stuttgart congress therefore exhorted: "The legal profession must enter the parties." However, homilies had little effect. Like other experts, attorneys ultimately wanted something unattainable—"a professional policy above parties," an *überparteiliche Standespolitik.*[81]

Although they had fewer deputies, secondary schoolteachers maintained and coordinated their representatives more effectively. Occasionally philologues could boast of a minister of culture such as former principal Boelitz, and their number in the Prussian Landtag—the center of cultural policy—was respectable (15–25). In lobbying parliamentary committees, the PhVb mobilized its members: "It is of utmost importance for us to use our personal contacts as much as possible for professional and educational policy initiatives of our association." Rejecting the formation of a separate bureaucratic party, the association encouraged teachers to run for office "so that our profession is represented as well as possible in all camps. The success of our entire work during the next years depends upon it." In Westphalia "a political advisory board," which was composed of elected pedagogues such as Dr. Goldmann (Center party) from all bourgeois parties, coordinated legislative efforts at salary hikes, and other initiatives, trying "to remove educational issues form party politics." To finance parliamentary campaigns like the struggle against the firing of officials, the PhVb also collected a regular war chest from its chapters.[82] Although philologues claimed neutrality and representation in all political camps, their Reichstag and Landtag affinities were distinct from the preferences of the growing number of primary-school pedagogues who doubled their Reichstag representation after 1918. Whereas three-fifths of the high school teachers belonged to the center-right bourgeois parties (Deutsche Volkspartei [DVP], Center, and DNVP), their grade school colleagues clustered in the socialist and democratic fractions of the Weimar coalition (with one-half), in spite of some religious ties to Center and DNVP. A 1926 survey of 500 politically active secondary schoolteachers reinforces this picture of center-right allegiance. Although only 3.8 percent of the philologues were involved in the SPD and 11 percent in the Deutsche Demokratische Partei (DDP), 18.3 percent chose the Center Party, and an impressive 30.4 percent belonged to Stresemann's DVP, with a sizable 27.8 percent also found in the nationalist-Protestant DNVP. Among sixty Westphalian teachers registered in parties in 1930, only one-tenth gravitated to the left (SPD, DDP), while two-thirds occupied the middle (Center, DVP) and one-quarter leaned to the right (DNVP).[83]

In contrast, engineers were more remote from the political process. Although even technicians supplied an occasional minister such as Walther Rathenau, they were drastically underrepresented in parliament, in spite of being more than ten times as numerous as lawyers. In certain "technical issues," the advice of the VDI carried considerable weight—but it was rarely employed for "professional" interests such as title protection. Even the architects with their campaign to create chambers and limit the term "master builder" *(Baumeister)* were more active. Party platforms had little to offer to most technicians who rejected the socialist class struggle and remained skeptical of the essentially Catholic religious identification of the Center party. By process of elimination, there remained the bourgeois middle parties, depending on progressive, industrial, or nationalist preferences. The weak links of engineers with the Weimar system through economic interest groups such as the Reichsverband der deutschen Industrie made them vulnerable to Nazi appeals in adversity. Hence half of the engineers in the Reichstag after 1918 were members of the *NSDAP*. Unable to reconcile an individual achievement ethic with collective caste aspirations, technicians appealed for a vague *Gemeinschaftsarbeit* during the mid-1920s. Their preference was a national pragmatism, willing to work within the republic only as long as it provided a viable framework for economic prosperity.[84]

The ideological outlook of professionals also depended on the responsiveness of the political system to their central concerns. For lawyers, the decisive issue was simultaneous admission of lower court attorneys to appellate courts. When their lot failed to improve with economic stability, AG advocates resumed their agitation: "Lower court lawyers, essential to a healthy administration of justice, are doomed to destruction unless something is done to remedy their material plight." Assuming that the general return of prosperity would eventually spread downward, the Prussian Ministry of Justice failed to budge, because it "consistently refused to have anything to do with this" issue. The association of district court lawyers therefore approached the Reichstag directly with a bill to improve their condition "in the interest of a popular administration of justice." However, when the open-minded Reich State Secretary of Justice Curt Joel consulted the states, Prussian Minister of Justice Zehnhoff unequivocally rejected any change.[85] Fearing that "polarization and division [might] break up the legal profession," the DAV desperately tried to mediate. However, the superior court lawyers dug in their heels against the "legal introduction of Simultanzulassung" and submitted a counterpetition. Although LG lawyers mobilized the chambers in which they had more votes as well as the Prussian Ministry of Justice, AG attorneys could count on some sympathy from the DAV board and the support of the DNVP, which was responsive to the desires of its rural lawyer constituency. When mediation broke down again, the paralyzed lawyers' association withdrew into formal neutrality, thereby indirectly favoring the status quo.[86]

In March 1925, DNVP deputy Otto Everling tried to break the deadlock by introducing a bill into the Reichstag to make simultaneous admission mandatory. However, in lengthy committee discussions on November 5 and 6, 1925, the Bavarian and Prussian governments opposed any change, the Center Party waffled, and the Socialists could not see any pressing need. Only the Democrats and, somewhat hesitatingly, the DVP went along. When Joel also failed to insist, the Everling bill was voted down by 14 to 10, but a milder version—calling for a joint admission decision of OLG and chamber presidents—survived.[87] Because neither side was satisfied with this outcome, the struggle over simultaneous admission continued with redoubled effort. Put on the defensive, the wealthier and more influential superior court attorneys argued that opening the gate would "not protect the interests of the administration of justice" but put them into economic jeopardy. In lengthy countermemoranda, the AG lawyers claimed that the experience of smaller states proved that it would facilitate litigation and lessen costs, not to mention improve their material lot. A Bavarian district court survey revealed an average of only 850 marks of receipts for 3 months—a sum on which no university graduate could hope to live. In spite of its "grave concerns about unrestricted simultaneous admission," the Prussian Ministry of Justice responded to Reichstag pressure by organizing a mediation session between representatives of both parties in January 1926. But agreement on raising the financial limit for lower court cases, sharing one-third of appellate fees, and handling admission petitions more leniently, foundered on the resolve of AG attorneys to insist on a legislative solution.[88]

The conflict continued to smolder until the political process imposed a solution from the outside. Unable to reconcile the opposites and embarrassed by its prior wavering, the DAV abdicated its leadership and clung to neutrality. However, the Reichstag broke the deadlock in the committee session of December 12, 1926, when Everling reintroduced his bill, claiming improved "litigation . . . , AG professional desires . . . , and economic interests." While the Prussian government emphasized "the completely unpredictable effect on the economic situation of LG lawyers," the Reich Ministry of Justice opposed the legislation less vigorously. The DNVP prepared its parliamentary strategy so well that the Socialists swung over to reform and the Center party overcame its scruples, producing a clear majority for unrestricted admission. In the final Reichstag debate on February 25, 1927, LG supporters managed to reinsert the requirement of OLG approval, but the substance of the law was an AG victory. Relieved, State Secretary Joel hoped that "this whole quarrel which was about to destroy the working ability of the legal profession may now be put to rest so that lawyers can regain that unity, necessary for them to remain a useful organ of the administration of justice."[89] Because attorneys had for two decades been unable to resolve this divisive problem themselves, the Reichstag finally dictated the needed reform, thereby restoring a measure of professional calm.

Even after some improvements in the fall of 1924, the crucial issue for secondary schoolteachers was inadequate pay (Table A.12). Philologue grumbling was borne out by the conclusion of a Reich Ministry of Finance study in January 1925 that "the salaries of middle and upper officials have been raised considerably less than the pay of lower bureaucrats." The shrinkage of the ratio between level III and XI of 1 : 4.9 in 1914 to 1 : 2.05 in 1920–1923 demonstrated that "higher training and better performance" were being devalued politically, because skilled workers' pay had risen 70.3 percent since 1897, in contrast to a mere 10.4 percent raise for higher officials! Propelled by restive members, the teacher association began to campaign through a special "economic policy section," headed by Adolf Bohlen, for "*sufficient* and *just* pay for all groups," which would restore prewar salaries and reaffirm the "merit principle" to differentiate between ranks.[90] Complicated by judges' desires for superior treatment, the coordinated complaints of the RhB and the regional philological associations about "the unfavorable income of the mass of philologues'' nevertheless created the impression that a special catch-up raise was needed to combat the ''danger of an economic and at the same time moral ruin.'' Direct pressure on individual parties, presentations to the Finance Minister Heinrich Köhler and concerted press appeals employed the political argument ''that a continuation of the present pay policy will drive officials into the arms of left or right-wing radicalism.'' After obtaining the sympathy of Minister of Culture Becker, the PhVb at its 1927 Dresden congress demanded not just a 25 percent raise but also real pay reform, restoring peacetime income. Because the new bourgeois cabinet was more receptive to professionals' demands, the Reichstag budget committee finally resolved on a basic restructuring in order to ''allow the groups of officials that standard of living to which they are entitled according to training, responsibility and performance.''[91]

A fierce struggle ensued over the implementation of this basic decision. With the warning, ''we face immediate economic collapse,'' the more numerous lower level officials proposed—in the name of ''social justice''—the principle of *Verzahnung,* which meant the overlapping of pay categories of the lower, middle, and higher service. Because four-fifths of the higher officials had only 258 marks left for food, clothing, and cultural needs each month, the Philologenverband insisted on approaching real prewar salaries and equality with legal bureaucrats.[92] Whereas the nonacademic officials demanded across-the-board increases to consolidate their gains, secondary schoolteachers sought a permanent revision to restore their prior advantages by rewarding superior achievement with greater pay and advancement possibilities. When the combined pressure of the DBB, left-wing parties, and the Ministry of Finance produced a more egalitarian second draft with functional supplements, the PhVb warned against ''declassing the philological profession,'' unless directors and Oberstudienräte were put into higher categories, base pay was raised by 600 marks and the probationers were credited with their full service.[93] Propelled by the sympathetic bourgeois DNVP and DVP, the Reichstag eventually agreed on an inversion of the classification scheme, putting Studienräte into ''group 2b'' with a normal range from 4800 to 8400 marks. But over the incensed protests of the higher level officials against ''the unbearable reduction of their salaries,'' the Prussian Landtag yielded to pressure of the SPD and the Christian trade unions (Adam Stegerwald) and lowered the entry bracket to 4400, while putting primary schoolteachers into ''group 4c'' between 2800 and 5000 marks, creating some salary overlap. Although ''the system change[d] more in favor of qualified officialdom,'' the December settlement in the Reich and Prussia seemed ''hardly pleasing'' when compared to the high hopes of the summer. Silesian, East and West Prussian, Rhenish, and Westphalian chapters thanked the national leadership for ''achieving all that was possible, given the situation and political constellation.'' However, Saxon philologues accused the PhVb of failing to obtain sufficient gains, an unrealistic charge, because greater obstinacy would have endangered the whole reform. Ironically, many philologues continued to talk of a ''salary-injustice,'' just when they had succeeded in reducing primary schoolteachers' pay from 74 percent (1920) to 61 percent of their own.[94]

The overriding concern of the engineers was the health of the German economy. In spite of the cliché that technicians were ''called upon to lead our economic life,'' their practical role was more modest, because most were white-collar employees rather than entrepreneurs. The VDI and VDDI therefore continually reported on "business questions" and the general economic climate in their journals. However, beyond the promotion of technological progress in such areas as rationalization or substitute raw materials, engineers had little if any collective voice in determining economic policy.[95] In their own mind, they contributed rather indirectly through innovation: "More than ever the leaders of our industry understand the lesson of technological development in the last decades, that every research result—even if it is initially remote from industrial work—thoroughly stimulates it and moves it into new, economically significant directions." However, translating technological leadership into professional power remained an elusive goal, because Weimar cabinets hesitated to create a "ministry of technology," concentrating all such government activities in one department. Minister Rudolf Oeser claimed that the Reich Ministry of Transport coordinating rail, ship, automobile, and air traffic after 1919, "provides a home for German technology and thereby energizes the economy." Though helping with the prestige of technology, this bureaucratic concentration could, according to disappointed practitioners in other areas, "not at all be considered the technical ministry which its advocates want."[96]

The recovery of normalcy facilitated a pragmatic rapprochement between the professions and the republic, but lingering problems limited its extent. In contrast to the initial chaos, the more stable Weimar years encouraged a shift in the ideological allegiance and the practice of professionals. Legislation defending the republic, curricular reform, and improvement of business conditions gradually pulled some experts out of their reserve. Intermittent efforts of bourgeois parties such as the DVP and DNVP to cultivate a professional clientele provided associations with important political links and individuals with a home within the republican structure. These growing ties led to a number of significant gains, such as the admission of district court attorneys to superior courts, the improvement of secondary schoolteachers' pay, and the concentration of technology in the Ministry of Transport. However, the painful adjustments of the stabilization process also hindered the psychological integration of practitioners. Ideological legacies of legal independence, cultural elitism, and technocratic pragmatism inspired resistance against SPD or DDP compulsion to democratize. Ironically, traditional professionals invoked their liberal heritage of autonomy for illiberal ends. The price of normalcy such as fee reduction, firing of teachers, and rationalization unemployment caused considerable resentment against the system that exacted it. Therefore, during stabilization, professionals learned to work within the republic without, in the main, embracing it emotionally.[97]

TOWARD REPUBLICAN PROFESSIONALISM

At the turn of the year 1928–1929, professionals viewed the future with more confidence than five years earlier. As a legacy of earlier crises, associations kept grumbling about "grave problems," but individuals were more at peace with themselves and their work. "A fresh wind is blowing through the legal profession," *Anwaltsblatt* editor Heinrich Dittenberger noted. "The encouraging fact

[is] that more and more colleagues interest themselves in professional questions.'' During 1928, the DAV therefore gave itself a new constitution, refurbished its business office, and debated professional ethics, trying to modernize some practices. With the resolution of the AG–LG quarrel over simultaneous admission, attorneys demonstrated a new professional vigor.[98] Teachers were similarly convinced that their enlightened traditionalism was producing positive results. The PhVb ''has known how to preserve what seemed alive, healthy and necessary for the future in the high school and yet understood how to show the way to new and higher goals, demanded by a different time.'' This constructive contribution allowed it to claim more influence in decision making as a neutral expert force: ''In our politically fragmented time, the apolitical professional association, unified through common interests and ideals, gains a special importance.'' Engineers were also gratified by ''the extent to which technical applications penetrate the circle of daily needs'' by expanding into ever newer areas. As ''gathering of the intellectual forces of German technology,'' the VDI took pride in ''keeping the technical conscience clear and awake'' and in ''securing for technology enough space to implement what it deems necessary.''[99]

With the return of a semblance of normalcy, the explicit political involvement of professional associations declined. Nonetheless, ''national'' gestures continued, such as the dedication of a VDI monument to the 581 engineers who had died in the First World War. Professionals did take a stand on internal issues in which their expertise gave them credibility and their interests were affected directly. The proliferation of legislation by emergency decree, for instance, led the extraordinary DAV convention in Berlin in 1925 to demand a return to more ordered legislative procedures. Similarly, teachers got involved in general youth questions and engineers sought to establish ''guidelines . . . and basic plans'' for such problems as road building. However, such issues were now discussed within the constitutional framework in a nonpartisan manner.[100] Cultural nationalism also inspired infrequent appeals in foreign policy questions, which were directed against the Treaty of Versailles. Foreign Minister Gustav Stresemann personally endorsed the special Saar issue in *Technik und Kultur* of the VDDI, hoping that it would be widely imitated. ''One cannot do enough to acquaint the broadest possible circles of the German people with the fate of the Saar area,'' because a widespread awareness of its separation was necessary for ''its reunification to which we have an elementary, natural right.'' To prepare for the *Anschluß* of German speakers outside of the 1919 frontiers, professional associations increasingly scheduled meetings in outposts such as Danzig or Vienna, demonstrating national unity and pride. As an element in foreign cultural policy, the PhVb mounted a regular campaign to support German schools abroad and about one-sixth of all philologues joined the pan-German Verein für das Deutschtum im Auslande (VDA). However, for the majority of academics, the conviction that ''Germany's fate transcends all professional problems,'' only justified peaceful revisionism.[101]

In the final analysis, the attitude of the professions toward Weimar democracy was less a republicanism of reason than of self-interest. The high price of normalcy encouraged centrist professionals to hesitate initially. However, eventually the recovery of economic and political stability improved prospects sufficiently to lead to greater individual acceptance. Collectively, the professional organizations were drawn into the democratic process by fighting for their interests in the parliamentary arena. Though frustrated in achieving all their goals, the associations nonetheless scored enough gains to prove of significant utility to their members. Moreover, prospects for the future looked generally encouraging, promising a continuation of the gradual integration of the apolitical majority. However, without a compelling vision, this *Interessenrepublikanismus* lacked emotional bonding to the republic, because it was essentially performance-oriented. Except for the committed democratic minority, most professionals warmed to Weimar as long as it delivered reasonably stable conditions for a rewarding practice. However, because a return to the imperial order was becoming ever less probable, those practitioners who felt materially or ideologically left out began to cast about for more radical right-wing alternatives.[102] How would this conditional loyalty hold up, when placed under unanticipated economic, social, and ideological strains?

4

The Breakdown of Liberal Professionalism

When the July 1932 election made the NSDAP the strongest party, professionals were forced to take notice of the Nazi challenge. Denouncing the "many undisciplined Jew-boys" in the lawyer chambers, Wilhelm Kube, the Nazi president of the Prussian Landtag, complained that "the majority of practicing attorneys has repeatedly demonstrated ethics which run fundamentally counter to the German sense of honor." Against such "lack of human and political decency," DAV chairman Rudolf Dix protested that advocates were a social and political "microcosm of the German people. I deeply regret that an NS deputy had to insult the entire German nation with this affront to one profession."[1] Less directly attacked, high school teachers debated Ernst Krieck's book on *Nationalpolitische Erziehung* with curious ambivalence. Concerned about the proposed reduction of secondary schooling and references to "philological arrogance," one reviewer, nevertheless, approved of its "original ideas." Opposed to leveling teacher training, other philologues accused the Nazi educational program of "superficiality . . . , insulting misrepresentations," and "pseudo-science," based on "willful and shallow philosophy."[2] In contrast, VDI engineers refused to be drawn into the debate, reaffirming their "duty of unconditional neutrality in religious and political questions." To a surprising extent, the professions ignored the rise of the Nazis, hoping that the threat would pass, if only they carried on their work.[3]

A growing minority of frustrated professionals, nevertheless, began to follow Hitler's call before 1933. As Prussian chairman of the NS Juristenbund, Dr. Roland Freisler charged that the DAV leadership had "no idea what the German people are like." Deploring the "Jewish shysters" in the legal profession, he complained that their "numbers are in inverse relation to their service to the law." With völkisch populism, he claimed that "Nazi jurists reject separate professional ethics, since in contrast to your chambers we know that there is only one sense of honor for a German, be he worker, peasant, soldier, technician, lawyer or doctor."[4] Some teachers like R. Murtfeld also defended Krieck's murky pedagogy, praising his program as scholarly, organic, timely, and political in the best sense:

''We 'philologues' should not fail to understand that our school work is subject to the laws of a new cultural policy which has to subordinate itself to high politics, the national struggle for meaning and living-space.''[5] Even engineers no longer remained immune to irrational currents, claiming with nationalist ardor: ''Only a strong will to live which overcomes petty strife and low egotism in a powerful national spirit will bring the German people back on top.'' In his 1933 New Year's reflection, VDI director Waldemar Hellmich observed an undefined but ''deep longing'' for ''spiritual recovery.'' Contrary to legend, National Socialism not only coerced the professions externally but also conquered them internally.[6]

Ever since January 1933, scholars have wrestled with the causes of the Nazi seizure of power. Like it or not, the *Machtergreifung* is the most important question of German history in the twentieth century. If anything, there are too many answers, depending on ideological preference. Contradicting each other, the general ''explanations'' such as fascism, totalitarianism, or anti-Semitism are metahistorical, stand outside of time and place, and function as credos, which are largely independent of evidence.[7] In contrast, political interpretations of the collapse of the republic or of the rise of the Nazi movement have become almost too specific and deal with a narrow set of influences, without probing the broader motivations behind politics.[8] Intellectual inquiries into the origins of Nazi ideology tend to be long on filiations of ideas but short on the reasons for their attractiveness.[9] The recently fashionable social approach has generated a wealth of hypotheses without completely convincing either. Marxist readings, stressing big-business money, state monopoly capitalism, or the bloc politics of interest groups, often confound cause with effect.[10] Liberal interpretations such as the ''lower middle-class thesis'' have been found wanting by fresh research that reveals broader Nazi appeals, typical of a *Volkspartei*.[11] Finally, economic analyses, focusing on ''the sociology of the slump,'' are stronger on policy decisions than on their impact on collective attitudes.[12] Though suggestive, such partial answers have one crucial failing: They are remote from the daily lives of the overwhelming majority of the people at that time![13]

To explain the nazification of the professions, one must focus more closely on their actual experience during the Depression years. Unfortunately, the existing literature is only moderately useful in this respect. While describing the desperate straits of many lawyers, Fritz Ostler refuses to discuss the reasons for the conversion of some attorneys to Hitler, implying that ''darkness'' fell upon them from the outside.[14] More self-critical, historians of education fasten on the ''social position and political consciousness of primary pedagogues'' rather than the ''national-völkisch'' outlook of secondary schoolteachers and their ambivalence about national socialism.[15] Recent investigations of engineers emphasize that the Nazis ''could appear as saviors in this situation'' without specifying precisely which technicians proved particularly susceptible.[16] The empirical as well as theoretical deficits of such accounts make it necessary to take another look at the impact of the great, multidimensional crisis of the republic's last years. Even if the term has lost its explanatory power through apologetic overuse, this dual economic and political ''crisis'' is a necessary starting point, because contemporaries considered their situation ''critical.'' Heinrich Dittenberger saw ''the crisis of attorneys [as] part of the German crisis,'' Wilhelm Bolle called ''the crisis concept . . . a favorite term of our age,'' and engineers simply talked about ''*the* crisis'' [emphasis added].[17] Instead of providing an easy answer, this pervasive atmosphere poses challenging questions: Precisely what material and psychological effect did the Great Depression have on the professions? Which radical alternatives arose from it to challenge liberal professionalism?

THE IMPACT OF THE GREAT DEPRESSION

When some ''economic slowdown'' became apparent in the fall of 1929, professionals were reluctant to confront the full extent of the ''general depression.'' Though aware that ''the current difficulties of the legal profession must in good part be explained by the overall plight of the nation,'' attorneys rarely tried to analyze its deeper causes and called for ''self-help,'' instead of devising political remedies.[18] Similarly, philologues preferred to interpret the crisis in cultural terms, and, when unable to deny the ''considerable deterioration in the financial situation of the Reich,'' they appealed to compassion but rejected ''saving money at the expense of public officials.''[19] More directly affected, technicians candidly confronted the ''decline of the world economy,'' discussing the impact of the Wall Street crash on German business as early as December 1929. ''We engineers have to look facts in the face'' Conrad Matschoß exhorted, but beyond work, simplicity, and a search for spiritual values, he had no remedies. ''The plight of our times is not primarily caused by the progress of technology, but rather by the frequent failure to make its results available to the economy in the right form.'' For engineers, the machine was not the reason for but the solution to unemployment, because it created more work than it eliminated.[20] Caught in an interest group perspective, most professionals underestimated the depression, misunderstood its causes, and protested pathetically when they were overwhelmed by it.

At first, practitioners carried on as usual, for instance trying to improve the quality of their training. Because of public complaints about declining achievements, lawyers ratified new guidelines for legal education in April 1929. The DAV wanted ''only capable and knowledgeable candidates to become judges and to have attorneys participate more strongly in academic and practical training.''[21] Denying ''criticism of the continued erosion of standards among graduates,'' philologues vigorously defended the ''academic character of the secondary school.'' Emphasizing the need for pedagogical instruction at the university, the PhVb claimed that only ''thorough scholarly study of one subject creates the foundation on which our professional ability can unfold.'' Instead of shifting training to the pedagogical academies for primary schoolteachers, ''the practical art of educating and teaching'' ought to be learned ''at that institution which fully demonstrates this task, namely the high school.''[22] Engineers also kept debating how to ''halt specialization, solidify scientific fundamentals, structure teaching more freely, limit the number of lecture or lab hours, ease transfers between institutions and make examinations more uniform.'' However, aside from some incremental progress at individual THs, the call for more practical economic or social instruction went largely unheeded because of more pressing concerns.[23]

Soon the deepening depression began to disrupt professional life through massive overcrowding. "There is hardly a lecture which is not filled to overflowing. . . . Class-rooms, seminars and institutes have run out of space," Wilhelm Dibelius described the situation at Berlin: "The incredible throng of students is about to explode the university, as higher learning and mass study are incompatible." By summer 1931, student numbers surpassed 138,000, an all-time peak. Because law enrollment had already declined slightly to 20,839, the university expansion was largely due to the growth of the faculty of philosophy which rose to 44,492! At the same time, students at technical colleges also increased to 23,749.[24] Contemporaries considered the threefold increase of high school graduations since 1914 responsible. The educational statistician Wilhelm Oberle blamed "the social and political transformation, the rise of the working class, the improvement of transportation, the support of the poor, the sharpening of economic competition," as well as the academization of primary schoolteaching. Long-range changes such as the increase in the numbers of female students to 18.65 percent and the effect of school reforms *(Deutsche Oberschule, Aufbauschule)* combined with the short-range effects of the depression "to keep students in school, since they cannot find a job." Overcrowding did not stem from prosperity, "but is a sign of need, as strange as that may seem."[25] Although shrinking birth cohorts began to reduce enrollment by some 4664 law and 10,459 philosophy students in the winter of 1932–1933, the academic public grew uncontrollably hysterical about ever greater numbers to come (Table A.1).

The return of overcrowding produced a renewed oversupply of professionals. Since the depression made jobs disappear and reduced public hiring, the excess of educated men and women led to severe unemployment. The steady rise of Prussian law trainees by about 1000 Referendare annually to a total of 10,065 in 1933 placed enormous pressure on admissions to the bar. Even if some 300 found places in the judicial administration, another 150 entered the general bureaucracy, and a few dozen went into business, most recent law graduates had little choice but to swell the ranks of attorneys. By January 1933, there were 19,440 advocates (with Danzig and the Saar), a 58.4 percent increase over 1921 (Table A.5a). Particularly frightening was the doubling of the annual growth rate from a 1927 low of 2.9 percent to a 1933 high of 6.5 percent with no end in sight. Women (all of 113) and retired or dismissed bureaucrats (a total of 899) made minor contributions to this forced expansion, but the bulk of the annual influx of 1000 came from new male practitioners. Because most of the newcomers were 27–28 years old and deaths were few (about 250 annually), attorneys were relatively young (median age of 45.5 years), thus creating only a small replacement demand. Whereas before the First World War there had been one advocate per 5500 people, now there was one solicitor for every 3360 potential clients, a drastic narrowing of the economic base. With 12 percent of salaried lawyers unemployed, attorneys wailed: "The flood is rising inescapably."[26]

Teachers were similarly hard hit. From a supplemental university census, the statistician Eduard Simon concluded that "21.9% of students strive to become a Studienrat; no other German profession is so popular." Because women constituted about one-third of pedagogical enrollment in Prussia, "employment in the high-school service is now the most frequent female career." More than half of the education students majored in modern foreign languages, mathematics, or natural sciences. "In no way does the demand correspond to the strong supply of young teachers which is to be expected for the next five to six years."[27] Actual figures support this grim assessment. The number of Prussian trainees rose consistently from less than 700 in the mid-1920s to 2202 men and 926 women in 1933. Instead of expanding list positions, the Ministry of Culture cut the number of *Anwärter* in half to 1146 and barred new acceptances after 1931. Although this reduction initially decreased probationers to 2132 (in 1930), the depression increased the number again to 4065, even without any employment prospects. The government reduced public hiring from 965 in 1929 to 4 (!) in 1933—thereby stranding those already promised a job (Table A.6b). Adding insult to injury, the cabinet also eliminated about 700 auxiliary teaching positions in 1932, leaving only 952 on the public payroll and terminating the other two-thirds without a Pfennig of severance pay. In spite of earlier reforms, the conjunction of overcrowding with depression drove "the plight of the young teachers" to unprecedented depths.[28]

Engineers also suffered from oversupply, even if the exact extent remains elusive. The appearance of articles in technical journals deploring overcrowding is one indicator that they were afflicted, although industrial employment was more flexible than admission to the bar or public hiring. Arriving at a realistic understanding of the problem is difficult because of the vagueness of the official census categories and totals. If government figures are anywhere near correct, then the virtual doubling of the listed number of engineers and technicians from 111,085 to 203,647 between 1925 and 1933 indicates an influx of about 11,570 graduates annually (Table A.4)! Such a massive surge of 132,562 new engineers in the short span of eight years had to strain the technical labor market during the best of times. In the depression, the annual graduation of one-quarter of an estimated 50,000 TH and technical school students meant "unemploy[ment] to a frightful extent; on average only about 20% find a position, 10% continue their studies, 20% take up some kind of work outside of their training and the remaining 50% have no income at all." The *VDI-Nachrichten* did not overdramatize the situation when warning: "It is no longer rare [to meet] Diplom-Ingenieure from the flophouse who do not know warm food and are happy about any kind of a job, making a few marks as dish-washer, cigarette salesman, or dancehall-partner."[29]

The professions reacted with alarm and anger to their predicament. "The strong exaggerations" and "sensationalist presentation" of the medical statisticians Leonhard Achner and Günther Müller, who warned that the 23,000–30,000 unemployed academics in 1931–1932 were doubling annually, created a "kind of panic" among the educated. Assuming the existence of about 350,000 professionals with 10,500 annual deaths or retirements, they projected that average yearly graduations of appreciably more than 20,000 would produce 120,000 unemployed by 1934! The dire prediction of the Ministry of Labor of a one-third "academic oversupply" was grist for the mill of cultural pessimists, who were ready to denounce the failure of Weimar educational reforms as "the inflation of higher schooling." Painstakingly, the philological statistician Georg Ried tried to correct this "misleading public impression," based on straight-line projections that ignored the beginning contraction of high school enrollments. Because numerous elementary errors such as "exaggerated graduation quotas" made them "worthless,'' these calculations were propaganda material for attacks on the entitlement system rather than scientific proof of an intractable excess.[30] Though with government support, the moderate Georg Keiser reassuringly concluded that overcrowding would disappear of its own accord, fear mongers such as the völkisch publicist Wilhelm Hartnacke dominated public opinion and robbed young people of hope.[31] Dividing practitioners according to educational philosophy, the debate on ''academic proletarianization'' pitted medical against philological interests in a struggle over which career would have to accept the surplus or bear the brunt of the necessary reductions.

Among lawyers, the 1929 DAV prize competition on measures ''to prevent legal overcrowding'' revealed growing sentiment for a *numerus clausus*.[32] The depression shifted opinion dramatically so that 64 of 106 local or provincial chapters now favored a general closure of admission for attorneys, 19 a waiting period of several years, and 16 a limitation of trainees. Nevertheless, the March 1930 DAV meeting once again divided nearly equally, with 56 delegates rejecting and 58 supporting a moratorium on access: ''Two world views confronted each other between which there was no bridge. It was a tragic drama.''[33] When the situation grew increasingly ''critical,'' the united chamber presidents issued an emphatic ''warning against the study of law'' in the spring of 1931. To alleviate ''already existing and threatening overcrowding,'' the chambers also drafted several bills calling for a ''three-year waiting period'' before bar admission and for a trainee *numerus clausus,* based on the ''projected need of the administration of justice'' in the future.[34] But in spite of the emergence of a professional consensus, the Ministry of Justice remained reluctant. Therefore, at the December 1932 emergency congress on ''the fate of attorneys,'' Freiherr von Hodenberg argued movingly that this existential threat could only be met through drastic legislative action. After a passionate debate, the delegates resolved ''unanimously that the destruction of the legal profession can only be avoided if the influx that has been rising for years is finally halted.'' Reversing long-cherished convictions by a lopsided vote of 127 to 19, lawyers ''demand[ed] first an immediately effective barring of admission for three years and eventually a limitation of access to the bar.'' Overcrowding finally forced a break with the tradition of the freie Advokatur—but the decision in favor of professional protectionism came politically too late.[35]

The magic formula with which secondary schoolteachers tried to weather the storm was ''selection'' and ''creation of work.'' Because new legal barriers would decrease high school enrollments and thereby reduce teaching opportunities, the Philologenverband counselled ''*Auslese* [selection] in the schools'' as well as universities. When the Ministry of Culture asked whether to select at the beginning, during, or at the end of training, Prussian philologists rejected barring university entry, although other states like Bavaria, Baden, Württemberg, Saxony, and Hesse were adopting a *numerus clausus*. Thinking meritocratically, liberal teachers preferred public warnings against the study of philology and tougher pupil testing to categorical prohibition of study. In lengthy discussions, philologues developed a catalogue of measures to ''regulate career access'' such as ''making promotion to high school senior more difficult,'' deflecting graduates directly into industrial work, sharpening selection at the university, and ''excluding unsuitable candidates during practical training.''[36] Under pressure from unemployed probationers, the

PhVb also insisted that the government "fulfill its moral obligation . . . to keep them from destitution." Once employed, Assessoren had a legal right to a job while trainees needed special aid. Better yet would be the "creation of work" by eliminating all nonacademic secondary schoolteachers, insisting on male parity in female schools, and the like. Unable to identify the necessary funds, the desperate philologues could only appeal for mutual aid and "hold the Prussian educational administration responsible for the fateful consequences of its indecision for the young who crowd unhindered into a hopeless career."[37]

Less hampered by bureaucratic regulation, engineers responded more cheerfully to their plight. In a strongly worded 1929 memorandum, the VDI polemicized against "the unhealthy overestimation of academic cultivation" and demanded "serious factual information about the true career prospects of engineers." Stressing "real achievements" over entitlements, technicians emphatically rejected "the foundation of new THs." Some individuals like E. Kothe also called for a *numerus clausus,* because the "other path to the engineering profession" through practical experience remained open.[38] More constructive was the creation of an *Ingenieurdienst,* a service "helping young engineers to gain practical experience." Started in November 1930 by VDI funds in Berlin, this concerted action of eighteen technical associations tried "to create employment possibilities in institutions, institutes, organizations and firms" so that young graduates could join the work force for several months. Eventually, this internship model proved so successful that the government started paying a subsidy and thus helped about 2500 beginning engineers to get a trial job that often turned into permanent employment.[39]

Another major consequence of the Great Depression was the impoverishment of many professionals. The "shrinkage of commerce and property has led to a decrease of all those procedures which require legal counsel and action." Although legal business increased to 1931, within two years it fell by one-half from 936.7 to 460.9 cases per capita (Table 2.1). In district court, debt collection decreased from 10.75 to 5.5 million cases, while financial litigation dropped from 496,155 to 134,849, and ordinary cases shrank from 3.09 to 1.84 million. Criminal prosecution also precipitously declined, while more and more cases had to be transacted under poor-law provisions (Table A.11a).[40] Oblivious to professional overcrowding, the government compounded the decrease of litigation by instituting economy measures in the administration of justice through the emergency decree of December 1, 1930. "It shatters the structure of court organization, undermines the preconditions for litigation, weakens legal protection, especially to the disadvantage of the poor, and finally destroys the material basis of the indispensable legal profession," the DAV wailed. The increase in the jurisdiction limit of Amtsgerichte to 800 marks cost the superior courts considerable business, while the reduction of poor-law fees by 10 percent diminished income from Prussian legal expenditures from 20.3 to 14.3 million marks between 1930 and 1932. To their chagrin, the same decree also subjected the free professions to the business tax *(Gewerbesteuer).*[41]

The contraction of work and further fee reduction (October 10, 1931) had a devastating effect on the economic condition of lawyers. "We are starving or we fear starvation," Ludwig Katz warned that overcrowding made the divisor too great and the shrinkage of business made the dividend too small. The chorus of perennial complaints about "the plight of attorneys" sounded increasingly desperate. Whereas in 1928 only 7 percent of lawyers earned less than 3000 marks per year, by 1931 16 percent fell short of the professional minimum, and by 1932 more than 30 percent could no longer make a decent living! In the five depression years, average attorney earnings were cut in half to 9490 marks, leaving a modest real income of 5220 marks compared to a salary of 10,000 marks for a judge! "The suffering is especially great in the large cities such as Berlin, Frankfurt, Cologne, Breslau, Essen and numerous others," where about half of the attorneys fell below the existential minimum. More and more lawyers were unemployed. In March 1930, the DAV placement service noted 434 applications compared to only 4 available jobs, and another observer estimated that 3300 advocates were out of work: "In several big cities attorneys have already been reduced to public welfare." Although some solicitors maintained a profitable practice and a minority continued to get along, most attorneys saw their income decline dramatically. Undoubtedly, the bottom third was being "proletarianized."[42]

As state officials, secondary schoolteachers were more secure—but they also presented an inviting target for budget cuts. In early 1930, a slump-induced shortfall of tax and customs revenue inspired "the plan of an emergency sacrifice" of public salaries to balance the deficit of unemployment insurance. Incensed by such "an unjust, one-sided burden on officials," the Philologenverband rejected the *Notopfer* proposed by Labor Minister Adam Stegerwald and Finance Minister Paul Moldenhauer as "impossible!" The "united defensive front of public officials" in all ranks, a hostile reception by the press, mass demonstrations, the intercession of the Reichsbund höherer Beamter with Chancellor Heinrich Brüning, and the unwillingness of the bourgeois parties to affront their constituency succeeded in postponing an across-the-board cut.[43] Because the cabinet could not force "deficit reduction through salary decrease" through the Reichstag, Brüning on December 1, 1930 imposed the pay cut for officials by emergency decree. The size of the sacrifice was a modest 6 percent, but the precedent was a dangerous "violation of article 129 of the constitution," threatening the principle of "well-earned rights" of the bureaucracy.[44] To the government rationale that "salary losses were compensated by price deflation," philologues replied that declining living costs did not ease their plight, because the worker-based index did not take higher cultural expenses into account. In spite of RhB warnings of "growing need and radicalization" and personal protests to the chancellor against the injustice of greater cuts for higher officials, the increasing public deficit led to another emergency decree on June 5, 1931, imposing an additional 4–7 percent reduction. "Officials lose up to one month's pay," the philologues fumed impotently while a broad spectrum of the press also condemned "the unjust distribution of burdens."[45]

Although the deepening fiscal crisis "made the lack of success of such sacrifices ever more apparent," pay cuts accelerated. As a result of industrial, urban, and union pressure, the cabinet authorized additional savings by the states to balance their budgets on August 24, 1931, precipitating new "catastrophic economies in Prussia." Promotions were frozen for 2 years and most salary supplements were canceled, although "shaken and desperate" Berlin philologues protested such "despotism by emergency decree."[46] The "heaviest blow" fell with the Prussian

Notverordnung of December 1931, cutting teachers' pay an average total of 20 percent and Assessoren more than 40 percent, while sending all 481 Studienräte more than 62 years of age into mandatory retirement! Not having been consulted beforehand, philologues considered themselves persecuted by such an "anti-social, illegal and willful" law and tried to challenge its provisions in court.[47] The final reduction was the Papen cabinet's dual "unemployment-aid" (6 percent for secondary schoolteachers) and compulsory loan (2.5 percent for married pedagogues) of August 1932. Although price deflation seemed to limit the objective loss of buying power to about 10 percent, teachers subjectively experienced these nominal 30–40 percent salary cuts as "deterioration of the *Mittelstand*" (Table A.12). Among the 690 dismissed Prussian Assessoren and the more than 2000 unemployed welfare recipients among probationary teachers (about 70 percent), these economies "left an ocean of desperation." In a scrupulous study of the living standard of higher officials, Adolf Bohlen revealed "a leveling of the salary pyramid to their detriment," a sinking of trainees "below badly paid workers," in short "a decline of culture." However, because officials could still "go on living, in a manner of speaking," the heaviest damage was psychological and political.[48]

Although "the income of engineers also deteriorated considerably," decrease of pay was less devastating than loss of employment.[49] Most directly affected by the business slump, technicians suffered the heaviest unemployment during the Great Depression. The job market for technicians practically collapsed, with open positions declining from about 1950 in the spring of 1927 to 194 in 1932 while job seekers increased from 515 to 1400 between the fall of 1928 and 1932 (Table A.13). By the year 1930 already 2500 Diplom-Ingenieure were out of work, and two years later more than 26 percent of the VDDI members were reputed to be jobless! The 1931 VDI report discussed "the great plight of the unemployed graduates of our THs," and one year later mentioned that "65% . . . remain without any possibility of work." Whereas the VDI warned of more than 20,000 jobless colleagues, the 1933 census listed an astounding 59,325 engineers or technicians as unemployed, at 32.6 percent the highest proportion among the embattled professions![50] For those reduced to the resources of their meager savings or to niggardly charity, deprivation was not only relative but also absolute.

Overcrowding and impoverishment fragmented the social status of professionals. While the fiftieth anniversary of the RAO celebrated the place of the legal profession in "the top social life of our nation," growing numbers of attorneys were losing the means to maintain a professional life-style. When "certain regrettable instances of corruption" revived old anti-lawyer prejudices, Rudolf Dix argued in a press conference: "We are conscious that we are only one part of the heavily suffering national community and feel obligated to share the plight of our fellow citizens." To counter the "impression of the lawyer as servant of capital who sells his valuable abilities to the highest bidder and neglects his social duties," he pointed to the creation of "collective legal defense bureaus" for the poor.[51] Teachers were similarly defensive about their public image. At the twenty-fifth anniversary of its founding, the PhVb celebrated the growing "recognition of the academically trained teachers among the other higher officials" as one of its great successes.[52] However, it increasingly encountered "the unpleasant stereotype of the German Oberlehrer," which had been created by "a literature of pedagogical criticism'' of famous authors like Heinrich Mann, Frank Wedekind, Erich Maria Remarque, or Ernst Glaeser. Philologues attributed this negative view to ''sentimental humanitarianism . . . dominant primitive sexuality . . . political polarization and especially the ill-fated entitlement system.'' Unwilling to resort to press propaganda, teachers preferred to create better ''pedagogical personalities'' in order to counteract criticism.[53] For technicians, the slump aggravated old status problems and created new ones. ''Too heavily weighs the present economic situation'' on engineers to celebrate the ''immense progress of technology'' at the seventy-fifth anniversary of the VDI ''with hopeful enthusiasm.''[54] Moreover, TH graduates still struggled to be recognized as regular, full members of the educated stratum, the so-called *Vollakademiker.* To charges of ''arrogance and caste spirit,'' they replied: ''One should finally also concede the same right to the Diplom-Ingenieure as to the other academic professions, namely to pursue their interests through their own association, and cease accusing them of false pride.'' The educated seemed to be losing more status than any other stratum.[55]

The depression also rendered professional practice more difficult. The rapid succession of emergency decrees created legal uncertainty, while the limitation of appeals and the protection of debtors—especially in the rural East—complicated litigation. Though initially multiplying economic disputes, the slump aggravated old complaints such as the barring of attorneys from labor courts or arbitration, bureaucratic hostility, and unlicensed competition from consultants.[56] One innovative response was specialization. Modernizers such as Sigbert Feuchtwanger supported the introduction of the *Fachanwalt* as a way to generate more business, but traditionalists like Arthur Oppenheimer resisted such ''unethical competition'' that would squeeze out the small attorney. The long-standing deadlock was broken when the 1929 Hamburg congress ''approved the public announcement of specialization'' for fields such as tax, copyright, state and administrative, international, or labor law (eventually also trade and social insurance questions). Though ''a step of self-help in difficult times,'' the cumbersome procedure of a five-year waiting period, chamber approval, and advertising curbs admitted only 39 specialists in 1930—hardly enough to revitalize legal practice in general![57] A more useful innovation was the creation of central collection agencies in Berlin and Leipzig for judgments which fell increasingly into default. In spite of traditionalist grumbling, this *Vollstreckungshilfe* with a card file and special investigators saved time and money, provided that there was something left to collect.[58]

While philologues welcomed the subsiding of school reform struggles, classroom teaching also suffered from economy measures. In the spring of 1931, the Prussian Ministry of Culture consolidated the double reduction of teaching hours for 45- and 55-year-olds in a single stroke at the age of 50, leading to ''a further barbaric overburdening'' of 5000 Studienräte. The uniform 25- or 23-hour load meant ''a ruthless exploitation of labor, an increased danger to health, [and] a heightened nervousness of instruction'' that decreased pedagogical effectiveness. Unable to withstand the pressure for savings completely, the Philologenverband suggested less harmful instructional economies such as ''limiting special electives,'' combining parallel courses, having only two entry classes per high school, reducing technical-artistic subjects, decreasing weekly hours, and dissolving marginal institutions. In Westphalia such mandated reductions resulted in the closing of two institutions and the loss of 5.9 percent pupils, 3.8 percent classes, and 3.9 percent teachers. In addition to "worsening working conditions," these economies steadily enlarged class sizes beyond the norm of 30 for the lower, 25 for the middle, and 20 for the higher grades, lengthened periods to 50 minutes, decreased weekly instruction hours to 30, suspended continuing education courses, and abolished trainee supplements, thereby "endangering teaching success." Surveying their experience in the republic, teachers concluded bitterly that they "were reaching the end of their energy." Falling disproportionately upon philologues, further cuts "threaten *a catastrophe of the high school.*"[59]

For engineering practice, the depression posed new economic challenges. Given the oversupply of graduates, the gravest problem was finding work at all, if necessary by opening up "new technological territory." Whereas engineers had traditionally been involved in construction, according to Waldemar Hellmich they were about "to conquer production" through efficiency training within the *Arbeitsgemeinschaft für Betriebsingenieure.* Although they had long designed investment goods, the lack of jobs was pushing an increasing number of graduates into the development of consumer products as well: "Beyond creating and manufacturing a diesel engine jet, [making] a teapot is slowly gaining acceptance as an engineering task." VDI initiatives in food industry, home appliances, or noise and dust reduction tried to devise fresh applications for technology. The slogan of *Ingenieurneuland* also applied to "the area of sales"—analogous to "channelling water flows"—into which technicians ventured only hesitantly. But the more technical a product, the more an engineer was needed. Finally, management—called problematically "the organic" area—was just emerging as a possibility. Expanding the boundaries of engineering practice required overcoming internal and external obstacles, not the least of which were psychological, because neither business nor bureaucracy was particularly eager to hire technicians. While carving out a job in an unlikely area like a sausage factory might be gratifying, many engineers were displaced from their traditional tasks and felt dissatisfied by having to toil for their bread in strange fields.[60]

The dislocation of the depression eventually created "a crisis of professional consciousness." According to the progressive attorney Sigbert Feuchtwanger, "a sum of capable practitioners is not yet a profession." The material problems had a deeper cause: "Lawyers are suffering from the 'absence' of a professional ideal." The "growing competition from outside and inside" increasingly led to ethical failures that made "a revision of the problematic lawyers' code necessary." Because the press reported more embezzlement and conflict of interest, there was general agreement on this diagnosis. However, how should one reform the legal profession to make it "a community which through systematic measures secures . . . the spiritual and material preconditions for individual freedom to work?"[61] One controversial suggestion was the liberalizing of fee schedules to make attorneys competitive with nonacademic legal consultants. Arguing for the preservation of "a special profession with its own consciousness and ethics," Albert Pinner rejected "simply joining the ranks of businessmen," since being a lawyer was "not primarily a trade but a service to justice." Because "this traditional view has artificially restricted our ability to compete," moderates pleaded for "reforming professional consciousness.'' More drastic proposals suggested a division into court and business attorneys in order to resolve ''the incongruence between legal organization and the general socio-economic structure.'' In spite of ingenious pleas for the modernization of ethics, the 1931 Leipzig congress rejected the liberalization of fees in debt collection by a vote of 82 to 28.[62] The polarization of attorneys between innovators and traditionalists also limited the reform of the honor court system to ''the elimination of the worst defects'' by tightening admission procedures and creating a lesser penalty—the reprimand.[63]

Among teachers, self-doubt manifested itself less in attempts to redefine their role than in efforts to reassert pedagogical authority. According to the revealing letters between the Latinist Otto Schumann and the Germanist Martin Havenstein, practical frustrations combined with intellectual vexations in a philippic against the ''cultural crisis of the age.'' Annoyed by ministerial reform directives, these outspoken schoolmen resented overburdening, criticized the influence of liberal politics on education, and ridiculed ''the lack of direction with which we are governed.'' To varying degrees both rejected youth-centered pedagogy, complained about the trivialization of cultivation, deplored the leveling mass tendencies, disapproved of contemporary literature, and even discussed Jewish lack of appreciation for German classics.[64] Other Protestant philologues criticized the hollowness of ''modern pedagogy'' and called for a return to ''discipline'' in the classroom. To reverse ''the dissolution of community and loss of values,'' the religion teacher Konrad Jarausch argued that ''all of our school work must be structured so as to combat this disintegration.'' Demanding ''a radical rejection of the dominant cult of the individual,'' he urged resubjecting youths to ''the natural bonds of family, tribe, people,'' and school in order to restore meaningful teaching and learning relationships. In the crisis atmosphere of the last Weimar years such neoconservative injunctions became popular, especially when clothed in the language of the *Volk*. Unable to provide a spiritual renewal, the PhVb demanded active government support to avert ''a mood even more dangerous than a sense of crisis, namely resignation, fatigue and a lack of trust.''[65]

Engineers dealt with the uncertainty of their self-image by intensifying their struggle for a cohesive Weltanschauung. Wilhelm von Pasinski argued for moving ''from technology to culture'' in order to escape the subordinate position among the educated. ''Especially the engineer is in danger of remaining a prisoner of the narrow circle of his professional duties without power or will to lift himself to higher horizons.'' The Swiss Aurel Stodola pleaded for an ennobled, hopeful realism, while Rudolf Plank propagated a ''metatechnology,'' fusing specialized knowledge with general culture and Conrad Matschoß called for an ''idealist technology of the future.''[66] By striving for meaning beyond the machine and for recognition beyond the factory, engineering became vulnerable to idealistic mystification. In a provocative reflection on ''changes in the centers of German culture,'' Fritz Reuter denounced the mechanistic world view as the matrix of materialism and called for a rededication in völkisch terms. The subsequent debate in *Technik und Kultur* accepted much of his indictment, also talking about a ''turning point,'' the need for stronger willpower, or the superiority of the ''Germanic spirit.'' Democratic engineers like Eugen Diesel believed that ''incredible nonsense is being written about technology'' and retained their faith in ''courageous and determined progress.'' However, the depression created enough self-doubt to allow irrational currents to enter this ''profession without [living] space.''[67]

In the long run, the depression also strained the organizational fabric of the professions. To counteract the ''regrettable disunity of representation,'' lawyers tried to integrate grass roots activity more firmly into the national DAV by consolidating the 157 local associations into one-third as many district groups. On the Reich level, attorneys created eight committees on civil law, civil procedure, criminal, public, international, insurance, and traffic law as well as on professional issues in order to formulate policy positions.[68] Because they resented the blocking of remedies by cliques of notables in better circumstances, suffering practitioners called for more representative elections to the national delegate assembly through lists with candidates who were ideologically distinctive. But in the summer of 1932, grumbling about unresponsive leadership led to the creation of a ''self-help association of German attorneys,'' which was spearheaded by the maverick Hans Soldan. Fearing the fragmentation of ''unity and resolve,'' Rudolf Dix retorted that failure did not stem from insufficient effort but ''from the conditions of the time and the lack of political clout and influence of the small group of attorneys.''[69] To increase their weight, lawyers also kept pushing for a Reichsanwaltskammer with wide competency, such as ''advancing the interests of German attorneys'' in public and government. In spite of some ministerial sympathy, this initiative—derided by critics as ''a reactionary idea—went nowhere and a more modest successor bill seemed not urgent enough to become law.[70] ''The critical situation of the legal profession'' did prompt one organizational reform, namely, the transfer of association headquarters to Berlin in order to have lawyer views more effectively represented in the capital. Appealing to ''organizational discipline,'' the DAV offered just enough possibility for internal change to keep most followers loyal. However, some dissidents dropped out, decreasing the share of its members among attorneys slightly from 82.5 percent in 1929 to 79 percent in January 1933.[71]

With fewer outlets for self-help, secondary schoolteachers had difficulty in coping with increasing organizational tensions. The erosion of ''professional civil service'' privileges made members restive, because the gap between calls for ''a hard, inflexible will and united action'' and actual results regarding pay or overburdening problems appeared to be widening. Hindered by the decentralization of cultural policy and the statutory exclusion of ''confessional or political interests,'' the PhVb could only work through ''establishing ties to other important interest groups and institutions . . . shaping the formation of public opinion [or] cooperating with appropriate offices,'' which was a slow and thankless task. The slump also made ''collaboration, codetermination and coresponsibility'' difficult, because the ministry grew hesitant to consult the PhVb, ''forcing it to criticize after the fact . . . [and] to resort to opposition tactics,'' a negative and unsatisfactory stance.[72] Frustrated by perceived inaction of the state leadership, provincial chapters began to voice public criticism and demand greater representation on the governing board and control over the executive committee. At the same time, clashes of interest between different ranks such as directors, regular teachers, girls' school pedagogues, and trainees strained internal harmony, because each group wanted preferential treatment. Whereas making the constitution more representative in 1930 reduced dissatisfaction, contentious issues such as the bankruptcy of the RhB bank due to mismanagement kept tempers flaring. In order to contain the "strong activism" of probationers within the association, the PhVb energetically championed their interests as long as these did not conflict with tenured teacher desires, such as the pensioning of sixty-year-olds. Although it managed to preserve unity and dues generated a national budget of about 95,000 marks, PhVb membership stagnated at about 30,000 because unemployed entering professionals grew reluctant to join.[73]

Among engineers, the depression had less impact on organization. When celebrating its seventy-fifth anniversary, the VDI presented itself as prosperous and influential, full of "faith in its own strength." With the 53 district associations, 1200 annual lectures, 11 glossy journals, a publishing house, about 30 topical committees, more than 40 sponsored research projects, and new members increasingly academic, the VDI was the epitome of a successful organization. The only sign of trouble was an 8.6 percent membership drop from a high of 30,788 in 1930 due to technical unemployment. Its secret was good management and the refusal to engage in any controversial issue that divided engineers as professionals.[74] In contrast, the VDDI, when looking back on 20 years in 1929, could see more obstacles to "the historical mission of German *Akademikertum*" than achievements, except for the preservation of the association with about 6000 members. Because neither title protection nor chambers were succeeding, the VDDI concentrated on raising the professional consciousness of Diplom-Ingenieure and on improving their training at the THs. The impact of the "German crisis" pushed academic engineers into redefining their task as strengthening the "national community." Frustrated in their professional aspirations, VDDI members were more susceptible to elitist calls for authoritarian leadership.[75]

The general socioeconomic slump triggered a specific crisis of the German professions. Latent since the First World War, it surfaced in the chaotic beginning of Weimar, abated without being cured during stabilization, and erupted fully during the Great Depression. Long incubation made for particular virulence, as the prevalent crisis mentality indicates. Induced by "reparations payments in gold, export increases, rationalization, unemployment insurance, and the depression," fiscal misery led to severe overcrowding, material impoverishment, and status loss through unemployment, a situation symbolized by the slogan of "academic proletariat." Secondary effects involved the disruption of training, complication of practice, unsettling of consciousness, and strains in organization, affecting virtually all areas of professional life in some way. Compared to the survival threat to unskilled laborers, the relative deprivation of professionals may seem mild. However, the bankrupt attorneys, the dismissed teachers, or the unemployed young engineers hardly thought so, being threatened in their professionalism, the core of self-esteem. Not the extent of the material suffering, but the ideological reaction to it was crucial. According to the perceptive Minister of Culture Adolf Grimme, "the psychological situation of the teachers is decisive." Among philologues, the depression "undermined the bases of our official position not only materially, but, what is worse, spiritually." The political effects of widespread anguish about "legal insecurity, erosion of trust, confusion of values and radicalization" depended on the remedies proposed by the associations as well as the responses of the governments to the plight. When "the hope for an economic revival died," professionals had run out of "magic solutions."[76] If liberal policies faltered, then which radical remedies might emerge?

THE RISE OF NAZI ALTERNATIVES

"The problem of superfluous and unemployed German academics has reached the stage of highest danger." In mid-1932, the student aid director Reinhold Schairer warned that "the fate of these tens of thousands hangs like an avalanche over the otherwise peaceful valley of academic professions. Their masses grow and nobody sees a way out."[77] However, it was not for want of ideas that the crisis of the professions proved so intractable. There was no dearth of short-term proposals such as public warnings against studying a certain subject or dissemination of information on career prospects, increased meritocratic selection during all levels of training, and self-help such as the Ingenieurdienst. Since they were essentially compromises between traditionalist inaction and reformist activism, these liberal measures were often implemented too timidly (like the Fachanwalt). Long-term solutions such as waiting for the arrival of smaller birth cohorts took too much time to produce visible results. Bickering about whether the high school, the university, or the profession itself should bear the brunt of the reductions undermined cooperation. Given the severe constraints of falling revenue and failing borrowing, appeals for increased state funding were exercises in futile rhetoric. Therefore, those most affected such as beginning, unemployed, or marginal practitioners felt abandoned by professional elites. Although it meant breaking with their liberal legacy, an increasing number of suffering academics called for protectionism, barring training or admission through a *numerus clausus,* imposing bureaucratic controls, or instituting technocratic leadership. Republican moderation did not work quickly enough to forestall calls for the return of an authoritarian professionalism.

Although national and state governments were keenly aware of the crisis of the professions, they acted too little and too late. From the beginning, associations bombarded their ministries with petitions and memoranda, outlining their plight. However, in the great storm of the depression, these little gusts were of small concern. Real and imagined budget constraints—enunciated in uncompromising terms by the Ministry of Finance—aggravated the problem instead of solving it. For instance, reductions in poor-law case reimbursements accelerated the impoverishment of legal professionals while teacher dismissals and hiring freezes for trainees created more unemployment when many pedagogues were already out of work. Bureaucratic procrastination needlessly postponed inexpensive remedies such as the Reichsrechtsanwaltskammer, which might have afforded some symbolic relief. Often not unsympathetic, individual officials were caught between the pleas of their clients and the exigencies of general politics. Because they had grown tired of repeated warnings about the price of political disaffection, the ministries—preoccupied with stronger constituencies—heeded the potential damage all too little. Claiming to be benevolent toward the professions, the last Weimar cabinets at best sponsored ineffective palliatives, such as improving career advising. President Friedrich Syrup of the national unemployment office reacted in typical fashion to the proposal for introducing a small make-work program, called *Akademikerhilfe,* for all graduates, not just engineers. Beyond voluntary labor service (FAD), "special support for a particular profession cannot be justified."[78]

A telling example of inertia was the government's response to overcrowding. Ever since 1835, the Prussian Ministry of Culture had followed the debate on the danger of "an academic proletariat" in newspaper articles, journal essays, and petitions. One such alarmist memorandum by Dr. E. Kelter concluded that there were 94 percent more law as well as 166 percent more philosophy students than necessary and counselled a drastic reduction of enrollment by two-thirds![79] To obtain an independent data base, the ministry in early 1930 sponsored the creation of a "Central Economic Office for University Studies and Academic Professions" that was to "clarify the important economic and cultural problems of the entitlement system and of academic overcrowding." Directed by Prof. Bernhard Harms at Kiel and funded with 80,000 marks annually, this research center found the "investigation of the selection, training and professional integration of students" more difficult than imagined, because an uncertain number of annual graduates could not be neatly matched with an even more elusive figure of jobs. Instead of making accurate predictions about "academic supply and demand," the institute produced popular pamphlets "on the situation of academic professions" such as doctors, dentists, and foresters, as well as a monograph on legal examinations. Although the *Volkswirtschaftliche Zentralstelle* tried to calm the overcrowding hysteria through accurate statistics, it was eventually swallowed up by cutbacks and right-wing political opposition to its "enlightened" approach. For professionals hit by the crisis, "scholarly" studies were cold comfort, because they legitimized the postponement of decisive action.[80]

Given the organizational structure of the Weimar Republic, only complex and prolonged negotiations between the ministries, professional associations, and economic interest groups could produce effective relief. The first discussion on overcrowding on June 2, 1930—sponsored by the Reich Ministry of Interior—emphasized redirecting pupils from higher education into jobs at a lower level. Another meeting reviewed possible steps to reduce graduation rates such as making training more expensive, tests harder, and work more attractive. On February 10, 1931, Prussia instituted sharper "pupil selection" while the Reich education committee propagated the introduction of a "differentiated Abitur."[81] To prevent youthful radicalization, in January 1932 Interior Minister Wilhelm Groener suggested "steering pupils away from higher education and facilitating their entry into practical occupations." Led by Eduard Hamm of the Deutscher Industrie- und Handelstag, the "placement" subcommittee tried to prod business into giving jobs to the 28.1 percent of secondary school graduates who did not want to continue a formal education as well as the 18.7 percent who were still undecided. Chaired by Prof. Fritz Tillmann of the Verband deutscher Hochschulen, the "selection" subcommittee (with the VDI but without the PhVb) discussed facilitating job entry with lower certification *(Mittlere Reife)* and reducing the number of graduates from schools and universities.[82] But since Prussia rejected "mandatory planning for intellectual cultivation" while Bavaria favored restrictions, it proved impossible to reach agreement among the German states. Eduard Spranger opposed the introduction of intermediate tests, compulsory curricula, or a *numerus clausus,* because "the university does not have the capacity to reduce the excessive number of students effectively." Similarly, officials called the pensioning of sixty-year-olds ineffectual, women professionals rejected reducing "female education" and careers for reasons of equality, while eliminating dual-wage earning proved practically difficult. Therefore, the overcrowding committee finally recommended less drastic solutions such as tougher high school selection coupled with a year of work in industry, or rural settlement. By the end of 1932, these expert debates had accomplished little beyond public warnings, job counseling, tightening of admission, retention, and graduation standards, and facultative enrollment limits in cramped institutes. The last Weimar cabinets failed to resolve overcrowding, because they were hampered by bureaucratic procrastination, democratic scruples, and interest group politics.[83]

The final effort at interprofessional cooperation against the crisis was similarly stillborn. Overcrowding and unemployment gave new urgency to Otto Everling's attempts to "unite German workers of the mind" on behalf of the DNVP. Most associations among free professionals (21 with 129,610 members), public officials (RhB with 95,000 followers), white-collar employees (4 with 47,000 subscribers), and others (representing another 52,000), joined his "protective cartel of German workers of the mind." However, the efforts of this comprehensive representation to "counter the immiserization of the cultural stratum" through job exchanges and tax relief produced disappointing results. Even founding a tighter "working group of academic professional associations" in late 1932 did not bring about that collaboration, "which has often been attempted but never achieved." It was well and good to intone with conviction before the press: "Decreasing and easing the professional crisis of German academics is a pressing and important task today." However, compiling a list of twenty-five demands that summarized academic frustration was easier than implementing them with effective action. This well-meaning DNVP deputy contributed to raising public consciousness about "the plight of the professionals" and to putting pressure on the bureaucracies. However, conflicting interests of individual professions, such as the rivalry between lawyers and engineers for technical public jobs, as well as competing desires of entering versus established practitioners prevented a common course.[84] Ultimately, the failure of liberal remedies, government solutions, and cooperative efforts paved the way for radical alternatives.

Collectivist or socialist prescriptions promised a more effective cure. Because free professionals were neither officials nor businessmen but "holders of a social office" in the public trust, Feuchtwanger advocated the "socialization of the legal profession" to secure its livelihood while preserving its autonomy.[85] Beginning to transform an individual practitioner into a *Kollektivanwalt,* the DAV-sponsored collection agency in Leipzig attempted "voluntary cooperation" for financial reasons. The Berlin guidelines for distributing poor-law mandates were similarly egalitarian, because "these may come to play the same role for attorneys as insurance cases for doctors." In larger cities, the spread of collective practice from "office sharing" to integrated partnerships as well as the introduction of free legal aid "for the poor without regard to occupation, religion or party membership" also seemed to point toward socialized law.[86] Against the resistance of most of their colleagues, younger teachers searched for collectivist remedies as well. Prodded by dissatisfied students, the Assessoren demanded "job creation" through "stretching work," which would be funded by savings from pay reductions. However, egalitarian *Arbeitsstreckung* appeared to the PhVb as ineffective and wrongheaded, since such "measures could be interpreted as a struggle against tenured philologues." After heated discussions with trainee representatives, the association rejected job sharing, because it would create the danger of "replacing professional officials with badly paid and dependent employees who can always be fired."[87] Some technicians were also fascinated by the Bolsheviks' gigantic electrification schemes, which created consulting opportunities in Russia and looked like socialist technocracy. Nonetheless, the bulk of engineers remained utterly "opposed to the class struggle."[88]

When the depression seemed to confirm Marxist predictions, a minority of professionals joined small but committed leftist groups. Because the DAV was relatively liberal, it took until March 1928 to found a "free association of democratic attorneys" under the auspices of Interior Minister Erich Koch-Weser. During a Reichstag soiree more than one hundred attorneys and chamber board members debated the DDP program and created a permanent organization so as to "meet an often felt need." Farther to the left were the 132 lawyers of the Rote Hilfe Deutschlands, such as Felix Halle, or Hans Litten who defended Socialists and Communists in political trials for modest fixed fees. Though vigorous and articulate attorneys like Max Hirschberg and Rudolf Olden worked hard to democratize the judicial system, splinter groups like the Association of Social-Democratic Jurists were too limited to present a viable alternative.[89] Among pedagogues, a small but active Republican Teachers' League competed with several socialist associations: The radical members of the Verband sozialistischer Lehrer were close to the USPD and KPD, while the moderates of the Arbeitsgemeinschaft sozialdemokratischer Lehrer were more in tune with the SPD, and there was even a teachers' union, renamed Allgemeine Freie Lehrergewerkschaft Deutschlands in 1928. Dominated by primary-school pedagogues, these leftist groups looked unattractive to all but a few academics for whom joining meant renouncing their professional standing among colleagues.[90] In the technical field, the "employees' union" ButaB lost almost half its members during the depression (down to 54,043) and no longer posed a serious challenge. In spite of the emergence of a sociology of intellectuals and the organization of a Verband Sozialdemokratischer Akademiker, Socialists failed to organize the professions, which they considered bourgeois and thereby beyond the pale.[91] At the same time, most professionals recoiled from socialist solutions because they were foreign to their milieu, ran counter to the ideas received in Gymnasium and university, required breaking with the social norms of the Bildungsbürgertum, and were incompatible with "professionalism" as defined by liberal elites.

At the other extreme, authoritarian solutions found increasing resonance among moderate practitioners. Restorative longings prompted attorneys to attempt prohibiting the competition of legal consultants, because their "often irresponsible and mostly uncontrolled activity . . . creates grave dangers for the public." Traditionalists criticized advertising as a violation of legal ethics and tried to use the honor courts in order to "police the profession." Because liberals dominated the

DAV and most chambers, authoritarian lawyers could at best retard innovations by invoking a somewhat twisted legacy of freie Advokatur.[92] Protectionist sentiment also induced pedagogues to try displacing their nonacademic colleagues. Claiming that 2756 music, sport, art, and other technical instructors were taking up their places, unemployed Assessoren insisted on restoring the "academic character of the secondary school" by pushing former seminarians back into lesser institutions. Similarly, philologues demanded that "the governmental preference for women must cease," thereby returning male teachers to girls' schools and keeping females out of boys' institutions. Eliminating the "unnecessary" earnings of married female teachers would create jobs for male breadwinners, while "double-dipping through second jobs" ought to be eliminated.[93] Not even engineers remained immune to authoritarian impulses. In 1931, the legal protection of the title *Baumeister* for master builders inspired the VDI to propose a British-style "engineering list," which would convey "the right to use the professional title 'engineer,' " based on VDI membership criteria of training and experience. However, the VDDI rejected this compromise as "fundamentally wrong," because "combining people of completely different educational achievements" afforded insufficient protection to TH graduates.[94]

A more radical challenge came from the völkisch fringes of the profession. Invoking the Lohengrin myth in his manual on the "mission of the attorney," Bremen lawyer Richard Finger propounded a populist vision: "As a German, the German lawyer has a German vocation for the German people and must strive for a German law." The "old Germanic ideal of a community of fate" would cure the materialist ills of "unjust capitalism" and lead to the "rebirth of German law." Because "the imperiled vital needs of the German people transcend currently valid law," Finger reasoned dangerously that "the German lawyer should work toward a true justice," dedicated to völkisch survival.[95] Similarly, the eugenic rantings of the Saxon school director Dr. Wilhelm Hartnacke warned that education mania equaled reproductive death. "The excessive, exaggerated and over-expanded education system of today" produced "a loss of the will to procreate" among the cultivated, thereby "murdering the future." Because talent was genetically limited, education should no longer be a pathway to mobility and women ought to return to their biological role, leaving only a few students, "suited for higher intellectual work." Seeing overcrowding, decadence, and political impotence as inextricably intertwined, Hartnacke called for a völkisch renewal: "Above all, we must get away from the excesses of formal democracy."[96] At the same time, engineers began to talk about the need to create "an elite which can dominate the dull mass through moral superiority." The self-evident collapse of capitalism and the ineffectiveness of political measures reawakened technocratic leadership aspirations. The prevalent "disorder and decay of all areas of public and private life" demanded reconstruction according to a different principle: "Renewal and recovery can only be expected from a truly corporate development." Such professional neocorporatism might finally turn the dream of "a strong, independent profession of academic engineers within the national community" into reality.[97]

Spawned in this authoritarian and völkisch milieu, the new Nazi associations that emerged during the depression were more successful than earlier right-wing affiliates. Attorneys became important for Adolf Hitler personally and the NSDAP collectively when both needed defense counsel in the frequent political trials that they provoked. One of the most able and ambitious solicitors was a young assistant at the Technical University of Munich, Dr. Hans Frank. A war veteran, this Bavarian lawyer's son had already become an enthusiastic follower of Hitler in June 1919 and entered the party and SA in 1923. On November 1, 1928, his case load having grown too heavy for one person to handle alone, twenty-nine lawyers who belonged to the party founded a League of NS German Jurists (BNSDJ) for "the advancement of the general aims of the NSDAP." Keeping street fighters out of jail and working for the seizure of power were complemented by professional aims: "In all legal issues concerning the party, its program or members, the League is empowered to take a position and to influence the development of German legal life ideally as well as practically from a NS perspective." According to Hitler's founding charge, the BNSDJ had a monopoly in legal party matters, but, as a result of Frank's scholarly interests, it strove for the renewal of law in general: "The plight of German law is a vital question for our time and a task in the forefront of our party activity." Prerequisites for membership were academic standing as demonstrated by "legal or administrative training and completion of one final examination" as well as party membership, indicating the league's political auxiliary status. In contrast to purely professional associations, the BNSDJ was run according to the Führer-principle, with essential powers reserved for Hans Frank who delegated them to *Gauobmänner* in the party districts. As the newspaper *Bayernkurier* dryly commented, by academic standards this was, indeed, "a strange creation."[98]

In spite of Hitler's notorious dislike for lawyers, the BNSDJ slowly began to grow after the party's public commitment to legality. Prodded by Frank, the Führer declared in a Leipzig courtroom after his 1930 electoral breakthrough: "I want to come to power legally within the constitution just as any other political party desires to do." Provoked by the cross-examination of Hans Litten, Hitler also abjured force in Berlin-Moabit during May 1931. In 1929, there were only 60 to 80 NS lawyers; a year later league membership crept up to 233; in 1931, numbers expanded to 701, by 1932 membership doubled to 1374, and by April 1933 there were roughly 1624 NS jurists.[99] Building upon this momentum, Frank managed to consolidate his organization in early 1930 by creating a national legal office within the political NSDAP leadership in Munich: "In order to transform the existing conditions fundamentally in a NS direction it is necessary . . . for one center to formulate standards in all areas of life so as to unify ethics, custom and justice in written law." This Reichs-Rechtsamt should "win the best racial and professional talent" for the BNSDJ and coordinate "legal defense" for the party. Moreover, it claimed a general role in the drafting of new legislation and in renewing "the chief legal areas of individual, racial, real estate, administrative, police, state, [and] community law."[100]

One of the first activities of the lawyer league was the production of a biweekly supplement to the party organ, the *Völkischer Beobachter*. After its October 1930 and March 1931 conferences in Leipzig, the BNSDJ expanded it into a new journal, called *Deutsches Recht* in order to "prepare, in the service of Adolf Hitler's movement, the way for the idea of German law, without which the

Third Reich cannot exist.'' In the first issue, Hans Frank rhapsodized programmatically about the ''awakening of German law.'' Castigating the decision on monetary revaluation, abortion combined with divorce practices, and the protection of the republic law, he played on traditionalist aversion to materialism, politicization, immorality, lack of honor, and excessive individualism. Claiming that ''German man is deeply alienated from his law,'' he held, in a classic summation of the anti-Semitic stereotype, the ''rootless, asiatic-oriental, crooked, intriguing, lying, sensationalist decadence-lawyers'' responsible. Long on resentment, Frank was short on prescriptions, beyond asserting: ''Whatever benefits the völkisch community shall be law.'' Reintroduction of the death penalty, forced sterilization—he was not squeamish about the ''brutal, yes even partly inhumane'' cure, which was required ''in order to save everything spiritual in one necessary stroke.'' For NS lawyers such as the racist Walter Luetgebrune, ''intellectual renewal'' implied the elimination of Jewish corruptions such as material ''greed,'' empty formalism, and alienation from a popular sense of justice. On a more mundane level, the *Deutsches Recht* also published job listings and promoted the third BNSDJ conference in November 1932.[101]

A corresponding Nazi teachers' organization emerged earlier but was formalized later. Its driving force was the primary-school pedagogue Hans Schemm from Bayreuth, who joined the party in 1923 and eventually became district leader *(Gauleiter)* for Upper Franconia. Unusually energetic and not content with his modest occupational role, he was a gifted orator who dabbled in laboratory science, continuing education, and Free Corps politics. During the 1926 NS party congress, he gathered a handful of teachers to discuss common interests, and in January 1927 twenty-three pedagogues from Bavaria, Saxony, and Thuringia formally convened in the Franconian city of Hof to organize a counterpart to ''the existing teacher associations which were led by socialists, democrats or political Catholics and protected the Weimar Republic.'' Building upon völkisch antecedents, this NS teachers' group pursued the following goals:

1. Energetic, ruthless struggle within the general organization of the NSDAP with the aim of conquering political power in the Reich and the states.
2. Ideological penetration of education, culture, religion, and art with Nazi ideals.
3. Creation of organizational and personal resources to consolidate and stabilize that transformation in the Reich and the states.
4. Struggle for academic teacher training.
5. Ruthless struggle against the largely liberal, Marxist and democratically infected teachers' organization in the states and the Reich.
6. Struggle against cultural Bolshevism on the broadest front regarding all areas of life.

Whereas the conquest of power and the renewal of German culture were political goals, the pleas for academic teacher training and the campaign against existing teacher associations concerned professional interests, revealing old frustrations of primary school pedagogues. Moreover, the ''struggle'' rhetoric sounded a more brutal nationalist note.[102]

After several further informal gatherings, the first official meeting of the National Socialist Teachers League (NSLB) took place at Hof on April 21, 1929. This time fifty pedagogues responded to the call to "create an activist core among teachers everywhere, ready to work unceasingly on mobilizing those forces which can guarantee the revival of our people." In an inspiring but vague speech, Hans Schemm stressed that the struggle for power had priority over the elaboration of an "NS educational ideal, the strong German ethical-religious character within a unified national community." As a result of tireless propaganda, the NSLB grew to 200 by the party congress of 1929, reached about 2000 by the end of 1931, jumped to 5000 in April 1932, and again doubled to more than 11,000 members by early 1933. More than two-thirds of the first 250 members were primary schoolteachers, more than nine-tenths were male, and less than one-tenth were trainees. Out of informal procedures emerged a bureaucratically staffed national office, relying on a cadre of Gauobmänner for individual districts. On January 19, 1931, the NSLB achieved a party monopoly in educational matters, because the controversy between Prof. Johannes Stark who supported and Wilhelm Hartnacke who opposed academic teacher training had sown confusion among adherents and in the profession: "Articles, brochures, and any kind of pronouncements, in which party members treat educational and school questions from a Nazi perspective, must be sent to the NSLB before publication."[103]

A crucial propaganda tool was the *Nationalsozialistische Lehrerzeitung*. First appearing in August 1929 "as [the] central organ of the NS educational idea," the journal rabidly attacked the progressive pedagogy of the SPD and ridiculed the religious goals of the Catholic Center party. Although denying the "neutrality" of the DLV, it tried to sketch a counterprogram of "education on a national and Christian basis" and conveyed news of the Nazi teacher movement. The NSLB received symbolic boosts when authorities such as the theoretician Prof. Ernst Krieck and the pedagogical leader Heinrich Scharrelmann converted to the cause. By April 1932, the NSLB was strong enough to organize a rally in the Berlin Sportspalast under the banner "Pestalozzi—Fichte—Hitler," so that "twenty-thousand German teachers [could] swear allegiance to Adolf Hitler." Invoking the nationalist educational tradition, "this meeting shall be a powerful demonstration of all German teachers against the destruction of culture, against the present system—a mighty protest against the disruption of any chance for education." Even if only 2000 or 3000 of those present were teachers, this Easter rally was the largest professional endorsement of the Nazi cause before 1933. Such success was all the more surprising because "the NSLB never focuse[d] its struggle on professional, bureaucratic, pay or hiring questions. Its will has always centered on the ideological penetration of German education, the fight for political power in the state and the cleansing of our cultural life from all Marxist destructive tendencies."[104]

A Nazi organization for engineers appeared later and proved more ephemeral than the other professional affiliates. Its guiding spirit was Diplom-Ingenieur Gottfried Feder, an inventor of ferrocement ships, a critic of "wage slavery," and an advocate of technical corporatism, who served as leading economic ideologue in the late 1920s. In his NS pamphlet series, the Catholic engineer Peter Schwerber tried to reconcile "National Socialism and technology" by transforming anticapitalism into racial anti-Semitism in order to free the creative power of technology from the fetters of money—"the suffocating Jewish-materialist embrace of our life elements." Another proponent of the nazification of engineering was the turbine specialist Franz Lawaczeck who called for abandoning big industry and returning to decentralized production in order to solve unemployment.[105] In August 1931 the technocratic Feder, pro-agrarian Lawaczeck, and antimodern architect Paul Schultze–Naumburg founded a "Fighting League of German Architects and Engineers" so as to gather technicians, "educate and school them in National Socialism," and "select leaders for the coming great political and economic challenges." Within a year, the KDAI counted 2000 members and later the NSBDT claimed that as many as 7000 technicians had been "old party members." With Hitler's blessing, the Munich party headquarters created an "engineering-technical section" (ITA) in order to "mobilize technology" in the service of the Nazi movement in November 1931. Down to the Gau level, these engineering offices were to make technical proposals to the political leadership—a novelty in party organization that demonstrated the technical fascination of the Nazis, who were otherwise so critical of modernity. Claiming that 71,000 technicians were jobless, NS engineering propaganda promised the "creation of work" and competing party authorities developed vast plans, ranging from autarchy through labor service, construction, decentralizing energy, rural settlement, and gigantic public projects. However, affiliation with Alfred Rosenberg's League for German Culture limited the success of the KDAI while fierce economic policy struggles fragmented the technical office.[106]

Which professions were particularly susceptible to Nazi appeals? Some indications emerge from a secondary analysis of Michael H. Kater's NSDAP *Hauptkartei* sample when compared to the 1933 census returns.[107] A subsample of "professionals" defined as tertiary graduates, "semiprofessionals" comprising less elevated occupations with postprimary training, and "protoprofessionals" indicating youths in secondary school or higher education, yielded 2429 cases among more than 21,000 entries drawn from all NS party members between 1925 and 1945 (Table 4.1).[108] The 1933 *Berufszählung* counted a total of 1,426,603 individuals in these categories, which serve as basis for an index of representation. Its narrow range reveals that membership in the NSDAP was surprisingly widespread. Because various characteristics canceled each other out, there is little difference between the professional and semiprofessional aggregates. However, the Nazis had less success with the clergy and female-held occupations (e.g., kindergarten teachers, lab technicians, druggists), although the legal consultant and judicial official numbers are too small to be reliable. About equally involved (ranging from 0.8 to 1.2 in the index) were most professionals such as lawyers, dentists, pharmacists, professors, philologues, chemists, engineers, or architects, and many semiprofessionals such as middle-level officials, lesser teachers, or other engineers. Within individual occupations, the nonacademic ranks (lower officials, hygienists, primary schoolteachers, and technicians) seem to have been a bit more eager to join. Among university graduates, foresters and veterinarians were particularly attracted, and judges, doctors, and legal or teaching trainees were overrepresented, indicating that agrarian, status, and generational motives played a key role.[109]

Which professionals entered the NSDAP disproportionately *before* 1933? While

Table 4.1. Nazi Proclivity of Professions, 1925–1945

Professional Category[a]	Percentage Sample	Percentage Population	Index
Professionals			
1. Clergy	0.25	2.82	0.09
2. Lawyers	1.28	1.35	0.95
Judges	0.98	0.73	1.34
Administrators	0.51	0.60	0.85
Trainees	1.15	0.84	1.37
3. Doctors	4.36	3.58	1.22
Veterinarians	0.68	0.44	1.54
Dentists	0.77	0.85	0.86
Pharmacists	1.03	1.28	0.80
4. Professors	0.51	0.51	1.00
Secondary schoolteachers	2.78	2.63	1.06
Trainees	0.26	0.19	1.35
5. Chemists	0.86	0.88	0.98
6. TH engineers	2.27	2.80	0.81
Architects	2.52	2.53	1.00
7. Foresters	2.30	1.50	1.53
TOTAL	22.54	23.50	0.96
Semiprofessionals			
2. Consultants	0.13	0.21	0.57
Judiciary officials	0.38	0.51	0.52
Administrative officials	27.52	25.86	1.06
3. Dental hygienists	2.27	2.17	1.05
Druggists	1.62	2.62	0.62
4. Trade teachers	3.34	3.35	0.99
Primary schoolteachers	16.29	14.25	1.14
Kindergarten	1.07	1.89	0.57
Journalists	0.98	1.21	0.81
5. Lab technicians	0.56	1.29	0.43
6. HTL engineers	8.53	7.71	1.11
Technicians	5.56	3.59	1.59
TOTAL	67.40	64.58	1.02
Protoprofessionals			
Students (higher education)	7.70	9.06	0.85
Pupils (secondary education)	2.60	2.89	0.89
TOTAL	11.95	10.30	0.86

[a]Numbers indicate professional field: 1, religion; 2, law; 3, medicine; 4, education; 5, chemistry; 6, engineering; 7, forestry.

only 37 or 1.5 percent of fanatics joined before 1930, another 304 or 12.5 percent jumped on the NS bandwagon up to the seizure of power (Table A.15). The demographic variables that can be drawn from the NS membership cards yield a clear pattern: The birth cohorts between 1899 and 1912, those 21 to 34 years old in 1933, were consistently more likely to be early enthusiasts. Prepower support came from rural regions of East Prussia, Schleswig–Holstein, and Mecklenburg, areas hit by the agricultural depression, and from central Germany (Thuringia, Saxony, Hanover, Hesse), where small industry suffered. Urban centers such as

Berlin or Munich were responsible for an overrepresentation in cities of more than 20,000 inhabitants. Converts to the movement among the professions before 1933 were even more predominantly male than their usual 11:1 preponderance. The social affinities are somewhat predictable. Nonelite professionals without doctorates were quicker to enter. Especially academics in agriculture, and somewhat also in the commercial or industrial sector as well as free professionals were more eager than state officials (for whom party membership was intermittently forbidden). More surprising is the proclivity of particular careers: Agricultural occupations such as veterinarians, foresters, and university-trained farmers joined early. Technical pursuits such as academic engineers, architects, and technicians flocked to Hitler before 1933, as did business graduates. Although confirming earlier analyses of the agrarian and youthful aspects of Nazi support, the susceptibility of engineers, confirmed by their Reichstag proclivity for the NSDAP (Table 3.2), raises new questions about the applied careers, because it runs counter to received wisdom of political neutrality among technicians.[110]

A closer look at the early joiners within a specific profession sharpens this profile of Nazi militants. Although the BNSDJ membership file did not survive the war, a list of the first 211 who had entered as of December 31, 1930 indicates the character of the founding cohort when compared to the pattern of non-NS lawyers in 1932 (Table A.16). Six or 2.5 percent were noblemen, a higher share than in the population. Moreover, three Jurists' League members were women, at 1.4 percent roughly twice as many as among attorneys in general! Geographically, the BNSDJ founders hailed disproportionately from Bavaria (as a result of Frank's influence) as well as from Saxony and Thuringia, with Prussia considerably underrepresented. Nonetheless, early activity centered in Munich, Berlin, Leipzig, and Dresden, in other words, in metropolitan areas with enough party members to found a special professional group. The NS jurists were surprisingly well educated, with more than half possessing the doctorate. Moreover, 8.1 percent were in higher positions, revealing some penetration of the elite, while only 5.2 percent held employment that was questionable for university graduates. Although some were dispersed in commerce and industry, more than half of the league's founders were free professionals, two-fifths officials, and one-seventh still in training. With 53.6 percent, lawyers were the strongest single group, followed by trainees with 14.2 percent, judges with 10.8 percent, higher officials with 10 percent, and businessmen with 4.8 percent. A second list of October 1, 1931 contains 253 names of lawyers and notaries only. While the posession of doctorates and superior court positions by two-thirds indicates modest success, these advocates were less likely to be DAV members and held virtually no professional offices. The liberal legal elite "utterly looked down upon them as loudmouths, ordinary demagogues, empty windbags and virtually complete ignoramuses." The early jurists' league, therefore, grew out of the frustrations of modestly successful attorneys rather than the resentment of bureaucrats.[111]

The more hierarchical teaching profession reveals additional divisions. A systematic 1 percent sample of the entire NSLB membership file yielded 4386 individuals, ranging from university professors down to nursery school teachers. An additional stratified sample increased the number of long-time Nazis, defined as pre-1933 party members, by 435 cases and—weighting to keep the overall proportion correct—boosted the size of the total to 13,596 cases (Table A.9).[112] In professional terms, there were enormous differences between 2.2 percent university faculty, 19.4 percent philologues (including private institutions and trainees), 11.5 percent middle or trade school instructors, 60.1 percent primary school pedagogues, and 6.8 percent kindergarten aides. Their places of work formed a layered pyramid, starting with 1.5 percent in tertiary institutions, 13 percent in secondary schools, 16 percent in middle and trade institutions, and the overwhelming majority of 67.9 percent on the primary school level or below. Professional cleavages were reinforced by demographic fractures. Catholics were generally underrepresented, especially in trade and high schools. Whereas only 3 percent of the university faculty was female, 21.8 percent of high school teachers and 34.5 percent of primary school pedagogues were women, in contrast to 55.7 percent trade school instructors and 93.9 percent kindergarten aides. Unlike the majority of male colleagues, women instructors were likely to be single. Secondary schoolteachers were even older (44 years) than junior college faculty, and primary school pedagogues (39 years) were more advanced in years than trade instructors, but kindergarten aides were quite young (24 years). While NS university personnel, trade and nursery school teachers tended to live in urban areas, most secondary school instructors came from mid-size towns, and primary school pedagogues were likely to be found in villages.[113]

The uniformity and breadth of nazification among educators is all the more surprising. The small pre-1933 share of 2.7 percent NSLB joiners and 2.9 percent long-time party members demonstrates that teachers were somewhat reluctant to get involved in an NS movement that occasionally cost them their job (Table A.17). However, the above-average SA and SS activism of these Old Fighters indicates the existence of a fanatical core.[114] The demographic pattern of NS support was similar to the proclivity of attorneys. Protestants as well as men were more likely to join early. Although even some of the older educators were not immune, the late-Weimar age group produced the highest share of NS enthusiasts. Moreover, villagers and pedagogues from middle-sized cities were more eager, while Berlin, north-central, and Bavarian educators were overrepresented. The social composition of Nazi fanatics remains controversial, because its interpretation depends on classification and involves old animosities of various teacher groups. Some contradictions dissolve upon discovering that conservative philologues often joined the party before 1933, while frustrated primary school pedagogues were more likely to enter the NSLB. Moreover, principals and others with authority felt freer to sign up. Finally, the existentially threatened trainees and beginners embraced the NSLB and the party disproportionately. A list of 301 NSLB members for sub-district Lower Silesia from December 31, 1932 contains 4.3 percent secondary schoolteachers, 11.9 percent middle and trade school instructors, 76 percent primary school pedagogues, and 7 percent teacher trainees.[115] Confirmed by the Reichstag pattern (Table 3.2), these findings correct claims that philologues were more eager to join before the seizure of power.[116]

To determine which factors disposed German teachers to become Nazis, the pattern of attraction must be analyzed in a multivariate fashion, focusing on NSDAP membership as dependent variable.[117] After missing and redundant data are eliminated, contingency tables of NSDAP membership with the remaining character-

Table 4.2. Main-Effects Model for NSDAP Membership among Teachers

Estimate[a]	Standard error	Parameter
−0.7089	0.1362	1
−0.6661	0.0886	religion (2)
−1.3090	0.1179	religion (3)
0.6133	0.0793	residence (2)
0.5775	0.1472	cohort (2)
0.8569	0.1406	cohort (3)
0.9749	0.1457	cohort (4)
0.4773	0.1729	cohort (5)
−1.3690	0.0975	sex (2)

[a]Deviance, $D = 62.38$. Degrees of freedom = 51.

istics yield six variables with an association of Cramer's V above .08. Dictated by the categorical nature of the data, a logit analysis of these independent variables produces proportional reduction of error coefficients of .234 for religion, .173 for gender, .155 for cohort, and .107 for residence. Marital status (.043) and professional title (.022) have such a small effect that they could be disregarded subsequently. Further analysis of the contingency table of the four strongest variables yields a nicely fitting baseline model with a significant deviance of 664.70 and a main-effects model that explains 90 percent of the variance (Table 4.2). A more detailed probe of pre-1933 joiners reinforces the importance of Protestant backgrounds, urban settings, youthfulness, and somewhat less so of male gender.[118] Although the limitations of the variation reinforce the Volkspartei thesis, this statistical model relativizes distinctions of education, rank, or salary by underlining the importance of demographic characteristics that separate various teacher categories.

Accentuated by the progressive policies of Weimar cabinets, such social cleavages both inhibited and accelerated the nazification of the professions. Though submerged in associational rhetoric, religion was one of the fundamental divides of German society that polarized professions internally and externally. Because one-quarter of the lawyers were Jewish, and were disproportionately clustered in the progressive urban elites, crucial tensions ran along anti-Semitic lines. Although professional contacts were usually correct, the BNSDJ did not hesitate to exploit the substantial social distance to and occupational envy of small-town Aryan practitioners. Because the minority of Jewish educators was much smaller, the NSLB rantings against cultural Bolshevism were less based on self-interest. Teachers were rather divided between Protestants and Catholics, with the latter underrepresented on the higher levels as a result of their much-discussed *Bildungsdefizit.* Although only primary schools tended to be religiously segregated, on the secondary level local hiring decisions involved proportional representation to ensure a correct ideological climate, segmenting the job market and creating Protestant resentment against Catholic pressure for equality. Except for occasional denunciations of Jewish capitalism, confessional prejudice played the least visible role among engineers. On the one hand, almost all Jewish practitioners rejected NS appeals; furthermore, Catholic subculture, organized by separate associations and oriented toward its own brand of authoritarian corporatism, proved somewhat impervious to Nazi pressure, much to the chagrin of zealous proselytizers. On the other hand, Protestant colleagues were susceptible to Hitler's siren call, because they felt threatened by Jewish or Catholic newcomers and identified their own national-conservative professionalism with "justice," "culture," or "technology" in general. An ugly undercurrent rather than an overt theme, anti-Semitism was most pronounced among attorneys who called for the restoration of "German custom" through a racial purge.[119]

The overcrowding hysteria of the early 1930s made gender into a divisive issue, exaggerating the numerical impact of female inroads into male domains. Exasperated by the doubling of their number during the Weimar Republic, traditionalist male lawyers held the couple of hundred distaff attorneys coresponsible for their plight. While philologues succeeded in fending off women from boys' schools, Weimar hiring practices increasingly turned girls' schools over to female directors and staff. Moreover, on the lower educational levels, the advance of women seemed inexorable. The exclusion of female colleagues from the PhVb, repeated board discussions, and countless articles testify to the depth of male resentment against this feminization of teaching. With only sixteen women having reached the *Diplom* by 1930, engineers could still concentrate on maintaining their sexist stereotype.[120] Because it took unusual dedication to study at the university, female professionals came from liberal and often Jewish milieus, making them more resistant to Nazi appeals. But frightened by increasing job competition and the change in sex roles—heralded by the arrival of "the new woman"—many males were ready to listen to NSLB promises to put females back into their domestic place. Imbued with *Männerbund* ideology, Nazi agitators loudly called for keeping women from studying, barring them from entering a profession or expelling married females (double-income) and even sole breadwinners from their chosen careers. For nationalist women, NS propagandists promised a restoration of their traditional role in a völkisch vein.[121]

Another reason for the rightward drift of the professions was "the plight of youth and the struggle of generations." By the year 1931, 550,000 young unemployed and 40,000 superfluous academics seemed to block all prospects for the future. Philologues recognized that youth's "appalling disinterest in intellectual issues [and] its increasing political radicalization are primarily caused by the lack of living space and the resulting dearth of work and careers." According to one teacher, typical reactions involved turning into a nervous and "weak aesthete," a Communist adventurer, a "practical man" ready to emigrate, a walking corpse, or an activist "who expect[s] salvation from a political upheaval" on the Right.[122] Older practitioners with firm political allegiances, which were largely formed during the empire, clung to their familiar convictions. However, disappointed with adult responses such as protectionism, industrial trial jobs, or volunteer labor service, the younger cohorts were especially susceptible to unscrupulous Nazi promises.[123] To exploit generational resentment, the NSLB made "the plight of the young teachers" a major dimension of its campaign for a *numerus clausus,* university entrance exams based on intelligence, and the prohibition of "female study." National Socialist students called for "compulsory pensioning," job sharing, reducing the teaching load, limiting class size, deacademizing primary schoolteacher training, and eliminating double incomes.[124] In the summer of 1932, a "young teachers' group" submitted a memorandum to the Reichstag that "revealed a frightening picture of external and internal suffering," thereby making entering pedagogues look to the NSLB for "the lifting of their plight." Unrestrained by responsibility or practicality, NS agitators made extreme demands in order to appeal to frustrated youths, thirsting not for talk but action. Although a few were radicalized by Communist critiques, many young professionals, fed up with the inadequacy of adult help, believed in Nazi promises.[125]

What made a small but growing minority of practitioners join the NS movement across all demographic divides?[126] Conforming to the "Old Fighter" myth, typical texts like Georg Kaiser's curriculum vitae refer to conversion ("at first I adhered to NS ideology spiritually"), violence ("my family was never sure of its life" as a result of Communist attacks), and job discrimination ("I had to wait for eight and a half years for a teaching appointment"). Taken collectively, such letters to NS affiliates suggest several motives: First, many professionals were, like the recent graduate Wolfgang Braun, economic victims. "Currently I have nothing, since my mother's small pension is hardly enough for her own support. State employment cannot be expected soon. Moreover, my home town demands repayment of my student loan."[127] Second, there were völkisch ideologues like Prof. Friedrich Kötteritz who felt "unable to adapt to the new state." Professional persecution hardened their fanaticism: "When . . . I was supposed to start in my new position at the Protestant Lyceum in Fulda, the Jews who have black-listed me decided in secret session to get rid of me. . . ." Third, marginal practitioners like lawyer Dr. Johann H. Böhmker, who barely managed to gain admission and lacked the talent to succeed, blamed their failure on "the system." Party and affiliate activity such as defense counsel or Gauspeaker brought them clientele, prestige, and the spoils of public office. Fourth, impressionable individuals like Fritz Ochs were sometimes swept off their feet by Nazi luminaries like Prof. Krieck, without fully understanding the consequences. Finally, an increasing number of opportunists like the Heidelberg University Prof. Emil Zirkel, a "popular and sociable party member," jumped on the bandwagon in 1932 when the Nazis were approaching power. However, frequent references to "disciplinary proceedings," dismissals, or "threats to existence" indicate that it took conviction born of deprivation, ideology, marginality, or naiveté for a professional to embrace the Nazi cause before 1933.[128]

National Socialist propaganda appealed to such frustrations by idealizing them. Pleading for "the unification of all types of pedagogues," teacher spokesman Hans Schemm was adamant about not following the usual Standespolitik: "Our highest goal is the renewal of the German school and not the struggle for salary or 'customary rights.' " Therefore, Nazi agitators invoked traditional values and denounced the "decline of the popular feeling of justice," the "disintegration of German culture," or the fettering of German technology by finance capital. In trying to capture nationalist resentment, they differed from other conservative groups by the violence and radicalism of their racist rhetoric, calculated to rouse those who had given up on moderate solutions: "All of you must come who are torn by the misery and despair of this decadent epoch and carry the burning faith and unshakable hope for a better German future in your hearts."[129] In spite of protestations of "idealism, not materialism," Nazi professionals knew the predicament of their colleagues well enough to offer job listings in the *Deutsches Recht* and the *NS Lehrerzeitung* as well as individual advice. Consoling the distressed with "the thought of the coming Third Reich," NSLB invitations to the April 1932 Berlin rally fused the professional plight with the cultural crisis:

> Through this grandiose demonstration we shall achieve the rescue of many a colleague from serious disciplinary proceedings and take a further step towards the seizure of power. In the interest of jobless young pedagogues, of eroding cultivation in the whole country, of our magnificent German culture and its future revival, every teacher is duty-bound to give his best effort.

For NS activists the professional struggle was essentially political. Appealing to an ideologically and socially frustrated minority, Nazi organizers wanted to transform practitioners "into educators in the German sense, Hitler's fighters [and] soldiers in education."[130]

COLLAPSE OF INTEREST REPUBLICANISM

Under the impact of the depression, liberal professionalism gradually crumbled. Through 1929, the Philologenverband remained committed "to educating youth to support the state and to respect the republic with its symbols" and resented the charge of antidemocratic attitudes. However, when tested by the professional crisis, this limited "loyalty to the state but not subservience to the parties" eroded, because it was based on self-interest rather than on emotional bonds. Although most teachers were "no saboteurs," they were "indifferent to the state and political questions."[131] Under massive rightist pressure, professional associations grew more nationalistic in foreign issues. At the tenth anniversary of the Treaty of Versailles, the PhVb enjoined "all members to join the struggle against the war guilt lie at every opportunity." The 1929 philologue meeting in Vienna—followed a year later by the engineers—was a none-too-veiled "demonstration for the *Anschluß* idea and cultural ties between Germany and Austria." In the heated discussion on the referendum against the Young Plan, the RhB vigorously defended the right of pedagogues to agitate against government policy.[132] Enthusiastically, teachers greeted the liberation of the Rhineland from foreign occupation in 1930 as an event "that can rekindle national feelings," since it proved: "A national will always leads to a national deed." While lawyers celebrated President Paul von Hindenburg's eighty-fifth birthday as "a symbol of those German forces which shall eventually guarantee national resurgence," engineers began to write articles on "the search for the best cruiser" or on "technical questions of civil defense." By raising excessive demands, tougher rhetoric boded ill for the reemergence of international links among the professions.[133]

Eventually, overcrowding, salary cuts, unemployment, deterioration of practice, and ideological reservations led many professionals to hold the republic responsible for their plight. In domestic questions, the associations therefore began to look toward authoritarian solutions. Reporting on the situation of lawyers in 1931, Heinrich Dittenberger deplored the twin "collapse of the economy and of the parliamentary system.'' At the end of 1932, some liberal leaders like Julius Magnus were beginning to see faint signs of hope for the improvement of ''the international situation and thereby the condition of our fatherland.'' However, the majority of practitioners instead dreamed of ''changing the system.'' An unsigned New Year's reflection in the *Philologenblatt* claimed that the ''partisan power state'' of Prussia had proved unable to create ''the preconditions for a spiritual renewal of the people.'' Excessive economizing almost ''liquidated'' the high school while ''the politicization of the entire public administration'' heightened strife. Though ''the complete failure of the democratic system of government . . . had reduced the public's fear of an authoritarian regime,'' the dilettantism and bureaucratization of the Papen and Schleicher cabinets was discouraging. Abolishing provincial school boards, militarizing youth, or aggravating the generational struggle only made the embattled philologues more anxious. In contrast, academic engineers denounced individual selfishness, called for an end to political stagnation, and demanded the beginning of ''a better economic attitude which is always and everywhere concerned with the common weal.'' Democracy and capitalism were discredited. Authoritarianism, claiming to solve the professional crisis, seemed full of risks, and beyond, beckoned völkisch promises. ''What we lack is the liberating deed.''[134]

In spite of its increasing popularity, professional associations refused to endorse National Socialism before 1933. At the December 1932 attorneys' congress, Freiherr von Hodenberg warned that ''the unity of the profession'' was endangered because ''some partisan or zealous colleagues want to impose one-sided attitudes and goals, perhaps even slight or affront the proponents of different convictions, whether this clash is purely political, ideological or racial.'' Clinging to its liberal heritage, the DAV reaffirmed ''the principle of unconditional justice for all.''[135] During the summer of 1932, the PhVb ''got in touch with'' the eugenics ideologue Hartnacke and NS Reichstag fraction chairman Wilhelm Frick in order to ascertain NSDAP educational views. On core issues such as the size, duration, and structure of the secondary school, pupil selection, teacher training, and educational goals, the philologues discovered that populist NS aspirations ''sharply contrasted'' with their own elitist program. Fearing ''new educational policy struggles,'' moderate teachers wanted to ''influence NSDAP decisions on school questions through colleagues active in the party.'' But instead of making some concession ''to the new political trend'' in filling PhVb offices, ''the majority of the board'' resolved ''that the neutral attitude of the professional association must be maintained in the future.'' By early 1933, disappointment with authoritarianism left philologues with nothing better than ''a firm defensive front'' and warnings of ''new dangers, lurking in the background.''[136] Though susceptible to appeals for Gemeinschaftsarbeit, engineers stopped short of endorsing the NSDAP as well. While the October 1932 declaration of the VDI emphasized responsibility to the Volk and ''true *Führertum* in technology and economy,'' it also ''warned against irresponsible prophets who talk the German people into an anti-technological mood.'' In December, Conrad Matschoß urged engineers to look forward to sound agriculture, plentiful jobs, and renewed spiritual values. Though NS phrases were seeping into technical discourse, not even a frustrated association such as the VDDI was willing to embrace the Nazi cause.[137]

Because of the disapproval of elites, Nazi professionals were forced to emerge in opposition to liberal professionalism. Understanding the frightful implications of the Nazi program, well informed experts like the Prussian lawyer Robert Kempner warned that *"boundless murderlust characterizes the blood-justice of the [coming] Third Reich."* But marginal practitioners who were dissatisfied with their careers disregarded such alarms, ready to risk a drastic alternative. Among scores of right-wing movements, the NSDAP presented the most radical program, charismatic leadership, and effective organization, blending specific vocational appeals with the general promise of national regeneration. Once attracted, völkisch professionals encountered like-minded colleagues and, to escape ostracism, infused their work with Nazi ideas, provided expert services to the party, or founded an appropriate NS league. Such academic party affiliates gradually developed into programmatic and organizational rivals to the established associations.[138] In exploiting practitioner frustrations, NS propaganda criticized the Jewish or Catholic professional leadership, railed against its failure to halt feminization, and denounced its domination by age and experience. Resentful of foreign influences and opposed to Weimar's modest reforms, NS professionals ridiculed the inadequacy of "liberal and Marxist" responses to their plight, urging more drastic remedies.[139] Nazi practitioners also offered a hazy vision of their own, which rejected real tradition in favor of a contrived past. Völkisch professionalism prided itself on being youthful and forward-looking in contrast to outworn liberalism. It made much of being egalitarian, including all occupational ranks into one community, thereby breaking with the hierarchical legacy. While promising practical solutions, it claimed to be idealistic in contrast to socialist or capitalist materialism. Finally, it also strongly appealed to nationalism, but in a new intolerant and activist key.[140]

Although Nazis made growing inroads into the professions before 1933, their absolute gains were still quite limited. If one assumes that three-fifths of BNSDJ members were attorneys, then about 5 percent of lawyers joined the NS affiliate before 1933. With more than 300,000 teachers and about 12,000 NSLB members, about 4 percent of pedagogues were Old Fighters. Similarly, when more than 200,000 engineers are compared to 7000 claimed prepower Nazis, about 3.5 percent of technicians followed Hitler's call. A NSLB survey of political leanings in Upper Silesia spotted only 18 of 281 teachers as Nazis (6.4 percent), in contrast to 9.6 percent "Marxists," 5.3 percent pacifists, 15.7 percent Democrats, and 6.4 percent Center Party supporters. Most pedagogues were apolitical officials (39.5 percent), and even German nationalists were more numerous (19.2 percent). Given the depth of the depression crisis, it is astounding that on the eve of the seizure of power, one-third of the professionals remained ideologically opposed and another third apolitical, while among the rest nationalist sympathizers outnumbered NS adherents by three to one![141] Trying to explain "why the educated, even the teachers, joined us so late," Hans Schemm argued that "Hitler had to break through a deep insulation barrier." Concretely, he named "intellectualism, materialism, new realism, the arrogance of so-called cultivation [and] specialization" as setting university graduates apart from the simple people. "Youth heard the bells tolling of a great völkisch time. The cultured adults had their ears stuffed with the cotton of a false *Bildung*." Widespread NS resentment of intellectuals suggests that professionalism provided some immunity to the Nazi virus: "Many a so-called educated man is not ready to bend his knees to the racial well of life and therefore dies of thirst in the dust of his files.'' The clash of cultural styles between academic sophistication and primitive emotionalism limited Nazi success among professionals: ''Many [had] studied their soul to death.''[142]

Those practitioners who did follow Hitler's call, nonetheless, had a nefarious impact beyond their small but rapidly growing number. Reaching about one of every twenty experts, NS league membership was bigger than the following of any other political professional affiliate, including the left. Moreover, the Nazi appeal extended to those nationalists who were willing to sympathize with the movement, support NS candidates, or even work for the party or SA without necessarily joining. Although they were by no means decisive in the seizure of power, Nazi practitioners contributed to victory in three significant ways: Some, like the teacher Dr. Martin Löpelmann, who criticized the shortcomings of the republic, facilitated the erosion of Weimar democracy and turned youths toward a radical illiberalism that transcended moderate authoritarianism. Pedagogues often wondered why the young were not content with traditional nationalism without understanding that they themselves had sown the seeds of this longing for something more heroic and extreme. Others, like the lawyer Dr. Roland Freisler, who joined the party in 1925, legitimated the NS movement socially for colleagues or neighbors in the upper and middle classes. Given the ruffian image of SA street fighters, making them *salonfähig* was no small feat. Societal acceptance made it possible for the cultivated to vote for Nazi candidates and to cooperate with them in countless professional and local offices. Others yet, like the *Oberingenieur* F. Vogel, offered crucial technical expertise, organization, and propaganda. Coming from a well-educated engineer, lectures on ''peasants, workers and the creation of jobs in the Third Reich'' were bound to impress the simple country folk in Bavaria more than yet another ''political'' speech. Because of the Nazis' rhetorical excesses, unruly character, and chaotic organization, the legitimation of antidemocratic activism, the creation of an aura of respectability, and the infusion of practical efficiency made an essential contribution to success.[143]

In the end, any attempt to comprehend the incomprehensible leaves behind an inexplicable residue. Perhaps the justifications of a leading convert might provide some clues on ''why I am a National Socialist.'' Explicitly citing the motto of the liberal student movement of the *Burschenschaft,* professor Julius von Negelein publicly announced his support for the NSDAP in the spring of 1932. ''We academics maintained HONOR by keeping the values of our ethical and spiritual culture pure. *Hitler* protects them against Bolshevik or Marxist attacks, especially against the destruction of family and religion.'' Nazism therefore promoted itself as an anticommunist solution to the cultural crisis. ''FREEDOM beckons us in the future as members of a powerful state after the elimination of pacifist efforts. Only where there is power, is there also freedom of thought and action. *Hitler* leads us to this freedom.'' National Socialist academics turned a lingering liberal heritage into a celebration of public might in order to reject the weak republic and the shame of Versailles. ''Regaining the FATHERLAND is the goal of every true academic. *Hitler* has rediscovered it as the fountainhead of völkisch energy, as the source of rejuvenation for the world.'' Finally, a sense of national mission, redefined in a völkisch, racist manner, propelled some professionals toward the Führer.

"Hitler's person unites political wisdom with ruthless willpower and spotless probity of character. A thousand years of history teach: *Such men deserve victory!*"[144] Fearing the collapse of their calling due to reform and depression, a growing minority of practitioners tried to save their profession by abandoning its liberal heritage and hitching it to the rising Nazi star.

II

PROFESSIONALS AS ACCOMPLICES

5

The Illusion of Reprofessionalization

The nazification of the professions was surprisingly swift. In October 1933, attorney leader Dr. Walter Raeke marveled about the successful ''coordination of the entire German legal profession, including economists, consultants as well as judicial and legally trained officials, in the BNSDJ after the Nazi revolution.'' Adolf Hitler had personally charged the lawyers' league with ''implementing the great future tasks of creating a German law and reforming the legal order.'' Accordingly, all law-related occupations, united in the ''legal front of the BNSDJ, shall be integrated as one professional group into the evolving corporate structure'' of the Third Reich. Jubilant about such a broad mission, NS militants welcomed with open arms the thousands of colleagues who had hitherto belonged to nationalist veterans' groups or bourgeois parties. However, in order to absorb the twentyfold surge of membership (to about 30,000 individuals), the league had to ''justify the Führer's trust through truest loyalty and most selfless cooperation in the NS renewal of law.'' Though not always going this smoothly, organizational coordination implied ideological indoctrination, a personnel purge, and tight discipline in exchange for a ''comfortable existence.'' Repeated in every occupation, such political-economic bargains opened the prospect of restored professional authority, material security, and national power under Nazi rule.[1]

Twelve years later in the bleak spring of 1945, such dreams of professionals lay in ruins. Except in an occasional oasis untouched by the war, practitioners had to work in bomb-gutted cities, fear for their lives from the approaching front, and struggle for food. In the chaos of last-minute SS brutality and dispirited surrender, party control ebbed, administration crumbled, and practice disintegrated.[2] Harassed by special courts (the infamous *Sondergerichte*), attorneys, if they found cases at all, had to defend soldiers no longer willing to fight (''deserters''), starving people scavenging for food (''parasites'') or desperate men trying to joke about the inevitable (''demoralizers''). Hindered by the destruction of schools, teachers had to instruct children who were exhausted from nightly bombing alarms and were often removed from their parents to safer districts (KLV) or youths manning anti-air raid defenses *(Flakhelfer)*. Frustrated by scarce raw materials and unsuitable substitutes, engineers had to keep faltering production going, supervise slave labor, and motivate requisitioned women, even if their products were unlikely to reach their destinations. When defeat appeared inevitable, professionals at the home front began to worry about survival and many wondered how they had gotten into this predicament. Some Nazi "supporters became undeceived through events," Carlo Schmid remembered the confusion. But "others whom I knew . . . as Nazi opponents, seemed to be prey to a kind of Hitler mystique."[3]

Historians have long pondered the paradoxical nature of the Third Reich. The Nazis deliberately used their marching columns to suggest unity, permanence, and invincibility. At the same time, socialist exiles (SOPADE) hoped that resentment against inhumanity, exploitation, and persecution would eventually bring the swastika down. Though ideologically opposed, the concepts of Fascism (elaborated by the Marxist Left) or Totalitarianism (developed by the liberal moderates) emphasize the monolithic nature of Nazi rule.[4] Because of the pervasive Führer cult and his colorful personality, much of the debate has centered on Hitler's own claim to centrality to the exclusion of questions about his social role.[5] Scholars preoccupied with anti-Semitic ideology, Hitler's domination over party or government, and NS foreign policy tend to stress the "intentionalist" quality of the Third Reich. In contrast, historians fascinated by the polycratic chaos in economic or domestic matters often emphasize the "functionalist" constraints on Nazi rule.[6] Therefore, "Hitler's social revolution" has remained controversial, with analysts disagreeing on whether the Nazis represented an essentially reactionary attempt to preserve the power of the old ruling classes or whether they modernized German society through their policies as well as their defeat.[7] Offering an alternative perspective to such general interpretations or recent local analyses, the professions provide a fresh case study of the nazification of the vital "intermediary structures" that bound together German society.[8]

COMPULSION OR SELF-COORDINATION?

In their own sphere, professionals encountered Hitler's seizure of power through the "coordination" of their associations. Not content with political power, the NS movement sought to capture social control of the nonpolitical infrastructure in order to imbue every citizen with its ideology. Taken from the March 31, 1933 law on the *Gleichschaltung* of the states with the Reich, the concept of "coordination" has become synonymous with the nazification of all aspects of life.[9] Contemporaries were stunned by the speed and extent of Nazi domination over a diverse country. In trying to account for this success, scholars initially stressed somewhat apologetically that outside compulsion left practitioners little choice but to comply. However, more recent critical writings suggest that a considerable element of "self-coordination" was necessary for such a quick and thorough takeover of the voluntary groups.[10] Existing accounts leave some confusion on a number of important issues: Precisely how were the Weimar leaders ousted by their Nazi challengers? What mixture of idealism and opportunism motivated professionals to jump on Hitler's bandwagon? Why were NS zealots successful in capturing the professions? While there is little doubt about the imposition of NS political control, the pattern, motives, and methods of social coordination have yet to be fully explored.[11]

For the professions, Gleichschaltung meant the takeover of national and local associations and their incorporation into larger Nazi fronts. By March 26, Hitler's election victory, the symbolic reconciliation with Hindenburg, and the Enabling Act had altered the political landscape so fundamentally that the once-liberal DAV felt compelled to welcome the new order publicly, while warning implicitly against excesses. To avoid absorption by the BNSDJ or by "Christian" nationalists, it called for special elections, because "the members should be given the opportunity to change their officers due to the general situation."[12] Pressed to expel the eleven Jewish attorneys among twenty-five board members, president Rudolf Dix unilaterally asked those in question "to lay down their offices" on April 7. Though deeply offended, all non-Aryans complied in "the interest of maintaining the independence of the DAV."[13] However, rhetorical appeals to "join the front of the national rising" were no longer enough. On April 25, Dix announced: "In order to link the DAV even more closely with the national parties behind the government, I have asked our Berlin colleague Dr. Voß to serve as a NS representative *(Vertrauensmann)* for the DAV until the new election of the board." The remaining lawyer leadership co-opted this former DVP Landtag deputy and recent Nazi convert as a token of cooperation so as to "safeguard specific lawyer ideals in this turbulent time." However, Hermann Voß was unwilling to protect the DAV against party demands and called for its entry into the BNSDJ, postponing elections until Jewish members would be disenfranchised: "According to the opinion of the Prussian Justice Minister, there is no room for the DAV alongside the BNSDJ." Though more independent-minded than German-national judges, many attorneys like Friedrich Grimm decided "to join the movement in order to create the national community which . . . Hitler seeks."[14]

Emboldened by such voluntary compliance, Nazi lawyers demanded the complete dissolution of the DAV. On May 5, the ambitious NS attorney and Prussian *Ministerialdirektor* Roland Freisler called for its immediate integration into the BNSDJ, threatening that he "could no longer tolerate the postponement of an overdue decision." On the next day, Reich Justice Commissar Hans Frank appointed Voß his deputy in matters of "transferring the DAV into the BNSDJ."[15] Nevertheless, Dix fended off a dissolution order for May 9 and held a last semi-legal DAV delegate meeting on May 18: "At stake is the incorporation of the German legal profession into the corporate structure of Adolf Hitler's Reich." Pressured into surrender, the DAV president explained his agreement to collective co-optation of attorneys into the BNSDJ to an agitated assembly: "The chairman of the Lawyers League has decided . . . that NSDAP party membership is not a precondition for joining, but that he will welcome all those who are so to speak of good German attitude and will." Because "a so-called unpolitical, neutral professional association . . . is no longer possible," it was better to comply, trusting Frank's assurances of continued "independence of the association" within the legal front. As "fighters against economization . . . , mechanization and atomization," lawyers could claim that "the corporate state of the Third Reich needs an independent, proud and, within national discipline, free attorney." Seeking to safeguard a nationalized heritage of freie Advokatur, the DAV "collectively joins the BNSDJ, in order to collaborate with it under Hitler's leadership in the formation of German law and the construction of the national state."[16]

The same process of intimidation and accommodation was repeated dozens of times in local chambers. The decisive battle was fought in Berlin, where 20 of the 33 combined lawyer chamber board members elected on February 7, 1933 were Jewish. Claiming that "Aryan" lawyers were not "equitably" represented and "Nazi fighters excluded," nationalists founded a counterorganization on March 22 and intimidated the board into resigning on March 28. Three days later the NS attorney Dr. Reinhard Neubert was appointed commissary director of the Berlin chamber. Because of the board's reservations about the national revolution, the Nazis replaced four-fifths of its members and promoted their followers to leadership positions, keeping only a few known nationalists to maintain some credibility.[17] Once the liberal Berlin bastion had fallen, Minister of Justice Hanns Kerrl demanded "the resignation of the chamber boards through negotiations," and the appointment of commissars in consultation with the BNSDJ or other national organizations. The "principle of Gleichschaltung also applies to the relationship between the administration of justice and the professional organization of attorneys." Only an open ballot by acclamation could restore public confidence in the legal profession.[18] Choreographed by Nazi commissars, these so-called April 22 elections resulted in resounding "majorities, bordering on unanimity" and by late May all chambers were firmly under NS control. "German attorneys in Prussia have proven through these elections that they want to work constructively in the spirit of the Nazi revolution." Because there had been less resistance than feared, Kerrl gloated: "As Prussian Minister of Justice I am glad to cooperate with such lawyers."[19]

The twenty-fifth lawyers' meeting at the national *Juristentag* in Leipzig in early October 1933 publicly heralded the completion of the Gleichschaltung. A typical uniformed mass demonstration celebrated the creation of the German "legal front" and incorporated lawyers and law-related professions into one professional association of legal occupations.[20] Rejecting the charge of "leveling," the BNSDJ business manager Dr. Wilhelm Heuber rationalized the fusion of different groups as "necessary cooperation in order to reach our common goal" by providing for legal professionals a comprehensive organization that was big enough not to be swallowed up in the German Labor Front (DAF). After the coordination, 4600 lawyers were individual and another 10,000 were collective members of the BNSDJ, amounting to about half of its membership in 1933. For the lawyers' league board member Erwin Noack, participation in the *Deutsche Rechtsfront* would enable attorneys, "as organs of administration of justice," to pursue their ideal aims and thereby overcome the professional crisis. Bluntly, SA leader Walter Luetgebrune warned that lawyers would have to serve "the welfare of the entire community" in order to survive in the Third Reich.[21] Because incorporation as Section Two into the BNSDJ made the DAV superfluous, this traditional association was dissolved in December 1933 in order to seize its two million-mark assets and control its journals. When the Nazi organ *Deutsches Recht* became the central lawyer publication, the lively *Anwaltsblatt* was allowed to lapse in March 1934, and the internationally renowned *Juristische Wochenschrift* was swallowed up five years later as well.[22] In order to preserve their profession, lawyers sacrificed their liberal tradition and vaunted autonomy with astonishing alacrity.

Because of their nationalist leanings, high school teachers seemed easy to co-opt as well. "True to their pioneering work for German culture and nationality," philologues greeted the national rising on March 22 as an opportunity for improving support for "the spiritual values of the German people." After he was beaten up by SA thugs in his apartment, the liberal PhVb chairman Felix Behrend turned his office over to the "old and convinced Nazi" *Stadtschulrat* Rudolf Bohm to whom the board "assigned a number of significant powers." The new leader warned, "it would be disastrous to hesitate in joining a popular movement which will be changing our nation for a long time to come."[23] Participating with other association chairmen in the national NSLB conference at Leipzig on April 8, Bohm was pleased by Hans Schemm's diplomatic declaration: "A spiritual and organizational coordination must take place, but this should be the result of negotiations and discussions." Hence the professional leaders "agreed without reservations to the political, cultural and philosophical principles of the present government and expressed their approval and active will to cooperate." When Schemm stressed "concepts such as race, defense, character and religiosity" as the core of "the new German education," most of the 4000 educators were reassured, because the NSLB demanded only "the dominance of NS Weltanschauung in all teachers' associations," not complete organizational control. With regional groups purging Liberals, Marxists, and Jews and electing NS colleagues, it appeared in May as if "virtually all educational organizations . . . have almost been completely coordinated in the sense of the new regime."[24]

In fact, the coordination of secondary schoolteachers turned out to be complicated and protracted. Conflict became inevitable when the "political fighting organization" of the NSLB sought to transform itself into a professional association, "bringing together all educators of NS Germany." Having nazified its constitution with the *Führerprinzip* and "Aryan" membership on May 31, the PhVb warned of the "grave danger that valuable organizations will be destroyed or atomized without being replaced by an organic whole that is not only externally but internally united and really alive."[25] On June 8, about 7000 demonstrating pedagogues, nonetheless, persuaded the leaders of forty-eight teachers associations to join the "German Educators' Community" in a "wonderful unification" ceremony at Magdeburg. However, unlike the egalitarian DLV (which sensed some affinity with the populist NSLB) and thirty-nine other groups, the PhVb did not disband voluntarily and agreed only to affiliate as a section with the DEG. Interested in gathering officials under his own influence, Reich Minister of Interior Wilhelm Frick cautioned by telegram that a well-structured organism would leave its parts "an independent life, making valuable expert work *(Facharbeit)* possible."[26] When the teachers' league continued to call for dissolution of the old associations, the philologues, having long fought a uniform profession, resisted in the name of the "scholarly character of the secondary school." However, massive intimidation by Nazi zealots like R. Knoop in Westphalia caused "a vexing conflict of conscience" and Pommeranian NS philologues criticized "continual foot-dragging." To restore discipline, the PhVb fired two overzealous provincial leaders and mobilized Frick and Minister of Education Bernhard Rust to warn publicly that "in wooing members the NSLB should eschew any moral or political pressure."[27]

The struggle between the unitary and corporatist alternatives to nazifying the teaching profession increased in vehemence during late 1933. On the one hand, Hans Schemm insisted on individual membership in the NSLB and rejected "organizational independence" for different teachers. On the other hand, professors, philologues, trade or commercial instructors, private philologues, and Bavarian educators founded a counterorganization on November 30, "since the NSLB has not followed the [Magdeburg] agreement, but identified itself with the DEG and threatened the associations with dissolution." Directed by the Bremen Senator Dr. Richard von Hoff, this new version of the "German Educators' Community" aimed at fulfilling its original function as a Nazi umbrella over separate associations, facilitating both their cooperation and safeguarding their independence.[28] Outraged by the suggestion "I should do the incredible and join the newly founded DEG with my NSLB," Schemm counterattacked by taking Rust (who had been turned around by Knoop) to Hitler: "The Führer expressed clearly that the total state can permit only one youth organization and only one educators' association, in other words, the NSLB." After fierce negotiations in the Ministry of Interior, both sides agreed to a compromise on December 8, which forbade the restoration of dissolved associations and underlined the NSLB monopoly "as the appropriate NS organization in the area of education." However, on the next day a press release claimed that the groups in the second DEG "remain[ed] untouched," indicating a division of labor between the ideological NSLB and the scholarly PhVb.[29] In late December, the "*Reichsfachschaft* of high school teachers" breathed a sigh of relief when Robert Ley, on Hitler's orders, decreed "that in future the members of all affiliates have to belong to the party" and it looked "like everything was ganging up on the NSLB."[30]

During the spring of 1934 the stalemate continued, with neither the remaining associations willing to disband nor the NSLB ready to accept anything less. Because "the totality of our state demands a unified community of educators under one leadership and that is the NSLB," Schemm's restless energy soon regained the initiative. "It just takes a bit longer with teachers than with lawyers." In early February, Minister of Interior Frick during an inspection tour to Thuringia hinted that he no longer opposed the dissolution of the local PhVb and was disinterested in organizational matters.[31] However, after a truce was proclaimed in April, negotiations made little headway, because the PhVb was only willing to join if it could maintain its identity—while the NSLB argued "that a 'Philologenverband' shall no longer be allowed to exist in name or in substance, only high school teachers." Its manager, SA member Georg Ried, typically complained: "There is no more talk of any autonomy, we are to be completely put under the thumb of the primary teachers who are already deluging us with friendly proposals about how to reform the high school." When philologues claimed that an exclusively political organization "leads invariably to intellectual deterioration," NSLB partisans countered: "Watch out for reactionaries!"[32] To make the teachers' league more attractive, Schemm instituted a special Section Two for high school "curricular work," which "conservative" philologues rejected as bureaucratic control. However, intent on gaining more membership dues, the NSLB was undeterred:

"The differences between pedagogues have disappeared and only one great educator type remains, the teacher of the German people, the instructor of our German youth and the shaper of our future."[33]

In spite of resolute philologue resistance, the united front of the second DEG began to crumble in the summer of 1934. First, Schemm lured the trade and commercial teachers into the NSLB fold by turning Section Six over to them and maintaining their old leadership.[34] Next, the NSLB overcame the reluctance of the particularist leader of the Bayerische Lehrerverein, Joseph Bauer, by conceding the continued autonomy of its social and retirement institutions. Moreover, the topical philological associations also fell into line, "happy to join the broad front of those collaborating in the renewal of our education and school."[35] Constant local pressure and the NSLB prohibition against double membership began to erode PhVb following "since we no longer see any possibility for effective work." An East Prussian survey claimed that in the spring of 1934 64 percent of the philologues had already joined the teachers' league and another 15 percent were double members, while only 17 percent clung to their professional association, and 4 percent belonged to neither.[36] Convinced that "the ripe fruit will shortly fall into our lap by itself," the NSLB continued to insist on complete surrender while the PhVb protracted negotiations in order to get better terms, thereby increasing personal animosities.[37] In despair, Bohm explained in public that he was only trying "to achieve a position for the secondary teachers which allows them to continue working for the aims and tasks of the high school, for their own further education . . . for the cultivation of their extensive foreign relations and for their ethical professional community." Due to this unauthorized protest, buttressed by a memorandum on the "purpose . . . of the high school," he was forced to resign.[38]

The final struggle, from late 1934 to early 1935, was brief and inglorious. For the sake of "pedagogical and scientific work," his ambitious successor *Oberstudiendirektor* Kurt Schwedtke pleaded for the PhVb's "incorporation as separate section . . . under its own leaders, own journal, independent financing and own business office." In spite of Rust's promise "to maintain its organizational autonomy," Schemm summarily broke off negotiations. When Schwedtke objected that the NSLB "prohibition of dual membership has thrown teachers into deepest psychological depression," ministry spokesman Martin Löpelmann answered disingenuously that this was "an associational legal matter in which I have no occasion to interfere." Outraged by this betrayal, Schwedtke, in the New Year's edition of the *Philologenblatt,* denounced "problematic adventurer types" as well as "the broad stratum of opportunists" as dangers to the Nazi revolution and counseled "a return to the sources of our ideals."[39] Such courageous but misguided idealism provoked a drastic response: "The publication of this article . . . has finally eliminated the leadership of the PhVb as negotiating partner for the NSLB, since every convinced National Socialist is revolted . . . by the unsurpassable impudence of these arguments which work as horror propaganda abroad." Accused of "reactionary spirit," Schwedtke was immediately expelled from the NSLB and suspended from his job, thereby silencing him professionally. The January issue of the *Philologenblatt* was impounded and in mid-February the journal ceased publication. The Reich Minister of Education also "forbade all teachers under him to participate in assemblies of the Dt. PhVb.'' Forced to choose between NSLB and their traditional home, dispirited philologues joined Section Two in large numbers, and on June 14, 1936 the tattered remnants finally dissolved the once-proud organization.[40]

Protected by an aura of technical expertise, engineers fared better in the Gleichschaltung than other professionals. On April 5, chairman Adolf Krauß assured the loyalty of the VDI and three weeks later he promised cooperation in an effusive birthday telegram to Hitler: ''Under the leadership of the national government, German engineers . . . are proud to be able to fight in the rebuilding front, created by you.''[41] In the decisive meeting on the morning of April 26, the board began to coordinate itself, hoping that the VDI could thereby ''assume the leadership in the restructuring of the professional representation of engineers.'' In a letter to Hitler, it promised to participate actively in fighting unemployment, securing raw materials, and contributing to rearmament. Moreover, the VDI founded a new committee to serve the goals of the national movement with scientific work. Without direct compulsion, the engineering association also expelled its Jewish officers.[42] However, at noon, the KDAI leader Gottfried Feder who had just absorbed the RDT, appeared with four followers, posted eight SA men at the doors, and demanded even more. Claiming authorization by Wilhelm Frick and Rudolf Heß, he called upon Krauß to resign and for himself to be appointed as chairman instead. Under threat that the party would name a commissar and abolish the VDI, the cowed board members drafted a letter of submission ''to the wish of the Reich government,'' which was based on Feder's leadership of the KDAI, the only NS-approved political organization for architects and engineers.[43]

Ironically, the survival of the nazified VDI was ensured by a more recent party member (since 1931), Heinrich Schult. Present at VDI headquarters in order to be co-opted as NS representative, this young AEG engineer called Feder's bluff for reasons of professional competence by appealing to Reich Economic Commissar Otto Wagener. When the latter intervened with Heß, he discovered that the cranky ideologue was not acting on Frick's orders and that adequate NS representation on the board would be enough. Because ''coordination had already been approved,'' the VDI in effect revoked its offer to Feder, while Krauß as well as five other members resigned so as to make space for a new board. Two lists therefore confronted one another in the decisive election of May 9, one KDAI slate led by Feder, and another mixed group headed by Schult, which also included the non-Nazi professor Georg Garbotz. When both sides appealed to him, Hitler uncharacteristically ruled that he did ''not want the election to take place under pressure. It concerns a scientific leadership group. It does not matter who is elected. We ought to stay out.'' Without party interference, Schult's slate won handily and election protests by the defeated fanatics were of no avail.[44] At the annual VDI meeting in late May, the new chairman reiterated in party uniform ''the German engineers' support for the new government.'' Rejecting KDAI attempts ''to influence the internal work of our association by force,'' Schult rather talked of electrical ''rectification,'' directing all energies toward a common goal, and proposed the soldier motto *Ich dien!* [I serve!] as a guideline for the future. Given limited autonomy, technology would gladly cooperate.[45]

The struggle for control of the technical professions between the nazified experts and the ideologues was far from over, however. As an organizational counterweight to the Feder-controlled RDT of 200,000 technicians, the VDI during June 1933 created a "Reich community of technical-scientific work," which pledged 60,000 higher technologists "to serve the Nazi economic order." This RTA consisted of five sections for engineering, electronics, construction, mining, and materials, composed of the relevant associations as well as the norms committee and the DATSCH.[46] Not giving up easily, KDAI militants founded a new journal, called *Deutsche Technik,* to liberate engineers "from materialist thought," hoping that "technical spirit shall largely determine the face of the emerging Third Reich."[47] When the KDAI tried to gain control by invading local chapters, Schult traveled to Munich and assured Heß personally of the loyalty of the VDI. On September 26, the Führer's deputy issued a written order, declaring that "after its incorporation into the Nazi front," the VDI possessed "the approval of the Reich party leadership." With its monopoly broken, the KDAI was not to "take over technical-scientific work by excluding its associations." With such unequivocal backing, Schult in early October unanimously pushed through the leadership principle, reduced the board to advisory status, and demanded proof of "Aryan" birth for new members. Moreover, he also succeeded in rejecting the smothering embrace of Ley's German Labor Front by agreeing to split membership fees.[48]

Because of their anti-Marxist and often illiberal ideology, academic engineers also "welcomed the political and spiritual transformation." During the national delegate meeting of March 11, the existing VDDI leadership was generally confirmed, and the Diplom-Ingenieur association, "as a matter of course, joyously put itself at the disposal of the new age. It did not have to change its tune and its constitution had to be altered in only a few points."[49] In June the VDDI aryanized itself, and in late July it adopted the obligatory Führerprinzip while keeping Prof. Friedrich Romberg as chairman. Intent on "organic incorporation" rather than amalgamation with the KDAI, the academic engineers "joined the Reichsbund Deutscher Technik" in order to escape long-standing VDI dominance.[50] As long as Feder accepted its claim to be "the only professional association of the academic-technical practitioners," the VDDI was delighted to become part of the "front of technology." However, in October 1933, party recognition of the VDI as "technical-scientific organization" in effect "ruptured the basis" of this unification of the "professional community," thereby jeopardizing the unified voice of technology in the Third Reich.[51]

The conflict between professional and political-technical associations began to be resolved during 1934. Shielded by Hitler's personal respect for technology and his reluctance to take on the industrialists, the VDI strengthened its position by the dissolution of the RDT, appointment of the new "inspector general for the *Reichsautobahn* Fritz Todt" as chairman of the RTA, and the prohibition of compulsion during the reorganization.[52] At the end of May, Heß cleared up the confusion by creating a unified "office of technology" in the party leadership, which was nominally directed by Gottfried Feder, but practically run by the long-time Nazi, highway builder, and car enthusiast Fritz Todt, who was thereby drawn into the NSDAP bureaucracy. At the same time, he dissolved the unsuccessful KDAI and transferred its membership to a new "National Socialist League of German Technology" (NSBDT) as the appropriate party organization of engineers. "This directive has brought us much closer together. All three components of the cooperation of technology, the Amt der Technik, the NSBDT and the RTA have been put into a single hand.'' Schult immediately welcomed the solution as ''facilitating constructive cooperation'' in the organic restructuring of the economy.[53] To end the rivalry of the technical associations, Todt in early August ''combined the business offices of the RTA and the NSBDT'' in the VDI house in Berlin, called Schult into the NSBDT, and sent party member Georg Seebauer into the RTA, thereby interweaving their leadership—much to the chagrin of the VDDI, which felt left out. Another step in the imposition of NS control was membership sharing between the NSBDT and the RTA by a Solomonic division of labor, with the former responsible for ''NS ideology'' and the latter ''for scientific work.''[54]

In the varied experience of lawyers, secondary schoolteachers, and engineers, the Gleichschaltung was a complex and prolonged process of self-coordination, collaboration, and compulsion. Internally, it began with loyalty declarations to the government of national concentration that were only a shade more eager than endorsements of earlier cabinets. With the Enabling Act, cooperation turned into co-optation of Nazi professionals as a show of goodwill and a protection against further demands. However, such Trojan horses insisted on a Nazi line, trying to secure association property and prepare fusion with the appropriate NSDAP affiliate. By the summer of 1933, every profession could claim, like the PhVb, that it ''corresponds in its structure to all demands of the NS state: it is led from top to bottom by Nazis; its goals are National Socialist; its constitution is based upon the leadership principle, the Aryan paragraph and the political principles of the NSDAP.''[55] Externally, the coordination required organizational integration into the Nazi network. The loosest form was incorporation into a ''front'' of law, education (DEG) or technology (DTV) under a common leadership, but with continued practical autonomy. Greater pressure was exerted in a corporatist arrangement in which the entire occupation was absorbed by a Nazi group, permitting the continuation of associational identity (VDI) in exchange for subordination to NS ideology. The tightest control came from a unitary solution, merging the prior group into an affiliate section collectively (retaining some sense of continuity as in the BNSDJ) or individually (obliterating all tradition as in the NSLB). With Weimar elites being ousted by nationalists and these in turn replaced by party zealots, coordination developed a seemingly unstoppable momentum of its own.[56]

The motives of the participants were decidedly mixed. Although a courageous few resisted, most liberal leaders were strangely resigned to the inevitable and stepped down voluntarily. By yielding, the Weimar leadership sought to assure the survival of the profession and preserve the associations and journals that it had struggled so hard to build. Nationalist board members stayed on and rejoiced either from elation about the ''national rising'' or from opportunism, serving as symbols of legitimacy. Troubled by modernization and worried about the socio-economic crisis, traditionalists longed for a restoration of professional authority but opposed NS populism and neo-heathenism. Trying to take over, overt and covert Nazis were animated by a blend of revenge or greed with the hope for a völkisch rebirth. Many Old Fighter militants also genuinely desired the building of a purified national and social professionalism. BNSDJ leader Hans Frank promoted ''the great idea of the renewal of legal life'' by ''restoring its roots in the

German people.'' Appealing to ''teachers to help make the rebirth perfect,'' Hans Schemm similarly stressed noble aims: ''Our meeting shall not be under the motto . . . profession . . . salary . . . or teaching load,'' because material questions would ''solve themselves'' in a true national community. For others, the Third Reich was the precondition for true, corporate professionalism. Gottfried Feder dreamed about having appropriately applied technology ''share state leadership and government decisions.''[57] Such idealistic rhetoric helped silence lingering doubts by concealing baser desires.

Confusing legal and extralegal methods also contributed to the success of coordination among the professions. The NS assault was often so improvised and piecemeal that it was difficult to resist. Pressure came simultaneously from national and local fronts, such as competing organizations, nazified ministries, or even employers. Sometimes posing as ''coordination commissions,'' Nazi zealots used a persuasive mixture of threats and enticements. On the one hand, they resorted to negative sanctions such as physical beatings, government orders, or job retaliation. On the other hand, they suggested positive rewards, such as career opportunities, party preferment, and other spoils. Because those practitioners—not singled out for persecution—quickly understood that they had to nazify, there was remarkably little outward resistance. Rather, struggles developed around the form and degree of Gleichschaltung, depending on a profession's closeness to politics (which allowed more latitude to engineers than to lawyers) and on the strength of its tradition (which made philologues resent the plebeian NSLB). The amount of autonomy that remained had much to do with the professionalism of an NS affiliate (which made the BNSDJ more successful than the KDAI) and with the potential allies within NS polycracy (that initially protected the PhVb). Finally, the timing of coordination also played a crucial role, with earlier ''supporters'' receiving better terms (e.g., female secondary schoolteachers) than later converts, especially after personal antagonisms had developed between parallel organizations (e.g., between PhVb and NSLB). Once the attraction of NS corporatism had evaporated, the new masters left ''little doubt that even the *Herrn* experts will have to prove their sincere will to work and that everything is to be judged by Nazi standards.''[58]

RESTORING PROFESSIONAL AUTHORITY

Misled by NS promises of a national rebirth, many practitioners greeted the Conservative–Nazi coalition with high hopes for a resolution of their crisis and a restoration of their authority. On February 8, lawyers met with the Minister of Justice Franz Gürtner to discuss ''an effective admission stop and a subsequent *numerus clausus* for attorneys'' as well as other relief measures. On February 18, philologues debated ''several proposals for the improvement of the distressed academic labor market'' and implored the new minister of culture ''to abandon unhesitatingly his senseless and mistaken economies.'' Engineers also clamored for ''overcoming unemployment and financially rehabilitating public administration so as to ease the burdens which oppress and throttle business and entrepreneurship.''[59] Beyond a ''return to solid work,'' Nazi zealots sought a more radical transformation of the professions. Unabashedly, Hans Frank called for a purge of "Jewish capitalists from the East" and a "fundamental cleansing of ideology." Similarly, Hans Schemm admitted to his district leaders that "we are moving in an unregulated area," implying that the NSLB was not bound by legal niceties in its pursuit of power in education. Finally, Gottfried Feder did not hide the antiliberal and anti-Marxist thrust of his economic policy.[60] Which of these only partly overlapping authoritarian or völkisch visions would govern professional practice in the first years of the Third Reich?

Initial measures of the government of national concentration such as the "law against the overcrowding of schools and universities" fulfilled expectations of decisiveness. In order "to restore normal working conditions," professional associations had for years demanded a *numerus clausus* (DAV), "an immediate regulation of the influx" (PhVb), or a sharper selection (VDI). On January 13, 1933, the faculty of Königsberg University proposed a one-year admission freeze, a two-tier high school diploma (with only superior performance allowing immatriculation), and a reduction in student aid. With presumably 40,000 graduates jobless, frightened experts, convening a week later in the Reich Ministry of Interior, agreed that "drastic changes in the present admissions procedure, even if mistaken, are preferable to inaction."[61] Another public warning was not enough, because "universities are generally reluctant to reject applicants for lack of space." When the medical student association demanded a *numerus clausus,* Minister of Education Bernhard Rust replied that restricting access to one field alone was "impracticable because of the overcrowding of all academic professions." Although the statistician Georg Keiser predicted an enrollment drop of 30–40 percent for the following three years, Nazi lecturers at Königsberg demanded by telegram "the immediate introduction of a *numerus clausus* for Jewish students," thereby injecting a racial note that the Nazi Student League had sounded since 1929.[62] Responding to overcrowding hysteria among the professions and to wishes of NS fanatics like Hartnacke, Reich Minister of Interior Frick endorsed a major admission reduction as an alternative to a general prohibition of study.

The law of April 25, 1933 ingeniously combined overcrowding curbs with anti-Semitic stipulations. Its general purpose of restoring the balance between educational supply and labor needs seemed innocuous: "In all schools . . . and universities the number of pupils and students is to be limited so as to assure thorough training and to meet the demand of the professions." According to an agreement negotiated between the states on February 15, high school graduates of insufficient promise were to be counseled against studying. Although they could not be formally excluded from the university, they were to receive no student aid and to be tested after three semesters before being allowed to continue.[63] The barely hidden anti-Semitic agenda surfaced in the warning that "the economic and intellectual influence of foreign elements in national life weakens the spiritual unity and the national power of the German people and state." The law therefore required Jewish matriculations to "stay below the percentage of non-Aryans in the German population," set at 1.5 percent, so as not to exceed 5 percent in any single faculty. With an officially estimated 4.71 percent share of Jewish students, this meant in effect a two-thirds reduction of access as well as a closing of their preferred careers (i.e., medicine with 7.6 percent and law with 7.3 percent).[64]

The final victims of exclusion were women. Deep-seated misogynist reflexes among Nazi activists as well as fear of competition from able females whose share was rising to about 20 percent of all students held women coresponsible for professional overcrowding. Therefore, the implementation instructions of the general law limited females to only 10 percent of male enrollment, thereby cutting their hard-won academic access more than in half.[65]

These brutal restrictions had drastic effects. During the Easter 1933 Abitur, 1360 of the 7470 successful graduates (120 failed) were discouraged from university study in Prussia. Because even this 18.2 percent reduction seemed too small, Wilhelm Frick set the national 1934 target for beginning students at 15,000 (allowing 8984 for Prussia). This *Hochschulvermerk* permitted only 15,919 of the high school graduates to continue (while rejecting 22,814), even less than the declining 1932 figure of 19,586 freshmen.[66] As if by magic, between the winter of 1932–1933 and the summer of 1935, university enrollment shrank from 92,601 to 57,001, while technical higher education contracted from 20,431 to 11,364! The 3950 Jewish students before the seizure of power dropped precipitously to 538 in the last official count of winter 1934–1935. The number of women was similarly reduced from 17,192 to 9645, declining to 16.9 percent of the student body.[67] For the professions, the decrease of first-year students to 13,449 (1933) and 7914 (1934–1935) promised dramatic relief from the pressure of beginners in the academic job market. With law enrollment falling from 18,364 to 7400, philosophy attendance sliding from 37,105 to 16,541, and technical inscriptions similarly collapsing between 1932 and 1935, only half as many college graduates would clamor for career entry four years later (Table A.1). Although the enrollment drop was largely due to the arrival of decimated First World War birth cohorts and the improvement in economic prospects, Nazi bureaucrats claimed the overcrowding law as a public relations success for those not excluded by it. By February 1935, student numbers had shrunk so far that the Ministry of Culture could discontinue issuing new target figures.[68]

To accelerate the process of Gleichschaltung, the Nazis ruthlessly purged the professions by delicensing racially or politically undesirable practitioners. Vengeful NS lawyers saw the victory of "the national movement" as an opportunity for settling old scores. Shouting *Juden raus!* [Jews out], on March 11, 1933 SA troops stormed the Breslau courts and chased Jewish judges and attorneys into the streets, badly injuring two lawyers. Pressured by the police chief, the Appellate Court president informed local attorneys five days later that he would henceforth admit only seventeen Jewish lawyers, setting a dangerous precedent by in effect disbarring 350 others! Although Hitler ordered "a stop to the disruption of the administration of justice," such "spontaneous" assaults spread to other towns such as Kassel, leading to the murder of several prominent lawyers who were political opponents.[69] Prodded by the BNSDJ, new rightist groups such as "a Christian-national lawyer association" of 100 Breslau attorneys "demand[ed] an immediate solution because of the preponderantly un-German lawyer-chamber." On March 23, 800 Berlin jurists founded a similar "League of national attorneys and notaries" which immediately called for the exclusion of Jewish colleagues.[70] Ironically, the legal instrument of disbarment was temporary suspension (introduced through emergency decree on March 22), which was long demanded by liberal reformers. Claiming that "the arrogant behavior of Jewish attorneys has created special outrage," Prussian commissar Hanns Kerrl on March 31 ordered the chambers "that only certain Jewish attorneys shall practice, generally corresponding to the proportion of Jews in the rest of the population." Anticipating the national boycott of Jewish stores, non-Aryans should no longer be deputized as poor-law defenders or as mandatory counsels.[71]

Temporary suspension was, however, not enough for Nazi fanatics. Though increasingly excluded from courtrooms, Jewish attorneys were still legally licensed. Therefore, many "Aryan" colleagues began to shun them (in Naumburg), local associations expelled them (in Magdeburg), and Christian-nationalist organizations argued that it was unethical to substitute for them (in Düsseldorf). For Prussia, Kerrl forbade the preparation of legal briefs by "not-admitted" attorneys and reiterated his other prohibitions on April 4.[72] When the states were trying to make the anti-Semitic boycott permanent (with Frank's Bavaria barring all Jewish attorneys from the courts), Reich Minister of Justice Gürtner forestalled complete exclusion by drafting a more moderate national law. Somewhat restrained by fear of an uproar abroad, Hitler asked the cabinet on April 7 "only to regulate what is necessary at this time. For attorneys a solution similar to the law on the restoration of professional civic service ought to be found," while doctors were to remain free. Rejecting a general *numerus clausus,* the government also extended disbarment to "non-Jewish attorneys, if these have been active as Communists." The law on "admission as attorney" revoked credentials for Jews, but on Field Marshal Hindenburg's insistence excepted those who, like Siegfried Neumann, had been admitted during the empire, fought in the war, or had fathers or sons who were killed at the front. During disbarment proceedings, attorneys were suspended so as to drive away their clients, even if they might eventually be readmitted. Beginning in April, the chambers purged their membership, spurred on by "Aryan" resentment against the "dominant position" of their Jewish competitors. Though critical of the "excessive number of Jews in public positions," Max Hachenburg warned against overreaction.[73] Undeterred, expulsions concentrated on those cities where Nazis deemed "the disproportion quite unbearable," but spread also to smaller towns, depriving 11.5 percent of all advocates (and 19.3 percent of all notaries) of their livelihood (Table 5.1)![74]

The purge of "active Communists" was equally ruthless and thorough. Already in March, Nazi fanatics complained that "known personalities from the SPD or KPD are still appointed notary public." Based on denunciations, local

Table 5.1. Purge of Jewish Lawyers in Prussia, 1933–1934

OLG district	Number of Lawyers	Jewish		Purged		Remainder	
		Number	Percentage	Number	Percentage	Number	Percentage
Berlin	3,890	1,880	48.3	721	18.5	1159	61.6
Frankfurt	607	275	45.3	121	19.9	154	56.0
Breslau	1,056	378	35.6	145	13.7	233	61.6
Königsberg	375	90	24.0	47	12.5	43	47.8
Others	5,886	750	12.7	330	5.6	420	56.0
TOTAL	11,814	3,373	28.6	1,364	11.5	2009	59.6

authorities expelled alleged "Communists," such as attorney "W," even if the information later turned out to be spurious. Several Prussian chambers drew up proscription lists (e.g., Berlin submitted thirty-three names), with defense of Marxists and opposition to the NS movement as typical "offenses." A national Ministry of Interior listing with 132 lawyers who had worked with the Marxist legal aid Rote Hilfe served as basis for persecution, even if Communists had often hired bourgeois attorneys in order to make their cases credible.[75] Predictably included in the April 7 expulsion law, Communists proved quite difficult to define in legal practice. As a nationalist bureaucrat, Reich Minister of Justice Franz Gürtner maintained that "an attorney's representation of Communist interests in the course of his professional duty should not in itself justify the assumption of 'Communist activity.' " However, as a fanatical Nazi, Prussian State Secretary Roland Freisler countered "that the voluntary defense of Communists in political cases is to be seen as Communist activity in principle." Although conservative jurists sought a clear ruling, which would be based on "the frequency . . . manner . . . or circumstances" of a defense, NS fanatics wanted an interpretation vague enough to allow the prosecution of all enemies. Construing representation of Marxists as "indirect support for the political goals of the Communist party," the Prussian Ministry of Justice asked the lawyer chamber to declare it unethical. In July 7, 1934, the Reichsrechtsanwaltskammer (RRAK) therefore announced that "an attorney shall not support subversive tendencies directly or indirectly," making voluntary representation of leftists unprofessional.[76]

When it became known that exceptions permitted three-fifths of the Jewish lawyers to continue their practice, mobs in Celle, Frankfurt, Hanover, and Duisburg once again used their fists to "cleanse" the courts. Over the protests of the League of Jewish Veterans (BJF) and conservative jurists, the board of the Berlin chamber on May 23, 1933 forbade "any professional association" with de-certified or still licensed Jewish attorneys, such as joint offices *(Sozietät),* which helped in circumventing expulsion or taking over case loads. Because zealots like Kerrl and Frank disbarred as many attorneys as possible, the first implementation order defined the exceptions more broadly. When Jewish lawyer leaders demanded that the Prussian Ministry of Justice protect their remaining rights, Freisler had to agree that admitted lawyers were fully equal, but Voß and Neubert rejected any compromise as "interference in the internal matters of a party organization."[77] Rampant confusion about what remained permissible forced the Reich Ministry of Justice to clarify the situation in negotiations with the state ministries during the summer. On October 1, the second implementation instruction assured that "Jewish attorneys remaining in office retain the full enjoyment of their professional rights and can demand that respect which they are owed as members of their professional community." However, at the same time, the BNSDJ formalized the exclusion of Jews from the lawyers' professional association, depriving them of a collective voice and of listing in the annual directory, thereby consigning them to inferior status.[78] Formally still free to practice, the surviving Jewish lawyers were, like Horst Berkowitz, squeezed out economically. "In this manner thousands of professional men . . . together with their families and their employees, were faced with certain ruin."[79]

High school teachers were similarly purged through the "law on the restora-

Table 5.2. Prussian Teacher Purge, 1933–1937

Rank	Number	Reason: Political	Race	Unreliability	Reassigned	Pensioned	Number affected	Percentage of total
Ministry	281	1	1	11	20	11	44	15.7
Other officials	2,576	2	10	70	154	123	359	13.9
Professors	3,776	2	340	47	—	89	478	12.6
Assistants	1,070	—	30	7	—	—	37	3.4
Art administrators	776	5	10	7	70	120	212	27.7
Philologues	5,626	14	275	230	943	1,119	2,581	45.9
Primary pedagogues	110,974	63	95	700	1,311	1,174	3,343	3.0
TOTAL	125,079	87	761	1,072	2,498	2,636	7,054	5.6

tion of professional public service'' of April 7, 1933. Suggesting by its title that it was intended to undo republican politicization, this measure in effect imposed political and racial conformity with a vengeance. Deploring the ''strong underrepresentation of NS forces in the work of the state,'' Prussian Prime Minister Herrmann Göring bluntly called for immediate ''elimination of all personalities that are not unobjectionable in terms of morals and character.'' Dismissing bureaucrats appointed by virtue of their Weimar party membership (paragraph 2), the comprehensive but vague law instituted the infamous ''Aryan paragraph'' (paragraph 3) that proscribed Jews, permitted the firing of ''politically unreliable officials'' (paragraph 4), and in lesser cases their ''reassignment'' (paragraph 5), or premature ''pensioning'' (paragraph 6) for administrative reasons (Table 5.2).[80] The implementation instructions of May 6 spelled out that the measure pertained to ''public school instructors,'' but not to Jewish pedagogues in their own institutions. Membership in a party other than the Communist did not constitute a crime unless ''an official has in word, writing or through other actions shown his hatred for the national movement, cursed its leaders or abused his office to persecute nationalist officials.'' Minister of Education Bernhard Rust not only went along, but also insisted on ruthlessness, because ''a stricter racial standard must be applied to teachers and educators of youth than to other officials.''[81]

The impact of the purge on teachers was greater than is commonly realized. All public educators had to fill out detailed questionnaires on their political leanings and racial origins, which were screened by a three-member commission—causing much fear and favoritism. Although reserving the final decision to himself, Bernhard Rust established special subsections within his ministry, which were headed by such trusted NSLB zealots as the notorious Martin Löpelmann for secondary schools. Especially principals and Oberstudienräte were replaced. Even widows living on pensions were not safe and the witch-hunters also cut the retirement pay of hated former ministers of education such as Grimme and Becker.[82] In Prussia, only fourteen philologues were dismissed as political appointees such as the pedagogical reformer and SPD member Friedrich Copei. Whereas anti-Semitic prejudice had made public careers difficult, 275 Jewish high school teachers were fired for racial reasons, like the respected Berlin German-language instructor Bruno Strauss. Moreover, political unreliability led to the sacking of 230 pedagogues, whereas 943 were transferred and 1119 retired prematurely such as the Cologne Gymnasium director August Altmeyer. Although only 3 percent of the primary schoolteachers were involved, a staggering 45.9 percent of Prussian state high school personnel was affected in some way by 1937: 5 percent were dismissed for racial and 4 percent for political reasons, whereas 16.8 percent were demoted and another 19.9 percent were pensioned off or relegated to primary schools. The philologues' resistance against the NSLB and their political visibility led to their being singled out. The purge was harshest in formerly Socialist Hamburg (12.6 percent), Prussia (5.6 percent), Bremen (5.3 percent), and Saxony (4.1 percent), in contrast to the Catholic Saar (.5 percent) and Bavaria (.8 percent), with the rest of the nation averaging 2.9 percent. Although most pedagogues continued to teach, such intimidation and the "legal corruption" of NS favoritism had a chilling effect.[83]

The anti-Semitic witch-hunt even spread to engineers, albeit more indirectly than to the other professions. Together with up to 800 technicians of Jewish descent, the 1443 engineers listed as religious Jews in the German census of 1933 made up around 1 percent of all practitioners. Except for public officials purged with the other occupations, technical academics depended upon the pleasure of their business employers who enjoyed some latitude in their decisions. Blocking hiring for Jewish students, the campaign of hatred pressured many companies into dismissing younger technicians even if some industrialists sought to keep their experienced personnel. Once fired, Jewish technicians rarely found new jobs and had little choice but to emigrate. Associations such as the VDI aggravated the predicament by adopting the "Aryan paragraph" for their officers in 1933 and requiring it for all members in 1935.[84] The effect of anti-Semitism upon VDI membership was startling. In contrast to the annual drop-out rate of around 900 between 1930 and 1937, as many as 1952 resigned in 1933, and once again 1775 left the VDI in 1936 after the Nuremberg laws (with deaths already subtracted). This membership drop suggests a sizable exclusion of Jewish colleagues, even if the category expulsion disappears from the annual reports after 1932. The number of German Jewish engineering emigrés in Israel (at least 160), England (more than 800), and the United States (ranging between 645 and 2818) also indicates that "technology" was somewhat less neutral than its leaders later claimed.[85]

The remaining professionals sought to restore their economic position through the machinery of the Third Reich. The attorney law of July 20, 1933 fulfilled some long-standing desires. Article 1 prohibited the admission of pensioned officials and retired judges, those dismissed in the purge as well as those deemed "incapable" or infirm. To keep disbarred lawyers from becoming legal consultants, Article 3 permitted the "court to reject representatives and advisors who engage in oral negotiations as a business," depending on legal need and individual aptitude. Since this measure "practically excluded the entire legal consultant occupation from . . . the courts," nonacademic counselors denounced it as a "class struggle law," benefiting readmitted Jewish attorneys. Though suggesting local leniency, the ministry, nevertheless, backed the professionals in aiming for "the gradual throttling" of their competitors.[86] Because "the plight of German lawyers is ever worsening," NSLB section leader Walter Raeke insisted on further restrictions in October 1934. A "general clause" should prevent admission, "if the personality of the applicant, according to his prior behavior, offers no guarantee that he will practice law in line with correct ethics.'' This arbitrary stipulation also effectively halted the licensing of women as lawyers. More controversial was the exclusion of syndics who were ''regularly dependent on or employed by a third party,'' because such ''ties are incompatible with the practice of the legal profession.'' Outraged, attorneys in leading industrial positions, interest group organizations, or legal departments of firms countered that lawyers would lose all connection to business and that their exclusion would ''not help alleviate the plight of the advocates.'' In spite of considerable industrial pressure, the law of December 20, 1934 barred syndics from civil suits and arbitration proceedings.[87]

Although attorneys failed to achieve complete closure, the partial elimination of competitors ultimately began to improve their income. Other measures, such as the admission of lawyers to labor courts beginning on January 20, 1934 actually expanded the field for legal practice. Only when the Nazi state had to absorb the cost, such as in poor-law reimbursements, did the new government become unsympathetic and actually reduce rates further.[88] Eventually, the combination of study limitation and anti-Semitic purge decreased the number of practitioners from about 19,208 in 1933 to 18,432 in 1934 and 18,780 in 1935 (due to 1364 new attorney admissions that year). However, improvements were limited by the gradual reduction of the case load. Eleven of thirteen indicators of legal business contracted between 1933 and 1935, with civil cases falling between 13.9 percent (debt collection) and 41.4 percent (financial and title questions), while criminal judgments decreased 12.2 percent and labor disputes sank 23.4 percent (Tables A.11a, A.11b).[89] Even though there were more than 5400 unemployed Assessoren, the favorable effects of the limitation of competitors, the elimination of Jewish colleagues, and an enlargement of their field gradually began to be felt for those with jobs. Between 1933 and 1935, the proportion of poverty-stricken practitioners with an annual income of less than 3000 marks decreased from 41.9 percent to about 25 percent. At the same time, average yearly receipts increased from less than 6500 marks in 1933 to 6900 marks in 1934 and to 9750 marks in 1935. Slowly, collaboration with the Nazi regime began to pay off for the majority of ''Aryan'' nationalist professionals.[90]

In spite of cosmetic corrections, the material situation of academic teachers improved less than expected in the early Nazi years. Philologues were ''overjoyed'' when Minister of Education Rust announced on April 12 that ''the schedules hitherto reduced by economy measures are to be restored to their old form.'' The resumption of 24,000 canceled class hours in Prussia required the rehiring of about 1000 secondary schoolteachers who had been dismissed. ''Through the elimination of Jewish and Marxist elements . . . further staff appointments are to be expected.'' Since married female teachers like Elisabeth Petri-Jarausch were encouraged to resign, 1844 probationers went back onto the Prussian payroll in temporary positions. However, it took until April 1935 for the permanent hiring freeze to be lifted for those public high school teachers, who are ''capable of molding youth into National Socialists.'' As a result of dropping enrollments, the number of tenured Prussian teachers, nevertheless, continued to shrink from 16,104 in 1931 to 13,830 in 1935. Since normal hiring was resumed only in 1936, probationer unemployment peaked at 20.3 percent (Table A.6b).[91] Philologues were also disappointed in their hope for a quick reversal of the late Weimar pay cuts.

Because the Nazi state needed funds for rearmament and public works, it kept the reductions in the name of patriotism without fear of public contradiction. Salary questions, once central to the *Philologenblatt,* disappeared from print after 1933. As a token concession, the Prussian tax withholding of June 8, 1932 was halved in April 1934 and completely eliminated in the following year. However, that correction brought only a minimal improvement of 2.5 to 5 percent (Table A.12). While regaining a measure of security, philologues were disappointed that the Nazis failed to reverse the "decline of their salaries."[92]

Because engineers had suffered severely during the depression, the subsequent reversal of their economic fortunes was dramatic. In the spring of 1933, the Reichsanstalt für Arbeitsvermittlung agreed to underwrite the private Ingenieurdienst with public funds, thereby helping young engineers to gain work experience for the nominal pay of three marks per week. One-fifth of the 4200 aspiring technicians, supported that year, managed to turn temporary positions into permanent jobs. The VDI engineering aid continued to dispense funds, but the number of monthly recipients decreased from about 235 in 1932 to 155 in 1934.[93] Charity became superfluous when the economic resurgence restored the labor market for engineers. Starting already in the summer of 1932, "the recovery picked up steam after the NS revolution" because of the creation of work and the restoration of "confidence in leadership." Available jobs listed by the VDDI rose from 64.7 per month in the second quarter of 1932 to 532 in the third quarter of 1935! At the same time, unemployment of VDDI members declined from about 11 percent to less than 2.5 percent (Table A.13). Although beginning pay was still a meager 120 marks per month, "in contrast to other academic specialties, the economic situation of young [technical] professionals has improved considerably." Only engineers over thirty-five years old found it difficult to reenter the work force, so that the Ingenieurdienst shifted its attention to several thousand older technicians in 1935. For the younger engineers, the limitation of educational access and economic recovery created "an increased demand . . . which cannot always be satisfied any longer."[94]

In contrast to gradual economic gains, the social status of professionals failed to improve in the Third Reich. Adolf Hitler himself resented all Akademiker, because from his Viennese failures he equated them with Jews and thought them unnatural. Having occasionally humiliated him in court, lawyers were especially suspect. "Those who spend their whole life defending crooks cannot be considered decent professionals." If anything, pedagogues were worse. "Only a certain type who is unfit for the struggle of the free professions becomes a teacher," the Führer repeatedly grumbled due to the "unpleasant recollections" of his own dropping out of school. Only engineers found favor as representatives of technological progress. Reflecting such prejudices, the NS leadership directory published in 1934 included only forty lawyers (three-fifth of whom were Old Fighters) and about twenty teachers (all of whom were zealots) in contrast to listing about seventy engineers (two-thirds of whom had not even joined the party). In Nazi circles, mere "civilians" seemed somehow less important than the ubiquitous uniforms of the NSDAP and the military. The prevailing Volksgemeinschaft ideology also equated the workers of the hand with those of the head and tried to close "the ill-fated gap" between "academic arrogance" and "proletarian uncouthness.'' To escape such leveling and maintain their privileges, professionals preferred attempts at ''corporate'' restructuring of society.[95]

Lawyers had to rebut charges of ''alienation from the people as well as arrogance.'' In Nazi eyes, the ''academically trained jurists of the liberal era stood outside the national community.'' Redefined as guardians of law, they were now to be called *Rechtswahrer,* thereby ''expanding the personal limits of the profession beyond the circle of the academically trained and beyond those involved in justice or administration.'' To distance themselves from the racial stereotype of the Jewish shyster and prove themselves as ''friend and patron of their clients,'' attorneys were compelled to ''offer free legal consultation to all poor German citizens.'' Hailed despite its Weimar roots as an example of German socialism, this NS-*Rechtsbetreuung* in more than 1200 local offices dispensed advice to hundreds of thousands of clients, often making litigation unnecessary. According to Raeke, ''the restored and growing trust of the less fortunate strata'' was ''the most beautiful reward for the Aryan lawyers assembled in the BNSDJ.'' To the sanguine Noack, party efforts to lessen the plight of young or underemployed attorneys proved that ''the Nazi state's increased confidence . . . has finally ended the period of suspicion and discrimination of lawyers.''[96]

In spite of Hitler's claim that the Nazis intended ''to educate men,'' teachers found long-standing prejudices against them redoubled. When pedagogues flocked into the NSDAP in during 1933, traditionalist colleagues accused them of being ''opportunists'' while suspicious Old Fighters called for special screening and indoctrination. ''Educators must no longer be free game for wild HJ leaders who believe in increasing their own authority by undermining the teachers' prestige in order to make themselves popular with the boys,'' NSLB leader Max Reiser complained to the national head office about the teaching ''profession being placed outside of the national community.'' Whereas Ernst Krieck castigated the ''triumphant chorus of reaction'' and ''philological arrogance,'' secondary school pedagogues argued that ''the people must show the teaching profession new and greater respect.'' In spite of repeated NSLB protests, pedagogues were a favorite target of NS satires in the press and the movies. No wonder that ''philologist circles are incensed about their Gleichschaltung with primary educators in the NSLB.'' Most secondary schoolteachers rejected the populist egalitarianism of the SA as leading to ''sad and dangerous half-education'' and pleaded for ''recognition of all honest and brave work.''[97]

In contrast, engineers saw the Third Reich as an opportunity to gain social esteem through the ''sovereignty of factual expertise.'' In Gottfried Feder's overblown technocratic vision, ''state leadership of the economy makes possible a return to its original principles, the constructive synthesis of single elements in a purposeful whole.'' In contrast to capitalist profit orientation or bureaucratic regimentation, the business recovery ''should be directed by technicians themselves.'' In such a noneconomic economy, engineers would gain new leadership roles free from traditional academic constraints. However, reality often fell short of these aspirations, because ''the engineering profession does not attract public interest.'' As a specialized expert, the technician appeared to be an economic problem solver rather than ''someone serving the entire community'' and therefore did not seem to be a real professional. But for Heinrich Schult, the vast tasks of

Nazi economic planning and rearmament provided engineers with fresh chances to ''elevate the engineering profession'' by working hard and conforming to the party line. At the 1935 VDI congress, Rudolf Heß underscored ''the importance which the new Germany places on technology'' and on NS engineers as ''the technical officer-corps of the German economy.''[98]

Whereas some practices continued much as before, other patterns changed considerably. Lawyers still dealt with clients but under an altered set of ethics, ''in accord with the views of the Third Reich.'' Responding to attorney wishes, the Ministry of Justice transferred honor court appeals from the Supreme Court to the national lawyers' chamber in order to tighten control of attorney behavior. In part, the new ''guidelines for the practice of the legal profession'' restated accepted custom through traditional injunctions to silence, honesty, financial probity as well as prohibitions of rate competition, fee sharing, success percentages, or advertisement. However, the rejection of specialization, dependence on outsiders, or association with nonlawyers (unless admitted into the BNSDJ) reversed some Weimar innovations. ''The attorney of German blood shall work on the great tasks of the nation in a [Nazi] spirit and shall involve himself in the NS movement and its organizations as much as possible.'' Thorough nazification meant that advocates must ''refuse to represent openly asocial and un-German legal ideas which contradict healthy popular feeling.'' This identification of advocates with their clients made defense of anyone defined as a national enemy dangerous. However, in the first years of the Third Reich, independent attorneys like Friedrich Grimm still succeeded in beating down some political accusations like the charges against Konrad Adenauer. Working for ''German'' justice also implied that ''joint practice of Aryan with non-Aryan lawyers is to be avoided in principle.'' The famous theoretician Carl Schmitt defended such ''general clauses'' as essential for the Nazi ''rule of law,'' thereby sanctioning a drastic warping of legal ethics.[99]

High school teaching revealed a similar mixture of tradition and Nazi insistence that ''the teacher must become different from what he was.''[100] Although outward uniformity was impressive, the internal quality of instruction depended on the particular school climate, which was determined by the director, faculty, pupils, and parents in a given town. Weimar reform efforts such as Fritz Karsen's school were summarily stopped, but less prominent progressives survived in remote places and some liberal institutions such as the *Französisches Gymnasium* in Berlin remained largely unaffected. Whereas much regular teaching continued as before, the introduction of the leadership principle decreased pedagogical autonomy and opened the door to petty arbitrariness, because initially ''the leaders do not know what actually is National Socialist.'' Compulsory politicization often engendered ''a mixture of informers, ignoramuses and criminals,'' which poisoned collegial relations through constant fear of denunciation. The officially decreed ''voluntary'' involvement in air raid protection, NS welfare, the teachers' league, and the constant collections also ''made hurrying up a principle . . . so that we have no time to think.'' Goaded on by ''HJ urchins who can dare to be fresh to an instructor,'' pupils grew more assertive, thereby undermining that pedagogical authority that the Third Reich was supposed to restore. With marching and patriotic ceremonies infringing on instructional and homework time, teachers began to complain ''about incredibly poor performance in the high schools. Instruction has become so superficial that one must be horrified by the educational level of the coming generation.''[101]

Under the vague heading of Gemeinschaftsarbeit, engineering practice shifted to the Nazi priorities of ''creating work for German citizens; forging new ties between people and land through settlement . . . ;'' reforming technical education, ''securing national supply from German soil; serving rearmament and thereby protecting German homes.''[102] Engineers could claim a large share of the credit for the propaganda victory in the ''battle of labor,'' because, as they proudly pointed out in a special edition of the *VDI-Zeitschrift,* all facets of technology had contributed to its success. The most highly touted project was the construction of new superhighways, the famous Reichsautobahnen, which created jobs for road engineers as well as several hundred thousand laborers in a mixture of technical futurism, military utility, and national prestige that appealed to Hitler personally. Another task involved the development of raw-material substitutes and energy sources to make Germany independent of foreign supplies. Settlement schemes also sought to break up urban squalor and improvement plans for agricultural machinery tried to make farm production more efficient.[103] Finally, revisionist Nazi foreign policy brought clandestine rearmament out in the open and made military technology once again an engineering favorite. However, in other important areas of rapid development such as computers or radar, the NS leaders simply missed the boat.[104]

Altered practice rested on a different conception of the role of the professions in the Third Reich. After some initial conflict between ''the will and spirit of our highest Führer'' and their consciences, most practitioners developed a new view of their duties, reconciling their ''tasks as Nazi'' and professional. For lawyers, Hans Frank redefined the purpose ''of justice as safeguarding the life of the people rather than securing the application of rules.'' In contrast to liberal individualism, Nazi legal thinkers stressed völkisch communitarianism, recognizing as law only ''what is suited to protect the substantive values of national and political existence.''[105] This racial collectivism fundamentally transformed the lawyer's charge from representing the client to becoming ''an advocate of justice'' in the people's interest. Nazi attorneys were supposed to think of themselves as ''servant[s] of the law and thereby as indispensable organ[s] of legal administration.'' Only while ''cooperating in the finding of justice through the court'' could the lawyer become ''a helper to his fellow countrymen in legal distress.''[106] In procedural practice, this altered perspective strengthened the powers of the judge while weakening the position of the attorney. Instead of an equal antagonist to the prosecutor, a lawyer was reduced to a subsidiary role and had to take great care not to seem to be obstructing popular legal sentiment. Consequently, practitioners considered ''the position of the defense in German criminal procedure difficult and thankless,'' because there was much distrust of incompletely nazified attorneys. In many ways, NS ideology was hostile to the very existence of lawyers, preferring arbitration to litigation. Therefore, protestations that the Third Reich needed ''free and independent attorneys'' in order to ''secure the prestige of German justice'' had a hollow ring.[107]

The Nazis also had considerable difficulty in developing a new role for philologues, because the NSLB propagated a single unified teaching profession. In contrast to the ossified scholar, Hans Schemm called for "a young fighter who moves forwards, and storms ahead; then he will also inspire youth to follow. . . ." Because in the Third Reich the school no longer primarily fostered learning, knowledge, or skills, but molded character, the new teacher had to be a gifted pedagogue, an *Erzieherpersönlichkeit,* firmly rooted in German nationality. "He must carry the spiritual values of his *Volkstum* not as antiquarian knowledge, bought by college fees, but as answers to questions posed by vibrant life."[108] However, the "inner renewal of the teaching profession" turned out to be difficult, because many academically trained teachers feared the "destruction of our proven cultural and scientific institutions in an excess of revolutionary enthusiasm." Although Rust's criticism of "the Marxist-democratic spirit of the empty comprehensive school" guaranteed the survival of academic secondary institutions, his demand for "educators above all," willing to march in closed ranks, left little room for a separate philological identity.[109] Curricular changes compounded the perplexity. Although the rediscovery of Germanic völkisch history could be seen as restoring national pride, the introduction of "racial science into teaching" appeared intellectually problematic. Nazi zealots repeatedly counseled educator–leaders "to tear down the paper walls" of bookishness: "If we philologues and the high school want to regain our importance for nation and state, we must get closer to the people than during the liberal era."[110] It is no wonder that traditionalist high school teachers reacted to the new demands with a certain "pedagogical defensiveness."

"The mission of engineers in the new state" had to be rethought in broadly national terms. Rudolf Heiss, the editor of a programmatic volume with this title, argued that Nazi altruism offered the solution to the "technical cultural crisis." Technicians should become the shocktroops of "psychological mobilization" in forging a national technology and healing the economic wounds left by liberal democracy. According to the murky theoretician Heinrich Hardensett, the Third Reich finally allowed engineers to escape the capitalist profit motive and to work in true idealism for the entire community, thereby rejecting Marxist perversions of socialism. They had to show the way in creating work, pacifying the strife between employers and workers, becoming "leaders of the men in their charge," and defending the fatherland with new arms.[111] Most technicians, while enjoying such praise of their importance, simply got on with their jobs, grateful for their steady work, but oblivious to the political demands of the new regime. Therefore, Nazi fanatics insisted on "educating the German engineer as a political man" in order to turn a capable expert into a politically conscious professional. For Fritz Todt, "in the Third Reich a specialist alone does not suffice for the tasks of technology, he must also be a dedicated Nazi." The redefinition of the engineering role aimed at the elusive combination of technical expertise with "Nazi attitude."[112]

In the organizational sphere, Nazi coordination fundamentally altered the professionals' sociability as well as their pursuit of common interests. Initial efforts at realizing neocorporate desires (e.g., through the appointment of some professional representatives to the Reichstag) were soon instrumentalized or overtaken by events. On March 18, 1933, the attorneys could finally welcome a national lawyers' chamber as a recognized official voice with quasi-governmental authority. Charged with "establishing a continuing relationship among the boards of the [local] chambers," the Reichsrechtsanwaltskammer was empowered to submit expert opinions to the government and to levy membership fees. However, under Reinhard Neubert's direction, this corporate self-government served to control lawyers by redefining ethics through subsidiary honor courts.[113] After the self-dissolution of the DAV on December 27, 1933, the attorney section of the BNSDJ became the "professional organization of German lawyers." Open to "every honest German attorney" of Aryan descent who was "not an enemy of the Nazi state," the BNSDJ consisted of judges, legal officials, professors, notaries, business lawyers, legal consultants, and trainees. Membership was essential for inclusion into the official attorney directory, because everyone not listed there was automatically suspect.[114] During 1934, the lawyer section completed its Gau organization, took over the social funds of the DAV, issued new "honor court" standards, and agitated for an improvement in the situation of entering professionals. After much discussion in March 1935, it issued a set of professional demands, such as introducing a special training period for attorneys, excluding unauthorized legal consultants, maintaining the combination of notary and advocate, allowing lawyers into labor courts, and continuing simultaneous admission of AG attorneys. In spite of some material gains and an impressive membership (82,807 by 1935), the league's emphasis on nazifying legal thinking and "controlling and increasing NS activity in the administration of justice" showed the limits of professional self-government in the Third Reich.[115]

Lacking a chamber of their own, philologues proved more difficult to organize in the NSLB. To make it attractive, Hans Schemm subdivided the teachers' league according to school types into seven sections for professors, secondary school faculty, middle school teachers, primary school pedagogues, special school instructors, commercial school tutors, and private educators. However, the PhVb's denunciation of Section Two as an "unnecessary duplication," the primitive tone of the NSLB press, and the double division into Gaue as well as twelve topical areas hampered effective organization.[116] During the summer of 1934, the reorganization of Section Two under Dr. Rudolf Benze from the Prussian Ministry of Education and the foundation of a special journal, *Die Deutsche Höhere Schule,* gradually gave it some credibility. Concentrating on "the appointment of reliable and capable Gau section leaders," Benze began "working towards a new NS-inspired instruction" in biology, sport, German, history, religion, geography, art, music, physics, math, foreign languages, and so on. However, because the NSLB lacked any conception beyond "a change in school spirit and educational content," the ministry continued to balk at turning the transformation of specific subjects over to the teachers' league. Reflecting the generational predicament, Section Two agitated strenuously for improving the lot of Assessoren, instituted a labor exchange, and tried to clarify their legal status. But rejection of "a union or professional strategy" made the NSLB ineffectual in bringing benefits to the established philologues who saw it as a vehicle for "teacher indoctrination with Nazi educational aims" rather than as a representation of their own interests.[117]

Complicated by fragmentation, the reorganization among engineers similarly combined professional aspirations with political manipulation. Long-standing VDDI hopes for title protection merged with the KDAI demand for "the professional incorporation of architects and engineers into the coming corporate state" in plans for a "Reich chamber of technology," such as Dr. Nonn's draft of November 1933. However, when Rudolf Heß authorized a joint VDI–KDAI committee to deliberate about "the organic merger of all technicians," its chairman Fritz Todt rejected "all overly hasty intermediate solutions" until a general scheme could be worked out. While Feder dreamed about a triple accord of labor front, economic corporation, and profession, VDDI leaders proposed that an engineering chamber "cultivate, extend and control the cultural field of *Ingenik*" by policing ethics, shaping training, cooperating with other professions, providing job counseling, gathering statistics, exploring new work areas, supervising the appropriate use of technology, advising government on legislation, and working with a new office of "state technology."[118] When Todt announced the continuation of preparations at the March rally of 7000 technicians, he warned that the self-selection of technical organizations first had to be complete. In a formal draft, VDDI chairman Romberg outlined as the purpose of a *Reichskammer der Technik*—divided into subject areas and specialist groups—"the creation of a unified attitude of technical practitioners," transforming liberal "private technology" into "state technology." According to *Deutsche Technik,* the Chamber of Technology—modeled on Goebbels' *Reichskulturkammer*—should "steer and direct the application of engineering correctly" instead of serving "professional interests."[119] However, in June 1934, the dissolution of the KDAI in favor of the NSBDT doomed the chamber plans. Although the VDDI kept insisting and the term lived on, Feder's eclipse, party disenchantment with völkisch corporatism, and VDI opposition stalled the realization of this aspiration of academic engineers.[120]

In spite of some marked disappointments, most practitioners interpreted the völkisch measures of the early Third Reich as a restoration of professional authority. Practitioners who had seen Hitler as "our *only* hope" for the return of order were willing to detect in the redefinition of their mission many traditional elements that outweighed radical NS innovations. Clearly, the Jewish, left-wing, and female victims of the Nazi purges grievously suffered the loss of their livelihood and sense of self. Lawyers bemoaned the decline in their social status, teachers grumbled about inadequate pay, both found their practice altered for the worse, and older professionals regretted the disappearance of their traditional associations. However, the majority of younger, male, nationalistic Germans had reason to be pleased. The "restoration of professional civil service" might be explained as a necessary removal of corrupt and threatening newcomers, producing career chances for the rest. Undoubtedly, lawyers and engineers were better off economically (and even teachers regained security). Technicians actually rose in social esteem and faced more challenging opportunities. Even organizational incorporation into a larger front might give the profession more influence, and lawyers gained their long-desired chambers at last. Despite the unsettling changes, many attorneys were better off, teachers resumed their national mission, and engineers faced brighter prospects after 1933. Unfortunate Nazi excesses could be rationalized as overenthusiasm: "Nothing is eaten as hot as it is cooked," one traditionalist teacher observed, seeking to downplay the reports of anti-Semitic brutality.

After considering resignation, even critical professionals stayed on due to a sense of responsibility: "Then I once again tried to give my best—for the sake of the children."[121]

FROM NATIONALIST TO NAZI PROFESSIONALISM

For university graduates, the transition from Weimar into the Third Reich was cushioned by the hope for "reprofessionalization." In contrast to the remembered stability of the empire, the prolonged spiritual and material crisis of the republic seemed to have led inexorably toward "deprofessionalization" through an erosion of traditional values and proletarianization. For all their anti-intellectualism, Nazi appeals suggested halting this deterioration by restoring authority for established practitioners and by creating career chances for entering professionals.[122] In contrast to Weimar politicization, the very title of the law on "the restoration of professional civil service" promised a return to bureaucratic professionalism, marked by order and stability. After years of indecisive legislative struggles, the new government also took drastic action against educational overcrowding. Preoccupied with survival, most practitioners cared little that the racial and political purge violated professional norms or that the quota system of admissions repealed hard-won academic opportunities. Silenced by corporate concessions such as the establishment of the Reichsrechtsanwaltskammer, the majority of practitioners acquiesced in the organizational coordination and personnel purge by the NS minority, confident that "even *Herr* Hitler will have to listen to the experts." During the crucial transition in the spring of 1933, enthusiasm for the national renewal encouraged a selective perception that ignored the fate of victims and the incipient warping of ethics. When NS transgressions proved not to be aberrations, the realization that reprofessionalization was an illusion came too late. According to a nationalist professional, "everything which I wished, strove for and recommended, is today so exaggerated, distorted and simplified, that I cannot want and approve it any longer."[123]

To all appearances, most professionals embraced Hitler's New Order with few scruples. In foreign policy, the national tradition simply continued. International lawyers explained that "Germany's resignation from the League of Nations is a legally and politically necessary consequence of the behavior of the other powers."[124] Because they had for years asserted that "the Saar remains German," professionals loudly celebrated the plebiscite victory in 1935.[125] In domestic issues the patriotic reflex persisted as well. At Hindenburg's death, regret at the loss of the popular field marshal turned into appeals for "an enthusiastic yes for the Führer and Chancellor Adolf Hitler" who was about to assume the presidency. Only the bloody SA massacre in the summer of 1934 "quite upset attorneys," while "Nazi enthusiasm among teachers" noticeably cooled and engineers were beginning to resent overwork. However, when Dr. Werner Pünder sued the Reich for the pension of the murdered Catholic leader Dr. Erich Klausener, the Gestapo arrested the courageous lawyer and his associate, thereby suppressing any legal challenge to SS illegality.[126] Within their own sphere, many experts supported Nazi policies as well. University graduates approved of "the unification of German law,'' the creation of one ''Reich Ministry of Science, Education and Public Instruction,'' and the policy of ''work and peace,'' because such measures realized old academic dreams.[127] In spite of widespread persecution, lawyers did not publicly contradict Carl Schmitt's claim that the Third Reich ''completely safeguards the principles of legality and order as the rule of law is generally understood.'' Protestations of scholarship notwithstanding, philologues uncritically accepted Rust's decree on ''pupil selection,'' stressing physical fitness, character, and race over intellectual achievement. Despite the bitter experience of a lost war, engineers failed to challenge massive rearmament that diverted resources from civilian projects. When the Röhm murders revealed Hitler's ruthless dictatorship, practitioners, having lost their voice through *Selbstgleichschaltung,* had little choice but to keep serving his cause.[128]

The penetration of Nazism into the professions was, nonetheless, incomplete. Even the dramatic increase in NS membership during 1933 through the ''March victims'' or the ''June bugs'' fell short of being all-inclusive. This opportunistic influx brought older, Rhenish, southwestern, degreed, and semiprofessional academics (as well as married, former DLV, and primary schoolteachers and east central Prussian, urban, professorial, government, shop floor, and machine engineers) into the party fold (Tables A.14–A.18). But Walter Raeke admitted in January 1935 that the BNSDJ consisted of only 14,400 of the 18,400 attorneys. With about 2900 Jews remaining, this still left 1100 Aryans ''who from the beginning were hostile to the League and should not be recruited,'' constituting an internal opposition. Because Fritz Wächtler, with habitual exaggeration, claimed 300,000 NSLB members by 1936, but failed to break them down into categories, the exact extent of philological participation remains elusive. However, the delayed entry dates on league file cards indicate that many secondary schoolteachers held out until 1935 due to ''deep ideological differences.'' Among engineers the KDAI proudly announced 10,000 followers in September 1933, but this miniscule Nazi share of the more than 200,000 technicians increased only slowly because of its dissolution and the continuation of the *Fachverbände* alongside the NSBDT.[129] Although the outlook of professionals shifted considerably, their reorientation did not go as far as Nazi zealots wanted. Clearly, the small band of Socialists and the somewhat larger group of Democrats among experts was eliminated from public discourse. Willing to reap its benefits, pragmatists went along with the new regime, but only minimally embraced the Nazi creed. Initially, traditional nationalists believed that they were in charge, but, disabused in the ensuing power struggles, they became bitterly ambivalent. ''We are weakened in our opposition not only by the feeling of near complete impotence, but also by our wholehearted approval and support of some things, such as the reintroduction of the draft.'' Although Nazi opportunists and fanatics now controlled the professions, they were often frustrated when trying to exact more than outward conformity.[130]

What kind of society did the Third Reich ultimately become for professionals? The Nazi ritual of uniformed marches, and mass meetings required the professions to prove their enthusiastic support. But in spite of public proclamations of ''momentous successes and laborious toil,'' leaders like Heinrich Schult knew that the monolith was a myth and ''our work is just beginning.''[131] Though removed from daily practice, the Führer did occasionally intervene by setting priorities based on his prejudices (against lawyers and teachers and for engineers) or in settling disputes such as those between pharmacists and druggists or dentists and dental technicians.[132] However, within the overall guidelines of ideology, professional organizations lived in a Darwinian world of struggle for survival, with success or failure dependent on one's allies in the party leadership, the Reich chancellery, the respective ministry, the economic interest groups, and so on. The extinction of the Philologenverband and the survival of the VDI are cases in point.[133] Therefore, the transition from nationalist to Nazi professionalism was a curious blend of reaction and social revolution. As far as it became a reality, the restoration of professional authority reaffirmed traditional patterns. However, the ruthless racist, political, and gender purge as well as the reshaping of professional ideology and practice showed the seriousness of NS revolutionary intent.[134] On balance, German professionals found the Third Reich neither as terrible as the critics predicted nor as glorious as the propagandists claimed. Making concessions to the new regime when necessary, most practitioners, relieved by the economic upturn and gratified by the recovery of national pride, simply plodded on. Only some of the most perceptive experts realized: "This time is as great a trial for true spirit and character as the World War was for bravery and manliness. Woe unto him who does not pass this test!"[135]

6

"Germanizing" the Professions

Professional life under Hitler has left a series of contradictory images. The initial self-portrait of success is colored by impressive uniformed demonstrations of "the unity of the legal profession and the idea of law in the Nazi Reich." This propaganda version is enhanced by powerful mass testimonials "that the front of German educators stands united and remains unshakable" and by ritualistic self-congratulations on the achievements of German technology through the "loyalty and cooperation of engineers."[1] In contrast, the later picture of failure is inspired by ubiquitous political fear and racial persecution. This negative portrayal rests on the protests of countless victims against Nazi perversion of law through "orderly arrests so as to torture people to death" that combined apparent legalism with the basest brutality. It also derives from the stultifying indoctrination of schools that tried "to mold the spirit of youth according to [NS] ideology," thereby "befogging their brains" with half-truths. Finally, it draws on the thinly veiled exploitation of white- and blue-collar workers through the yellow union of the German Labor Front and the constant decline of real wages.[2] Focusing on the bloody dialectic between the arrogant Nazi masters and the suffering victims, these complementary pictures constitute the official postwar recollection of the Third Reich.

Though enshrined in scholarship, the Manichaean view is seriously incomplete, because it fails to reflect the personal memories of the majority of German professionals. Not always duped by official pomp, most university graduates remember the Third Reich neither as fanatic Nazis (some having conveniently forgotten) nor as persecuted resisters (others did not survive). When surfacing in occasional oral recounting or in nostalgic memoirs (on "how much fun we had in the Hitler Youth"), their recollections point to a more humdrum private existence that tried to ignore the dangerous political domain. Although they will rarely admit it, many older Germans think of prosperity and unity, of a new sense of national pride, and perhaps even of the glorious adventure of making war in distant places. Often this favorable view confuses personal happiness, such as first love, with public policy, mistakenly crediting Hitler with achievements for which the Nazis were not responsible.[3] Because it is rarely subjected to conscious scrutiny, this remembrance tends to be selective, stressing the return of "law and order" over "temporary" SA transgressions, emphasizing the restoration of pedagogical authority over chaotic HJ activism, and highlighting the recovery of work over labor regimentation. Suffering, if admitted at all, is restricted to the bombing raids, the postwar expulsion, and economic chaos. In spite of an overwhelming preponderance of critical public verdicts, positive private recollections live with surprising tenacity in popular memory.[4]

This discrepancy between scholarly interpretation and personal remembrance has created a dangerous neorevisionism that trivializes the experience of the Third Reich. Unlike earlier disputes on foreign policy,[5] the unfulfilled German longing for national pride and identity in the mid-1980s fueled a return to putative tradition, which was articulated by Michael Stürmer and enshrined in new museums in Bonn and Berlin, while in the German Democratic Republic the need for a pedigree restored the Prussian past to unexpected respectability.[6] To resolve the incongruity between private recollection and public image, the respected diplomatic historian Andreas Hillgruber called for empathy "with the concrete fate of the German population in the East and with the desperate and sacrificial exertions of the German army" against the Russian onslaught in 1944–1945.[7] In a similar vein, the idiosyncratic Fascism specialist Ernst Nolte ruminated on "the past that will not pass away" and called for introducing shades of gray into black-and-white evaluations of the Third Reich. Claiming that the mass murder of the Jews was not all that singular, he suggested provocatively that the genocide might have been an anticipatory defense against Asiatic destruction with *Klassenmord* preceding *Rassenmord*.[8] These academic challenges to the uniqueness of the holocaust created a public storm when the outraged philosopher Jürgen Habermas denounced them as "grossly apologetic tendencies."[9]

In the ensuing "quarrel," German historians passionately debated the historical, ethical, and political implications of the Third Reich. Largely centered on the German media, it ostensibly revolved around the critical consensus on the Nazi era and the moral singularity of the holocaust. The discussion was complicated by arguments over the war in the East as well as Central Europe's geopolitical position in the world.[10] Beyond the dominance of the negative orthodoxy, the heated exchanges implicitly involved such concrete stakes as hegemony over the historical profession and the control of public memory.[11] Within the Federal Republic of Germany, the controversy focused on the current political implications of the troubled past as legitimizing either NATO vigilance or peaceful coexistence. Abroad in Israel or the United States, the moral issues of judging the genocide of millions of Jews, Poles, Gypsies, and so on, predominated.[12] Stripped of its political overtones, this *Historikerstreit* has posed the fundamental question of the legitimacy of historicizing the Third Reich: Does the memory of the victims demand a metahistorical condemnation of the perpetrators, or does it instead call for the scrupulous reconstruction of the experience of *all* the people in the NS system, including the seemingly uninvolved bystanders? The dilemma is profound: Looking for the ordinary in extraordinary times risks belittling the suffering. Fastening upon the extreme runs the danger of misunderstanding the regular.[13] The abnormal normality of the Nazi years suggests the need for careful historicization, limited by a critical stance toward the ambiguous role of the professions.

NAZIFICATION OF PERSONNEL AND PRACTICE

In the spring of 1936, the Nazis, who were firmly in organizational control, faced the difficult task of transforming the professions into their own image. After the initial enthusiasm of the ''national rising'' had cooled, the remaking of professional theory and practice turned out to be a complicated and protracted challenge. First, many NS fanatics wanted to complete the Aryanization of personnel by purging their remaining Jewish colleagues. Second, fascist theoreticians sought to develop a coherent vision of ''German'' professionalism out of the amalgam of conservative traditions and völkisch departures. Third, the new masters needed to find ways to disseminate their model to beginners through education as well as to established practitioners through retraining. Fourth, the party elites tried to enforce the changed standards through positive rewards or negative sanctions (honor courts). Impressed by global theories of Fascism or Totalitarianism, historians initially assumed that content corresponded to NS appearance. However, recent research has brought to light a discrepancy between Nazi organizational dominance and the professionals' search for a ''technical,'' apolitical realm, governed by other criteria such as efficient performance.[14] These conflicting interpretations raise the question: How successful were the Nazi leaders in ''germanizing'' legal, teaching, and engineering practice?

As a first step, the nazification of the professions required the completion of the racial purge. National Socialist zealots agitated for the economic boycott of the remaining Jewish veterans or old practitioners and the rescinding of their pensions. Considering Jews ''utterly unfit'' for rendering German justice, Minister of Justice Franz Gürtner conceded that the selection of poor-law attorneys ''will have to depart from the consideration that an Aryan party expects the appointment of an Aryan lawyer.''[15] The infamous Nuremberg laws of September 15, 1935 discriminated further against Jewish professionals by limiting citizenship to racial Germans. The creation of two inferior classes of mixed descent, pejoratively known as *Mischlinge,* and Jews (i.e., of at least one-half Jewish birth and religion) effectively excluded ''all Jewish officials with their pension,'' thereby purging the last teachers who had escaped so far. The stripping of citizenship rights also meant ''that notaries who are Jews in this sense must resign''[16] and that additional non-Aryan engineers were fired. On February 6, 1936, the Ministry of Justice permitted German attorneys to refuse representing Jewish clients as incompatible with ''their duties as party members'' or BNSDJ leaders. When some ''three-quarter German'' attorneys of mixed descent protested against their déclassé professional status, the minister intimated that they might still serve as court-appointed defenders, but refused to reinstate them in general. To eliminate the remaining 2552 solicitors, a 1936 ''scholarly'' conference resolved that ''in the future it shall be impossible for Jews to speak in the name of German law.'' In July 1937 the remaining teachers of mixed descent were also fired, since they were considered "unsuitable for the profession of educating German youths." Formally only removing the last exceptions for officials, the Nuremberg laws hastened the economic ruination and social ostracism of the non-Aryan professionals, who were defined as racially inferior.[17]

Not content with gradual displacement, NSRB lawyers continued to demand the complete elimination of the final 1753 legally admitted Jewish competitors. In 1938, RRAK president Reinhard Neubert enviously complained about "the relatively high number of Jewish lawyers with big incomes," even if "Aryan" attorneys in Berlin earned almost twice as much in 1936 (14,795 versus 7963 marks). Although the ministry resisted NSRB pressure, an April 1938 exploratory discussion between justice officials and lawyer leaders reached "full agreement that Jews in the sense of the Nuremberg laws . . . are to be excluded from the legal profession as soon as possible." Licensing a limited number of "Jewish client representatives" could both support disbarred colleagues from its proceeds and provide the Jewish population with legal protection.[18] Because only 480 of the 2100 Viennese lawyers were "Aryan," the Austrian *Anschluß* provided further impetus for disbarment and a May 4 meeting settled on the term "legal consultant" for Jewish defenders. On June 28, 1938, the Reich Ministry of Justice sent a draft exclusion law to the Führer's deputy Heß for approval, arguing that "as in the medical occupations, the final clarification of the Jewish problem in the legal profession appears ready for a solution. . . ." Ten days later, Martin Bormann officially agreed. However, the remaining Jewish lawyers protested this renewed injustice through Dr. Julius Fließ. Invoking the guarantee of equality of October 1, 1933, these veterans and old attorneys "opposed any regulation which . . . would limit the practice of a part of the lawyers or create distinctions in the legal position of attorneys."[19]

Unimpressed, Justice officials continued drafting exclusionary rules that flatly asserted: "The legal profession is closed to Jews." However, on the basis of the common "war experience," the elderly Field Marshal August von Mackensen pleaded with the minister to stop "destroying the existence of veterans, even if they are Jewish." When the medical leadership disbarred Jewish physicians in July, NSRB spokesman Erwin Noack emphatically demanded that "we also 'cleanse' ourselves of Jews." On August 28, Franz Gürtner forwarded the final copy to Hitler for his official signature.[20] Incredulous, Jewish attorneys could only ask "that the appointment of Jewish consultants be speeded up as much as possible." On September 9, Gürtner informed the cabinet of the pending suspension of the remaining Jewish attorneys, except for 172 legal consultants whose special designation would mark them as Jews. Although Hitler signed the order on September 27, Bormann asked for a postponement of the announcement "during the duration of the present high international tension." On October 15, the *Deutsche Nachrichtenbüro* finally released the headline: "No more Jewish attorneys!" With one stroke of the pen another 10 percent of lawyers lost their livelihood. Exceptionally zealous, the Munich Gestapo arrested "about half of the Jewish attorneys," confiscated their papers and sent many to the notorious Dachau concentration camp. When on December 19, 1938 Rudolf Heß forbade any party or affiliate member to represent non-Aryan clients, the persecuted Jewish minority was left virtually without defense. The NSRB militants, however, crowed: "Long hatched by the lawyer section, the plan of the final elimination of Jewish attorneys has become a reality.''[21]

Bereft of their jobs, the political and racial victims of ''germanization'' faced a terrible choice: Either they could struggle on, trusting that the storm would blow over, or they could emigrate into an unknown and often unfriendly outside world. Especially veterans like Felix Hecht who had shed their blood for the fatherland or intellectuals like Siegfried Neumann who felt culturally German were reluctant to leave, thinking of the Nazis as a passing aberration. Some older practitioners with sufficient means, like Eugen Schiffer, could simply retire and prepare their memoirs. However, professionals in the prime of life could only practice under incredible difficulties. Primarily chosen from among wounded war veterans, legal consultants had to return up to 90 percent of their earnings beyond 300 marks per month to subsidize disbarred colleagues, carry special identification, and not hire Aryan secretaries younger than 45.[22] To make ends meet, Jewish professionals in some larger cities organized aid committees for their suffering colleagues. Their less fortunate peers were displaced into inferior occupations, such as running an emigration service, like Robert Kempner. Carrying on in a reduced but related job could prove dangerous, because the lawyer chambers prosecuted unauthorized legal advisors such as Ludwig Bendix. In most cases, waiting for a better day meant economic deprivation and social isolation, because Aryan associates and clients all too quickly turned away. Bureaucratic chicanery and intermittent police brutality made life difficult, while few long-standing colleagues showed any solidarity. The lawyer–playwright Siegfried Neumann quipped bitterly: ''The racial question *[Rassenfrage]* has turned out to be a financial question *[Kassenfrage]*.'' Jewish professionals were systematically restricted to representing Jewish clients, teaching in Jewish high schools (such as in Berlin), or working for Jewish businesses, threatened by compulsory Aryanization. The decreasing size of the Jewish community and the continual escalation of Nazi persecution made staying on at best a temporary solution.[23]

With fewer tangibles and less intangibles to lose, younger professionals preferred to emigrate. Not only were they vigorous enough to build up a new existence elsewhere, but they were also less attached to Germany and more open to Zionist ideas. When they could no longer bear the organized contempt, especially the women urged: ''We must get out, whether we want to or not. If not for our own sake, then for the children.'' Often flight was precipitated by a threatening arrest, SA plunder, or Gestapo beatings, or it could also be required as condition of release from a concentration camp. A first wave of academics fled directly after the seizure of power, because, like Alfred Apfel or Franz Neumann, they were marked as political opponents. A second group of university jurists such as Rudolf Isay or Rudolf Callmann left Germany after the passage of the Nuremberg laws, resentful of the growing racial harassment and aware that their future looked bleak. A third cohort, containing such famous lawyers as Max Hachenburg and Ernst Fraenkel, escaped after the *Kristallnacht* pogrom in November 1938 dispelled the last illusions about so-called legality. Teachers like Fritz Ollendorf also emigrated in large numbers with the gradual closure of separate Jewish schools. ''It is as if a nightmare were lifted, as if I could breathe freely once again,'' an unnamed pedagogue observed when crossing the German border. ''And yet I am afraid of the future in a strange country.'' For experts emigration was especially difficult, because their skills and credentials were largely not transferable. Only a few attorneys such as Heinrich Kronstein repeated their training in another system and succeeded in passing the bar examination. Dependent on language and culture, secondary schoolteachers had much difficulty securing white-collar employment. While engineers might transfer their expertise, foreigners were not always in demand. Aside from a few stellar exceptions, most professionals had to leave their possessions or friends behind and start over again in a country where their cultural entitlements were not recognized.[24]

Far more tragic than deprivation or expulsion were incarceration and death. After the shock of the Nazi seizure of power, some leading professionals like the star defender Max Alsberg or the leading radio engineer Walter Schäfer committed suicide. Many practitioners who had aroused the enmity of NS potentates were ''beaten to death,'' like lawyer Dr. Max Plaut. Others who could not believe the indignities, such as the attorney Bruno Marwitz, ''died from a broken heart.'' Those former professional leaders who passed away of natural causes, like Adolf Heilberg, remained publicly unlamented and unmourned so as to obliterate their contributions. Hundreds of opposition or Jewish professionals were intermittently locked up in camps where many perished, like the former editor of the *Juristische Wochenschrift* Julius Magnus. More than their colleagues who were disbarred in 1933, the nationalist veterans and long-standing professionals who continued to practice until November 1938 were caught up in the final holocaust from 1940 until the end of the war. Committed to fighting for their clients, especially legal consultants and community leaders like Otto Hirsch—the former director of the ''representation of Jews in Germany''—died in the concentration camps.[25] While a few fortunate individuals like the teacher Jizchak Schwersenz survived in the underground, many more perished like the pedagogue Julia Cohn, even on the eve of liberation. When Aryan practitioners observed the disappearance of their Jewish colleagues, most excused persecution as an ''unfortunate incident'' or ''regrettable exception,'' and failed to understand it as typical of general Nazi attitudes. Instead of protesting, the pedagogue Theresa Kurka admitted: ''We did not ask about it.'' Even if it were possible to compile exact figures for all the ruination, expulsion, incarceration, and killing, the human suffering perpetrated in the name of racial purification remains immeasurable and indescribable. As a result, the nazified professions were not only smaller, but also intellectually impoverished.[26]

''Germanizing'' professional ideals proved difficult, because it presupposed a coherent vision, which was rarely found in NS ideology. Intent on ''reorienting German law,'' Hans Frank created an Academy for German Law as a think tank in which judicial theorists could produce a Nazi recodification. However, the priority of the party (''law is the written will of the *Führer*''), pragmatic concerns of the government, and administrative inertia resisted a broad redefinition.[27] Nonetheless, legal rhetoric changed profoundly in the Third Reich. Instead of imported Roman or French law, NS theorists clamored for a ''German community law,'' based on the eternal values of ''blood, soil, honor, defense and work!'' Breaking with the liberal tradition of legal individualism, Frank polemically announced: ''Right is whatever is good for the people.'' In contrast to centuries of abstraction, law should serve ''vital [national] needs,'' because ''living justice supersedes formal law.'' One such imperative was the ''racial protection'' of the population through the Nuremberg laws in order to safeguard biological inheritance. Another corollary was the reversal of the traditional *nulla poena sine lege* into ''no crime without a punishment.''[28] Such warping of legal principles rendered hollow gains in ''popularity, speed [and] arbitration'' or any claimed reduction in criminality figures. In the ominous words of SS leader Reinhard Heydrich, ''the struggle against the enemies of the state'' such as Jews, Communists, Freemasons, and ''politicizing church officials'' took precedence over traditional notions of legality. In fighting these ''opponents of the racial, ethnic and spiritual substance of our people,'' the secret police stretched the definition of ''protective arrest'' *(Schutzhaft)* while in political cases the party considered itself above legal challenge. Instead of being a right of its own, law turned into ''a typical instrument of order of the German ethnic community'' in the Third Reich.[29]

The redefinition of justice had profound implications for the role of the lawyer. ''Revolutionizing everyday practice'' required the elaboration of a new mission based on general NS principles. ''No attorney will become a master of his profession without respecting Nazi ideology as correct and valid,'' an advice pamphlet for law students proclaimed. In order to avoid litigation, the solicitor was supposed to become ''a councillor to his ethnic comrade,'' helping him ''intelligently, effectively and equitably.'' When conflicts could no longer be mediated, ''the lawyer aids the court *and* his client in seeking the law'' by becoming ''an organ of the administration of justice.''[30] While preserving an important functional purpose, this redefinition as a ''servant of justice'' created countless conflicts of conscience between an attorney's duty to the state and his responsibility to the accused individual. National Socialist lawyers tried to gloss over the dilemma by making ''the search for truth and justice'' their central mission: ''In short, his professional duty consists of representing, in the interests of his client, what the attorney considers true and just in the given case.'' Whereas some claimed that ''an effective defense is now needed more than ever before,'' others argued that ''a groundless appeal'' would ''run diametrically counter to the attorney's task of being a guardian of law.'' Even if ''an ethnic comrade'' who violated community norms required special assistance, the tendency to treat the accused as guilty until proven innocent threw the very purpose of advocacy into doubt. The NS conception of lawyer duties as ''legal mediator between judge and people'' was inherently self-contradictory.[31]

Teaching was similarly ''germanized'' in rhetoric and structure. While NSLB and Hitler Youth pressed for a total renewal, the Ministry of Education and most philologues tried to maintain the efficacy of instruction, albeit in a different key. According to Section Two leader Karl Frank, ''we no longer have to form men, stuffed with knowledge, but physically healthy, racially conscious, independent, responsible, decisive Germans of good character who are intimately rooted in the blood and soil of their home and actively participate in the living rhythm of their nationality.'' Nazified education did not favor the mind, but stressed a healthy body and sound character. German training should engage youth actively with new pedagogical methods such as ''teaching through work.''[32] To implement such aims, the high school was fundamentally restructured in 1937. ''Shortening the nine-year secondary school to eight years for important population policy reasons'' created more manpower for rearmament and allowed earlier childbearing. A new "German Upper School" became the "main type," but this was in effect an old *Oberrealschule* based on English and Latin with separate natural science and language tracks. At the same time, the Gymnasium (with Greek and English) survived as an exception, while a few *Aufbauschulen* were maintained for talented primary-school pupils. Because "the common education of the sexes contradicts NS educational spirit," boys and girls were once again separated into different institutions. Given the priority of politics over pedagogy, the *Deutsche Oberschule* "has the task of forming the Nazi man with its proper means but in cooperation with the other pedagogical forces of the nation" such as the HJ or the family. This "confusion between drill and education" prompted one German teacher to warn of the danger of cultural decline: "Today true German learning is in jeopardy by those who continually trumpet it."[33]

Because "a school is worth only as much as its teachers," NS zealots tried hard to refashion the conception of the educator. Admitting that "I am a Nazi first and only then a philologue," Karl Frank demanded "that all pedagogues who want to work constructively in the high schools of Adolf Hitler's Reich must share this view." Because ideological indoctrination was central, "in the NS state no one can work as teacher or educator who is not capable of thinking and feeling as a Nazi." The "internally renewed, so to speak reborn teachers" should not be traditional subject specialists but rather genuinely popular "educator leaders," transmitting the eternal values of the national community. Teaching by personal example, the NS pedagogue "ought to be a model for his pupils and students in every respect, not just intellectually but also, as much as possible, personally and physically." Whereas philologues continued to pay lip service to the traditional triad of "scholarly teacher . . . educator . . . official," the NS emphasis on the educator as "model for the individual and leader of the whole" devalued academic learning. Although younger teachers might enjoy camaraderie with their charges and more flexible teaching methods, the concept of "formation education" largely robbed philologues of their distinctive intellectual mission. Instead, "the uniform teacher type" was supposed to lead youth in general beyond the doors of his school.[34]

Engineering was nazified with even greater enthusiasm. Although NSBDT ideologues and technical pragmatists differed in emphasis, their practical cooperation in prestige projects such as the "people's car" (VW) generated mutual respect. According to Fritz Todt, the "total revolution" required that technology "should also be oriented towards" National Socialism. Instead of being international, engineering had a racial base: "The motor, which has made possible all of modern technology, is a German creation." These Nordic roots also lifted engineering beyond material concerns so that critics could finally "recognize its higher cultural mission." Moreover, the Third Reich freed technology from the bondage of bureaucracy and industry: "In the center of NS economic striving stands neither money nor capital, but solely production."[35] Never shy about purported or real accomplishments, Nazi engineers celebrated the success of "the German economy under NS leadership," rhapsodizing the new superhighways as "streets of a technical perfection and beauty which the world has never seen." In contrast to earlier regimes, engineers saw "technology as a central buttress of the Third Reich" and believed that it ''has never before been as much approved as by the Führer.'' Together with the economic recovery, greater Nazi respect contributed to a redefinition of technology in a racial, irrational, and militaristic sense.[36]

The rhetorical recasting of the engineer's role was therefore easy. ''National Socialism has given new life to the engineering profession,'' one zealot claimed without fear of contradiction. The traditional self-image of engineers could be nazified with only minimal change, if one heroized technicians like Prof. Otto Streck as

> fighters for form with material and power; makers, shapers, builders, organizers; men with practical will to creative action; mortal enemies of skepticism; people of joyful resolve; strivers for quality plus marketability . . . ; users of raw materials and tools; leaders and molders of workers in the shop; all those who ask: ''What shall be'' and ''How shall it look!''

Larger than life and committed to action, engineers should mediate between capital and labor by being ''counsellors and leaders of men.'' Moreover, in ''the soldier engineer'' the Hitler state created ''a new type of technician,'' fusing fighting character with expertise in a novel synthesis. Instead of a narrow ''one-sided specialist,'' the Nazi engineer was to be a politically committed, broadly aware problem solver, finally claiming his sociopolitical leadership role. Declaring war on the apolitical expert, NS technical propagandists sought instead to transform the engineer into ''a general of technology in the service of the nation.''[37] In spite of such strident pronouncements, the student advice pamphlet sponsored by the University of Berlin made no mention at all of politics.[38]

Such ''germanized'' ideals were disseminated through training and retraining. Pinning their hopes on the coming generation, NS gatekeepers vigorously screened future professionals by preferring HJ alumni, requiring labor service, and insisting on SA membership. To select ''the best according to character, loyalty, ability and accomplishment,'' the Ministry of Justice restructured the legal curriculum in July 1934. ''During the first two semesters, students will be introduced to the völkisch foundations of scholarship,'' a NS lecturer explained. ''Courses on race and kin, ethnology, and pre-history shall . . . deepen and solidify their [earlier] communal experience.'' In subsequent semesters, emphasis was to shift from Roman to Germanic law, because knowledge of national legal history was essential for ''later participation in the shaping of German law.''[39] All Prussian trainees then had to attend the ''Gemeinschaftslager Hanns Kerrl'' in order ''to test their character in a camp community for eight weeks'' and ''to keep physically and mentally fit through sport'' before entering a streamlined three year practical apprenticeship. In a technique borrowed from the Youth Movement, ideas were to be reshaped more effectively in a camp environment, when young professionals were removed from home. Such crude paramilitary methods often failed to overcome ''lack of political interest'' and sometimes rather ''alienated part of the Referendare from National Socialism.'' Although Hans Frank protested several times with Rudolf Heß and the NS Student League criticized the camp, the ministry maintained the requirement but improved its academic tone. More successful was local indoctrination through practical working groups.[40]

Transforming the older practitioners was even more difficult, because they were not as impressionable. On the one hand, Nazi professionals used existing institutions, such as professional journals, to propagate their new role. Traditional occasions such as the national lawyer meetings were also appropriated: "The German *Juristentag* 1936 documented the complete victory of National Socialism in the area of law."[41] On the other hand, the Nazis also invented new methods such as the ubiquitous *Schulung,* which meant ideological "schooling" in meetings and camps. To train the indoctrinators, the BNSDJ gathered the Reich section leadership and the Gau lawyer leaders in special conferences beginning in 1934–1935.[42] In the summer of 1936, the NSRB also succeeded in obtaining from Heß the official charge for "the ideological Schulung of the lawyers in the German legal front." National and regional courses and camps were to stress "the NS racial idea," work through "communal education" preferably in *Lager,* admit "only suitable lawyers" who were motivated, "thoroughly treat the history of the movement and the life of the Führer," and engage in physical exercise. Although state officials could simply be ordered to "volunteer," it apparently proved difficult to generate much enthusiasm for this indoctrination among the majority of attorneys.[43]

The nazified teacher role was propagated with similar methods. National Socialist students called for "reducing, concentrating and deepening" the curriculum, while theorists like Ernst Krieck demanded methodological grounding and unification of all teacher training at the university. In the year 1936, the pedagogical academies were upgraded into colleges for teacher education *(Hochschulen für Lehrerbildung),* which were charged with "the political and physical training of future instructors" in a völkisch, pedagogical, and practical vein.[44] Because philologues resented losing their academic standing, in 1937 Minister of Education Rust decreed a compromise, which required future high school teachers to spend their first two semesters at a HfL for "orientation towards a unified political-ideological goal" and selection through practical experience. Actual academic instruction in a major subject and two minor fields continued to take place during a six-semester university course in the traditional faculty of philosophy. Against NSLB opposition, practical training remained at individual school seminars, which were consolidated into district centers that were to emphasize concrete, political tasks.[45] National Socialist fanatics also suggested that the state examinations be recast to stress political commitment over intellectual attainment: "It is more necessary to be conversant with important Nazi writings than with specialized pedagogical literature." From 1937 on, individual states like Thuringia began to sponsor trainee camps for "ideological indoctrination," providing five weekly hours of NS theory, eight hours on race, defense, chemistry, and ethnology, as well as eight hours of sport and some introduction to teaching.[46] In the Third Reich, teacher training therefore became a hybrid of indoctrination and scholarly instruction.

The reeducation of the educators already in the schools was complicated, because the Ministry of Education and the NSLB competed for control. On the one hand, Bernhard Rust authorized special "national-political" courses by established continuing-education centers such as the Zentralinstitut für Erziehung und Unterricht. On the other hand, active NSLB districts like Westphalia created their own *Schulungslager* and required members to attend. Problems arose over re-

Table 6.1. Indoctrination of German Teachers

	Year							
	1934	1935	1936	1937	1938	1939	1941	1942
Number	23,882	35,057	44,284	45,009	35,813	30,455	57,257	59,163
Cumulative percentage	6.6	16.2	28.4	40.8	50.6	59.2	74.9	91.8

leased teaching time and general jurisdiction, when the NSLB tried "to go far beyond the ideological indoctrination which is its task." Teacher league methods were often so primitive and physically revolting (threats that recalcitrants ought to be shot) that the minister insisted on "making sure that such incidents do not happen again." Unwilling to subsidize a system of NSLB indoctrination centers with his own scarce funds, Rust, in February 1936, gladly accepted a division of labor that left "NS-political indoctrination of all teachers" to the league, but retained continuing education in academic fields for the ministry.[47] Involving only about one-fifteenth of the teachers up to that time, mass indoctrination started in earnest in 1935. A year later, Fritz Wächtler could point to the existence of 57 camps and emphasize reaching out to non-NSLB members. By the year 1937, Schulung involved two-fifths of all German pedagogues and thereafter a systematic three-tier structure emerged: general A-indoctrination during the summer, B-Schulung for propagandists, and special C-training in the national center at Donndorf for the elite (Table 6.1). Locally, teacher retraining revolved around numerous lectures, combining "ideological indoctrination and scholarly improvement."[48]

Among engineers the dissemination of Nazi professional ideals proved difficult, because technical practice seemed remote from ideology. To break with "the system of deifying youth, of growing effete cosmopolitan green-house plants," Prof. Georg Garbotz propagated "the coordination of technical education" in a simplified, authoritarian curriculum. In 1934, the leader of German students, Dr.-Ing. Oskar Stäbel, called for "political and labor-service indoctrination" of academic youth, but concerned professionals countered "that above all performance must be decisive." Using complaints about quality of technical expertise, the Nazi Student League (NSDStB) in 1936 suggested a fundamental restructuring of higher technical education, by shortening prior schooling and instituting "an appropriate intermediate step" of *Fachschule* instruction followed by TH study. Because the prestigious DATSCH opposed such a drastic recasting and growing manpower needs militated against experiments, the only result was some broadening of access for technical school graduates. Though ever more practical, training remained largely unchanged and unideological.[49]

In spite of much talk about "ideological Schulung of engineers," the results of technopolitical indoctrination were unimpressive. In late April 1935, the technicians' league conducted the first Reich camp for its leaders in order "to cement the political leadership of the NSBDT within the technical associations." Organized by the energetic Stäbel, the retraining of "the engineer as political man" initially concentrated on small NS cells and on young technicians through combining ideology with problem solving. After June 1937, the engineering elite was indoctrinated at the castle Plassenburg as, for instance, in January 1938 when 75 NSBDT leaders discussed "the unity of technical education." During four day courses in this romantic setting, engineers were supposed to coalesce into "a sworn community" through sport, flag raising, lectures on "ideology and technology," discussions on race and nature, hiking through the forests, driving on the new Autobahn, and a few friendly beers. The late consolidation of the NSBDT and the division of labor, which left specifically technical tasks to the old organizations like the VDI, meant that engineering indoctrination was more limited in scope and reached a smaller number of professionals than the Schulung of lawyers and teachers.[50]

Enforcement of the germanized roles involved both incentives and sanctions. As carrot, Nazi professional affiliates consistently sought to promote their members into leading positions and claimed the right to be heard with a written opinion in personnel matters. When the NSRB intimated that Reinhard Neubert did not "appear to enjoy the confidence of the party," the incumbent president of the RRAK could win reappointment only with ministry support.[51] As stick NS fanatics used the professional honor courts to police practitioners. When lawyer leader Walter Raeke insisted in 1934 "that personal desires and individual excuses are less important than professional interests," the new supreme EGH of the RRAK insisted on outward respect for party and state. For instance, it fined attorneys for "derisive comments about the Hitler salute," expelled Jewish lawyers for similar criticism, and reprimanded Aryan attorneys who still associated with them. Beginning in 1938, the honor court required positive engagement for the Nazi government: "Support for the German state leadership in its great world-political decisions is the professional duty of every German lawyer." Excessive zeal in defending a political enemy was construed as "utter lawlessness" and as transgression of professional freedom! When the racist rag *Der Stürmer* attacked an attorney for addressing a Jew with *Herr Doktor,* even RRAK president Neubert objected. However, by extending supervision to the private domain and applying bureaucratic standards as "a state court," the lawyers' EGH sanctioned the "germanized" reinterpretation of professional ethics to a shameful extent.[52]

Nazi teachers enforced "German" standards through personnel policy. A central instrument were party recommendations, judging the suitability of a candidate for every career step: "I believe . . . that teacher Herbert Abel supports NS ideas, but he will not draw the *final* consequences from this ideology," because he "comes from a strictly ultramontane family," one typical letter of reference *(Beurteilung)* read. At issue was always "political reliability." Once tagged as "a SPD stalwart" like Schulrat Dr. Ahrens or as "a Communist" like Assessor Heinrich Albert, one had virtually no chance for advancement. Representatives of "the staunchest Catholicism" such as Elfriede Kamp and teachers of mixed descent were also subject to discrimination.[53] In contrast, meritorious party service often brought rewards. When he got into financial difficulties, Otto Abel asked for a transfer to a better post: "In return I promise to become a zealous activist for the NSLB in your district." After the Austrian refugee Dr. H. Adam "lost his position because of his support of the NSDAP," German ministries tried to find new employment for him. In countless letters, Old Fighters asked for compensation for their personal and professional sacrifices for the Hitler cause. Because zealots like

Max Feight "cannot understand that the same officials are to decide about their career as before," some regional NSLB groups forwarded entire "lists of proposals for preferred promotion of teachers who served the national movement well." Although the ministries clung to professional standards, appointment to important positions such as principal (Fr. Sichermann) required a clean bill of political health, thereby exerting a none too subtle pressure for conformity.[54]

Exclusion from the NSLB and bureaucratic punishment reinforced conformity as well. Denunciations frequently initiated some kind of official procedure. In March 1936, Willy Sichting complained about "the manner in which religion is taught at the local Gymnasium," criticizing *Oberstudienrat* Goebel's effort "to construe a contradiction between church and state." Like Ernst Ohlhof, one could be denied admission into the NSLB for having been a Freemason. Or, like K. Skorczyk, one might be expelled from the teacher's league "since your remaining in the PhVb means that you have not taken a clear and unmistakable position on the NSLB."[55] Graver still was official action. When Oberlehrer Max Zöllinger showed himself recalcitrant by not "voluntarily" contributing to collections, failing to fly the swastika, and keeping his son out of the *Jungvolk,* it was "recommended that he be transferred as punishment." Obviously, daring to criticize the Third Reich publicly would bring on retribution. When Max Abresch ridiculed the Bund deutscher Mädel (BdM) by singing a popular ditty, calling the blue-skirted and white-bloused girls "complete air-heads," he was fined 250 marks. Sometimes party connections could save a culprit, such as teacher Oelmann, who, when accused of sexually molesting girls in the *Berufschule,* claimed that these charges were politically motivated. In other instances, incontrovertible testimony that drunken NS leaders had beaten up a critical teacher like Josef Sippel was ignored and the victim dismissed! If one were fortunate like Adolf Voigt, then private sarcasm against the Nazis might be overlooked or party overzealousness (e.g., a NS teacher's concentration camp threat against school director H. Otto) might lead only to a fine.[56] On the whole, the NSLB and the bureaucracy used their considerable power to insist on strict observance of Nazi conduct.

Among engineers the enforcement of "German" behavior faced greater obstacles, because white-collar employees were not easily policed. When an official appointment was involved, such as a TH professorship for Herrmann Alker, "suitability reports" were required. However, private employers tended to be more interested in "capable performance" than in ideology. Frequently, Old Fighters such as Hans Alzinger, who had belonged to the party since the early 1920s, claimed to have "lost [their] job due to [their] political attitude." Even when a *Kreisleiter* recognized "a certain responsibility to help a party comrade" whose radio shop had gone bankrupt, it was easier to assist if a public broadcast position was open than to place him in private industry.[57] Membership in the NSBDT could be denied to undesirables such as to "non-Aryans" (whose cards were pulled in July 1937) or even to three-quarter "Aryans" like Dr. Ing. Fritz Fried. Old political opponents like H. Pieper were also barred on the grounds that "there is quite an enormous difference between also-nationalists and National Socialists." Though not crucial for economic survival, lack of NSBDT membership did mean exclusion from official lists of consulting engineers and public or party patronage. Some city engineers, such as Paul Lippert, were dismissed "as enemies of the movement,'' but others, such as Julius Schwalm, managed to survive in industry by ''endorsing the aspirations of the new state'' after having been fired as member of the Republican teachers' league. Engineers therefore had greater latitude to escape compulsion, because traditional civil crimes had to be involved before the Gestapo would intervene.[58]

In the second half of the 1930s, the ''germanization'' of the professions was a greater external than internal success. The personnel purge was ruthlessly completed in both a political and racial sense. Building on nationalist rhetoric, professional roles were redefined in harsher völkisch terms. Nazi standards were systematically disseminated through revised curricula and elaborate retraining schemes for practitioners. Moreover, conformity was enforced through career rewards as well as frequent punishment. National Socialist professionals gloated about these undeniable ''accomplishments,'' but perceptive leaders sensed that the complete control, which the ''totality principle'' demanded, continued to elude them. Although Jewish competitors had been eliminated, a hard core of ''Aryan'' professionals proved recalcitrant while the apolitical majority remained apathetic. Even if it was easy to redefine professional principles in a general way, the renewal of the substance of German law, education, or technology turned out to be frustrating and time-consuming. While students and practitioners could be required to participate in indoctrination camps, this compulsion proved somewhat counterproductive, because they were known as ''a real waste of time.'' Although the party could enforce outward compliance among lawyers and teachers more than among engineers, it was difficult to win the inner allegiance of professionals. Ironically, increasing efforts to nazify society made professionalism once again attractive as a neutral space, free from political constraint.[59]

THE SPOILS OF COLLABORATION

Against the pressure of indoctrination, many practitioners struggled to maintain a measure of professionalism during the Third Reich. Though often warped and misappropriated, older traditions such as ''free advocacy'' continued to set certain limits. The need for competence ensured the survival of a modicum of technical expertise. Pressing problems such as a shortage of experts required effective solutions, even if these ran counter to ideology. Finally, the internal dynamics of scientific development initiated changes irrespective of NS guidance. In many nonpolitical areas, practitioners therefore retained some freedom of choice among conflicting party demands and professional imperatives. In trying to resolve this conflict, they could either become zealous NS experts and advance quickly or support uncompromising standards and risk being shunted aside. Instead of taking a clear stand for or against the regime, most practitioners energetically pursued their careers, which they rationalized as their duty while making minimal concessions to party demands. Not just a result of compulsion, their collaboration was a response to creative opportunities, offered by the apparent return of normal practice conditions. When the Third Reich visibly improved daily work and life, ideological injunctions such as the ''ten basic demands for the new German engineer,'' were accepted more easily. Although promising rich professional spoils, this implicit Faustian bargain was to exact an unexpected price in ethical corruption and political conformity.[60]

Professional training illustrates the tension between ideology and competence in the Third Reich. Whereas most of the traditional curriculum continued to be taught by a ''germanized'' faculty, research became less important than ''practical application of knowledge.'' State examinations began to emphasize practice over theory in order ''to train excellent scientific experts who are capable of solving the great tasks posed by our völkisch destiny.'' For students beginning in the fourth semester, departmental study groups *(Fachschaften)* combined indoctrination with professional instruction in ''lively and responsible discussions of the new questions'' of Nazi scholarship. Similarly, the propagandistic national vocational contest sought to inspire students through prizes, fee reduction, or publication to develop NS professional projects. ''In the *Reichsberufswettkampf* German students test themselves in the solution of scientific tasks as National Socialists.'' With the help of zealous faculty members, they wrestled with ''political and racial'' problems, such as the Jewish influence on culture or the development of raw-material substitutes for autarchy.[61] Finally, academic subculture was drastically restructured by the creation of a Reich student leadership and the abolition of ''archaic'' corporations in favor of NS *Kameradschaften.* Unable to dispense with expert instruction, Nazi leaders supplemented it ideologically with study groups, vocational contests, and compulsory associations to instill their spirit into unenthusiastic future practitioners. Yet with minimal outward compliance, some students could still receive competent training.[62]

As a result of NS restriction and regimentation, higher education enrollment virtually collapsed. Between winter 1935–1936 and summer 1938, the drop in student numbers continued, with university attendance sinking from 60,148 to 41,069, less than two-fifths of its peak of 1931! Law inscriptions declined precipitously from 8026 to 4275, while matriculations in the faculty of philosophy shrank from 17,760 to 12,240. Much reduced already, TH engineering studies slid from 11,794 to 9347 in 1937 (Table A.1). Some causes of this unprecedented contraction of professional training were structural (such as the one-quarter decrease in the 18- to 25-year-old birth cohort between 1932 and 1939). However, others, such as the additional 12 percent shrinkage of high school graduations or the two-fifths decline in willingness to study due to improved economic prospects, resulted from NS policies that delayed university entrance through the mandatory labor service (fourth-fifths of all freshmen) and the compulsory draft.[63] In contrast to Volksgemeinschaft rhetoric, social access to the professions narrowed during the Third Reich. Not only were students older (the inscription age rose from 19.72 to 21.16), but they also tended to be more urban (only 10.7 percent came from villages), more classically trained (almost two-fifths graduated from a Gymnasium), and more male (85.97 percent). In spite of propaganda claims about increased aid, the share of students from academic families once again grew from 25 percent in 1933 to 29.4 percent in 1939, while the percentage from the propertied bourgeoisie modestly rose to 12.5 percent. The century-long trend of increasing educational opportunities for children from the middle and lower classes was clearly reversed.[64]

Initially, the professions welcomed the easing of the labor market. Because the peak class of 1931 had finished its studies by the mid-1930s, the number of graduates began to decline steadily thereafter. Whereas in law 3459 candidates passed the first state examination in 1935, only 986 did so by 1939, and doctoral degrees dropped from 1484 to 903. In philology, the number of successful examinees similarly shrank from 3124 in 1932 to 1803. Technische Hochschule diplomas also decreased from 3006 to 2430, while HTL graduations were more than cut in half to about 4000 a year. The fall in student numbers was moderated somewhat by more lenient examinations and fewer dropouts, which produced higher relative graduation rates.[65] With a reduced influx, the remaining unemployed beginners were gradually absorbed. Whereas the rising number of law probationers (Table A.5b) led to sharper government selection, between 1936 and 1937 the number of jobless Assessoren fell from 1066 to 378, leaving only a hard core of women and males beyond 40 years of age for the NSRB placement service.[66] Among teachers, the decrease of incoming trainees was offset by the slowness of Prussian hiring (400 annually), so that the ranks of probationers actually grew more crowded from 5803 to 7679. However, four-fifths of the Assessoren were now employed, with 5448 in full-time jobs. The drop in appointment age from about 40 to 33.5 "visibly improved the general mood, so that everyone looks into the future with optimism."[67] In spite of several thousand jobless older technicians, by 1936 the technical labor market was, with over 500 open positions per month, "more favorable than in 1928," making for the "best prospects" in years (Table A.13).[68]

After a fleeting balance in supply and demand, the Third Reich faced a growing, self-induced deficit of academic manpower. Beginning in 1936, numerous advertisements demonstrated that the same "technicians who only a few years ago had no jobs . . . are now in great demand." By the late 1930s, the "engineering shortage" amounted to 18,500 graduates. For philologues, cautious statisticians predicted in 1938 that "a deficit . . . is certainly to be expected," because some specialties were beginning to run short. Even in the chronically oversupplied legal career, by 1939 officials talked of "a lack of judges [as] a danger for the administration of justice."[69] Hampered by their overcrowding fixation, Nazi leaders responded to the fiasco of manpower planning by shortening secondary schooling to eight years in order to "provide supply for the army and the university," virtually doubling the pool of potential students for 1938. To hasten graduation, the government also cut the TH course to six semesters against professorial advice and pressured other faculties to reduce study time.[70] Simultaneously, NS planners unleashed a vigorous campaign to attract prospective professionals. When the Luftwaffe could not get enough technicians in 1936, the Ministry of Science coined the slogan "Germany needs capable engineers!" A year later, the NSBDT proclaimed before 2500 HJ boys in Munich: "Youth, technology is calling you!"[71] Certain ideological biases had to be jettisoned as well. Women were once again encouraged to study and unreliable officials, who had previously been weeded out, were gradually rehired.[72] Active recruitment halted the university decline at 40,716 and increased engineering enrollment to 12,287 in 1939, shifted freshmen preferences from philology (5.9 percent) or law (5.0 percent) toward technology (21 percent), but not even financial inducements could restore the former luster to professional careers.[73]

When the supply dried up, the economic situation of the professions began to improve. By 1935, lawyers still felt distressed enough to agitate for a *numerus clausus,* some form of legal insurance, modeled after the health funds, or an "increase in the field of practice." Although agreeing with the NSRB and RRAK that the situation was "catastrophic," the Ministry of Justice preferred rather to regulate admissions, reduce the influx, and prod the elderly into retirement.[74] Because Gürtner believed "that the attorneys' plight can only be relieved by a reduction in the influx," the December 13, 1935 law introduced another level of practical training after the second state examination: Every prospective lawyer had to be apprenticed in an attorney's office for a trial year, followed by three years as a semi-independent *Anwaltsassessor,* remunerated by a modest but guaranteed fee. Whereas practitioners rejoiced about the temporary suspension of access, trainees grumbled about the extension of training, their exploitation for 200 marks, and the uncertainty of admission at the age of 35![75] Eventually the reduction in practitioners began to increase attorney income. Between 1935 and 1939, the number of lawyers continued to decline from 18,780 to 14,734 because of the purge of 1611 Jewish colleagues in 1938 and the decrease of admissions to the bar from more than 1000 to 141. Although legal business also dropped off, "the available work-load is shared by a smaller number of participants so as to create more traffic for each individual and thereby augment average income" (Table 2.1).[76] By the year 1936, attorney receipts recovered to 10,800 marks, second only to the 12,500 marks earned yearly by doctors. However, about one fifth still fell below the "existential minimum" of 3000 marks in 1937 and some "emergency districts" had substantial numbers earning less than 2000 marks. Although RRAK president Neubert continued to demand a further "decrease in practitioners," his own figures indicate that average attorney income rose to 12,000 marks by 1938![77] Using overcrowding fears to impose an unparalleled reduction of their numbers, Aryan attorneys gradually regained not just security but prosperity.

In contrast, high school teaching was "hardly materially attractive" in the second half of the 1930s. In spite of a "drastic instructor deficit," produced by rapid aging of the staff, economic issues could not be discussed because of NSLB insistence on a "unitary teacher type." Although the Brüning cuts were maintained, philologues received some relief when their scales were switched from the Prussian to the Reich standard in 1936, raising nominal beginning pay from 4400 to 4800 marks annually. On 188 marks a year per weekly hour of instruction, auxiliary teachers faced considerable hardship, because they were rarely assigned more than 15 periods. However, the lot of the Assessoren improved somewhat with a married probationary teacher in a medium-sized city taking home 370 marks monthly, which was enough for a modest life-style. When finally promoted to Studienrat, a married philologue in a medium-sized town started with 398 marks monthly, because housing and family allowances compensated for the cuts, and could eventually hope to rise to 671 marks. According to the Führerprinzip, high school directors were strongly rewarded for nazifying their institutions by raising their starting salary from 5600 marks all the way to 7000 marks (with the ceiling increased to 9700 marks). With 47 percent of all lawyers still earning less than 6000 marks in 1937, teacher incomes were adequate, especially when considering the financial security of a state official and the vested pension rights. However, many philologues grumbled because earnings fell short of the late imperial or Weimar levels. The Nazis "have violated especially the two Achilles heels of the teachers—the issues of pay and vacation."[78]

Although technical professionals profited from economic recovery, NS restrictions limited the extent of their gains. Massive rearmament and public works "greatly increased the importance of engineers," because of the much lamented shortage of technical personnel. However, the Nazi wage and salary freeze meant that incomes could be augmented only through overtime, which was widespread after 1936. Although labor mobilization expressly forbade changing jobs for improving pay, in 1937 the Reich Labor Office exempted technical occupations not only for the sake of business profits but also for "professional development." In the same year, the "new fee scale" for consulting engineers was revised upward in order to "do justice to the important and responsible work of this profession." Since raises were permitted only for "productivity gains," industrial companies began to resort to "special bonuses," which eventually surpassed the increasing deductions and "voluntary" contributions. At the prestigious electrical firm Siemens, the beginning pay for Diplom-Ingenieure of a meager 250 marks a month in 1936 was barely better than the 200 marks of legal probationers and less than the starting salary of teachers. In 1938 the Berlin VDI claimed that "average incomes of the free engineers are not favorable compared to other professions." When Georg Franzius asserted that technicians in business received, "one might say, almost princely" pay, VDDI leader Karl-Friedrich Steinmetz ridiculed this claim. In the absence of comprehensive statistics, one can only surmise that income of technicians passed predepression levels in 1936–1937 and increased further without meeting the expectations of its recipients.[79]

In spite of greater material rewards, the status of professionals scarcely improved during the second half of the 1930s. When 12 percent of high school graduates selected the military and 34 percent business careers in a 1936 NSDStB survey, Reich Labor Office President Friedrich Syrup urged choosing one of the professions as "a state-political necessity."[80] A "young lawyer" leader in Baden also complained about ill-informed press attacks: "Especially the legal careers have lost prestige and continue to do so." Within the BNSDJ leadership, Walter Raeke admitted "the difficult position of the attorneys vis-à-vis the 'dynamic forces' " of the Third Reich. "Moreover, lawyers are treated suspiciously and rudely by many party offices." Security service (SD) reports agreed that "the position of the attorneys has not improved." Because the anti-Semitic *Stürmer* identified all advocates with Jews, Hans Frank promised at the 1939 congress that with "the impurities removed" by the final purge, "the prestige of attorneys will continue to rise."[81] As a symbolic antidote to this loss of social esteem, the NS government reinstated honorary titles on July 1, 1937. Deserving lawyers could become *Justizrat,* engineers or architects *Baurat,* and physicians *Sanitätsrat.*[82] Though pleasing to chosen practitioners, such concessions could hardly dispel the ideological disregard and practical distaste for the professions in the Third Reich.

Teachers felt more unappreciated than ever. Frustrated by "the continual defaming of the profession and its work," many fled into other careers, such as the 83 Swabian primary school pedagogues who turned to the army (21), public or party service (11), business (5), or further training (45). In the year 1939, the

NSLB journal reprinted twenty-one advertisements of educators who were looking for commercial jobs: "Studienassessor, 28 years, chemistry (state examination with distinction), physics, mathematics, single, experienced organizer, typist and stenographer, seeks position in industry. . . ." An average of about 300 Prussian probationers annually left their career between 1933 and 1939, transferring especially into the burgeoning military school system.[83] Pedagogues were embittered because "the teaching profession can still be subjected to public ridicule." Much of the criticism came from the Hitler Youth, which tried to "determine the rules for school-education by itself" without any recourse to the NSLB. Stung by repeated "insults to all teachers," some educators started making "defensive speeches for their profession [emphasizing] that many were reserve officers, Old Fighters or had been killed in the war." Although endorsing "healthy school jokes," the NSLB press office dared criticize the *Völkische Beobachter:* "We emphatically reject those articles in the daily press which can only be called professional slander and exert a baneful influence." Because of repeated party criticism of schools and pedagogues, secret SD reports summarized in 1938: "The teachers' mood is influenced by the feeling that the state bureaucracy does not support the educators sufficiently in their efforts to be appreciated."[84]

Engineers continued "to struggle tenaciously for recognition." In public they complained about "disrespect" and in private they resented lack of "esteem, social rank and possibilities for personal development." Disliking the dependence of a lifelong "employee relationship in industry," they objected to the "subaltern position of army engineers" and the lack of technical influence in local and state administration.[85] In response to the agitation for "legal protection of the engineer title," Fritz Todt tried to define the term for NSBDT membership in 1936—albeit rather along inclusive VDI than exclusive VDDI lines. Technische Hochschule and higher engineering school graduates were accepted unquestionably, as were dropouts or technical middle-school leavers, if they could show four or five years of "engineer-like activity." Exceptions for "unusual achievements in creative engineering" were to be allowed, based on at least eight years of practical experience. In 1939 "consulting engineers" were protected through the establishment of an official list.[86] The NSBDT also waged a press campaign to create "more respect for the men of technology," arguing: "It is impermissible that artistic knowledge is socially accepted, but technical competence is placed on a lower level." To assuage this "inferiority complex," the Nazi leadership reassured engineers through praise for the "great achievements of German technology." On September 12, 1938 Fritz Todt, Ferdinand Porsche (VW), and Wilhelm Messerschmitt and Ernst Heinckel (airplanes) received the second "German national prize for art and science" at the Nuremberg party rally. "Through these four national prize winners, the Führer honors all of German technology."[87]

In the last prewar years, practice presented a bewildering mixture of frustrations and opportunities. To compensate for the litigation decline, Franz Gürtner appealed with indifferent success to the Ministries of Interior or Labor and the German Labor Front to cease "unjust attacks against a whole profession" and to admit attorneys to their proceedings.[88] In the February 1936 lawyer code, syndics managed to reassert most of their previous rights, while legal consultants gained readmission on the basis of "selection and need." In 1937, notaries separated from lawyers "in principle" with their own section and chamber, creating hardships for smalltown lawyers whose major source of income was notarizing wills and property transactions.[89] When the NSRB recognized "business trustees" on the basis of a separate examination, lawyers countered with a specialized "Fachanwalt for tax law" and fought the auditing monopoly by declaring tax advising incompatible with accounting.[90] Whereas civil practice continued largely unchanged, Nazi antilawyer bias made defending criminal clients more difficult. In spite of the protests of the Ministries of Justice or Interior, the RRAK, and the BNSDJ, the Gestapo practically excluded lawyers from "protective custody" cases. In courtrooms with competent judges, attorneys could still exploit the vagueness of the new legal principles in order to help their mandates by psychological astuteness. Even Jewish consultants occasionally managed "small triumphs of justice." However, spectacular successes brought down party censure and zealous district attorneys often intimidated nationalist judges. Judicial unpredictability made pleading a tight-rope act that could at any moment end in a disastrous fall. Therefore, some advocates became uninvolved "extras" in the legal drama, but others with more "civil courage" dared to play a contrary role.[91]

Teaching also continued to be difficult. Whereas foreign visitors paid tribute to "a number of advantages" of the German school, embittered émigrés denounced the "decline of higher schooling in the Third Reich." Classes were large, teaching loads remained heavy, and the reduction of secondary school training to eight years left less time to present subject material. Therefore, the ministerial directive on "education and instruction" urged concentration on essentials by teaching "through reasoning" and learning through doing. Making for livelier classrooms, this reorientation "towards the needs and demands of the present" produced a mixed curriculum of traditional content and NS ideology.[92] For history, the pan-German professor Dietrich Schäfer sketched new priorities of "racial science" and völkisch character, emphasizing prehistory, geopolitics, and the will of great men: "Race, space and time, blood, soil and tradition, people and state are becoming the bases of a German völkisch history which leads from the past of the home, family and tribe to national and world history and makes man both rooted and cosmopolitan." In frequent NSLB conferences, specialists tried to transform nationalist instruction into nazified didactics on touchy subjects such as "the treatment of the Jewish question in historical instruction of the middle and upper grades." To "educate young Germans in NS attitude and thinking," the revised *Lehrplan* selected topics like the fruitless Italian campaigns of Emperor Barbarossa and introduced lessons on the "blessings of the Nazi period" in order to instill "an organic conception of history."[93] Although limitations of teaching time made the reworking of the curriculum difficult, the NS grip on instruction gradually tightened. Many "teachers were deeply depressed, since they were robbed of all pedagogical freedom and autonomy." Having "to indoctrinate and stultify youths against their will," philologues "work[ed] without any professional pride."[94]

If one can believe their vibrant journals, then engineers were more enthusiastic about those daily tasks that "bore the stamp of the new era." However, the vague imperative of Gemeinschaftsarbeit that sought to combine "joyous work with performance" was not easy to implement. The economic buildup of the Four-Year Plan and the acceleration of rearmament necessitated a production increase that could only be achieved by raising productivity, once reserve labor and resources had been committed. Though eliminating unnecessary losses, motivating workers, and optimizing procedures were technical tasks, they also put more pressure on engineering work. While improving morale, the campaign for job safety and beautification created costs that could only be justified if productivity grew.[95] Nazi technicians sought to evade the contradiction by stressing prestige projects that promised real or vicarious benefits for everyone. The design of a ''people's car'' (VW), claiming to make transportation generally available for less than 1000 marks, demonstrates how popular technology was used to stabilize Nazi rule. Airplane construction had more direct military overtones, but the competition for world-speed records added a sporting element. The erection of monumental public buildings was supposed to manifest the triumph of NS ideology in stone. Less glamorous was the development of raw-material substitutes that were intended to extend the resource base. . . .[96] There were countless challenges, competitions, and battles that promised rich rewards, as long as engineers were willing to overlook the regimentation and militarization of their work.

The self-image of the professions wavered between new NS demands and older traditions. The 1936 code redefined the lawyer as ''the qualified, independent representative and advisor in all legal matters,'' elevating him to quasi-bureaucratic status: ''His profession is no trade, but a service to the law.'' Nonetheless, Hans Frank kept invoking the legacy of the ''free attorney'' as ''an essential part of an independent administration of justice'' and all attempts to eliminate the attorney's position ''as paid representative of the public'' failed due to lack of sufficient funds. Similarly, a NSLB spokesman claimed that ''as civil officers of our people, teachers consider it their sacred duty to form the growing generation into capable followers of Adolf Hitler and his ideology.'' However, clinging to the heritage of scholarship, ministerial guidelines defined ''the peculiarity of the higher school [as] striving for its educational goals by means of cognition.'' Although demanding lively presentation and practical relevance, they admitted that philologues still needed to be ''intellectual types'' capable of ''thorough knowledge and ability.'' Finally, Fritz Todt argued that being ''an expert is not enough for technical tasks, one must also be a convinced Nazi.'' However, in celebrating its eightieth anniversary, the VDI reaffirmed the primacy of ''technical-scientific work,'' proudly surveying its numerous subgroups that wrestled with concrete problems. Even a politicized engineer had to be able to design a working machine: ''Tell Goebbels that in our factory we do what we want!''[97] Because the Nazis changed ideological vocabulary more than practical tasks, considerable traces of traditional self-perception survived.

In the organizational competition of the late 1930s, NS affiliates served as instruments of control rather than as representatives of practitioner aspirations. During the 1936 congress, the League of NS German Jurists (BNSDJ) changed its name to NS League of Guardians of Law (NSRB) in order to get rid of the negative legalistic connotation: ''As jurists we began, as Nazis we have triumphed and as Rechtswahrer we shall march into the history of the Third Reich.'' At the same time, the NSRB promised a ''professional guarantee'' of ''a certain ideological as well as substantive qualification of its members.''[98] The attorney section also tried to deliver material improvements by working ''on an old-age pension which includes widow and invalid support as well as secures an existential minimum for active lawyers,'' to be set at 3600 marks annually. Because 90 percent of lawyers older than 65 were still active, something needed to be done, but insufficient funds and the outbreak of the war shelved the proposal.[99] Although the benefits of joining remained negligible, the NSRB could boast of more than 104,000 national members, comprising four-fifths of all ''guardians of law'' in Berlin. While less zealous than the 45 percent NSDAP medical doctors, about 25 percent of the listed advocates joined the party by 1936. Hailing more from Protestant provinces, Nazi lawyers were less titled, more often notaries, and younger, and were clustered in the middle ranges of simultaneously admitted and superior court attorneys. In contrast, the elite and the bottom ranks, especially in Catholic regions, chose to remain uninvolved (Table A.16). The bulk of practitioners who only belonged to the league was less enthusiastic, because the NSRB made participation in the free legal advising system mandatory, thereby reducing their income. The league's expansion also meant that attorneys who had made up over half of the founders now only accounted for one-fifth of all inscriptions, decreasing their organizational weight. ''The interest of the members in the work of the League was small,'' the SD reported in 1938, because ''its activity is practically unimportant.'' Even Hans Frank complained ''that the NSRB is being completely ignored'' and one-tenth of the lawyers refused to join the league at all.[100]

Among teachers, the NSLB sought to combine ''ideological struggle and substantive scholarly work.'' After Schemm died in a plane crash, Thuringian Education Minister Fritz Wächtler took over the reins in December 1935 and pushed for more vigorous regional and national organization.[101] To attract philologues, Section Two intensified its topical work, blending ''ideological indoctrination and subject matter training.'' In numerous lectures such as ''Humanism and National Socialism'' or ''Adolf Hitler as Educator,'' NS teachers sought to win their colleagues over to the new perspective. The actual curriculum was nazified in topical working groups that tried go ''beyond [conveying] knowledge so as to awaken NS consciousness in the pupils.'' By engaging scholarly interests, the *Arbeitsgemeinschaften* were modestly successful in ''accomplishing the indispensable subject work in terms of methods and materials.'' Aside from regular monthly meetings, there were also topical conferences (e.g., in mathematics and sport) and camps.[102] Nonetheless, ''the mood among Section Two members remains unsatisfactory,'' NSLB leader Gliemann reported in 1937. ''Everywhere there are complaints about the poor performance of the pupils which partly results from the unreasonable and excessive time demands of the HJ.'' Too much mandatory volunteering and ''the overloading of the colleagues through diverse meetings'' also hampered NSLB activities. ''Embittered about some ministerial measures'' such as the reduction of secondary schooling to eight years, slow promotions, and low municipal pay, many young philologues resented that their ''energies are not fully and correctly used for the construction of the Third Reich.'' Therefore, the Section Two leadership campaigned for ''the improvement of the economic and social plight of the Studienassessoren'' through acceptance into officer training, the elimination of the dual list system, and increased hiring.[103]

Formally, the NSLB penetrated the teaching profession quite deeply, enrolling 299,445 members by November 1938 (Table 6.2). Reaching 37.1 percent, the

Table 6.2. NSLB Penetration of German Teachers in 1938

Section	Number of Members	Percentage	Number of Teachers	Percentage	NSLB Share (Percentage)
Professors	1,840	0.61	6,678	1.85	27.6
Philologues	41,210	13.76	47,749	13.24	86.3
Middle school	9,790	3.27			
Primary school	208,650	69.68	198,553	55.04	110.0
Special school	5,860	1.90	8,497	2.26	69.0
Trade school	23,445	7.83	49,142	13.62	47.7
Kindergarten	8,650	2.89	24,753	6.86	34.9
TOTAL	299,445		335,372		89.3

pedagogues' NSDAP membership was considerably higher than among lawyers because of bureaucratic pressure. Compared with Old Fighters or opportunists, peacetime converts were more often female, Catholic, rural, Bavarian, Saxe-Thuringian, or Austrian, and philological, showing that power allowed the party to reach out into hitherto-reluctant milieus. Fresh graduates without prior affiliation also entered in large numbers (Table A.7). With 41,210 members in Section Two, most philologues joined the NSLB, but their influence was limited, because they accounted only for one-seventh of the total. Whereas educators in the highest or lowest levels (professors and kindergarten teachers) were reluctant, primary-school pedagogues were especially zealous (many *Fachlehrer* classified as trade teachers also belonged here). However, 92,123 members failed to subscribe to the official NSLB organ and in Thuringia only 38 percent of the philologues received *Die Deutsche Höhere Schule.* In spite of formal and informal pressure, one-tenth of the educators steadfastly refused to join at all. Beneath the surface unanimity lingered considerable resentment and alienation. "For the teacher, the NSLB does not at all have the same meaning as his earlier association which was at once a union and a source of further professional training." The informants of the SOPADE gleefully reported "continual heavy frictions between pedagogues and the HJ as well as between them and the NSLB."[104]

Though delayed, the ultimate NSBDT victory in the "restructuring of German technology" was complete. After several false starts, Heß elevated Fritz Todt's office into a *Hauptamt für Technik* in November 1936, in order to ensure "the political use of technology" through the politicization of engineers.[105] On March 7, 1937, "the recognized technical organizations [were] united in the NSBDT," thereby granting it a monopoly. "The NSBDT decides collectively on the solution of all common tasks of German technicians, especially questions of technical indoctrination and professional concerns." Unlike in law or education, the traditional associations were not abolished, but rather called upon to "continue their technical-scientific work" under NSBDT control. Consolidated from eighty-four into sixteen, the specialized groups were combined into five NSBDT sections on: (1) machine technology and general engineering (VDI), (2) electricity, gas, and water (VDE), (3) chemistry (VDCh), (4) metallurgy and mining (VDEh), and (5) construction (DGfB).[106] Celebrating the synthesis of expert tradition and political revolution in the Berlin Sportspalast, Fritz Todt charged 12,000 enthusiastic technicians with "advancement of technical-scientific work; education and indoctrination of members in the use of German technology according to the demands of people or state; and support of highest achievement, identification and maintenance of professional duties and honor.''[107] In May 1938, the VDI unanimously chose Todt as new chairman in order to ''remove the last doubt about the political leadership of the expert organizations.'' Though reserving ''superior direction'' for the party, he was willing to allow some ''freedom and joyous independence'' to technical groups, because he ''recognized'' their value to Nazi rule.[108] Fulfilling an old engineering dream, the unification of technology spelled doom for purely professional associations. When the 10,000 member VDDI was classified as a ''white-collar association'' according to the 1937 union property liquidation law, the German Labor Front tried to swallow it up in September 1938. A Gestapo warning that ''the VDDI hinders the undisturbed construction of the Third Reich'' forced it to sever ties with its journal *Technik und Kultur*. Although appeals to the Ministry of Interior won temporary reinstatement, corporate self-nazification ultimately proved insufficient and the VDDI had no choice but to disband in July 1939.[109]

By the fall of 1937, the NSBDT could claim 81,000 members, about one-third of all German technicians. Amazingly enough, a full 27 percent of all NSBDT members also joined the NSDAP. These 21,000 Nazis were but one-tenth of Todt's estimated 220,000 technicians, indicating a lower involvement level than among teachers and lawyers. However, when one compares this participation with those 108,817 practitioners who subscribed to a technical journal, engineers were hardly neutral, because every fifth active professional belonged to the party! If the few surviving DAF membership cards of technicians are any indication, then Nazi engineers were younger, more likely to come from the Ruhr and north central Germany, or to be urban, educated (TH and doctorate), government-employed, and auxiliary activist than the rest (Table A.18). Though reaching fewer owners and managers, the party members apparently constituted an elite within the technical professions. Among the general NSBDT members, 48 percent were mechanical engineers (showing VDI dominance), 13 percent electrical, 14 percent chemical, 8 percent mining, and 17 percent construction specialists. Because 65 percent were employees, 15 percent public officials, 12.5 percent self-employed, and 5 percent pensioned, league joiners largely represented the dependent white-collar engineers in business and bureaucracy. With more than half having attended a TH and more than two-fifths graduated from a technical school, NSBDT activists were somewhat more exclusive than technicians in general.[110] Although the technicians' league controlled power over the professionals, the survival of technical-scientific associations retained the possibility of some apolitical sociability on the local chapter level. The remaining organizations prospered so much through the consolidation of smaller specialty groups that the VDI increased its membership from 28,140 to 46,761 in 1939. Moreover, about two-thirds of the technicians had no direct NS affiliation at all!

Although the rewards of collaboration fell short of NS boasts, most professionals' lives improved more than critics were willing to admit. No doubt, the destruction of traditional student groups, the labor shortage, the erosion of social status, the shrinkage of legal practice or complication of teaching, the conflict of self-images, and organizational compulsion were disappointing. However, the shift to practical training, the restoration of career chances, the improvement of income, the design opportunities for engineers, and the consolidation of technical associations generally outweighed such frustrations. To be sure, the "limitation of the defense" made courtroom work more difficult for lawyers. "Lack of respect" for knowledge, classroom disruptions, and compulsory volunteer work frustrated philologues with "this unculture." Raw-material shortages, constant overtime, and missing manpower also complicated engineering. But modest real improvements coupled with immodest Nazi claims made professionals believe that real stability was returning for the first time since the empire. Many experts could point with pride to actual accomplishments in their field, such as a decrease in spurious litigation, more youth-oriented teaching methods, and countless technical innovations. Whereas NS fanatics took the credit for any such success, apolitical practitioners tolerated indoctrination as long as it did not interfere too much with their work. An aware minority "consciously opposed Hitler," criticizing his "anti-Semitic racial superstition, the Nazis' personnel policy . . . the unleashing of uneducated and uncultured youth and the suppression of truth." However, the majority of "easy-living" professionals, though unsure where the voyage would go, was willing to enjoy the ride.[111]

ABNORMAL NAZI NORMALITY

In early 1939, Nazis looked back on the "germanization" of the professions with satisfaction: "What a change has taken place during these six years in law and its representatives," Reinhard Höhn enthused at the pan-German lawyer congress in May. "Perhaps the greatest transformation . . . has occurred among attorneys," turning shady manipulators into "lively and popular guardians of law" who worked in harmony with judges and prosecutors. Karl Frank claimed a similar improvement in the role of philologues. "More than ever, we teachers and educators of German high schools . . . face the task of energetically shaping the future leaders of Germany in the spirit of the NS movement, shoulder to shoulder with parents, HJ and the dominant educational force of the entire nation, the NSDAP." Engineers saw their responsibility increased and their work endowed with higher meaning. "We live in an age, at once romantic and made of steel," Joseph Goebbels rhapsodized at the opening of the Berlin automobile exhibition: "National Socialism has succeeded in removing the soulless character of technology and in filling it with the rhythm and hot impulse of our time." Outwardly, the "germanization" of the professions seemed complete.[112] Inwardly, there was still much "discontent with everyday life, though no fundamental opposition" for lack of a compelling alternative. Upset by Hitler's unprecedented ruthlessness, some courageous attorneys like Paul Ronge, teachers like Heinz Grupe, or engineers like Manfred von Ardenne retained sufficient professional, moral, and political integrity to view the system as organized abnormality. However, intent on enjoying its rewards, the ordinary majority of experts accommodated itself to the new normality and willingly collaborated in the construction of the Third Reich.[113]

The astounding success of Nazi foreign and domestic policy consolidated the loyalty of experts to the regime. During the remilitarization of the Rhineland in

March 1936, lawyers justified the overthrow of the Treaty of Versailles by a higher "national right to live," claiming that the "Nazi struggle for truth, justice and honor serves world peace." In April 1938, teachers watched the century-old dream of the Austrian Anschluß come true: "In an incomparable historical deed, the Führer has created this [greater] Reich, broken down artificial barriers and brought 10 million Germans home into nation and state." A year later, engineers gloated about the "enormously superior" conquest of Czechoslovakia and applauded the construction of the *Westwall* as deterrent against aggression.[114] At home, practitioners supported the "national peace policy" in repeated plebiscites: "Through another vow of unshakeable loyalty, German lawyers shall express their thanks for the new tasks and aims, established by the Third Reich." The recovery of strength added sincerity to the rituals of gratitude at Hitler's birthday as well.[115] Within their own sphere, professionals followed Nazi directives without visible scruples. Prominent lawyers ranted against "free masons and Jews as patrons and coordinators" of the "enemies of the state," demanding "merciless combat against them." History teachers affirmed the bases of NS ideology by explaining the "new German man," the structure of the Third Reich, the "renewal of German culture," the return of prosperity, colonialism, and "Bolshevism as world enemy." Similarly, engineers promoted the "Four-Year Plan" and the militarization of the economy, in order to get ready for the coming struggle for survival. To skeptics, such frantic public acclamations only served to silence private doubts.[116]

Pleased with the extension of their own sphere, professionals welcomed the "liberation" of their Austrian and Sudeten colleagues. With many early supporters (such as 470 pre-June 1933 NSLB members) hailing from the new Gaue, NS affiliates proudly celebrated the "unification of the greater German national soul," because 50,000 new teachers and 25,000 technicians promised sizable membership gains. Hoping to share the economic and political dynamism of the "free, strong and united greater Germany," pan-German Austrians enthusiastically cooperated in the coordination of their associations.[117] However, for Jewish practitioners, the Anschluß had more sinister implications, because it introduced anti-Semitic measures on March 31, 1938 that disbarred about 700 Viennese lawyers alone. Resenting the continuation of the remaining 900 veterans or old practitioners, 480 attorneys of "German blood" called for an additional removal of 200–300 eastern Jews. The final racial purge of December 1938 dealt harshly with lawyers of mixed descent and extended the proscription of Communists to "all who have been active as enemies of the Nazi movement." Only in Vienna were some Jewish attorneys allowed to remain beyond the 83 consultants "for a transition period," since a three-quarter personnel reduction would have imperiled the administration of justice. By the end of the year, the number of Austrian attorneys had shrunk from 3307 to 1677 and Sudeten lawyers decreased from more than 1000 to about 500! Austrian secondary schoolteachers also faced dismissals or reassignments while the Aryan paragraph was extended to NSBDT engineers.[118]

Divergent historical structures, however, resisted the fusion of professions. Although the Reich's legal training could be imposed, the homogenization of practice turned out to be complicated, because Austrian attorneys claimed unlimited access to courts, demanded freedom of movement, and objected to "bureaucratization." When the Ministry of Justice tried to extend the national lawyer code, different customs such as nonlocalization, the absence of legal consultants, and the combination of law and notariate had to be respected in order to avoid the impression of "one-sided incorporation." Although the RRAO was introduced in the Sudeten areas on March 31, 1939, its extension to Austria broke down when Frick and Bormann demanded the immediate elimination of "the attorney trainee service" for eugenic reasons.[119] Although the reduction of German secondary schooling to eight years formally replicated the Austrian *Mittelschule,* the purge of Jewish and Catholic influence on the curriculum proved difficult, because there was little enthusiasm for compulsory reorientation. When appeals to become "priests of Nazi faith and officers of Nazi service" grew tiresome, the NSLB initials were popularly translated as "*n*odding, *s*ilencing, *l*aughing, and *p*aying."[120] For engineers, the Anschluß created the challenge of "bringing Austria up to the Reich standard as quickly as possible" by extending the Autobahn network to Vienna and building a grand shipping route on the Danube. Because Austrian TH graduates outnumbered the middle-school technicians, they had succeeded in obtaining a legal monopoly to the title of "engineer" and long "promoted the pan-German idea." Ironically, incorporation into the Reich cost them their prerogatives (e.g., higher status and chambers), while nonacademic technicians gained recognition through broader membership criteria of the NSBDT.[121]

In retrospect, the experience of most professionals during the late 1930s has assumed a kind of golden glow, coloring personal recollections, literary reconstructions, and film collages. Half a century later, Nazi indoctrination has come to seem faintly ridiculous while racial and political persecution appears so distasteful as to be entirely repressed. The adventure of the war and the postwar dislocation have obscured the very real disappointments and frustrations of practice in the Third Reich. Instead, a positive image of domestic stability and prosperity, of national pride, and diplomatic success forms a subterranean, but nonetheless powerful countercurrent to the official condemnations of the Nazi period.[122] This mainstream nostalgia is factually wrong and politically dangerous. The secret police reports of 1939 are full of criticisms that "the situation of the attorneys has not improved," complaints about "the further deterioration of the prestige of the teaching profession," and grumbling about "the lack of essential engineers."[123] But the opposite view of some antifascist activists and holocaust scholars, portraying the Third Reich as an unrelenting nightmare for all its citizens, is equally mistaken. Compared to the crisis-ridden 1920s, German practitioners did feel a sense of material improvement and psychological recovery that made them willing to pay the price of the plebeian and disagreeable aspects of Nazi rule. More disturbing than positive or negative Third Reich stereotypes is the realization that precisely the accommodation of most practitioners to abnormal NS normality made the frightful dialectic between perpetrators and victims possible. For responsible experts, the ethical dilemma was irresolvable. Maintaining professional standards did create an apolitical refuge and serve persecuted clients, curious pupils, and trusting customers. But such competent performance also helped to support dictatorship at home and aggression abroad.

7

Deprofessionalization in the Third Reich

''The die has been cast! The German people are rallying for the struggle of right against wrong,'' Hans Frank justified the outbreak of the Second World War in September 1939: ''The Führer has left no stone unturned to help justice triumph peacefully. Now it must be won by arms.'' To bring the implications home to each practitioner, he added: ''The aim of your fight during the Nazi revolution has turned into the German nation's struggle for survival. I expect everyone to do his duty where the leadership of the NS Reich puts him.'' The majority of professionals greeted such appeals with a distinct lack of enthusiasm, remembering the suffering that patriotic rhetoric had brought them a quarter century before. Therefore, Nazi propagandists argued that reactionary ''England has frivolously started the war,'' stressing that ''we march into battle under incomparably better circumstances than in 1914. . . . Versailles did not conclude but only interrupt the war, and now it must be finished!''[1] Once again professionals faced military conscription or service on the ''home front.'' NSRB functionary Wilhelm Heuber called upon attorneys to ''substitute voluntarily for your comrades'' in order to safeguard their existence. Philologue chairman Karl Frank exhorted teachers to uphold morale and be ''inspired by soldier spirit.'' The VDI journal asked engineers ''to forge the sharpest weapons, make the best tools and cast the loveliest bells'' to celebrate the soldiers' ''victorious return to a free, beautiful and great Nazi Germany!''[2]

For five and three-quarter years professionals struggled from euphoric victory through frustrating stalemate to agonizing defeat. Initially, NS activists claimed a share of the credit: ''The incredibly rapid advance of the armies testifies not only to the incomparable achievements of German arms, but also to the high state of our technology.'' In the second year, the ''amazing and momentous successes of our Führer's superior genius'' seemed to promise ''a victorious conclusion to the fight against the plutocratic world of England.''[3] However, by 1942, Nazi propagandists were compelled to admit that the ''icy grip of the Russian winter has forced a temporary halt,'' requiring ''increased sacrifices, greater work and even more severe trials.'' A year later, the much-conjured final victory began to recede, bringing ''instead of desired peace, an extension of the war of unbelievable proportions; undiminished and successful, Germany is fighting with its allies on near endless land fronts and on all oceans.'' In January 1944, a note of desperation began to creep into appeals for ''hearts of steel [and] faith in victory.'' Castigating ''the hegemonic aspiration of subhumanity incorporated in the Jews,'' Nazis sought to rouse practitioners to greater defensive exertions by warning of the ''animalistic hatred [of] our enemies.'' By 1945 defeat was so imminent that NS leaders no longer bothered to rally their subordinates. There remained only the eerie silence of death and destruction. Civilians experienced the war in three distinctive stages: limited disruption during victory, increasing strains imposed by total warfare, and chaotic collapse at the end.[4]

In retrospect, German professionals recall their involvement in Hitler's war with deep ambivalence. Compelled to apologize for their actions, many older practitioners seek to disassociate themselves from racial conquest and emphasize national self-defense instead. ''During this dark time not all Hanoverian attorneys took complete leave of their senses, but attempted to cling to proven virtues so as to prevent the worst.'' The rationale of trying to make the best of a bad situation served to justify the ''resolute pursuit of professional tasks,'' even if efficient performance prolonged the struggle and thereby increased the suffering. Haunted by guilt, many nonpolitical experts protest their subjective sincerity in order to retain some defiant pride in their achievements at the front or at home.[5] In contrast, émigré professionals and especially younger scholars tend to condemn all collaboration with the Third Reich as immoral. To the outraged critics, it matters little whether practitioners were carrying out their duties in order to help the people or to support Nazi policies. ''In spite of being tied to NS laws, even the lawyer who applied them had some freedom which permitted a minimum of humanity''—but used such discretion all too rarely. In terms of objective results rather than subjective intent, it seems that without any direct threat to life or limb many professionals ''became instruments of a criminal system'' that abused their goodwill and personal decency.[6] This clash of apologetic and accusatory views clouds the picture of the professions' actual role in the war.

Emotional undercurrents also complicate the theoretical debate on the continuation of professionalization in the Third Reich. Michael Kater has unearthed much evidence that medicine flourished as an academic field because of the need for doctors at the front. The destruction of ambulatory clinics, the establishment of a medical monopoly, and the breaking of the power of the health insurances *(Krankenkassen)* suggest that the Nazis allowed doctors to gain dominance through ''physician-controlled services.''[7] Other researchers claim that psychology (and psychotherapy) progressed from a scholarly subject to a profession during the Third Reich: ''It could become a firmer academic discipline, institute its own training and examination, and institutionalize the first psychological occupational career.'' In the narrow sense of institutionalization, power, and prosperity, the fighting brought gains for some groups of practitioners: ''Since the outcome of the war depended last but not least on technical performance, the engineers almost automatically made progress with their striving for professionalization.''[8] Against such a favorable view argue the countless Nazi victims who suffered the ''reversal of healing and killing'' during the shameful ''participation of physicians in mass murder.'' According to Robert Lifton, the collaboration of the experts in the holocaust rather demonstrates moral corruption: ''Genocide requires two groups of people: a professional elite that formulates and supervises the killing, and professional killers who kill.'' Numerous complaints of frustrated generals, bureaucrats, or scientists attest to a warping of ethics, a deterioration of standards, and a loss of autonomy. Broader criteria and a comparison of several occupations seem to suggest instead a creeping ''deprofessionalization,'' beginning in 1933, but accelerating after 1939.[9]

PROFESSIONS AT WAR

Ostensibly dedicated to peaceful pursuits, the professions became, nevertheless, directly involved in the war effort. The military struggle not only called many practitioners to arms, but also mobilized the remaining experts at home, depending on the relevance of their specialty to national defense. Although all belligerents instituted disruptive emergency measures, Nazi zealots tried to use the opportunity to reorient the lives of professionals more drastically. First, many experts were drafted into the army or the labor service during successive stages of escalation toward total war. How did these academics react to the removal from their career and brutalization of their lives in uniform? Second, the mobilization and war conditions fundamentally restructured the parameters of practice at the home front. What effect did the new burdens such as simplification of procedures, erosion of quality, or enlarged responsibility have on those who escaped the military? Third, NS propagandists never tired of explaining that exceptional wartime circumstances required changing the content of professional work. How did the militarization of practice and the racial radicalization of professional codes affect the quality of practitioner services? Fourth, by doing their job, university graduates contributed physically and intellectually to the war effort of the Third Reich. Did they apply war law, indoctrinate children, or build weapons primarily for Hitler's conquests or for their own self-defense?[10]

For professionals under forty, the Second World War meant above all military service on the front. Because ''preparations for the continuation of legal business in case of general mobilization'' had begun several months *before* September 1939, ''a great number of lawyers was called up already in the first days'' of the fighting. But initial Blitzkrieg victories allowed some demobilization until the attack on the Soviet Union once again required full manpower, putting 65 percent of the probationers and 35 percent of established practitioners into uniform. By the summer of 1942, the NSDAP chancellery asserted that ''more than 7000 lawyers are serving under colors, sacrificing their lives and possessions to the fatherland,'' while Reinhard Neubert claimed ''almost 8000 soldiers,'' with three decorated by a *Ritterkreuz* and 240 dead.[11] In January 1943, total war mobilization threatened the remainder by demanding the ''registration of all men and women for tasks of national defense,'' as long as they were not ''doing an essential job.'' However, the lawyer chamber and Ministry of Justice asked for their exemption as ''necessary organs of the administration of justice,'' because the judiciary needed the preservation of "a sufficient number . . . of defense attorneys, tax advisers, consultants of weapons companies and advocates for litigation requiring counsel." After the Stalingrad defeat, lawyers born after 1900 could no longer be shielded from the army, although some might be turned into judges or prosecutors. Predictably, old Nazi enemies were defined as nonessential, such as "Mischlinge of the first degree, those with Jewish relatives, and practitioners whose subversive behavior has been determined by a court."[12]

Combing out additional professionals for military or civilian service created vexing problems. In Saxony, an anti-intellectual Gauleiter designated all superfluous attorneys for "manual labor," because "they have never really worked and should learn it now." The Reich Ministry of Justice quickly protested that such practice "violates fundamental rules of planning" and demanded more suitable placement according to their training and status.[13] By summer 1943, 45.4 percent of lawyers served at the front, and by September 1944 merely some 7000 continued to practice. Though finding few additional soldiers, the total war recruitment netted another 1551 attorneys for labor service and some 300 for transfer as judges, so that only about two-fifths of the peacetime complement remained.[14] Nevertheless, a secret police report considered the "intended indirect purge . . . a failure" because nonconformists could use their importance to the war effort to escape being requisitioned. Labor offices had difficulty finding suitable jobs for lawyers in the bureaucracy or war industry, thereby "preventing a manpower success." Finally, the forced recruitment of specialists "created serious discontent in attorney circles" because of insecurity over conditions and misassignments. By January 1945, the desperate military situation necessitated the call-up of the last reserves among professionals. Although in Dresden only 515 of the original 1283 practitioners still practiced, the ultimate "escalation of total war" demanded the conscription of another 250, leaving merely one-fifth of the original number! Now all men in their forties and fifties had to go and some over sixty were drafted, even if their use "proceed[ed] very slowly." By early 1945, only old and sick practitioners remained to be dragooned into the *Volkssturm* in a vain attempt to defend the crumbling Reich.[15]

Philologues faced similar obligations, although bureaucratic employment provided more security and control. In the 1939 mobilization, "many professional comrades of Section Two also exchanged school-work for *Wehrmacht* service." In May 1940, about "a third to a quarter" of the 12,689 Prussian Studienräte and "approximately half" of the 5260 probationary teachers "were called to military duty," making for about 6000 educator soldiers. Assuming the same proportion of the 35,697 male high school pedagogues in the Reich, the total number of secondary school instructors in uniform during 1940 is likely to have been about 12,000. This estimate is borne out by a list of 100 Thuringian trainees that shows that three-fifths were soldiers. By January 1942, "75,000 German educators have taken up weapons, in other words, one-third of the male comrades of all age-groups," one NSLB functionary claimed: "Teachers are proud of their five Ritterkreuz winners. *Innumerable pedagogues,* among them one thus decorated, *have fallen on the field of honor,* tens of thousands are wounded."[16] Even with some curriculum simplification, "the drafting of a large share of the available teachers" strained regular instruction and made it difficult to find additional soldiers in subsequent mobilizations. The demands on pedagogues for volunteer work were so great that in July 1943 the Reich Ministry of Education felt forced to decree "that education is to be considered an essential task which must continue to be fulfilled even under conditions of total war." While younger philologues were drafted in roughly the same numbers as lawyers, the designation of schooling as vital to the war saved the rest from additional labor duty until they had to dig trenches in the futile final struggle.[17]

Their central role in arms production shielded engineers better from military service, especially when they worked for large firms. Because the initial draft made few exceptions, the *VDI Nachrichten* sent a special greeting to the "thousands of you out at the front," above all TH students and young professionals. Directing "high-quality specialist" workers, engineers in uniform supervised separate "technical troops" in order to restore power, water, transportation, and industry immediately behind the battlefield.[18] However, Fritz Todt's assurance that "the war forced upon us finds the men of technology at their place" implied work in armament factories. After an April 1940 agreement, "a large number of militarily fit engineers remained in industry by order of the army," because technical experts "are more than ever supposed to be the driving force behind our armaments efforts." In the spring of 1942, Albert Speer safeguarded essential manpower through a special designation as "crucial worker" and called for more volunteers "for the solution of technical war tasks." Seeking to tap "the enormous reserves for total war mobilization," the VDI in early 1943 once again appealed to "the sense of responsibility of engineers." Instead of imposing compulsion, Speer put technicians in charge of manpower conscription by requiring every factory with more than 300 workers to appoint a "labor service engineer." Generally "resented by managers" as bureaucratic interference in production, these *Arbeitseinsatz-Ingenieure* were none too effective except in protecting themselves.[19]

Maintaining "the fighting spirit of drafted" practitioners required the provision of adequate support for their families. Free food, uniforms, medical care as well as military pay and front-line supplements might suffice for the men in uniform, but they could not safeguard an academic life-style for those left at home who were reduced to welfare without additional resources. As a result of the "great concern and deep depression" of attorneys, the government eventually agreed to base aid on "the prior living conditions and the peace-time income of dependents." Together with supplements for rent, educational expenses, a servant's wage, and a more liberal interpretation of the guidelines, this subsidy system, starting at 40 marks (for the first 100 marks) and rising to 200 marks (for anything more than 580 marks) monthly, improved the situation of the dependents of free professionals "for the short term." Lawyer chamber attempts to remove the remaining inequities foundered on the resistance of the Ministry of Interior.[20] In November 1940, the Reichsrechtsanwaltskammer imposed a "special contribution" on its members in order to create an "equalization fund" for returning soldiers "who have to begin totally or partially anew after the war." Because this surcharge of 75 percent on receipts of more than 20,000 marks annually raised only a few hundred thousand marks from profiteers, it appeared to many attorneys as "something of an insult." In 1943, Reinhard Neubert decreed a graduated dues increase, peaking at 8 percent for all incomes of more than 50,000 marks annually. Later in 1944, some of the 5 million marks accumulated was disbursed to alleviate the "bad situation of drafted lawyer trainees."[21] In contrast, teachers, as public officials, were able to collect their military pay and to receive their peacetime salary—slightly reduced by a war surcharge—plus any unearned income. Permanent business employees such as engineers could apply to local "family-aid" for the difference between their military receipts and their prewar income, thereby maintaining their status and job security.[22]

In contrast to propaganda claims, the military experience of most professionals was less than heroic. Whereas some looked sharp in uniform as reserve officers, other academics were "a picture of woe" as incorrigible civilians. Those serving as garrison in fortresses or in occupied territories could enjoy army life while others who were more directly involved in the fighting suffered frightfully. Much depended on the example of the officers and the tone of the unit. Because of a greater understanding of the likelihood of anonymous death, the "front experience" of the Second World War lost virtually all of its chivalrous romance. Although danger remained exciting and comradeship comforting, many professionals sensed the incredible human cost in the hollow eyes of the defeated prisoners or fleeing civilians. The intoxicating march through Poland and France tended to reinforce a feeling of superiority of German order and *Kultur*. However, personal observation of the achievements of conquered countries often contradicted NS propaganda, which began to lose credibility when the tide of battle turned in 1942. Abandoning Hitler's dreams of glory, professionals continued fighting out of a misplaced sense of responsibility for their own people. However, chance images, such as three hanged Jews in Łódź, left nagging questions about the justice of the German cause. Many educated soldiers were also affronted by the crude tone of the barracks as well as the waste of military duty, especially when they were assigned to paperwork in the orderly room.[23]

Those practitioners not maimed, killed, or captured, faced a loss of professional identity during life at the front: "I have painfully felt how my intellect is gradually shrivelling up," reflected one philologue. Being completely cut off from news and culture, except for an occasional classical music broadcast, was generally brutalizing. Only long letters home or an occasional visit to one's place of work during leave brought relief. Some experts such as doctors were fortunate to be assigned to a military version of their civilian calling. Lawyer Paul Ronge was deputized to a military court as a stenographer. Teacher Konrad Jarausch was sometimes used as a drill instructor for recruits. Diplom-Ingenieur Martin Vogel built pontoon bridges and coastal fortifications with engineering troops. A select few could even hope to serve in related capacities in the military government of a conquered country. However, much military work was "pointless" and academic graduates soon lost touch with their civilian pursuits, which grew ever more unreal and remote. The mobility of much of the fighting made it difficult for professional associations to maintain contact with their members in uniform. "All the time I think about how life and work are to continue in the future; but with the continual unrest . . . I do not find an answer." In spite of strenuous attempts to keep in touch with peacetime work, the years of training and of fighting made men "tired of everything," wishing for a transfer home and for peace. Eventually the "nameless suffering'' around them led some perceptive professionals to rediscover ''true human brotherhood'' in friend and foe alike.[24]

The war fundamentally transformed working conditions for those professionals who remained at home. To make do with less available labor, a battery of measures restructured both civil and criminal procedure in September 1939. At the district courts, single judges now decided all cases; lower courts appealed directly to superior district courts; the limits for initial jurisdiction and for later appeals were increased considerably; furthermore, judges were empowered to proceed with ''free discretion.'' To preserve morale, all soldiers were also ''protected'' from collection of debts and foreclosure. Even if lawyers resented this curtailment of their advocacy possibilities, civil litigation continued to deteriorate.[25] Anticipating ''a coming reform,'' criminal practice similarly eliminated lay judges, the jury system, and intermediary appeals. Along with ''a considerable extension of special court jurisdiction,'' procedure was simplified by ''limiting mandatory counsel, speeding up adjudication . . . freeing the collection of facts, limiting appeals,'' and so on. Finally, the government claimed a right of ''extraordinary objection'' to a sentence and made jurisdiction dependent on ''the severity of the anticipated punishment.''[26] The appointment of the fanatical Georg Thierack as justice minister and the proclamation of total war in 1942–1943 further eroded the position of lawyers. To prevent the postponement of all civil suits, attorneys argued that soldiers wanted divorces, determinations of racial origin, eviction of renters, and child support resolved. However, the new criminal procedure rules of 1944, seeking to ''save manpower to the limit of the possible,'' strengthened the role of the prosecutor once again. The war reinforced judicial and bureaucratic hostility to lawyers, because their arguments appeared as complications that should be dispensed with during an emergency—even at the risk of some mistakes.[27]

The institutional parameters of teaching were also drastically restructured. In early 1940, the Ministry of Education simplified the curriculum so ''as to satisfy the demand for teachers . . . facilitate the organization of instruction and establish a unified and stronger basis for the militarily important subjects.'' Reduced overall, class schedules still contained five weekly hours of sports, four of German (plus three in history, and two in geography, art, or music), but only four in mathematics and two in biology (with two of physics and chemistry added in the upper grades) and four periods of English and Latin instruction. ''Since the high schools have only seven and one half years available any more, everything nonessential had to disappear from the curriculum in order to obtain the best performance,'' NSLB Section Two leader Karl Frank justified the abolition of tracking and religion.[28] During 1941, a ''special examination'' was introduced to allow ''war participants'' with at least six years of secondary schooling to obtain a high school diploma by demonstrating ''sufficient intellectual ability for entrance into higher professions.'' Although Bernhard Rust tried to insist on uniform national standards for the ''promotion of high school pupils,'' the army demanded that everyone who had completed six years and military service was to be admitted to the university. In early 1944, the Ministry of Culture accepted the shortening of instruction by ordering that the material for the last three years ought to be ''condensed into two school terms'' in order to release students more quickly to the front. Struggling tenaciously for academic standards, philologues were less successful in maintaining requirements in the Second than during the First World War. Moreover, the benefits of curricular simplification and greater "teacher latitude" were outweighed by increased hours and larger class sizes.[29]

The "technical war" similarly transformed the framework of engineering work. During wartime, it was clear that everything "which does not serve struggle, perseverance or victory must be postponed!" Concentration on essential war production meant that "everywhere in the economy, energies and materials must be directed to the war effort and everything else must be dispensed with." Such military priorities required the closing of non-war-related industries and the massive transfer of labor and technical experts to armament production after some retraining in DAF courses. If it seemed not "decisive for the war," then basic research, such as the development of computers, generally stopped.[30] Although service industries for civilian needs in food or clothing had to be maintained, much engineering work was redirected toward "weapons development." Technicians proudly claimed that "the German engineer has handed the soldier the weapons with which he could be victorious." Running the war economy presented special technical challenges in "leading and employing work comrades," in "retraining and female labor," as well as in "transforming production." In short, "through his appearance, action and ingenuity the engineer shall enliven and galvanize war production so that he fully proves himself as leader of the inner front. . . ." While reducing the autonomy of lawyers and teachers, the fighting strengthened the role of expert technicians within the economy.[31]

The war also militarized the content of professional practice. Combatting the enemy at the home front required "exceptional stipulations which regulate the behavior of citizens according to domestic security needs." According to Frank, the Nazis "from the beginning structured legal principles in such a way that nothing had to be changed in case of war." Recognizing the importance of morale due to the domestic collapse of 1918, the military forbade "undermining the will to fight" while the government proscribed "listening to foreign radio stations" in order to eliminate the effect of hostile propaganda. Another decree against *Volksschädlinge* called for "increased protection against criminal elements," classified as plunderers, air raid violators, and saboteurs. Moreover, friendly intercourse with prisoners of war was strictly forbidden.[32] The criminal code revision of September 1941 introduced the death penalty for "dangerous habitual criminals" (such as sexual offenders) and made it mandatory for murderers, who were defined as a special type by "motives, result or purpose of deed." At the same time, punishments were raised for numerous other offenses such as "usury" or "misuse of legal documents." For "subhumans" in the East such as Poles and Jews, Roland Freisler developed a separate criminal law—based "on the general and comprehensive duty to obey"—which added new offenses to the already lengthy German catalogue. To "meet the need for protection of our Reich and people in its current struggle for survival," the notorious People's Court stretched traditional sedition law so far as to proscribe intent and attempt rather than actual acts. By criminalizing nonconformist behavior and elevating trivial offenses into major crimes, the "general clauses" and barbaric punishments of martial law *(Kriegsrecht)* rendered defense exasperatingly difficult.[33]

The fighting similarly intensified the militarization of instruction. "We shall educate our boys into soldiers, our entire nation shall feel and think militarily." Already on May 24, 1939, the German Supreme Command ordered the army to exert greater influence on education through special liaison "officers for school questions." Such "military spiritual training" meant especially drilling in "obedience and discipline" in order to prepare youths for armed service.[34] Moreover, it required instilling a willingness to fight, a *Wehrwillen* that did not just blindly follow orders but volunteered in a "martial spirit" of loyalty and honor. It also implied conveying military information—detailed *Wehrwissen* about services and weapons—helpful to future soldiers. More successful than overt military instruction was the covert introduction of war themes into regular subjects, from German (the Nibelung saga) to mathematics (solving ballistic problems) and languages (explaining England's reasons for starting the war). Building endless airplane or battleship models appealed to youthful imagination and role play. Celebrating fresh victories or past sacrifices such as the Langemarck slaughter was also effective. Most persuasive was the daily discussion of the fighting, written down in a war diary by the upper grades: "With great enthusiasm [every boy] will learn the heroic deeds of our submarines or cruisers and the momentous successes of our Luftwaffe." In November 1940 Rust rejected additional militarization, because political questions had been sufficiently integrated into the high school curriculum, especially in history and geography.[35]

The technical nature of the warfare redirected engineering "towards the front and the battle." In January 1940, Fritz Todt proclaimed: "The work of German technology serves the army, navy and airforce no less than the home economy. During this time, the German engineer has no other duty than to be a soldier at his job!" The top priority was weapons development and production. "The victories of our Messerschmidt fighters and Heinkel bombers, the successes of the U-boats, the superiority of our tanks and our anti-aircraft guns not only gratify those who constructed these instruments of war but also excite the entire nation, especially the young." Instead of resting on laurels, it was essential "to keep our technical advantage" and to create new weapons to counter the developments of the enemy. New applications continually emerged such as medical technology to care for wounded soldiers at the front or orthopedic technology to supply artificial limbs at home.[36] Because weapons had to be produced quickly and efficiently, "mass rationalization" needed to reach a new scale in order to increase productivity. In 1943 the mobilization for total war posed "the great challenge" of doing more with even fewer raw materials, less skilled labor, and decreased energy allotment. In spite of ideological scruples, the need to "increase efficiency and production" led inevitably to "more division of labor" and automation. The militarization of engineering therefore focused research on weapon design and shifted production to arms manufacture at any cost.[37]

Within their sphere, the professions made considerable contributions according to the relevance of their expertise to the war effort. Attorneys collaborated by applying martial law. "Understandably, formal law takes a back-seat when a war begins," Hans Frank explained the change of priorities while insisting that "in spite of all necessities the community believes ideally in the justice of its leadership." According to secret police reports, "the population follows the [criminal] cases against violators of the war economy especially attentively." It was crucial for morale that "the courts are willing and able to implement justice without regard for the position of the accused" and the fiction of legal fairness be maintained. However, because the public tended to demand harsh punishments, attorneys faced a difficult task in defending without "irresponsibly and biasedly taking the culprits' side" and thereby "creating an uproar."[38] In civil law, private tort suits increased as a result of the "greater abrasiveness of the population because of the tension" and unusual circumstances of the struggle. In the year 1943, the Ministry of Justice appealed to the public and the attorneys to "avoid legal quarrels and keep peace!" With the establishment of special German courts in Poland beginning in 1939, some attorneys also served as guardians of imperial legal control: "The German attorney in the Government General represents German culture as organ of administration of justice in an advance post in the German East." Rarely involved in military cases, attorneys rather enforced domestic conformity by applying wartime criminal codes and maintaining civil order, even when they were just doing their "professional" duty. On the whole, lawyers were powerless to prevent the escalation of punishment which meted out 16,000 civil and 25,000 military death sentences during the Third Reich, an appalling 26.5 times more than during the preceding quarter century![39]

Teachers contributed to popular morale by "propaganda support of all war-tasks, posed for educators and schools." In the national struggle for existence, "the school [was] also an important part of the 'domestic front'." Ernst Holler exhorted his colleagues in 1940: "During the war every philologue should be especially conscious that in an important way he helps shape the will of the nation." By stressing unity of resolve and equality of burdens, educators were to maintain the warlike spirit and "psychological resistance" of soldiers and people. Concretely that meant assisting in "the publication of news, reports, articles and flyers in the daily press" and "relaying relevant radio broadcasts" in order to expose the nefarious designs of the enemy and justify Nazi imperial policies.[40] "Cooperation in tasks important for the war" also implied ceaseless activism *(Einsatz),* such as organizing extracurricular competitions for pupils on the naval and eastern struggle, volunteering for collections of waste materials or healing herbs, taking on nightly air raid or fire brigade duty, signing up for agricultural work or other bureaucratic duty during vacation, and accepting reassignment to occupied territories in order to create a "völkisch wall" of defense: "In the new German East real colonial work must be done" by spreading Kultur through education. The remaining teachers formed the backbone of social service associations, because among NSLB members, 11.3 percent belonged to the welfare (NSV), 8.2 percent to the civil defense (RLB), and 2.2 percent to the women's front (NSF), in contrast to only 6.9 percent who were in the SA, 1.9 percent in the BdM, and 1.3 percent in the HJ. Whereas merely 3 percent held higher charges, 18 percent filled lower leadership roles in the NSLB and other groups (Table A.17).[41]

Engineers were more immediately engaged in the military struggle by organizing the war economy. As a result of his success with the superhighways and the border defenses, Fritz Todt was appointed "Reich Minister for weapons and munitions" on March 20, 1941 in order to "concentrate efforts and improve performance." The long-time dream of a ministry of technology thereby became a reality, albeit in military form. By cooperating in about sixty topical committees *(Fachausschüsse)*, engineers materially helped in the conversion to war production and in the increase of productivity in a "flexible armament economy." The VDI took the lead in discussing substitute raw materials, saving energy in production, simplifying and standardizing design, and finding ways to improve productivity. Countless conferences, exhibitions, guidelines, and flyers sought to disseminate new methods of solving standard problems, occasionally even drawing upon war experiences for civilian use.[42] Karl Saur's sweeping plans for total NSBDT control of technology lost momentum when Albert Speer's appointment as minister elevated a nonideological architect who was less interested in the engineers' professional advance. The practical consequence of the stalemate in the East was the demand for an "immediate increase in production" by "getting the best possible armament performance out of human labor and available resources." Indeed, the growth in weapons manufacture between 1940 and 1944 was impressive: The number of tanks increased more than tenfold, the figure for automatic weapons rose 4.6 times, the output of military planes multiplied 4.2 times, and the amount of munitions grew 3.8 times. In contrast to the peripheral participation of lawyers and teachers, the engineers made a vital contribution to the German war effort.[43]

The racial struggle drew professionals ever deeper into the vortex of the holocaust. In contrast to a considerable number of doctors, few lawyers, teachers, or engineers personally perpetrated the mechanized mass extermination in their professional capacity. Although almost one-third of the SS officer corps consisted of students and graduates—many with law degrees—academics tended to hold honorary commissions and members of the security apparatus were by and large legal bureaucrats. Some SS attorneys like Horst Bender were nonetheless instrumental in drawing up deadly decrees; some racist pedagogues ideologically prepared the killers in the NAPOLAs or Adolf Hitler Schools; furthermore, some inhumane engineers designed the lethal machinery. Because the annihilation was largely carried out in occupied territories in the East, the great majority of practitioners, like millions of Germans, "simply looked away," preferring not to see what might disquiet.[44] But, in the final solution, no bystanders were entirely innocent. Lawyers repeatedly encountered the consequences of anti-Semitic measures and either helped Jewish clients or profited from their distress. Teachers repeatedly faced Jewish or mixed-race pupils in their classes, either treating them humanely or ostracizing them. Not infrequently, armament engineers employed "Jewish manpower" along with slave laborers or POWs, apparently troubled more by its cost ineffectiveness than by moral scruples.[45] For the thousands of victims among professionals, the war marked the last stage of their indignity. Admission as "legal consultant" did not shield Jewish attorneys from deportation, and the practice of some 200 Mischlinge or "Aryan" lawyers married to Jews became ever more circumscribed. When the remaining Jewish schools closed in June 1942, unemployed teachers could only wait with their former students for the inevitable. By assuming a new gentile identity, a few Jewish engineers did survive, shielded by understanding employers.[46] Although countless individuals showed compassion, most German practitioners, by doing their duty without protest against Nazi barbarism, became guilty of an insidious kind of complicity.

The Second World War therefore involved professionals more directly than the Great War one generation earlier. Superficially, there were many parallels: A similar proportion of practitioners was drafted into the military and many others were compelled into civilian service. The remainder somehow struggled on at the home front under trying conditions. However, closer inspection also reveals significant differences. Although the Blitzkrieg strategy initially isolated civilians from the fighting, the subsequent escalation toward total war was more complete. The bloodshed lasted more than a year longer and reached civilians more massively through political persecution or racial extermination and saturation bombing. Experts in uniform more completely lost their professional identities, because academic outreach attempts were more feeble than between 1914 and 1918. Because the Nazis were less restrained by tradition, professional practice at home was transformed more drastically by wartime measures. Moreover, modern propaganda methods in radio and film made it possible to militarize work more thoroughly. Although some party experts or industrial engineers saw the fighting as an opportunity, the majority of practitioners in law and education experienced it as a deterioration of professional status and disruption of their individual lives. Personal sacrifices seemed worthwhile as long as German troops were advancing and creating a greater Reich in which professionals might play a larger role. However, once Hitler's racial fanaticism began to defeat their fatherland, many practitioners started to wonder where following the Führer might lead them in the end.

THE WARPING OF PROFESSIONALISM

The indirect impact of the Second World War on the professions was as profound as it was contradictory. The exceptional nature of the situation created a confusing mixture of opportunities and threats. In order to determine whether professionalization advanced or declined between 1939 and 1945, several crucial issues need to be clarified: Were wartime measures a temporary distortion or the logical culmination of Hitler's policies? Clearly emergency responses common to all belligerents, Nazi radicalization toward a racial "SS state," and technical problem-solving imperatives often clashed with one another. Because initial victory (1939–1941), military stalemate (1942–1943), and impending defeat (1944–1945) produced different institutional arrangements and psychological reactions, any discussion must keep the timing of decisions in mind. Generalization should also take into account that various groups within a profession were affected in distinctive ways and that different occupations had conflicting experiences. Which criteria are to be used in judging professional dynamics? If certification, prosperity, and power are seen as decisive, then some groups are likely to have made demonstrable gains. However, when competence, ethics, and autonomy are considered crucial, the losses stand out more starkly.[47] The ambiguities and complexities of wartime professional behavior that ranged from cynical collaboration in the holocaust to humanitarian idealism make any assessment difficult: Did the final phase of the Third Reich foster or warp professionalism?

One indication of a growing malaise among experts was the steep decline of educational standards. The continual grumbling of philologues about the ignorance of their charges was borne out by the 28 percent wrong answers to thirty basic information questions of 1938 labor service draftees. During the war, complaints about gaps in elementary knowledge of primary school pupils reached such a crescendo that even the secret police agreed that "the erosion of school standards is becoming an ever more serious problem" nationwide. From all over the Reich, the Ministry of Education was deluged with warnings "that the great drop in achievements will do grave harm." Scathingly, the provincial president of Saxony listed such "extracurricular reasons" as HJ activism, excessive outside demands, public denigration of the school, uncooperative parents, and such internal causes as frequent interruptions, failure of concentration, lack of homework, and the missing ninth year. Stung by army criticism, Bernhard Rust acknowledged these "real difficulties," but he did not dare challenge the "false attitude" of his NS colleagues that lay behind them.[48] Under the euphemistic heading "improving performance in the high school," instructors publicly admitted the drop in achievement: "We must reawaken respect for thorough and patient work in the young and denounce anyone as vermin who opposes us in this." In an NSLB Gau leader conference, pedagogues suggested reducing course content, employing new teaching methods, concentrating on essentials, and using the limited time more effectively. Because war measures had gutted the curriculum, appeals for a "sharper selection and promotion of a work ethic" were bound to founder on the hostile "attitude of the young." Even ministerial directives for "safeguarding of school education within the framework of total war measures" were of little avail, because decrees could hardly restore learning to higher priority.[49]

Professors similarly complained about the drop in the performance of university students. Whereas jurists mentioned "the well-known fears of a deterioration of general training," technical experts deplored the "reduction of competence of young engineers" as a danger for war production. "We cannot and must not go on like this!" protested the engineering professor and old fighter William Gürtler to Hitler in March 1940: "If you don't intercede, the whole coming generation of young technicians will go to the devil." Their many new "social and national duties" necessarily meant that students' "purely professional performance declines." Military service and compression of the curriculum into six semesters left too little time for study: "If the training level was untenable before, we now experience a catastrophic drop in mastery of information."[50] The ensuing cabinet consultation by the Reich chancellery yielded a disturbing unanimity of complaints, since neither Education Minister Rust nor Student Leader Gustav Adolf Scheel denied the erosion of standards. The Army High Command especially castigated "the ever greater decline of knowledge, of logical thinking and clear expression as well as the decreasing command of the German language in word and speech." Only the causes of the deterioration were controversial, because their frank analysis would have uncovered the bankruptcy of Nazi educational policy. Because Chancellery Chief Heinrich Lammers did not dare present it to the Führer, this devastating verdict only led to the return from trimesters to semesters, and some reduction of extracurricular obligations. Hence, "the training level continue[d] to slip" so that students did "not even possess the most basic information" and lacked "the essential ability to concentrate as well as the necessary degree of logical thinking."[51] In order to improve the "intellectual quality of young professionals," the conference of university rectors recommended preparatory courses and more practical training, such as legal "practitioner workshops," pedagogical discussion groups, and technical internships. In the long term, this collapse of standards was bound to have, as Rust himself admitted, "catastrophic consequences for the performance of the professions."[52]

Another sign of trouble was the decrease in the number of students, who were discouraged from entering professional careers by their "extraordinarily bad prospects." During the call-up of 1939, enrollment in the old Reich dropped precipitously from an already low figure of 56,667 to an even lower 36,934 in the winter of 1939. After the early victories, the demand for "academic professionals" led to a reopening of institutions so that attendance recovered to 49,702 because of more liberal military leaves (winter 1940). However, the attack on the Soviet Union once again produced "a not inconsiderable drop in enrollment" to about 41,000 by the summer of 1941, before the stalemate allowed a recovery to 52,344 during the following winter. The increasing need for cadres pushed student numbers to a wartime peak of 64,783 in 1943–1944, but the total war mobilization depressed attendance to 55,495 in the following summer, before it entirely collapsed in the final winter. The curves of specific fields parallel the overall trend except for a surge in draft-exempt medicine, the surprising stability of teaching, and a greater fall in law and engineering (Table 7.1). In order to provide some new experts, male freshmen were allowed to enroll in three registration periods in the winters of 1940, 1941–1942, and 1942–1943 with 10,147, 15,026, and 12,646 students, respectively. Army cooperation was crucial, because 47.5 percent of the males were reassigned to study while another 11.2 percent were on training leaves during the summer of 1942. But after the Normandy invasion, almost all high school graduates, beginning students, and higher semesters in law and philosophy—except in the sciences—were drafted to military or labor service. When seventy-seven faculties had to close, while fifty-eight others stayed open only for advanced students, training virtually came to a halt.[53]

This enrollment decline drastically transformed the composition of future professionals. To resupply overburdened practitioners at all, the Nazi government was forced to renounce its prejudice and permit women to study in large numbers: "Concerning the strong increase of female students, current reports indicate that due to the enormous manpower deficit of experts it is quite useful that the great

Table 7.1. Professional Training during the Second World War

Year	Law	Teaching	Engineering	Percentage of 1939
1939	4,555	7,978	12,287	100
1939–1940	2,826	5,202	6,184	57.3
1940 (2nd Trimester)	2,978	8,009	7,112	72.4
1940–1941	2,981	9,076	6,955	76.6
1941	2,561	8,000+	5,609	65.1
1941–1942	4,578		9,950	
1942	2,820	8,000+	7,090	72.2
1942–1943	4,391		10,060	
1943			6,675	
1943–1944	3,625	12,156	8,516	97.9

gaps among men are to a certain degree filled by women,'' especially in medicine and teaching. By the year 1943, it became necessary to recruit female students actively, because ''it is imperative that more women study'' to compensate for the loss of manpower through war deaths. The defeat of sexism by labor needs was startling: While women constituted only 11.2 percent of higher education students in 1939, they represented 46.7 percent by 1943–1944. According to fragmentary evidence for the summer of 1944, three-quarters of the remaining enrollment was female! No longer completely immune, misogynist fields still proved difficult, because law only increased its 2.5 percent female share to 16.4 percent. In contrast, philological studies owed their popularity to women not only in the humanities (increasing from 35 percent to 82.5 percent) but also in the sciences (11.5 percent to 66.3 percent). Technical aversion against women, which ridiculed the Fräulein Ingenieur in print, hampered the recovery of engineering numbers. As a result of the stereotype of ''men of technology,'' women merely expanded their share from 2 percent to 17.4 percent, mostly in peripheral subjects like chemistry.[54] The enrollment decrease and feminization of inscriptions reinforced the Nazi trend toward social exclusivity. Professional self-recruitment remained at 28.2 percent, and the share of the propertied middle class stayed at 11.6 percent so that two-fifths of the new matriculations in 1941 once again stemmed from the upper middle reaches of society (Table A.2).[55]

Coupled with the delayed effects of the earlier enrollment drop, the wartime fluctuations aggravated the shortage of skilled labor. Although 986 law students passed the first state examination in 1939, only 281 did so a year later while those successful in the second *Staatsexamen* dropped from 3429 to 297 by 1942! At the same time, the number of doctorates in law decreased from 903 to 492 (Table A.5b). Prospective secondary schoolteachers fared little better, because new philological Referendare declined from 1803 (1939) to 922 (1940), while the number of doctor of philosophy recipients was cut in half (Table A.6b). Successful Diplom-Ingenieure sank even more precipitously from 2430 to 914, whereas in the United States the annual output was estimated at about 20,000![56] With the number of trainees shrinking from 5076 to 3290, lawyers complained about ''a great dearth of guardians of law,'' while teachers deplored the lack of replacements (due to mass retirements), and engineers discussed the ever greater shortage of fresh recruits. By early 1943, observers from all fields agreed ''that *the deficit of academic professionals is becoming a central problem,*'' not just because of war-induced contractions but due to ''the declining trend in the choice of educated callings by the young.'' According to an alarmist SD report, ''we count on a lack of 50 to 80,000 experts in a few years,'' and especially in technology and teaching more than half of the jobs were expected to go begging. Trying to upgrade quality, manpower planning needed to increase the number of high school graduates and make those professions ''with special shortages'' more lucrative and prestigious.[57]

In spite of efforts to increase supply by simplifying training and certification, the number of professionals steadily declined throughout the war. Every profession sought to attract entrants by propaganda, such as the NSBDT campaign for ''youth and technology'' in June 1944. Technical correspondence courses or legal ''soldier letters'' attempted to bridge the gap between the front and the university, while special courses allowed "mature" soldiers to gain a high school certificate.[58] In November 1939, the Ministry of Education reduced degree requirements, cutting the number of semesters to six, and dropping the HfL year, much to the relief of philologues. Bernhard Rust simplified the first state examination by canceling the "written thesis" and by taking "personal character and political performance" into account. Moreover, he reduced the training period before the second Staatsexamen to two years for lawyers and to one year for teachers, while in early 1941 he eliminated the Abitur for primary school pedagogues who thereby lost their academic status. As a result of special wartime circumstances, attorneys reluctantly acquiesced in the reduction of their Anwärterdienst to one year, losing most of their hard-won overcrowding defense.[59] Despite lessening hostility to the admission of women, the number of lawyers continued to drop throughout the war. Because each year 161 more attorneys left than entered the profession, their racially decimated total shrank from 14,913 in early 1939 to 14,193 in 1943. In contrast, the nominal number of Prussian philologues increased from 13,795 to 15,375 between 1939 and 1941, because annual hiring doubled from 586 to 1150. But Rust's plan to create more permanent positions in the spring of 1942 foundered on the "quite thin incoming cohorts" after the reserves of probationers were exhausted. Because many Studienräte were close to retirement, even male institutions began to hire female auxiliary instructors, pensioned educators were reemployed, and many politically disciplined pedagogues were reinstalled, if they were willing to swear their loyalty. For engineers, the demand grew so great that "technical students have ten to twenty good positions fall effortlessly into their lap," thereby "unfavorably influencing the performance of future engineers."[60]

Material inequality among professionals also increased during the struggle. Depending on career (some callings were rewarded more), gender (males did better), time (everything grew worse toward the end), place (cities had more opportunities), service (civilians were more affluent), politics (NS connections helped), battle (damage was more widespread in border areas), and luck (where bombs fell), practitioners profited or suffered from the fighting. "An effect of the reduction in business is the unfavorable and steadily deteriorating situation of the attorneys, reported uniformly from the whole Reich." A chamber survey of 1941 income elicited 12,631 responses that revealed a growing disparity: With 9.6 percent reporting less than 1000 marks, 12.8 percent less than 3000 marks, and another 14.7 percent less than 6000 marks, more than one-third of the attorneys were badly off. Earning between 6000 and 15,000 marks, the solid middle (38.1 percent) made a respectable living. However, 29.6 percent benefited by war profits handsomely, with 2.4 percent urban (e.g., Berlin, Leipzig) and eastern lawyers making more than 50,000 marks a year! The poor were the lawyers serving at the front (one-quarter sent no returns at all!), partially inactive practitioners older than 70 years of age (4.1 percent), and attorneys from smaller towns (e.g., Darmstadt, Bamberg) or overcrowded districts (e.g., Düsseldorf, Dresden). In 1942, among 636 Hamburg NSRB lawyers, 29.2 percent paid no dues at all as soldiers, 30.7 percent made less than 5000 marks, 20.6 percent earned a respectable 10,000 marks, and 19.5 percent received a healthy income of more than 15,000 marks. Figures for seventeen attorneys from the wealthy Danzig district revealed an average net income of 13,177 marks for the first *half* of 1942. When in 1943 the "abuse" of freely negotiated criminal fees threatened "to impair the prestige of the entire profession," the Ministry of Justice imposed upper limits, while the RRAK pleaded for peer review of excessive charges in order to stem profiteering.[61]

Dependent on fixed and modest state salaries, philologues were subject to hidden wartime inflation instead. Though complaining about the "evident underestimation of the teaching profession," secondary schoolteachers took some satisfaction in maintaining their lead over primary school pedagogues in their 1940 salary restructuring, which extended the niggardly Prussian scale to the rest of the Reich (Table A.12). In spite of slight pay increases, young people were uninterested in teaching because "these professions have not kept up with the development of other careers in their basic endowment, their later economic return and public prestige." If anything, teachers left their calling for more attractive occupations (1314 in 1941) because of "lack of advancement possibilities, bad pay and public disregard." One drafted pedagogue proposed a simple solution to the shortage: "First, more respect; second, more money!"[62] In contrast, the great demand for technical experts inflated earnings in spite of NS attempts to freeze wages. Interested in "mobilizing performance reserves through appropriate rewards," companies and individuals collaborated in a complex system of evasions, based on piece rates, profit sharing, overtime, special premiums, reassignments, and so on. Young researchers literally "fled out of science," because they could "multiply their university salaries in industry." In the year 1943, the typical income of an "experienced practitioner" at the Baildonhütte was 600 marks base pay and 136 marks premium, in other words, 8832 marks annually. The vehemence with which Todt condemned "the irresponsible practice" of corporate raiding and "excessive demands" for better pay suggests that engineering incomes rose considerably during the war.[63]

The social prestige of the professions, nevertheless, continued to erode during the fighting. The SS journal, *Schwarzes Korps,* fueled public resentment against attorneys by "exposing" such cases as the zealous defense of a hoarder by lawyer Dr. Gröpke as "professional *Paragraphenschusterei.*" As a result of this pressure, the Celle honor court condemned the unfortunate attorney to payment of 5000 marks because of his "service to illegality." The SS journalist, Gunther d'Alquen, complained that "the far-reaching disturbance, caused by such attorneys," undermined popular morale and demanded unquestioning allegiance to Nazism. Emphasizing that 95 percent of the guardians of law were doing their duty, RRAK leader Reinhard Neubert countered that the "use of expressions like shysters and hired guns which besmirch the entire legal profession in the eyes of the population goes too far."[64] In spite of appeals for self-discipline, the SS journal continued to vilify attorneys as "paid coolies" or "troublemakers" and recommended cleaning up "the whole breed of small dirt-throwers and sewage-rats" by assignment to the front. Justice Undersecretary Franz Schlegelberger protested with Martin Bormann that "these allegations constitute an unjustifiably general and formally deprecating criticism of an entire profession which threatens to have undesirable effects upon the national community."[65] Claiming that the public was less hostile to lawyers than often assumed, Justizrat Heinrich Ehlers reluctantly admitted that "attorneys are . . . much too often subject to silly caricature, foolish misrepresentation in film, play and literature as well as cheap object of malicious or thoughtless criticism.'' In contrast to their former ''high esteem,'' the legal professions were beginning to experience ''a crisis'' during the war.[66]

Philologues had to contend with widespread derision. ''Today the figure of the German educator is becoming a welcome substitute for the erstwhile clown,'' one instructor in uniform complained about the public's failure to understand ''that teachers also have a professional honor.'' In countless newspaper articles, stories, plays, films, radio broadcasts, and cabarets, pedagogues were the butt of cheap jokes. When the NSLB charged that his portrayal of a teacher as a ''malicious billy goat'' went beyond normal humor, Bruno Brehm replied: ''Instead of getting excited about such judgments, your profession would do well to ponder how they come about.''[67] Educators were also outraged that the film *Eine unentschuldigte Stunde* ''casts a completely false light on the teaching vocation so that it is considered barely good enough to be joked about and ridiculed in public.'' Because ''pedagogical authority will be diminished in the eyes of the pupils,'' the Reich press office issued a directive against deprecating teaching, the NSLB journal published a series of counterexposés, and Walter Fischer edited a volume of appreciative essays on former educators.[68] When attacks continued, NSLB leader Fritz Wächtler demanded a more comprehensive defense:

> Ridiculing the teaching profession endangers the authority of state and school, undercuts the success of instruction, destroys educator morale and willingness to work for the national community, makes it harder to attract teachers, is undignified towards foreign countries and signifies a cultural disgrace towards colleagues at the front and fallen comrades as well as towards new Nazi pedagogues. In terms of national politics, this condition is a grave danger which can only be overcome through quick and radical measures by the state and the party.

Although Goebbels ordered ''the steady caricaturing of teachers in all public media'' to cease, poking fun at educators was too deeply ingrained to be stopped by executive fiat or by strenuous NSLB efforts.[69]

In contrast, the war offered opportunities to improve the status of engineers. Although technicians had a ''second-class position'' in the military, Albert Speer's appointment as armament minister ''placed the calling and the prestige of the engineer onto a new level in the social order and more precisely in the hierarchy of occupations and professions.''[70] The NSBDT section for ''professional questions'' zealously watched over the title Ingenieur, opposing the creation of ''sound engineers'' and the ''promotion of employees to engineers by firms'' to evade the pay freeze, because inappropriate ''business, personal and other reasons play a great role.'' Instead, Gebhard Himmler tried to differentiate the ''professional designation'' technician (at once more comprehensive and inferior) from the appellation engineer, creating for the latter a special NSBDT procedure, to be based on ''achievement, character and political attitude.'' Applicants with ''inferior or no training'' might gain the coveted diploma, if they could ''prove at least eight years of engineer-like work'' or ''extraordinary contributions'' to technology. Even the lack of political credentials might not be fatal, because the NSBDT was willing to turn lukewarm technicians into fervent Nazis.[71] Starting with 14 cases in 1939, this certification quickly expanded to 175 applicants in 1940, approved more than 300 engineers in 1941, and registered 519 in 1942 so that there were 1183 new "NSBDT engineers" by May 1943. In spite of a clearer demarcation of the lower border toward "masters, technicians and lab workers," tensions continued between graduates of technical institutes and higher schools. However, NSBDT engineers congratulated one another on the technicians' growing "legitimacy," and recognition within the national community.[72]

The fighting also disrupted professional practice. Lawyers vigorously defended their field when their "business contracted" faster than their number due to "a sharp decline of litigation, the creation of occupational legal advising and other measures." When many districts reported a reduction of 20 to 30 percent by early 1940, Roland Freisler appointed some attorneys as judges, tried to place them in other government departments—especially in the East—and attempted to defend their title against misuse.[73] Because advocates were being "pushed out of the area of tax and business advising," the ministry created chamber representatives for the 1200 tax lawyers and forbade joint practice with accountants as a conflict of interest. In May 1941, the RRAK changed the term from "specialist in tax law" to the simpler "tax consultant" and founded an Institute for Applied Law in Berlin to improve training. Unable to prevent the emergence of a separate occupation of *Steuerberater,* attorneys now saw corporate syndics as important allies in professional competition.[74] Efforts to exclude lawyers came to a head in June 1943 when Martin Bormann complained that attorneys increasingly "interfere in matters beyond their competence," such as intervening in "debates between party offices with citizens," draft issues, economic disputes, or labor service problems. Appalled by this "far-reaching limitation of legal practice," Reinhard Neubert protested that "questions of fact and law blend" and claimed the right of "advice and representation before *all* offices," because shady "interest representatives" would otherwise emerge. Unsympathetic to solicitor problems, Georg Thierack reassured Bormann that the party could decide on when to admit lawyers and that draft and labor service questions were not legal matters, only defending economic activities as "somewhat traditional." After further pressure, the ministry prohibited draft representation, reduced the attorneys' role in party matters largely to advising, and limited economic or labor practice to "difficult questions," sanctioning a further restriction of legal practice.[75]

Working conditions for lawyers deteriorated as well. Much of the business of the remaining attorneys consisted of mandatory substitution for drafted colleagues. For established practitioners, it was an onerous duty that involved considerable travel and brought little reward because the receipts went to their colleagues' families. For probationers, deputizing was an opportunity to gain experience, but the practice continued to belong to the returning veteran. Although the profession claimed to be 30 percent oversubscribed, local shortages of attorneys forced lawyers from neighboring districts or industrial firms to provide legal services.[76] The wartime expansion of SS powers also made criminal defense more difficult. Because the police generally resisted an attorney's unrestricted access to his client's files, it became increasingly difficult to create a defensive case. Unsympathetic to the legal duty of confidentiality, the secret service tried to coerce practitioners into assisting the prosecution, even sending uncooperative solicitors to concentration camps. One Old Fighter wondered how attorneys could advise clients when party organs were clearly "above existing law," and another attorney warned that arbitrary police measures "endanger the healthy sense of justice." When the security forces complained about legal objections to "interrogation methods," Minister of Justice Thierack reminded attorneys of their duty to cooperate without generalizing "possible reservations about the correctness of confessions." Increasingly, lawyers refused to take dangerous criminal cases, claiming ill health, "overwork," insufficient pay, lack of access to jailed clients, preconceived judgments, and "political reasons," such as party or police censure. Legal defense became a deadly contest between a merciless state machinery and a few courageous advocates who managed the internal contradictions of the Nazi system. Although exceptional men like Horst Berkowitz, Dietrich Güstrow, or Paul Ronge occasionally successfully defended an accused client, war conditions favored the prosecution and escalated punishments brutally, thus meting out "crying injustice."[77]

Teachers similarly had to defend their pedagogical authority against the continuing encroachments of the Hitler Youth. Arguing that formal instruction "has completely failed in the crucial question of German education," the HJ demanded political and personal training, because "the school is not supposed to educate, only to transmit knowledge!" To eliminate persistent local frictions, Bernhard Rust and HJ chief Arthur Axmann agreed, in January 1941, on reserving mornings for instruction and turning afternoons over to the HJ and the parents (with two days entirely free of homework), while limiting trips to vacation periods. Among teachers, "the prevailing impression was that the school was 'retreating' before the HJ and giving up important methods of school-education." Neither the introduction of a special Hitler Youth teacher nor the establishment of HJ camps to recruit pedagogues was able to bridge the gap between youthful activism and adult instruction.[78] Tension increased again when the Bavarian ministry announced the creation of a Hitler Youth class leader in May 1942 to help improve discipline by "carrying the HJ spirit" into the school. "The intended measure will merely create bad blood without having any positive effect," NSLB head Wächtler fumed, suggesting that "the HJ ought to encourage love for learning in its own ranks to make up for its sins (knowledge is power!!!). The school will only be able to fulfill its task if it is left alone by the HJ." The NSLB protested with the party chancellery that putting class leaders on a level with teachers would create "quite an unclear legal situation" and "trigger widespread resentment and outrage among pedagogues," because it was "incompatible with their professional honor." The struggle between scholarly philologues and the uniformed HJ continued during the war, because it not only derived from generational tensions but also involved fundamental power over the classroom in examination and grading in which no compromise was possible. Clashes might be avoided if HJ educators dominated a school or if a resolute principal managed to fend off interference. However, with neither the Hitler Youth nor the teachers about to yield, in the majority of cases conflict was inevitable and endemic.[79]

Maintaining regular instruction during war conditions was frustrating. Increasingly, provincial reports began to warn of "the disintegration of scholarly teaching," because schoolbooks and supplies began to disappear, there was no heat in the winter, and classes were often cancelled or taught by substitutes while pupils were constantly collecting trash, healing herbs, and mushrooms, or assisting in the harvest. No wonder that pedagogues grumbled in print: "The war has rendered professional teaching more difficult through the merging of classes, the increase in the work load and the growth of extracurricular demands." Educators had to volunteer for countless duties such as helping with rationing cards, participating in voluntary associations, writing reports, or leading collections:

> Often filling out some forms and statistical surveys is considered more important than teaching young people. One should remember that today instruction is already gravely impaired [by] lack of teachers due to the vacancy of tens of thousands of positions, military service of a high proportion of educators, aging of the profession from lack of newcomers, insufficient supply of teaching and learning materials, cancellation of classes through bombing alarms and coal vacations, inconsistency of curriculum and textbooks, etc.

Maintaining discipline also grew more difficult. A dangerous "bitterness, disgust, pessimism and resignation . . . dominate large circles of teachers" because of the widespread "disregard for intellectual work." The more perceptive philologues viewed the intellectual erosion of their instructional efforts as "dequalification."[80]

Particularly disruptive was nighttime bombing. Not only did air raids destroy school buildings, homes, and factories, but they also delayed the beginning of instruction by several hours on the following morning with both pupils and teachers irritable from lack of sleep. In late 1940, Rust agreed to send urban children into less endangered rural areas in a voluntary *Kinderlandverschickung,* and urged educators to cooperate with the NSV and HJ in charge (Table 7.2). By the spring of 1944, some 329 high schools were involved, 15 percent of the total with 22.1 percent of all pupils and one-quarter of the remaining staff (while another 15.9 percent of the students was relocated privately). Although regular teachers like Alfred Ehrentreich accompanied the children, camp conditions were often problematic, there were continual frictions with party offices, and—ministerial injunctions notwithstanding—instruction became quite irregular. Many philologues were reluctant to participate in the KLV, since it disrupted their pedagogical work and complicated their personal life. Finally, the drafting of sixteen to seventeen-year-old boys as air-defense helpers *(Flakhelfer)* often undermined teaching in the upper grades, even if their service occasionally included some class hours.[81]

Table 7.2. High School Relocation, Spring 1944[a]

Origin of Institution	Number	Destination	Number
Berlin	135	Bohemia	44
Rhine	55	Pomerania	37
Westphalia	54	Bavaria	34
Bavaria	19	Saxony	27
Württemberg	17	Württemberg	27
Others	49	Others	124

[a]Number of camps	Pupils	HJ leaders	Teachers	Family homes
3,128	147,432	5,408	7,601	106,002

Although the war challenged technical ingenuity, it rendered engineering work more difficult. Because of Germany's limited resources, the key task was "to increase productivity" through "rationalizing production" by "complete elimination of manual labor." In practice, streamlining production proved a laborious task. To make up for the lack of raw materials, Fritz Todt in early 1940 appealed for "collecting all the unused metal in factories and workshops" as a birthday present to Hitler. The VDI propagated the substitution of "wood and coal as solid fuels" for motor vehicles in order to stretch limited oil reserves. Instead of supervising skilled workers, technicians now had to instruct unskilled women, motivate reluctant slave laborers, and drive on badly treated prisoners of war.[82] Allied bombing also complicated engineering efforts. Not only did air raids require extensive protection of factories, public buildings, or homes as well as tenacious rebuilding of damaged production capacity, but they also necessitated the physical relocation of entire plants into safer rural areas, which caused much disruption for everyone involved. All these tasks demanded endless overtime, because, as Robert Ley warned in May 1941: "Drones and slaves have no right to live in Nazi Germany and we want to eliminate both from our community." Whereas physical laborers received extra rations, white-collar personnel got only normal allocations that were ever shrinking. By the year 1943, the SD registered an increasing number of reports "about the decline of intellectual vigor and productivity of mental workers (e.g., teachers, professors, lawyers, officials, doctors, technicians)." Working to the limit of their ability, engineers were especially susceptible to deficiency symptoms such as performance loss, lack of concentration, fatigue, and irritability.[83]

The war heightened the conflict between Nazi demands for ideological conformity and professional traditions of ethical autonomy. After an initial honor court amnesty, strengthening the home front necessitated tighter supervision of the judiciary, since "diverse ill-considered statements of defense attorneys" were having a "negative effect on morale." When the SS attacked advocates in the *Schwarzes Korps,* increasing disciplinary power through temporary suspension was no longer enough: "It goes without saying that a lawyer who has misbehaved will no longer be allowed to practice his profession."[84] Although Neubert warned that "the demands of scrupulous representation of clients should not lead to transgressions," the ineffectiveness of such self-discipline prompted bureaucratic intervention in June 1941: "If an attorney endangers important political matters by violating his duties, the Minister of Justice can temporarily or permanently forbid him to practice his profession, irrespective of any other action."[85] When "grave infractions" continued, the last vestiges of autonomy were abolished. Complaining about "the lack of ideological firmness of some attorneys," Deputy Justice Minister Schlegelberger in July 1942 suggested "more severe punishment by honor courts . . . closer political coordination of the views of all solicitors," and "the expulsion" of unsuitable practitioners. Nonetheless, the SD continued to report "a not inconsiderable number of cases which show that lawyers have not yet brought their practice into accord with war necessities" by defending "criminals of war, enemies of the state." To preserve "a healthy, self-governing legal profession," the RRAK issued another "serious warning to [its] professional comrades" to "endorse the Führer's work without reservations."[86] Fearing "that the survival of attorneys is endangered if they are not brought closer to the state," the Ministry of Justice drafted a law ''eliminating old, economically weak'' practitioners as well as ''tightening honor courts through participation of judges.''[87]

In spite of attorney resistance, ''the assumption of discipline by the state'' proved inevitable. NSRB leader Heinrich Droege protested that the ''emasculation of the chamber system'' made many lawyers ''doubt the future of their profession and arouse[d] bitterness and resentment.'' Similarly, Justizrat Ehlers argued that ''limiting free advocacy so as to eliminate it in effect'' would be ''a very big *mistake,''* because the people needed ''the assurance or at least the partial illusion, that there is an office in the legal system which, endowed with a certain autonomy, can serve as receiver, safety-valve and mouthpiece of private cares and wishes.'' However, obsessed with profiteering, partisanship, and negative publicity, Minister of Justice Thierack considered state ''leadership and supervision of attorneys'' essential for solving ''the crisis of the legal profession.''[88] In December 1942, Martin Bormann demanded stricter control, because ''instances in which the actions of lawyers in civil and criminal litigation must be criticized have increased considerably.'' Citing twenty-two ''exemplary cases of how a lawyer should not practice his profession,'' Hitler's henchman castigated ''the complete failure of the honor courts'' and insisted on ''a tight, severe, and unified discipline'' and additional indoctrination. Hastening to comply, the Ministry of Justice proposed an age limit of sixty-five (without retirement plan), OLG supervision of the chambers, and ''the transfer of control to the administrative courts which already rule on duty violations of . . . judges and notaries for the duration of the war.'' Proclaimed on March 1, 1943, this revision of the attorney code abolished cherished autonomy, purportedly in order to ''preserve the freedom of advocacy.'' Because the new provisions, such as mandatory pensioning, were to be applied ruthlessly against ''political and ideological'' deviants, even Neubert admitted that they ''strongly trouble lawyers.''[89]

This ''sharpest conceivable vote of no confidence'' deepened the ''grave crisis of confidence of the legal profession.'' When the supervising courts recommended suspensions more frequently, attorneys ''suffer[ed] from the bitter feeling of no longer being an equal partner in the administration of justice.'' Disposed toward leniency in cases of shady dealings, transvestism, deafness, or divorce tampering, the Saxon OLG president recommended expulsion because of a Jewish wife, dishonesty, unscrupulousness, carelessness, freemasonry, greed, and lack of competence.[90] To counter the impression ''that the legal profession is dying out,'' NSRB leaders insisted on the ''indispensability of lawyers'' and argued that the loss of formal autonomy ''restored the inner freedom'' of advocates from dependence on a client. Reassuring practitioners that ''attorneys remain a free profession,'' Georg Thierack criticized profiteering as well as individualism and emphasized ''strengthening the will to victory'' by harsh criminal punishments and suppression of civil litigation. ''The new and difficult challenges of crimes against the war . . . , the prohibition of intercourse with prisoners and the [proper] treatment of foreigners, Poles and Eastern workers'' could only be met by stronger control.[91] Therefore, the ministry demanded notification of disciplinary steps and ordered OLG presidents to keep a tight rein on unruly lawyers. To communicate the ''goals of the judicial leadership'' and guarantee ''strict coordination'' of practice, Minister of Justice Thierack in October 1944 issued the first and only ''lawyer letter,'' which was full of negative examples of excessive pleading and prolonging cases. Instead of retreating into the safety of civil law, competent attorneys should volunteer to ''defend enemies of the state and popular parasites'' in such a manner as to speed victory.[92]

Though less liberal in tradition, secondary schoolteachers also experienced an increasing conflict between indoctrination and instruction. Pondering ''the war and professional ethics,'' Otto Nehring argued that the Third Reich changed the content as well as process of education, thereby ''not destroying, but transforming'' the teacher's role. The new wartime tasks strained even the idealism of ''true pedagogues'' by the derogatory ''manner of justifying the constant compulsion [to volunteer] which had to undermine professional morale.'' Coupled with references to the drop in standards, this candid admission by a devoted Nazi demonstrates widespread teacher discontent during the summer of 1944, stemming less from the rehiring of dismissed ''unreliable'' colleagues than from the ''disturbance of instruction by the war.''[93] Émigré appeals to ''renew German education in the spirit of democratic pedagogy and real humanism'' hardly reached practitioners. However, in spite of zealous persecution by Nazi superiors, lingering religious, socialist, or Jewish countertraditions provided some alternative perspectives and personal networks of support. The Gestapo characterized nonconformist teacher Ernst Faust as ''an incorrigible griper and trouble-maker who poisons the souls of children . . . with corrosive ideas,'' creating ''the impression of wanting to fight against the Nazi state.'' Eventually, the steady deterioration of teaching conditions through the KLV or air defense duty and ever more blatant indoctrination made philologues doubt the possibility of serving both the transmission of knowledge and the instilling of NS ideology. ''Especially the best educators show psychological weariness and bitter resignation.''[94]

In contrast, engineers were less vocal about their frustrations with the Nazi system. Occasionally some would grumble about overwork and insufficient food. ''It is clear that under these circumstances, many engineers cannot understand why the mechanic next to them receives more food while they themselves remain empty-handed.'' Moreover, technicians resented bureaucratic red tape and party control. According to the SD, ''the pay-freeze and [prohibition] of changing jobs [were] circumvented'' frequently, much to the chagrin of those who were left out. As ''men of action,'' engineers were also incensed when a promising invention such as the creation of an ''insulation hose from scrap materials'' was vetoed by a rigid superior. Others hid from the draft in consulting ''engineering-bureaus,'' which were occupied with projects of questionable priority. A courageous few like Fritz Graebe took pity on their Jewish workers and tried to save them from extermination by requisitioning them as essential to the war effort. Because the NSBDT switched from indoctrination to practical problem solving after 1943, it only rarely censured a colleague such as Kurt Schumann who had been punished for ridiculing the government and the army. Although engineers increasingly chafed at the rapid deterioration of their working conditions, few technicians held the Nazi regime responsible for their predicament. ''When will we strike back, if our engineers, technicians and workers are only now working on the weapons which we need to retaliate?'' one exasperated Ruhr engineer pondered after a devastating air raid in the summer of 1943. ''I am afraid that our counter-attack will come too late.'' At most, the realization of economic inferiority encouraged occasional defeatism.[95]

The war also circumscribed the influence of NS professional affiliates. When the NSRB resumed activity in 1940, the RRAK consistently failed ''to consult the section head for attorneys'' in controversial questions. In adjudicating the struggle between lawyer league and chamber over ''sole organizational competence,'' Franz Schlegelberger reserved ''the final consultation of the political authorities'' for his own ministry.[96] Personally put in charge by Hitler, Georg Thierack ordered the NSRB to retreat from legal policy and to concentrate on ''comprehensive leadership of men and, most immediately, the care of drafted colleagues and of fallen soldiers' families.'' This February 1943 reorientation robbed the league of political purpose, and functionaries were ''distressed that professional questions are no longer to be treated at all.''[97] The proclamation of total war further reduced NSRB power. Considered ''indispensable for the ideological orientation of German lawyers,'' the league escaped complete shutdown, but Thierack simplified its structure into ''three columns for justice, administration and finance or business'' in the summer of 1943. With dues suspended, the NSRB turned its annual budget of 4,187,000 marks over to the party treasury, and slashed its personnel from 187 to 67 full-time employees, because future activities were to be carried out by volunteers.[98] Limited ''chiefly to indoctrination,'' the league saw its ''most important task as *leading the members towards the NS movement*'' in order to overcome the crisis of the legal profession. To guarantee ''unified NS legal practice'' through an ''applied Nazi ethics,'' discussions dealt candidly with frustrations, such as exclusion by the bureaucracy, practice of Mischlinge, defense of parasites or traitors, access to files, pension plans, and so on. By March 1944, 142 weekend workshops reached 4197 NSRB members, among them 570 attorneys, while 28 day meetings drew in another 1898 with 210 lawyers and evening sessions attracted an even bigger number.[99] After the emasculation of the league, membership declined to 99,866 in 1944, including 12,132 attorneys, and 5767 lawyer–notaries.[100]

The struggle of the NSLB for survival was even less successful. A lengthy memorandum on its ''tasks and achievements during the war'' tried to make the teachers' league seem indispensable. With the slogan, ''everything for victory!'' Fritz Wächtler charged the NSLB to ''involve all of school life in the great war experience,'' as well as to ''mobilize all forces among the educators . . . for the performance of vital war tasks.'' The philologue section busied itself with

> increased introduction of military education into individual subjects; [meeting] army demands . . . for pupil selection . . . ; measures against the decline of standards . . . ; collection of experiences about the effect of the high-school reform . . . ; evaluation of newly introduced textbooks . . . ; the issue of foreign languages . . . ; the question of merging both types of girls' schools; discussion of important and pressing school and instructional questions; educational support of German populations abroad; [and] caring for aspiring high-school teachers, especially young comrades in uniform.

In order to ''deepen and secure NS attitudes'' as well as prepare educators for their greater leadership tasks, wartime indoctrination focused on the political situation, "the new European order," the German national and racial structure, and "ideology and school."[101] Between 700 and 800 flag ceremonies, discussion groups, and weekend workshops reached more than 57,000 teachers in 1941 and 1942. However, high school instructors remained reluctant, constituting only 17.5 percent of 895 Gau-speakers, while less than one-third subscribed to their journal *Die Deutsche Höhere Schule*. NSLB pressure to "volunteer" for nightly air raid duty in the school, collection of "food from the forest," and teaching evacuated children did little to enhance its popularity. In spite of considerable assets (48 million marks in 1943), the teachers' league failed to pay taxes (owing 1,284,000 marks for 1937–1938) and Wächtler's personal extravagance forced it into party receivership in 1941. Bormann peremptorily suspended the NSLB beginning in February 18, 1943, allowing only a skeleton staff of 22 to continue ministering to 362,855 nominal members. Although the bureaucracy was delighted to have its party rival shut down, philologues thereby lost the last remnant of collective representation.[102]

In contrast, the NSBDT prospered in the Second World War. The appointment of Fritz Todt as "Inspector General" of the Four-Year Plan and Armament Minister in the spring of 1940 assigned political and industrial technicians an important role in the committees that coordinated the war economy. In a plan for a "Higher Office for Technology and Economics," Karl Saur developed a blueprint for extensive technocratic powers in 1941. To compensate for the paper shortage, the NSBDT Reich speaker system sought to blend "the latest information" on armament techniques with more thorough indoctrination through "continuing education and professional training." Reaching 385,000 participants, 553 approved speakers delivered more than 1800 lectures in late 1941, with about 10 percent of the 5434 talks in the first half of 1942 directly addressing political themes. The NSBDT section for "professional questions" continued mobilizing free professional technicians, safeguarding the title of consulting engineers, supplying "technical experts," and providing a modicum of services.[103] Less interested in ideology than performance, Albert Speer consolidated the NSBDT into ten "technical-scientific associations" within five *Reichsfachgruppen* and tightened supervision over affiliates through a new constitution in late 1942. The technicians' league survived the "total war" cuts better than other groups, losing only its *Die Deutsche Technik* while keeping the leading VDI journals. However, its refusal to act as an "interest group in supporting its members" made the NSBDT notoriously unsuccessful in attracting the majority of practitioners. Among 2357 engineers in 66 local groups of Gau Upper Bavaria, only 444 joined the league, indicating "that two-thirds are outside of our ranks." More associational life took place in the "technical-scientific" affiliates such as the VDI, the membership of which soared close to 60,000 by 1944. Ironically, the demands of warfare put priority on apolitical problem solving, thereby guaranteeing the survival of some associational latitude in the technical professions.[104]

Though offering exciting challenges, the protracted war ultimately had a negative effect on professionals. Once the disruption of mobilization had been overcome, practice contracted or expanded according to military necessity and Nazi policy. Some developments such as the reintroduction of tax law, the turn to more flexible pedagogy, and some technical innovations (e.g., television) occurred independent of the fighting or of NS rule. In other instances, such as the return of women to the universities and to limited professional roles, the imperatives of the struggle demanded that NS ideology be compromised. Performance pressure, growing more desperate with total war, devalued indoctrination and created new freedom from SS control. However, many wartime measures also represented an anticipatory realization of longheld Nazi desires, which could be more easily instituted during a national emergency. For instance, the shift of political repression outside of the regular judicial system, the deintellectualization of instruction, and the instrumentalization of technology for genocide were accelerated through the special circumstances that muzzled dissent. For some careers, especially medicine or engineering, and individuals within others, such as SS lawyers or military instructors, the Second World War offered rewarding opportunities for a time. However, when the *Wehrmacht* began to retreat and fighting reached the home front, practice became frustrating and began to disintegrate. For most professionals, such as attorneys or teachers, the carnage impaired standards, created personnel shortages, imposed material hardship, fostered status insecurity, complicated practice, corroded ethics, and destroyed association. By partly advancing but largely hampering expert work, Hitler's war fundamentally warped professionalism.[105]

PROFESSIONALISM INSTRUMENTALIZED

After five years of struggle, few professionals doubted the outcome of the war, because frantic defensive efforts were becoming a "farce." With the Red Army advancing into German territory, "the greatest national catastrophe" threatened "each family and individual with the severest consequences." In the summer of 1944, training virtually came to a halt, when 15,560 student-soldiers were recalled to active service, and 4393 males and 26,403 females drafted to civilian duty. With two-thirds of the students gone, university classes were cancelled and orderly examination ceased a few months later. While state officials continued to receive some pay, many white-collar employees were laid off and free professionals saw their income vanish because of the contraction of litigation except for disputes about air raid damage.[106] "The bombing terror" increasingly disrupted practice. In those "cities, where most of the offices were downtown, attorneys were unable to function" when their files were lost. With many school buildings destroyed or requisitioned as hospitals and refugee centers, teaching had to be suspended, because pupils had largely been evacuated, were engaged in labor service, or tried to fight the invaders as HJ cannon fodder in the Volkssturm. Even if it reduced red tape, the destruction of factories, transport, and communication eventually overwhelmed the engineers' improvisation talents, bringing production to a halt.[107] Once the fighting reached German soil and food grew scarce, educated people "realized that the war was lost." Some fatalists started to live only for the day; the disheartened or compromised prepared for suicide; others began to plan for a future after Hitler. Still seeking "to combat defeatism," the NSRB was shut down on October 1, 1944, making it even harder to "keep the guardians of law politically in line."[108] Although some zealots sought to maintain morale by meting out death sentences, Nazi authority dissolved in chaos even before the

Allied troops arrived. Instead of inspiring desperate defense, looming defeat unleashed an unseemly scramble for survival.

The war accentuated the political divisions among professionals. A small band of ideological fanatics, who happened also to be university graduates, marks one extreme on the continuum between unquestioned allegiance and implacable hostility to Hitler. Men like Roland Freisler, Hans Schemm, or Georg Feder were more National Socialists than professionals. Because their motivation was primarily political, these Old Fighters took pride in their party work and resolved the increasing tension between ideology and professionalism unhesitatingly in favor of the former.[109] A second limited group of enthusiasts sincerely believed in both National Socialism and professionalism, valiantly trying to reconcile them with each other. The last leader of the Philologenverband Kurt Schwedtke, VDI chairman Heinrich Schult, or RRAK president Reinhard Neubert propagated both "unreserved dedication to the work of the Führer" and the preservation of a "healthy, self-governing legal profession." Although these practitioners defended their calling internally against zealots, they helped enforce the nazification of their colleagues externally, thereby suffering a persistent role conflict.[110] More numerous were the opportunists to whom the Third Reich offered intoxicating career chances. Not that their embrace of the Führer need have been totally cynical. However, the national renewal also promised to remedy, in Albert Speer's words, "the persistent stagnation of my professional life." Though prominent, these latecomers saw their Nazism as well as their expertise as means to success rather than as ends in themselves. Finally, there were the traditional nationalists like Franz Gürtner who supported an authoritarian professionalism. Once allied with Hitler, such members of the old elite stayed on, ostensibly to prevent the worst, even if continuing in office meant compromising their convictions.[111]

The attitude of the majority of practitioners is more difficult to fathom, because their forced outward compliance often masked inner reservations. The largest group were the unthinking collaborators, a curious mélange of "*Mitläufer,* profiteers, cowards, credulous idiots, [and] superficial" people. Formally members of the appropriate professional affiliate and sometimes nominally belonging to the NSDAP *(Karteimitglieder)* as a kind of camouflage, these men were content to carry on as long as the government provided suitable conditions for their work. Some experts like the Hamburg school administrator Fritz Köhne even played a dangerous double game of formal complicance and informal integrity. Recurrent Nazi complaints about practitioner apathy indicate that their ideological convictions tended to be only skin deep. Prevalent in law and education, such Mitläufer shaded over into neutral professionals who were preoccupied with technical tasks and largely oblivious to party demands. Growing ideological pressure and deteriorating practice pushed many to withdraw into "professionalism" as a kind of nonpolitical refuge, according to the motto: "Try to get through this time without getting your hands or your conscience dirty." Such experts sought to preserve a small corner of objectivity within the irrational system by maintaining nonpolitical standards in the courts, the classroom, or the factory, deciding case by case between the demands of competence and NS ideology. A final cluster were the practitioners who risked working in the system, without necessarily being enamored of the Nazis, in order to express their own creativity. Often at the peak of their professional powers, they were willing to make "some sacrifices" of their principles to advance their chosen field, regardless of the political use of their expertise. No matter what their secret feelings, such specialist collaborators, through competent performance, contributed to the prolongation of the war and indirectly facilitated the holocaust.[112]

Beyond this mute mass, a growing number of professionals rejected Hitler's policies in their private life, work place, and sometimes even in public. Many university graduates disassociated themselves from the plebeian Nazi style by creating a personal cultural sphere. In conversation, the use of irony, of *double entendre,* or excessive compliance could break the spell by ridiculing NS pretensions—much to the exasperation of fanatics who found it difficult to prove disloyalty. Drawing on ethical traditions, other practitioners tried to resist within their professional domain. At the risk of disbarment, some attorneys, like Dietrich Güstrow, honestly defended their clients in politicized cases; at the risk of expulsion, some teachers, such as Otto Schumann, intrepidly pursued the truth and tried to transmit "true culture" instead of indoctrinating their pupils; at the risk of being sent to a concentration camp, some engineers, like Julius Braun, rationally questioned the outcome of the war.[113] When it became clear that professional integrity could not halt the impending defeat, a courageous few went even so far as to join the political resistance. Either they were inspired, like the Marxist teacher Kurt Adams (Hamburg) and the Protestant philologue Elisabeth Forck (Bremen), by strong ideological commitment. Or they drew, like the international lawyer Helmut James von Moltke and former advocate Peter Graf York von Wartenburg, the cofounders of the "Kreisau circle," upon ethical convictions centered in their professionalism to reject Hitler's travesty of justice. Most of those who dared prepare the overthrow of Nazi rule, such as the Catholic lawyer Josef Müller or the Socialist teacher Adolph Reichwein, paid with their lives for the realization that professionalism and National Socialism were essentially incompatible. Among the eighty-three left-wing parliamentarians who were murdered, there were four lawyers and two teachers, but no engineers. Because resistance professionals tended to be sincere patriots, they especially suffered, in the words of an anonymous poet, from "being called traitor[s] in this brazen time."[114]

In spite of tightening control, the defeat ultimately shattered Hitler's hold on professionals. At first the militarization of life and the surprising victories consolidated the power of NS zealots over the professions. However, when the attack on the Soviet Union froze in its tracks during the winter of 1941, perceptive experts like Fritz Todt began to realize that the Third Reich was losing the production race and demanded peace. The growing chasm between professional ideals and NS practice led even the fanatic Hans Frank to warn publicly that the national community needed to be founded upon law. Although the party still attracted young, female, rural, or semiprofessionals, established practitioners grew weary of NS appeals, except for an occasional engineer (Tables A.14–A.17).[115] When ever more massive bombing raids brought destruction to the home front in 1943, opportunists such as Paul Kleinewefers "began to have the first doubts about a favorable outcome of the war for Germany." Crushing defeats made collaborators less pliable, encouraged critics to obstruct party desires, and inspired the desperate July 20, 1944 assassination attempt upon Hitler, which failed because "the faith in the demonic personality is still too strong." Disturbed by rumors of SS atrocities and losses of loved ones, realists despaired of saving their country from the catastrophe while optimists still hoped "something will happen to prevent this end." By the spring of 1945, the failure of the "miracle weapons" to stem the Allied onslaught led to "a galloping crisis of confidence in the leadership" responsible for the impending defeat. "The deep disappointment of abused trust creates a feeling of sadness, dejection, bitterness and rising anger among the people." With fanatics isolated and idealists dispirited, the majority of opportunists, collaborators, or apolitical practitioners at last joined the private, professional, and political critics in deserting the discredited regime.[116]

Did the Third Reich, by design or default, "enormously advance professionalization?" Undoubtedly doctors gained greater dominance over patients, psychologists and psychotherapists "established professional and institutional status," and engineers obtained more social esteem and influence. The prior impetus toward professionalization continued in some careers (e.g., primary school pedagogues), while specific Nazi policies such as the reduction of the sickness funds, the creation of a diploma in psychology, or the public honors for technology favored useful expert groups. Coupled with nationalist appeals, these concrete advantages presented powerful incentives for collaboration with the regime.[117] However, if unqualified, such a positive image of NS professionalization can be seriously misleading. Advances in the knowledge, wealth, or organizational power of professions between 1933 and 1945 were fragile, often to be reversed by the Second World War, which cannot be disassociated from Hitler's policies. Moreover, professionals could only prosper individually or collectively as long as they did the bidding of their Nazi masters—a favor that could be revoked at a moment's notice when conflicts arose. Finally, the ethical price for such gains was appalling: Were not the infamous euthanasia, concentration camp experiments, and eugenic sterilizations, the fitness testing of soldiers for the front, or the building of engines of death and destruction a perversion of expertise? In the midst of the crumbling Reich, the philologue Otto Schumann blamed a mixture of "idealism and honest stupidity, laziness, herd mentality, opportunism, worship of success, weakness, cowardice, fear and common ambition" for the collaboration of professionals that led "to this terrible and inescapable misery."[118]

A broader and more morally sensitive perspective suggests that Hitler's rule led to deprofessionalization instead. Although experts were essential to the Third Reich, they were instrumentalized for inhuman ends, eventually losing many of their prized privileges as well as their autonomy and *Berufsethos,* which formed the core of their professional self-esteem. From being essential partners, lawyers were reduced to serving as minor cogs in an administration of injustice. From imparting knowledge, philologues were restricted to indoctrinating in a school system that "educated" pupils in anti-intellectualism. From advancing human welfare through technology, engineers were redirected toward designing machines for mass maiming and killing. The Nazi war not only led to a deterioration of practitioners' lives, but also fundamentally subverted the ethical purpose of professionalism. Improperly trained beginners, experts serving at the front, women doing men's work without male rewards, political opponents laboring in the concentration camps, and Jewish colleagues awaiting death were especially deprofessionalized. Instead of affecting just some dimensions like the Weimar crisis, the Nazi system impaired professionalism categorically: Training standards declined, certification produced a manpower shortage, economic remuneration fell short of increased work, academic status lines were blurred, practice was hindered, ethics were warped, and free association destroyed. While letting capable experts survive, NS policies stripped the educated occupations of the essence of their "professionalism." Though sharing regimentation and exploitation with other blue- or white-collar workers, professionals were more profoundly affected by being deprived of the scientific knowledge, autonomous practice, altruistic ethics, and collective self-government that made them special. It was precisely the illusion of völkisch *re*professionalization that rendered Nazi *de*professionalization so pernicious.[119]

8

Perils of Professionalism

In the grim spring of 1945, German professionals faced a defeat that was "so immense as to be unprecedented in history." Anti-Fascists welcomed liberation as "a hopeful and passionately desired new beginning," while many practitioners were "above all glad that everything was over, the fear of the Nazis and the bombing-raids." To nationalists the "nearly unimaginable chaos" left by the Third Reich appeared to confirm Oswald Spengler's gloomy prediction of the decline of the West.[1] "Far more than human lives, artistic monuments, buildings, streets and bridges were destroyed by over a decade of dictatorship and tyranny, by the war with its intolerable sacrifices and suffering and by the collapse which halted government, administration and judiciary." The gravest damage was not physical, but psychological. "Popular respect for justice had been severely harmed, the sense of right and wrong, the ability to discriminate between good and evil, what was allowed and forbidden, had more or less been lost." Education had been deformed into stultifying indoctrination and technology degraded into an instrument for killing. Confronted with unparalleled material destruction, professionals also encountered frightful intellectual devastation. Although their expertise survived largely unscathed, complicity with Hitler's rule had eroded the ethical basis of their calling. But as the jurist Karl Bader put it, this chaos also provided a creative opportunity: "We must start anew, begin completely afresh in constructing the foundations of law, legislation, judiciary and administration. There is nothing which can just be continued."[2]

To prevent a recurrence of the disaster, rebuilding the professions required a painful examination of what had gone wrong. From the Nuremberg prison, discredited leaders like Hans Frank, Baldur von Schirach, and Albert Speer tried to disassociate NS "ideals" from their gruesome results.[3] Traditional practitioners saw the Nazi era as a "misfortune," which had been imposed from the outside, and argued that—beneath massive external changes—their inner spirit "generally kept its integrity" during the dark years. Somewhat ashamed, more candid participants admitted that lawyers had been reduced to "covering up evident injustice," but were reluctant to admit their own contribution to this predicament. Only a critical minority was willing to confront the deeper warping of professionalism through racism, abuse of competence, and "the glorification of one party and the strengthening of a totalitarian regime."[4] To purge the professions of the incorrigibles, the victors pursued "the overriding goal of *de*nazification, *de*militarization and *de*nationalization." Burned by Nazi politics, moderate practitioners opposed forced democratization and withdrew from politics into private neutrality. Professionals who were ambivalent about their role in the Third Reich called for a return to the proven traditions of the past, which could be found "in a 'spiritual' world" of highest culture, deriving from the Greeks. Because privatism and idealism had been helpless against Hitler's hordes, critical professionals instead demanded "a passionate endorsement of democracy" and a "basic commitment against reaction and militarism" as preconditions for a renewal. Obsessed with guilt, one philologue warned: "I hope we have now finally learned our lesson!"[5]

The historical debate about the nature of the rebuilding after 1945 has produced a similar clash of opinions. Conservative scholars who view the Third Reich as an aberration tend to stress the new departures and the sincerity of democratization. Liberal historians emphasize the "restoration" climate of the Adenauer years, while radicals talk about "missed opportunities" for socialization or reunification.[6] Compared to this burgeoning general discussion, the postwar professions have attracted little attention beyond preliminary chronicles. Establishment apologists usually stress that the "zero hour" wiped the slate clean and called forth heroic efforts at reconstruction. Moderate scholars speak of a "resumption of the pre-1933 tendencies," without always explaining the implications of a return to Weimar arrangements. Foreign or younger critics are more likely to castigate the continuation of personnel, rhetoric, and policies that perpetuated Nazi patterns well into the postwar years. These conflicting interpretations of continuity or change raise the issue of the professions' ability to learn: Did restoration of authoritarian traditions, pragmatic problem solving, or a genuine new beginning dominate after 1945? By necessity, postwar practice blended the removal of Hitler's debris with the reconstruction of the physical setting and the recovery of intellectual integrity. In a confusing mixture of remorse and avoidance, atonement and apologetics, professionals tried to wrestle with the meaning of their troubled experience in the first half of the present century.[7]

REBUILDING THE PROFESSIONS

For many experts the long-awaited peace brought greater hardship than the war itself. The imperative of survival in a devastated country made practitioners "almost despair of the multitude of tasks." The division of Germany into four occupation zones created a confusing multiplicity of jurisdictions, "a chaos in educational policies," and a return to barter and black market trading.[8] At first, courts, schools and many factories were simply closed while the occupiers decided what to do with law, education, and industry. Control Council directive No. 24 removed all Nazi party members from leading positions in public office, (such as school administration), semi-public authority (such as lawyer chambers) and private industry (such as managers). After denazification screening, the military government readmitted 21 attorneys in Berlin in June 1945, and many courts began working again with their own lawyers in the fall. Most high schools reopened in September with skeleton staffs of untainted teachers, and factories, reconverted to civilian use, similarly resumed production piecemeal.[9] As a result of the "destruction, migration, and traffic" disruption, working conditions were deplorable. Lawyers lacked "rooms, personnel, supplies, and telephones," while philologues struggled with overcrowded classes, missing textbooks, and malnourished children, and engineers had to "clear the rubble" before resuming production.[10] The pressing need for food and shelter gave the restoration of professional activity priority in the short run. Standards needed to be reestablished, labor supply rebalanced, economic security and social prestige regained, practice returned to normal, moral direction recovered, and organizations refounded. However, for the full recovery of professionalism in the long term, it was crucial to democratize the outlook and behavior of experts more thoroughly than a generation before. To set the professions permanently free, training had to be infused with a new spirit, compromised personnel removed, Nazi practices rooted out, and political allegiance redirected toward unfamiliar liberty.

A semblance of order slowly emerged out of disjointed occupation directives, practitioner coping, and collective initiatives between 1945 and 1949. Professional training largely returned to Weimar patterns while keeping a few additions of practical merit of the Third Reich. Partly voluntarily, partly opportunistically, and partly under compulsion, universities purged the most notorious Nazi professors, expelled heavily compromised students, and slowly eliminated racist distortions from the curricula and examination prerequisites. Special wartime measures such as reduced requirements or shortened study times were rescinded, and supplementary courses tried to bring poorly trained veterans or anti-Fascist housewives up to prewar standards. In law, the principle of "completely unified instruction and examination of all future higher judicial and administrative officials" was reaffirmed, Roman law returned to prominence, and economics courses were deemphasized initially. The first state examination assumed a more academic character while the three-year practical training period was maintained. In education, philologues urged "a combination of true scholarship and regard for study plans" in order to reconcile freedom and efficiency as prerequisite for the elevated mission of the higher schools. In spite of pressure for an accelerated graduation, a thorough two year "practical-pedagogical" training in seminars and schools appeared essential as preparation for "the fruitful and responsible work as teacher and educator." Caught between the imperative of general cultivation and the explosion of technical specialties, engineers resorted to prior requirements while escaping their dilemma through "treating related subjects together" in paradigmatic problems. When exceptions for veterans were eliminated and material conditions improved, the removal of obvious Nazi corruptions and the willingness of postwar students to work hard gradually returned academic standards to traditional excellence.[11]

In spite of tougher requirements, students flocked to the universities. Happy to exchange uniforms for civilian clothes, returning veterans created "an enormous rush for study places" in the few institutions that were open. From several thousand in the fall of 1945, enrollment quickly rose to 94,566 by the summer of 1948 and continued to increase to 123,000 by the winter of 1955–1956, overtaxing the often damaged facilities and prompting renewed warnings against academic overcrowding. Resuming Weimar growth on a smaller territory, this expansion pushed the relative participation of the 18- to 25-year-old age group from 0.72 percent in 1937–1938 to 1.77 percent by 1949 and more than 2 percent by the mid-1950s. Legal studies continued to be popular with around one-fifth of the enrollment, humanities students (many of them future teachers) increased to 18 percent, while engineers enlarged their share to 14 percent. Nevertheless, the student body became somewhat more elitist. Expellees and refugees constituted about one-third, only 5 percent came from the countryside, and Protestants reasserted their overrepresentation, while the number of women fell back to a mere 16 percent. The share of students from academic homes rebounded from 26.4 percent to 32.4 percent between 1949–1950 and 1962–1923, whereas those students from affluent backgrounds returned to one-fifth of the total enrollment. Even though children from working-class families increased to 6 percent, lower-middle class recruitment still sank to less than one-half, which was the lowest level during the century. In spite of considerable growth in inclusiveness, the participation rate in German higher education fell behind other advanced countries and the composition of the student body returned to Wilhelmian patterns, which corresponded to the reassertion of the traditional curriculum.[12]

In the year 1945, the academic labor market looked bleak. After the initial massive demand for competent specialists had passed, numerous veterans, refugees, and widows competed with the remaining practitioners for the few available jobs. Readmission to legal practice depended on not only political clearance but also local need: one-tenth of the schools remained closed and there was not enough revenue for hiring teachers; only firms that had survived bombing, dismantling, or inflation could use engineers. By the year 1950, the number of West German lawyers had risen to 11,818, one-third more than within the same territory in 1931 (Table A.5). This increase prompted demands for the reintroduction of a *numerus clausus* or at least the restoration of the Anwaltsassessor training period in order to stem the tide.[13] If the situation of the North Rhine Westphalian philologues is any indication, then the about 20 percent war losses initially required the employment of 30.8 percent women and 16.1 percent trainees among 6570 full-time faculty. However, the education career soon became overcrowded with the "return of thousands of POW pedagogues" and the arrival of millions of refugees, amounting to one-fifth of all instructors by 1950. Therefore, teachers clamored for the founding of new schools and the resumption of hiring in order to avoid "the danger of an academic proletariat" for trainees in "most dire economic straits." To make room, the Bundestag decided in 1950 that female officials could be dismissed if their economic support was assured, thereby suspending the fundamental right of sexual equality.[14] Many technicians had to "change jobs or residence and inestimable numbers, expelled from their homes, vegetate[d] without real work wherever they found some shelter." In the year 1950, one of every ten engineers was still unemployed, many worked outside of their immediate field, others emigrated, and older technicians faced particularly hard times (Table 8.1).

After the currency reform overcame the immediate crisis, war losses and Nazi

Table 8.1. Unemployment among Technicians[15]

Year	Unemployed	Work Force	Percentage
1926	8,868	99,779	8.38
1932	94,306	292,227	32.27
1937	7,313	350,000 est.	2.09
1950	21,941	240,836	9.11
1954	8,262	282,630	2.92

planning mistakes created an age-specific demand. In large firms like the former IG Farben, "only a few old comrades" were left, because "the others had been killed or burned, were dead or denazified." There was much talk about a lack of potential leaders because "the middling cohorts are missing" with some estimates of casualties at almost 50 percent among men 20 to 40 years old. Reinforced by the return of prosperity, the unchecked rise in enrollment increased the number of lawyers to 15,643 by 1955, approximately a one-third expansion in five years! Reaching almost 30 per 100,000 of the population, this number of attorneys exceeded even the overcrowding peak of 1933. Since one half of the pedagogues were older than 55, replacement hiring absorbed many probationers, while public efforts to improve instruction increased the corps of secondary schoolteachers from 28,872 to 34,848 between 1950 and 1955. Even this one-fifth rise in half a decade could not keep abreast with growing pupil figures that pushed the student/teacher ratio to 1:22.25. Record graduation rates returned the number of technicians to about 300,00 in 1950 and continued to swell it thereafter. However, the demand for skilled manpower increased even faster so that unemployment virtually disappeared and there was a "pronounced shortage of engineers." Therefore, women were eventually rehired, refugees slowly integrated, and even dismissed Nazis largely reinstated, when exonerated by a general amnesty in 1951.[16]

The deplorable material situation improved gradually but unevenly. Because of the fragmentation of law, normal litigation resumed haltingly while inflation and currency reform once again depleted savings. "The condition of the attorneys is extremely precarious," H. Dittenberger complained about overcrowding and shrinking practice. Lawyers therefore campaigned for "an immediate increase in all fees, appropriate to the changed circumstances." Revision of the official scales and increasing business activity soon produced greater rewards. In spite of habitual complaints about insufficient returns, the average annual income of attorneys rose to 18,000 DM by 1954.[17] Initially, secondary schoolteachers also faced "unprecedented hardship," lacking basic food, while working in "cold rooms, inadequate light and tattered clothes." The Brüning cuts remained in force until 1950, but a year later price increases prompted a 20 percent supplement in order to keep the "relationship between wages and salaries" constant. In order to ease "the plight of the intellectual strata," philologues agitated for the restoration of "a just real value of salaries," claiming that their buying power had fallen 50 percent from the mid-1920s. Rejecting a separate teacher scale, they also demanded continued equality with judges, because their "net income hardly increased during one generation." Further adjustments in 1954–1955 raised take-home pay to 124.8 percent of the 1927 level, almost restoring real earnings to the peacetime stan-

Table 8.2. Structure of Postwar Engineers

Parameter	Percentage of Total Engineers	Parameter	Percentage of Total Engineers
Level of Training		*Type of Practice*	
TH	31	Research	9
HTL	57	Design	29
Other	11	Production	23
Unknown	1	Sales	10
Monthly Income (marks)		Management	16
Less than 400	3	Consultancy	5
More than 400	25	Other	8
More than 750	25	*Firm Size (Number of Employees)*	
More than 1000	24	Fewer than 20	6
More than 1500	22	Fewer than 100	12
Employment Status		Fewer than 500	23
Independent	16	More than 500	59
Bureaucrat	5	No Information	1
Employed	71		
Pensioned	5		
Other	3		

dard.[18] Because technical experts were in great demand for the rebuilding of devastated Germany, by the late 1940s'' it was not too difficult for young engineers to obtain a starting position.'' In the year 1947 an experienced designer earned 400 marks per month, and by 1950 average beginning pay started at 300 marks. Eventually, the economic miracle *(Wirtschaftswunder)* improved technical salaries so that by the mid-1950s they approached European levels of about 800–1000 DM monthly (Table 8.2).[19]

The discrediting of the military and the politicians allowed professionals to regain much of their imperial prestige, even if practitioners were slow to realize this change. When Professor K. Bader asserted, ''German lawyers suffer from an inferiority complex,'' Judge Schürholz replied: ''Compared to whom should we feel 'inferior'?'' As before, ''negative stereotypes about jurists [were] widespread in the population,'' emphasizing their hairsplitting, formalism, and otherworldliness. However, by championing popular freedom, attorneys began to reattain ''an intellectual and political position that corresponds to the best West European traditions.''[20] Philologues continued to feel unappreciated. Because it was determined by pupils and parents, other professionals and professors, primary schoolteachers, the Left, and the media, their public image was ''shockingly comic and intellectually light-weight.'' Lack of respect for ''the dignity of our profession'' made educators ''feel [that] they serve a lost cause'' and retreat into a realm of ''idealist, humanist, individualist ideas.'' However, public desire for restoring educational excellence also allowed academic teachers to appear as ''carriers and mediators of culture,'' who were endowed with a ''special responsibility'' for the future. Although incessantly complaining about the lack ''of economic and social esteem,'' philologues succeeded to a remarkable degree in ''putting their shaken social position'' onto a ''new foundation.''[21] Though praised by the Nazis, engineers still chafed at their "mistaken image" as "excessively materialistic" specialists. According to a 1956 survey, only 13 percent were content with their "social prestige," 60 percent partly dissatisfied, and one quarter were decidedly unhappy, with four-fifths convinced that their work was not sufficiently rewarded. While some admitted their own shortcomings, many others instead blamed technical ignorance or the disdain of others. Because they still did not enjoy title protection, members were encouraged to list the abbreviation "VDI" after their name to let it be known that they had "the right to be called engineer." Eventually, the visible contribution of technicians to the physical rebuilding and a somewhat modernized conception of cultivation led to a greater acceptance of academic engineers into the charmed circle of university graduates. Therefore, in postwar stratification studies, professionals occupied a secure place below the economic and bureaucratic elite in the upper middle to middle class.[22]

After the initial chaos had been overcome, professional practice normalized. The detritus left by Hitler's Reich, SS persecution, Allied bombing, mass flight, and expulsion created a host of new problems to be resolved. The prosecution of NS war criminals in the Nuremberg trials and the local courts as well as hundreds of thousands of denazification hearings required much legal defense. Other postwar measures such as the currency reform or the equalization-of-burdens law *(Lastenausgleichsgesetz)* produced fresh bureaucratic thickets that promoted litigation, once rising prosperity made competent counsel affordable. The restitution law, trying to return pillaged property to its erstwhile owners and to compensate Jewish survivors for their suffering, produced much contention and a chance for some refugee attorneys to resume their practice.[23] Though refounded as a "free profession," lawyers vigorously strove to "work against the further narrowing of their field of activity." In spite of general democratization, there were surprisingly few attempts by the lay public to break their court monopoly after 1945. Instead, the reintroduction of the specialist for tax law restored specialization in the economic area, which was necessary for competition with accountants. Attorneys also lobbied with determination against their exclusion from the labor courts as an abridgment of the rights of potential clients. In the year 1953, DAV President Emil von Sauer could proudly report: "What lawyers have desired in vain since 1890 has finally been achieved!" Against union opposition, advocates had been admitted to the *Arbeitsgerichte* for disputes of more than 300 DM, which was more than a symbolic victory.[24]

Teachers had some success in their struggle for improved working conditions. In the immediate postwar years, "overcrowded classes, substituting for collapsing colleagues and increased work-loads made new demands on their powers which hardly suffice[d] for bare survival." Whereas primary school pedagogues struggled against the reimposition of church control, philologues agitated for "the conservation of professional public service" and uniformity in treatment in order to achieve "personal and legal security" against political dismissal. In exchange for the restoration of traditional officials' privileges, the Philologenverband offered to forego the right to strike and joined the bureaucratic Beamtenbund rather than the socialist trade union confederation (DGB).[25] More assertive against bureaucratic control, many teachers also opposed lay supervision through elected local school boards as a threat to their professional authority. However, most philologues were willing to accept stronger parent associations and pupil councils as long as these limited themselves to "social tasks." With material resources increasing, educators complained more loudly that "the space problem in high schools" created "unbearable working conditions." For instance, the lack of non-Nazi schoolbooks required the reprinting from old plates of editions from the late Weimar period until new texts could be written. When improving revenues allowed the construction of new facilities and the hiring of additional staff, "the overcrowding of classes and the overburdening of teachers" gradually decreased.[26]

"The rebuilding pose[d] special challenges for engineers." Technicians needed to find practical solutions for removing thousands of tons of rubble, and for resuming production with scarce raw materials, broken-down communications, and a checkered labor force of former soldiers and women. At the same time, they had to plan for future demands so that cities would remain habitable, combining some conservation with much clearing for new traffic needs. Once again, exposed to the free flow of ideas, engineers could catch up with scientific breakthroughs elsewhere, although whole areas of prior activity (such as airplane construction) were now prohibited. The loss of domestic resources redirected "engineering work [towards] export," because the economy could prosper only by becoming competitive on the world market through further rationalization. Exposed to tough outside competition, many small firms failed when their ersatz products such as fiberboard suddenly became useless, once real wood was again available. With one-tenth doing research and more than half working in design or production, engineers expanded into management (16 percent) and sales (10 percent). By becoming more knowledgeable in business considerations, technicians tried to regain some control over their own work. Because three-fifths of technicians belonged to firms with more than 500 employees, many managers stressed the importance of a good "social climate" in the factory, postponing traditional labor antagonism in the common task of rebuilding. Inspired by "a feeling of togetherness and dedication to reconstruction," engineers took special pride in their contribution to the postwar revival.[27]

In reaction to NS compulsion, the self-image of attorneys returned to the hallowed tradition of the freie Advokatur. Though more highly compromised (with 47 percent belonging to the NSDAP), judges refused to admit their complicity, whereas the less tainted advocates tried to learn from their collaboration. In both the Allied perspective and "good German liberal-democratic" tradition, the lawyer could only "serve to prevent government injustice" as an independent professional. From a purged version of the 1936 code through a series of occupation-sponsored state laws between 1946 and 1948 to federal deliberations beginning in 1949, West German lawyers tried to redefine the concept of "free advocacy" as a higher service above a mere trade. The result was neither a chamber-dominated nor a bureaucracy-dependent system, but a return to the Weimar practice of a free profession, which was regulated by the state (e.g., in admission standards and fee questions) but self-governing in chambers, honor courts, and associations. The substantive decisions of the *Ehrengerichte* also resumed pre-NS practice by allowing some innovative specialization but continuing to proscribe contingency fees *(Erfolgshonorare)*. After a considerable struggle, the German attorney recaptured "his pivotal mediating role between his client and the court, equally tied to his party and the law, only bound by his sense of responsibility and the living ethics of his profession.'' In the Soviet-occupied zone of Germany the few carefully screened attorneys followed a different tradition in forming ''socialist lawyer collectives.'' Western antitotalitarian individualism proved irreconcilable with Soviet-inspired collectivism, thereby rupturing the unity of the profession.[28]

In rethinking their mission, secondary schoolteachers settled on an updated version of the traditional educator–scholar–official role. Never fond of the Nazi claim of a ''unified teaching career,'' philologues followed less reeducation or school reformer suggestions than their own desire to ''maintain and infuse with new spirit the proud, memorable edifice of our high school, constructed over four centuries.'' Instead of leveling differences with primary school colleagues, they demanded ''a special teaching profession, trained at the university.''[29] As ''mediators between the small band of researchers and the broad stratum of the cultivated,'' philologues saw themselves as central guardians of the embattled continuity of culture, be it in its classical, modern, or scientific guise. Their principal challenge was the ''cultivation'' of character in a higher conception of humanity through ''absolute and historical spiritual-ethical values.'' To prepare pupils for Wissenschaft, secondary schoolteachers promoted a ''special kind of scholarly'' instruction, which was based on their own reception of the research discourse. Serving ''such a non-utilitarian, ideal task,'' philologues demanded ''the security . . . of professional public service,'' while at the same time calling for more freedom from bureaucratic control. ''Without thorough scientific training, the pedagogue and the youth-movement activist fail to do justice to the Gymnasium,'' mused Dr. Walter Dederich about conflicting imperatives: ''The overextended office-holder only lives for the moment and has no time to qualify himself further . . . and perhaps the scholar lacks a true relationship to youth and therefore a suitable echo.''[30]

Surprisingly enough, the engineers undertook the most searching reexamination of their profession. In May 1947, VDI board member Waldemar Hellmich courageously reflected on their coresponsibility for the recent catastrophe. Spurred by the explosion of the atom bomb, a far-ranging discussion suggested the development of ''a technical conscience'' to control the use of inventions to the benefit rather than detriment of humanity.[31] The resulting ''credo of the engineer,'' promulgated at the 1950 VDI meeting at Kassel, stressed ''reverence for values beyond knowledge'' and ''humility before the all-powerful'' creator; dedication to ''the service of mankind'' in honor, justice, and impartiality; ''respect for the dignity of human life,'' irrespective of origin, class, or ideology; rejection of technical abuse in ''loyal work for human ethics and culture''; collegial cooperation for ''the sensible development of technology''; and finally, placing ''professional honor above economic advantage,'' while striving for well-deserved recognition.[32] In a series of conferences on such issues as ''man and work'' or ''the transformation of man through technology,'' engineers discussed the moral implications of their calling with surprising candor. A self-critical minority had realized: ''Technical-economic thinking which is all too easily confused with the striving for utility and gain must be governed by a humane *professional ethics* which is so wide-spread and well founded that it can help set the limits of the practical application of technical possibilities.'' Chastened by complicity with the Third Reich, thoughtful engineers struggled for a broader self-conception, combining technical expertise with social responsibility.[33]

After the suppression of Nazi affiliates, professional associations gradually reemerged, largely following the Weimar pattern. When the occupation authorities reluctantly relaxed their control of discipline, the traditional division into corporate self-government and pursuit of collective interests reasserted itself among attorneys. Since it proved impossible to organize jurists comprehensively, lawyers reestablished their chambers as private associations in the U.S. zone and as autonomous corporations in the French territory, while the chamber presidents of the British sector met to consult in February 1946. The extension of this "association of lawyer chambers" to the entire Federal Republic in September 1949 provided a collective organization, exercising compulsory supervision over practitioners. Voluntary associations for sociability and discussion reemerged as well during 1946 and 1947 in the northwest. Against bureaucratic suspicion, Emil von Sauer succeeded, on September 26, 1948, in refounding the Deutsche Anwaltverein, which was dedicated to "the maintenance, cultivation and advancement of the professional and economic interests of attorneys." The first postwar congress at Coburg in June 1949 breathed a vigorous democratic spirit, and the following meetings at Wiesbaden (1951), Lübeck (1953), and so on, debated burning professional and legal issues with the blessing of the Ministry of Justice.[34] Specialized attorney publications also reemerged with the *Neue Juristische Wochenschrift* in October 1947 and the *Anwaltsblatt* in July 1950. Though reaching fewer members than before, the federal DAV reestablished its Aid Fund and reasserted its role as chief spokesman for attorney interests.[35]

Propelled by resistance and émigré impulses, teachers also groped for associational renewal. By 1946, primary school pedagogues had already begun to organize across religious, sexual, and educational barriers to promote democracy and social reform, attracting numerous secondary school colleagues into a comprehensive association in some regions. Founded in January 1947, this "General Association of German Teachers" (ADLV) joined the trade union movement as *Gewerkschaft Erziehung und Wissenschaft* (GEW) in July 1948, while maintaining organizational identity, an independent school policy, and special bureaucratic rights.[36] As a result of "the terrible experiences . . . with the NSLB," most philologues preferred to reestablish a separate association of their own, first locally (1946) and later regionally (1947). To defend scholarly training "against the threatening danger" of dilution, state groups combined into a national Philologenverband on September 25, 1947 for "advancing the general professional, legal, economic and social condition of high school teachers." Now also accepting female colleagues and reaching out to refugee educators, the PhVb sought to resume its "illustrious tradition" in the journal *Die höhere Schule*. Opposing political experimentation, Chairman Dr. Erdmann urged "above all . . . quiet for the work of the school," academic training for philologues, and "an improvement of the economic and social situation of the staff." The first postwar congress at Bonn in 1951 documented its public reemergence when Federal President Theodor Heuss, Chancellor Konrad Adenauer, and Cardinal Joseph Frings blessed the secondary school's special mission of conserving culture.[37] Rejecting the "educational class struggle" of the GEW for a unified school and single type of teacher, the philologues in 1952 joined with religious, middle, and trade teachers in a Gemeinschaft Deutscher Lehrerverbände (GDL), which was dedicated to pedagogical pluralism. Although a significant minority left for the GEW, the reconstituted PhVb attracted three-quarters of the philologues and once again became their collective voice.[38]

After spurning labor alternatives, engineers resurrected their "technical" association as well. At first, the VDI seemed doomed when the provisional Berlin business office, operating amidst the ruins, was closed in November 1945 due to its former NSBDT affiliation. However, local branches resumed activity in the British zone and 17 chapters met in Düsseldorf to refound the VDI regionally in September 1946 with statutes purged of Nazi perversions. Self-consciously, the majority of engineers rejected the union-sponsored "Chamber of Technology" of the Soviet zone as well as similar plans of Rhenish consulting engineers: "In the future the VDI will continue to abstain from all purely professional questions and see its chief aim as high-level technical-scientific work."[39] Led by Hans Bluhm, the VDI restarted publication of its newsletter *VDI Nachrichten* in March 1947 and succeeded in reissuing its prestigious journal *VDI Zeitschrift* in January 1948. Resuming annual meetings in September 1947, it joined other associations in reestablishing a Deutsche Verband technisch-wissenschaftlicher Vereine "for the promotion of technical research" and refounded its numerous topical committees and working groups. Rapidly rising membership enabled the VDI to build a new house in Düsseldorf, extend its organization over the whole Federal Republic in 1949, sponsor national and international congresses, and reclaim its traditional place as the organizational focus of technology. In spite of the persistence of tensions between different types of engineers, widespread sentiment for "title protection" and more aggressive pursuit of economic interests did not lead to the return of a separate association for academic technicians after 1945.[40]

In contrast to the unquestioned restoration of professionalism, the success of democratization continued to remain in doubt. Because of disagreement on the extent and direction of the necessary changes between anti-Fascists and neotraditionalists, it proved difficult to reform training. Whereas the quality of instruction improved dramatically, political initiatives that could be derided as "impractical" had little appeal after the excessive politicization of the Third Reich. Since citizens in a democracy needed "cultivation beyond specialization," a revitalized *studium generale* attempted to convey social, political, and ethical orientation. However, achievement pressures directed most students toward maximizing their examination chances and the internal renewal of the curriculum was slow and uneven. Although many professors simply glossed over the Third Reich, some committed teachers like the jurist Carlo Schmid, the pedagogue Eduard Spranger, or the technician Rudolf Plank sought to infuse their subject with fresh spirit, calling, for example, for "scientific humanism as philosophical basis for the engineer."[41] The restoration of student self-government (AStA) and the founding of progressive associations were promising departures. "Somewhat exhausted after all these years," sober and yet enthusiastic, the postwar cohort was a curious mixture of surviving veterans, refugees, women, and former HJ members. Although "they were plagued by hunger, imprisonment, bombing, loss of family and poverty," youths were eager to study after having waited so long: "Spiritually hungry, students [were] open to rethinking their personal as well as general public situation due to the earthquake of the moral order.'' However, with the return of normalcy, this anti-Fascist solidarity evaporated in the desire for private careers and students grew conformist, even restoring their somewhat tainted corporations such as the *Burschenschaft*.[42]

The cleansing of personnel turned out to be equally complicated. Though high on the list of Allied priorities, bureaucratic denazification was haphazard and incomplete. The Nuremberg war crime trials failed to extend to ordinary professionals, except for involving four dozen defense lawyers, led by Rudolf Dix. Because Hans Frank was indicted for his crimes against the Polish people, the jurist case concentrated on the partly reluctant collaboration of Ministry of Justice officials and did not touch ordinary attorneys. With Baldur von Schirach accused for the HJ, educators were neither prominent nor implicated enough in Nazi atrocities to be tried. In spite of their role in war production, engineers were only indirectly affected by the prosecution of Albert Speer and the industrial trials of firms like IG Farben, because ''technicians'' were considered too unpolitical to be held responsible.[43] Though identifying several million erstwhile Nazis, American dismissals and German trials had little success in separating real NS criminals from nominal collaborators because of the confusion of aims (general or individual punishment) and the inadequacy of methods (bureaucratic questionnaires and citizen *Spruchkammern*). In practice, the review boards often began with minor Nazis, postponing the reckoning with the elite. Although public scrutiny and censure were unpleasant, culprits were usually reinstated after token atonement, if colleagues attested to their personal decency. ''Each attorney could only resume practice, once he had been checked and readmitted.'' Unfortunately, ''the application and implementation of these measures varied considerably among different districts,'' so that the British rule limiting former Nazis to 50 percent was quickly breached due to the acute manpower shortage. While up to three-quarters of the teachers were initially dismissed in some areas, the desperate need for instructors necessitated the rehiring of all but the one-tenth that was too heavily tarnished. Among engineers the purge was most superficial, because they were least identified with Nazi policies.[44]

During its gradual abatement between 1948 and 1950, denazification began to turn into rehabilitation. Because the flagrant miscarriages of justice perpetrated by judges went unpunished, attorneys could hardly be held to a higher standard. The blanket prohibition against admission of NS lawyers no longer appeared in the 1949 regulations of the British zone so that even former party members could resume their practice. Benefitting from concern for veterans and refugees, dismissed teachers were reinstated in 1951 because of the infamous paragraph 131 of the Basic Law, which mandated the rehiring or pensioning of 150,000 purged public officials except for major war criminals. In October 1948, an internal investigation concluded that the VDI had resisted militarist and capitalist pressures: ''If in the years from 1933 to 1945, specific external concessions were made to party demands, they did not touch the core of our work and attitudes'' and were only intended ''to preserve the association as a whole.''[45] Although denazification succeeded in barring leading NS politicians from public life, it failed to deal with the more subtle collaboration of the professions and proved unable to prevent continuity in personnel. Internment, interrogation, or dismissal interrupted the careers of former Nazis and gave democratic forces a head start, but non-political former collaborators quickly shunted aside anti-Fascists and most exiles were not called back. Eventually the manpower needs of rebuilding and the Cold War facilitated the reintegration of all but the most exposed criminals. Leading Third Reich professionals, like the lawyer Friedrich Grimm, the educator Wilhelm Hartnacke, and the engineer Heinrich Schult not only resumed practice but also returned to notoriety.[46] Even if overt Nazi rhetoric quickly disappeared, the covert influence of "immanent National-Socialism" that built upon corrupted older traditions lingered on in countless mental habits and figures of speech. Concentrating on the worst offenders and rehabilitating the lesser Mitläufer avoided the establishment of neo-Nazism, but prevented a thorough renewal of expert personnel and ideology.[47]

Effective democratization also required the reorientation of professional work. Because the occupation powers preferred German officials to free professionals, lawyers had to struggle long to reunify nine separate postwar laws into a *Bundesrechtsanwaltsordnung* (BRAO) in 1959. Building upon the rules of the British zone, the chamber draft of 1949 envisaged "unusually far-reaching, nearly unlimited powers" for the federal chamber, *Bundesrechtsanwaltskammer* (BRAK). Because it provided no guarantee against political corruption, "this aim did not find the approval of most judicial administrations," which preferred to strengthen bureaucratic supervision, especially through disciplinary courts.[48] The eventual compromise between chambers, DAV, Ministry of Justice, and the parties balanced "attorney autonomy with necessary state control" in the formula: "The lawyer is an independent organ of the administration of justice," and "the designated autonomous counsel and representative in all legal matters." Although the chamber was entitled to advise the ministry, admission had to be denied "'if an applicant illegally fights against the free democratic constitution." The honor court was continued, but given state status, localization maintained, and simultaneous admission limited to superior courts. Although some innovations such as mandatory Anwaltsassessor training disappeared, others such as syndics continued. The "pragmatic law" balanced bureaucratic, corporate, and associational impulses in order to "allow much space for the free, self-governing initiative of attorneys." Suspicious of socialist collectivism and liberal individualism, the BRAO's "freedom bound by law" exemplified Chancellor Konrad Adenauer's conservative democracy.[49]

Pressed to restructure their schools, secondary schoolteachers countered with the promise of "internal reform" that would retain their institutions while infusing them with a new spirit. Occupation authorities tried to reeducate the educators in special courses, combining subject information with ideological retraining to rehumanize instruction. When Socialists accused them of being "reactionary," philologues stressed the superior cultural mission of the high school, the necessity of selection by achievement, and the importance of an idealist outlook. Although they were willing to "reorient history teaching" away from nationalism toward reconciliation, secondary schoolteachers remained skeptical of civics propaganda. Rejecting the "slogan" of democratization as nefarious politicizing, the PhVb called for greater teacher participation in bureaucratic decisions instead.[50] To avoid the "dismantling of the high-school" by reducing its length, it complained about "the splintering of the educational system in the Federal Republic" through ill-considered and uncoordinated state reforms. Warning that primary schoolteacher demands for a "comprehensive school" would lead to "a decline of our cultural level," philologues campaigned for a restoration of academic achievement through "uniform and independent higher schools," combining "tradition *and* progress." In the Düsseldorf agreement of February 1955, the state cultural ministers largely accepted PhVb wishes for separate identity of the secondary school, the collective name of *Gymnasium* for classical, modern, and scientific types, and the nine-year course as the norm, even if they made English the dominant language and did not rule out exceptions.[51] The success of the philologues' struggle indicates that professional restoration, modified by concessions in method, was the dominant path of postwar democratization in a traditional key.

In spite of their reexamination of ethics, engineers rarely discussed reforming actual practice. The emphasis on subject expertise and prevailing employment by large capitalist firms led to the continuation of a problem-solving mentality that did not challenge the framework or internal structure of work. Allied pressure for decartelization could be denounced as an attempt to stifle the competition of large German firms. Specialist groups such as the Arbeitsgemeinschaft deutscher Betriebsingenieure resumed their topical debates almost unchanged after 1945. Instead, postwar unemployment put a premium on achieving the longstanding desire of "securing protection for the title of 'engineer'," because its holders were instrumental in producing goods, leading workers, and safeguarding against malfunction. Vigorous VDI lobbying, supported by other technical groups, led to the introduction of a protective bill by the CDU/CSU in 1953, limiting the term to graduates of the THs, the higher technical schools, honorary degree holders, and foreigners with equivalent training, as well as exceptional practitioners with at least six years of experience. Lurid examples of the dangerous consequences of misuse that substantiated the "elemental necessity" of legal prohibition against misappropriation won the legislative day in 1957.[52] Although there were passing references to "occupational diseases" resulting from technology, the emerging "labor sociology" was more interested in efficiency of production than in rethinking the engineering role. Whereas it provided a critical perspective on the social implications of the machine, the impressive general discussion about "man in the force-field of technology" yielded few reform impulses for actual engineering work.[53]

What did professionals learn politically from their catastrophic involvement in the Third Reich? As a reaction to the charge of collective guilt, confused practitioners continued to cling to some national feeling, tempered by slow recognition of the excesses of nationalism. While censorship prevented public railing against the defeat, recurrent tensions with the occupation forces fostered a sense of German "community of fate." Lawyers criticized Control Council measures and resented the introduction of Anglo-American legal procedures. Philologues resisted the imposition of foreign patterns under the name of "reeducation," because they threatened to destroy the elitist structure of the Gymnasium. Furthermore, engineers protested that the dismantling of industry had "catastrophic consequences" for nutrition and rebuilding.[54] Unable to prevent the fragmentation of the "fatherland," professionals tried to preserve the unity of their calling by criticizing the drastic restructuring in the Soviet zone, which hampered the restoration of legal practice, politicized teaching, and nationalized industrial production. After the blockade in 1948–1949, the professions also embraced Berlin as symbol of German destruction ("an atmosphere of ruins and rubble"), division ("a tragic island fate"), and determination to rebuild ("hopeful initiatives"): "The VDI meeting in Berlin shall testify to the undestroyed and indestructible bond between German engineers in the West and their colleagues in the East."[55] With the nation discredited, many professionals endorsed the "emerging European community," because it promised to end the old enmity to the West. For resurgent German industry, the European Coal and Steel Community offered a "common market for expanding business, increasing employment and raising the standard of living." Supported by numerous student exchanges, "serving the great task of European unity" provided a transpersonal meaning for practice. Although reunification dreams and repatriation claims clouded foreign policy rhetoric, the double defeat suggested to most professionals that even an imperfect peace was preferable to renewed war.[56]

Though outwardly impressive, the democratization of internal attitudes remained incomplete. Initially, many professionals adopted a "wait-and-see attitude," and reformers were frustrated that "restorative forces still have a preponderance." However, eventually Bonn's chancellor democracy was surprisingly successful in achieving "democratic legitimacy" as "provisional all-German constitution," because the Basic Law responded equally to the longing for participation and leadership.[57] Within this framework, the majority of practitioners concentrated on economic rebuilding, while remaining politically apathetic. Troubled by "the loss of our possessions and honor," experts sought redemption in work and tried to regain self-respect and international recognition through superior performance in their own sphere. The pride resulting from the successful *Wiederaufbau* helped consolidate allegiance to the regime while the prosperity of the "free-market economy" deflected the initial social reform impulses into limited equalization-of-burden programs.[58] A minority took democracy literally and tried to apply the bill of rights in political practice. When the cabinet rejected a referendum on the draft, the "committee against remilitarization [and] for a peace treaty" appealed to lawyers to refuse to follow "orders from above." The GEW also warned against rearmament and opposed the reflex anti-Communism of the Cold War. But the prestigious *NJW* argued that "whoever attacks the constitutional order oversteps the borders of his guaranteed rights." In contrast to Weimar, the postwar political struggle took place *within* and not *against* the constitution, even when that document was used to justify an unpopular policy. To the recurrent question, "have we learned enough" from the Nazi disaster? lawyer Wolfgang Heintzeler replied perceptively: "Things have improved, but we must remain vigilant."[59]

After 1945, most professionals pragmatically accepted the democratic system, although their emotional commitment was less than complete. With the Kaiser's death and Hitler's suicide, there were few alternatives to Adenauer's conservative authority, because draconian Soviet rule discredited socialism in the eastern zone of Germany. In economic and tax issues, the Federal Republic also proved responsive to the desires of the professionals as articulated by the Federal Association of Free Professions of 1949 that lobbied for about 150,000 lawyers, doctors, architects, accountants, and so on. Leading West German politicians drawn from the professions such as Justice Minister Thomas Dehler, Culture Minister Christine Teusch, or Transport Minister Hans-Christoph Seebohm repeatedly addressed national meetings. Less tarnished than bureaucrats, attorneys provided three-quarters of the postwar ministers of justice in the German states.[60] Because experts "apparently desire security more than freedom," the bourgeois coalition government did its best to provide material prosperity, winning adherents by economic performance. Even if professionals remained reluctant to join parties, Bonn's political landscape provided an ideological home for many attorneys in the liberal program of the FDP, for philologues in the Christian humanism of the CDU, and for engineers in the capitalism of the free-market economy. A minority of leftist practitioners leaned to the socialist nationalism of the SPD. However, the spectrum contracted toward the middle, because the large nationalist camp had dwindled to the few incorrigible neo-Nazis, while virtually none followed the Communist cause. Ironically, the greater postwar trauma of 1945 made the Federal Republic look attractive by comparison. Although older professionals never completely came to terms with their feelings of guilt, younger practitioners learned from their bitter NS experience: "In a liberal bourgeois state, the attorney will always find a good home." For the professions as a whole, it took the post-1968 questioning of collaboration taboos to make this lesson completely sink in.[61]

THE TRAVAILS OF GERMAN PRACTITIONERS

On balance, the experience of German professionals in the first half of the twentieth century was hardly a success story. The paradox of their high competence and shameful collaboration in Nazi crimes has been difficult to explain. Impressed by the prevalence of cultural despair, intellectual historians stress the irrational neoconservatism of the cultivated, but slight the socioeconomic underpinnings of their malaise.[62] Obsessed with the antimodern bent of many mandarins, historians of education emphasize the "illiberalism" of professors and students, although they have yet to trace its impact on their working lives.[63] Troubled by the peculiarity of German development, sociopolitical historians allege a deficit of bourgeois civic virtues, while their critics point to considerable evidence of middle-class hegemony.[64] Fascinated with the elusive Bildungsbürgertum, social historians analyze its erosion, but find it difficult to define its borders and ideology beyond a shared cultural style.[65] Specific studies of the role of the professions in the Third Reich have also remained inconclusive. The dichotomy between apologists of "forced" cooperation and critics of "voluntary" compliance oversimplifies the complexity of choices and accommodations. Moreover, the dialectic of perpetrators and victims ignores the overwhelming number of practitioners between these extremes, which allowed the Nazis to proceed.[66] A more comprehensive explanation of their contradictory fate therefore raises vexing questions of theory, history, and ethics.

A modified professionalization approach can help bring the travails of German college graduates between 1900 and 1950 into clearer focus. While introducing an

Anglo-American notion creates some difficulties of its own, the close resemblance of the aspirations of the akademische Berufsstände to the rhetoric of self-governing "professions" makes this transposition not only feasible but also fruitful, because its implicit comparative perspective illuminates a whole range of behavior, which would otherwise remain unintelligible. By providing analytical criteria, this theoretical perspective moves beyond chronicling individual careers to probing common patterns of development not just for the classical free professions, but for all occupations based on higher learning. Its dual emphasis on knowledge and market focuses on the interaction between culture and structure, which is crucial to the reconstruction of the lives of ordinary practitioners.[67] However, the Central European context requires modifications that in turn broaden the original concept of professionalization, which was preoccupied with practitioner autonomy. Instead of arising from spontaneous association, the German professions were largely created "from above" through state examinations, governing certification and entrance into practice. However, because the state loomed larger, they strove for autonomy from its smothering embrace and tried to utilize its legislative and educational machinery for their own aims, for example in neocorporate chambers. Both drawing on and struggling to escape from bureaucratic regulation and capitalist control, German professionalization should be seen as an effort to establish a tenuous middle ground of expert self-determination coupled with legal protection against competition. The Central European case also suggests that the process can be reversed, because "mature professions" might be "deprofessionalized" through socioeconomic crises or repressive policies.[68]

Compared to one another, Central European academic occupations developed a distinctive character that proved remarkably persistent. Though closely resembling their western colleagues, German lawyers were overshadowed by the more numerous public officials and judges. Although they received the same scholarly and practical training, better law graduates sought to enter the higher bureaucracy, middling students went into the judicial service, and—with some exceptions based on tradition or background (opportunities for Jewish lawyers)—less competitive jurists tended to become attorneys. Unlike the stiff entrance examinations for the civil service or judiciary, admission to advocacy was open, making the number of lawyers directly dependent on the fluctuations of law enrollment. Supported by a court monopoly and regulated by a fixed-fee schedule, income ranged widely, with clever attorneys becoming wealthy, ordinary advocates making a prosperous living, but some of the less adept just barely scraping by. Their social status was also mixed, because attorneys ranked below the higher officials, but belonged to the local notables because of their respectable origins, their association with business as well as their active civic involvement. Though autonomous, practice was controlled by a code of ethics and policed by honor courts that encountered increasing difficulty because of the shift from litigation or notary duties to commercial activities and corporate employment. In spite of considerable state dependence, lawyers drew from general bourgeois values an occupational ethos of "free advocacy," which stressed their guardianship of individual freedom against the government. This tension between bureaucratic models and aspirations for independence led to a dual organization of mandatory lawyer chambers—endowed with regulatory powers—and voluntary associations such as the Deutscher Anwaltverein. As prominent members of the Bildungsbürgertum, attorneys were generally liberal and led middle-class parties in demanding greater personal and collective rights.[69]

Although secondary schoolteachers were higher officials, they also achieved a considerable degree of professional standing as guardians of neohumanist cultivation. In contrast to their primary school competitors, philologues were trained at the university in scholarship rather than in pedagogy and constituted the majority of philosophical faculty graduates. Through successive state examinations and public hiring, the bureaucracy controlled entry into the teaching career without much input by practitioners. Based virtually exclusively on employment in a state or municipal high school system, philologue income was modest but secure, supplemented by housing or family allowances and by guaranteed pensions. Lower than legal officials or free professionals, the social status of secondary schoolteachers gradually improved when their salaries reached judicial pay and they obtained the coveted title of Studienrat, even if their recruitment was less exclusive and they remained the butt of literary jokes. Although practice, such as the size of the teaching load, was tightly regulated by the government, philologues aspired to pedagogical autonomy, the freedom to decide how to implement the curriculum in the classroom. Their self-image was a curious blend of scholarly, bureaucratic, and educational imperatives that emphasized the importance of their contribution to German culture. In spite of consistent attempts to gain a foothold in the Ministry of Culture, secondary schoolteachers failed to establish chambers and had to be content with the formation of a vocal pressure group, the Philologenverband. Due to greater state control, high school instructors tended to be nationalist and conformist in their politics and supported bourgeois parties of the Center and Right. However, especially when compared to their American counterparts, German philologues were more "professional" in almost every regard.[70]

Least successful in professionalizing were the engineers. Because they were fragmented by specialty and position as public officials, consulting engineers, and white-collar employees or entrepreneurs, technicians had great difficulty carving out a unified calling. In spite of the promotion of the THs to university rank and the rapid progress of technical knowledge, academic engineers had to compete for the same jobs with graduates of technical middle schools and gifted practitioners without formal training. Industrial insistence on cheap labor kept the Diplom-Ingenieure from gaining market control, leaving them at the tender mercies of enrollment fluctuations and business cycles. Although successful owners or managers could become wealthy, most salaried technicians received a more modest income and many were vulnerable to unemployment in economic crises. In spite of widespread admiration for technology, middle-class recruitment, and authority over workers on the factory floor, engineers were only reluctantly accepted into the Bildungsbürgertum because of their lack of classical cultivation. Although technical "expertise" provided some autonomy, their practical problem solving was usually directed by bureaucrats, clients, or managers, subjecting them to non-technical considerations of public policy, personal taste, or financial return. As compensation, engineers developed an ethos of technical progress, combining knowledge with action in order to advance human welfare through material improvement. Although engineers rallied to promote technology as early as the mid-nineteenth century, the VDI could not develop into a full-fledged professional association, since the clash of interests between professors, entrepreneurs, and employees prevented the formation of a united front in occupational issues that pitted one against the other. Because of the technicians' apolitical self-image, neither the unionizing ButiB nor the professionalizing VDDI succeeded in attracting more than a minority of their colleagues. Although German engineers were more formally trained than their Anglo-American counterparts, full recognition as professionals continued to elude them until after the Second World War.[71]

Across their respective fields, lawyers, philologues, and engineers shared a number of characteristics that set them apart as professions. Not only did they generally belong to the elusive Bildungsbürgertum, but by 1900 they also had developed a number of special professional traits: As graduates of institutions of higher learning, they possessed a liberal education, a core of scientific knowledge, and a body of practical skills. As holders of state-certified credentials, they claimed a market monopoly for their services, even if they were not always able to enforce it completely. Based on recognized expertise, these occupations demanded higher material rewards and aspired to a superior social status as Akademiker. In contrast to manual jobs, they expected autonomy of practice, with their "professional" decisions reviewed not by clients or employers, but by peers in a system of self-discipline. To justify such privileges, these callings embraced an ethos of public service, which was linked to central social values such as law, knowledge, and progress. In pursuit of this Berufsstandespolitik, they formed voluntary associations or compulsory chambers to advance their simultaneously altruistic and egotistic goals within the political system. Although not every academic vocation fully achieved these aims, all struggled with great determination for further professionalization, exhibiting a remarkable continuity of aspirations across political upheavals. Because they competed with each other for scarce resources (such as lawyers and engineers for the recognition of patents), they rarely cooperated with each other. Employment differences between officials, free practitioners, or white-collar employees prevented the formation of a united front of professionals. However, the very rivalry of academic callings demonstrates that they considered themselves related, because all sought to imitate the lead profession, be it law or medicine.[72]

Perennially encountering similar problems, German practitioners responded with related "professional" strategies. While favoring the introduction of some practical experience, they zealously insisted on the necessity of academic credentials against less-trained competitors such as technicians or primary schoolteachers. When faced with overcrowding, many called for market closure either by legal monopoly or by admission restrictions (e.g., *numerus clausus,* limits on the number of women), thereby exaggerating subsequent manpower shortages. Intent on maintaining a high standard of living, professionals resorted to lobbying the government or parliament for increased litigation, salary raises, or business prosperity rather than forming class-conscious and strike-bound trade unions, which they considered "unprofessional." To maintain their superior social status, associations vigorously combatted the negative stereotypes of lawyers as shifty shysters, teachers as petty tyrants, and engineers as uncultured boobs. Against encroaching client control, government regulation, or business dominance, they sought to safeguard the autonomy of their practice by self-discipline in cases of corruption. To sway the public, professionals also projected an elaborate ethos of service, claiming to combine altruistic motives with high technical competence. In order to compensate for their limited number, experts organized to an astounding degree (i.e., more than 90 percent of lawyers and teachers) as interest groups in the political struggle. Willing to borrow at times from bureaucratic, labor, or political strategies, professionals, nonetheless, preferred academization, closure, lobbying, publicity, self-discipline, projection, and voluntary association.[73]

To control their professional field, Central European experts fought similar battles against the pressures emanating from the university, their clients, and the state. As a basis of the claim to privilege, academic knowledge became increasingly problematic after the turn of the century. Under attack from modernist currents, neohumanist cultivation had eroded through philological drudgery so that it provided a veneer rather than a substantive ethos. The explosion of scientific research fragmented knowledge and made it ever harder to master a corpus of specialized *Fachwissen*. Practical training grew more important for professional socialization, thereby imperiling cultural competence and closure claims. During the Weimar Republic, laymen and social reformers increasingly challenged the considerable professional dominance over clients established in the empire. The Nazi party promoted the ascendancy of ideology over competence, and after 1945 expert authority was only partly restored because businessmen became more powerful. Although the legal, cultural, and technical bureaucracy retained a remarkable continuity, the drastic regime changes disoriented the relations between the professions and the state. Each upheaval unleashed a fierce redistribution struggle among practitioners, their nonacademic competitors, and clients. At the same time, overcrowding, unemployment, salary cuts, or losses of prestige made government intervention ever more pivotal for the survival of a viable professionalism. In contrast to the prevalent wage orientation of other social groups, professionals campaigned in order to preserve academic credentials, maintain dominance over clients, and use state policy to gain market control. The interaction between expert strategies, institutional counterpressures, and larger sociopolitical forces determined the pattern of professional development.[74]

In the first half of the twentieth century, four types of professionalism successively emerged in Germany, roughly corresponding to the changes of political regime. Although the traditional academic callings had existed since the Middle Ages, their government-sponsored professionalization through the introduction of a series of state examinations and the regulation of their practice culminated in the liberal founding decade of the Second Reich. Newer occupations of higher education graduates such as engineers tried to follow the successful model of jurists in order to achieve professional status as well. By combining bureaucratic approval and academic credentials with autonomous practitioner action, the *neocorporate professionalism* of the empire took advantage of particular sociopolitical opportunities while responding to specific threats. Lawyers used the arrival of national unification, rendering the creation of a uniform judicial system and legal profession imperative. Secondary schoolteachers drew strength from the rapid expansion of formal schooling, making educators more numerous and important. Engineers thrived on industrial expansion, requiring ever higher degrees of technological expertise. But bureaucratic control and the rise of organized capitalism also created considerable obstacles. Heavily regulated, attorneys had some difficulty maintaining their independence against jurists in public or judicial service. Directly employed by state or local government, philologues had much trouble asserting pedagogical autonomy. Dominated by industrialists, engineers had a hard time controlling their labor market.[75]

To advance their occupation within the status hierarchy of an increasingly dynamic society, academic vocations developed a neocorporate *(berufsständisch)* strategy. Lawyers created compulsory bar associations as representative organs of self-discipline, which were complemented by the voluntary organization of the DAV (1871). Teachers transcended their school type parochialism and in the Philologenverband (1904) formed a powerful professional association to influence the Ministry of Culture as well as the Landtag. Engineers supplemented the technical advocacy of the Verein Deutscher Ingenieure (1856) with the unionist Bund technisch-industrieller Beamter (1904) and academic-protectionist Verein Deutscher Diplom-Ingenieure (1909). The resulting neocorporate professionalism lobbied the state to establish a freie Advokatur in 1879, which made attorneys into a free profession, accessible to everyone trained to become a judge. It also pressured the government into raising teacher salaries to parity with judges in 1909 and to grant a higher title such as the Studienrat in 1917. Finally, it succeeded in forcing the Ministry of Culture to academize engineering training with the reorganization of Technische Hochschulen in 1900. Although claiming independence from the bureaucracy, the professions of the empire nonetheless rejected the full implications of "free field" competition by asking for government protection of credentials and a service monopoly. Establishing a German pattern of professionalization, this neocorporate strategy suffered from increasing internal strains such as overcrowding or elitism even before the First World War put its achievements into general jeopardy.[76]

The *interest group professionalism* of the Weimar Republic sought to adapt the professions to the challenge of a new, democratic environment. By discrediting authoritarian practices, the collapse of the empire led to some reduction in bureaucratic control, diminution of elite power, improvement of access for women or disadvantaged social strata, and modernization of practice. However, calls for lay participation in the courts, reform of school structures or curricula, and opening access to technical credentials were viewed as threatening to undo professional achievements. To fend off outside pressures, professionals turned their associations into vigorous interest groups, capable of cooperating directly with the respective ministry, establishing broader coalitions (e.g., Reichsbund höherer Beamter in 1919), infiltrating political parties, and appealing to public opinion through the Verein für Sozialpolitik. However, the initial chaos of Weimar, postwar overcrowding, proletarianization caused by hyperinflation, traditional self-conceptions, and inadequate organization blocked a positive identification with the new state. Therefore, interest group professionalism was an unstable compromise between partial democratization and neocorporate traditions, responding to the unleashing of collective struggles.[77]

Even during the halcyon years of the republic, regaining professional stability proved difficult, because legal cost cutting, the firing of 10 percent of the teachers, and technical rationalization unemployment prevented a full recovery. In spite of admission of lower court lawyers to district courts, teacher salary gains in 1927, and resurgent engineering activity, the liberalization of the professions remained tenuous, because it grew out of self-interest rather than intellectual conviction or emotional commitment. Through renewed overcrowding, impoverishment by salary cuts, and unemployment of 40,000–50,000 professionals, the Great Depression created a pervasive sense of "professional crisis," which was experienced as a collapse of the legal order, academic standards, and technological progress. When liberal remedies such as competition and selection failed, the majority of professionals rejected collective cures and turned to neoconservative prescriptions such as barring the entry of beginners—promising to restore hierarchical security. Spurred by personal hardship and inspired by nationalist rhetoric, a Protestant and male minority of the blocked younger generation sought salvation in even more drastic Nazi alternatives. Although NS inroads were limited, those marginal academics who followed völkisch appeals contributed disproportionately to Hitler's success. Closer to western patterns than to neocorporate traditions, interest group professionalism was repudiated because insurmountable socioeconomic problems confirmed ideological reservations against its apparent license.[78]

The *instrumentalized professionalism* of the Third Reich stemmed not just from Nazi compulsion but also from practitioner collaboration. Hitler's seizure of power provided Old Fighters, men, racists, and youths with a mandate to "coordinate" their associations and an opportunity to eliminate their competitors. Claiming to restore professional authority, NS fanatics stripped political opponents and Jewish colleagues of their livelihood, while discriminating against women and the elderly. Greater government powers allowed more radical remedies, and the economic recovery—fueled by rearmament—solved the overcrowding crisis. Whereas many welcomed the return of prosperity, the price of recovering a semblance of normalcy was steep. Not only were the professions purged, but practitioners also lost their cherished autonomy. Moreover, mission and practice were thoroughly nazified through endless indoctrination and vigilant discipline. Despite some grumbling about regimentation, evident material gains, partial openness to modern methods, and a sense of national revival seemed to make some sacrifice of professional integrity worthwhile during the early Third Reich.[79]

The illusion of reprofessionalization was dispelled when it became painfully clear that the professions did not regain self-determination, but were more thoroughly subjected to outside control than ever before. Those NS idealists who tried to develop a völkisch professionalism and insist on Nazi performance were bound to be disappointed in the long run. The "germanization" of theory and practice turned out to be a mirage, because Hitler's hordes would not be contained within the bounds of a völkisch law, education, or technology. The emergence of the SS police state removed ever larger areas of law from "professional" judgment, turned education from enlightenment into indoctrination, and used technological innovation not for humanitarian progress but for mechanized extermination and industrialized warfare. Moreover, the mobilization and destruction of the Second World War eroded academic standards, disrupted labor supply, imposed material hardship, fostered status insecurity, complicated practice, generated ethical conflicts, and destroyed the last remnants of association. Even if a modicum of expertise survived the Third Reich and the professions suffered less material hardship than other social strata, the result of the partly forced, partly voluntary cooperation was disastrous. In spite of institutional gains for some occupations such as engineers and groups within others such as physical education teachers, instrumentalization generally destroyed professionalism by ruining the very qualities that set it apart.[80]

The flight into a kind of *neoprofessionalism* in the Federal Republic was largely a response to the experience of the Third Reich and to the immense devastation left by Hitler's adventures. With the crushing defeat of the Wehrmacht, problems initially loomed larger than possibilities. The untold physical destruction, the decimation of the ranks of male practitioners, and the disruption of normal civil intercourse endangered the very survival of the professions. The taint of collaboration with an inhuman regime produced a moral disorientation, while the loss of national unity made for a myriad of regional measures that fragmented uniformity of practice. However, the collapse also offered a chance to cast off Nazi repression, to cleanse corrupted traditions, and to fashion a new, purified professionalism. Military occupation policies encouraged not only pragmatic problem solving but also sponsored democratic reforms, based on their own, less contaminated professional legacy.[81]

First individually and then collectively, professionals reclaimed their expertise. The pressing problems of postwar reconstruction put a higher premium on rebuilding training, restoring manpower supply, recovering prosperity and prestige, redirecting practice, and refounding associations than on engaging in ideological soul-searching. By the early 1950s, these efforts led to a gradual reprofessionalization—an Indian summer of the expert, so to speak—allowing practitioners to recover their competence and authority to a surprising extent. However, democratization was less complete, because the purge of NS personnel and the reorientation of work proved difficult. Except for an incorrigible few, most academics overtly distanced themselves from the Nazi past, even if some NS patterns survived covertly. Resuming Weimar's departures, a minority openly confronted the professions' complicity with Nazi crimes and called for drastic democratic or socialist reform. However, the bulk of practitioners preferred to return to neocorporate traditions of the empire, which were modified somewhat in the light of their chastening experience. Formally democratic, the uneasy neoprofessionalism in the Federal Republic was consolidated by the spectacular success of the economic miracle, which prevented a full renewal.[82]

This troubled evolution of the German professions had political implications for the Bildungsbürgertum in particular and society at large. On the one hand, professional allegiances depended on structural factors, such as their relationship to the state. Having begun as quasi officials, attorneys nonetheless saw themselves as defenders of individual freedom in the administration of justice. Compelled to present prescribed curricula, secondary schoolteachers claimed some classroom autonomy in implementing official guidelines. Except for a few technical bureaucrats, engineers worked in an economic marketplace, subject to the power of their employers in large firms. Lawyers claimed to advance the rule of law *(Rechtsstaat)* and teachers to guard culture *(Kulturstaat),* while engineers developed an ideology of technological progress. On the other hand, the experts' politics were determined by their actual situation at any given time. Because it affected material circumstances and practice conditions, a specific government policy toward justice, education, or technology was perceived either as favorable or hostile. The responsiveness of a cabinet to articulated professional interests shaped their outlook to a considerable degree. Although the bureaucracy expected the courts, schools, and factories to follow certain policies, professional associations tried to influence the ministries as well as bourgeois legislators to obtain their aims. During the four drastic regime changes, this complex interaction led to a fundamental restructuring of the professions, with practitioners partly the instigators and partly the victims of development. This strong interdependence with the state made for an ideological opportunism that saw the empire as favorable, was frustrated with the Weimar Republic, initially welcomed the Third Reich but eventually grew disillusioned, and grumbled about the Federal Republic before gradually coming to like its pro-expert policies.[83]

Their narrow interest orientation made professionals disastrously susceptible to shifts in general political development. Never completely uniform, the professions fell within the *bildungsbürgerlich* spectrum, albeit with special accents governed by their particular work experience. Lawyers were usually more libertarian, teachers tended to be more statist, and engineers were often more apolitical than other members of the educated middle class. With sociopolitical upheavals tipping the balance between them, several basic outlooks competed for the allegiance of professionals: Bureaucratic authoritarian traditions clashed with liberal elitist views, which were opposed by democratic lay and socialist collective currents, while the populist, völkisch, and racist countertradition started as a marginal rivulet, before swelling into an irresistible stream. During the empire, state-oriented elders were superseded by the liberal founding fathers of professionalism, who were subsequently challenged by their illiberal sons, who in turn were confronted by their neoliberal or imperialist offspring. In the Weimar Republic, the dialogue evolved beyond centrist pragmatists toward polarity between democratic reformers and authoritarian reactionaries. Dramatically shifting toward the völkisch fringe, the Third Reich discourse involved Nazi zealots, apathetic collaborators, and various kinds of covert or overt resisters. Reversed in the other direction, the professional debate of the Federal Republic pitted democratic idealists against neutral experts and lingering traditionalists, not to mention closet Nazis. In putting their special interests above the common weal, practitioners bartered away their ethical standards for material security and failed to defend the rule of law, the integrity of culture, and the humanity of technology as prerequisite for their work. When they used their autonomy to serve themselves above all, the professions made themselves "unfree."[84]

How exceptional was the corruption of German professionalism in the twentieth century? In many ways the fate of professionals in the Soviet Union presented an anticipatory reverse mirror image that discredited left-wing solutions. As progressive zemstvo reformers, established professionals helped bring about the February revolution of 1917 and supported the Provisional Government. Though endorsed by the radical intelligentsia of unemployed students, the Bolsheviks in their egalitarian fervor initially attempted to abolish the professions completely, because they distrusted bourgeois liberals. When such disestablishment proved counterproductive to competence, they created "collegia" of practitioners as collectives to handle all remuneration and to police practice, while the greatly increased numbers of higher education graduates diluted professional consciousness.[85] The Italian case foreshadowed the Nazi experience more directly. Massive educational overcrowding and professional unemployment in the early 1920s led many academics to follow Mussolini's call. Whereas the Gentile reform reduced access to professional training, practicing professionals were forced into Fascist corporations (70,000 by 1928 and 152,000 by 1940). Although managing to avoid party membership, advocates lost control over their credentials, self-government, and autonomy while having to struggle for an adequate livelihood within the corporate state.[86] These disappointing Bolshevik or Fascist solutions ought to have served as a warning against Nazi promises. However, during the existential crisis, totalitarian threats to professionalism seem not to have been heeded elsewhere.

Other Central European professionals reacted similarly to their German colleagues against the educational overcrowding of the late 1920s. As an International Student Service study of professional unemployment shows, in Austria the surplus of academics from the former Habsburg Empire led to a cessation of legal and teacher hiring in the second half of the 1920s, which meant that about 600 graduates a year could not find jobs. Economically distressed and ideologically fragmented, considerable numbers of these professionals (such as 470 secondary schoolteachers) had already joined NS auxiliaries like the NSLB *before* 1933 and continued to do so until 1938 in spite of prohibitions. Such internal preparation for the Anschluß closely resembled German self-nazification and paved the way for the fusion of the two professional systems thereafter. In Hungary, with one-sixth of all professionals unemployed in 1928, the economically depressed doctors demanded state control of the health market in order to prohibit the private competition of their Jewish colleagues, while the technocratic engineers moved from corporatism to anti-Semitism. But the more courageous and liberal lawyers resisted all attempts at proscription and managed to save the great majority of Jewish attorneys, demonstrating that similar economic problems do not necessarily lead to identical ideological reactions. However, in Japan the rising proportion of graduates without jobs to more than one-half by 1931 is likely to have reinforced their fierce nationalism. The League of Nations observer Walter Kotschnig feared that the crisis of the professions was leading especially the young to "join . . . the vanguard of revolution" toward the Right in other countries like Rumania (Iron Guard), France (Croix de Feu), and even in Holland.[87]

The peculiar *Sonderweg* of these Central European professions becomes apparent when compared to Western Europe. Although the socioeconomic depression also produced ideological disorientation and led some intellectuals to embrace Communist or Fascist programs, the overwhelming majority of western professionals clung to the parliamentary system and did not betray their humanitarian ethics. Not that they were necessarily better than their German colleagues. However, the structural and situational constellation differed. With greater distance from the state and more autonomy, English professionals developed stronger liberal loyalties. The higher resilience of the democracies managed to contain the antidemocratic currents before they could threaten the legitimacy of the system. The overcrowding problem was also less severe in countries where the entitlement system was not as pronounced. While there was much debate about individualist versus collectivist solutions, the discussion did not call into question the political order as such. Based on their greater self-control, the professions had more success with exclusionary strategies (such as the barring of foreigners in France), thereby protecting existing practitioners. After 1933 they could, as in Sweden, learn from the German disasters and pursue more effective remedial policies, such as improved vocational guidance. Therefore, related professional problems did not merge with general political resentment to the same nefarious degree. The more fortunate resolution of the professional crisis in Western Europe suggests that, in spite of similar pressures elsewhere, the Central European debacle, though explicable, was not inevitable.[88]

PROFESSIONALS AND LIBERTY

Ultimately, the corrosion of German professionalism stemmed from a separation from its liberal roots. Although academic occupations had existed since the Middle Ages, their professionalization during the nineteenth century was one of the proudest achievements of the educated middle class. Lawyers could flourish when the rule of law was assured and civil rights limited state power; secondary schoolteachers could advance when cultivation implied higher learning in educational institutions; engineers could prosper when technical progress became part and parcel of general human improvement. The emerging professional ethos had a largely liberal core: Certified competence, meritocratic pay and prestige, autonomous practice, ethical discipline, and collective self-government were noneconomic versions of central *bürgerliche* values. Liberal parties played a crucial role in establishing "free advocacy" in 1879, in increasing philologue pay, and in upgrading technical training.[89] However, in the last decades of the empire, unexpected tensions emerged between the professions and liberalism. Many practitioners had always been suspicious of the dangers of unrestrained competition and turned to other political parties. Beginning with the overcrowding crisis of the 1880s, professionals increasingly called for state protection and regulation. At the same time, the rapid expansion of the size of the professions and the dynamics of scientific specialization undercut their ethical commitment.[90] Therefore, the disruptions of the First World War and the disappointments of the Weimar Republic made many professionals repudiate their liberal legacy and openly embrace illiberalism. Ironically, the democratization efforts of radical intellectuals after 1918 led to an authoritarian backlash. More and more experts just wanted to practice their specialty without outside interference. When by 1933 liberal solutions failed to cure the chronic crisis, all too few professionals were willing to cooperate in developing more effective democratic or socialist remedies. Discarding basic liberties along with political Liberalism, traditionalist practitioners hoped that authoritarian reprofessionalization would set everything right, while völkisch zealots dreamed of the birth of a new Nazi professionalism.[91]

This attempt to save the professions by abandoning their outmoded ethical moorings exacted a frightful price. Instead of having their authority restored, in the Third Reich professionals found themselves "coordinated," politically and racially purged, and ideologically "germanized" as never before. Clearly some groups such as Nazi zealots or opportunists and some occupations such as doctors and engineers profited from collaboration. No doubt, considerable scientific and practical progress continued under Hitler's rule, even if engineering patents dropped by one-quarter.[92] But the clients "treated" by Nazi professionals suffered grievously in the courts, schools, or factories, not to mention those people victimized in the concentration camps, euthanasia clinics, and the like. The professions lost the very qualities that distinguished them, when competence declined, certification became haphazard, their material and social position deteriorated, autonomy vanished, ethics were corrupted, and free association became proscribed. Only during the crushing defeat of the Nazi armies did some chastened practitioners rediscover what they had lost in trying to save themselves. In troubling reflections about their complicity, German professionals concluded from "Third Reich tyranny" that freedom of advocacy was "an ethical question," requiring "everyone to share political responsibility." To turn "subjects" into "citizens," educators must "struggle against any authoritarian trend" and defend the freedom of speech as a precondition for teaching. Instead of trusting in rationality, specialization, and technology, engineers should aspire to "reverence for the unknowable," universality, and the "spirit of noble humanity."[93]

The experience of the German professions in the first half of this century shows that highly competent expertise alone has been found wanting. Its disastrous deformation in the Third Reich suggests that professionals are terribly vulnerable to socioeconomic crises and political instrumentalization. In order to benefit the public as well as the practitioners, professionalism must be more than a selfish instrument for material gain. Only as an altruistic service to humanity, anchored in ethical commitment, and protected by basic civil rights, can professions make their full contribution to individual and collective welfare. Through largely self-inflicted disasters, some sobered survivors came to understand this essential connection between professionalism, social responsibility, and liberty.[94]

APPENDIX A
STATISTICAL TABLES

with
Eric John Yonke

In contrast to the plethora of figures on education, statistics on the professions are fragmentary. Because numbers played a central role in the political debate at the time, lawyers and teachers more than engineers assiduously collected them, often assisted by census officials. However, scholars have made little systematic use of such information, perhaps because they suspected its reliability or lacked a conceptual frame of reference. In order to grasp the outlines of professional evolution, it is essential to establish accurate long-term time series that describe basic parameters. So as to probe the relationship between professionalization and other sociopolitical changes, it is equally imperative to create structural indicators that can be employed analytically. While the preceding text contains brief snapshots of specific problems, this appendix presents long-range statistics on broad developments as quantitative underpinning for the entire study.

Among the many problems suggested by professionalization theory, five aspects of professional history are particularly important. Tables A.1–A.3 deal with academic training, social selection, and financial aid in order to illuminate the changing number and composition of future practitioners. Tables A.4–A.7 portray the overall growth of the professions and the increase in individual careers, with supplementary data on beginning professionals that shed light on labor market dynamics. Tables A.8–A.10 probe the occupational structure of attorneys, secondary schoolteachers, and engineers in order to understand their internal conflicts. Tables A.11–A.13 focus on the elusive material situation of the sample professions by looking at the civil and criminal case load for lawyers, official salary figures for philologues, and the unemployment pattern of engineers. Finally, Tables A.14–A.18 address the Nazi proclivity of experts through cross-tabulations on NSDAP membership patterns of students, professionals, and the three exemplary careers.

Much useful information can already be gleaned from printed statistics, especially if selected and recombined. The governmental censuses of occupations between 1907 and 1950, which were published in the relevant volumes of *Statistik des Deutschen Reichs,* offer five cross sections (Table A.4), posing particular difficulties in the classification of technical careers (Table A.7). The annual *Sta-*

tistisches Jahrbuch contains frequent updates on judicial and educational figures (Tables A.5, A.6, A.11, and A.12), which have been surprisingly neglected until now. Drawn from these sources were the university statistics, presented in Hartmut Titze's handbook on *Das Hochschulstudium* (Tables A.1, A.2, A.6b), and recalculated in four-semester averages here. Topical studies such as Johannes Müller's investigation of judicial tests, Charlotte Lorenz's compilation of state examinations, or Axel Nath's analysis of teaching careers also provide valuable time series (Table A.5b). Finally, professional journals intermittently publish useful information on unemployment (Table A.13) or association membership that supplements official figures (Tables A.5–A.7). Though usually authoritative, these published statistics must be used with caution. They often break down during wartime or end abruptly in the Third Reich, use problematic or shifting categories (as for technicians), rest on a changing territorial base *(Großdeutschland* versus Federal Republic), and do not address some of the most important issues.

In order to answer more detailed and complex questions about the professions, it was therefore necessary to create fresh tables from primary data sets. For this purpose, the membership files of educational and professional associations were the central source. In order to probe NS academic priorities, a sample was drawn from the loan cards of the *Reichsstudentenwerk,* which was the central German student aid institution. Because the overall contours of the RSW file have already been explored by Gerhard Arminger [*HSR* 30 (1984): 3ff], while Michael H. Kater has analyzed the medical faculty *(Doctors Under Hitler,* Appendix), it sufficed to select 12 percent of the cases from law, teaching, and engineering ($N=1436$). Each card lists the amount or date of borrowing and also shows a student's birthplace and date, his or her father's occupation, parents' residence, and, after 1932, involvement in various Nazi organizations. Though clearly not representative of all future professionals, this data set offers interesting insights into financial aid policy (Tables A.3a and b) as well as into scholarship students' Nazi affinity (Table A.14).

Establishing the relative degree of complicity of each profession required a comparison with all others. Fortunately, Prof. Kater was kind enough to make accessible the notebooks of his systematic sample of the NSDAP *Hauptkartei* from the Berlin Document Center [see his explanations in *GG* 3 (1977), 451ff, and *The Nazi Party,* p. 13ff]. Selecting the professionals (with full academic training), semiprofessionals (some postsecondary education), and protoprofessionals (students, pupils, trainees) from his more than 21,000 entries yielded 2429 cases for secondary analysis. Though somewhat rudimentary, the information on the party membership cards sheds light on gender, birth cohort, residence, title, and career, which confirms well-known patterns on sex or age, but challenges other interpretations such as the thesis of the nonpolitical character of engineers (Tables 4.1 and A.15).

For the legal profession, the DAV membership directory proved invaluable [*Verzeichnis der Rechtsanwälte, Notare und Gerichtsvollzieher* (Leipzig, 1924, 1932, 1936)]. In order to compare across time, a systematic 5 percent sample was drawn for 1924, 1932, and 1936, consisting of 2967 individuals. Though scanty on social background, these registers list place of practice, advanced degree, and type of court. A persistence variable trying to assess professional longevity could be computed as well (Table A.8). The 1936 directory also designated NS party members with an asterisk, allowing a comparison between Nazi and non-NS attorneys. In addition, the names of the founding members of the BNSDJ plus a couple of dozen other pre-1933 joiners have survived in the Federal Archives (NS 16). This list offers regional distribution, degree, and legal career, allowing for a contrast with the 1932 DAV directory (Table A.16).

The core of this quantitative analysis is the NSLB data base. The Berlin Document Center has preserved the entire teachers' league file in 451 drawers, with each holding about one thousand individuals, amounting to more than 400,000 total members. Selecting the first ten cards from each drawer yielded a systematic 1 percent sample of 4386 cases, independent of alphabetical distortion (which is essential since names vary regionally, by religious affiliation, and the like). Because it only produced 143 pre-1933 joiners, this sample was extended by 435 additional Old Fighters, selected randomly, and the rest of the data set weighted by a factor of 3.04 (in order to keep the same proportion), resulting in 13,596 cases overall. Each card holds an extraordinary amount of information, ranging from birthplace and religion to type of teaching job, marital status, and prior teacher association membership. Also included are NSLB and NSDAP numbers and dates as well as entries on other NS affiliates, allowing the construction of about twenty-five variables, half of which are fairly complete. Because the NSLB comprised more than nine-tenths of all teachers in the 1930s (Table 6.2), this data set allowed a comprehensive reconstruction of professional stratification (Table A.9), and of Nazi proclivities (Table A.17). So as not to burden this study with too much statistical detail, a more complex logit model has been published separately in the *Journal of Interdisciplinary History* (with G. Arminger, "The German Teaching Profession and Nazi Party Membership" 29 [1989]: 197–225).

Ironically, data on engineers proved frustratingly elusive, because occupational boundaries were too fluid to allow precise figures. For the internal structure, the VDI membership directories of 1913, 1929, and 1952 proved helpful [*Mitgliederverzeichnis des VDI* (Berlin, 1913, 1929, Essen, 1952)]. A systematic sample of every twentieth entry yielded 4420 cases, representing the limited number of VDI members concentrated in mechanical engineering rather than technical professionals in general. The scanty listing yields information on gender, urbanity, region, degree, occupation, and employment sector (Table A.10). The only primary source on the engineers' relationship to National Socialism are the few surviving DAF cards of NSBDT members, which were alphabetically interleaved with the NSLB file. Combined with the technicians found in the teacher sample, a search of every forty-fifth drawer produced 181 entries, amounting only to a small splinter of the entire NSBDT. However, the DAF *Adrema* cards contain much detail on regional distribution, occupational level, and economic sector as well as marital status, birthdate, NS involvement, and professional affiliation. Unfortunately, the uncertain relationship of this splinter to the whole makes any results suggestive at best (Table A.18).

To facilitate comparison, table design and categories have been standardized as much as possible. For the sake of consistency, long-term time series seemed preferable to short-term fragments, even if that meant resorting to information from Prussia rather than staying with data from the Reich exclusively. Although the discreteness of the data often required transformation, much effort went into maintaining essential dividing lines while condensing it into usable aggregates. In order to permit checking, sources have always been indicated. Moreover, categories and headings are explained in some detail the first time they appear. Finally, specific problems in particular figures are pointed out in additional notes. Filling the gaps in the record required much labor and was only sometimes crowned with success. In other instances, a measurable indicator (e.g., legal case load or technical unemployment) had to substitute for a desired category (such as income). Fragmentary figures that did not allow tabulation are directly presented in the text.

The backwardness of statistics on professions made it necessary to put a premium on data compilation. By providing basic documentation, the following tables sketch the rough outlines of professional development and conflict for German lawyers, teachers, and engineers. However, in the creation of indexes, the comparison of structures with cohorts, and the cross-tabulation of characteristics with Nazi involvement, this appendix also tries to suggest fruitful directions for more complex analysis (see Chapter 4, pp. 100–104).

Table A.1. Students in Professional Training: Four-Semester Averages[a]

Year	Law	Teaching	Engineering	Total Students	Per 100,000
1900–1901	9,919.50	10,037.00	11,288.00	50,450.67	90.07
1902–1903	10,932.75	11,153.00	12,362.75	54,798.50	94.16
1904–1905	11,656.50	12,298.00	12,016.50	58,089.00	96.98
1906–1907	11,773.50	14,172.50	11,500.00	62,053.00	100.56
1908–1909	11,212.75	17,061.75	11,078.50	66,614.25	105.24
1910–1911	10,672.00	20,340.00	10,938.25	72,087.25	110.66
1912–1913	10,445.25	22,438.50	11,026.25	77,473.00	116.39
1914–1915[b]	8,866.25	19,351.00	10,265.00	31,231.00	46.07
1916–1917	11,231.50	21,424.00	11,070.50	30,055.50	44.66
1918–1919	15,880.50	25,387.75	15,639.75	80,054.25	123.44
1920–1921	18,749.25	22,431.00	22,296.50	118,239.25	190.29
1922–1923	22,006.75	19,944.50	25,463.00	120,234.00	193.61
1924–1925	17,034.75	16,633.50	21,570.50	92,440.00	147.77
1926–1927	19,246.00	22,815.00	20,854.50	98,035.25	153.58
1928–1929	22,394.25	32,460.50	21,523.00	117,874.75	182.55
1930–1931	20,273.25	35,991.25	22,649.00	132,354.75	202.82
1932–1933	15,774.25	26,450.50	18,938.50	118,734.75	181.33
1934–1935	9,202.75	14,863.25	12,637.00	85,974.00	129.05
1936–1937	5,477.00	9,790.00	10,084.00	69,326.50	102.58
1938–1939[c]	4,146.50	7,477.00	9,952.00	51,672.00	75.29
1940–1941[d]	3,176.00	8,768.00	7,215.50	53,216.00	76.20
1942–1943[e]	3,473.00	13,200.75	8,334.06	60,138.00	86.08
SS 1944[f]				55,495.00	79.43
1948–1949[g]	12,046.00	34,018.00	15,273.50	104,177.50	211.75
1950–1951	12,680.50	33,805.50	18,427.00	114,302.00	227.43
1952–1953	12,175.00	33,238.75	21,234.25	116,462.75	227.89
1954–1955	14,301.25	36,537.25	22,453.25	124,710.75	239.23

Source: Data from H. Titze, ed., *Das Hochschulstudium in Preußen und Deutschland 1820–1944* (Göttingen, 1987), Table 1; Statistisches Bundesamt, *Statistisches Jahrbuch für die Bundesrepublik Deutschland* 1 (1952): 71; 2 (1953): 96; 3 (1954): 94; 4 (1955): 94; 5 (1956): 96; 6 (1957): 96.

[a]Explanation of headings: law, *Juristische Fakultät;* teaching, *Philosophische Fakultät* minus nonteaching subjects; engineering, Technische Hochschulen; total students, all postsecondary enrollment; per 100,000, postsecondary enrollment compared to population.

[b]Actual students in 1914 were fewer than 40,000 and in 1918 fewer than 25,000 [see F. Schulze and P. Ssymank, *Das Deutsche Studententum* (Munich, 1932), pp. 453]. Total students taken from W. Albert, *Materialien zur Entwicklung (HIS)* (Hanover, 1969), p. 98, 18.

[c]Total students taken from *HIS,* p. 98.

[d]See Titze, *Hochschulstudium,* Table 3.

[e]See Ch. Lorenz, *Die Entwicklung des Fachstudiums während des Krieges* (Berlin, 1944), Table 2.

[f]See J. Pauwels, *Women, Nazis, and the Universities* (Westport, 1984), p. 153.

[g]Figures to 1955 include Berlin, based on summer semester averages.

Table A.2. Social Structure of Future Professionals: Four-Semester Averages

	Percentage of Women in Faculty				Percentage of Gymnasium Graduates[a]				Percentage from Academic Families[b]			
Year	Lawyers	Teachers	Engineers	University	Lawyers	Teachers	Engineers[c]	University	Lawyers	Teachers	Engineers[d]	University
1900–1901					99.83	61.48	25.76	82.05	30.39	20.08	22.42	25.09
1902–1903					96.73	65.08	21.04	80.06	29.09	19.46	22.57	24.15
1904–1905					88.89	71.12	23.52	74.82	28.10	16.87	22.09	22.69
1906–1907			0.05				28.92					
1908–1909[e]	0.23	4.79	0.14	2.99	83.93	69.73	27.44	72.01	27.90	15.85		21.70
1910–1911	0.35	7.64	0.40	4.43	78.95	63.66	27.68	69.00	29.56	14.43		21.17
1912–1913	0.51	9.91	0.57	5.57								
1914–1915	0.87	14.27	0.86	7.79								
1916–1917	1.09	16.36	1.65	9.48								
1918–1919	2.04	15.70	1.73	9.43								
1920–1921	3.06	16.93	1.32	9.44								
1922–1923	3.45	18.69	1.61	10.17								
1924–1925[f]	2.90	20.43	1.61	11.18	58.07	37.80		46.32	25.01	20.00	23.70	22.60
1926–1927	2.80	25.43	2.01	12.89	54.00	38.09		46.18	24.69	16.33		21.90
1928–1929	4.13	25.13	2.63	15.48	49.00	34.19		44.19	25.10	14.00		21.30
1930–1931	5.75	26.38	3.83	18.25	44.84	31.50		40.45	27.06	14.08	18.70	21.63
1932–1933[e]	5.34	26.96	4.42	18.11	42.55	29.88		39.04	28.00	14.45	22.18	22.36
1934–1935[g]	2.90	27.72	3.35	16.46					28.80	21.50	21.67	22.01
1936–1937[g]	1.55	27.88	2.43	15.54								26.31
1938–1939	1.15	24.66	2.33	15.56								27.23
1940–1941[g]	3.50	44.36	7.27	26.29					25.58	22.79	19.50	27.92
1942–1943[h]	14.82	56.22	17.05	44.21								

Source: Data from H. Titze, ed., *Das Hochschulstudium in Preußen und Deutschland 1820–1944* (Göttingen, 1987), Tables 3, 6, 7, 29, 34–43, 46–48, 50–63, 94, 98, 101–106, 116, 120, 124–126, 134, 136, 138.

[a]Percentage of male Prussian students with classical secondary training.

[b]Percentage of male Prussian students from university-educated families (after 1933, all German students).

[c]Figures for 1900–1910 are for TH Karlsruhe; see *Badische Hochschulstatistik,* p. 122.

[d]Figures for 1900–1905 are for TH Karlsruhe; see *Badische Hochschulstatistik,* pp. 272–73.

[e]Percentage of women from academic families: 1908–1909 = 45.27; 1924–1925 = 32.53; 1932–1933 = 32.25; 1941 = 39.36.

[f]Percentage Gymnasium trained women: 1924–1925 = 10.44; 1932–1933 = 4.60.

[g]For social origin, see Ch. Lorenz, *Zehnjahres-Statistik des Hochschulbesuchs* (Berlin, 1944), Tables XVIa, XVIb. Figures in the university column are based on entering students.

[h]Ch. Lorenz, *Die Entwicklung des Fachstudiums während des Krieges* (Berlin, 1944), Table 2.

Table A.3a. Financial Aid for Professional Training: Distribution of Financial Aid

	Four-Semester Averages								
Parameter[a]	To 1929	1930–1931	1932–1933	1934–1935	1936–1937	1938–1939	1940–1941	1942–1944	Average[b]
Demographic									
Percentage female		6.8	11.3	7.0	2.7	5.6	6.8	23.1	7.3
Over age 24	45.8	35.3	40.1	47.2	47.8	53.7	58.6	47.6	51.3
Birthplace size									
Rural	25.0	31.0	22.6	31.1	24.3	24.2	29.2	17.0	25.8
Town	37.5	33.6	45.1	36.7	46.4	41.6	40.6	50.8	42.0
City	37.5	35.3	32.3	32.2	29.3	34.2	30.2	32.3	32.3
Social Origin									
High official	17.4	17.4	16.8	22.1	21.3	23.3	18.4	23.4	20.4
Free professional	17.4	18.3	14.8	11.6	12.2	10.8	15.3	9.4	13.2
Propertied *(Besitz)*	4.3	12.2	11.3	5.0	5.9	5.1	4.2	7.8	6.9
Old middle class	43.5	24.3	27.0	25.6	23.2	24.6	21.6	28.1	25.0
New middle class	4.3	20.9	18.0	24.1	23.2	21.7	26.8	15.6	21.7
Working class	13.0	7.0	12.1	11.6	14.2	14.4	13.7	15.6	12.9
Faculty									
Law	96.0	47.0	40.2	44.7	42.9	43.8	43.8	36.9	43.9
Teaching	4.0	38.5	39.5	34.2	25.8	24.2	15.1	29.2	28.4
Engineering		14.5	20.3	21.1	31.6	32.0	41.1	33.8	27.7
Financial Aid									
Length[c]		18.8	21.4	20.6	28.1	49.5	68.2	41.5	35.4
Amount[d]	1032.0	550.0	500.0	480.0	600.0	500.0	593.0	600.0	550.0
Percentage of total	1.7	8.2	17.9	13.9	17.9	22.5	13.4	4.5	100.0

Source: Data from Reichsstudentenwerk files, consisting of a 12 percent systematic sample of law, philosophy, and engineering students, based on the surviving personal file cards of grantees from 1923 to 1944.

[a]Birthplace size: rural, population under 5000; town, between 5000 and 100,000; city, over 100,000. Financial aid: length, percentage of students with less than 1 year of aid; amount, median amount of aid received (in marks).

[b]Marginal average for the data set. It is not the row average.

[c]Length in months.

[d]Amount in marks.

Table A.3b. Financial Aid for Professional Training: Distribution of Aid by Faculty

	Weimar (1923–1932)				NS Period (1933–1938)				War (1939–1945)			
Parameter[a]	Law	Teaching	Engineering	Total	Law	Teaching	Engineering	Total	Law	Teaching	Engineering	Total
Demographic												
Percentage female	3.2	15.0	0.0	7.0	1.5	18.0	1.0	6.3	2.3	38.0	2.0	9.2
Over age 24	31.7	41.0	46.7	37.7	40.2	52.0	51.7	46.8	54.4	52.6	63.9	57.6
Birthplace size												
Rural	19.2	39.0	11.1	25.2	25.6	33.8	19.2	26.4	24.3	30.4	22.8	24.9
Town	40.8	34.0	55.6	40.7	40.1	37.8	47.3	41.3	43.9	46.9	42.2	43.9
City	38.4	27.0	33.3	33.3	34.3	28.5	33.5	32.4	31.8	22.8	34.3	31.0
Social Origin												
High official	17.5	19.0	20.0	18.5	21.8	20.2	20.0	20.8	26.8	15.2	16.7	20.7
Free professional	20.0	9.0	13.3	14.7	18.2	4.8	10.5	12.1	15.5	13.9	12.5	14.1
Propertied (*Besitz*)	15.0	4.0	11.1	10.2	11.5	0.9	5.5	6.7	6.0	2.5	5.6	5.1
Old middle class	31.7	31.0	20.0	29.4	25.2	24.6	26.5	25.3	20.2	20.3	22.9	21.2
New middle class	10.8	23.0	28.9	18.5	14.8	29.8	25.0	22.0	20.8	25.3	25.0	21.2
Working class	5.0	14.0	6.7	8.7	8.5	19.7	12.5	12.9	10.7	22.8	17.4	15.6
Financial Aid												
Length	12.0	22.0	24.4	17.8	22.3	25.9	33.0	26.2	68.8	55.7	64.4	64.6
Amount	665.0	485.0	430.0	572.0	600.0	505.0	500.0	538.0	600.0	530.0	500.0	540.0
Percentage of total	46.3	37.0	16.7	18.8	43.5	29.9	26.6	53.2	43.1	19.7	37.2	28.0

Source: Data from Reichsstudentenwerk set (see Table A.3a).

[a]For explanation of headings, see Table A.3a. Since missing values were less than 2 percent, they were deleted from the computations.

Table A.4. Growth of the Professions

Profession[a]	1907	1925	1933	1939	1950
Law					
Judges[b]	9,289	9,361	10,450	16,987	15,048
Attorneys/Notaries	8,608	13,886	19,364	19,091	13,553
Consultants	—	—	3,104	—	996
Referendaries	—	—	14,801	7,391	—
Total	17,897	23,247	55,005	51,788	29,597
Teaching					
Professors	5,100	4,958	7,272	7,352	5,706
Secondary[c]	35,339	40,985	37,935	51,020	28,783
Trade	12,065	17,030	48,399	53,427	29,617
Primary	187,485	208,801	206,011	215,670	147,680
Private	—	1,816	10,765	9,121	6,802
Kindergarten	—	22,547	27,281	26,850	28,702
Total	277,153	296,137	337,663	363,440	247,390
Engineering					
Architects	45,978	44,977	78,868	126,993	88,535
Chemists	5,800	10,574	12,696	16,932	15,503
Engineers[d]	45,916	111,085	175,947	266,457	176,887
Technicians	—	—	27,700	51,588	19,490
Total	97,694	166,636	295,211	461,970	300,415
TOTAL	392,744	486,018	687,879	877,198	577,402
Percentage of work force	1.6	1.5	2.1	2.6	2.6

Source: Data from the professional censuses as transcribed by the VASMA Project. The 1907 figures are from the *Statistik des Deutschen Reichs* (Berlin 1910), Vol. 202, and the *Statistisches Jahrbuch* 30 (1909): 287, and 35 (1914). See W. Kleber and A. Willms, *Historische Berufszählungen. Datenhandbuch* (Mannheim, 1981), Tables BZ.25.TO2. DAT3.X, BZ.33.TO2.DAT1, BZ.39.T12.DAT1, BZ50.TO1.DAT4.

[a]Explanation of professional titles: judges, *Richter* and *Staatsanwälte;* attorneys, *Rechts-* and *Patentanwälte* as well as *Notare;* councillors, *Rechtskonsulenten;* referendaries, *Regierungs-* and *Gerichtsreferendare;* professors, *Hochschullehrer* and *-rektoren;* secondary, *Studienräte* and *-direktoren;* trade, *Fach-* and *Berufsschullehrer;* primary, *Mittel-* and *Volksschullehrer;* private, *Privat-* and *Hauslehrer;* kindergarten, *Kindergärtner;* architects, *Architekten, Bauingenieure,* and *-techniker;* chemists, *Chemiker* and *Lebensmittelchemiker;* engineers, all combinations with *-ingenieure* and *-techniker* except for technicians, which are *Vermessungs-* and *Chemotechniker.*

[b]Judges from *Statistisches Jahrbuch* (Berlin), 45 (1926): 436.

[c]Teaching figures for 1924 from *Statistisches Jahrbuch* 43 (1923): 397. The 1933 philologue figure apparently lists only the academically trained.

[d]The 1907 engineering figure includes all "*Ingenieure und Techniker,*" but understates the total, because it omits owners and managers.

Table A.5a. Increase in Attorneys: German Lawyers

Year	Total	Change Rate[a]	Per 100,000	DAV Members[b]	DAV Percentage[c]
1880	4,091		9.07	1,492	36.97
1891	5,317	29.97	10.80	3,043	57.23
1901	6,800	27.89	12.13	4,676	68.76
1911[d]	10,817	59.07	16.75	8,248	76.25
1913	12,297	13.68		9,574	77.85
1915	13,024	5.97	19.20	10,576	81.20
1917	12,393	−4.84		10,105	81.63
1919	12,030	−2.93	19.13	9,753	81.07
1921	12,276	2.05	19.87	9,707	79.67
1923	12,729	3.69			
1924	12,531	−1.56		10,190	81.32
1925	13,537	8.03	21.43	10,746	79.38
1926	14,308	5.70		11,472	80.18
1927	14,894	4.10		12,052	80.92
1928	15,329	2.92		12,533	81.76
1929	15,846	3.37		13,070	82.48
1930	16,416	3.60	25.22	13,508	82.29
1931	17,184	4.68		14,122	82.18
1932	18,036	4.96		14,651	81.18
1933	19,208	6.50	29.09	15,178	79.02
1934	18,432	−4.21			
1935[e]	18,780	1.89	28.08	14,400	76.68
1936	17,897	−4.70			
1937	17,109	−4.40			
1938	17,041	−0.01			
1939[f]	14,734	−13.54	21.26		
1940	14,561	−1.17	20.85		
1941	14,359	−1.39			
1942	14,193	−1.16	20.31	12,132	85.48
1950	11,818		23.64		
1951	13,125	11.06	25.98		
1952	14,028	6.88	27.58		
1954	15,107	7.69	29.12		
1955	15,643	3.54	29.86		

Source: Data from *Statistisches Jahrbuch* 14 (1891): 135; 24 (1901):162; 40 (1919): 224, and alternating years thereafter. From 1938 to 1942, see "Betrifft Jahresstatistik über die Personalbewegung bei den Rechtsanwälten" in the Ministry of Justice files. Totals for 1950–1955 are from *Abl* 5 (1955): 84. Population figures from *HIS,* 18. DAV Membership from *DAV Jahresbericht 1931* (Leipzig, 1931): 40; *Abl,* Jan. 1932 and Jan. 1933.

[a]Rate of change from previous year.

[b]Members of the Deutsche Anwaltverein.

[c]DAV members among all attorneys.

[d]DAV lawyer figures for 1911 = 10,844; 1913 = 12,324; 1915 = 12,544.

[e]Membership of lawyer section of NSRB. See *DR* 5 (1935): 74f; "Mitgliederstand vom 1. 10. 44," BA, NS 16, No. 44.

[f]Greater Germany totals: 1939 = 16,817; 1940 = 16,713; 1941 = 16,498; 1942 = 16,348.

Table A.5b. Increase in Attorneys: Prussian Law Graduates[a]

Year	State Exam I	Percentage of Failures	Trainees	State Exam II	Percentage of Failures	Probationers
1901	1,263	25.9	4,949	705	18.4	1,820
1902	1,335	24.9	5,308	773	17.7	1,979
1903	1,418	27.6	5,709	756	19.6	2,065
1904	1,460	26.8	6,148	853	19.8	2,209
1905	1,503	25.6	6,511	864	18.3	2,198
1906	1,727	25.3	6,990	1,027	15.6	2,272
1907	1,604	28.9	7,160	1,109	17.8	2,470
1908	1,679	28.9	7,512	1,103	18.3	2,534
1909	1,475	29.4	7,662	1,185	18.3	2,661
1910	1,508	28.8	7,667	1,321	18.3	2,934
1911	1,441	30.4	7,579	1,289	21.0	3,241
1912	1,328	30.7		1,212	24.3	
1913	1,196	32.8	7,114	1,245	22.5	3,479
1914	1,986	14.8		1,511	16.0	
1915	465	6.4	6,113	674	11.0	3,848
1916	309	7.8		292	14.9	
1917	238	11.5	5,665	221	14.7	4,065
1918	214	6.1		222	13.0	
1919	565	8.1	5,040	712	12.6	3,611
1920	1,129	13.8		1,086	13.1	
1921	1,490	18.7	3,959	1,091	17.7	1,849
1922	1,396	24.0		822	26.5	1,731
1923	1,219	29.5	4,152	847	22.8	1,958
1924	1,217	28.0	4,085	909	21.1	2,168
1925	1,316	30.4	4,354	896	21.3	2,313
1926	1,380	30.2	4,629	935	21.1	2,229
1927	1,634	33.0	5,147	948	19.0	2,120
1928	1,910	32.1	5,932	1,064	19.0	2,210
1929	2,171	34.8	6,642	1,280	16.2	2,411
1930	2,687	31.6	7,005	1,346	20.7	
1931			8,163	1,390	21.9	3,051
1932	2,088	31.8	9,235	1,564	21.8	3,433
1933	2,846	25.4	10,065	2,340	13.5	3,855
1934	2,692	21.1	9,456	2,699	12.0	4,382
1935	3,459	19.0	8,568	3,418	9.7	5,402
1936	2,428	18.5		2,841	10.2	
1937	1,938	17.6	7,302	2,757	12.6	
1938	1,396	16.1	6,254	2,456	14.8	
1939	986	13.6	5,076	3,429	10.0	
1940	281	10.5	3,782	1,493	8.7	
1941			3,720	954		
1942			3,421	297		
1943[b]			3,290			

Source: Data from Joh. Müller, *Die Juristischen Prüfungen im Deutschen Reich seit 1900* (Berlin, 1932), pp. 8–12; *Statistisches Jahrbuch für das Deutsche Reich* 14 (1891): 135; 24 (1901): 162; 40 (1919): 224, and alternating years thereafter; Ch. Lorenz, *Zehnjahres-Statistik des Hochschulbesuchs und der Abschlußprüfungen* (Berlin, 1943) Vol. 2, p. 92ff; and D. K. Müller *et al.*, "Modellentwicklung," p. 65f.

[a]Explanation of Headings: State exam I, II, number passing the first and second state examinations, respectively; trainees, *Referendare;* probationers, *Assessoren.*

[b]For the postwar period the number of state examinations was 2,729 in 1952, 2,794 in 1953, 2,851 in 1954 and 2,049 in 1955.

Table A.6a. Increase in Secondary Schoolteachers: German High School Pedagogues

Year	Total[a]	Percentage Female	Number of Schools[b]	Number of Students	Student/Teacher Ratio	Percentage PhVb Members
1911	35,339[c]	26.56	2,515	662,105	18.74	
1922	40,959	26.69	2,930	722,714	17.64	89.90[d]
1926	45,099	25.23	2,602	821,286	18.21	90.98
1931	44,915	24.38	2,474	787,828	17.54	
1935	42,499	25.21	2,326	673,975	15.86	
1936	42,727	24.70	2,319	672,073	15.73	
1937	43,013	24.43	2,282	670,895	15.60	
1940	42,769	23.15	2,240	666,652	15.59	
1950	28,872[e]	31.03	1,488	620,488	21.49	
1951	29,527	31.23	1,471	643,085	21.78	74.51
1952	31,551	31.41	1,512	681,628	21.60	
1953	32,706	31.51	1,541	728,098	22.26	
1954	34,114	31.57	1,553	763,462	22.38	
1955	34,848	31.93	1,572	775,320	22.25	

Source: Data from *Statistik des Deutschen Reichs* 40 (1919): 320; 43 (1923): 330; 46 (1927): 447; 51 (1932): 425; 55 (1936): 539; 56 (1937): 577; 57 (1938): 601; 59 (1941): 639; *Statistisches Jahrbuch für die Bundesrepublik Deutschland* 1 (1952): 64; 2 (1953): 88; 2 (1954): 86; 3 (1955): 86; 4 (1956): 86; 5 (1957): 89; *Phbl* 28 (1920): 508; 33 (1925): 593.

[a] All secondary schoolteachers of male and female schools.

[b] Number of male and female secondary institutions.

[c] Of the 1911 total, only 22,098 were university graduates.

[d] For 1921, the membership of the PhVb was about 27,000, whereas by 1926 it had reached 30,902. The membership percentage was calculated by subtracting female teachers from the total, and comparing the association members with 30,027 academically trained male teachers in 1921 and 33,965 in 1926. In 1919, 96.05 percent of male Prussian philologues teaching in boys' schools belonged to the PhVb. Only 86 percent of probationers and 63 percent of trainees were members. Moreover, merely 66.86 percent of male philologues working in girls' schools joined the PhVb. See also Rainer Bölling, "Zum Organisationsgrad der deutschen Lehrerschaft," in M. Heinemann, ed., *Der Lehrer und seine Organisation* (Stuttgart, 1977), p. 130.

[e] Percentages of total who were refugees: 1950, 16.52 percent; 1951, 17.93 percent; 1952, 18.33 percent; 1953, 18.09 percent; 1954, 17.48 percent; 1955, 18.00 percent.

Table A.6b. Increase in Secondary Schoolteachers: Prussian Philologues[a]

	Tenured		Probationers		Trainees		Instructors	
Year	Total	Percentage Female	Total	Percentage Female	Total	Percentage Female	Total	Percentage Female
1900	6,979		693		376		688	
1901	6,642		683		385		700	
1902	7,466		340		478		602	
1903	7,782		204		662		677	
1904	7,932		165		871		842	
1905	8,239		130		1,030		987	
1906	8,564		124		1,134		1,008	
1907	8,924		125		1,279		1,121	
1908	9,384		169		1,475		1,245	
1909	9,837	0.1	235		1,651		1,328	
1910	10,258	0.1	356	2.0	1,901	0.7	1,354	
1911	10,617	0.3	540	2.2	2,201	0.7	1,432	
1912	11,031	0.4	886	1.7	2,454	1.1	1,526	
1913	11,340	0.5	1,375	2.8	2,540	1.4	1,622	
1914	11,658	0.6	1,909	0.4	2,584	1.7	1,706	1.1
1915	11,314	0.7	2,654	1.6	1,882	3.2	1,804	4.8
1916	11,216	0.9	2,704	1.8	1,803	4.3	2,049	5.7
1917	11,149	1.6	2,950	2.3	1,459	8.0	2,230	7.5
1918	11,129	2.2	3,072	2.4	1,250	12.4	2,361	8.8
1919	12,001	2.7	3,299	2.3	1,041	21.5	2,953	6.8
1920	12,073	3.1	3,504	2.1	1,258	18.9	2,747	7.7
1921	12,680	7.8	3,953	4.0	1,063	23.1	2,690	7.5
1922	12,962	7.9	4,315	5.3	979	27.7	2,579	7.7
1923	12,984	8.0	4,642	10.2	794	31.1	2,510	10.1
1924	12,011	8.5	4,853	17.8	674	32.3	2,804	13.3
1925	12,055	8.8	4,960	19.9	687	31.4	3,837	15.0
1926	12,605	9.4	4,540	21.6	688	28.6	3,964	16.7
1927	13,111	10.0	4,150	22.3	703	27.5	3,785	16.1
1928	14,648	10.8	3,126	25.5	761	31.7	3,075	17.6
1929	15,431	11.4	2,433	27.1	1,001	30.5	2,640	19.2
1930	15,947	11.9	2,132	30.3	1,479	29.9	2,400	20.6
1931	16,104	12.2	2,365	33.6	2,016	28.0	1,873	24.6
1932	15,560	12.4	3,088	33.5	2,781	28.7	952	23.2
1933	15,299	12.4	4,065	32.8	3,128	29.6	1,919	21.6
1934	14,439	11.9	4,964	30.2	3,024	29.0	2,286	19.4
1935	13,830	11.8	5,803	30.1	3,100	30.5	2,756	21.8
1936	13,895	11.6	6,378	31.3	3,063	30.0	2,955	22.7
1937	13,784	11.7	7,061	32.2	2,739	27.1	3,831	24.5
1938	13,651	11.9	7,458	31.8	2,386	28.5	5,105	26.9
1939	13,795	11.9	7,679	31.5	1,884	31.5	5,745	29.4
1940	14,497	12.5	7,387	32.8	1,782	34.4		
1941	15,416	13.4	6,916	36.8	1,188	12.4	2,731	72.1

Source: Data from A. Nath, *Die Studienratskarriere im Dritten Reich* (Frankfurt, 1988), p. 305ff.

[a]Explanation of headings: tenured, *festangestellte wissenschaftliche Lehrer;* probationers, Studienassessoren; trainees, Studienreferendare; instructors, *wissenschaftliche Hilfslehrer.*

Table A.7. Development of Engineers[a]

Specialization	1907	1925	1933	1939	1950
Architecture					
Architects, construction engineers	45,978	44,977	78,868	126,993	88,535
Chemical					
Chemists			12,696	16,932	15,503
Chemotechnicians			18,393	32,089	5,949
Total[b]	5,800	10,574	31,089	49,021	21,452
Nautical					
Engineers and technicians	2,413	6,153	8,112	8,406	1,465
Land Survey					
Engineers			5,362	6,164	4,538
Technicians			9,307	19,499	13,541
Total[b]	8,399	8,304	14,669	25,663	18,079
General					
Electrical		19,318	30,907	55,466	37,869
Mining/metallurgy	6,994	7,925	16,492	21,494	7,652
Mechanical	28,110	36,985	64,749	123,467	59,600
Other specialties[c]		15,229	18,622	7,482	9,396
Nonspecified[d]		17,271	31,703	43,978	56,367
Total[b]	35,104	96,628	162,473	251,887	170,884
TOTAL	97,694	166,634	295,211	461,970	300,415

Source: Data from VASMA Project (see Table A.4); Statistisches Reichsamt, *Statistik des Deutschen Reichs,* Vols. 203 (Berlin, 1910), 402 (Berlin 1927); 470, part 2(2) (Berlin, 1937); *Statistisches Jahrbuch der Bundesrepublik Deutschland* (1953), p. 120; Ch. Lorenz, *Abschlußprüfungen* (Berlin, 1943), p. 70f; M.-L. Heuser and W. König, "Tabellarische Zusammenstellungen zur Geschichte des VDI," in *Technik, Ingenieure und Gesellschaft* (Düsseldorf, 1981), pp. 560–61.

[a]The fluidity of the technical terminology complicated the determination of the total number of engineers as well as of their specialties. No accurate figures exist for TH, HTL, or other technicians. One indicator for the growth of engineering is the number of successful *Diplom* examinatins at the TH:

Year	Number of Successful *Diplom* Exams	Year	Number of Succesful *Diplom* Exams
1932	2712	1939	2430
1933	2985	1940	1294
1934	3099	1941	914 (First trimester)
1935	3006	1952	2403
1936	2662	1953	2931
1937	2622	1954	3324
1938	2305	1955	3485

Another valuable indicator is the rise in VDI membership (calculated in 3-year averages):

Time Period	Average VDI Membership	Time Period	Average VDI Membership
1899–1901	15,111	1929–1931	30,595
1902–1904	17,855	1932–1934	29,034
1905–1907	20,738	1935–1937	36,252
1908–1910	23,419	1938–1940	46,579
1911–1913	24,215	1941–1943	56,667
1914–1916	24,299	1944	60,000
1917–1919	24,438	1947–1949	14,269
1920–1922	25,703	1950–1952	23,197
1923–1925	29,243	1953–1955	29,350
1926–1928	29,759		

[b]Total within general field.

[c]*Sonstige Ingenieure der Energieumwandlung und der Stoffverarbeitung.*

[d]*Ingenieur und Techniker ohne Angabe einer Fachrichtung.*

Table A.8. Structure of Attorneys

Parameter	Percentages			
	1924	1932	1936	Average
Demographic				
Percentage female	0.0	0.5	1.2	0.5
Region				
East-central Prussia	16.8	16.6	17.4	16.9
Berlin	16.3	18.0	11.6	15.8
Rhine–Ruhr (western Prussia)	14.2	14.9	19.8	15.9
Bavaria	11.7	11.5	11.4	11.6
Saxony–Thuringia	13.4	12.7	12.9	12.9
North-Central[a]	13.5	13.4	15.6	14.0
South-West[b]	14.1	13.0	11.3	12.9
Residential size				
Rural	9.4	9.3	6.9	8.7
Town	16.4	20.7	18.2	18.9
City	74.2	70.0	74.8	72.4
Professional				
Doctorate	43.7	48.7	53.1	48.4
Titled (Justizrat)	15.7	9.9	4.7	10.2
Notary	46.5	40.9	35.4	41.1
Type of court of practice				
District	16.7	18.5	4.0	14.2
District and superior	14.7	14.8	27.3	18.0
Superior	41.2	52.0	52.9	49.1
Superior and regional superior	12.4	0.4	—	3.8
Appellate	14.7	14.0	15.4	14.6
Supreme	0.2	0.3	0.3	0.3
Associational				
DAV Member	62.7	80.8	58.4	69.8
Persistence[c]				
1924	100.0	48.2	31.9	
1932	51.8	100.0	56.9	
1936	28.3	43.1	100.0	

Source: Data from *Verzeichnis der Rechtsanwälte, Notare und Gerichtsvollzieher* (Leipzig, 1924, 1932, 1936).

[a]Schleswig-Holstein, Mecklenburg, Lübeck, Hamburg, Hanover, Brunswick, and the area between the Weser and Ems Rivers.

[b]Baden, Württemberg, Hesse, Hesse-Nassau.

[c]Persistence in the profession, appearing in more than one register. Years indicate percentage of attorneys with first appearance in the registry of attorneys for that year.

Table A.9. Structure of the Teaching Profession[a]

Parameter	Level of School[b] Higher	Secondary	Middle and Trade	Primary	Special	Average
Demographic						
Percentage female	3.0	21.8	55.7	34.5	93.9	37.8
Median age	42.0	44.0	38.0	39.0	24.0	
Married	69.5	61.0	38.6	55.7	3.2	51.8
Catholic	58.1	36.9	33.5	40.8	37.9	39.3
Residential size						
Rural	9.0	16.1	22.5	48.3	34.4	37.3
Town	31.3	45.5	32.7	25.6	26.4	30.4
City	59.7	38.3	44.8	26.1	39.1	32.3
Region[c]						
East-central Prussia	8.5	18.0	19.4	23.1	16.3	20.9
Berlin	6.7	6.7	6.4	3.9	7.6	5.1
Rhine–Ruhr	9.6	17.8	17.7	17.5	15.0	17.3
Bavaria	13.8	11.1	4.6	8.5	11.4	8.9
Saxony–Thuringia	24.1	17.7	16.6	12.7	18.2	14.7
North-Central	8.2	5.4	12.4	8.4	6.5	8.1
South-West	7.8	13.9	12.5	14.5	14.6	14.1
Austria	21.3	9.3	10.3	11.4	10.4	11.0
Professional						
Doctorate	48.3	13.5	2.7	0.4	0.0	4.3
Pensioned	5.3	9.5	3.8	7.2	0.3	6.7
Association[d]						
Philologue	8.3	19.4	0.0	0.0	0.0	3.9
Specialist	5.3	7.1	16.2	6.8	1.0	7.5
DLV[e]	0.0	6.8	10.1	28.9	1.0	19.9
Religious	0.0	0.6	2.8	8.5	0.0	5.6
Women's	0.0	2.2	7.9	3.6	5.8	3.9
Political	0.0	0.0	0.2	0.2	0.0	0.1
None listed	86.3	63.9	62.8	51.9	92.2	59.0
Cohort[f]						
Empire	15.7	16.9	9.8	13.7	1.0	13.0
Late empire	27.4	28.8	22.7	19.5	3.0	20.7
Early Weimar	31.5	22.3	25.2	30.4	6.8	26.6
Late Weimar	22.4	23.1	29.2	20.5	28.2	22.6
Third Reich	3.0	8.8	13.0	15.9	61.0	17.0
Sector[g]						
University/TH	100.0	0.0	0.0	0.0	0.0	
High school	0.0	76.8	23.2	0.0	0.0	
Middle/trade	0.0	0.0	79.9	20.3	0.0	
Primary school	0.0	0.0	4.2	95.8	0.0	
Special	0.0	0.0	0.0	35.3	64.7	
Percentage of total	2.2	19.4	11.5	60.1	6.8	

Source: Data from NSLB membership sample, BDC.

[a]Teachers from Austria, the Sudetenland and the Warthegau produced certain peculiarities, such as the overrepresentation of Catholics on the university level.

[b]Higher includes universities, THs, etc. Special comprises kindergarten and special education.

[c]For regions covered, see Table A.8.

[d]Association membership.

[e]Deutscher Lehrerverein and regional affiliates.

[f]Period of entry into the profession: empire, entered before 1905; late empire, entered before 1915; early Weimar, entered before 1925; late Weimar, entered before 1935; Third Reich, entered after 1935.

[g]There is some dispersion of titles according to place of work.

Table A.10. Structure of the Engineering Profession

Parameter	1913	1929	1952	Average
Demographic				
Percentage male	100.0	100.0	100.0	100.0
Residential size				
Rural	6.6	4.3	3.2	4.7
Town	29.6	28.3	36.8	31.1
City	63.4	67.3	60.0	64.0
Region[a]				
East-central Prussia	12.6	13.1		9.2
Berlin	10.8	10.8	3.2	8.7
Rhine–Ruhr	21.3	23.4	38.0	26.9
Bavaria	7.4	7.8	15.2	9.8
Saxony–Thuringia	10.3	10.4		7.4
North-Central	10.3	12.1	24.0	14.9
South-West	11.8	12.8	18.0	13.9
Austria	2.8	2.5		1.6
Other	12.7	7.1	1.6	7.2
Professional				
Degree[b]	20.2	31.2	31.2	27.8
Occupation				
Owner or partner	7.9	7.7	4.4	6.8
Firm director or manager	13.1	19.0	15.2	16.1
Professor or other government official	6.9	6.5	6.0	6.5
Production supervisor	8.0	14.0	15.2	13.0
Engineer	56.9	49.0	53.6	52.8
Technician or inspector	7.2	3.9	5.6	5.4
Sector				
Reich or state government	7.9	6.8	4.8	6.6
City or local government	8.1	11.7	7.6	9.4
Architecture	0.4	0.8	1.2	0.8
Mining/Metallurgy	8.1	7.4	4.4	6.8
Chemical and/or Electrical	3.3	3.2	6.0	4.0
Large (heavy) industry	29.2	32.3	38.0	33.0
Small business	2.8	5.5	6.8	5.0
None listed	40.2	32.2	31.2	34.4
Percentage of total	31.2	40.5	28.3	

Source: Data from the *Mitgliederverzeichnis des Verein deutscher Ingenieure* (Berlin, 1913, 1929), (Essen, 1952).

[a] For regions covered, see Table A.8.

[b] Percentage with doctorate or Diplom-Ingenieure. Of those listed in this row, 15.7 percent were Diplom-Ingenieure in 1913, and 20.9 percent in 1929.

Table A.11a. Legal Business: Civil Cases in District Court

Year	Debt Collection[a]	Titles and Checks[b]	Arrests	Regular Cases	Total	Index
1891–1895	2,055,151	171,332	56,571	1,344,101	3,627,155	100.0
1896–1900	1,918,102	182,892	49,085	1,504,622	3,654,701	100.8
1900–1905	2,007,055	242,431	49,201	1,832,752	4,131,439	113.9
1906–1910	2,081,969	273,176	62,162	2,183,064	4,660,371	126.8
1911	2,659,982	319,173	74,813	2,477,310	5,531,278	152.5
1913[c]	3,251,444	328,305	77,627	2,570,687	6,228,063	171.7
1914[d]	2,860,876	309,597	63,924	2,156,867	5,391,264	148.1
1915	1,782,989	120,883	29,833	1,150,362	3,084,067	85.0
1916	1,485,218	12,161	21,407	642,543	2,161,329	59.6
1917	990,240	6,194	18,803	488,464	1,503,701	41.5
1918	821,802	3,452	21,568	448,447	1,295,269	35.7
1919	1,290,239	5,638	45,281	754,179	2,095,337	57.8
1920[e]	1,700,171	5,794	72,404	916,899	2,695,268	74.3
1921	2,456,068	15,323	91,174	1,184,283	3,746,848	103.3
1922	2,010,156	7,584	105,321	1,080,374	3,203,435	88.3
1923	791,458	2,386	118,610	922,789	1,835,243	50.6
1924	3,426,898	83,189	107,209	1,255,586	4,872,882	134.3
1925	6,654,735	382,898	118,851	1,040,853	8,197,337	226.0
1926	7,542,563	429,622	114,592	1,246,743	9,333,520	257.3
1927	7,542,563	288,852	101,385	1,019,165	8,951,965	246.8
1928	8,403,715	378,163	102,681	1,054,775	9,939,331	274.0
1929	9,361,218	435,321	107,212	2,831,856	12,735,607	351.1
1930	10,101,149	440,198	113,669	3,699,364	14,354,380	395.7
1931	10,750,271	496,155	130,633	3,090,643	14,467,702	398.8
1932	8,203,641	293,708	132,523	2,730,668	11,360,535	313.2
1933	5,500,039	134,849	111,996	1,843,663	7,590,547	209.3
1934	4,979,874	85,041	97,736	1,689,760	6,852,411	188.9
1935	4,734,937	79,135	80,118	1,988,224	6,882,414	189.7
1936	6,699,641	73,981	68,342	1,826,409	6,668,373	183.8
1937	4,515,821	63,885	59,155	1,654,952	6,293,773	173.5
1938	3,994,405	51,499	52,042	1,435,057	5,533,003	152.6
1939	3,065,310	33,391	41,056	1,090,980	4,230,737	116.6

Source: Data from *Statistisches Jahrbuch* 14 (1891): 135; 24 (1901): 162; 40 (1919): 224, and alternating years thereafter until 1941–1942.

[a] Dunning letters and foreclosures.

[b] Property and financial disputes.

[c] No figures for 1912.

[d] Between 1914 and 1918 excluding Colmar and Posen.

[e] Between 1920 and 1934 excluding Saar.

Table A.11b. Legal Business: Civil Cases in Superior Court

Year	Marital Disputes and Divorces	Titles and Checks[a]	Arrests	Regular Cases	Total	Index
1891–1895	11,416	56,834	14,417	145,779	228,446	100.0
1896–1900	13,924	61,027	16,748	168,670	260,369	114.0
1901–1905	18,535	78,231	20,966	227,127	344,859	150.9
1906–1910	24,024	82,868	29,467	274,715	411,074	179.9
1911	28,048	43,390	30,301	194,835	296,575	129.8
1913	30,494	42,743	33,617	204,392	311,246	136.2
1914	26,086	40,204	30,166	178,927	275,383	120.5
1915	17,552	18,202	18,325	139,674	193,753	84.8
1916	22,680	6,594	16,467	104,064	149,805	65.6
1917	25,556	5,978	17,002	99,873	148,409	65.0
1918	35,570	6,529	24,179	123,693	189,971	83.2
1919	74,214	10,658	66,722	262,505	414,099	181.3
1920	70,909	19,803	97,590	409,350	597,652	261.6
1921	61,505	30,180	85,488	330,065	507,238	222.0
1922	55,277	16,421	94,555	343,210	509,413	222.9
1923	52,877	10,390	118,115	341,865	523,247	229.0
1924	54,466	93,230	69,869	275,679	493,244	215.9
1925	55,373	125,108	74,789	353,354	608,624	266.4
1926	59,666	83,364	68,299	363,159	574,488	251.5
1927	59,924	46,210	64,970	289,276	460,380	201.5
1928	62,000	60,498	66,743	305,950	495,191	216.8
1929	63,713	67,118	69,456	319,899	520,186	227.7
1930	65,940	56,317	69,742	320,393	512,392	224.3
1931	64,175	37,224	64,388	240,286	406,073	177.8
1932	67,123	13,515	55,380	156,921	292,939	128.2
1933	69,426	5,530	51,885	104,523	231,364	101.3
1934	77,892	3,786	49,388	94,903	225,969	98.9
1935	82,481	3,129	47,493	89,805	223,208	97.7
1936	84,429	5,171	58,477	122,634	270,711	118.5
1937	83,117	5,969	45,506	126,384	260,976	114.2
1938	96,227	5,260	35,391	117,575	254,453	111.4
1939	90,637	3,991	10,044	89,371	194,043	84.9

Source: Data from *Statistisches Jahrbuch,* as in Table A.11a.

[a]Property and financial disputes.

Table A.11c. Legal Business: Criminal Cases in District Court

Year	Court Orders[a]	Private Actions[b]	Misdemeanors	Felonies	Capital Offenses[c]	Total	Index
1891–1895	475,703	95,335	240,270	314,176	42,171	1,167,655	100.0
1896–1900	486,671	108,413	221,693	344,513	45,291	1,206,581	103.3
1900–1905	523,533	119,294	233,442	374,608	51,320	1,302,197	111.5
1906–1910	529,893	134,834	222,340	424,241	56,361	1,377,669	118.0
1911–1914	506,992	128,274	175,878	380,108	55,110	1,246,868	106.8
1915	316,756	72,363	83,133	260,576	39,254	772,082	66.1
1916	495,865	64,735	62,512	251,095	43,239	917,446	78.6
1917	783,186	59,042	44,501	279,318	51,982	1,218,029	104.3
1918	969,958	69,408	36,145	187,514	55,155	1,318,180	112.9
1919	774,513	100,980	42,529	215,699	79,653	1,213,374	103.9
1920	1,063,324	140,144	61,487	324,299	100,068	1,689,323	144.7
1921	902,170	162,510	80,787	286,816	87,807	1,520,090	130.2
1922	869,753	169,070	93,469	278,769	88,795	1,499,856	128.4
1923	1,004,907	175,239	73,956	363,019	88,344	1,705,465	146.1
1924[d]	694,186	106,584	126,011	163,383	44,803	1,418,709	121.5
1925	892,830	124,284	199,268	236,698	74,933	1,528,013	130.9
1926	878,568	122,386	180,709	254,139	73,710	1,509,512	129.3
1927	831,677	116,958	147,244	240,256	69,914	1,406,049	120.4
1928	831,447	113,633	140,072	227,833	70,155	1,383,140	118.4
1929	786,451	111,787	115,021	182,196	71,330	1,266,785	108.5
1930	781,822	117,414	115,414	235,761	77,106	1,327,517	113.7
1931	720,592	105,199	98,682	222,287	75,271	1,222,031	104.7
1932	695,025	81,895	65,489	172,860	72,114	1,087,383	93.1
1933	643,257	84,963	61,342	184,801	56,851	1,031,214	88.3
1934	563,055	78,686	52,007	154,226	51,380	899,354	77.0
1935	648,881	84,251	54,000	114,974	26,099	928,205	79.5
1936	528,324	73,074	46,042	98,701	24,118	770,259	66.0
1937	530,265	72,688	42,642	109,973	23,269	778,837	66.7
1938	406,722	59,699	36,322	84,866	20,263	607,872	52.0
1939[e]	334,884	52,493	32,254	88,049	20,784	528,464	45.3

Source: Data from *Statistisches Jahrbuch,* as in Table A.11a.

[a] Applications for the issuing of a court order.

[b] Charges initiated by private individuals.

[c] Capital cases tried before a jury.

[d] Because of the change in the *Gerichtsverfassungsgesetz* (*RGBL* 1924, 15), the number extends only from April 1, 1924 to December 31, 1924, hence the total was multiplied by 4/3 to compute the index.

[e] The German Reich without the Sudetenland.

Table A.12. Salaries of Secondary Schoolteachers (in Marks)[a]

Year	Starting Salary	Monthly Salary Ceiling	Average Pay	Cost of Living Index Based on 1913–1914	Real Wages
1913	358.0	708.0	533.0	100.0	533.0
1923[b]	242.0	307.0	274.5		
1924[c]	298.5	384.5	341.5	130.8	261.1
1926	452.0	642.0	547.0	142.1	384.9
1927[d]	504.0	834.0	669.0	147.9	452.3
1928	524.0	854.0	689.0	151.7	454.2
1931[e]	475.0	785.0	630.0	136.1	462.3
1932	400.0	661.0	530.5	120.6	439.9
1936	386.0	661.0	523.5	124.5	420.5
1940	429.0	709.0	569.0	130.1	437.4
1941	475.0	785.0	630.0	133.2	472.9
1951	584.0	974.0	779.0	211.6	368.1
1953	708.5	1138.5	923.5	211.6	436.4
1956	783.0	1253.0	1018.0	220.3	462.1

Source: Data from Chapter 9 of the *Statistisches Jahrbuch für das Deutsche Reich,* 42 (1921–1922); 59 (1941–1942), and Chapter 21 of the *Statistisches Jahrbuch für die Bundesrepublik,* beginning with 1951.

[a]Calculated for married Reich officials of salary level XA or 2C2 in major cities; entries are only for those years when salary changes were listed.

[b]Condition on December 1.

[c]In June 1924 the starting salary was 394 marks and the top pay was 560 marks. In November the figures were 405.5 and 577 marks, respectively, whereas in December they had risen to 441.5 and 628 marks.

[d]For October, with one child.

[e]For teachers with one child. In July 1931 the beginning salary was 433 marks and the top pay was 734 marks.

Table A.13. Engineering Unemployment

Year	Quarter	Number of Open Positions: Total	Mechanical	Electrical	Number of Referral Requests: Applicants	Unemployed	Percentage Unemployed
1924	I	600					
	II	780					
	III	710					
	IV	1300					
1925	I	1780	840	380			
	II	1576	790	310			
	III	1144	600	210			
	IV	790	400	120			
1926	I	674	225	102			
	II	938	273	124			
	III	1027	321	188			
	IV	1399	520	250			
1927	I[a]	1850	692	315	1075	750	70.0
	II	1950	754	259	925	650	70.2
	II	1750	612	342	850	500	58.3
	IV	1710	650	330	725	425	58.6
1928	I	1750	690	380	525	200	38.1
	II	1710	630	440	600	225	37.2
	III	1500	560	280	515	250	48.5
	IV	1320	550	240	650	300	46.2
1929	I	1230	490	240	650	325	50.0
	II	1330	450	210	625	325	52.0
	III	1550	490	190	600	300	50.0
	IV	900	390	150	725	250	37.5
1930	I	820	370	140	900	250	27.8
	II	650	280	90	1100	275	25.0
	III	500	180	60	1240	350	28.2
	IV	410	170	70	1300	475	36.5
1931	I	400	170	80	1250	650	52.0
	II	340	120	60	1400	675	48.2
	III	250	80	40	1350	800	59.3
	IV	210	70	40	1325	850	64.1
1932	I	211	60	40	1300	875	67.3
	II	194	50	40	1225	900	73.5
	III	238	70	40	1375	1075	78.2
	IV	384	120	60		1100	78.6
1933	I	382	130	50	1300	1075	82.7
	II	410	150	70	1275	1050	82.3
	III	450	180	60	1200	950	79.2
	IV	536	220	80	1025	800	78.0
1934	I	933	380	180	800	525	68.6
	II	1068	480	180	725	350	48.3
	III	1233	600	180	600	275	45.8
	IV	1204	590	190	475	225	47.4
1935	I	1430					
	II	1560					
	III	1595					
	IV	1558					
1936	I	1560					

Source: Data from *ZVDDI* 26 (1936): 14, 66, 113; 27 (1936): 21.

[a]Estimates based on graph 2 in *ZVDDI* 26 (1935): 14, column B.

Table A.14. Nazi Proclivity of Students

	Membership Date[b]					Affiliation[c]				
Parameter[a]	Non-NS	Pre-1933	1933	Peace	War	NSDAP	SS/SA	NSDStB	Auxiliary	Average
Demographic										
Percentage female	52.9	2.9	12.5	26.9	4.8	14.4	0.0	22.1	12.5	7.2
Birth cohort										
Pre-1907	77.6	5.5	7.9	6.1	3.0	15.8	10.3	2.4	2.4	11.6
1907–1910	56.1	11.4	25.9	6.1	0.5	22.7	23.4	2.8	1.9	30.0
1911–1914	14.8	14.4	45.5	22.4	2.9	38.6	35.3	9.1	6.7	38.5
1915–1918	18.0	11.2	18.0	44.4	8.3	43.9	17.1	19.0	9.8	14.4
Post-1918	32.1	0.0	11.6	30.8	25.6	28.2	12.9	24.4	7.7	5.5
Region										
East-central Prussia	37.4	10.4	31.6	16.5	4.1	28.0	25.5	10.2	4.1	25.4
Berlin	42.4	16.3	23.9	15.2	2.2	31.5	22.9	5.4	5.4	6.4
Rhine–Ruhr	35.3	7.9	37.7	16.7	2.3	27.4	28.4	9.8	6.5	15.0
Bavaria	39.2	11.3	32.0	14.4	3.1	27.8	27.8	9.3	8.2	6.8
Saxony–Thuringia	35.2	17.5	25.8	14.2	1.7	29.2	23.3	9.2	1.7	8.4
North-Central	40.8	8.3	35.3	18.8	2.3	34.6	25.6	4.5	5.3	9.3
South-West	30.5	7.9	41.1	18.5	2.0	36.4	30.5	6.0	2.6	10.6
Austria	17.8	21.7	14.0	38.8	7.8	44.2	24.1	10.9	9.3	9.0
Other	46.2	6.2	10.0	23.8	13.8	30.0	13.1	9.2	6.2	9.1
Birthplace size										
Rural	35.2	9.5	30.4	20.3	4.6	32.8	23.6	7.9	5.4	25.8
Town	34.4	11.3	31.1	18.6	4.5	31.6	27.3	8.8	5.3	42.0
City	38.4	12.6	26.2	19.1	3.7	29.9	23.3	9.1	5.0	32.2
Social Origin										
High official	36.5	12.8	26.0	19.1	5.6	32.6	27.5	5.6	6.6	20.4
Free professional	39.8	11.3	28.0	15.6	5.4	29.0	22.6	10.8	2.7	13.2
Propertied	44.9	8.2	31.6	10.2	5.1	29.6	22.4	8.2	3.1	6.9
Old middle class	36.8	13.9	30.3	16.4	2.5	30.6	23.5	7.1	6.8	25.0
New middle class	31.3	11.1	30.0	23.5	4.2	32.9	27.3	9.4	3.9	21.7
Working class	32.4	4.9	33.5	25.8	3.3	30.2	24.1	14.3	6.6	12.9
Academic Area										
Law	36.2	14.5	27.0	17.2	5.1	35.3	27.1	5.1	3.8	43.8
Teaching	43.1	8.6	27.2	19.4	1.7	23.3	23.1	9.8	6.9	28.4
Engineering	28.6	8.8	34.7	22.4	5.5	33.2	24.6	13.3	5.5	27.7
Total Aid										
>2,000	61.0	6.8	17.1	12.3	2.7	16.4	21.5	4.8	5.5	10.2
>6,000	32.9	10.4	28.5	23.2	4.9	65.2	51.7	20.0	11.0	49.4
>10,000	33.8	11.7	31.0	17.4	6.0	61.8	50.9	20.5	10.7	22.0
<10,000	33.0	15.2	36.0	14.8	1.1	63.2	50.4	10.5	7.5	18.4

(continued)

Source: Data from Reichsstudentenwerk set, see Table A.3a.

[a]For amplification of headings, see Tables A.3a and A.8.

[b]Data listed by students for membership in any NS organization. Non-NS represents students who were not party members.

[c]Highest NS organizational affiliation. Because most students joined more than one Nazi group, this category is hierarchically arranged with NSDAP membership ranking higher than SS entry, etc. For example, if someone belonged to the party and the SS, he or she appears under the NSDAP figure, but if the person joined the SS and the NSDStB, then he or she is included under the SS percentage, etc. NSDStB = NSDStB and ANST; Auxiliary = NSV, NSF, HJ, BDM, etc.

Table A.14. Nazi Proclivity of Students (*continued*)

	Membership Date[b]					Affiliation[c]				
Parameter[a]	Non-NS	Pre-1933	1933	Peace	War	NSDAP	SS/SA	NSDStB	Auxiliary	Average
National Socialist Background										
Entry										
Weimar[d]	96.7	1.5	1.5	0.4	0.0	2.6	6.0	0.0	0.0	18.8
Peace	21.9	16.9	44.6	16.5	0.1	34.7	37.8	5.8	6.0	53.2
War	21.9	7.0	19.0	37.2	15.0	44.1	13.5	20.2	7.2	28.0
Affiliation										
NSDAP	6.9	27.2	33.9	27.4	4.7					31.3
SS	10.6	9.1	43.9	30.3	6.1					4.6
SA	13.4	6.5	64.7	13.0	2.4					20.3
NSDStB	4.0	3.2	24.0	51.2	17.6					8.7
Auxiliary	9.3	13.3	26.7	41.3	9.3					5.2
Percentage of Total[e]	36.1	11.2	29.2	19.2	4.2	31.3	24.9	8.7	5.2	

Source: Data from Reichsstudentenwerk set, see Table A.3a.

[a]For amplification of headings, see Tables A.3a and A.8.

[b]Data listed by students for membership in any NS organization. Non-NS represents students who were not party members.

[c]Highest NS organizational affiliation. Because most students joined more than one Nazi group, this category is hierarchically arranged with NSDAP membership ranking higher than SS entry, etc. For example, if someone belonged to the party and the SS, he or she appears under the NSDAP figure, but if the person joined the SS and the NSDStB, then he or she is included under the SS percentage, etc. NSDStB = NSDStB and ANST; Auxiliary = NSV, NSF, HJ, BDM, etc.

[d]The 1.5 percent appearing in the pre-1933 and 1933 columns represent students who borrowed money between 1931 and 1934.

[e]The average for nonaffiliated students was 29.9 and its pattern generally followed the non-NS party members. The 6.9 percent who belonged to the party among the unaffiliated did not have a membership number and could therefore not be classified according to date.

Table A.15. Nazi Proclivity of Professionals

	NSDAP Membership				
Parameter	Pre-1933	1933	Peace	War	Average
Demographic					
Percentage female	4.4	3.7	7.4	17.5	8.1
Cohort					
Pre-1871	1.2	2.8	0.7	0.8	1.4
1871–1880	5.9	12.0	6.4	5.5	7.7
1881–1890	12.6	21.8	18.9	17.9	18.6
1891–1900	21.7	26.0	24.6	18.1	23.2
1901–1910	47.8	30.1	33.2	24.0	32.4
1911–1920	10.9	7.3	16.2	17.7	13.3
Post–1920	0.0	0.0	0.1	16.0	3.5
Region[a]					
East-central Prussia	21.1	20.3	21.6	18.7	20.5
Berlin	10.9	5.3	5.1	6.7	6.3
Rhine–Ruhr	11.1	25.0	22.1	14.5	19.7
Bavaria	8.8	9.8	9.2	5.1	8.4
Saxony–Thuringia	16.1	12.4	12.2	21.3	14.8
North-Central	16.7	10.8	14.3	5.7	11.8
South-West	10.0	15.2	9.8	9.7	11.3
Austria	5.3	1.2	5.7	18.3	7.1
Residential size					
Rural	26.9	33.1	32.6	36.0	32.7
Town	27.6	29.2	29.5	26.9	28.6
City	45.4	37.6	38.0	37.1	38.7
Professional					
Doctorate	7.0	9.9	7.4	7.2	8.0
Free professional[b]	12.9	13.7	11.1	8.2	11.5
Occupation					
Lawyer	17.6	27.3	33.8	31.0	29.1
Teacher	12.9	26.6	26.3	25.3	24.3
Engineer[c]	23.8	17.7	16.9	23.8	19.6
Status within occupation[d]					
Elite	3.2	6.7	5.0	5.1	5.3
Academic	47.8	41.4	37.4	35.4	39.6
Semiprofessional	49.0	51.9	57.6	59.4	55.0
Percentage of total	14.0	28.2	36.2	21.6	

Source: Data from a secondary analysis of M. Kater's NSDAP membership set, extracting 2429 professionals from over 21,000 party members. See M. H. Kater, "Quantifizierung und NS-Geschichte," *GG* 3 (1977): 451–84.

[a] For amplification of headings, see Table A.8.

[b] Percentage whose social and economic status is free professional. The entire data set included doctors, pastors, and students, as well as lawyers, teachers, and engineers.

[c] Includes chemists, architects, and engineers.

[d] Status: elite, top standing within profession; academic, middle range of occupation; semiprofessional, in training and semiacademic ranks.

Table A.16. Nazi Proclivity of Attorneys

Parameter	BNSDJ Founders[a]	1932 Attorneys[b]	NSDAP Members[c]	Nonmembers[d]
Demographic				
Percentage female	1.3	0.6	0.0	0.6
Region				
East-central Prussia	12.8	16.8	19.1	16.5
Berlin	7.1	18.1	16.5	15.7
Rhine–Ruhr	7.5	14.6	17.6	15.7
Bavaria	28.8	11.8	9.6	11.9
Saxony–Thuringia	23.5	13.0	11.9	13.1
North-Central	8.0	12.8	15.2	13.8
South-West	8.8	12.8	10.1	13.3
Austria	3.5			
Residential size				
Rural	8.4	8.9	9.6	8.6
Town	30.1	39.1	36.7	37.7
City[e]	61.5	52.0	53.8	53.7
Professional				
Doctorate	55.8	49.1	49.4	48.3
Titled (Justizrat)		10.4	3.4	11.2
Notary		39.6	46.8	40.2
Type of Court of Practice[f]				
District		19.7	5.4	15.5
District and superior		13.7	27.1	16.6
Superior		51.3	55.6	47.9
Superior and regional superior		0.5	0.5	4.2
Appellate		14.3	10.9	15.1
Supreme		0.3	0.3	0.3
Associational				
DAV Members		80.4	69.3	69.9
Entry[g]				
1924			43.7	30.9
1932			41.3	17.9
1936			15.0	6.6
Total Number	226	1207	387	2580
Percentage of Total	100.0	40.7	13.0	87.0

Source: BNSDJ data from the remaining NSRB files at the BA Coblenz, NS 16. Other data from the *Verzeichnis der Rechtsanwälte*. See Table A.8.

[a]The first 211 BNSDJ members plus 15 lawyers who joined the NSDAP before 1933.

[b]Attorneys taken from the 1932 register who did not appear in the 1936 register as members of the NSDAP.

[c]Attorneys who appeared in the 1936 register and were listed as NS party members.

[d]Entire data set excluding party members.

[e]Among the BNSDJ founders, 45.6 percent came from cities with a population of more than 500,000.

[f]The BNSDJ set did not list the type of court, but it did give professional titles that could be categorized as follows: lawyers, 56.6 percent; judges, 10.6 percent; higher court officials, 9.3 percent; lower court officials, 4.4 percent; Referendare, 13.3 percent; not active in legal profession, 5.7 percent.

[g]Earliest edition of the register in which the NSDAP member appeared. For further explanations see Table A.8.

Table A.17. Nazi Proclivity of Teachers

Parameter	Non-NS	NSDAP[a] Pre-33	NSDAP[a] 1933	NSDAP[a] Peace	NSDAP[a] War	NSLB[b] Pre-33	NSLB[b] 1933	NSLB[b] Peace	NSLB[b] War	Average
Demographic										
Percentage female	44.2	12.9	9.5	37.2	73.5	12.3	31.2	40.3	62.7	37.8
Median age	39.0	35.0	39.0	38.0	23.0	37.0	41.0	34.0	29.0	39.0
Married	39.6	68.6	77.6	54.9	15.2	72.0	60.0	39.3	33.2	51.8
Catholic	36.7	16.1	22.6	73.7	39.4	11.7	30.7	56.0	61.5	39.1
Residential size										
Rural	33.7	35.1	49.9	58.0	55.9	28.4	35.2	33.3	52.4	37.3
Town	31.3	32.7	27.2	28.2	23.5	32.9	30.6	31.5	28.7	30.6
City	35.1	32.2	23.0	13.7	20.6	38.7	34.2	35.2	18.8	32.1
Region										
East-central Prussia	20.8	21.8	25.0	6.2	12.1	28.4	25.4	15.5	12.3	20.9
Berlin	5.6	7.3	3.2	2.1	0.0	13.0	6.2	3.5	1.9	5.1
Rhine–Ruhr	17.5	9.8	19.2	6.9	27.3	10.1	22.2	12.9	7.2	17.2
Bavaria	9.1	10.1	7.0	11.5	3.0	4.6	7.2	14.7	5.8	8.8
Saxony–Thuringia	12.1	22.5	17.6	48.9	33.3	18.0	12.1	8.9	32.8	14.7
North-Central	8.0	12.4	9.6	2.1	0.0	11.6	10.8	5.1	3.1	8.2
South-West	14.0	8.8	17.4	3.7	15.2	8.1	16.0	11.8	11.6	14.0
Austria	12.9	7.3	1.0	18.5	9.1	6.1	0.1	27.7	25.2	11.1
Professional										
Doctorate	4.2	4.8	4.3	5.7	0.0	6.2	3.3	7.1	2.5	4.2
Pensioned	7.8	3.0	2.3	6.4	0.0	2.0	6.3	8.7	5.6	6.7
Association										
Philological	3.7	5.1	6.0	0.0	0.0	6.2	5.1	3.3	0.0	3.9
Special	6.9	12.2	11.2	1.6	0.0	12.9	11.5	2.1	0.8	7.6
DLV	15.7	31.6	42.6	5.0	2.9	26.3	29.6	9.8	0.0	20.0
Religious	5.6	0.8	6.5	4.1	0.0	1.4	9.1	1.3	0.0	5.6
Women's	4.7	1.3	1.2	0.0	0.0	1.4	6.3	1.1	0.1	3.9
Political	0.1	0.0	0.3	0.0	0.0	0.0	0.2	0.0	0.0	0.1
None	63.3	49.1	32.2	89.2	97.1	51.8	38.2	82.5	99.0	59.0
Cohort										
Empire	14.4	7.6	9.2	7.1	0.0	10.2	16.3	10.7	5.2	13.0
Late Empire	20.7	17.2	23.5	16.3	2.9	23.6	25.2	15.7	11.9	20.8
Early Weimar	24.5	30.1	36.7	26.8	11.8	36.6	32.8	18.7	14.7	26.6
Late Weimar	21.3	38.2	27.5	19.7	8.8	27.3	22.1	27.3	16.0	22.5
NS Period	19.0	6.8	3.2	30.1	76.5	2.3	3.5	27.6	52.3	17.0
Title										
Higher	2.1	3.6	2.3	3.9	0.0	1.7	1.1	3.8	2.9	2.1
Secondary	20.1	22.4	15.7	20.9	2.9	22.7	17.2	26.3	16.0	19.4
Middle/Trade	11.7	10.9	10.3	12.6	8.8	11.4	12.0	10.5	11.2	11.5
Primary	58.0	60.8	70.9	59.0	55.9	64.2	67.2	47.8	53.6	60.2
Special	8.0	2.3	0.9	3.7	32.4	0.0	2.5	11.5	16.3	6.8
Other NS Involvement[c]										
SS	0.5	2.5	0.8	0.0	0.0	0.8	0.8	0.4	0.1	0.6
SA	5.4	16.2	14.6	2.7	0.0	10.6	10.2	1.6	0.0	7.0
Auxiliary[d]	18.9	23.2	39.1	11.3	17.5	27.2	30.2	8.9	11.4	22.0
Percentage of total	77.4	12.8	69.4	14.4	3.4	2.7	57.1	24.7	15.6	100

Source: Data from NSLB membership cards, BDC. See Table A.9.

[a]NSLB members who were also party members.

[b]NSLB members only.

[c]Listed membership in another Nazi organization.

[d]Other NS groups such as the NSF or NSV. See also Table A.9.

Table A.18. Nazi Proclivity of Engineers

Parameter	Non-NS	NSDAP[a] Pre-33	1933	Peace	War	NSBDT	Average
Demographic							
Percentage male	100.0	100.0	100.0	100.0	100.0	100.0	100.0
Married	78.8	59.1	100.0	93.9	81.3	83.5	82.3
Cohort							
Pre-1871	7.7	0.0	0.0	0.0	0.0	3.2	3.4
1871–1880	19.2	9.1	28.6	4.3	14.3	15.8	14.3
1881–1890	21.8	13.6	28.6	34.0	21.4	24.1	24.6
1891–1900	25.6	45.5	28.6	44.7	42.9	34.2	34.9
1901–1910	16.7	27.3	14.3	17.0	14.3	17.1	17.7
Post-1910	9.0	4.5	0.0	0.0	7.1	5.7	5.1
Region							
East-central Prussia	15.0	18.2	42.9	14.3	31.3	19.5	18.8
Berlin	13.8	27.3	0.0	14.3	6.3	13.4	13.8
Rhine–Ruhr	11.3	9.1	21.4	24.5	12.5	11.8	15.5
Bavaria	6.3	9.1	0.0	6.1	6.3	6.7	6.1
Saxony–Thuringia	12.5	9.1	7.1	4.1	12.5	9.1	9.4
North-Central	10.1	4.5	7.1	26.5	12.6	14.0	13.8
South-West	11.3	18.2	14.3	2.0	6.3	8.0	9.4
Austria	16.3	4.5	0.0	2.0	6.3	8.5	8.8
Urban	53.8	68.2	64.3	65.3	50.1	58.5	59.1
Professional							
TH	38.8	36.4	50.0	53.1	37.5	42.1	43.1
University	13.8	27.3	14.3	12.2	31.3	15.9	16.6
Doctorate	27.6	50.0	28.5	42.9	25.0	32.9	34.3
Occupation							
Owner or partner	7.5	0.0	0.0	4.1	0.0	4.9	5.0
Director	28.8	31.8	21.4	26.5	31.3	26.8	28.2
Professor	13.8	27.3	28.6	22.4	43.8	20.7	21.5
Production	23.8	4.5	21.4	18.4	6.3	19.5	18.2
Engineer	18.8	31.8	28.6	14.3	12.5	20.7	19.3
Tech/Insp.	5.0	4.5	0.0	10.2	0.0	4.9	5.5
Sector							
Reich/state govt.	16.3	18.2	28.6	24.5	31.3	20.7	21.0
City/local govt.	8.8	36.4	35.7	20.4	12.5	18.9	17.7
Architecture	1.3	9.1	0.0	2.0	0.0	1.8	2.2
Mine/Metall.	13.8	4.5	21.4	12.2	6.3	11.6	12.2
Chem./Electr.	5.0	18.2	0.0	14.3	6.3	7.9	8.8
Large industry	40.0	9.1	14.3	22.4	43.8	30.5	29.8
Small business	1.3	0.0	0.0	0.0	0.0	0.6	0.6
None listed	13.8	4.5	0.0	4.1	0.0	7.9	7.7
Associational							
VDI	29.5	38.1	21.4	26.5	6.3	25.3	27.0
NS affiliate							
SS/SA	11.4	36.4	7.1	40.8	31.4	25.6	23.7
NSV	23.8	27.4	42.9	32.7	31.3	31.1	28.7
Other	1.3	4.5	7.1	4.1	6.3	3.0	3.3
NSBDT	90.0	86.4	85.7	91.8	100.0		90.6
Percentage of total	44.2	12.2	7.7	27.1	8.8	90.6	

Source: Data from 181 Deutsche Arbeitsfront/NSBDT membership cards, BDC.

[a]Pre-33, all party members under number 1,550,000; 1933, numbers between 1,550,000 and 2,400,000; Peace, between 2,400,000 and 5,300,000; War, over 5,300,000. See Table A.10.

APPENDIX B
A NOTE ON SOURCES

with
Ingrid Rehm Richards

The source materials for a history of the German professions in the first half of the twentieth century are rich but uneven. As highly educated people, professionals expressed their concerns vocally and tended to keep a written record. However, the NS rupture in organizational continuity complicated preservation, the Second World War destroyed many files, and the subsequent partition of Germany led to the scattering of the remainder. The very volume of written records often ensured the survival of routine semipublic papers in contrast to rare handwritten drafts on confidential matters, which tended to vanish. Because they were produced by organizations, such remains also shed more light on group decisions than on individual motives. Only intermittently allowing a detailed event narrative, this imbalance suggests an exemplary analysis of broader structural patterns that is based on the systematic layering of evidence from different sources in order to compensate for its imperfections. The excess of information on some issues and dearth on other questions is both an obstacle to and a challenge for historical reconstruction that requires a brief explanation of the evidential basis of this study.

Unfortunately, most of the records of the professional associations were lost during Hitler's war. Whereas no DAV files have survived, a few fragments from the lawyer chambers are still at the German Federal Archives. Although the central PhVb materials disappeared, remnants can be found in the RhB documents in the Central State Archives in Potsdam and most of the regional Westphalian papers are deposited at Bochum University. Similarly, only traces of the written VDI tradition have been preserved at its headquarters in Düsseldorf. However, some of the records of the NS affiliates are still extant at the BA in Koblenz. Although the NSRB and NSBDT collections are slight, somewhat more material is available on the NSLB. Moreover, some teachers' league and technicians' league correspondence has been kept in alphabetized form at the Berlin Document Center, together with their membership files.

Voluminous government deposits largely compensate for this deficit, because they record both official views and professional aspirations. The Prussian Ministry of Justice files, located in the archives in Berlin Dahlem and Merseburg, contain much material on lawyer questions, codes, chambers, and the like. The Reich

Ministry of Justice records, which are divided between Koblenz and Potsdam, similarly provide ample documentation on NS policy as well as attorney reactions. Prussian Ministry of Culture archives in Dahlem and Merseburg also offer much useful information on teacher issues, school problems, salary quarrels, and so on. Though somewhat less complete, the education records in the Reich Ministry at Potsdam yield substantial clues to NS decisions and pedagogue responses. The Central State Archives also contain some late-Weimar material on school questions, unemployment, or the Reich Economic Council. However, engineers lacked a single responsible ministry and technical officials were more interested in the solution of practical problems than in professional issues. Therefore, their mosaic must be pieced together from educational sources, Ministry of Interior records, and so on, thereby necessarily making the picture less complete.

Printed journals are a copious source for the history of the professions, because they carefully comment on all significant developments. Enjoying a wide readership and a long tradition, these *Verbandszeitschriften* informed the association membership, formulated collective demands through internal debate, and lobbied with the public or government. Produced and edited by prominent professionals, such publications were generally accurate, candid, and representative. By discussing work and politics from the perspective of the practitioner and fostering a certain public image, they played a central role in the formation of the identity of the professional. Lawyers subscribed to the prestigious *Juristische Wochenschrift* (1874–1939), presenting a mixture of scholarly reflection and practical commentary, and to the more mundane but informative *Anwaltsblatt* (1913–1934), which concentrated on DAV affairs. In the Third Reich, the *Deutsches Recht* (1931–1944) took over, but after the war both the *NJW* (1947–) and *Abl* (1950–) were revived. For comparative reasons the *Deutsche Richterzeitung* and official *Deutsche Justiz* are also of some interest.

Secondary schoolteachers looked to the *Philologenblatt* (1892–1935) for the vigorous representation of their interests, while the *Monatsschrift für das höhere Schulwesen* had a more academic tone. During the Nazi years, the *Deutsche Höhere Schule* (1934–1944) became the organ of NSLB Section Two, whereas after the war the *Höhere Schule* (1948–) continued the earlier philologue tradition. The viewpoint of primary school pedagogues was presented in the DLV-sponsored *Allgemeine Deutsche Lehrerzeitung* and also dominated the NSLB organ *Reichszeitung der Deutschen Erzieher* (1931–1944). However, the countless *Fachzeitschriften* on pedagogy or specific topics, such as *Schule und Evangelium* (coedited by K. Jarausch beginning in 1933), rarely commented on general issues. Engineers regularly perused the *Zeitschrift des Verbands Deutscher Ingenieure* (1856–1945) for new technical information and occasional professional discussions, while the *VDI Nachrichten* (1920–1945), renamed *RTA,* provided more association news. For the competing academic technicians, the *Zeitschrift des Verbands Deutscher Diplom-Ingenieure* (1909–1942), retitled *Technik und Kultur,* was the central reference point, because it promoted "professionalization." In the Third Reich, the *Deutsche Technik* (1933–1943) conveyed the official NSBDT position. The great number of specialized technical journals usually did not address broader concerns. After the war, the VDI publications returned *(VDIN* 1947– , *ZVDI* 1949–), if anything in a glossier format than before.

Though not always reliable, autobiographies and memoirs flesh out the monochrome official picture with colorful subjective recollections. Surprisingly, attorneys were most loquacious, producing a spate of atmospheric and anecdotal narratives that convey the problems of free legal practice from the empire to the postwar period. Political and racial victims of the Nazis more often put pen to paper than regular practitioners [W. Heintzeler, *Der rote Faden* (Stuttgart, 1983)], while party lawyers generally remained silent [except for the prolific F. Grimm, *Mit offenem Visier* (Leoni, 1969)]. Among the many gripping accounts, most informative are the books by or on A. Apfel, *Behind the Scenes of German Justice* (London, 1935), C. Riess, *Der Mann in der schwarzen Robe. Das Leben des Strafverteidigers M. Alsberg* (Hamburg, 1965), R. Bendix, *Von Berlin nach Berkeley* (Frankfurt, 1985), U. Beer, *Versehrt, Verfolgt, Versöhnt: Horst Berkowitz* (Essen, 1979), D. Güstrow, *Tödlicher Alltag* (Berlin, 1981), M. Hachenburg, *Lebenserinnerungen eines Rechtsanwalts* (Stuttgart, 1978), R. Kempner, *Ankläger einer Epoche* (Berlin, 1986), H. Kronstein, *Briefe an einen jungen Deutschen* (Munich, 1967), S. Neumann, *Nacht über Deutschland* (Munich, 1978), and P. Ronge, *Im Namen der Gerechtigkeit* (Munich, 1963).

Although they often wrote on educational issues, philologues were curiously reluctant to recall their professional experience. Only P. Mellmann, *Geschichte des Deutschen Philologen Verbandes* (Leipzig, 1929), and F. Behrend, "Erinnerungen an die Tätigkeit des Philologen Verbandes," *HS* 7 (1954), 165ff, comment on their organizational role. Although biographies concentrate on pedagogical reformers rather than on classroom teachers, the Schumann–Havenstein correspondence, edited by N. Hammerstein, *Deutsche Bildung?* (Frankfurt, 1988) is revealing. The works on or by V. Wehrmann, ed., *Friedrich Copei 1902–1945* (Detmold, 1982), A. Ehrentreich, *Pädagogische Odyssee* (Weinheim, 1967), J. Gutmann, *Von Westfalen nach Berlin. Lebensweg und Werk eines jüdischen Pädagogen* (Haifa, 1978), and P. Hartig, *Lebenserinnerungen eines Neuphilologen* (Augsburg, 1981) are also useful. Moreover, manuscript autobiographies in the Kempowski collection by H. Grupe ("Die böse Zeit—wie ich sie erlebte," KA 121), F. Herrmann ("Der Wüstenprediger," KA 230), W. Pflughaupt ("Lebenserinnerungen," KA 733), and R. Stöver ("Spurensuche," KA 71) as well as by B. Jarausch ("Geschichte einer schlesisch-märkischen Familie," in the author's possession) proved informative. Finally, engineers were virtually mute. If they wrote at all, they either reported as inventors [M. von Ardenne, *Ein glückliches Leben für Forschung und Technik* (Berlin, 1973), K. Zuse, *Der Computer, mein Lebenswerk* (Munich, 1970)] or as entrepreneurs [P. Kleinewefers, *Jahrgang 1905* (Stuttgart, 1977)]. However, the manuscripts by Klaus Friedrich (KA 508) and Martin Vogel ("Martin Vogel's höchst unbedeutende Memoiren," KA 1384) provide illuminating detail. The published SOPADE articles [*Deutschland-Berichte der SOPADE* (reissued, Frankfurt, 1980)] and SD reports (H. Boberach, ed., *Meldungen aus dem Reich* (Herrsching, 1984)] offer some contextual help as well.

In transition from amateur accounts to systematic scholarship, the history of the Central European professions is beginning to show analytical promise. Although the writings about law, education, and technology are voluminous, few titles deal with the professionals who practiced these pursuits. [For bibliographical examples see L. Gruchmann, *Justiz im Dritten Reich* (Munich, 1988), H. Scholz,

Erziehung und Unterricht unterm Hakenkreuz (Göttingen, 1985) or the "*Verzeichnis der zitierten Schriften,*" in K.-H. Ludwig, ed., *Technik, Ingenieure und Gesellschaft* (Düsseldorf 1981), pp. 611–632]. Association, practitioner, and regional publications tend to be parochial, nostalgic, and apologetic chronicles, all too often afflicted with the *Festschrift* syndrome. During the last decade, several outside impulses have began to liven up this stagnant field. The general concern of social scientists with problems of contemporary professions [E. Freidson, *Professional Powers* (Chicago, 1986), M. S. Larson, *The Rise of Professionalism* (Berkeley, Calif., 1977), R. Collins, *The Credential Society* (New York, 1979), to name just a few] has raised important questions about their earlier development. The comparative interest of Anglo-American social historians in continental patterns has created a fresh appreciation of the state-dominated variants of professionalization [G. Geison, ed., *Professions and the French State 1700–1900* (Philadelphia, 1985), J. Kocka and W. Conze, eds., *Bildungsbürgertum im 19. Jahrhundert* (Stuttgart, 1985), A. Heidenheimer's forthcoming volume on the state and the professions, and M. Burrage and R. Torstendahl's collection of essays on *Professions in Theory and History* (London, 1990)]. Finally, the gradual public realization of professional collaboration in Nazi atrocities has initiated a reexamination of their record during the Third Reich [R. Lifton, *The Nazi Doctors* (New York, 1986), the journal *Kritische Justiz,* pedagogical studies like *Heil Hitler, Herr Lehrer* (Berlin, 1983), and J. Herf, *Reactionary Modernism* (Cambridge, 1984)]. The first results of this reawakening are evident in Charles McClelland's forthcoming book on the rise of the German professions as well as in G. Cocks and K. Jarausch, eds., *German Professions 1800–1950* (New York, 1990).

Although older works still serve as essential references, a theory-based, comparative, and critical history of German professions in the twentieth century has just begun to emerge. For lawyers, the anniversary volume by F. Ostler, *Die deutschen Rechtsanwälte 1871–1971* 2nd ed. (Essen, 1982) remains useful, while D. Rüschemeyer, *Lawyers and their Society* (Cambridge, Mass., 1973), may serve as a comparative introduction. Recent studies by K. Ledford, "A Social and Institutional History of the German Bar in Private Practice, 1878–1930," (diss. Baltimore, 1988); S. König, *Vom Dienst am Recht. Rechtsanwälte als Strafverteidiger im Nationalsozialismus* (Berlin, 1987), and H. Siegrist's forthcoming study of *Advokaten und Bürger* in Germany, Switzerland, Italy and France offer more theoretical inspiration and empirical detail. For teachers, R. Bölling has provided a slim overview in *Sozialgeschichte der deutschen Lehrer* (Göttingen, 1983) and a substantial monograph on the DLV, *Volksschullehrer und Politik* (Göttingen, 1978), while A. Nath has just completed a fine analysis of *Die Studienratskarriere im Dritten Reich* (Frankfurt, 1988). However, aside from the F. Hamburger dissertation on "Lehrer zwischen Kaiser und Führer" (Heidelberg, 1974), W. Feiten, *Der NSLB: Entwicklung und Organisation* (Frankfurt, 1981), and various essays in M. Heinemann's collections, *Der Lehrer und seine Organisation* (Stuttgart, 1977) as well as *Erziehung und Schulung im Dritten Reich* (Stuttgart, 1980), and individual articles by H. Titze such as "Die soziale und geistige Umbildung des preussischen Oberlehrerstandes von 1870–1914," 14. Beiheft of the *ZfP* (Weinheim, 1977), p. 107ff, there is no general history of the philologues. For engineers, the best summary are the articles in the 1981 VDI *Festschrift, Technik,*

Ingenieure und Gesellschaft (Düsseldorf, 1981). The dissertations by C. Gispen, "Technical Education and Social Status" (Berkeley, 1983) which has just appeared as *New Profession, Old Order* (Cambridge, England, 1989) and J. C. Guse, "The Spirit of the Plassenburg" (Lincoln, Neb., 1981) and the books by K.-H. Ludwig, *Technik und Ingenieure im Dritten Reich* (Königstein, 1979), and G. Hortleder, *Das Gesellschaftsbild des Ingenieurs,* 2nd ed. (Frankfurt, 1970) are also essential. Morris Beatus' dissertation on the "Academic Proletariat" (Madison, Wis., 1975) still offers useful information on the overcrowding problem during the Weimar Republic.

These efforts, complemented by other recent work, demonstrate that the social history of university graduates is coming of age. H. Siegrist's reader on *Bürgerliche Berufe* (Göttingen, 1988) provides comparative perspective, while some impressive single profession studies concern doctors [C. Huerkamp, *Der Aufstieg der Ärzte im 19. Jahrhundert* (Göttingen, 1986), M. H. Kater, *Doctors Under Hitler* (Chapel Hill, 1989)], dentists [W. Kirchhoff, ed., *Zahnmedizin und Faschismus* (Marburg, 1987)], psychiatrists [G. Cocks, *Psychotherapy in the Third Reich* (New York, 1985)], or psychologists [U. Geuter, *Die Professionalisierung der deutschen Psychologie im Nationalsozialismus* (Frankfurt, 1984)]. Recently, the growing interest in everyday history *(Alltagsgeschichte)* has begun to inspire a spate of critical studies, largely based on oral history. For instance, the journal *Kritische Justiz* has edited a series of dissenting lawyer portraits in *Streitbare Juristen* (Baden-Baden, 1988). Teacher initiatives have produced institutional histories [O. Geudtner *et al.*, eds., *"Ich bin katholisch getauft und Arier"* (Cologne, 1985)], local analyses [U. Hochmuth and H.-P. de Lorent, eds., *Hamburg: Schule unterm Hakenkreuz* (Hamburg, 1985)], and oral histories [M. Klewitz, *Lehrersein im Dritten Reich* (Weinheim, 1987), and L. van Dick, *Oppositionelles Lehrerverhalten, 1933–1945* (Weinheim, 1988)]. Engineers have also started to preserve the memory of victims through interviews [W. Mock, *Technische Intelligenz im Exil, 1933–1945* (Düsseldorf, 1986) and Y. Gelber and W. Goldstern, *Vertreibung und Emigration deutschsprachiger Ingenieure nach Palästina, 1933–1945* (Düsseldorf, 1988)]. These new findings on the problematic behavior of professionals have begun to reach the general public through the remarkable exhibitions on Nazi terror [R. Rürup, ed., *Topographie des Terrors* (Berlin, 1987)] and the judiciary in the Third Reich [Bundesminister der Justiz, ed., *Im Namen des deutschen Volkes: Justiz und Nationalsozialismus* (Cologne, 1989)]. If it becomes more theoretically oriented, comparatively aware, and critically inspired, then the professional perspective will yield even richer insights into the exceptional or ordinary lives of people in the past.

NOTES

CHAPTER 1

1. R. Dix, "Erklärung des Deutschen Anwaltvereins," *Abl* 20 (1933): 89. Cf. H. V. Schubert, "Die Anwaltschaft im Neuen Staat," *DR* 3 (1933), No. 1. To save space, footnotes combine several references, with quotations or paraphrases cited in order of appearance and additional literature separated by cf. or see also.

2. Appeal by the new leader Bohm, "An die deutschen Philologen" on April 1, 1933, *Phbl* 41 (1933): 181ff. On March 22 the Philologenverband claimed that it had always championed "national education" and endorsed the loyalty declaration of the RhB of March 18. *Ibid.*, 100ff.

3. "Von den deutschen Ingenieuren an den Herrn Reichskanzler," *VDIN* 13 (1933), No. 18. German terms have been translated whenever possible. Where their special connotation required retention, they have initially been italicized and subsequently treated as English words.

4. R. Dix and Dr. Voß, "An die Mitglieder des DAV" (urging them to join the NSDAP unless they were already in the DNVP or the *Stahlhelm), Abl* 20 (1933): 129f.

5. The professions' confrontation with their own past after 1945 has yet to be explored systematically. The anniversary histories' denial of guilt has in turn spurred an overly-generalized indictment of all professional activity after 1933.

6. J. J. Linz, "Some Notes toward a Comparative Study of Fascism in Sociological Historical Perspective," in W. Laqueur, ed., *Fascism: A Reader's Guide* (Berkeley, 1976); P. Aycoberry, *The Nazi Question: An Essay on the Interpretations of National Socialism* (New York, 1981); and I. Kershaw, *The Nazi Dictatorship: Problems and Perspectives of Interpretation* (London, 1985).

7. J. Becker, "Die Zerstörung einer 'Republik Wider Willen'," in *1933. Fünfzig Jahre danach* (Munich, 1983); and M. Broszat *et al.*, eds., *Deutschlands Weg in die Diktatur* (Berlin, 1983); versus J. Kocka, "Ursachen des Nationalsozialismus," *Aus Politik und Zeitgeschichte* 25 (1980): 9–24.

8. R. Hamilton, *Who Voted for Hitler?* (Princeton, N.J., 1982); T. Childers, *The Nazi Voter* (Chapel Hill, N. C., 1983), and many articles by J. Falter, such as "Radikalisierung des Mittelstandes oder Mobilisierung der Unpolitischen?" in P. Steinbach, ed., *Probleme politischer Partizipation im Modernisierungsprozess* (Stuttgart, 1982), p. 438ff.

9. M. H. Kater, *The Nazi Party: A Social Profile of Members and Leaders, 1919–1945* (Cambridge, Mass., 1983), and M. Jamin, *Zwischen den Klassen. Zur Sozialstruktur der SA Führerschaft* (Wuppertal, 1984).

10. L. E. Jones, *German Liberalism and the Dissolution of the Weimar Party System, 1918–1933* (Chapel Hill, N.C., 1988); and D. Abraham's controversial *The Collapse of the Weimar Republic: Political Economy and Crisis,* 2nd ed. (New York, 1986).

11. F. K. Ringer, *The Decline of the German Mandarins* (Cambridge, Mass., 1969); H. Döring, *Der Weimarer Kreis* (Meisenheim, 1975), and G. Giles, "National Socialism and the Educated Elite in the Weimar Republic," in P. Stachura, ed., *The Nazi Machtergreifung* (London, 1983), p. 49ff.

12. M. H. Kater, *Studentenschaft und Rechtsradikalismus in Deutschland 1918–1933* (Hamburg, 1975); G. Giles, *German Students and National Socialism* (Princeton, N.J., 1985); K.H. Jarausch, *Deutsche Studenten 1800–1980* (Frankfurt, 1984).

13. F. Ostler, *Die deutschen Rechtsanwälte, 1871–1971* (Essen, 1971); M. Heinemann, ed.,

Der Lehrer und seine Organisation (Stuttgart, 1977); and K.-H. Ludwig, *Technik und Ingenieure im Dritten Reich* (Königsstein, 1979).

14. C. Huerkamp, *Der Aufstieg der Ärzte im 19. Jahrhundert. Vom gelehrten Stand zum professionellen Experten* (Göttingen, 1986); M. H. Kater, "Professionalization and Socialization of Physicians in Wilhelmine and Weimar Germany," *JCH* 20 (1985): 677–701; and F. Kudlien, ed., *Ärzte und Nationalsozialismus* (Cologne, 1985).

15. A. J. LaVopa, "The Language of Profession: Germany in the late 18th Century" (Ms., Princeton, N.J., 1980). See H.-J. Daheim, *Der Beruf in der modernen Gesellschaft* (Cologne, 1967) and A. H. Hesse, *Berufe im Wandel. Ein Beitrag zum Problem der Professionalisierung* (Stuttgart, 1968).

16. W. Conze, "Beruf" in O. Brunner *et al.*, eds., *Geschichtliche Grundbegriffe* (Stuttgart, 1972), Vol. 1., pp. 490–506; and A. J. Heidenheimer, "Professions, the State and the Police(y) Connection," (Ms., St. Louis, Mo., 1983). Cf. E. Tatarin-Tarnheyden, *Die Berufsstände, ihre Stellung im Staatsrecht und die deutsche Wirtschaftsverfassung* (Berlin, 1922).

17. Most German professional journals contain a section on *Standesfragen,* discussing general professional problems. C. McClelland, "Zur Professionalisierung der akademischen Berufe in Deutschland," in W. Conze and J. Kocka, eds., *Bildungsbürgertum im 19. Jahrhundert* (Stuttgart, 1985), Vol. 1, p. 233ff; H.-E. Thenorth, "Professionen und Professionalisierung," in Heinemann, ed., *Lehrer,* p. 457ff.

18. From the voluminous literature see only T. Heuss, "Organisationsprobleme der 'freien Berufe'," in *Festschrift für Lujo Brentano* (Munich, 1916), p. 237ff; S. Feuchtwanger, *Die Freien Berufe. Staatsamt oder Sozialamt?* (Königsberg, 1929); V. Deneke, *Die Freien Berufe* (Stuttgart, 1956) and *idem, Klassifizierung der freien Berufe* (Cologne, 1969); or H. Kairat, *"Professions" oder "Freie Berufe"?* (Berlin, 1969).

19. R. Vierhaus, "Umrisse einer Sozialgeschichte der Gebildeten in Deutschland," *Quellen und Forschungen aus Italienischen Archiven und Bibliotheken* 60 (1980): 395–419; R. Vondung, *Das wilhelminische Bildungsbürgertum* (Göttingen, 1977); H.-J. Henning, *Das Bildungsbürgertum in den preußischen Westprovinzen* (Wiesbaden, 1972); and W. Conze in the first part of the introduction, in Conze and Kocka, eds., *Bildungsbürgertum im 19. Jahrhundert,* Vol. 1, p. 10f.

20. Because there is no historical analysis of the concept, one can turn only to dictionaries such as *Der große Brockhaus* of 1893. F. Ringer's notion of "mandarin" analyzes a group of professors in the faculty of philosophy and *not* all university graduates. Cf. S. Liedman, "Institutions and Ideas: Mandarins and Non-Mandarins in the German Academic Intelligentsia," *Comparative Studies in Society and History* 28 (1986): 119ff.

21. For example, R. Lepsius, "Kritik als Beruf. Zur Soziologie der Intellektuellen," *Kölner Zeitschrift für Soziologie und Sozialpsychologie* 16 (1964): 75–91; and T. Geiger, *Aufgaben und Stellung der Intelligenz in der Gesellschaft* (New York, 1975 repr.). Although there are numerous works on revolutionary Russia, Jürgen Kuczynzki's *Die Intelligenz* (Cologne, 1987) remains only a suggestive fragment.

22. For instance, A. M. Carr-Saunders and P. A. Wilson, *The Professions* (Oxford, 1933). This classification impulse characterizes a good deal of the literature, such as P. U. Unschuld, "Professionalisierung im Bereich der Medizin," *Saeculum* 25 (1974): 251–76.

23. T. Parsons, "Professions," in *International Encyclopedia for the Social Sciences* (New York, 1968), Vol. 12, p. 545; D. Bell, *The Coming of Post-Industrial Society* (New York, 1976), p. 374; still echoing in H. Perkin, *The Rise of Professional Society in England Since 1880* (London, 1989).

24. E. Freidson, *Profession of Medicine* (New York, 1970); M. S. Larson, *The Rise of Professionalism: A Sociological Analysis* (Berkeley, Calif., 1977); and B. Bledstein, *The Culture of Professionalism* (New York, 1976). Cf. M. S. Larson, "Professionalism: Rise and Fall," *International Journal of Health Services* 9 (1979): 607–27.

25. R. Collins, *The Credential Society* (New York, 1979); R. Spree, *Soziale Ungleichheit vor Krankheit und Tod* (Göttingen, 1981), p. 138ff; R. Murphey, *Social Closure: The Theory of Monopolization and Exclusion* (Oxford, 1988).

26. E. Freidson, *Professional Powers* (Chicago, 1986), p. 35f; and C. Tilly, *As Sociology Meets History* (New York, 1981). Cf. G. Geison, ed., *Professions and the French State, 1700–1900* (Philadelphia, 1984).

27. R. Torstendahl, "Essential Properties, Strategic Aims and Historical Development: Three Approaches to Theories of Professionalism," in M. Burrage and R. Torstendahl, eds., *Professions in Theory and History* (London, 1990).

28. D. Rueschemeyer, "Professional Autonomy and the Social Control of Expertise," in R. Dingwall and P. Lewis, eds., *The Sociology of the Professions* (London, 1983), p. 38ff, pleads for "comparative historical and intercultural studies."

29. Huerkamp, *Aufstieg der Ärzte,* p. 14ff. Cf. A. Abbott, *The System of Professions* (Chicago, 1988), p. 3ff.

30. G. Geison, "Introduction" to his *Professions and Professional Ideologies in America* (Chapel Hill, N.C., 1983), p. 3ff.

31. Kocka's part of the common introduction with Conze to the volume on *Bildungsbürgertum im 19. Jahrhundert,* Vol. 1, p. 16ff.

32. In contrast to M. S. Larson, "The Rise and Fall of Professionalism" (Ms., Philadelphia, 1986) and F. K. Ringer's methodology in his forthcoming comparative study of French and German *Bildung,* this investigation focuses on the perspective of practitioners.

33. M. Burrage, K. Jarausch, and H. Siegrist, "An Actor-Oriented Framework for the Study of the Professions," in *Professions in Theory and History.* Instead of elaborating yet another model, the just-mentioned discussion seeks to draw from theoretical criteria a number of questions for the historical analysis of mature professions.

34. K. H. Jarausch, "The Crisis of the German Professions, 1918–1933," *JCH* 20 (1985): 379–98. In order to link the questions more closely to theory, it proved necessary to treat testing/certification/admission as a separate category and to distinguish a dimension of practice (based on autonomy and work quality).

35. D. Light *et al.,* "Social Medicine versus Professional Dominance: The German Experience," *American Journal of Public Health* 76 (1986): 78ff; H. Siegrist, "Gebremste Professionalisierung," in *Bildungsbürgertum im 19. Jahrhundert,* Vol. 1, p. 301ff; as well as Jarausch *et al.,* "Framework."

36. K. H. Jarausch, "Die Not der geistigen Arbeiter: Akademiker in der Berufskrise, 1918–1933," in W. Abelshauser, ed., *Die Weimarer Republik als Wohlfahrtsstaat* (Stuttgart, 1987), p. 280ff, *Beiheft* 81 of *VSWG;* and "The Perils of Professionalism: Lawyers, Teachers and Engineers in Nazi Germany," *GSR* 9 (1986): 107–37. Cf. *idem,* "The Old 'New History of Education': A German Reconsideration," *HEQ* 26 (1986): 225–41.

37. Because the state-employed German *Juristen,* such as higher officials or judges, are better analyzed in terms of bureaucracy, this study only deals with free professional attorneys. D. Rueschemeyer, *Lawyers and their Society: A Comparative Study of the Legal Profession in Germany and the United States* (Cambridge, Mass., 1973).

38. The very tension between academic and nonacademic teachers presents important professionalization conflicts. R. Bölling, *Sozialgeschichte der deutschen Lehrer* (Göttingen, 1983), is a good survey.

39. In spite of particular attention to *Diplomingenieure,* much of the text will deal with engineers in general, because technical work tended to obliterate the distinction in training. G. Hortleder, *Das Gesellschaftsbild des Ingenieurs. Zum politischen Verhalten der technischen Intelligenz in Deutschland,* 2nd ed. (Frankfurt, 1970).

40. The continuity discussion, initiated by F. Fischer, should more profitably be reframed on this individual level of persistence and adaptation. For the term see H. Cord Meyer, *The Long Generation: Germany from Empire to Ruin 1913–1945* (New York, 1973).

41. H. Titze *et al.,* "Bildungsauslese und akademischer Berufszugang" (Ms., Göttingen, 1987); C. E. McClelland's forthcoming study of the rise of the German professions; and G. Cocks and K. H. Jarausch, eds., *German Professions, 1800–1950* (New York, 1990).

42. Huerkamp, *Aufstieg der Ärzte,* p. 254ff; and D. Skopp, "Auf der untersten Sprosse: Der *Volksschullehrer* als 'Semi-Professional' im Deutschland des 19. Jahrhunderts," *GG* 6 (1980): 383ff.

43. Stenographic report of the *Verhandlungen des XX. Deutschen Anwaltstags zu Würzburg,* Sept. 22 and 23, 1911, in PrGStA Da, Rep. 84a, No. 102.

44. Spree, *Soziale Ungleichheit,* p. 138ff; C. Huerkamp, "Die preußisch-deutsche Ärzteschaft als Teil des Bildungsbürgertums," in *Bildungsbürgertum im 19. Jahrhundert,* Vol. 1, p.

358ff; and C. McClelland, "Professionalization and Higher Education in Germany," in K. H. Jarausch, ed., *The Transformation of Higher Learning* (Chicago, 1983), p. 306–20.

45. H.-U. Wehler, *Das deutsche Kaiserreich, 1871–1918* (Göttingen, 1973), now in English translation (Leamington Spa, England, 1985), versus D. Blackbourn and G. Eley, *The Peculiarities of German History: Bourgeois Society and Politics in Nineteenth Century Germany* (New York, 1984), and the collection edited by J. Dukes and J. Remak, *The Other Germany* (Boulder, Colo., 1987).

46. An empirical approach seems more promising than further arguments by R. Fletcher, "Recent Developments in Western German Historiography," *GSR* 7 (1984): 451ff; J. N. Retallack, "Social History with a Vengeance?" *ibid.*, 423ff; or R. G. Moeller, "The Kaiserreich Recast," *JSH* 17 (1984): 655–83.

47. A. Weißler, *Die Geschichte der Rechtsanwaltschaft* (Leipzig, 1905), p. 573ff; E. Fuchs during the Rechtsanwaltstag 1911, see *Verhandlungen des XX. Anwaltstags.* Cf. Ostler, *Rechtsanwälte,* p. 11ff; H. Siegrist, "Public Office or Free Profession? The German Attorney in the Nineteenth and Early Twentieth Centuries" in Cocks and Jarausch, eds., *German Professions, p. 45ff.*

48. For example, *Justizrat* Boyens, "Sind Reformen zur Vorbildung der Juristen nötig?" *JW* 40 (1911), Suppl. to No. 15; and the discussion at "Der XX. Deutsche Anwaltstag in Würzburg," *ibid.*, No. 16. Cf. G. Dilcher, "Das Gesellschaftsbild der Rechtswissenschaft und die soziale Frage," in Vondung, ed., *Das wilhelminische Bildungsbürgertum,* p. 53ff.

49. Noest and Nitze on "Überfüllung des Anwaltstandes," *JW* 40 (1911): 619ff. H. Titze *et al.*, *Das Hochschulstudium in Preußen und Deutschland, 1820–1944* (Göttingen, 1987), 86f. Cf. D. Rueschemeyer, *Juristen in Deutschland und in den USA* (Stuttgart, 1976), p. 155ff.

50. "Ergebnis der Umfrage über die Einkommensverhältnisse der Rechtsanwälte" (Leipzig, 1914), Suppl. to Vol. 1 of the *Abl.* In 1911, Landsberg mentioned 5000–6000 Marks as average annual income at the Anwaltstag, while Kassler disputed this figure as too high. "Empfehlen sich gesetzgeberische Maßnahmen gegen eine Überfüllung des Anwaltstandes?" Suppl. to *JW* 40 (1911): 672ff.

51. A. Müller, "Der Justizratstitel," *JW* 412 (1913): 363f; H. Dittenberger, "Kritiker der Anwaltschaft," *ibid.*, p. 397; and Fuchs in *Verhandlungen des XX. Anwaltstags.* K. H. Jarausch, *Students, Society and Politics in Imperial Germany: The Rise of Academic Illiberalism* (Princeton, N.J., 1983), pp. 141ff and 322ff, indicates that more than 40 percent of the Bonn law students were recruited from elite families. The Celle figures are recomputed from K. Ledford, "A Social and Institutional History of the German Bar in Private Practice," (Diss. Baltimore, 1988), p. 377.

52. Hans Oelert, "Memoiren eines Rechtsanwalts," KA, p. 728; and M. Hachenburg, *Lebenserinnerungen eines Rechtsanwalts und Briefe aus der Emigration* reissued by J. Schadt (Stuttgart, 1978). Figures from Reichsjustizamt, *Deutsche Justiz-Statistik* 16 (1915): 23ff.

53. Statements by Landsberg and Dr. Fuchs (Berlin) at the 1911 *Juristentag,* see *Verhandlungen des XX. Anwaltstags.* Cf. various *Ehrengerichtsordnungen.*

54. For regional studies see: H. Huffmann, *Geschichte der Rheinischen Rechtsanwaltschaft* (Cologne, 1969), p. 136ff; W. Hülle, *Geschichte der Oldenburgischen Rechtsanwaltschaft* (Oldenburg, 1977); R. Göhmann, "150 Jahre Advokaten- und Rechtsanwaltsverein Hannover," in *Festschrift zur 150 Jahrfeier des Rechtsanwaltsvereins Hannover, 1831–1981* (Hannover, 1981), p. 1ff; and P. Heinrich, *100 Jahre RAK München* (Munich, 1979).

55. "Was wir wollen," *JW* 1 (1872): 1–2; "Zum 25jährigen Jubiläum der Hülfskasse für Rechtsanwälte," *ibid.*, 39 (1910), No. 7; and H. Dittenberger, "Bericht über die Geschäfte des deutschen Anwaltvereins in den Jahren 1910 und 1911," Suppl. to *JW* 40 (1911), No. 16. Cf. Weißler, *Geschichte der Rechtsanwaltschaft,* p. 560ff; and Ostler, *Rechtsanwälte,* p. 3ff.

56. *Verhandlungen des XX. Anwaltstags, passim;* Noest, "Die Umfrage der Vereinigung rheinisch-westphälischer Rechtsanwälte," *JW* 42 (1913): 809ff; and D. K. Müller and others, "Modellentwicklung zur Analyse von Krisenphasen im Verhältnis von Schulsystem und staatlichem Beschäftigungssystem," *ZfP* 14. Beiheft (Weinheim, 1977): 65f. See Huffmann, *Rheinische Rechtsanwaltschaft,* p. 145ff; and Hülle, *Oldenburgische Rechtsanwaltschaft,* p. 105ff.

57. V. Berger, "Freizügigkeit und Simultanzulassung" (AG memorandum for the DAV), *JW* 42 (1913), Suppl. to No. 13; M. Goldschmidt, "Simultanzulassung," *ibid.*, p. 831ff. Cf.

K. F. Ledford, "Simultaneous Admission and the German Bar, 1903–1927," in Cocks and Jarausch, eds., *German Professions, p. 252ff.*

58. *Verhandlungen des XXI. Deutschen Anwaltstags zu Breslau,* Sept. 12 and 13, 1913, in PrGStA Da, Rep. 84a, No. 102. The Friedländer report presented the conclusions of a special DAV commission.

59. Quotes from Landsberg and Bassermann in the 1911 discussions, *Verhandlungen des XX. Anwaltstags.* See Ostler, *Rechtsanwälte,* p. 59ff.

60. F. Paulsen speech on "Das höhere Schulwesen in Deutschland, seine Bedeutung für den Staat und für die geistige Kultur des deutschen Volkes und die sich daraus ergebenden Folgerungen für die Stellung des höheren Lehrerstandes," Darmstadt, April 8 and 9, 1904. Cf. J. C. Albisetti, *Secondary School Reform in Imperial Germany* (Princeton, 1983) and *Schooling German Girls and Women* (Princeton, 1988) as well as A. La Vopa, "Specialists Against Specialization," in *German Professions,* p. 27ff.

61. For the evolution of the *Prüfungsordnung* cf. Ch. Führ, "Gelehrter Schulmann—Oberlehrer—Studienrat. Zum sozialen Aufstieg der Philologen," in *Bildungsbürgertum im 19. Jahrhundert,* Vol. 1, p. 417ff and A. Nath, "Zugangsnormierung der preußischen höheren Lehramtskarriere," (Ms., Göttingen, 1987).

62. Titze *et al., Hochschulstudium,* p. 86ff; and H.-G. Herrlitz and H. Titze, "Überfüllung als bildungspolitische Strategie. Zur administrativen Steuerung der Lehrerarbeitslosigkeit in Preußen 1870–1914," *Die deutsche Schule* 68 (1976): 348ff.

63. P. Mellmann, *Geschichte des Deutschen Philologen-Verbandes* (Leipzig, 1929), p. 140, and H. Morsch, *Das höhere Lehramt in Deutschland und Österreich* (Leipzig, 1905).

64. Paulsen in his 1904 speech, and Bismarck quoted in "Oberlehrerverein und Oberlehrertag," *Pädagogisches Wochenblatt für den akademisch gebildeten Lehrerstand Deutschlands,* 11 (1902), No. 47. Figures from *Preußische Statistik,* Vol. 236 (1911), p. 136f and Jarausch, *Students, Society and Politics,* p. 146ff.

65. Paulsen in his 1904 speech, No. 60, and Bölling, *Sozialgeschichte,* p. 30ff. See *Dienstanweisung für die Direktoren und Lehrer an den höheren Lehranstalten für die männliche Jugend* (Berlin, 1910).

66. Paulsen in his 1904 speech; Mellmann, *Geschichte des Deutschen Philologen-Verbandes,* p. 108; and speech by Prof. Keller on "Aufgabe des Lehrers—eine Kunst auf gelehrter Grundlage," at the Eisenach meeting, April 16 and 17, 1906, *ibid.,* p. 114f.

67. "Deutscher Oberlehrerverband," *Westfälischer Merkur,* Oct. 11, 1903; Mellmann, *Geschichte des Deutschen Philologen-Verbandes,* p. 91ff; and figures calculated from the "Teilnehmerliste" of the founding conference, April 8 and 9, 1904, ZStA Me, Rep. 76 VI, Sekt. 1, Gen. z, No. 205, Vol. 1. Cf. S. Müller, "Die Verbandsinteressen der Lehrer an den höheren Schulen am Ende des 19. Jahrhunderts," in Heinemann, ed., *Lehrer,* p. 235ff.

68. "Erster Deutscher Oberlehrertag," *BT,* April 9, 1904; association statutes; marginalia by "R" June 29, 1906; and clippings on the biennial meetings in ZStA Me, Rep. 76 VI, Sekt. 1, Gen. z, No. 205, Vol. I. It took until 1910 for the Prussian Ministry of Culture to send its first observer.

69. Althoff to Rheinbaben, June 24, 1907; Lortzing, *Denkschrift über die Gleichstellung der Oberlehrer mit den Richtern* (Berlin, 1907) and debate in the Prussian Landtag on April 13, 1907, in ZStA Me, Rep. 76 VI, Sekt. 1, Gen. z, No. 61, Vol. XXXI. Cf. *ibid.,* No. 159, comparing the mortality of teachers and judges.

70. Althoff to Rheinbaben, June 26, 1907; H. Schröder, *Zur Gleichstellung der höheren Beamten in Preußen, insbesondere der Philologen und der Justiz* (Gelsenkirchen, 1907); Hintzpeter to William II, Nov. 4, 1907; Holle to Rheinbaben, Nov. 16, 1907; joint Holle–Rheinbaben votum to the Ministry of State, Nov. 20, 1907; debate of the Herrenhaus, March 30, 1908; *Normaletat* of June 5, 1909, all in ZStA Me Rep. 76 VI, Sekt. 1, Gen. z, No. 61, vol. XXXI.

71. Mellmann, *Geschichte des Deutschen Philologen-Verbandes,* pp. 109, 118, 137f; Bölling, *Sozialgeschichte,* p. 38f.

72. For the professor title see Althoff note on Sept. 27, 1904 in ZStA Me, Rep. 76 VI, Sekt. 1, Gen. z, No. 28, Vol. IV; Block speech at the 1906 Weimar meeting, *ibid.,* No. 205, Vol. I; Kalisch and Schuster, *Ist eine einheitliche Titulatur für den deutschen höheren Lehrerstand erwünscht?* (Stuttgart, 1905); Trott to Ministry of State, April 4, 1913, PrGStA Da, Rep.

90, Vol. 563. Cf. Mellmann, *Geschichte des Deutschen Philologen-Verbandes,* pp. 112, 116, 123–27, 131f.

73. W. von Humboldt, "Über Prüfungen für das höhere Schulfach," in *Werke in fünf Bänden* (Darmstadt, 1964), Vol. 4, p. 240ff. Reinhardt note, April 14, 1914 and greeting in Munich ZStA Me, Rep. 76 VI, Sekt. 1, Gen. z, No. 105, Vol. I; O. Hintze, *Beamtentum und Bürokratie,* ed. by K. Krüger (Göttingen, 1981), p. 63. Cf. H.-E. Thenorth and E. Keiner, "Schulmänner—Volkslehrer—Unterrichtsbeamte," *IASL* 6 (1981): 198–222.

74. Rector Barkhausen of the TH Hanover to the Ministry of Culture, Dec. 10, 1897 in ZStA Me, Rep. 76 Vb, Sekt. 1, Tit. 5, No. 7, Vol. I. P. Lundgreen, *Techniker in Preußen während der frühen Industrialisierung* (Berlin, 1975); and L. U. Scholl, *Ingenieure in der Frühindustrialisierung* (Göttingen, 1978).

75. K.-H. Manegold, *Universität, Technische Hochschule und Industrie* (Berlin, 1970); for the lower levels Cf. C. Gispen, *New Profession, Old Order: Engineers and German Society, 1815–1914* (Cambridge, England, 1989).

76. TH Hanover to Bosse, Feb. 16, 1895; Frank note of March 21, 1896; *Standesinteressen der Deutschen Ingenieure* (Munich, 1897) and William II rescript, Oct. 11, 1899, in ZStA Me, Rep. 76 Vb, Sekt. 1, Tit. 5, No. 7, Vol. I. Cf. C. Gispen, "Selbstverständnis und Professionalisierung deutscher Ingenieure," *Technikgeschichte* 50 (1983): 34ff.

77. Titze *et al., Hochschulstudium,* p. 27ff; and Gispen, "Engineers in Wilhelmian Germany," in Cocks and Jarausch, eds., *German Professions, p. 104ff.*

78. Schwarz, "Statistik der Deutschen Diplom-Ingenieure 1899–1909," *ZVDDI* 1 (1910): 309ff; and Gispen, "Selbstverständnis," p. 57.

79. R. Jaeckel, *Statistik über die Lage der technischen Privatbeamten in Gross-Berlin* (Jena, 1908), and A. Günther, *Die deutschen Techniker, ihre Lebens-, Ausbildungs- und Arbeitsverhältnisse* (Leipzig, 1912), presenting the results of 11,500 questionnaires of the Deutsche Techniker Verband. Memorandum of the Verband der deutschen Technischen Hochschulen, May 1905, ZStA Me, Rep. 76 Vb, Sekt. 1, Tit. 5, No. 7, Vol. I. Cf. Gispen, *Engineers and German Society,* p. 200f.

80. C. Nipkow, "Der Mißbrauch der Bezeichnungen 'Ingenieur' und 'Architekt' in Deutschland," *ZVDDI* 7 (1916): 128ff; H. Herkner, "Berufs-, Standes und Klasseninteressen, sowie die Organisationen zu deren Vertretung," *ibid.* 1 (1910): 177ff. The 1900–1905 figures of the *Badische Hochschulstatistik* 1911 are more useful than L. Cron, *Glaubensbekenntnis und höheres Studium* (Heidelberg, 1900). Cf. A. Günther, *Deutsche Techniker,* 5ff and G. Fiedler, "Soziale Herkunft und höhere technische Ausbildung," in W. Kertz, ed., *Projektberichte zur Geschichte der Carolo-Wilhelmina* (Braunschweig, 1987), Vol. 3., pp. 121–34.

81. There is little evidence on what engineers actually did. For some glimpses see J. Kocka's pioneering *Unternehmensverwaltung und Angestelltenschaft am Beispiel Siemens 1847–1914* (Stuttgart, 1969).

82. Figures in Table 1.2 from *Statistisches Jahrbuch für den Preußischen Staat* 8 (1910): 53. Cf. C. Matschoß, "Aus der Geschichte des VDI," in *VDI, 1856–1926* (Berlin, 1926); and G. Fiedler, "Beruf, Qualifikation und Arbeitssituation von Ingenieuren im Kaiserreich," *Projektberichte* 1 (1985): 87–96.

83. W. König, "Die Ingenieure und der VDI als Großverein in der wilhelminischen Gesellschaft 1900 bis 1918," in *Technik, Ingenieure und Gesellschaft. Geschichte des VDI, 1856–1981* (Düsseldorf, 1981), pp. 235–287, is the best summary. For the background, cf. Gispen, *Engineers and Germany Society, passim.*

84. K. F. Steinmetz, "Der 'Butib' und der 'VDDI'," *ZVDDI* 1 (1910): 420ff; F. Junge, "Großkapital und Technik," *ibid.,* 4 (1913): 386f. Cf. J. Johnson, "Academic, Proletarian, . . . Professional? Shaping Professionalization for German Industrial Chemists, 1887–1920," in Cocks and Jarausch, eds., *German Professions, p. 123ff.;* and Gispen, *Engineers and German Society,* pp. 223–312.

85. A. Lang, "Die Techniker in der modernen Staatswirtschaft," *ZVDDI* 1 (1910): 1ff; Anonymous, "Die Berechtigung der Standesorganisation," *ibid.,* p. 68f; A. Lang, "Ein Jahr VDDI," *ibid.,* p. 333ff. Cf. Gispen, *Engineers and German Society,* pp. 313–331.

86. Reichel and Lang (VDDI) petition to the Ministry of Culture, June 21, 1910, for title

protection; ministerial acceptance of the title for internal purposes, Sept. 13, 1911 and so on, in ZStA Me, Rep. 76 Vb, Sekt. 1, Tit. 5, No. 7, Vol. I.

87. A. Lang, "Jahresbericht 1913," *ZVDDI* 5 (1914): 165ff; C. Weihe, "Technische Erziehung," *ibid.*, 6 (1915), No. 19; M. W. Neufeld, "Die Akademiker in den Technischen Vereinen und Verbänden," *ZVDDI* 8 (1917): 82ff; and V. Clark, "Anglo-American Models and German Professionalization: The Case of the Private Architect," in Cocks and Jarausch, eds., *German Professions, p. 143ff.*

88. Statement by E. Fuchs at the 1911 bar association meeting, No. 47. Cf. H. Siegrist, "Professionalization with the Brakes on: The Legal Profession in Switzerland, France and Germany," *Comparative Social Research* 9 (1986): 267–98.

89. P. Mellmann, speech at the 1912 secondary teachers' congress in Dresden, in *Geschichte des Deutschen Philologen-Verbandes,* p. 171. H. Titze, "Die soziale und geistige Umbildung des preußischen Oberlehrerstandes von 1870 bis 1914," 14. Beiheft of the *ZfP* (Weinheim, 1977), p. 107ff.

90. Reichel to Trott, March 20, 1917 (petitioning for title protection) versus Höfle to minister June 27, 1917 (objecting for the DTV) in ZStA Me, Rep. 76 Vb, Sekt. 1, Tit. 5, No. 7, Vol. II. Cf. Gispen, "Professionalisierung," p. 59f.

91. K. H. Jarausch, "The German Professions in History and Theory," in *idem* and G. Cocks, eds., *German Professions, p. 9ff.* Cf. the essays by D. Light, A. Engel, and C. Timberlake on the American, British, and Russian professions in Jarausch, ed., *Transformation of Higher Learning,* pp. 293–365.

92. Light *et al.*, "Social Medicine versus Professional Dominance," p. 78ff, and *idem,* "Comparing Health Care Systems: Lessons from East and West Germany," in P. Conrad and R. Stern, eds., *The Sociology of Health and Illness* (New York, 1985). Cf. R. Stichweh, "Professionen und Disziplinen," in K. Harney *et al.*, eds., *Professionalisierung der Erwachsenenbildung* (Frankfurt, 1988).

93. A. J. Heidenheimer, "Comparing Status Professions: The Evolution of State-Profession Relationships of Lawyers and Physicians in Britain, Germany and the US" (Ms., St. Louis, Mo., 1987). Not even J. Kocka's perceptive introduction and C. McClelland, "Zur Professionalisierung der Akademischen Berufe in Deutschland," in *Bildungsbürgertum im 19. Jahrhundert,* pp. 16 ff, 233ff, are entirely free from this stereotyping.

94. Siegrist, "Gebremste Professionalisierung," in *Bildungsbürgertum im 19. Jahrhundert,* p. 327ff and Rueschemeyer, *Lawyers and their Society,* p. 146ff.

95. H.-E. Thenorth, "Lehrer in Preußen. Zur Geschichte professioneller Lehrertätigkeit" (Ms., Frankfurt, 1983) moves beyond earlier assertions about the "unity" of the teaching profession on all levels. S. Müller, "Verbandsinteressen der Lehrer," in Heinemann, ed., *Lehrer,* p. 244f, speaks only of "semiprofessionalization" because his analysis breaks off before the decisive steps took place.

96. C. Gispen's conceptual "introduction" to his book *Engineers and German Society.* In contrast to Sweden, management did not try to use professionalization as strategy for engineers' subservience. Cf. R. Torstendahl, "Engineers in Industry 1850–1910: Professional Men and New Bureaucrats," in *Science, Technology and Society in the Time of Alfred Nobel* (Oxford, 1982), p. 253ff.

97. This characterization employs a historical Central European meaning of "corporatism" as calling for a sociopolitical order based on *Berufsstände.* The prefix "neo" indicates the postliberal thrust of the attempt to reintroduce premodern elements into high industrial society. Cf. K. van Eyll, "Berufsständische Selbstverwaltung," in *Deutsche Verwaltungsgeschichte* (Stuttgart, 1985), p. 78ff.

98. J. J. Sheehan, *German Liberalism in the 19th Century* (Chicago, 1978), p. 19f; Jarausch, *Students, Society and Politics,* p. 399ff; and R. Chickering, *We Men Who Feel Most German* (Boston, 1984).

99. E. Auerbach, "Der Anwaltstand und der Liberalismus," *FZ,* May 3, 1914; Mertens to Bülow, June 10, 1909, ZStA Me, Rep. 67 VI, Sekt. 1, Gen. z, No. 61, Vol. XXXI; and O. Vent, "Krieg und Ingenieurwissenschaft," *ZVDDI* 6 (1915), Nos. 7 and 8. Among imperial Reichstag deputies, free professionals were mostly found in liberal parties, higher officials started

as conservatives and moved toward the middle, while entrepreneurs tended to be National Liberals. H. Best, "Politische Modernisierung und parlamentarische Führungsgruppen in Deutschland, 1870–1918," *HSR* 13 (1988): 63ff.

100. G. Eley, "Educating the Bourgeoisie: Students and the Culture of 'Illiberalism' in Imperial Germany," *HEQ* 26 (1986): 287ff; H.-U. Wehler, "Wie bürgerlich war das deutsche Kaiserreich?" in J. Kocka, ed., *Bürger und Bürgerlichkeit im 19. Jahrhundert* (Göttingen, 1987); and K. H. Jarausch, "The Crisis of the Bildungsbürgertum in the First Third of the Twentieth Century," appearing in H. Schulte, ed., *The Tragedy of German Inwardness? Antirationalism in German Culture, 1870–1933* (Hamilton, Ont., 1990).

CHAPTER 2

1. "Der Kriegszustand und die Reichsgesetzgebung," *JW* 43 (1914), No. 15. Cf. K. Vondung, ed., *Kriegserlebnis* (Göttingen, 1980) and R. Stromberg, *Redemption by War* (Lawrence, Kansas 1982).

2. "An die deutschen Diplom-Ingenieure!" *ZVDDI* 5 (1914): 355. The history of the professions during the war is virtually unexplored. Cf. J. Kocka, *Klassengesellschaft im Krieg 1914–1918* (Göttingen, 1973).

3. "Zum neuen Jahre," *JW* 47 (1918): 1f. Cf. K. Jarausch, *The Enigmatic Chancellor: Theobald von Bethmann Hollweg and the Hubris of Imperial Germany, 1856–1921* (New Haven, Conn., 1973) and B. Sösemann, ed., *Theodor Wolff. Tagebücher 1914–1919* (Boppard, Germany, 1984), 2 Vols.

4. H. Grupe, "Die Böse Zeit—wie ich sie erlebte," KA, 121.

5. R. Schiffers, ed., *Der Hauptausschuß des Deutschen Reichstags 1915–1918* (Düsseldorf, 1981), Vol. 2, pp. 1060–64, Vol. 3, pp. 1231–33; E. Ludendorff, ed., *Urkunden der Obersten Heeresleitung über ihre Tätigkeit 1916/18* (Berlin, 1920), pp. 67, 79, 268ff. Cf. K. Jarausch, "German Students in the First World War," *CEH* 17 (1984): 310ff.

6. Official matriculation figures are fictitious, because high school graduates were allowed to enroll without being able to attend. Revised numbers from H. Titze, *Das Hochschulstudium in Preußen und Deutschland, 1820–1944* (Göttingen, 1987), pp. 29 and 168. According to J. Schwarz, *Studenten in der Weimarer Republik* (Berlin, 1971), pp. 20–57, 409ff, tertiary enrollment dropped from 79,225 to 17,089 in 1916 before returning to 25,079 in 1918.

7. "Die Technischen Hochschulen . . . im Sommer des 2. Kriegsjahres 1916," *ZVDDI* 7 (1916): 125; Jarausch, "German Students in the First World War," p. 318ff. For the experience of a Jewish student–soldier, cf. S. Neumann, *Nacht über Deutschland* (Munich, 1978), p. 16ff.

8. Figures from *JW* 48 (1919): 401, and *Phbl* 26 (1918): 410, 432, and 27 (1919): 528. "Die unbesetzten Oberlehrerstellen an den höheren Lehranstalten in Preußen," *ibid.*, p. 286.

9. A. Kaufmann, "Vom klagenden Anwaltstande," *Der Tag,* Jan. 3, 1917; P. Albers, "Wirtschaftliche Kriegsnot der Notare und Anwälte," *BT,* Oct. 16, 1915; "Die Notlage der Anwaltschaft," *VZ,* June 2, 1916; and F. Ostler, *Die deutschen Rechtsanwälte, 1871–1971* (Essen, 1971), p. 112ff.

10. "DAV," *VZ,* April 17, 1916; "Verhandlungen der Vertreterversammlung des DAV" PrGStA Da, Rep. 84a, Vol. 106; H. F. Abraham, "Die wirtschaftliche Stärkung des Anwaltstandes," *Norddeutsche Allgemeine Zeitung,* March 20, 1918; M. Friedländer, "Zur Notlage der Anwaltschaft," *JW* 47 (1918): 196ff. Cf. Ostler, *Rechtsanwälte,* p. 109ff and A. Apfel, *Behind the Scenes of German Justice* (London, 1935), p. 43ff, for a reluctant profiteer.

11. G. Strutz, "Die 'Proletarisierung' der höheren Beamten," *Phbl* 26 (1918): 196f, and further articles in *ibid.* by J. Müller, p. 284f, and Hergt, p. 357ff. The foundation of the Bund höherer Beamter on Oct. 8, 1918 was a result of this frustration. *Ibid.*, p. 403.

12. A. Lang, "Die Diplom-Ingenieure und der technische Arbeitsmarkt im Kriege," *ZVDDI* 5 (1914): 381ff. Cf. J. Kocka, *Klassengesellschaft im Krieg, 1914–1918* (Göttingen, 1973), p. 71ff.

13. R. Bendix, *Von Berlin nach Berkeley* (Frankfurt, 1985), p. 102ff. Ostler, *Rechtsanwälte,* p. 135ff.

14. Trott to Ministry of State, April 4, 1913; Schmidt-Ott to Ministry of State, Oct. 29,

1917, and Jan. 27, 1918; proclamation of the *Reichs- und Staatsanzeiger,* Jan. 27, 1918, in PrGStA Da, Rep. 90, Vols. 563 and 564. Cf. "Beschlüsse des Vertretertages der preußischen Philologenvereine zur Neuordung der Amtsbezeichnungen . . ." and "Zeitungsschau," *Phbl* 26 (1918): 65ff.

15. C. Nipkow, "Der Mißbrauch der Bezeichnungen 'Ingenieur' und 'Architekt' in Deutschland," *ZVDDI* 7 (1916): 128ff; A. Lang, "Die Regelung des Zivilingenieurberufes in Deutschland," *ibid.*, p. 115ff; *idem,* "Der Rechtsschutz der Bezeichnung 'Ingenieur' im Deutschen Reiche," *ibid.*, 8 (1917): 73ff; and R. Skutsch, "Der Schutz des Ingenieurtitels und der VDI," *ibid.*, 81ff.

16. Ostler, *Rechtsanwälte,* p. 105ff; A. Lang, "Die Diplom-Ingenieure und das heimatliche Wirtschaftsleben während des Krieges," *ZVDDI* 5 (1914): 363ff.

17. "Beschlüsse von Anwaltskammern und Anwaltsvereinen aus Anlaß des Krieges" *Abl* 1 (1914): 113f. "Zur Ausführung des Gesetzes über den vaterländischen Hilfsdienst," *ibid.*, 4 (1917): 3ff. Ostler, *Rechtsanwälte,* p. 127, claims that only few lawyers actually served. Cf. G. Feldman, *Army, Industry and Labor in Germany 1914–1918* (Princeton, N.J., 1967), p. 172ff.

18. J. Magnus, "Die Anwaltschaft im Dienste der Aufklärung des neutralen Auslandes," *Abl* 1 (1914): 112f; and E. Schott, " 'Kriegsstunden' in der Schule," *Phbl* 22 (1914): 697ff. Bruno Jarausch, "Aufsätze" (Ms., Berlin, 1914). E. M. Remarque, *All Quiet on the Western Front* (Boston, 1930) presents a literary portrayal of *Oberlehrer* chauvinism. Other lawyers defended prisoners of war: W. Grimm, *40 Jahre Dienst am Recht* (Bonn, 1953), p. 24ff.

19. "An die deutschen Rechtsanwälte!" *Abl* 1 (1914): 109; "Im Kampfe für das Vaterland sind folgende Kollegen gefallen," *ibid.*, p. 110f. A. Biese, "Luther, Goethe und Bismarck. Eine Schulansprache in schwerster Zeit," *Phbl* 26 (1918), No. 41/42.

20. K. Schwabe, *Wissenschaft und Kriegsmoral* (Göttingen, 1969); and K. H. Jarausch, "Die Alldeutschen und Bethmann Hollweg: Eine Denkschrift Kurt Riezlers aus dem Jahre 1916," *VfZG* 21 (1973): 435–68.

21. DAV members declined 7.7 percent from 10,576 (1915) to 9,758 (1919), while the VDI membership contracted from 24,725 (1914) to 23,798 (1917). "Geschäftsbericht des DAV 1923/4," in PrGStA Da, Rep. 84a, Vol. 106, and M.-L. Heuser and W. König "Tabellarische Zusammenstellungen zur Geschichte des VDI," in Ludwig, ed., *Technik,* p. 559ff.

22. *Justizrat* Werner, "Die Hülfskasse im Jahre 1916/17," *Abl* 5 (1918): 8ff; "Verhandlungen der Vertreterversammlung des DAV zu Eisenach, May 20, 1917," PrGStA Da, Rep. 84a, Vol. 106. J. Magnus, "Die soziale Organisation der Anwaltschaft," *VZ,* May 25, 1918.

23. M. Neufeld, "Die Akademiker in den technischen Vereinen und Verbänden," *ZVDDI* 8 (1917): 82ff; K. F. Steinmetz, "Der deutsche Ingenieur im 20. Jahrhundert," *ibid.*, 9 (1918), No. 5 and 6. "Die Kriegssitzung des Mitteleuropäischen Verbandes akademischer Ingenieurvereine," *ZVDDI* 7 (1916): 114f.

24. Dr. Noest, "Zur anwaltlichen Notlage," *Abl* 4 (1917); 53ff; Dr. M. Drucker, "1918 und später," *ibid.*, 5 (1918): 4ff; J. Norenberg, "Das Unterrichtswesen nach dem Weltkriege," *Phbl* 26 (1918): 297f; and A. von Rieppel, "Ingenieur und öffentliches Leben," *ZVDI,* 61 (1917): 987ff. Cf. König, "Die Ingenieure und der VDI," in Ludwig, ed., *Technik,* p. 279ff.

25. E. Schott, "Zum Abschluß der Kriegsstunden," *Phbl* 26 (1918): 419.

26. Apfel, *Behind the Scenes,* p. 42, claims that he was radicalized; Bendix, in *Von Berlin,* p. 107, realized the need for reforming his profession.

27. K. Link, "Zur Sammlung der Geister in unserm Berufsstande," *Phbl* 26 (1918): 404f. Cf. Hagen Schulze, *Weimar. Deutschland 1917–1933* (Berlin, 1982), p. 155ff; P. D. Stachura, *The Weimar Era and Hitler 1918–1933* (Oxford, 1977); and D. Orlow, "1918/19: A German Revolution," *GSR* 5 (1982): 187–203.

28. G. Hollenberg, "Bürgerliche Sammlung oder sozialliberale Koalition?" *VfZG* 27 (1979): 392ff. Bibliographies and collections ignore the professions. G. P. Meyer, *Bibliographie zur deutschen Revolution 1918/19* (Göttingen, 1977); J. Flemming *et al.*, eds., *Die Republik von Weimar,* Vol. 2, *Das sozialökonomische System* (Königstein, 1979).

29. E. Umbach, "Der Oberlehrerstand und die neue Zeit," *Phbl* 26 (1918): 419f. For the effect of revolutions see M. Burrage's forthcoming book on lawyers in France, Russia, the United States, and Britain.

30. O. Flechtheim, "Karl Liebknecht: Parlamentarier und Revolutionär," in Kritische Justiz,

ed., *Streitbare Juristen* (Baden-Baden, 1988), p. 117ff; "Kundgebung der volkswirtschaftlichen und technischen Organisationen," *ZVDDI* 9 (1918): 128. The ButiB "welcome[d]" the revolution without reservation and urged engineers to enter the socialist labor unions, "Die Revolution und der Bund der technisch-industriellen Beamten," *ibid.*, 9 (1918): 132.

31. "Berliner Rechtsanwälte im Arbeiter- und Soldatenrat," *BT*, Nov. 14, 1918; and "Bund höherer Beamter," *Phbl* 26 (1918): 403f.

32. On Nov. 15 Fr. Ebert assured public officials that their salaries would be paid. "Erklärung der Reichsregierung über die Rechtsansprüche der Beamten," *Phbl* 26 (1918): 411; Dec. 4, 1918 decree, quoted by C. Seeligmann, "Die Oberlehrer zu Beginn der Weimarer Republik" (Ms., Bielefeld, 1987). Cf. W. Elben, *Das Problem der Kontinuität in der deutschen Revolution* (Düsseldorf, 1965), p. 83.

33. "Berliner Rechtsanwälte im Arbeiter- und Soldatenrat" indicates that Dr. Thiele and E. Fuchs were deputized by the lawyers' assembly. The role of professionals in the various revolutionary councils has been slighted by historians. Cf. E. Kolb, *Die Arbeiterräte in der deutschen Innenpolitik 1918–1919* (Düsseldorf, 1962).

34. Quotations from press clippings in G. Schreiber, *Die Not der deutschen Wissenschaft und der geistigen Arbeiter* (Leipzig, 1923), p. 127ff. Cf. R. Rürup, *Arbeiter-, Soldaten- und Volksräte in Baden 1918/19* (Düsseldorf, 1980), pp. LXXXII and 137; and E. Kolb, *Regionale und Lokale Räteorganisationen in Württemberg 1918/19* (Düsseldorf, 1976), pp. 6, 115 for the Stuttgart council, which represented 8000 participants!

35. "Landesverein akademisch gebildeter Lehrer Gothas," *Phbl* 27 (1919): 65, 88; T. Körner, "Der neue Lehrerrat in Hamburg," *ibid.*, p. 357; and A. Maurer, "Der Lehrerrat zu Frankfurt am Main," *ibid.*, p. 454. Haenisch letter of April 5, 1919, insisting on comprehensive councils, ZStA, Me, Rep, 76 VI, Sekt. 1, Gen. z, Vol. 269; and rescript Aug. 14, 1919, WPhV, G12, 79.

36. Report, speeches, and resolutions of the Dec. 22, 1918 meeting of 300 attorneys, PrGStA Da, Rep. 84a, 10351. Cf. *Justizrat* Werner, "Die Anwaltschaft und der Frieden," *Abl* 5 (1918): 92ff.

37. Dr. Stölzl, "Schulreform im freiheitlichen Geiste," *Wilmersdorfer Zeitung*, Nov. 26, 1918; "Und die höhere Schule? Vorschläge zu ihrer Reform," *Vorwärts*, Nov. 17, 1918.

38. Prof. Skutsch, "Braconiden," *ZVDDI* 10 (1919): 1f.

39. M. Hachenburg, "Zum neuen Jahre!" *JW* 48 (1919): 1ff; and B. Marwitz, *Die Sozialisierung und die Rechtsanwaltschaft* (Berlin, 1919).

40. A. Bohlen, "Ein Redekampf um die Einheitsschule," *Phbl* 27 (1919): 158ff; "Hauptversammlung des Westfälischen Philologenvereins," *ibid.*; and "Die Stellung der Oberlehrer zur Einheitsschulfrage," *ADLZ* 48 (1919): 172. Cf. F. Hamburger, "Lehrer zwischen Kaiser und Führer. Der deutsche PhVb in der Weimarer Republik" (Diss., Heidelberg, 1974).

41. Appeal in the *ZVDI*, 62 (1918): 887; *ibid.*, 63 (1919): 224, 712; and *ibid.*, p. 322ff. Cf. E. Viefhaus, "Ingenieure in der Weimarer Republik: Bildungs-, Berufs- und Gesellschaftspolitik 1918 bis 1933," in Ludwig, ed., *Technik*, p. 289ff.

42. "Freie Vereinigung für Recht und Sozialismus," *JW* 48 (1919): 427. This question has yet to be researched among lawyers, since Ostler, *Rechtsanwälte*, p. 212, only mentions a Republikanischer Anwaltsbund in passing. Cf. B. Schulz, *Der Republikanische Richterbund, 1921–1933* (Frankfurt, 1982).

43. Viefhaus, "Ingenieure in der Weimarer Republik," p. 292ff.

44. Invitation to Haenisch, Oct. 1, 1919; "Leitsätze" of Sept. 18, 1919; Haenisch to BeS, Oct. 23, 1920 and other material in ZStA Me, Rep. 76 VI, Sekt. 1, Gen. cc, Vol. 9. Cf. "Denkschrift des Bundes entschiedenener Schulreformer unter den akademisch gebildeten Lehrern und Lehrerinnen an deutschen Schulen über sofort durchführbare und nur geringe Kosten erfordende Reformen im Schulwesen," *Phbl* 27 (1919): 198ff. and W. Böhm, "Lehrer zwischen Kulturkritik und Gemeinschaftsutopie: Der BeS," in Heinemann, ed., *Lehrer*, p. 191ff.

45. "Erster deutscher AG-Anwaltstag," *Mitteilungen für AG-Anwälte* 12 (1921), No. 10; Dr. Hawlitzky, "Die Bewegung der AG-Anwaltschaft," *Abl* 19 (1920): 115ff; "Sitzung des Vorstandes des DAV," *ibid.*, p. 228f; "Simultanzulassung," *ibid.*, 9 (1921): 32ff; and "Verein deutscher LG-Anwälte," *ibid.*, p. 129ff. Cf. K. F. Ledford, "Simultaneous Admission and the

German Bar, 1903–1927,'' in G. Cocks and K. H. Jarausch, eds., *German Professions* (New York, 1990), p. 252ff.

46. *Justizrat* Baumeister to Radbruch, April 27, 1922; Radbruch to the state justice ministries, Nov. 3, 1922; Zehnhoff to Radbruch, Nov. 28, 1922, all in PrGStA Da, Rep. 84a, Vol. 71. Cf. Ostler, *Rechtsanwälte,* p. 183ff.

47. Figures from A. Nath, ''Der Studienassessor im Dritten Reich,'' *ZfP* 27 (1981): 281ff. Cf. Hübner, ''Die Notlage der Gerichtsassessoren,'' *JW* 48 (1919): 214f, for the same problem in law.

48. ''Eine Unterredung im preußischen Unterrichtsministerium,'' *Phbl* 26 (1918): 408f; ''Anstellung und Beschäftigung der aus dem Heeresdienst entlassenen Studienassessoren,'' *ibid.*, p. 410; ''Engerer Zusammenschluß der Studienassessoren und -referendare Preußens,'' *ibid.*, 27 (1919): 18f. Judging from a note about wartime relocation and the disappearance of volumes before 1943, it is likely that the voluminous Prussian ministerial records on the *Assessoren* question were destroyed.

49. ''Empfang von Studienassessoren im Ministerium für Wissenschaft . . .'' *Phbl* 26 (1918): 106; ''Dringende Forderungen des Verbandes der Studienassessoren und Studienreferendare Preußens,'' *ibid.*, p. 140f; G. Noteboom, ''Gibt es noch eine Notlage der nicht fest-angestellten Philologen in Preußen?'' *ibid.*, p. 320f; and ''Verband der Studienassessoren und Studienreferendare Preußens,'' *ibid.*, p. 511.

50. *Justizrat* Werner, ''Die Anwaltschaft und der Frieden,'' *Abl* 5 (1918): 98; ''14. Vertreterversammlung zu Braunschweig . . . 1922,'' *ibid.*, 9 (1922): p. 23f; G. Radbruch, *Der innere Weg* (Göttingen, 1961), p. 114; and Ostler, *Rechtsanwälte,* p. 169ff. Cf. J. Stephenson, ''Women and the Professions in Germany, 1900–1950,'' in Cocks and Jarausch, eds., *German Professions*, p. 270ff.

51. J. C. Albisetti, ''Frauen und die akademischen Berufe im kaiserlichen Deutschland,'' in R.-E. Joeres *et al.*, eds., *Frauen in der Geschichte* (Düsseldorf, 1985), Vol. 6., p. 286ff. Figures from A. Nath, *Die Studienratskarriere im Dritten Reich* (Frankfurt, 1988), p. 305ff. Antifeminism served to separate philologues from the increasingly female primary schoolteachers. Cf. J. Schneider, ''Volksschullehrerinnen,'' in Cocks and Jarausch, eds., *German Professions, p. 85ff.*

52. B. Amedick, ''Über die Aufnahme weiblicher Mitglieder in die Philologenvereine,'' *Phbl* 28 (1920): 222; ''Beschlüsse des preußischen Philologentages,'' *ibid.*, 30 (1922): 354; board minutes, June 24, 1922; and ''Die verheiratete Lehrerin,'' *ADLZ* 51 (1922): 201f. Cf. R. Bölling, *Sozialgeschichte der deutschen Lehrer* (Göttingen, 1983), p. 95ff; and C. Huerkamp, ''Frauen, Universitäten und Bildungsbürgertum,'' in H. Siegrist, ed., *Bürgerliche Berufe* (Göttingen, 1988), p. 200ff.

53. Although there was a trickle of female technical students, gender discrimination was not seriously discussed by engineers, perhaps because their misogynist stereotype sufficed to frighten off all applicants. K. F. Steinmetz, ''Weibliche Ingenieure,'' *ZVDDI* 10 (1919): 55.

54. H. Heinemann, ''Rechtspflege im neuen Deutschland,'' *JW* 48 (1919): 172; *Justizrat* Schulze, ''Der Segen der Güte,'' *ibid.*, 49 (1920): 1006f; ''Erklärung,'' *ibid.*, 51 (1922): 4. Cf. Radbruch, *Der Innere Weg,* p. 113; and Ostler, *Rechtsanwälte,* p. 148ff.

55. J. Johnson, ''Academic, Proletarian, . . . Professional? Shaping Professionalization for German Industrial Chemists, 1887–1920,'' in Cocks and Jarausch, eds., *German Professions,* p. 123ff.

56. ''Verfügung des preußischen Ministeriums für Wissenschaft . . . betreffend den Geschichtsunterricht usw.,'' *Phbl* 26 (1918): 409f. For Haenisch's handwritten drafts of ''An die Lehrer und Lehrerinnen der höheren Lehranstalten,'' and the resistance of officials, teachers, or the public see ZStA Me, Rep. 76 VI, Sekt. 1, Gen. z, Vol. 265. Cf. F. Behrend, ''Erinnerungen an die Tätigkeit des PhVb,'' *HS* 7 (1954): 195; and A. Ehrentreich, *Fünfzig Jahre Erlebte Schulreform* (Frankfurt, 1985), p. 36f.

57. ''Verfügungen der preußischen Unterrichtsverwaltung'' to the teachers and pupils concerning religious instruction, *Phbl* 26 (1918): 420ff. For the ensuing controversy and the rescinding of the decrees, cf. G. A. Ritter, ed., *Die deutsche Revolution 1918–1919. Dokumente,* 2nd ed. (Hamburg, 1975), p. 277ff.

58. "Abänderung der preußischen Dienstanweisung," *Phbl* 27 (1919): 157; drafts and correspondence for "Konferenzordnung für die höheren Lehranstalten," July 3, 1922, ZStA Po, Rep. 49.01, 4353. For more material, cf. ZStA Me, Rep. 76 VI, Sekt. 1, Gen. z, No. 17, Vol. V; A. Bohlen circular, June 19, 1922, in WPhV, A10, 52, and letters in *ibid.*, G1, 77.

59. "Schulforderungen des DLV," *Phbl* 26 (1918): 411f. Cf. R. Bölling, *Volksschullehrer und Politik. Der DLV, 1918–1933* (Göttingen, 1978).

60. "Zusammensetzung der Reichsschulkonferenz," *Phbl* 28 (1920): 256; "Vertretertag des Vereinsverbandes akademisch gebildeter Lehrer Deutschlands zu Kassel . . . 1919," *ibid.*, 27 (1919): 625ff; "Die Reichsschulkonferenz," *ibid.*, pp. 242–56; and Behrend, "Erinnerungen," p. 165ff. Cf. *Die Reichsschulkonferenz 1920* (Leipzig, 1921, repr. 1972) and H.-J. Heydorn, *Zur Bildungsgeschichte des Deutschen Imperialismus* (Munich, 1973), Vol. 2.

61. "Von der Reichsschulkonferenz," *Phbl* 28 (1920): 282–88; "Bilanz der Reichsschulkonferenz," *ibid.*, 421ff; "Verhandlungen des Ausschusses für Lehrerbildung auf der Reichsschulkonferenz," *ibid.*, 29 (1921): 145ff; "Lehrer und Oberlehrer," *ADLZ* 48 (1919): 693ff, and 69 (1920), 325. Cf. C. Führ, *Zur Schulpolitik der Weimarer Republik* (Weinheim, 1972), p. 45ff; Seeligmann, "Die Oberlehrer zu Beginn der Weimarer Republik," and Bölling, *Sozialgeschichte,* p. 105ff.

62. Dr. Friedländer, "Die Organisation der Rechtsanwaltschaft," *JW* 48 (1919): 408–10; "Juristiche Gesellschaft Berlin," *ibid.*, p. 427ff; "Zum Anwaltstag," *ibid.*, p. 623ff; "Sitzung des Vorstandes des DAV," *Abl* 6 (1919): 53; "Beschlüsse des außenordentlichen Deutschen Anwaltstags zu Leipzig . . . 1919," *ibid.*, p. 95ff. "Die Strafrechtgruppe des DAV," *ibid.*, p. 48f.

63. H. Scheid, "Was kann der PhVb aus der gewerkschaftlichen Arbeiterbewegung lernen?" *Phbl* 27 (1919): 173ff; W. Brinkwerth, "Zum Ausbau der Standesorganisation der preußischen Philologen," *ibid.*, pp. 407ff and 417ff; A. Bohlen, "Berufs- und Standesorganisation," *ibid.*, p. 529ff; "Vorläufige Satzungen des Preußischen Philologenvereins" and other material in ZStPo, Rep. 70 Re. 1, 435; *Satzung des Westfälischen Philologenvereins* (n. p., after 1925); and Bohlen circular Oct. 14, 1919, WPhV, A10.52.

64. Mellman to Haenisch, May 19, 1920; ministry to Prussian PhVb, April 12, 1920; Becker to PhVb, April 14, 1921, all in ZStA Me, Rep. 76 VI, Sekt. 1, Gen. z, No. 205, Vol. I; and Behrend, "Erinnerungen," p. 185ff.

65. K. F. Steinmetz, "Gewerkschaft der Diplom-Ingenieure," *ZVDDI* 10 (1919): 25ff; "Ordentliche Ausschußsitzung 1919," *ibid.*, p. 103ff; E. H. Schulz, "Das Arbeitsnachweisgesetz," *ibid.*, 12 (1921): 17ff; K. Fried, "Die Organisationsfrage der akademischen Ingenieure," *ibid.*, p. 110ff; and R. Stahlschmidt, "Der Ausbau der technisch-wissenschaftlichen Gemeinschaftsarbeit 1918 bis 1933," in Ludwig, ed., *Technik,* p. 347ff.

66. Voß to Saxon teachers, *Bericht über die 38. HV des PhVb der Provinz Sachsen,* June 23 and 24, 1922 in ZStPo, Rep. 70 Re. 1, 433.

67. E. Auerbach, during the "Verhandlungen des Außerordentlichen Anwaltstags zu Leipzig . . . 1919," *JW* 48 (1919): 217; Dr. Ofner, "Kriegshilfe für Kollegen," *ibid.*, p. 30; M. Oppenheim, "Zur Frage der Kriegsteilnehmer," *ibid.*, p. 172; G. Noteboom, "Landesverlust und Zukunftsaussichten der Studienassessoren in Preußen," *Phbl* 27 (1919): 533ff.

68. H. Dittenberger, "Die Leipziger Tagung," *Abl* 9 (1919): 97–107; "Entwürfe zu Verordnungen: über die Kriegsfürsorge. . . ; über die Gebühren und Auslagen in Armensachen; über die Rechtsberatung Minderbemittelter. . . ," *JW* 48 (1919): 606ff; Anwaltskammer Königsberg, "Eingabe an das Justizministerium," *ibid.*, p. 924. Cf. the DAV correspondence and the drafts of the Ministry of Justice, in PrGStA Da, Rep. 84a, Vol. 10351.

69. M. Beatus, "Academic Proletariat: The Problem of Overcrowding in the Learned Professions and Universities during the Weimar Republic, 1918–1933" (Diss. Madison, Wisc., 1975), p. 44ff. Figures in Table A.1 from Titze, *Hochschulstudium,* 26ff, 41ff, 72. Cf. K. H. Jarausch, *Deutsche Studenten 1800–1980* (Frankfurt, 1984), p. 129ff.

70. D. K. Müller, *Datenhandbuch zur deutschen Bildungsgeschichte* (Göttingen, 1988), Vol. 1, p. 207ff; and Jarausch, *Deutsche Studenten,* 131f. For the cyclical aspects, cf. H. Titze and others, "Der Lehrerzyklus. Zur Wiederkehr von Überfüllung und Mangel im höheren Lehramt in Preußen," *ZfP* 31 (1985): 97ff.

71. Letter from Ministry of Justice, July 15, 1920, PrGStA Da, Rep. 84a, Vol. 71; Neuman

Nacht über Deutschland, p. 50; "Verbandsnachrichten, *ZVDDI* 12 (1921): 182. Figures from D. K. Müller *et al.*, "Modellentwicklung zur Analyse von Krisenphasen im Verhältnis von Schulsystem und staatlichem Beschäftigungssystem," *ZfP* 14. Beiheft (Weinheim, 1977): 65ff; A. Nath, "Der Studienassessor," p. 281ff; and R. Bölling, "Lehrerarbeitslosigkeit in Deutschland im 19. und 20. Jahrhundert," *Archiv für Sozialgeschichte* 27 (1987): 233.

72. Niedieck, "Numerus clausus für Juristen," *JW* 49 (1919): 440 and Ostler, *Rechtsanwälte,* p. 164f. Zehnhoff's June 13, 1922 draft letter to the Saxon justice minister refers to "the feared further overcrowding of the legal profession." ZStA Da, Rep. 84a, Vol. 71.

73. "Gegen die Gründung neuer Hochschulen," *VDIN* 2 (1922), No. 12; "Die Not der staatlichen höheren Maschinenschulen," *ibid.*, No. 15; "Überfüllung. . . ," *ZVDDI* 11 (1920), No. 23/4.

74. W. Oberle, "Zur Überfüllung der Oberlehrerlaufbahn," *Phbl* 27 (1919): 32; G. Noteboom, "Schulreform und Anstellungsaussichten der Studienassessoren," *ibid.*, p. 54ff; W. Oberle, "Aussichtslosigkeit des Philologiestudiums," *ibid.*, p. 405ff; Buchrucker, "Warnung vor dem Eintritt in unsern Beruf," *ibid.*, p. 157; and R. Jahnke in "Aus den Verhandlungen der Preußischen Landesversammlung," *ibid.*, 28 (1920): 32ff.

75. E. Simon, "Hilfslehrertum und scheinbarer Assessorenmangel in Preußen," *Phbl* 28 (1920): 281f; and "Zur Frage des Numerus Clausus bei den preußischen Philologen," p. 394f; A. Ackermann, "Die Einführung des Numerus Clausus in Preußen," *ibid.*, p. 395ff; board minutes, the Westphalian PhVb, Oct. 1 and 18, 1920 as well as July 23, 1923 circular, WPhV, A10, 52. See Vahlen to Ministry of Finance, Oct. 5, 1934, ZStA Po, Rep. 49.01, Vol. 7 and Nath, "Der Studienassessor," p. 290f.

76. "Wirtschaftliche Umschau," *ZVDI* 67 (1923): 501ff; this monthly column *(ibid.*, pp. 700, 1066ff, etc.) clearly mirrors contemporary inflation analysis. Cf. A. Wichert *et al.*, "Die Inflation als Problem der Mechanik," *ibid.*, p. 1073ff. Cf. O. Büsch and G. Feldman, eds., *Historische Prozesse der deutschen Inflation 1914 bis 1924* (Berlin, 1978), and subsequent volumes such as *The Adaptation of Inflation* (Berlin, 1986).

77. F. Eulenburg, "Die sozialen Wirkungen der Währungsverhältnisse," *Jahrbücher für Nationalökonomie und Statistik* Part 3, 67 (1924): 748–94. "Even if pay and salaries are tight," VDI chairman G. Klingenberg believed that "everyone working in industry finds bread and livelihood." "Die Scheinblüte der deutschen Industrie," *ZVDI* 66 (1922): 735. Cf. N. Stern, "Aus Beruf und Leben," *ZVDDI* 12 (1921): 136f; and "Briefe eines Ingenieurs," *ibid.*, 13 (1922): 176f.

78. "Sitzung des Vorstandes des DAV," *Abl* 7 (1919): 54ff; and "Die Vereinbarung von Teuerungszuschlägen," *ibid.*, p. 187ff. Cf. Ostler, *Rechtsanwälte,* p. 155ff.

79. "Eingabe des DAV zu dem Entwurfe des Gesetzes über Teuerungszuschläge zu den Gebühren für Rechtsanwälte," *Abl* 7 (1919): 158ff; and "Das Gesetz über Teuerungszuschläge," *ibid.*, p. 195f.

80. "Aus der Vereinstätigkeit," *Abl* 9 (1921): 52f; *ibid.*, p. 104f; and "Gesetz betreffend die Gebühren der Rechtsanwälte. . . ," *ibid.*, p. 107ff. For a comparison between the government draft and the DAV proposal see "Vorarbeiten," *ibid.*, p. 113ff. "Aus der Vereinstätigkeit," *ibid.*, 10 (1922); 3ff, reports on seventy-eight chambers' reactions. Cf. M. Hachenburg, *Lebenserinnerungen eines Rechtsanwalts und Briefe aus der Emigration,* reissued by J. Schadt (Stuttgart, 1978), p. 75ff.

81. "Die Vergütung der Anwaltstätigkeit," *Abl* 10 (1922): 177f; "15. Vertreterversammlung des DAV," *ibid.*, p. 187f; "Aus der Vereinstätigkeit," *ibid.*, p. 221f; "Notanwaltstag Weimar," *ibid.*, pp. 22f and 91–110; "Entwurf einer Gebührenordnung für Rechtsanwälte," *ibid.*, p. 56ff; "Aus der Vereinstätigkeit," *ibid.*, p. 133ff. See Zelter, "Richternöte und Anwaltnot," *JW* 49 (1920): 680ff.

82. Total number of civil cases (district and superior court) and criminal cases (district court only, because the number of higher cases was negligible), calculated from Tables A.11a and A.11b. Cases per capita were computed by dividing total cases by number of lawyers.

83. "Aus der Vereinstätigkeit," *Abl* 11 (1923): 151f; "Stellungnahme des DAV zu dem Entwurf eines Gesetzes über die Gebühren . . . ," *ibid.*, p. 161; "Aus der Vereinstätigkeit," *ibid.*, p. 170ff; "Gesetz über die Gebühren der Rechtsanwälte und der Gerichtskosten," *ibid.*, p. 172f; "Zur neuen Gebührenordnung," *ibid.*, p. 187f. C. Spohr to Prussian Ministry of Jus-

tice, Aug. 3, 1923; Berlin resolutions, Aug. 9, 1923, PrGStA Da, Rep. 84a, Vol. 71; Beatus, "Academic Proletariat," p. 75f. For a beginning lawyer, this "was the most difficult time of my life." Neumann, *Nacht,* p. 62.

84. "Kasseler Beschlüsse," *Phbl* 27 (1919): 628, 642; J. Irmer, "Die Studienassessoren und der neue Entwurf der Besoldungsordnung für Preußen," *ibid.*, 28 (1920): 124; G. Buschbell, "Die Vergütung für Ausbildung der Studienreferendare," *ibid.*, p. 150; Haenisch circular, Oct. 4, 1919; memorandum of negotiations of Jan. 22, 1920, and so on, in ZStA Me, Rep. 151, IC, No. 7879f. Cf. Bölling, *Sozialgeschichte,* 116ff.

85. F. Grebe, "Die Oberlehrer in der preußischen Besoldungsordnung," *Phbl* 28 (1920): 187; "Zur neuen Besoldungsordnung für die preußischen Beamten," *ibid.*, p. 256f; protest "An die Preußische Landesversammlung," *ibid.*, p. 493; "Die endgültige preußische Besoldungsreform," *ibid.*, 29 (1921): 2ff; and W. Bolle, "Regierung und Parteien in ihrer Stellung zur Besoldung," *ibid.*, p. 81f. For the assignment of primary schoolteachers into group VII and secondary schoolteachers into group X cf. ZStA Me, Rep. 76 IIa, Sekt. 55, Gen. 1, Vol. XI, as well as Beiheft C and *ADLZ* 49 (1920): 322f.

86. A. Rathke, "Wie lange noch?" *Phbl* 29 (1921): 377; S. Mauermann, "Zur unzureichenden Besoldung der Philologen," *ibid.*, p. 398ff; and "Die wirtschaftliche Notlage des Philologenstandes," *ibid.*, 30 (1922): 255f.

87. *Statistisches Jahrbuch für das Deutsche Reich* 42 (1921–1922): 310; 43 (1923): 311; and 44 (1924–1925): 286; reports on "Stand der Besoldungsaktion," Dec. 12, 1921 to circular, Nov. 7, 1923, WPhV, A10, 52; "Vorschläge des RhB zur neuen Besoldungsreform," *Phbl* 30 (1922): 47; W. Bolle, "Vom Preußischen Philologentag," *ibid.*, p. 305ff; "Der preußische Oberstudienrat," *ibid.*, 31 (1923): 253; "Die neuen 'Gold'-Gehälter," *ADLZ* 52 (1923): 501. Cf. Beatus, "Academic Proletariat," p. 68f; and A. Kunz, *Civil Servants and the Politics of Inflation in Germany, 1914–1924* (Berlin, 1986), p. 76f.

88. See K. H. Jarausch, *Students, Society and Politics in Imperial Germany: The Rise of Academic Illiberalism* (Princeton, N. J., 1983), p. 160ff, and M. Kater, "Professionalization and Socialization of Physicians in Wilhelmine and Weimar Germany," *JCH* 20 (1985): 677ff.

89. "Zum neuen Jahre!" *JW* 49 (1920): 1ff; A. Mellmann, "Aufruf," *Phbl* 28 (1920): 72. A. Müller appealed to this problem-solving spirit, "Durch welche Mittel muß die deutsche Industrie der Veränderung ihrer Produktionsbedingungen Rechnung tragen?" *ZVDI* 64 (1920): 1ff.

90. H. Dittenberger, "Rechtsanwalt und öffentliche Meinung," *Abl* 10 (1922): 51. Cf. G. Zapf, *Wandlungen der deutschen Elite* (Munich, 1965), p. 48ff.

91. "Philologen sind Akademiker 2. Klasse," *Phbl* 30 (1922): 72f; "Beschlüsse des Vertretertages des Preußischen PhVb zu Kassel," *Phbl* 27 (1919): 641f; "Zur Neuordnung der Amtsbezeichnungen für Philologen," *Phbl* 28 (1920): 164f. For the title struggle cf. PrGStA Da, Rep. 90, Vol. 564. According to Paul Hildebrand, it took "special idealism" to become an *Oberlehrer* before the war and "now it seems to be getting worse." See "Die Tragikomödie der Oberlehrer," *VZ*, Feb. 4, 1919.

92. Dr. Mo, "Diplom. Melkknecht," *VDIN,* Feb. 15, 1921; C. Matschoß, "Technik und Presse," *ibid.*, Dec. 21, 1921; Br., "Der Techniker in der Stadtverwaltung," *ZVDI* 64 (1920): 141; "Ingenieure im höheren Verwaltungsdienst," *ibid.*, p. 563f; "Techniker in der Verwaltung," *ibid.*, p. 851; and "Ingenieur und kommunale Wirtschaft," *VDIN,* Dec. 13, 1922.

93. Dr. Freiesleben, "Rechtsanwälte oder Fachanwälte?" *Abl* 7 (1920): 76ff; F. Alexander,"Rechtsanwälte oder Fachanwälte?" *ibid.*, p. 18ff; "Beschlüsse der Vertreterversammlung des DAV zu Leipzig," *ibid.*, p. 170ff; H. Dittenberger, "XII. deutscher Anwaltstag," *ibid.*, p. 175ff; and the report of Dr. Fischer in *JW* 49 (1920): 808ff.

94. E. Dihle, "Die Vorbildung der Oberlehrer," *ibid.*, 28 (1920): 1ff; minutes of a meeting in the Ministry of Culture, Oct. 16, 1917, and other material in ZStA Me, Rep. 76 VI, Sekt. 1, Gen. z, No. 180, Vols. III–IV; protocol of PhVb session, Jan. 25, 1920, WPhV, S42, 238. Cf. *Der Philologe* (Berlin, 1919), p. 19ff, and R. Bölling, "Die Ausbildung der Lehrer an höheren Schulen in Preußen," *IZEBF* 20 (1983): 159ff. Cf. N. von Hammerstein, ed., *Deutsche Bildung? Briefwechsel zweier Schulmänner* (Frankfurt, 1988), p. 15ff.

95. Rösing, "Die Zurücksetzung der Technik in der alten deutschen Marine," *ZVDI* 48 (1920): 230ff; "Ingenieur und Maschine in Spenglers 'Untergang des Abendlandes,' " *VDIN,* Oct. 25, 1922; W. von Moellendorf, "Wirkungsgrad," *ZVDI* 64 (1920): 853f; the new title

Technik und Kultur of the *ZVDDI,* "Zum Geleit!" 13 (1922): 1; and C. Weihe, "Technik und Kultur," *ibid.,* p. 2f. Cf. Viefhaus, "Ingenieure," p. 296ff.

96. M. Friedländer, "Die Organisation der Rechtsanwaltschaft," p. 408ff; "Juristische Gesellschaft Berlin," *ibid.,* p. 427ff. Cf. PrGStA Da, Rep. 84a, Vol. 34, for the annual chamber reports. K. van Eyll, "Berufsständische Selbstverwaltung," in *Deutsche Verwaltungsgeschichte* (Stuttgart, 1985), Vol. 4, p. 66f, neglects professional chambers. Cf. C. Maier, *Recasting Bourgeois Europe* (Princeton, N. J., 1975).

97. Reports in *ZVDI* 65 (1921): 82ff, 104f, 508; "Versammlung des Vorstandsrates am 25. Juni, 1921," *VDIN,* Oct. 26, 1921: 46f. Cf. Viefhaus, "Ingenieure," p. 308f.

98. Baltzer to Haenisch, May 15, 1919; Schmidt to Haenisch, June 3, 1919; Haenisch instruction, Aug. 14, 1919; constitution of Berlin teacher council, March 27, 1919; Bolle to Haenisch, Oct. 1, 1919, and so on in ZStA Me, Rep. 76 VI, Sekt. 1, Gen. z, Vol. 269.

99. "Leitsätze und Beschlüsse," *Phbl* 27 (1919): 626; Verband sozialistischer Lehrer to Haenisch, Dec. 12, 1919; Kawerau to ministry, Sept. 27, 1919; Hoffmann memorandum, Dec. 1, 1919; Jahnke to Nägler, Oct. 15, 1919; and marginal note on Feb. 24, 1922; Bolle to ministry, Jan. 5, 1923, all in ZStA Me, Rep. 76 VI, Sekt. 1, Gen. z, Vol. 269. Cf. Boelitz letter, Jan. 30, 1920; "Vorläufige Satzungen der Philologen Kammer," WPhV, G12, 79; and "Gewerkschaftliches Denken," *ADLZ* 50 (1921), No. 13.

100. "Unabsetzbarkeit und Unabhängigkeit der Richter," *Abl* 10 (1922): 55; "Arbeitsgemeinschaft freier geistiger Berufe," *ibid.,* 8 (1920): 139. Cf. the *Reichswirtschaftsrat* material in ZStA Po, Rep. 04.01, Vol. 464.

101. "Bund höherer Beamter," *Phbl* 26 (1918): 403, 423; Blohn, "Großorganisationen und Splitterorganisationen," *ibid.,* 28 (1920): 397; P. Mellmann, "Alte und neue Ziele des Vereinsverbandes," *ibid.,* 29 (1921): 210ff. Cf. letter of April 3, 1920 and other RhB material in ZStA Po, Rep. 70 Re. 1, Vols. 435 and 436; Bohlen circular, July 20, 1921, WPhV, A10, 52, and Kunz, *Civil Servants,* p. 134ff.

102. "Deutscher Verband technisch-wissenschaftlicher Vereine," *VDIN,* Oct. 12, 1921; C. Wendt, "Zur Klassifikation der technischen Vereine und Verbände," *ZVDDI* 8 (1917): 89ff. Viefhaus, "Ingenieure," p. 311ff.

103. "Zusammenschluß der akademischen Berufsstände," *Deutsche Tageszeitung,* Nov. 17, 1918; "Der Reichsausschuß der akademischen Berufsstände," *ZVDDI* 10 (1919): 7; A. Pinkerneil, "Die Zukunftsaufgaben der akademischen Berufsverbände," *ibid.,* p. 81ff; H. Böttger, "Deutsche Zentralstelle für Berufsberatung der Akademiker," March 10, 1918, and petition of Oct. 23, 1923 in ZStA Me, Rep. 76 Va, Sekt. 1, Tit. 1, Vol. 38. Cf. the series on *Die akademischen Berufe,* edited by A. Pinkerneil.

104. Schreiber, *Die Not der deutschen Wissenschaft, passim;* and "Reichsausschuß akademischer Berufsverbände," *JW* 48 (1919): 430.

105. A. Weber, *Die Not der geistigen Arbeiter* (Munich, 1923), text and transcript of discussions in Vol. 163 of the *Schriften des Vereins für Sozialpolitik.* The debates remained diffuse because the topic "is new and relatively rarely analyzed." Cf. the voluminous material by L. Sinzheimer in *Die geistigen Arbeiter* (Munich, 1922), Vol. 152 of the same *Schriften.*

106. For the *Reichswirtschaftsrat* debates see ZStA Po, Rep. 04.01, Vols. 464, 467, 475–76; and Hachenburg, *Lebenserinnerungen,* p. 184ff. Cf. K. H. Jarausch, "Die Not der geistigen Arbeiter: Akademiker in der Berufskrise, 1918–1933," in W. Abelshauser, ed., *Die Weimarer Republik als Wohlfahrtsstaat* (Stuttgart, 1987), p. 280ff.

107. C. Siehr, "Ein Fortschrittsprogramm für den Anwaltverein in 14. Punkten," *JW* 49 (1920): 676ff, and S. Feuchtwanger, *Die freien Berufe* (Munich, 1922) demonstrate that the professional plight could be a spur to reform ideas.

108. J. Magnus, "Zum neuen Jahre!" *JW* 53 (1924): 81f; and K. Steinmetz, "1923," *ZVDDI* 14 (1923), No. 23 and 24. Cf. the New Year's reflections in the *Phbl* and the "Chronik" in the *ZVDI* 68 (1924), No. 1.

109. Beatus, "Academic Proletariat," p. 105ff.

110. Hachenburg, "Zum neuen Jahr!" p. 1ff; O. Mayer, "Zur vorläufigen Reichsverfassung," *JW* 48 (1919): 209f; Thiele letter, Sept. 16, 1920, ZStA Po, Rep. 70, Re. 1, 436; E. H. Schulz, "Die Stellung des VDDI im heutigen Staate," *ZVDDI* 13 (1922): 3ff; and E. Haes, "Um den Achtstundentag," *ibid.,* 14 (1923): 18.

111. H. Breitgoff *et al.*, "Theorie und Praxis der 'Arbeitsgemeinschaft sozialdemokratischer Lehrer und Lehrerinnen' 1919–1922," in D. Krause-Vilmar, ed., *Lehrerschaft, Republik und Faschismus 1919–1933* (Cologne, 1978), p. 25ff; C. Seeligmann, "Der Deutsche-Republikanische Lehrerbund," *Jahrbuch des Instituts für deutsche Geschichte* 8 (1979): 365ff; and *idem*, "Vorläufer des nationalsozialistischen Lehrerbundes (NSLB)," *Lehrer:* 305ff.

112. E. Feder, "Der Vertragsbruch von Versailles," *ZVDI* 64 (1920): 1080f; Mellmann, "Aufruf," *Phbl* 28 (1920), p. 10; "Gegen Entente Willkür!" *ZVDI* 64 (1920): 532; "Zum Bauverbot von Dieselmotoren," *VDIN,* Dec. 20, 1921; "An die Techniker der Welt!" *ZVDI* 64 (1920), Nov. 6.

113. "Aufruf des Deutschen Anwaltstages and the Rechtsanwälte aller Länder!" *JW* 52 (1923), Feb. 15, and *Abl* 10 (1922): 17; "Westfalens Ingenieure!" *ZVDI* 67 (1923): 73; "An die deutschen Ingenieure," *ibid.*, p. 121; K. Steinmetz, "Ruhr," *ZVDDI* 14 (1923): 13, 69, and so on. Cf. the board minutes of the Westphalian PhVb, June 18, 1923ff, WPhV, A10, 52 and *ADLZ* 52 (1923); 50.

114. Bundesjustizministerium, ed., *Vom Reichsjustizamt zum Bundesministerium der Justiz* (Cologne, 1977); F. Stein, "In Sachen des Anwaltstandes," *JW* 50 (1921): 609f.

115. B. Laudien, "Der Minister Haenisch und die Oberlehrer," *Schlesische Zeitung,* Oct. 23, 1919; Behrend, "Erinnerungen," p. 165ff; material in ZStA Me, Rep. 76, Sekt. 1, Gen. z, No. 265; and Bohlen circular, July 12, 1923 and board minutes, Sept. 28/9, WPhV, A10, 52.

116. K. Friedrich, "Der falsche und der rechte Weg," *ZVDDI* 14 (1923): 69f; Viefhaus, "Ingenieure," p. 301ff; Dr. Hawlitzky petition for the AG attorneys to the Prussian Ministry of Justice, Aug. 30, 1923, in PrGStA Da, Rep. 84a, Vol. 71.

CHAPTER 3

1. VDI, "Bericht über das Geschäftsjahr 1924/5," *VDIN,* March 25, 1925; J. Magnus, "Zum neuen Jahre!" *JW* 56 (1927): 1f; W. Bolle, "Rückblick und Ausblick,' *Phbl* 37 (1929): 1ff.

2. H. Dittenberger, "Die Aufgaben des Jahres 1926," *Abl* 13 (1927): 1ff; "1927," *ibid.*, 14 (1928): 1ff; and "Jahresabschluß," *ibid.*, 15 (1929): 2f. Cf. J. Magnus, "Zum neuen Jahre!" *JW* 58 (1929): 1ff and H. Dittenberger, "Die deutsche Rechtsanwaltschaft im Jahre 1928," *ibid.*, 11ff.

3. "Schulabbau," *Phbl* 32 (1924): 18f; W. Bolle, "Rückblick und Ausblick," *ibid.*, 36 (1928): 1ff; R. Haas, "Arbeiten und nicht verzweifeln!" *VDIN,* Jan. 27, 1926; and C. Köttgen, "Zum Jahreswechsel," *ibid.*, Jan. 2, 1929.

4. S. Zweig, *Die Welt von Gestern* (Vienna, 1952), p. 289, and N. Preradovich, "Zum Bewußtsein der Zeitgenossen 1924–1929," in H.-J. Schoeps, ed., *Zeitgeist der Weimarer Republik* (Stuttgart, 1968), p. 107ff. Cf. M. L. Hughes, *Paying for the German Inflation* (Chapel Hill, N C., 1988), p. 181ff; L. E. Jones, "Inflation, Revaluation and the Crisis of Middle Class Politics," *CEH* 12 (1979): 143ff, and T. Childers, *The Nazi Voter* (Chapel Hill, N. C., 1983), p. 50ff.

5. F. Ostler, *Die deutschen Rechtsanwälte, 1871–1971* (Essen, 1971), p. 196ff; R. Bölling, *Sozialgeschichte der deutschen Lehrer* (Göttingen, 1983), p. 120ff; and E. Viefhaus, "Ingenieure in der Weimarer Republik: Bildungs-, Berufs- and Gesellschaftspolitik 1918 bis 1933," *Technik,* p. 289ff.

6. Hagen Schulze, *Weimar. Deutschland 1917–1933* (Berlin, 1982), pp. 39ff, 287ff; and E. Kolb's introduction and the documentation by J. Fleming, *Die Republik von Weimar* (Königstein, 1979), 2 Vols.

7. "Ausbildungsordnung" Aug. 17, 1923 and other material in ZStA Me, Rep. 76 Va, Sekt. 1, Tit. VII, No. 8, Vol. XXI, and "Reichstag," *JW* 51 (1922): 422ff. Cf. E. Fuchs, "Rechtsfakultäten und Weltwende," *ibid.*, 48 (1919): 4ff; "Hebung des geistigen Standards der Referendare," *ibid.*, 51 (1922): 157f; and A. Levy, "Die Wiederherstellung des 7. Ausbildungsjahres," *Abl* 15 (1928): 240. Cf. U. Beer, *Horst Berkowitz* (Essen, 1979), p. 39ff, and H. Kronstein, *Briefe an einen jungen Deutschen* (Munich, 1967), p. 75ff.

8. E. Otto, "Volksbildner und Philologe," *ADLZ* 53 (1924): 671; "Die neue preußische Lehrerbildung," *ibid.*, 54 (1925): 705; "Zur Neuordnung der Lehrerbildung," *ibid.*, 56 (1927):

595; E. Meyer, "England und die Hochschulbildung der Lehrer," *ibid.*, 55 (1926): 49. Cf. E. Boehm, *Der Streit um die Lehrerbildung* (Radebeul, 1926) and WPhV, S42, p. 238.

9. "Zum Entwurf einer Neuordnung des Vorbereitungsdienstes für die Oberlehrer in Preußen," *Phbl* 27 (1919): 568; J. Wagner, "Zur Frage der pädagogischen Ausbildung der Philologen," *ibid.*, 33 (1925), No. 14; K. Kesseller, "Zur Frage des pädagogischen Universitätsstudiums der Philologen," *ibid.*, 36 (1928): 451; "Die Beschlüsse des X. Verbandstages des Deutschen PhVb," *ibid.*, 35 (1927): 440. Cf. A. Ehrentreich, *Fünfzig Jahre Erlebte Schulreform* (Frankfurt, 1985), p. 45ff; P. Hartig, *Lebenserinnerungen eines Neuphilologen* (Augsburg, 1981), p. 24ff.

10. H. Aumund, "Die Hochschule für Technik und Wirtschaft," *ZVDI* 65 (1921): 137ff; and "Die Entwicklung der Reform der TH," *ibid.*, 1179ff; "Die Stellung des VDI zu der Denkschrift des Prof. Aumund," *ibid.*, 507ff; *Diplomprüfungsordnung für die Preußischen Technischen Hochschulen* (Berlin, 1922); "Hochschulreform," *VDIN*, June 21, 1922; and Becker to minister of commerce, May 30, 1922, in ZStA Me, Rep. 76 Vb, Sekt. 1, Tit. 5, No. 2, Vol. XI. Cf. *ZVDI* 63 (1919): 1089 and 64 (1920): 140f, 1008f.

11. G. Lippart, "Entwicklung und Stand der Praktikantenfrage," *ZVDI* 71 (1927): 993ff; R. Bosch, "Die praktische Ausbildung des Ingenieurs," *VDIN*, March 14, 1928; G. Heidebroek, "Fortbildungskurse für Ingenieure," *ZVDI* 70 (1926): 965; and "Hochschulkursus Darmstadt," *VDIN*, Nov. 18, 1928; Cf. R. Locke, *The End of Practical Man* (Greenwich, Conn., 1984), and Viefhaus, "Ingenieure," p. 320ff.

12. Figures from H. Titze, *Das Hochschulstudium in Preußen und Deutschland, 1820–1944* (Göttingen, 1987), pp. 28ff, 88ff, 172f, and D. K. Müller, *Datenhandbuch zur deutschen Bildungsgeschichte* (Göttingen, 1988), p. 209. Cf. M. Beatus, "Academic Proletariat: The Problem of Overcrowding in the Learned Professions and Universities during the Weimar Republic, 1918–1933" (Diss., Madison, Wisc., 1975), p. 149ff.

13. P. Lundgreen, *Sozialgeschichte der deutschen Schule im Überblick* (Göttingen, 1981), Vol. 1, p. 146f, and K. H. Jarausch, *Deutsche Studenten 1800–1980* (Frankfurt, 1984), p. 131ff.

14. Boelitz letter, Aug. 21, 1924, ZStA Me, Rep. 76 Va, Sekt. 1, Tit. VII, No. 8, Vol. XXI, and "Bewegung der Zahl der Anwälte im Deutschen Reich," *Abl* 15 (1928): 110f.

15. "Warnung vor dem juristischen Studium," *Abl* 15 (1928): 115; L. Chodziesner, "Die Not unseres Standes und was unserm Stande not tut," *ibid.*, 54; F. Weyrauch, "Gedanken zum Numerus Clausus," *ibid.*, p. 56f; Dr. Recken, "Ein neuer Gedanke zur Beseitigung der Anwaltsnot," *ibid.*, p. 166; Dr. Noest, "Numerus Clausus!" *ibid.*, p. 194ff; and *Justizrat* Carstens, "Soll der Überfüllung des Anwaltstandes durch Zulassungsbeschränkungen gesteuert werden?" *ibid.*, p. 250.

16. R. Grau, "Soll der Überfüllung des Anwaltstandes durch Zulassungsbeschränkungen gesteuert werden?" *Abl* 15 (1928): 279ff; H. Dittenberger, "Die Frankfurter Abgeordnetenversammlung," *ibid.*, p. 351ff; and "Stenographischer Bericht über die 22. AV" (printed as manuscript, Leipzig, 1928), p. 7ff.

17. K.-H. Ludwig, *Technik und Ingenieure im Dritten Reich* (Königstein, 1979), p. 39. K. Steinmetz, "Eine neue Hochschule in Sicht?" *ZVDDI* 15 (1924): 12; *idem*, "Mangel an jungen Ingenieuren?" *ibid.*, 19 (1928): 197; and W. von Pasinski, "Von der Technik zur Kultur: Ein Beruf ohne Raum," *ibid.*, 20 (1929): 180ff.

18. "Preußische Anwärterordnung," *Phbl* 31 (1923): 124ff; "Zum Numerus Clausus der Studienassessoren," *ibid.*, 176ff. Cf. F. Behrend, "Der NC für die Studienassessoren in Preußen," *ibid.*, p. 169ff; "Protest der Philologen gegen den NC für Studienassessoren," *Deutsche Tageszeitung*, April 19, 1923; and "Numerus Clausus," *Vorwärts*, April 17, 1923; versus "Neuorientierung des Lehrerstandes," *VZ*, April 14, 1923 and "NC für Studienassessoren," *BT*, April 14, 1923; and B. Jarausch, "Geschichte einer schlesisch-märkischen Familie," (Ms, Berlin, 1960), p. 68ff.

19. Figures from Preußischer PhVb, *Das höhere Schulwesen Preußens 1914 und 1922* (Leipzig, 1922); A. Nath, "Der Studienassessor im Dritten Reich," *ZfP* 27 (1981): 283f and *Die Studienratskarriere im Dritten Reich* (Frankfurt, 1988), p. 305ff. Cf. the material in WPhV, U2, 392. By the year 1927 29,702 primary schoolteachers, i. e. 27.1 percent were unemployed. Cf. Bölling, "Lehrerarbeitslosigkeit in Deutschland," *Archiv für Sozialgeschichte* 27 (1987): 237.

20. E. Simon, "Steht ein Mangel an preußischen Philologen bevor?" *Phbl* 33 (1925): 49ff;

W. Alexander, "Mangel oder Überfluß an Nachwuchs in der preußischen Philologenlaufbahn?" *ibid.*, p. 395; G. Proebsting, "Beschäftigungsaussichten für den Philologennachwuchs in Preußen," *ibid.*, 34 (1926): 129ff; "Der scheinbare Assessorenmangel in Preußen und seine Gründe," *ibid.*, p. 225f; "Fast 10,000 künftige Studienräte auf preußischen Universitäten," *ibid.*, 36 (1928): 33ff; Preußischer PhVb circular, Feb. 23, 1927, WPhV, B42, 542; and Deutscher PhVb board minutes, Feb. 24, 1928, *ibid.*, B43, 543.

21. "Dreizehnte Verordnung über die Gebühren der Rechtsanwälte," *Abl* 11 (1924): 9ff, as well as "Aus der Vereinstätigkeit," *ibid.*, p. 6f. See "Aus der Vereinstätigkeit," *Abl* 12 (1925): 103 and "Abbau der Armenrechtsgebührenerstattung," *ibid.*, p. 105ff. Cf. Ostler, *Rechtsanwälte,* p. 190ff.

22. "Denkschrift über die Frage einer Herabsetzung der Rechtsanwaltsgebühren," *Abl* 13 (1924): 9ff; "Entwurf eines Gesetzes über die Gerichtskosten und die Gebühren der Rechtsanwälte," *ibid.*, p. 114f; "Gesetz über die Gerichtskosten und Gebühren der Rechtsanwälte," *ibid.*, p. 185ff.

23. "Zur Lage der Anwaltschaft," *Abl,* 13 (1926): 259ff; and "Die Lage in der Rechtspflege und die Lage der Anwaltschaft," *ibid.*, p. 282ff; "Das neue Kosten- und Gebührengesetz," *ibid.*, 14 (1927): 47ff; *Wirtschaft und Statistik* 12 (1932): 242f; and Beatus, "Academic Proletariat," p. 166.

24. Protocol of the Staatsministerium session, Oct. 16, 1923; Luther to Boelitz, Oct. 18, 1923; and ministerial deliberations in ZStA Me, Rep. 76 VI, Sekt. 1, Gen. b, No. 32, Vol. I. F. Behrend, "Beamtenabbau und höhere Schule," *Phbl* 31 (1923): 349f; G. Meinshausen, "Assessoren und Abbauverordnung," *ibid.*, p. 350f; "Verordnung zur Herabminderung der Personalausgaben des Reichs vom 27. Oktober 1923," *ibid.*, p. 351ff.

25. PhVb petition, Nov. 12, 1923, and Lande report, Nov. 16, 1923 in ZStA Me, Rep. 76 VI, Sekt. 1, Gen. b, No. 32, Vol. I; "Beamtenentrechtung," *Phbl* 31 (1923): 365f; "Gegen die Zerstörung der deutschen Schule," *ibid.*, p. 366; "Entscheidungstage," *ADLZ* 53 (1924): 13ff; "Der Abbau der Schulen," *BT,* Dec. 13, 1923; "Kulturabbau?" *Berliner Börsen Zeitung,* Nov. 28, 1923; "Beamtenabbau und Schule," *Neuland,* Nov. 20, 1923; "Sozialdemokratie und Beamtenabbau," *Vorwärts,* Nov. 21, 1923, and so on.

26. Boelitz interview with *Die Zeit,* Jan. 4, 1924; Lande note of a conference with the PhVb leaders in late Nov. 1923; Boelitz to Luther, Dec. 11, 1923, and so on in ZStA Me, Rep. 76 VI, Sekt. 1, Gen. b, No. 32, Vol. I. "Eingabe an die Landtagsfraktionen betreffend die Personal-Abbau Verordnung," *Phbl* 32 (1924): 21f; notes on an interministerial conference in late Feb. 1924 and on the cabinet decision, Feb. 22, 1924, ZStA Me, Rep. 76 VI, Sekt. 1, Gen. b, No. 32, Vol. II.

27. W. Schramm, "Die Preußische Personal-Abbau-Verordnung und das höhere Schulwesen," *Phbl* 32 (1924): 49ff; text of the final version, *ibid.*, p. 55ff. Boelitz to Luther, Feb. 23, 1924; Boelitz to PSKs, Feb. 28, 1924; Günther's note on discussion with PSK representatives in March 1924 all in ZStA Me, Rep. 76 VI, Sekt. 1, Gen. b, No. 32, Vol. II. Cf. "Abbaukämpfe," *ADLZ* 53 (1924): 121ff.

28. "Zur Durchführung des Abbaus und der Schulreform in Preußen," *Phbl* 32 (1924): 97. Lande travel report, May 1, 1924; Jahnke note, Sept. 3, 1924 (sixty-four directors dismissed); Lande justification, Sept. 5, 1924, ZStA Me, Rep. 76 VI, Sekt. 1, Gen. b, No. 32, Vol. II. "Übersicht über den Abbau der Lehrkräfte an den öffentlichen höheren Lehranstalten nach dem Stande vom 1. 12. 1924," *ibid.*, Vol. III.

29. A. Söhring, "Der Personalabbau im Volksschulwesen und die Fürsorge für die Abgebauten," *ADLZ* 35 (1924): 493ff; and board minutes, May 10, July 12, 1924, WPhV, A10, 53. The *numerus clausus* and the firing produced shortages in some subjects while generally there was an oversupply. E. Simon, "Zur gegenwärtigen Lage von Nachfrage und Angebot in der preußischen Philologenlaufbahn," *ibid.*, 34 (1926): 308ff.

30. "Aus der Praxis der Rationalisierung," *VDIN* (1925), No. 12; "Der Ausbau des Reichskuratoriums für Wirtschaftlichkeit," *ibid.*, Dec. 30, 1925. G. Schlesinger, "Brennende Probleme der Betriebsorganisation und ihre natürliche Lösung," *ZVDI* 68 (1924): 459ff; and VDI, "Bericht über das Geschäftsjahr zwischen den Hauptversammlungen 1926/27," *VDIN,* 1927. Cf. Viefhaus, "Ingenieure," p. 332ff.

31. C. Este, "Vom Arbeitsmarkt für Diplom-Ingenieure," *ZVDDI* 18 (1927): 71f, 115f,

188f; *ibid.*, 19 (1928): 8f; K. Steinmetz, "Vom Arbeitsmarkt für Diplom-Ingenieure," *ibid.*, pp. 68f, 118ff and so on. Cf. N. Stern, "Kritische Betrachtungen zum 'Ford-Buch'," *ibid.*, 16 (1924): 112ff.

32. "Die Ingenieurhilfe im Jahre 1920 und ihre weiteren Ziele," *ZVDI* 65 (1921): 705ff; "Aufruf zur Linderung der Not unter den stellungslosen Ingenieuren," *VDIN*, June 30, 1926. Cf. ZStA Po, Rep. 39.03, Vols. 180ff, and Beatus, "Academic Proletariat," p. 164.

33. Dr. K. Kaßler, "Zur Frage der Anwaltstitel," *Abl* 14 (1927): 69f; Jessen, "Neue Anwaltstitel?" *ibid.*, p. 8f; "Nochmals Rechtsanwaltstitel," *ibid.*, p. 197ff; "Führung früherer Amtsbezeichnungen bei Ausübung des Anwaltsberufes," *Abl*, 12 (1925): 168ff; and *ibid.*, 13 (1926): 135f. Cf. Ostler, *Rechtsanwälte*, p. 195f.

34. Dr. Schlechtriem, "Anwalt und Presse," *ibid.*, p. 270ff; R. Fürst, "Zur Betätigung von Rechtsanwälten in der Tagespresse," *ibid.*, 14 (1927): 276ff; and K. Alexander, "Anwaltschaft und Presse," *ibid.*, 15 (1928): 101f. Cf. C. Riess, *Der Mann in der schwarzen Robe. Das Leben des Strafverteidigers M. Alsberg* (Hamburg, 1965), p. 209ff.

35. P. Mellmann, "Standesfragen der deutschen Philologenschaft," *Phbl* 35 (1927): 409ff; and A. Bohlen, "Der Philologe im Staat," *ibid.*, 34 (1926): 380f, as examples of numerous complaints.

36. For the long struggles between PhVb (Nov. 22, 1924), the cultural bureaucracy (Nov. 27, 1924), and the Ministry of Finance, see ZStA Me, Rep. 76 VI, Sekt. 1, Gen. z, No. 276, Vols. Iff. Cf. W. Lohse, "Gleichstellung," *Phbl* 33 (1925): 413ff; E. Loewenthal, "Die Groß-Berliner Philologen und die Besoldungspolitik des Verbandes," *ibid.*, 34 (1926): 748ff; and Preußischer PhVb circular, Feb. 2, 1927, WPhV, B42, 542.

37. "Die Amtsbezeichnung 'Studienrat' in Preußen," *Phbl* 33 (1925): 790f; "Akademiker und Nichtakademiker an den höheren Schulen Preußens," *ibid.*, 34 (1926): 629ff; "Vorstandssitzung des Preußischen PhVb," *ibid.*, p. 725f; and "Zur Frage der Amtsbezeichnung," Nov. 18, 1926, WPhV, K5, 105.

38. K. Steinmetz, "Zur Einschätzung der Technik," *ZVDDI* 18 (1927): 17f; and "Ingenieurkammer," *ibid.*, pp. 139ff, 191ff; VDI, "Versammlung des Vorstandsrates," *VDIN*, May 20, 1925; "Bericht über das Geschäftsjahr 1925/26," *ibid.*, May 1926; and "66. Hauptversammlung," *ibid.*, July 10, 1927.

39. Kaefes, "Diplom-Titel," *ZVDDI* 18 (1927): 218ff; K. Steinmetz, "Falsche Diplom-Ingenieure," *ibid.*, 19 (1928): 45ff; and "Der rechtliche Schutz der Bezeichnung Ingenieur im Deutschen Reiche," *ibid.*, 20 (1929): 31ff, 84ff, 110ff. Cf. "65. Hauptversammlung des VdI in Hamburg," *VDIN*, 1926, No. 29; VDI, "66. Hauptversammlung," *ibid.*, July 1927; and "67. Hauptversammlung," *ibid.*, Aug. 8, 1928. See Viefhaus, "Ingenieure," p. 310f.

40. "Beschlüsse der 18. Vertreterversammlung des DAV," *Abl* 12 (1925): 54; "Beschlüsse der 19. Vertreterversammlung des DAV," *ibid.*, 13 (1926): 113; "Anwälte im Nebenberuf," *ibid.*, p. 115; Jessen, "Anwälte im Nebenberuf," *ibid.*, 14 (1927): 44ff; Dr. Lehmann, "Beamte im Amte, abgebaute Beamte, Notare, Rechtsanwälte," *ibid.*, p. 121ff, and Ostler, *Rechtsanwälte*, p. 194f.

41. Dr. Knoepfel, "Ein Vorstoß der Rechtskonsulenten," *Abl* 13 (1926): 70; "Die Preußischen Verwaltungsrechtsräte," *ibid.*, p. 284f; Dr. Hawlitzky, "Gegen das Rechtskonsulententum," *ibid.*, 14 (1927): 270f; H. Dittenberger, "Preußische Verwaltungsrechtsräte," *ibid.*, p. 249f, and Ostler, *Rechtsanwälte*, p. 186ff.

42. "Zum Arbeitsgerichtsgesetzentwurf," *Abl* 13 (1926): 142; "Aus der Vereinstätigkeit," *ibid.*, p. 312f; "1927," *ibid.*, 14 (1927): 1ff. Cf. Kronstein, *Briefe*, p. 112ff, and Ostler, *Rechtsanwälte*, p. 179ff.

43. For details see "Die Überbürdung der Philologen," *Phbl* 35 (1927): 177ff. Conference in ministry, March 31, 1922, and other material in ZStA Me, Rep. 76 VI, Sekt. 1, Gen. z, No. 140, Vol. III; Boelitz to Ministry of Finance July 4, 1923; H. Richert, "Betrifft die Arbeitszeit der Philologen," Dec. 4, 1923; Boelitz decree of March 12, and Lande explanation Sept. 3, 1924, *ibid.*, Vol. IV.

44. "Entschließungen des deutschen Hochschultages," *Phbl* 33 (1925), No. 12; Becker speech in Landtag, May 7, 1926, *ibid.*, 34 (1926): 296ff; W. Krebs, "Überlastung," *ibid.*, 35 (1927), No. 1; "Die Verbandsvertreter beim Minister," *ibid.*, p. 97; "Ein wichtiger Beschluß zur Pflichtstundenfrage," *ibid.*, p. 312, and "Neue 'Erleichterung' unserer Arbeitslast," *ibid.*, pp.

749. Cf. the conference of the Prussian PhVb with Minister Becker, Jan 31, 1927, WPhV, B42, 542.

45. "Die barbarische Überlastung der Philologen," *Phbl* 36 (1928): 129; "Ein erster Schritt," *ibid.*, p. 707; "Die höhere Schule im preußischen Staatshaushalt," *ibid.*, 37 (1929), No. 1. Another bone of contention was the 50-minute class period, ZStA Me, Rep. 76 VI, Sekt. 1, Gen. z, No. 234, Vol. II. Cf. R. Engelsing, *Der literarische Arbeiter* (Göttingen, 1976), p. 67.

46. F. Neuhaus, "Die Normung in Deutschland," *ZVDI* 68 (1924): 1065ff; W. Hellmich, "Zehn Jahre deutscher Normung," *ibid.*, 71 (1927): 1525ff; "Angelegenheiten des Vereins," *ibid.*, 68 (1924): 664; and "Befohlene Gemeinschaftsarbeit," *VDIN* (1924), No. 4. Cf. P. Lundgreen, "Technisch-wissenschaftliche Vereine zwischen Wissenschaft, Staat und Industrie, 1860–1914," *Technikgeschichte* 46 (1979): 181ff.

47. O. Kienzler, "Fließarbeit, eine neue Form der Betriebstechnik," *ZVDI* 71 (1927): 300f; "Ziele und Tätigkeit des VDI," *ibid.*, p. 716; Dipl.-Ing. Kaefes, "Von dem Weg zu den leitenden Stellen," *ZVDDI* 15 (1924): 23. Cf. R. Stahlschmidt, "Der Ausbau der technisch-wissenschaftlichen Gemeinschaftsarbeit 1918 bis 1938," Ludwig, ed., *Technik,* p. 348ff.

48. Introductory essay on "Deutsches Reich," in J. Magnus, ed., *Die Rechtsanwaltschaft* (Leipzig, 1929), with quotes from pp. 8, 9, 10, 13, 18, 21, 34. Cf. L. Levin, "Die Festgabe für Adolf Heilberg," *JW* 57 (1928): 1113ff, as well as the actual *Festschrift* for the conflicting self-conceptions of lawyers in the late 1920s.

49. "Aus der Vereinstätigkeit," *Abl* 11 (1924): 8f; draft proposal of insurance scheme, *ibid.*, p. 15ff; "Aus der Vereinstätigkeit," *ibid.*, p. 32; and H. Dittenberger, "17. Vertreterversammlung des DAV," *ibid.*, pp. 59ff. Cf. Ostler, *Rechtsanwälte,* p. 200f.

50. "Aus der Vereinstätigkeit," *Abl* 12 (1925): 83, 145, 167.

51. "Das Versicherungsgesetz für Rechtsanwälte," draft with Cahn and Minden memoranda, *Abl* 13 (1926): 26–55; H. Dittenberger, "Die 19. Vertreterversammlung," *ibid.*, p. 118ff; and the stenographic report of the "19. Vertreterversammlung des DAV" (printed as manuscript in Leipzig, 1926), pp. 14–58.

52. See the file on "Die Förderung der Lehrer im wissenschaftlichen Streben" in ZStA Me, Rep. 76 VI, Sekt. 1, Gen. z, No. 180, Vol. III. W. Klatt, "Der Erfurter Verbandstag," *Phbl* 34 (1926): 343ff, with various speeches on school reform; "Richtlinien für die Lehrpläne der höheren Schulen Preußens," *ibid.*, 33 (1925): 225f; W. Klatt, "Deutscher Philologentag," *ibid.*, p. 421f. Cf. "Bericht der GA Sitzung," Oct. 31, 1927, WPhV, B45, 545; Ehrentreich, *Fünfzig Jahre,* p. 54ff; and Hartig, *Lebenserinnerungen,* p. 45f.

53. W. Bolle, "Die höhere Schule als Spiegelbild des modernen Geisteslebens," *Phbl* 36 (1928): 355ff; Havenstein to Schumann, March 25, 1932 in Hammerstein, ed., *Deutsche Bildung?* (Frankfurt, 1988), p. 49; A. Bohlen, "Die Verbandspolitik nach dem Danziger Philologentag," *ibid,* 371ff; board minutes Oct. 2, 1924, Feb. 6, 1925, and July 5, 1928, WPhV, A10, 53. Cf. F. Kreppel, "Der Lehrer in den zwanziger Jahren," H. Schoeps, ed., *Zeitgeist,* p. 124f; and Ehrentreich, *Fünfzig Jahre,* p. 116ff.

54. K. Steinmetz, "Die Technik im Reiche der Geisteswissenschaften," *ZVDDI* 21 (1929): 3ff; K. Seyderhelm, "Technik, ein Grundpfeiler der Kultur," *ibid.*, 18 (1927): 41ff; C. Weihe, "Zu guter Letzt," *ibid.*, 20 (1928): 209ff. Weihe ran a regular review column, called "Kultur-Umschau," because "it is important for the evaluation of technology, technical work and thereby technicians, to investigate the relationship between technology and other areas of culture. . . ." See "Zum Abschied" *ibid.*, 19 (1928), No. 12.

55. A. Stürzenacker, "Die Schönheit des Ingenieurbaues," *ZVDI* 68 (1924): 1113ff; and R. Riemerschmid, "Kunst und Technik," *ibid.*, 72 (1928): 1273ff. Cf. "Romantische Technik," *VDIN,* Dec. 21, 1927; "Kunst und Technik," *ibid.*, Jan. 2, 1928; and Gosebruch, "Kunst und Technik," *ibid.*, July 4, 1928.

56. F. Dessauer, "Weltsinn der Technik," *ZVDI* 70 (1926): 1f; R. Planck, "Naturwissenschaft und Technik," *ibid.*, 72 (1928): 837ff; C. Weihe, "Die Philosophie der Technik," *ZVDDI* 18 (1927): 73ff, 97ff; and S. Marold, "Techniker und Weltanschauung," *ibid.*, p. 101ff. Cf. J. Herf, *Reactionary Modernism* (Cambridge, Mass., 1984), p. 152ff.

57. H. Dittenberger, "Bemerkung zu den Anträgen auf Satzungsänderung," *Abl* 11 (1924): 38ff; "Satzungsänderungen," 12 (1925): 35; H. Dittenberger, "Die 18. Vertreterversammlung des DAV," *ibid.*, p. 62f.

58. "Entwurf einer Wahlordnung," *Abl* 14 (1927): 127f; "Reichswahlvorschläge für die Wahlen zur Vertreterversammlung des DAV," *ibid.*, p. 214f. Cf. Dittenberger, "Aus der Vereinstätigkeit," *Abl* 14 (1927): 261; "Entwurf einer Satzung des DAV," *ibid.*, 15 (1928): 91ff; "Zur neuen Satzung," *ibid.*, p. 196ff; "Satzung des DAV," *ibid.*, 215ff.

59. "Reichsanwaltskammer," *Abl* 15 (1928): 174f; and "Notwendigkeit, Aufgaben und Organisation einer Reichsanwaltskammer," *ibid.*, p. 290ff. See Ostler, *Rechtsanwälte*, p. 222ff.

60. E. Hassel, "Aus der Praxis der Verbandsarbeit," *Phbl* 36 (1928): 761; A. Bohlen, "Ein Jahrzehnt im Reichsbund," *ibid.*, p. 758ff; and "Entstehung und Tätigkeit des Schulausschusses des Verbandes deutscher Hochschulen," *ibid.*, 34 (1926): 10ff.

61. Boelitz to Bolle, April 20, 1923, ZStA Po, Rep. 49.01, 4353. Cf. board minutes, Feb. 20 and June 26, 1926, WPhV, A10, 53; P. Mellmann, "Standesfragen der deutschen Philologenschaft," *Phbl* 35 (1927): 409ff; and A. Bohlen, "Die Verbandspolitik nach dem Danziger Philologentag," *ibid.*, 36 (1928): 371 for three examples.

62. F. Ohlmüller, "Ein Besuch beim VDI," *VDIN*, March 2, 1927; and "67. Hauptversammlung des VDI in Essen," *ibid.* (1928), No. 23; "Die Arbeiten des VDI im Jahre 1927/28," *ibid.*, Aug. 8, 1928. Cf. Stahlschmidt, "Ausbau der Gemeinschaftsarbeit," p. 347ff.

63. F. Romberg, "Uber den Stand unserer Verbandsarbeit," *ZVDDI*, 18 (1927): 5ff; "Diplom-Ingenieur-Tagung 1927," *ibid.*, p. 197f; "Die Ausschußtagung 1927," *ibid.*, p. 211ff. The 1926–1927 annual report gives the share of TH graduates among new VDI members as 55.2% in contrast to 16.3% HTL graduates and 18.5% with practical experience. *VDIN*, March 30, 1927. Though large (89,056), the ButaB was generally ignored.

64. Dosenheimer, "Die deutsche Richterschaft und die Revolution," *DRZ* 11 (1919): 12–16; F. Riss, "Jahresbilanz," *ibid.*, p. 1–6; and R. Bendix, *Von Berlin nach Berkeley* (Frankfurt, 1985), p. 152ff. See Ostler, *Rechtsanwälte*, p. 182 and G. Fieberg, ed., *Im Namen des deutschen Volkes. Justiz und Nationalsozialismus* (Cologne, 1989), p. 18ff.

65. The debate between the left deputies Hoffman, Rosenfeld, or Brodauf and the bourgeois representative Kahl in the Reichstag on Feb. 23 and 24, 1922 is reprinted in *JW* 51 (1922): 422ff; "Der sechste deutsche Richtertag in der Kritik," *DRZ* 17 (1925): 71ff; and "Vertrauenskrisis—Genesungskrisis," *ibid.*, 18 (1926): 322ff. Cf. W. Hoegner, *Der Politische Radikalismus in Deutschland, 1919–1933* (Munich, 1966), p. 144ff.

66. Dr. Weiß, "Der Kampf um das Recht und der deutsche Richterstand," *DRZ* 17 (1925): 309ff; E. Müller-Meiningen, "Zuverlässige Richter in der deutschen Republik," *ibid.*, p. 422ff; and Dr. Oertel, "Die Sicherung der richterlichen Unabhängigkeit," *ibid.*, p. 566f; versus E. Eyck, "Kritik an der deutschen Rechtspflege," *JW* 55 (1926): 1130f. L. Ebermayer, *Fünfzig Jahre Dienst am Recht* (Zürich, 1930), p. 176ff.

67. M. Reichert, "Das deutsche Richtertum," *JW* 58 (1928): 13ff. The same author "categorically rejected" the journal of the republican lawyer's league, *Die Justiz*, in *DRZ* 18 (1926): 21ff. See "Justiz und Republik," *ibid.*, p. 28ff; W. Simons, "Richtertum und Sozialismus," *ibid.*, p. 149f; and "Angriffe auf die Weimarer Verfassung," *ibid.*, p. 271ff.

68. A. Friedländer, "Der 19. Band der Entscheidungen des Ehrengerichtshofs," *Abl* 13 (1926): 224; J. Magnus, "Juristische Wochenschrift," *JW* (1924): 442; Dr. Siehr, "Der Deutsche Anwaltstag," *ibid.*, 54 (1925): 1338; and *Außerordentlicher Anwaltstag zu Berlin* (Berlin, 1925). Cf. Bendix, *Von Berlin*, p. 162ff, F. Grimm, *Politische Justiz, die Krankheit unserer Zeit* (Bonn, 1953), p. 37ff, and S. Quack, "Paul Levi (1883–1930). Politischer Anwalt und sozialistischer Politiker," in Kritische Justiz, ed., *Streitbare Juristen. Eine andere Tradition* (Baden-Baden, 1988), p. 131ff.

69. R. Heydeloff, "Strafanwalt der Rechtsextremisten. W. Luetgebrune in der Weimarer Republik," *VfZG* 32 (1984): 373–421; A. Apfel, *Behind the Scenes of Justice* (London, 1935), p. 199ff; Riess, *Der Mann in der Schwarzen Robe*, p. 19ff; Grimm, *Politische Justiz*, p. 51ff. Cf. H. Hannover, *Politische Justiz—1918 bis 1933* (Bornheim, 1987).

70. Boelitz decree, July 1, 1922; DNVP interpellation, July 5, 1922; PSK Hanover to ministry, July 14, 1922; PSK Stettin to ministry, July 8, 1922; Boelitz draft decree, July 18, 1922; Mellmann to ministry, Sept. 19, 1922 in ZStA Me, Rep. 76 VI, Sekt. 1, Gen. z, No. 285; and newspaper clippings in WPhV, U10, 394. "Reichsgesetz über die Pflichten der Beamten zum Schutze der Republik," *Phbl* 39 (1922): 395f.

71. "Die Zukunft des deutschen Unterrichts. Eine Unterredung mit Minister Boelitz," *BT*,

Aug. 20, 1922; Boelitz decree, Dec. 23, 1922, lifting controls on pupil membership in political associations; more stringent guidelines of the Thuringian Ministry of Education, Aug. 5, 1922, and so on, in ZStA Me, Rep. 76 VI, Sekt. 1, Gen. z, No. 285.

72. PSK report, Nov. 10, 1922; Latrille note, Oct. 2, 1923; PSK Münster report, Nov. 1, 1923; PSK Breslau report, May 10, 1924, in ZStA Me, Rep. 76 VI, Sekt. 1, Gen. z, No. 264, Vol. II. Fülle to Bohlen, Sept. 13, 1922, WPhV, XX.1, 360. B. Jarausch, "Tagebuch," Aug. 14, 1922.

73. Becker decree, Aug. 29, 1925, ZStA Me, Rep. 76 VI, Sekt. 1, Gen. z, No. 264, Vol. II; "Entpolitisierung?" *Phbl* 34 (1926): 487f; "Erklärung des Preußischen PhVb," *ibid.*, p. 583; "Zur Erklärung des Preußischen PhVb," *ibid.*, 35 (1927): 39f; "Das Recht der freien Meinungsäußerung und der politischen Betätigung der Lehrer," *ibid.*, p. 82f; stenographic report of the Landtag discussions, May 6, 1926; "Staatsbürgerliche Erziehung," *Kath. V. Nachrichten,* April 27, 1927; and C. Seeligmann, "Die Oberlehrer zu Beginn der Weimarer Republik" (Ms., Bielefeld, 1987), p. 38f.

74. Dr. Bohner, "Protest der Jugend," *BT,* Aug. 15, 1928; Prof. Pflug, "Protest der Jugend?" *Tag,* Aug. 21, 1928; W. Hartke, "Ein Wort zur Verständigung," *BT,* Aug. 22, 1928; "Die Jugend feiert die Verfassung," *Vorwärts,* Aug. 22, 1928; and conservative critiques "of the abuse of immature youths for partisan purposes" under "Zeitungsschau," *Phbl* 36 (1928): 525ff.

75. "Preußischer Philologenverband," *Phbl* 36 (1928): 597f; and Becker's speech in the Prussian Landtag, reprinted *ibid.*, p. 723ff; Cf. board minutes, Sept. 22, 1928, WPhV, A10, 53.

76. H. Deiters (for the Republican Teachers' League), "Die Beamtenpolitik in ihrem Verhältnis zur Staatspolitik," *Phbl* 34 (1926): 600; W. Hohmann, "Die Philologen und die Staatspolitik," *ibid.*, 36 (1928): 680f; and V. Hirsch (for the Deutschnationale Lehrerbund), "Staat und Beamtenverbände," *ibid.*, p. 681f. Cf. Seeligmann, "Oberlehrer," p. 27ff.

77. "Bekenntnis des Reichskanzlers zur Technik," *VDIN,* May 20, 1925; S. Hartmann, "Technischer Fortschritt und Politik," *VDIN,* Oct. 19, 1927; and C. Matschoß, "Das Deutsche Museum," *ZVDI* 69 (1925): 609ff.

78. Prof. Brix, "Der deutsche Straßenbau," *ZVDI* 72 (1928): 613; R. Eisenlohr, "Über den Röhnsegelflug-Wettbewerb 1926," *ibid.*, 70 (1926): 1406ff; E. Everling, "Aufgaben der Luftfahrt," *ibid.*, 72 (1928): 1393f; Oskar von Miller, "Technik und Gemeinden," *ibid.*, 70 (1926): 1505ff. The political dimension of engineering practice has yet to be analyzed.

79. "Der VDDI," *ZVDDI* 16 (1924): 10ff; K. Friedrich, "Der Verband und seine Arbeit," *ibid.*, p. 113ff; and K. F. Steinmetz, "Der Einfluß der technischen Akademiker auf die Führung im Staat," *ibid.*, 20 (1928): 94ff. Cf. Viefhaus, "Ingenieure," p. 304f.

80. Figures in Table 3.2 from the Reichstag member data-set, compiled by H. Best and W. H. Schroeder at the Center for Historical Social Research, Cologne. Cf. H. Best and R. Ponemereo, eds., *Datenhandbuch. Abgeordnete deutscher Nationalparlamente. Reichstag 1867–1918* and *Reichstag 1918–1933* (Cologne, 1987). This extensive collection supersedes M. Schwarz, *MdR. Biographisches Handbuch der Reichstage* (Hannover, 1965), pp. 139ff, 531ff and *Reichstags-Handbuch* (Berlin, 1907 to 1933). Cf. Ostler, *Rechtsanwälte,* pp. 102, 145, 196, and correspondence between the DDP, DVP, and the DAV, "Zum Arbeitsgerichtsgesetz," *Abl* 14 (1927): 57f.

81. Dr. Wrzeszinski, "Anwaltsnot und staatspolitische Betätigung der Anwaltschaft," *Abl* 15 (1928): 8f; and K. Siehr, "Zum Stuttgarter Anwaltstag," *ibid.*, 14 (1927): 200f. Cf. O. Rothbarth, "Die Stellung des Anwalts in der Öffentlichkeit," *ibid.*, 28 (1928): 182f; and "Aus der Vereinstätigkeit," *ibid.*, 83, 116.

82. "Entpolitisierung?" *Phbl* 34 (1926): 487. Bohlen to Goldmann, Nov. 13, 1921; Bohlen to Fülle, Oct. 24, 1922; protocols of the "Politische Beirat," n.d.; February 23, 1923; April 24, 1926, WPhV, XX1, 360; Drepper to Bohlen, Feb. 9, 1924; "Reichstagswahl am 4. Mai, 1924"; Wendroth to Bohlen Oct. 27 and Tigges to Bohlen, Oct. 31, 1924; "Unsere Sammlung zum Kampfschatz," Jan. 29, 1924, all in WPhV, B34, 417.

83. E. Hassel, "Schulmänner und Universitätslehrer im Preußischen Landtag," WPhV, XX1, 360; "Schulmänner im neuen Reichstag," *Phbl* 33 (1925): 153ff; "Der neue preußische Landtag," *ibid.*, 36 (1928): 403ff; "Der neue Reichstag," *ibid.*, p. 435ff and *ADLZ* 57 (1928): 474.

Westphalian figures computed from 120 surveys (showing one-half active in the school council, one-fifth in the church or city government) in WPhV, HY24, 685. Bölling, *Sozialgeschichte,* p. 131f.

84. The engineering journals offer few clues to the political preferences of engineers. Cf. C.-F. von Siemens, "Gemeinschaftsarbeit und deutsche Industrie," *VDIN,* July 4, 1923; Prof. Klingenberg, "Gegenwartsfragen der Technik," *ibid.,* June 4, 1924; K. Wendt, "Zeitfragen des Ingenieurberufs," *ibid.,* June 30, 1926; and K. Steinmetz, "Baumeister," *ZVDDI* 18 (1927): 61f. By focusing on ideology and neglecting the practical dimensions of engineering J. Herf's arguments in *Reactionary Modernism,* p. 152, remain tentative.

85. Celle AG attorney petition, Oct. 10, 1924; H. Raabe to Zehnhoff, Oct. 1924; "Gesetzentwurf zur Linderung der Not der AG Anwälte," Sept. 1924; Berndt marginalia, Oct. 14, 1924; Joel inquiry, Oct. 27, 1924; Zehnhoff to Joel, Nov. 21, 1924, all in PrGStA Da, Rep. 84a, Vol. 72. Cf. H. Raabe, "Das Ende der deutschen AG Anwaltschaft," *JW* 53 (1924): 900ff. K. F. Ledford, is sketchy on the final resolution of the problem in "Simultaneous Admission and the German Bar, 1903–1927," in G. Cocks and K. H. Jarausch, eds., *German Professions* (New York, 1990), p. 252ff.

86. "Aus der Vereinstätigkeit," *Abl* 11 (1924): 167f; *ibid.,* 12 (1925): 8f, 16, 31. "Stenographische Niederschrift über die Mitgliederversammlung des Vereins deutscher LG Anwälte," April 5, 1925; petition of the LG association, Dec. 1924, in PrGStA Da, Rep. 84a, Vol. 72. Cf. the DAV documentation, *Um die Simultanzulassung* (Leipzig, 1925), 2 Vols. for the internal negotiations.

87. Excerpt of Reichstag stenographic report, March 17, 1925; and protocol of the Reichstag commission discussion, Nov. 5 and 6, 1925, in PrGStA Da, Rep. 84a, Vol. 72. Cf. *Mitteilungen der AG Anwälte* 16 (1925), April–May; "Zur Simultanzulassung," *Abl* 12 (1925): 168; "Der Vorstand des DAV und die SZ," *ibid.,* 13 (1926): 64ff, 140ff, 178f.

88. LG lawyer K. Kaßler to Zehnhoff, Nov. 27, 1925; Hawlitzky to Zehnhoff, Nov. 25, 1925, with AG memoranda of May, June, and Nov. 1925; Zehnhoff to Joel, Jan. 4, 1926; ministerial memorandum about the AG–LG negotiating session, Jan. 23, 1926, all in PrGStA Da, Rep. 84a, Vol. 72. Ostler, *Rechtsanwälte,* p. 186, is too perfunctory.

89. DAV presidium to Zehnhoff, March 15, 1926; Zehnhoff to Joel, April 8, 1926; stenographic report of the Reichstag Commission session of Dec. 4, 1926, and other material in PrGStA Da, Rep. 84a, Vol. 72. Excerpts from the final Reichstag debate are in Vol. 73. Cf. "Aus der Vereinstätigkeit," *Abl* 14 (1927): 66f.

90. Reich Ministry of Finance "Denkschrift über die Entwicklung der Besoldung der Reichsbeamten von 1897 bis Dez. 1924," Jan. 19, 1925; and Bolle (RhB) memorandum on "Was fordert die höhere Beamtenschaft zur Besoldungsfrage," Feb. 12, 1925, in ZStA Me, Rep. 76 IIa, Sekt. 55, Gen. 1, Vol. XVII. Cf. Bohlen's reports to the Westphalian board meetings, March 27, 1926, Dec. 15, and so on, WPhV, A10, 53; Bolle to Saxon PhVb, Jan. 8, 1927, *ibid.,* B42, 542; and *ALDZ* 55 (1926): 717. Cf. J. Becker, ed., *Heinrich Köhler. Lebenserinnerungen* (Stuttgart, 1964), pp. 251–64.

91. "Vorstandssitzung des Preußischen PhVb," *Phbl* 34 (1926): 726f; Bolle to Becker, Nov. 25, 1926; Grzezsinski to Becker, Dec. 31, 1926; Becker to Höpker-Aschoff, March 7, 1927, in ZStA Me, Rep. 76 IIa, Sekt. 55, Gen. 1, Vol. XIX. "Die höheren Schulen im Hauptausschuß des preußischen Landtags," *Phbl* 35 (1927): 113ff; "Vorstandssitzung des Preußischen PhVb," *ibid.,* p. 305ff; and A. Bohlen, "Wege der Besoldungsreform," *ibid.,* p. 449ff. Cf. Deutscher PhVb circular, Jan 13, 1927; Bohlen circular, Feb. 10, 1927, and letter to party members, and so on in WPhV, B38, 538; as well as A. Mellmann, *Beamte, Staat und Wirtschaft* (Berlin, 1926), distributed in 40,000 copies!

92. Soziale Arbeitsgemeinschaft Deutscher Beamtenverbände to Becker, May 14, 1927, ZStA Me, Rep. 76 IIa, Sekt. 55, Gen. 1, Vol. XIX; "Denkschrift des Preußischen Beamtenbundes," Oct. 24, 1927; cabinet sessions on Sept. 20, 28, 1927, and so on, *ibid.,* Vol. XX. Cf. Bohlen circular, May 28, 1927, and Schnitzler to Köhler, July 19, 1927, WPhV, B38, 538.

93. A. Bohlen, "Auf dem Wege zur Entscheidung," *Phbl* 35 (1927): 609ff; and "Der verbesserte preußische Regierungsentwurf," *ibid.,* p. 653ff; "Der Preußische PhVb zur neuen Regierungsvorlage," *ibid.,* p. 669f; "Die Einstufung der höheren Beamten in Preußen," *ibid.,* 670f; and A. Bohlen, "Besoldungsgrundsätze in Reich und Ländern," *ibid.,* p. 685ff.

94. *Preußisches Besoldungsblatt,* Dec. 12, 1927; Becker to Ministry of Finance, Dec. 31, 1927, with *Stellenplan;* Prussian Landtag stenographic report, Dec. 13, 1927, and so on, in ZStA Me, Rep. 76 IIa, Sekt. 55, Gen. 1, Vol. XXI. Max Engel, "Die Protestkundgebung der höheren Beamten Preußens in Berlin," *Phbl* 35 (1927): 800ff; "Das Ergebnis der Besoldungsreform im Reich und in Preußen," *ibid.,* p. 813ff; and A. Bohlen, "Die deutschen Philologen nach der Besoldungsreform," 36 (1928): 582f. Cf. PrPhVb circulars, Dec. 2, 1927, and Jan. 11, 1928; Ismer to Bolle, Jan. 28, 1928 and reply of Feb. 14, WPhV, B45, 542, and W. Patch, "Class Prejudice and the Failure of the Weimar Republic," *GSR* 12 (1989): 35ff.

95. "Diplom-Ingenieur-Tagung 1926," *ZVDDI* 18 (1927): 3. The annual VDI reports began with a section on business while the *ZVDI* and the *ZVDDI* carried columns on "Wirtschaftsfragen," which reported news rather than discussed decisions. The VDI journal *Technik und Wirtschaft* focused on rationalization rather than economic policy.

96. "Reichsbahn und Technik," *VDIN,* Oct. 1, 1924; Dr. Cremer, "Der Ingenieur im Reichshaushalt für 1929," *ibid.,* Feb. 13, 1929. Cf. J. Salzwedel, "Die Aufgaben des Reichsverkehrsministeriums," *Deutsche Verwaltungsgeschichte* 4: 260ff.

97. In contrast to Beatus, "Academic Proletariat," p. 179, who talks about a negative "barricade mentality."

98. H. Dittenberger, "Aus der Vereinstätigkeit," *Abl* 16 (1929): 4f. Cf. "Entwurf einer Satzung des DAV," *ibid.,* 15 (1928): 91ff; H. Dittenberger, "Zur neuen Satzung," *ibid.,* p. 196ff; "Satzung des DAV," *ibid.,* p. 215ff; and Buß, "Fachanwaltschaft, Reklame und Organisation," *ibid.,* p. 288f.

99. Bolle (?), "Rückblick und Ausblick," *Phbl* 37 (1929): 1ff; "Der VDI und seine Arbeiten im Jahre 1928/29," *VDIN* No. 23, 1929; C. Köttgen, "Zum Jahreswechsel," *ibid.,* Jan. 2, 1929.

100. "Übernahme des Kriegerdenkmals im Vereinshause," *ZVDI* 68 (1924): 592; "Beschlüsse des außerordentlichen Anwaltstages zu Berlin," *Abl* 12 (1925): 53; Brix, "Der deutsche Straßenbau," *ZVDI* 72 (1928): 613. Cf. J. Goldschmidt, "Gesetzesdämmerung," *JW* 53 (1924): 245ff and W. Alterthum, "Die wirkliche deutsche Rechtsnot," *Abl* 12 (1925): 116f.

101. G. Stresemann, "Zum Geleit!" *ZVDI* 19 (1928): 157ff; Deutscher PhVb board minutes of Aug. 21 and Sept. 29, 1928, in WPhV, B46, 546; Bohlen, "Die Verbandspolitik nach dem Danziger Philologentag," *Phbl* 36 (1928): 371; E. Tatarin-Tarheyden, "Die 6. Tagung der Vereinigung der deutschen Staatsrechtslehrer in Wien zur Begrüßung," *JW* 57 (1928): 1017f.

102. "Rede des Ministerialrates Grimme," *Mitteilungen des Philologenvereins der Provinz Hannover* 10 (1928): 96ff. Cf. K. Jarausch, "The Decline of Liberal Professionalism," in *idem* and L. Jones, eds., *In Search of a Liberal Germany* (Oxford, 1990).

CHAPTER 4

1. "Offener Brief des Präsidenten des DAV an den Abgeordneten des Preußischen Landtags Herrn Kube," *Abl* 19 (1932): 224; "Erklärung der Vorstände der deutschen Anwaltskammern vom 5. Juli 1932," *ibid.,* p. 224f.

2. B. Wiese, "Nationalpolitische Erziehung," *Phbl* 40 (1932): 420f; and W. Strauß, " 'Nationalpolitische Erziehung' und höhere Schule," *ibid.,* p. 468f. Cf. the controversy between J. Kühnhold and Dr. Benze in *Mitteilungen des Philologenvereins der Provinz Hannover,* July–Aug. 1932.

3. Statement by the editorial board of the *VDIN,* "Jahreswende—Zeitenwende?" Feb. 1933.

4. "Schreiben des Landtagabgeordneten Rechtsanwalt Dr. Freisler-Kassel an den Präsidenten des DAV," *Abl* 19 (1932): 226f.

5. "Vom Bildungsprogramm des Nationalsozialismus," *Phbl* 40 (1932): 216f; R. Murtfeld, " 'Nationalpolitische Erziehung' und höhere Schule," *ibid.,* p. 548f; W. Strauß, " 'Nationalpolitische Erziehung' und höhere Schule," *ibid.,* 41 (1933): 18ff.

6. "Eine Kundgebung der Ingenieure," *VDIN,* Oct. 19, 1932; W. Hellmich, "Jahreswende—Zeitenwende?" *ibid.,* Jan. 4, 1933.

7. This aspect is responsible for much of the inconclusiveness of the debates. Cf. T. S. Hamerow, "Guilt, Redemption, and the Writing of German History," *AHR* 88 (1983): 67.

8. As introduction to the vast literature see M. Broszat *et al.*, eds., *Deutschlands Weg in die Diktatur* (Berlin, 1983), p. 42ff.

9. G. L. Mosse, *The Crisis of German Ideology* (New York, 1964) and J. Petzold, *Die Demagogie des Hitlerfaschismus* (Berlin, 1982).

10. D. Abraham, *The Collapse of the Weimar Republic* (Princeton, N.J., 1981) versus H. A. Turner, *German Big Business and the Rise of Hitler* (New York, 1985); and Feldmann versus Abraham in *CEH* 17 (1984): 159–293.

11. Special *CEH* issue on "Who Voted for Hitler?" 17 (1984): 3–85 with contributions by R. Hamilton or T. Childers and J. Falter *et al.*, eds., *Wahlen und Abstimmungen in der Weimarer Republik* (Munich, 1986).

12. K. Borchardt, "Zwangslagen und Handlungsspielräume in der grossen Wirtschaftskrise der frühen dreißiger Jahre," *Jahrbuch der Bayerischen Akademie der Wissenschaften* (Munich, 1979), p. 85ff; and H. James, *The German Slump* (Oxford, 1986).

13. D. Peuckert, *Volksgenossen und Gemeinschaftsfremde* (Cologne, 1982), p. 22ff.

14. F. Ostler, *Die deutschen Rechtsanwälte 1871–1971* (Essen, 1971), p. 229. More sketchy is D. Rüschemeyer, *Juristen in Deutschland und in den USA* (Stuttgart, 1976), p. 171f.

15. W. Breyvogel, *Die soziale Lage und das politische Bewußtsein der Volksschullehrer 1927–1933* (Königstein, 1979); D. Krause-Vilmar, ed., *Lehrerschaft, Republik und Faschismus 1919–1933* (Cologne, 1978), p. 7ff; J. Erger, "Lehrer und Nationalsozialismus," in M. Heinemann, ed., *Erziehung und Schulung im Dritten Reich* (Stuttgart, 1980), Vol. 2, p. 206ff; versus H.-C. Laubach, "Die Politik des PhVb im Reich und in Preußen während der Weimarer Republik," in Heinemann, ed., *Lehrer*, 249ff as well as F. Hamburger, "Pädagogische und politische Orientierung im Selbstverständnis des Deutschen PhVb in der Weimarer Republik," *ibid.*, p. 263ff.

16. K.-H. Ludwig, *Technik und Ingenieure im Dritten Reich* (Königstein, 1979), p. 72f; E. Viefhaus, "Ingenieure in der Weimarer Republik: Bildungs-, Berufs- und Gesellschaftspolitik 1918 bis 1933," in Ludwig, ed., p. 338f, and J. Herf, *Reactionary Modernism* (Cambridge, England, 1984), p. 187f.

17. Dittenberger, "Zum neuen Jahre," *Abl* 18 (1931): 1ff; W. Bolle, "Rückblick und Ausblick," *Phbl* 38 (1930): 1ff; "Zur Krise," *ZVDDI* 22 (1931): 95. For the overuse of the term cf. *Deutschlands Weg*, 104ff.

18. Dittenberger, "Zum neuen Jahre," *Abl* 17 (1930): 1ff; 18 (1931): 1ff; 19 (1932): 1ff. Cf. D. Petzina, *Die deutsche Wirtschaft in der Zwischenkriegszeit* (Wiesbaden, 1977), p. 96ff.

19. W. Bolle, "Rückblick und Ausblick," *Phbl* 38 (1930): 1ff; A. Bohlen, "Unter dem Druck der Finanznot," *ibid.*, p. 145ff; W. Bolle, "Enttäuschungen und Hoffnungen," *Phbl* 39 (1931): 1ff; "Eine erschütternde Jahresbilanz," *ibid.*, 40 (1932): 1ff; and K. Jarausch, "Volksnot," *SE* 5 (1930–1931), p. 244.

20. "Niedergang der Weltkonjunktur," *VDIN*, Dec. 11, 1929; C. Matschoß, "1932," *ibid.*, Jan. 6, 1932; W. Hellmich, "Das Jahr 1930," *ZVDI* 75 (1931): 139ff; E. Heidebroek, "Maschine und Arbeitslosigkeit," *ibid.*, 76 (1932): 1041ff; and W. von Pasinski, "Ist die Technik die Ursache der Arbeitslosigkeit?" *ZVDDI* 22 (1931): 100ff.

21. Dittenberger, "Aus der Vereinstätigkeit," *Abl* 16 (1929): 142; "Richtlinien für die Reform der Juristischen Vor- und Fortbildung," *ibid.*, p. 159ff; and R. Busch, "Die Verlängerung des Universitätsstudiums für den künftigen Anwalt," *ibid.*, p. 270ff.

22. A. Bohlen, "Um die Zukunft des Akademikertums," *Phbl* 37 (1929): 161ff, 177ff; "Minister Dr. Becker zur Volksschullehrerbildung," *ibid.*, p. 217ff; "Denkschrift des Preußischen PhVb und der Philologen Fakultät der Universität Berlin über die Universitätsausbildung für das höhere Lehrfach," *ibid.*, p. 537ff; Ried circular, May 16, and Deutscher PhVb board minutes, June 28, 1929, WPhV, B46, 546. Cf. Preußischer PhVb draft principles, *ibid.*, B43, 543.

23. O. Ammann, "Die Ausbildung an den Bauingenieurabteilungen der deutschen TH," *ZVDI* 74 (1930): 561ff; Dr. Harm, "Die praktische Ausbildung des Studierenden," *ibid.*, p. 1531; and H. Krieger, "Zur Reform der deutschen TH," *ZVDDI* 21 (1930): 54f, 132f. The VDI rejected the academization of vocational schoolteacher training. G. Lippart, "Der industrielle Nachwuchs in der Berufsschule," *VDIN*, Jan., 23, 1929.

24. W. Dibelius, "Die Überfüllung der Universität," *Phbl* 38 (1930): 265ff; H. Titze, *Das Hochschulstudium in Preußen und Deutschland, 1820–1944* (Göttingen, 1987), pp. 30f, 88f; P.

Lundgreen, *Sozialgeschichte der deutschen Schule im Überblick* (Göttingen, 1981), Vol. 1, p. 146; and "Besuch der deutschen TH und Bergakademien im Winterhalbjahr 1930/31," *ZVDI* 75 (1931): 943.

25. W. Oberle, "Zur Frage des verstärkten Zustroms zu den höheren Schulen," *Phbl* 37 (1929): 721ff; Dibelius, "Die Überfüllung der Universität," *ibid.*, 38 (1930): 265ff; "Studenten ohne Raum," *ZVDDI* 20 (1929): 38ff.

26. Dittenberger, "Bewegung der Zahl der Anwälte im Deutschen Reich," *Abl* 17 (1930): 78ff; 18 (1931): 37ff; 19 (1932): 71ff; 20 (1933): 75ff; W. Schweer, "Die gegenwärtige und künftige Altersgliederung der deutschen Rechtsanwälte," *ibid.*, 18 (1931): 268ff; "Die Aussichten des juristischen Studiums," *ibid.*, 19 (1932): 70f; M. Beatus, "Academic Proletariat: The Problem of Overcrowding in the Learned Professions and Universities during the Weimar Republic, 1918–1933" (Diss., Madison, Wisc., 1975), p. 221.

27. E. Simon, "Der philologische Nachwuchs Deutschlands und die Besuchszahlen der höheren Lehranstalten im Lichte der deutschen Hochschulstatistik," *Phbl* 38 (1930): 353; and W. Kullnick, "Nachwuchs und Bedarf an Studienräten in Deutschland," special supplement of the *Deutsche Hochschulstatistik* (Berlin, 1930).

28. "Die Not des Nachwuchses," *Pbhl* 39 (1931): 179f; A. Nath, *Die Studienratskarriere im Dritten Reich* (Frankfurt, 1988), p. 187ff; and R. Bölling, "Lehrerarbeitslosigkeit in Deutschland im 19. und 20. Jahrhundert," *Archiv für Sozialgeschichte* 27 (1987): 233.

29. H. Sikorski, "Der Besuch der deutschen Hochschulen," *VDIN*, May 15, 1929; "Zur Berufsstatistik der deutschen Ingenieure," *ibid.*, Dec. 10, 1929; "Arbeitslose Absolventen," *ibid.*, March 11, 1931; K. Steinmetz, "140,000 Ingenieure," *ZVDDI* 21 (1930): 70.

30. For example, Dr. Achner, "Der Arbeitsmarkt der geistigen Berufe," in *Arzt, Hochschule und Krankenhaus,* Sonderdruck of No. 2, 1932, and G. Müller, "Arbeitslosigkeit bei den Akademikern," *Ärztliche Mitteilungen* 34 (1930): 731ff. versus G. Ried, "Übertreibungen und Zahlenphantasien im Kampf gegen die Überfüllung der Hochschulen und höheren Schulen," *Phbl* 40 (1932): 177ff, 185ff; "Entstellungen und Tatsachen," *ibid.*, p. 389ff; and F. Behrend, ed., *Vom Sinn und Unsinn des Berechtigungswesens* (Leipzig, 1929). Cf. Beatus, "Academic Proletariat," p. 220f.

31. G. Keiser, "Das Hochschulstudium in Deutschland im Sommersemester 1931 unter besonderer Berücksichtigung der Studienratswissenschaften," *Phbl* 39 (1931): 733ff; versus W. Hartnacke, *Bildungswahn—Volkstod!* (Munich, 1932). Cf. H. Titze, "Akademische Ausbildung und Beschäftigungssytem im 20. Jahrhundert" (Ms. Göttingen, 1983).

32. "Preisausschreiben," *Abl* 16 (1929): 1; Dr. L. Levin, *Schutz der freien Rechtsanwaltschaft* (Leipzig, 1930); Dr. Kottmeier, "Zulassungsbeschränkungen?" *Abl* 16 (1929): 145ff; and L. Katz, "Gedeih und Verderb der Anwaltschaft," *ibid.*, p. 212ff, are but a few illustrations.

33. "Aus der Vereinstätigkeit," *Abl* 16 (1929): 228; "Einführung von Zulassungbeschränkungen," *ibid.*, p. 323ff; Dittenberger, "25. Abgeordnetenversammlung des DAV," *ibid.*, 17 (1930): 103ff; A. Pinner, "Nachdenkliches zur AV," *ibid.*, p. 105; *Stenographischer Bericht über die 25. AV* (Leipzig, 1930). Cf. Ostler, *Rechtsanwälte,* p. 213ff.

34. "Warnung vor dem juristischen Studium," *Abl* 18 (1931): 102; "Aus der Vereinstätigkeit,"*ibid.*, p. 76; "Entwürfe von Gesetzen zur Änderung der Rechtsanwaltsordnung und über den juristischen Vorbereitungsdienst," *ibid.*, p. 118ff; "Aus der Vereinstätigkeit," *ibid.*, p. 321.

35. "Lage und Schicksal der deutschen Anwaltschaft!" *Abl* 19 (1932): 369; "Beschlüsse der 29. Abgeordnetenversammlung des DAV zu Berlin," *ibid.*, p. 371; "Vorläufiger Bericht über die 29. AV," *ibid.*, p. 372ff; and *Stenographischer Bericht über die 29. AV* (Berlin, 1932). Cf. Ledford, "The German Bar in Private Practice," p. 311ff.

36. Preußischer PhVb, "Vorstandssitzung am 8. Feb. 1930," *Phbl* 38 (1930): 129ff; "Wann soll die Auslese für die Studienratslaufbahn erfolgen?" *ibid.*, p. 728ff; "Der Preußische PhVb zur Auslese für die Studienratslaufbahn," *ibid.*, 39 (1931): 33ff; W. Bolle, "Leitsätze des PhVb zur Nachwuchsfrage," *ibid.*, 40 (1932): 268. Cf. Westphalian debate on Dec. 13, 1930, WPhV, A10, 53.

37. F. Behrend, "Erinnerungen an die Tätigkeit des PhVb," *HS* 7 (1954): 194f; A. Schlothauer, "Sparprogramm und Assessorennot," *Phbl* 39 (1931): 530ff; W. Bolle, "Anwärterprob-

lem und Berufspolitik,'' *ibid.*, 40 (1932): 265ff; ''Entschließungen des 6. Preußischen Philologentages,'' *ibid.*, p. 505f; board minutes, April 25, June 17, Nov. 23, 1931, WPhV, A10, 53; A. Nath, ''Der Studienassessor im Dritten Reich,'' *ZfP* 27 (1981): 297f.

38. Stg, ''Neue TH?'' *ZVDI* 73 (1929): 472f; ''Neue TH,'' *VDIN* (1929), No. 8; and E. Kothe, ''Der andere Weg zum Ingenieurberuf,'' *ibid.* (1930), No. 16.

39. ''Arbeitslose Absolventen,'' *VDIN,* March 11, 1931; ''Helft den stellungslosen Absolventen!'' *ibid.*, May 20, 1931. Cf. the reports in ZStA Po, Rep. 39.03, Vol. 183, and Viefhaus, ''Ingenieure,'' p. 336f.

40. Dr. Knöpfel, ''Entwicklung des anwaltlichen Tätigkeitsfeldes nach der Reichsstatistik,'' *Abl* 17 (1930): 377ff; and Fr. H. von Hodenberg in *Stenographischer Bericht über die 25. AV,* p. 8ff.

41. ''Zur Verordnung des Reichspräsidenten vom 1. Dez. 1930,'' *Abl* 17 (1930): 345ff; Dittenberger, ''Die Notverordnung vom 1. Dez. 1930 und die Anwaltschaft,'' *ibid.*, p. 352ff; *Stenographischer Bericht über die 25. AV,* p. 9, and Ostler, *Rechtsanwälte,* p. 202ff.

42. L. Katz, ''Gedeih und Verderb der Anwaltschaft,'' p. 213; Dr. Thalheim, ''Über die Einkommenslage der deutschen Rechtsanwälte,'' *JW* 61 (1931): 3497; and *ibid.*, 62 (1932), Nov. issue; *Statistik des Deutschen Reichs,* Vol. 482 (Berlin, 1936), p. 16f; *Stenographischer Bericht über die 25. AV,* pp. 11f, 28; Dr. Münster, ''Notlage der deutschen Anwaltschaft,'' *JW* 61 (1932): 623f; ''Arbeitsamt der deutschen Rechtsanwaltschaft,'' *ibid.*, 59 (1930): 698; Beatus, ''Academic Proletariat,'' 222f.

43. ''Verhängnisvolle Kürzungspläne,'' *Phbl* 37 (1929): 577f; A. Bohlen, ''Unter dem Druck der Finanznot,'' *ibid.*, 38 (1930): 145ff; *idem,* ''Vor einem neuen Sparprogramm,'' *ibid.*, p. 321ff; and ''Die Antwort auf den Notopferplan: Unmöglich!'' *ibid.*, p. 369f; ''Pressestimmen zum Notopferplan,'' *ibid.*, p. 378ff; ''Der RhB beim Reichskanzler,'' *ibid.*, p. 408; A. Bohlen, ''Vor der Entscheidung über das Notopfer,'' *ibid.*, p. 433ff; and H. Brüning, *Memoiren 1918–1934* (Stuttgart, 1970), p. 173f.

44. ''Finanzierung durch Gehaltskürzung,'' *Phbl* 38 (1930): 593; ''Entschließungen des 5. Preußischen Philologentages,'' *ibid.*, p. 649; A. Bohlen, ''Gehaltskürzung durch Notverordnung,'' *ibid.*, p. 769ff; ''Der Verlauf der Preissenkungsaktion,'' *ibid.*, p. 785f; and Brüning, *Memoiren,* p. 209f.

45. ''Gegen den Unfug der Gehaltskürzung!'' *Phbl* 39 (1931): 289; ''Entschließungen und Beschlüsse des 12. Verbandstages des Deutschen PhVb,'' *ibid.*, p. 337f; A. Bohlen, ''Vor der dritten Gehaltskürzung,'' *ibid.*, p. 353ff; and ''Die Notverordnung,'' *ibid.*, p. 369ff. Cf. Bohlen circulars, Feb. 12, June 2, 10, 1931, and Monje RhB report, May 8, 1931, WPhV, B40, 540.

46. ''Vor schweren Eingriffen,'' *Phbl* 39 (1931): 529; ''Katastrophale Sparmaßnahmen in Preußen?'' *ibid.*, p. 545; ''Schützt den Beamten noch das Recht?'' *ibid.*, p. 573; ''Notverordnung gegen die höhere Schule,'' *ibid.*, p. 561f; ''Protest der Großberliner Philologenschaft,'' *ibid.*, p. 563f; A. Bohlen, ''Notverordnungs-Willkür,'' *ibid.*, p. 621ff. Bohlen circulars, July 6, Aug. 10, 31, 1931, WPhV, B40, 540. Cf. Deutscher Städtetag, *Selbsthilfe der deutschen Städte* (Berlin, 1931) and *Geschäftsmann und Beamter* (Darmstadt, 1931).

47. E. Brüser, ''Revision der Kürzungspolitik tut not!'' *Phbl* 39 (1931): 645f; ''Der schwerste Schlag,'' *ibid.*, p. 721; W. Bolle, ''Eine erschütternde Jahresbilanz,'' *ibid.*, 40 (1932): 1ff. Bohlen reports, Sept. 1, 1931 ff, WPhV, B40, 540; board minutes, Jan. 21, 1932, *ibid.*, A10, 53 and F5; and Brüning, *Memoiren,* p. 371ff.

48. ''Schärfster Kampf gegen die fünfte Gehaltskürzung,'' *Phbl* 40 (1932): 269; Preußischer PhVb, ''Sitzung des Gesamtvorstandes,'' *ibid.*, p. 274f; ''Entschließungen des 6. Preußischen Philologentages,'' *ibid.*, p. 505f; A. Schlothauer, ''Sparprogramm und Assessorennot,'' *ibid.*, 39 (1931): 530ff; and ''Schrumpfung und Überfüllung,'' *ibid.*, 40 (1932): 176ff; and A. Bohlen, *Die Lebenshaltung der höheren Beamten* (Leipzig, 1932). Figures from Nath, ''Studienassessor,'' p. 283f.

49. Unfortunately, no figures are available. Cf. O. Hollbach, ''Die Lage der Ingenieure,'' *Die Lage der akademischen Berufe* (Berlin, 1932).

50. K. Steinmetz, ''Vom Arbeitsmarkt der Diplom-Ingenieure,'' *ZVDDI* 21 (1930): 160ff; *ibid.*, 24 (1933): 13f; ''Das Jahr 1931,'' *ZVDI* 76 (1932): 391ff; annual report for 1932, *VDIN,* March 1, 1933; and B. Gleitze, ''Die Berufszählung der technischen Berufe,'' *ZVDI* 79 (1935): 1342f.

51. R. Dix, "Das Festbankett der Berliner Anwaltschaft," *Abl* 16 (1929): 37f; J. Magnus, "Zum neuen Jahre!" *JW* 59 (1930): 1ff; and *ibid.*, 60 (1931): 1f; Thalheim, "Einkommen," *ibid.*, p. 3497f; "Pressekonferenz des DAV," *ibid.*, p. 161f.

52. P. Mellmann, "25 Jahre Deutscher Philologenverband," *Phbl* 37 (1929): 337ff.

53. W. Hohmann, "Der Philologe im Spiegel der öffentlichen Meinung," *Phbl* 39 (1931): 103ff; and Preussischer PhVb, "Berufspolitisches Programm," *ibid.*, p. 472f.

54. "Weihe des Denkmals in Alexisbad," *ZVDI* 75 (1931): 665f; Dr. Köttgen, "75 Jahre VDI," *ibid.*, p. 801ff.

55. W. Schwenke, "Sind Diplom-Ingenieure 'Vollakademiker'?" *ZVDDI* 21 (1930): 51f; K. Steinmetz, "Standesdünkel—Kastengeist," *ibid.*, p. 165; T. Geiger, *Die Soziale Schichtung des deutschen Volkes* (Stuttgart, 1932).

56. S. Neumann, *Nacht über Deutschland* (Munich, 1978), p. 71ff; H. Dittenberger, "Die Lage der Rechtsanwaltschaft," *Akademische Berufe;* and Ostler, *Rechtsanwälte,* p. 202ff.

57. A. Oppenheimer, "Fachanwaltschaft?" *Abl* 16 (1929): 47f; *Stenographischer Bericht über den 24. Deutschen Anwaltstag Hamburg* (Leipzig, 1929); "Fachanwaltschaft," *Abl* 17 (1930): 50; "Aus der Vereinstätigkeit," *ibid.*, p. 163; A. Pinner, "Die Fachanwaltschaft als wirtschaftliches Problem," *ibid.*, p. 219f; "Richtlinien für die Fachanwaltschaft," *Abl* 18 (1931): 12f.

58. A. Besser, "Die Berliner Vollstreckungshilfe," *Abl* 18 (1931): 87f; *idem,* "Das Reich der tausend 'Aber'," *ibid.*, p. 196ff; and "Die Vollstreckungshilfe," *ibid.*, p. 341ff, for further reports.

59. "Weitere Verstärkung der barbarischen Belastung," *Phbl* 39 (1931): 129; Preußischer PhVb, "Berufspolitisches Programm," *ibid.*, p. 472; G. Müller, "Die berufliche Lage bei den Philologen," *Akademische Berufe;* board minutes, Nov. 28, Dec. 13, 1930, July 30, 1931, and resolution of Feb. 20, 1932, WPhV, A10, 53. Cf. R. Engelsing, *Der literarische Arbeiter* (Göttingen, 1976), p. 68f.

60. "140,000 Ingenieure," *VDIN,* Jan. 29, 1930; W. Hellmich, "Ingenieurarbeit," *ZVDI* 75 (1931): 1ff; Hettner, "Vom Ingenieurneuland," *VDIN,* Dec. 23, 1931; and W. Hellmich, "Ingenieurneuland in der Verwaltung," *ibid.*, March 16, 1932.

61. S. Feuchtwanger, "Idee und Wirklichkeit in der deutschen Anwaltspolitik," *JW* 61 (1932): 1091ff; Siehr, "Anwalt, Volk und Staat," *Abl* 16 (1929): 229f; "Der 25. Band der Entscheidungen des EGH," *ibid.*, 19 (1932): 124f. Cf. Ledford, "The German Bar in Private Practice," p. 224ff.

62. R. Bauer, "Götzendämmerung im Anwaltstand," *Abl* 17 (1930): 55f; A. Pinner *et al.*, "Zur Frage der Gebührenlockerung," *ibid.*, p. 318ff; H. F. Abraham, "Gebührenlockerung und Zweiteilung der Anwaltschaft," *ibid.*, p. 369f; R. Bauer, "Zur Frage der Gebührenlockerung," *ibid.*, 18 (1931): 21f; "Beschlüsse der 27. Abgeordnetenversammlung," *ibid.*, p. 105; and Dittenberger, "27. AV," *ibid.*, p. 111f.

63. "Reform der RAO. Denkschrift nebst Gesetzentwurf und Begründung," *Abl* 17 (1930): 231ff; Dittenberger, "26. AV des DAV," *ibid.*, p. 313ff.

64. N. Hammerstein, ed., *Deutsche Bildung?* (Frankfurt, 1988), p. 15–54; F. Behrend, "Die Entwicklung der deutschen Schulpolitik seit der Reichsschulkonferenz," *Phbl* 37 (1929): 341f; A. Bohlen, "Wirtschaftsabbau—Kulturabbau," *ibid.*, 40 (1932): 540.

65. K. Jarausch, "Moderne Pädagogik und Disziplin," *Phbl* 39 (1931): 356ff; *idem,* review of W. Farber, *Die Schule in Staat und Volk* (Berlin, 1931), in *SE* 6 (1931–1932): 52f; *idem,* "Die Kulturpädagogik und der wirkliche Mensch," *ibid.*, 222ff; "Schulpolitische Tendenzen der Gegenwart," *Phbl* 40 (1932): 507; W. Bolle, "Rückblick und Ausblick," *ibid.*, 38 (1930): 1ff; Hamburger, "Pädagogische und politische Orientierung," p. 264ff.

66. W. von Pasinski, "Von der Technik zur Kultur," *ZVDDI* 20 (1929): 99ff; 180ff; A. Stodola, "Gedanken zu einer Weltanschauung vom Standpunkte des Ingenieurs," *ZVDI* 75 (1931): 1228; R. Plank, "Die Stellung der Technik im Rahmen moderner Kultur," *ibid.*, p. 641ff; C. Matschoß, "Vom Sinn der Technik," *ibid.*, 76 (1932): 23f.

67. F. Reuter, "Wandlungen in den deutschen Kulturzentren?" *ZVDDI* 20 (1929): 222ff, and rejoinders, *ibid.*, 21 (1930): 46ff; and *ibid.*, 22 (1931): 2ff; H. Blüher, "Kulturwende und Ingenieur," *ibid.*, 21 (1930): 169ff; A. Nägel, "Technik in der Wirtschaftskrise," *ZVDI* 76 (1932): 329ff; E. Diesel, "Zum gerechten Urteil über die Technik," *VDIN,* July 6, 1932; and K. M. Wild, "Vom Sinn der Technik," *ibid.*, Oct. 19, 1932.

68. K. Kaßler, "Zur Frage der Bezirksgruppen," *Abl* 16 (1929): 162f; "Änderung der Satzung des DAV," *ibid.*, 17 (1930): 257f; "Die Ausschüsse des Vorstandes des DAV," *ibid.*, 16 (1929): 192ff.

69. R. Bauer, "Die Abgeordneten," *Abl* 18 (1931): 237f; Hawlitzky, "Die Wahlen," *ibid.*, p. 263f; "Reichswahlvorschläge für die Wahlen zur AV des DAV 1931," *ibid.*, p. 258f; "Verzeichnis der Mitglieder der AV," *ibid.*, 19 (1932): 155f; "Vereinsnachrichten," *ibid.*, p. 257ff; P. Posener, "Verbandsdisziplin," *ibid.*, p. 319f.

70. R. Robinow, "Reichsanwaltskammer," *Abl* 16 (1929): 124ff; "Beschlüsse der 23. AV des DAV," *ibid.*, p. 138f; "Aus dem Vereinsleben," *ibid.* 19 (1932): 159f; "Entwurf eines Gesetzes über die Reichsrechtsanwaltskammer," *ibid.*, p. 170f.

71. Dittenberger, "26. AV des DAV," *Abl* 17 (1930): 313f; "Beschlüsse der 28. AV des DAV," *ibid.*, 19 (1932): 114 (on the close vote of seventy-nine to sixty-five); Dittenberger, "Die Tagung der AV," *ibid.*, p. 121f, and *Bericht über die Geschäfte des DAV* (Leipzig, 1931), p. 40.

72. P. Mellmann, "50 Jahre Preußischer PhVb," *Phbl* 39 (1931): 611ff; A. Bohlen, "Die Standespolitischen Aufgaben des Deutschen PhVb," *ibid.*, 38 (1930): 345ff; G. Ried, "Wirkungsmöglichkeiten und Wirkungsgrenzen des Deutschen PhVb," *ibid.*, p. 506ff; W. Bolle, "Enttäuschungen und Hoffnungen," *Phbl* 39 (1931): 1ff.

73. Preußischer PhVb circular, Feb. 20, 1930; WPhV, "Das Stimmrecht der AGs in den Verbandskörperschaften," March 26, 1930; Preußischer PhVb, "Vorstandssitzung am 30/31. Mai," WPhV, U55, 549; board minutes, Aug. 1, 1929, Jan. 17, Feb. 24, 1930, Nov. 23, 1931, in WPhV, A10, 53; Preußischer PhVb, "Bericht über die Sitzung des GV Ausschusses am 20. 6. 1930," *ibid.*, B43, 543; G. Ried, "Entstellungen und Tatsachen," *ibid.*, p. 389ff. Cf. Nath, "Studienassessor," p. 302.

74. C. Köttgen, "75 Jahre VDI," *ZVDI* 75 (1931): 801ff; C. Matschoß, "VDI Geschäftsbericht 1932," *VDIN*, (1933), No. 9; R. Stahlschmidt, "Der Ausbau der technisch-wissenschaftlichen Gemeinschaftsarbeit 1918 bis 1938," *Technik*, p. 347ff; and Heuser-König," Tabellarische Zusammenstellungen," in Ludwig, ed., *Technik*, p. 559ff.

75. "Diplom-Ingenieur-Tagung 1929," *ZVDDI* 20 (1929), No. 6; "20 Jahre VDDI," *ibid.*, p. 122ff; "Berichte des Verbandsvorstandes," *ibid.*, p. 129f; "Von der ordentlichen Ausschusstagung 1930," *ibid.*, 21 (1931): 24ff.

76. Bohlen analysis in board meeting, Feb. 29, 1932, WPhV, A10, 53; memorandum on "Aussprache über Fragen des höheren Schulwesens," May 8 and 9, 1931, ZStA Po, Rep. 49.01, 4568; Altendorf quoted in circular 19 of 1932, *ibid.*, Rep. 70 Re. 1, 457; "Der Staat in der Vertrauenskrise," *Phbl* 40 (1932): 391f. Cf. M. Kater," "Physicians in Crisis at the End of the Weimar Republic," in P. Stachura, ed., *Unemployment and the Great Depression in Weimar Germany* (London, 1986), pp. 49–77.

77. R. Schairer, *Die akademische Berufsnot. Tatsachen und Auswege* (Jena, 1932). He proposed postponing study by a year of compulsory work, a sabbatical for professionals to create demand, as well as sharper selection. Cf. Schairer to Grimme, Aug. 21, 1930, ZStA Me, Rep. 76 Va, Sekt. 1, Tit. VII, Vol. 122. Cf. K. Jarausch, "The Decline of Liberal Professionalism," in *idem* and L. E. Jones, eds., *In Search of a Liberal Germany* (Oxford, 1990), pp. 261–286.

78. For example, DAV to Prussian Ministry of Justice, Feb. 2, 1928, "Die Notlage der Rechtsanwaltschaft und die Mittel zu ihrer Abhilfe," in PrGStA Da, Rep. 84a, No. 106. For the Akademische Berufsberatung cf. ZStA Po, Rep. 15.01, Nos. 2691f or ZStA Me, Rep. 76 Va, Sekt. 1, Tit. I, No. 38; and for the Akademikerhilfe, ZStA Po, Rep. 39.03, Nos. 189f.

79. Löwe memorandum, Dec. 9, 1930, "Die zahlenmäßige Entwicklung des Hochschulstudiums . . ."; Bund angestellter Akademiker der technisch-naturwissenschaftlichen Berufe petition, Nov. 2, 1931; E. Kelter, "Denkschrift über das Problem der Überfüllung der Hochschulen und der akademischen Berufe," n.d., in ZStA Me, Rep. 76 Va, Sekt. 1, Tit. I, No. 7, Vol. I. Cf. *ibid.*, No. 7A for a clipping file.

80. "Eine volkswirtschaftliche Zentralstelle für Hochschulwesen," *Kölner Zeitung*, Feb. 3, 1930; "Satzung der VWZfH," spring 1930; "Aufzeichnung über Arbeitsplan und Mittelbedarf der VWZfH im Rechnungsjahr 1931/2"; Grimme to finance minister, Aug. 21, 1930; Kickhöffel to Kähler, Dec. 19, 1932; pamphlet series *Zur Lage der akademischen Berufe;* J. Müller, "Die

juristischen Prüfungen im Deutschen Reich seit 1900,'' ZStA Me, Rep. 76 Va, Sekt. 1, Tit. VII, No. 121.

81. Invitation of Reichsministerium des Inneren, June 27, 1930 and report of meeting of July 2, ZStA Me, Rep. 76 Va, Sekt 1, Tit. VII, No. 123; ''Niederschrift über die 9. Sitzung des Ausschusses für das Unterrichtswesen im RdI vom 10. Feb. 1931,'' ZStA Me, Rep. 76 Va, Sekt. 1, Tit. I, No. 7, Vol. II. Cf. Nath, *Studienratskarriere*, p. 183ff.

82. W. Groener circular, Jan. 2, 1932; H. Richert note of Feb. 3, 1932; Pellengahr summary of the Jan. 23 meeting; ''Niederschrift der 2. Sitzung des Ausschusses für die Frage der Überfüllung der Hochschulen und die Arbeitsbeschaffung der Jugendlichen'' in ZStA Me, Rep. 76 Va, Sekt. 1, Tit. VII, No. 122; and report on the RdI session of Jan. 23, 1932 in ZStA Me, Rep. 76 Va, Sekt. 1, Tit. I, No. 7, Vol. II.

83. Grimme to RdI, May 23, 1932; ''Bericht über die Verhandlungen der deutschen Hochschulkonferenz in Dresden;'' Grave to Grimme, June 28; and Prussian ministry circular, Oct. 28, 1932 in ZStA Me, Rep. 76 Va, Sekt. 1, Tit. 1, No. 7, Vol. II; overcrowding committee, ''Entwurf einer Denkschrift für das RdI,'' July 15, 1932 with contributions by Spranger, Heidebroek, Weinstock, Schairer, Löffler, Niessen, Bäumer, and Sikorsky; final draft of the memorandum by Schairer, Nov. 9, 1932, in ZStA Me, Rep. 76 Va, Sekt. 1, Tit. VII, No. 122.

84. O. Everling, *Der Zusammenschluß deutscher Geistesarbeiter* (Berlin, 1930); *idem, Von Wert und von der Not der geistigen Arbeit* (Berlin, 1932); and *idem, Akademische Berufsverbände und akademische Berufsnot* (Berlin, 1933). Cf. the cartel's report for 1931 and constitution in ZStA Me, Rep. 76 Va, Sekt. 1, Tit. VII, No. 122.

85. S. Feuchtwanger, *Der Staat und die freien Berufe. Staatsamt oder Sozialamt?* (Königsberg, 1929); and ''Grundsätzliches zur Frage der Selbsthilfe,'' *JW* 61 (1932): 1091ff. R. Bendix, *Von Berlin nach Berkeley* (Frankfurt, 1985), p. 181ff, slights his father's legal socialism.

86. For example, Dr. Jacobson, ''Das Gebot der Stunde,'' *Abl* 16 (1929): 19ff; ''Gutachten zur Genossenschaftsfrage'' by M. Krauel and Dr. Ihde, *ibid.*, p. 48ff; ''Zur Verteilung der Armensachen,'' *ibid.*, 17 (1930): 24ff; ''Gestaltung des Sozietätsverhältnisses,'' *ibid.*, p. 154f; Dr. Katinszky, ''Hausanwalt—Anwalthaus?'' *ibid.*, 19 (1932): 54f; ''Rechtsauskunftsstelle des Leipziger Anwaltvereins,'' *ibid.*, 18 (1931): 344ff.

87. Preußischer PhVb, ''Sitzung des Gesamtvorstandes vom 18. März 1932,'' *Phbl* 40 (1932): 149ff; ''Sitzung des Gesamtvorstandes am 11./12. Juni 1932,'' *ibid.*, p. 273ff; ''Leitsätze des Deutschen PhVb zur Nachwuchsfrage,'' *ibid.*, p. 268; ''Entschliessungen des 6. Preußischen Philologentages,'' *ibid.*, p. 505f; and W. Siedentrop, ''6. Preußischer Philologentag in Potsdam,'' *ibid.*, p. 529. Cf. board minutes, Feb. 29 and May 13, 1932, WPhV, A10, 53.

88. G. Cleinow, ''Neurußland und Deutschland,'' *ZVDDI* 19 (1928): 60f; Dr. Fleming, ''Die Ausbaupläne der russischen Elektroindustrie,'' *ibid.*, 20 (1929): 139; Prof. Dettmar, ''Deutsche Technik und Industrie in Sowjet-Rußland,'' *VDIN*, Aug. 21, 1929; ''Von der ordentlichen Ausschußtagung 1930,'' *ZVDDI* 22 (1931): 24f; and K. Zuse, *Der Computer, mein Lebenswerk* (Munich, 1970), p. 26ff.

89. ''Demokratische Anwalts-Vereinigung,'' *VZ*, March 6, 1928; Menzel of the Reich Ministry of Interior to the Nachrichtendienststellen of the states, Dec. 31, 1931 with fee schedule and list of names. Ostler mentions neither group in *Rechtsanwälte*. For further biographical information see Kritische Justiz, ed., *Streitbare Juristen*, pp. 153–203.

90. H. Breitgoff, ''Theorie und Praxis der 'Arbeitsgemeinschaft sozial-demokratischer Lehrer und Lehrerinnen' (AsL) 1919–1922,'' in Krause-Vilmar, ed., *Lehrerschaft*, 25ff; W. Stöhr, *Lehrer und Arbeiterbewegung* (Marburg, 1978); Bölling, ''Lehrerschaft, Schulpolitik und Arbeiterbewegung in der Weimarer Republik,'' *Archiv für Sozialgeschichte* 21 (1981): 602ff; and Ch. Seeligmann, ''Der Deutsche Republikanische Lehrerbund in der Weimarer Republik,'' *Jahrbuch des Instituts für deutsche Geschichte* 7 (1979): 365ff.

91. J. Kocka, *Die Angestellten* (Göttingen, 1981) p. 144ff. Ludwig, *Technik*, does not bother to mention it. Cf. F. Walter, ''Der Verband Sozialdemokratischer Akademiker'' (Ms., Detmold, 1987). For association membership figures cf. the *Jahrbuch der Berufsverbände*, a *Sonderheft* of the *Reichsarbeitsstatistik* for 1920, 1925, and 1930, Vols. 22, 30, and 52.

92. ''Aus der Vereinstätigkeit,'' quoting from a bill to outlaw legal consultants, *Abl* 19 (1932): 284; R. Bauer, ''Reklame,'' *ibid.*, 16 (1929): 290ff; and S. Feuchtwanger, ''Gedanken über die Grenzen der Wirksamkeit der Standespolizei,'' *ibid.*, p. 175ff.

93. "Die höhere Schule den Philologen," *Phbl* 40 (1932): 128f; Preussischer PhVb, "Sitzung des Gesamtvorstandes am 11. und 12. June 1932," *ibid.*, p. 773ff; "Entschließungen des 6. Preußischen Philologentages," *ibid.*, p. 505; "6. Preußischer Philologentag in Potsdam," *ibid.*, p. 531.

94. "Angelegenheiten des Vereins. Das Jahr 1931," *ZVDI* 76 (1932): 391ff; C. Matschoß, "VDI Geschäftsbericht 1932," *VDIN* (1933), No. 9; F. Romberg, "Zum Jahresschluß," *ZVDDI* 24 (1933): 1ff.

95. Dr. Richard Finger, *Die Sendung des Rechtsanwalts* (Munich, 1930), pp. 9f, 15f, 26, 44, 48, 90f, 140.

96. Hartnacke, *Bildungswahn—Volkstod!* This diatribe originated in a lecture for the German Society for Racial Hygiene, held at Munich University in Feb. 1932. Hartnacke's warnings were discussed even by engineers: "Bildungswahn," *VDIN* (1932), No. 35. Cf. *idem, Die Überfüllung der akademischen Berufe* (Dresden, 1932): and K. Jarausch, "Naturgrenzen geistiger Bildung," *SE* 7 (1932–1933): 95ff.

97. A. Nägel, "Technik und Wirtschaftskrise," *ZVDI* 76 (1932): 320ff; H. Hardensett, "Die Techniktheorie des technischen Menschen," *ZVDDI* 24 (1932): 3ff; and Romberg, "Zum Jahresschluß," *ibid.*, p. 1ff. Cf. Herf, *Reactionary Modernism*, p. 180ff.

98. H. Frank, *Im Angesicht des Galgens* (Munich, 1953); "Aufruf!" *VB*, Nov. 13, 1928; "BNSDJ," *Bayern-Kurier*, both in BA, NS 16, No. 112. Cf. N. Frank, *Der Vater. Eine Abrechnung* (Munich, 1987), p. 27ff; and K. Willig, "The Theory and Administration of Justice in the Third Reich" (Diss., Philadelphia, 1975), p. 334ff.

99. Frank, *Angesicht*, pp. 70, 84ff; H. Düx, "Hans Litten," *Streitbare Juristen*, p. 193f; membership list of Jan. 1, 1931, BA, NS 16, No. 112. Other figures from Willig, "Theory and Administration of Justice," p. 335f. Not all jurist party members joined the league.

100. Frank, *Angesicht*, p. 87; Rechtspolitische Abteilung to G. Strasser, July 2, 1932, BA, NS 16, No. 112.

101. M. Reiter, "Zur Einführung," *DR* 1 (1931): 1f; H. Frank, "Erwachen des Deutschen Rechts," *DR* 1 (1931): 3ff; F. Mößmer, "Eherecht," *ibid.*, p. 20ff; "Stellenvermittlung," *ibid.*, p. 152; G. Lind, "Deutsche Rechtsnot," *ibid.*, 2 (1932): 9ff; "3. Reichstagung des BNSDJ," *ibid.*, p. 225ff. Cf. H. Heydeloff, "Staranwalt der Rechtsextremisten," *VfZG* 23 (1984): 373ff.

102. Schemm memorandum, "Der NSLB, seine Gründung, sein Wirken und Wachsen, seine Bedeutung und die ersten schulpolitischen Maßnahmen nach der Machtergreifung" (summer 1933), IfZG Archive. P. G. Herrmann, *Zehn Jahre NSLB* (Munich, 1939), p. 9ff. Cf. W. Feiten, *Der NSLB. Entwicklung und Organisation* (Frankfurt, 1981), p. 40ff; and C. Seeligmann, "Vorläufer des NSLB," in Heinemann, ed., *Der Lehrer*, p. 305ff.

103. The confusion about the founding date results from Herrmann's 1939 publication, which was designed to praise Schemm's successor Wächtler, while the 1933 memorandum clearly mentions 1927 as "the birth hour." Feiten, *NSLB*, p. 43f. Membership numbers from the NSLB file in the BDC and profile from "Die ältesten Mitglieder des NSLB," *RDE* (1936), No. 1. Cf. Bressler to Schemm, "Notwendigkeit der Hochschulbildung der Volksschullehrer," Dec. 17, 1930, versus Dr. K. Zimmermann, "Nationalsozialismus und Lehrerbildung," and other material in BA, NS 12, No. 640.

104. H. Schemm, *Denkschrift*, "Der NSLB," points E–S; "Unsere deutsche Schule, ein Schacherobjekt der Schwarzen und Roten," *RDE* (Nov. 1930), No. 5; Schemm, "Vorankündigung," BA, NS 12, No. 620; NSLB, "Rundschreiben No. 8, *ibid.*, No. 780; Feiten, *NSLB*, p. 46ff; "NS Lehrer tagen," special issue of *RDE* (1932), No. 5. Cf. H. Scharrelmann, *Goldene Heimat* (Hamburg, 1908).

105. P. Schwerber, *Nationalsozialismus und Technik. Die Geistigkeit der NS Bewegung* (Munich, 1930); F. Lawaczeck, *Technik und Wirtschaft im Dritten Reich. Ein Arbeitsbeschaffungsprogramm* (Munich, 1932). Cf. J. C. Guse, "The Spirit of the Plassenburg: Technology and Ideology in the Third Reich" (Diss., Lincoln, Neb., 1981); and Herf, *Reactionary Modernism*, p. 192f.

106. Ludwig, *Technik*, p. 73ff; and Guse, "Plassenburg," p. 37–84. Few primary sources on the KDAI have survived.

107. M. H. Kater, *The Nazi Party. A Social Profile of Members and Leaders 1919–1945* (Cambridge, Mass., 1983). His sampling method is described in "Quantifizierung und NS-

Geschichte: Methodologische Überlegungen über Grenzen und Möglichkeiten einer EDV-Analyse der NSDAP-Sozialstruktur von 1925 bis 1945," *GG* (1975): 472ff. Cf. *Volks-, Berufs- und Betriebszählung vom 16. Juni 1933,* Vol. 453 of the *Statistik des Deutschen Reichs* (Berlin, 1933).

108. I would like to acknowledge Prof. Kater's generosity in making this important source available. In contrast to *Nazi Party,* which selected 15,343 complete cases from the first 18,255 individuals, the present analysis used all entries in his notebooks.

109. The accuracy of the index rests on the exactness of the dividend and the divisor. The census identifies many professions unambiguously, but blurs other distinctions such as TH versus HTL engineers. Many of the officials under "semiprofessionals" are actually university graduates, but it was impossible to disaggregate the total according to education. The engineering numbers represent estimates. In coding occupations, the census instructions were followed for reasons of comparability and consistency. Because it was impossible to find census figures for academic farmers (16), *Diplom-Volkswirte* (26), or trainees (59), 101 cases had to be omitted.

110. Kater, *Nazi Party,* pp. 32ff, 51ff, for the older literature. Ludwig, *Technik,* p. 106f, claims that "engineers . . . should not have been overrepresented in the NSDAP." The data were statistically processed with SPSS/PC. For the methodology cf. K. Jarausch, *Quantitative Methoden in der Geschichtswissenschaft* (Wiesbaden, 1985).

111. "BNSDJ Mitgliederverzeichnis per 1. Jan. 1931," BA, NS 16, No. 112; BNSDJ, "Mitgliederverzeichnis vom 1. Okt. 1931," NSDAP Hauptarchiv, Folder 1868, Reel 90, Frame 93f. Cf. K. Jarausch, "Jewish Lawyers in Germany, 1848–1938: The Breakdown of a Professional Symbiosis," forthcoming in *Yearbook of the Leo Baeck Institute* (1990).

112. The NSLB cards in the BDC are in 451 alphabetized metal drawers, each averaging approximately 1000 cards, indicating a total Third Reich membership of about 450,000. The first ten cards of every drawer were photocopied and transformed into an SPSS file, thereby assuring each letter of the alphabet an equal chance of representation. The stratified pre-1933 sample was created by pulling out all such cases in every forty-fifth drawer. To keep the proportion of post-1932 members correct, the number of later Nazis was multiplied by the appropriate factor.

113. Of the sample, 6.7 percent were pensioned, while 40.6 percent of the teachers were still single. The *Oberlehrer* present a particular problem, because this traditional term for academic secondary schoolteachers began to migrate downward after the introduction of the *Studienrat.*

114. "Disziplinarurteil gegen Lehrer X wegen Zugehörigkeit zur NSDAP," *DR* 1 (1931): 106ff. "Beteiligung eines Beamten an der NSDAP begründet ein Dienstvergehen," *Phbl* 39 (1931): 300.

115. NSLB Untergau Niederschlesien, "Mitgliederverzeichnis aufgestellt am 31. Dez. 1932," BA, NS 12, No. 1068.

116. W. Breyvogel, "Volksschullehrer und Faschismus," in Heinemann, ed., *Lehrer,* 317ff; and Kater, "Hitlerjugend und Schule im Dritten Reich," *HZ* 228 (1979): 606ff. The latter's figure of 2.1 percent pre-1933 members is too low, because it is not based on the population at risk, in other words, those NSLB birth cohorts who were old enough to be teachers before 1933!

117. For full documentation and detailed statistical explanation cf. K. Jarausch and G. Arminger, "The German Teaching Profession and National Socialism: A Demographic Logit Model for Nazi Party Membership," *Journal of Interdisciplinary History* 20 (1989): 197–225.

118. The values for "religion" are (1) Protestant, (2) Catholic, (3) none; for "residence," (1) rural, (2) urban; for "cohort," (1) empire, (2) late empire, (3) early Weimar, (4) late Weimar, (5) Third Reich; for "sex," (1) male, (2) female. In this procedure the coefficients vary between −3 and +3 while the direction of the relationship is indicated by plus or minus. The first category of each independent variable is always used as the reference point.

119. H. Frank, "Erwachen des Deutschen Rechts," *DR* 1 (1931): 3ff; S. Neumann, *Nacht über Deutschland,* p. 52f; K. H. Jarausch, *Students, Society and Politics in Imperial Germany: The Rise of Academic Illiberalism* (Princeton, N.J., 1983), p. 95ff; and discussions during the colloquium on "Sozialstruktur und politische Konflikte in Deutschland," edited by H. Best as *Politik und Milieu* (St. Katharinen, 1989).

120. Seven passed in machine building and nine in electronics. Cf. H. Harnisch-Niessing,

"Frauen in der Technik," *ZVDDI* 17 (1930): 146f, and I. Knott-ter Mer, "Die Frau als Ingenieur," *VDIN*, June 11, 1929.

121. H. Förster, "Um Stellung und Beruf der Frau," *RDE* (1932), No. 7; R. Evans, "German Women and the Triumph of Hitler," *JMH* 48 (1976): DA IV; C. Huerkamp, "Frauen, Universitäten und Bildungsbürgertum," *Bürgerliche Berufe*, p. 200ff; and J. Stephenson, "Women and the Professions in Germany, 1900–1945," in G. Cocks and K. H. Jarausch, *eds., German Professions* (New York, 1990), p. 270ff.

122. W. Bolle, "Rückblick und Ausblick," *Phbl* 38 (1930): 1ff; G. Müller, "Die seelische Lage unserer Jugend angesichts der verzweifelten Berufsaussichten," *ibid.*, 39 (1931); and W. Bolle, "Not der Jugend und Kampf der Generationen," *ibid.*, p. 709ff. Secondary schoolteachers were particularly sensitive to generational resentment because they encountered it daily in their pupils.

123. P. Jessen, "Anwaltjugend," *Abl* 16 (1929): 266ff; "Reichsbund Deutscher Referendare," *JW* 58 (1929): 567f; "Entschließungen des 6. Preußischen Philologentages," *Phbl* 40 (1932): 505; E. Kothe, "Denen, die nach uns kommen," *VDIN*, Dec. 11, 1931; "Für die Jungingenieure," *ibid.*, Dec. 23, 1931; "Forschung im freiwilligen Arbeitsdienst," *ibid.*, Aug. 10, 1932. Cf. Nath, *Studienratskarriere*, p. 233ff; and W. Heintzeler, *Der rote Faden* (Stuttgart, 1983), p. 24ff.

124. NSLB to A. Hörmann, Aug. 14, 1931, BA, NS 12, 640; memo of the Philologische Fachschaft at Leipzig, Nov. 23, 1931, BA NS 12, No. 790. H. Mommsen, "Generationskonflikt und Jugendrevolte in der Weimarer Republik," T. Koebner *et al.*, eds., *Der Mythos Jugend* (Frankfurt, 1985), p. 50ff; M. Kater, "Generationskonflikt als Entwicklungsfaktor in der NS-Bewegung vor 1933," *GG* 11 (1985): 215ff. The cohort approach has difficulty in defining temporal boundaries, addressing changes in generational tension and incorporating the economic dimension.

125. R. Zeiser, "Die Reichsjunglehrerschaft beim Eintritt in das Wintersemester 1932/3," BA, NS 12, No. 640; "Ein Kennzeichen des Systems: Das 'Assessoren-Elend'," *RDE* (1931), No. 3. In the Weimar crisis, social and political issues were more important for the young than wartime psychological problems. Cf. P. Loewenberg, "The Psychohistorical Origins of the Nazi Youth Cohort," *AHR* 76 (1971): 1457ff.

126. Because the just-mentioned model explains only the variance equivalent to a multiple-regression coefficient of 0.374, the rest of the effect needs to be interpreted through qualitative factors. Urbanity and residence largely play a facilitating role, because they suggest where the Nazis made inroads into the professions (such as cities where there was a critical mass and regions where the movement as a whole was strong), rather than why they did succeed.

127. G. Kaiser, "Politischer Lebenslauf," Oct. 16, 1938, BDC, NSLB file; W. Braun to NSLB, July 22, 1932, BA, NS 12, No. 636. Ever since Theodore Abel's research on *The Nazi Movement: Why Hitler Came to Power* (New York, 1938), historical social scientists have been trying to separate fact from fiction. Cf. P. Merkel, *Political Violence under the Swastika* (Princeton, N. J., 1975).

128. "Lebenslauf des Professors Dr. Kötteritz," Aug. 16, 1931, BA, NS 12, No. 640; F. Ochs to NSLB, Jan. 15, 1934, and c.v. of Emil Zirkel, in BDC, NSLB file. For persecution see F. Düssel or M. Haberl, *ibid.*, as well as the c.v. of engineer Hans Alzinger and the petition of A. Schweizer, May 12, 1935, *ibid.*, NSBDT file. Cf. L. Stokes, "Professionals and National Socialism," *GSR* 8 (1985): 449ff.

129. Schemm, *Denkschrift*, points S and T; Reiter, "Zur Einführung," *DR* 1 (1931): 1f; "Vorankündigung, Reichstagung des NSLB," BA, NS 12, No. 620.

130. Schemm, "NLSB Rundschreiben No. 8," March 1, 1932, BA, NS 12, No. 780; and NSLB to Professor Kötteritz, Aug. 31, 1931, *ibid.*, No. 640.

131. "Zu den Vorgängen in Goslar," *Phbl* 37 (1929): 657; "Staatsgesinnung—Staatserziehung—Staatsfeiern," *ibid.*, pp. 473, 693ff. In the Goslar scandal, the PhVb protested against Minister Becker's claim that pupil chauvinism derived from "the failure of school and family," thereby protecting the nationalists who were coresponsible. Cf. Lande in "Fragen des höheren Schulwesens," ZStA Po, Rep. 49.01, 4568.

132. Deutscher PhVb board minutes, March 16 and 17, 1929, WPhV, B46, 546; Westpha-

lian board minutes, Dec. 6, 1929, *ibid.*, A10, 53; material in WPhV, J9, 596; PhVb to Ministry of Culture, Jan. 9, 1929, ZStA Po, Rep. 49.01, 6581; Oskar von Miller, "Von Österreichs Ingenieurarbeiten," *ZVDI* 74 (1930): 1285; "Deutsche Ingenieure in Wien," *VDIN*, Sept. 24, 1930.

133. "Befreites deutsche Land!" *Phbl* 38 (1930), No. 27; "Zu Hindenburg's 85. Geburtstag," *Abl* 17 (1930): 280; W. Schmidt, "Die Suche nach dem besten Kreuzer," *ZVDI* 75 (1931): 367f; and E. Gossow, "Technische Fragen des Luftschutzes," *ibid.*, 76 (1932): 41ff. Whereas engineers had no scruples about foreign contacts, lawyers and philologues just began to be readmitted into international associations when such cooperation became inopportune. Bohlen circular, April 20, Deutscher PhVb board minutes, Aug. 30, 1929, WPhV, B46, 546; Behrend, "Erinnerungen," p. 216.

134. Dittenberger quoted in DAV, *Stenographischer Bericht über die 28. AV vom 16. und 17. April 1932* (Leipzig, 1932), p. 8f; J. Magnus, "Zum neuen Jahre;" *JW* 62 (1933): 1ff; [W. Bolle?], "Systemwechsel?" *Phbl* 42 (1933): 1ff; F. Romberg, "Zum Jahresabschluss," *ZVDDI* 24 (1933): 1ff.

135. Hodenberg speech in *Stenographischer Bericht über die 29. AV*, p. 18. J. Magnus appealed for national unity, but stressed "the high legal values of justice and freedom." "Zum neuen Jahre!" *JW* 62 (1933): 1ff.

136. Westphalian board minutes, April 30 and Sept. 17, 1932, WPhV, A10, 53; H. Förster, "NS und die 'höhere Schule'," *RDE* (1932), No. 3, and "Offener Brief," *ibid.*, No. 9; "Zumutungen," *Phbl* 41 (1933): 49f; Preußischer PhVb, "Sitzung des Geschäftsführenden Vorstandes," *ibid.*, p. 50f; Behrend, "Erinnerungen," p. 217. F. Hamburger, "Lehrer zwischen Kaiser," p. 278, fails to do justice to this defensive professionalism.

137. "Eine Kundgebung der Ingenieure," *VDIN*, Oct. 19, 1932; C. Matschoß, "Die Galoschen des Glücks," *ibid.*, Dec. 28; F. Romberg, "Zum Jahresschluß," *ZVDDI* 24 (1933); 1ff. Herf, *Reactionary Modernism*, p. 152ff, glides over these reservations.

138. E. von Repkow [pseudonym for R. M. Kempner], *Justizdämmerung. Auftakt zum Dritten Reich* (Berlin, 1932); Willig, "Theory and Administration of Justice," p. 334ff; Feiten, *NSLB*, p. 40ff; and Ludwig, *Technik*, p. 73ff. The links between overcrowding and Nazism are more complex than Beatus, "Academic Proletariat," p. 261ff, asserts. T. Childers' study of "The Social Language of Politics in Germany," forthcoming in the *AHR*, emphasizes the occupational focus of NS appeals.

139. M. Kater, "The Nazi Physicians' League of 1929," in T. Childers, ed., *The Formation of the NS Constituency* (London, 1987), pp. 147–81.

140. H. Schemm, in BA, NS 12, No. 967. Cf. H. Friedmann, in broken English: "The NSLB was thought [of] as NS organization of fighters, which ought to fill the life of education of Germany with the ideas of the national socialistic view of the world and to struggle against the old unions of teachers which were led partly in the marxistic, for the greatest part however, in liberalistic and confessional manner," In "The organization of the NS Union of Teachers," BA, NS 12, No. 620.

141. Figures from above organizational discussion and the 1925 as well as 1933 censuses. "Verzeichnis" in four pieces, BA, NS 12, No. 780. The lists contain revealing comments about "NS-haters," "dangerous" colleagues, with "convictions according to need," as well as "democrat-pacifists" or "national officials." Three entries could not be classified. According to Kater, "NS Physicians," p. 171, every tenth doctor belonged.

142. Bayreuth speech by Schemm in the spring of 1933 after the Potsdam garrison church ceremony, points 22–24, BA, NS 12, No. 967. These complaints caution against overinterpreting elite support for the NSDAP. The case of the university town Göttingen indicates that mixed lower middle class districts embraced the Nazis rather than professorial (DNVP) neighborhoods. F. Hasselhorn, *Wie wählte Göttingen?* (Göttingen, 1983).

143. Schemm, *Denkschrift*, point L; F. Ostler, "Rechtsanwälte in der NS-Zeit," *Abl* 33 (1983): 50ff; Heydeloff, "Staranwalt," p. 402ff and papers by F. Vogel, such as "Gewählt wird Adolf Hitler" of April 23, 1932; "Meine Themen zur Reichstagswahl," or "Arbeiter und Bauern und Arbeitsbeschaffung im Dritten Reich," all in BDC, NSBDT file Vogel.

144. Dr. Julius von Negelein, ord. Univ. Prof. Erlangen, "Weshalb ich ein Nationalsozialist

bin?'' BA, NS 12, No. 780. Cf. A. Faust, ''Professoren für die NSDAP,'' in Heinemann, ed., *Erziehung und Schulung im Dritten Reich* (Stuttgart, 1980) p. 31ff.

CHAPTER 5

1. W. Raeke's speech, Hitler's letter to Frank, May 30, 1933, and Dr. Heuber's figures are in R. Schraut, ed., *Deutscher Juristentag 1933* (Leipzig, 1934), pp. 7–12, 46ff.

2. For some diary excerpts and letters cf. M. Schmid, ed., *Wiedergeburt des Geistes: Die Universität Tübingen im Jahre 1945* (Tübingen, 1985), p. 165ff. See K. H. Jarausch, ''1945: The Burden of the Past and the New Start'' (Ms., Chapel Hill, N. C., 1985).

3. See, for example, D. Güstrow, *Tödlicher Alltag* (Berlin, 1981), p. 187ff; P. Kleinewefers, *Jahrgang 1905,* 2nd ed. (Stuttgart, 1977), p. 128ff; and C. Schmid, *Erinnerungen* (Bern, 1979), p. 209ff.

4. As introduction to a vast literature cf. W. Laqueur, ed., *Fascism: A Reader's Guide* (Berkeley, 1976); C. J. Friedrich, ed., *Totalitarianism* (New York, 1964); W. Sauer, ''National Socialism: Totalitarianism or Fascism?'' *AHR* 73 (1967): 404ff; and P. Aycoberry, *The Nazi Question: An Essay on the Interpretations of National Socialism* (New York, 1981), p. 109ff.

5. See the standard biographies by A. Bullock, *Hitler: A Study in Tyranny* (Harmondsworth, England, 1969); J. C. Fest, *Hitler* (New York, 1974); and the psychohistorical studies by G. L. Waite, *The Psychopathic God* (New York, 1977), and R. Binion, *Hitler and the Germans* (New York, 1976). An exception is M. H. Kater, ''Hitler in a Social Context,'' *CEH* 14 (1981): 243ff.

6. See the controversy between K. Hildebrand and Hans Mommsen in W. J. Mommsen, ed., *Der 'Führerstaat': Mythos und Realität* (Stuttgart, 1981), pp. 43ff and 73ff, or K. Hildebrand, *Das Dritte Reich* (Munich, 1980), p. 123ff, versus M. Broszat, *The Hitler State* (London, 1981).

7. D. Schoenbaum, *Hitler's Social Revolution* (New York, 1966) and R. Dahrendorf, *Society and Democracy in Germany* (Garden City, N.Y., 1967), versus the GDR literature cited in K. Jarausch, ''East German Views of Fascism: Some Ironies of History as Politics,'' forthcoming in R. Koshar, ed., *After Forty Contentious Years: The Two Germanies Since 1945* (1991). For a recent summary cf. I. Kershaw, *The Nazi Dictatorship* (London, 1985), p. 130ff.

8. R. Koshar, ''From *Stammtisch* to Party,'' *JMH* 59 (1987): 1–24.

9. Still fundamental, K.-D. Bracher, *Die Deutsche Diktatur* (Cologne, 1969). Cf. *idem et al.,* eds., *Nationalsozialistische Diktatur, 1933–1945* (Bonn, 1983).

10. F. Ostler, *Die deutschen Rechtsanwälte, 1871–1971* (Essen, 1971), p. 229ff, versus B. Reifner, ''Freie Advokatur oder Dienst am Recht,'' in H. Fangmann, ed., *Recht, Justiz und Faschismus* (Cologne, 1984), p. 49ff; R. Bölling, *Sozialgeschichte der deutschen Lehrer* (Göttingen, 1983), p. 136ff; and K.-H. Ludwig, *Technik und Ingenieure im Dritten Reich* (Königstein, 1979), p. 109ff.

11. D. L. Anderson, ''Historians and Lawyers: On Writing the History of Law in the Third Reich,'' *Research Studies* 50 (1982): 119ff. Cf. A. Beyerchen, *Politics and the Physics Community in the Third Reich* (New Haven, Conn., 1977); G. Cocks, *Psychotherapy in the Third Reich* (New York, 1985); and M. H. Kater, *Doctors Under Hitler* (Chapel Hill, N.C., 1989).

12. ''Aus der Vereinstätigkeit,'' *Abl* 20 (1933): 51ff; Dix, ''Erklärung des DAV,'' *ibid.,* p. 89; ''Neuwahlen,'' *ibid.,* p. 90; ''Aus der Vereinstätigkeit,'' *ibid.,* p. 93ff; ''Neuwahlen im DAV,'' *VZ,* March 27, 1933. Cf. Fieberg, ed., *Justiz und Nationalsozialismus* (Cologne, 1989), p. 89ff.

13. H. Göppinger, *Die Verfolgung der Juristen jüdischer Abstammung durch den Nationalsozialismus* (Villingen, 1963), p. 42ff, and Ostler, *Rechtsanwälte,* p. 230f.

14. Dix, ''Vereinsnachrichten,'' *Abl* 20 (1933): 129; Voß appeal, *ibid.,* p. 130; Dittenberger, ''Aus den Vereinsnachrichten,'' *ibid.,* p. 132; and Voß to Freisler, May 3, 1933, PrGStA Da, Rep. 84a, Vol. 106. Cf. F. Grimm, *Mit offenem Visier* (Leoni, 1969), pp. 116–23; and I. Müller, *Furchtbare Juristen* (Munich, 1987), p. 44ff.

15. Voß to Freisler, May 8, 1933; Frank to Voß, n.d., in PrGStA Da, Rep. 84a, Vol. 106; G. Buchheit, *Richter in roter Robe* (Munich, 1968), p. 24ff. Cf. Ostler, *Rechtsanwälte,* p. 232.

This pressure shows H. Frank to have been less of a defender of legality than his memoirs claim: *Im Angesicht des Galgens* (Munich, 1953), p. 169f.

16. "Beschlüsse der AV vom 18. Mai, 1933," *Abl* 20 (1933): 137; "Ansprache des Präsidenten Dix," *ibid.*, p. 140ff; and Ostler, *Rechtsanwälte,* p. 232f. Dix had to defend himself against charges of unconstitutionality by pleading "a supralegal emergency." Cf. the nationalist Seeger to Kerrl, May 17, 1933, PrGStA Da, Rep. 84a, Vol. 106.

17. *Bericht des Vorstandes der Anwaltskammer zu Berlin 1933* (n.p., n.d.). For other local cases see König, *Vom Dienst am Recht. Rechtsanwälte als Strafverteidiger im Nationalsozialismus* (Berlin, 1987), p. 37f.

18. Kerrl circular, March 31, 1933; Kerrl to Prussian administration of justice, April 11, 1933, and further material in PrGStA Da, Rep. 84a, Vol. 35. Ostler, in *Rechtsanwälte,* p. 235f, underrates this compulsion.

19. Kerrl to Neubert, May 19, 1933; Ministry of Justice circular, May 23, 1933; "Protokoll über die außerordentliche Kammerversammlung vom 22. Mai 1933," where a NS speaker claimed "inner agreement between lawyers' professional tasks and the aims of Chancellor Adolf Hitler"; and other material in PRGStA Da, Rep. 84a, Vol. 35.

20. "Deutsche Rechtsfront," *Abl* 20 (1933): 153; "Organisation der deutschen Anwaltschaft im neuen Reich," *ibid.*, p. 193ff. See Frank, *Im Angesicht,* p. 171f, for Hitler's speech on custom and international law.

21. Quotations from Heuber, figures from Raeke, and citations from Noack and Luetgebrune in Schraut, *Deutscher Juristentag,* pp. 46ff, 86f, 94f, and 105f. Cf. Heydeloff, "Staranwalt," p. 410ff.

22. "Organisation der deutschen Anwaltschaft im neuen Reich," *Abl* 20 (1933): 193ff; "An alle Empfänger des Mitteilungsblattes," *ibid.*, 21 (1934): 13; Ostler, *Rechtsanwälte,* p. 236f. After the distinguished Jewish editors J. Magnus and M. Hachenburg were fired, the content deteriorated under H. Frank's editorship.

23. Deutscher PhVb, "Im Dienst der nationalen Aufbauarbeit," *Phbl* 41 (1933), No. 12; "Vorsitz im Deutschen PhVb," *ibid.*, p. 154; Deutscher PhVb, "An die deutschen Philologen," *ibid.*, Nos. 15 and 16; "Die Organisationen in der Zeitenwende," *ibid.*, 180f. Professional associations should no longer be interest groups, but, led by "responsible *Führer,*" ought to work for the common weal. W. Bolle resigned as Prussian chair on April 7, 1933. F. Behrend, "Erinnerungen an die Tätigkeit des PhVb," *HS* 7 (1954): 217.

24. "Weckruf an alle deutschen Erzieher," *RDE* (1933), No. 5; E. Jagala, "Reichstagung des NSLB in Leipzig," *Phbl* 41 (1933): 197; "Organisationen in der Zeitenwende," *ibid.*, p. 181; H. Schemm, circular, May 2, 1933, *ibid.*, No. 10; protocols of April 25, May 12, 1933, WPhV, A10, 53, and material in unnamed file. Cf. W. Feiten, *Der NSLB. Entwicklung und Organisation* (Frankfurt, 1981), p. 55ff; and U. Hochmuth and H.-P. de Lorent, eds., *Hamburg: Schule unterm Hakenkreuz* (Hamburg, 1985), p. 12ff.

25. NSLB to H. Baumgärtel, April 13, 1933, BA, NS 12, No. 861; R. Bohm, "Stand der Verhandlungen über die Schaffung einer DEG," *Phbl* 41 (1933): 225ff; "Programmatische Erklärungen des preußischen Unterrichtsministers Rust," *ibid.*, p. 229; Bohm circular, May 27, 1933, WPhV, 388, 525. Cf. H. Küppers, "Zum Gleichschaltungsprozeß der öffentlich organisierten Erziehung in den Jahren 1933/4," in Heinemann, ed., *Erziehung und Schulung* 2:232ff.

26. "Vertreterversammlung des Deutschen PhVb am 31. Mai 1933," *Phbl* 41 (1933): 272f; "Die Gründung der DEG," *ibid.*, p. 271f; "Organisation!" *ibid.*, p. 293f; and W. Pipke, "Die Geschichte der Reichsfachschaft VI" in BA, NS 12, No. 1496, pp. 3ff, 18ff. Cf. "Vereinbarung über die Eingliederung des DLV in den NSLB" *ibid.*, No. 879; "Der Preußische Lehrerverein in der Grenzmark," *ADLZ* 62 (1933): 286f; clippings, WPhV, 388, 525; and Schemm speeches and NSLB organization plans in the July 1933 issue of *RDE*.

27. Frick to education ministers of the states, Oct. 18; Schwedtke to the Westphalian branch, Sept. 20; and Schemm memorandum, Dec. 7, 1933, in BA, NS 12, No. 1133; Pipke, "Geschichte," p. 6ff; "Die Eingliederung des Deutschen PhVb in die DEG," *Phbl* 41 (1933): 380f and 425ff, 443ff. Cf. the "Vermerk" of Oct. 19, and so on in ZStA Po, Rep. 49.01, No. 6698; Eilers circulars, Sept. 18f, WPhV, n. N; Wiese-Bohlen letters, Aug. 3, 15, 1933, *ibid.*, pp. 338, 525; and "Bundesnachrichten," *RDE*, Sept. 1933.

28. Troge to trade schoolteachers, Oct. 3, 1933, in Pipke, "Geschichte," p. 22f; Schemm

to Frick, Oct. 30, 1933, BA, NS 12, No. 1133; "Besprechung in Berlin am 30. Nov. 1933," and "Vorläufige Satzung der DEG," *ibid.*, No. 637. Cf. "Die Aufrechterhaltung des Deutschen PhVb verstößt nicht gegen den NS Totalitätsgedanken," *Phbl* 41 (1933): 485ff, and "Schaffung der DEG," or "Dank an den Reichsminister des Innern," *ibid.*, No. 49.

29. Schemm memorandum, Dec. 7, 1933, BA, NS 12, No. 1133; Pipke, "Geschichte," p. 40ff, with another compromise of Dec. 12, 1933; "Die organisatorische Lage," *Phbl* 41 (1933): 569f. See Schmitt to Frick, Nov. 30, 1933, and related material in ZStA Po, Rep. 49.01, No. 6698, and Eichenauer circular, Dec. 12, 1933, WPhV, n. N.

30. "Von der Reichsleitung des NSLB Bayreuth wird bekanntgegeben"; memorandum on "NSLB und DEG" and "Verfügung," BA, NS 12, No. 1133; "Endgültige Organisationsverfügung der PO für den NSLB," *Rhein–Ruhr,* Feb. 1934, p. 27. Pipke, "Geschichte," p. 45f; and "Ergebnis der Beratungen im RdI am 9. Jan. 1934," *Phbl* 42 (1934): 25f. Cf. the conciliatory letter by R. von Hoff to Schemm, Dec. 27, 1933, BA, NS 12, No. 1132; and Bohm circular, Jan. 10, 1934, WPhV, n. N.

31. Pipke, "Geschichte," p. 45ff; NSLB to Wottin, Jan. 3, 1934, BA, NS 12, No. 549; Schemm memorandum, "Der NSLB—seine Geschichte, seine organisatorische Entwicklung und die daraus resultierende Stellungnahme zur gegenwärtigen organisatorischen Lage," BA, NS 12, No. 1133; Papenbrook, "Eine eindeutige Antwort des Reichsinnenministers Dr. Frick," *Der Erzieher* (1934), No. 3; "Unterlagen zur Besprechung im RdI am 19. Jan. 34," BA, NS 12, No. 637. Hoff to Schemm, March 3, 1934, demanded the transformation of the associations into sections under their old leadership as price for fusion. BA, NS 12, No. 1133.

32. Bohm to Schemm, April 11, 1934, and reply, June 29; Benze to Schemm, April 4, 1934, and "Entwurf einer Vereinbarung über die Eingliederung des Reichsverbandes der Lehrer an höheren Schulen in die Gesamterzieherorganisation," BA, NS 12, No. 869; Georg to Rose Ried, May 18, and R. Ried to Hitler, May 19, 1934, *ibid.*, No. 1133; "Der Stand der organisatorischen Verhandlungen zwischen dem Deutschen PhVb und dem NSLB," *Phbl* 42 (1934): 181ff; "Gebt acht auf die Reaktionäre!" *Erzieher im Braunhemd* (1934), No. 3; and Dr. Geipel telegram, n.d., in BA, NS 12, No. 637.

33. Benze to NSLB section leaders, May 7, 1934, and "An die Amtswalter der Fachschaft II im NSLB," BA, NS 12, No. 1132; versus "Zur organisatorischen Lage," *Phbl* 42 (1934): 299f, and Brandenburg PhV circular of Nov. 7, 1933, BA, NS 12, No. 1133. Cf. Schemm, "Geleitwort," Oct. 20, *DHS* 1 (1934): 1, and Benze, "Fachschaftsarbeit in der Fachschaft 2," *RDE* (1934), No. 8.

34. Schemm to Schmitt, Feb. 14, 1933; and Troge to Schmitt, June 21, 1934, with text of the agreement in ZStA Po, Rep. 49.01, No. 6698. Cf. the details in Pipke, "Geschichte," p. 55ff.

35. Bauer to Bormann, Feb. 23, 1936, BA, NS 12, No. 870; "An unsere Leser," *SE* 8 (1934): 281f; P. Hartig, *Lebenserinnerungen eines Neuphilologen* (Augsburg, 1981), p. 57. Cf. the sketchy Küppers, "Gleichschaltungsprozeß," p. 242f, and Feiten, *NSLB,* 65f, with Hamburger, "Lehrer," p. 294f.

36. Raatz report on "Organisationsverhältnisse der ostpreußischen Lehrer," ZStA Po, Rep. 49.01, No. 6698. Papenbrook to Kolb, July 13, 1934, BA, BS 12, No. 1132, opposed concessions because the Thuringian PhVb retained only 100 from among 1500 previous members. Cf. resignations in WPhVb, V22, 364.

37. Benze to Schemm, Oct. 21, 1934, with memo on "Eingliederung des Deutschen PhVb in den NSLB"; draft press releases; and Griepentrog to Roder, May 5, 1934: "In our national interest, Bohm must be rendered harmless." BA, NS 12, No. 869. Cf. Bohm to Schemm, Nov. 3, 1934, rejecting the demand for "prior dissolution" and pointing to personal antipathies of Benze, BA, NS 12, No. 1133.

38. Bohm to Rust, Dec. 6, 1934, in circular 1, 1935, of PhVb, BA, NS 12, No. 869. "Kundgebung des Großberliner Philologenverbandes," *Phbl* 42 (1934): 537; and Bohm, "Mitteilung," as well as Schwedtke, "Dank an Oberschulrat Bohm," *ibid.*, p. 549f. The NSLB leadership had long tried to silence Bohm through excluding him from the teachers' league and involving him in a series of party discipline cases. Bormann to Schemm, Dec. 27, 1933, BA, NS 12, No. 1133. Cf. R. Bohm, ed., *Höhere Schule—wozu?* (Leipzig, 1934).

39. Schwedtke to Löpelmann, Dec. 19, 1934 and Jan. 12, 1935; Löpelmann to Schwedtke,

Jan. 7 and 8, 1935, as well as concluding text by Schwedtke, Jan. 14, 1935, in BA, NS 12, No. 869. For a detailed report cf. the circulars of the Bayerischer Philologenbund, Nos. 57, 60, and 71 in BA, NS 12, No. 1132.

40. Schwedtke, "Besinnung," *Phbl* 43 (1935): 1ff. Although the NSLB was not mentioned, "the hidden and camouflaged, but clearly expressed insult to all Old Fighters, and the covertly phrased attacks on party and state" were all too well understood, in "Schreiben einer Gauorganisationsstelle vom 20. Jan. 1935," and Schwedtke's circular No. 2, Jan. 29, 1935, BA, NS 12, No. 869. Cf. H. Friedmann, "Auf dem Wege zur Ganzheit," *DHS* 2 (1935): 117ff; "Aus dem NSLB ausgeschlossen," *ibid.*, p. 119; and "Verbot der Beteiligung an den Versammlungen des PhVb," *ibid.*, p. 157. See Hoff to Schemm, May 20, 1936, BA, NS 12, No. 1132.

41. A. Krauß, "Die deutschen Ingenieure," *VDIN* 13 (1933), No. 14; "Der VDI an den Herrn Reichskanzler," *ibid.*, No. 18. Cf. G. Hortleder, *Das Gesellschaftsbild des Ingenieurs. Zum politischen Verhalten der technischen Intelligenz in Deutschland,* 2nd ed. (Frankfurt, 1970), p. 114f.

42. The accounts by A. F. Manning, "Der VDI und der Nationalsozialismus," *Acta Historica Neerlandica* 2 (1967): 163ff; Ludwig, *Technik,* p. 109ff; and *idem,* "Der VDI als Gegenstand der Parteipolitik 1933 bis 1945," in *Technik,* p. 407ff, substantially agree. Cf. also W. Mock, *Technische Intelligenz im Exil, 1933–1945* (Düsseldorf, 1986), p. 57ff.

43. H. Schult, "Ergänzungen zur Chronik des VDI 1933–1938" (Berlin, 1939) and other material in the VDI archives. Cf. G. Feder, "Die Aufgaben der Technik beim Wiederaufbau der Deutschen Wirtschaft," *ZVDDI* 24 (1933): 93ff, and *Der Deutsche Staat auf nationaler und sozialer Grundlage,* 5th ed. (Munich, 1932). See B. M. Lane, *Architecture and Politics in Germany, 1918–1945,* 2nd ed. (Cambridge, Mass., 1985), p. 174f; and J. C. Guse, "The Spirit of the Plassenburg: Technology and Ideology in the Third Reich" (Diss., Lincoln, Neb., 1981), p. 90ff.

44. Note in BA, Bestand Schumacher, No. 280; "Wahlen und Beschlüsse der Versammlung des Vorstandsrates am 9. Mai 1933 in Berlin," *ZVDI* 77 (1933): 603. Manning, "Der VDI und der NS," p. 175ff; Ludwig, "Der VDI als Gegenstand," p. 409ff; and Guse, "Plassenburg," p. 96ff.

45. "Die deutschen Ingenieure am Bodensee," *VDIN* 13 (1933), No. 22; "Der Vorsitzende auf der 71. Hauptversammlung," *ibid.*, No. 23; "Das Bekenntnis der deutschen Ingenieure zur neuen Staatsführung," *ZVDI* 77 (1933): 725ff.

46. "Angelegenheiten des Vereins," *ZVDI* 77 (1933): 724; and "Reichsgemeinschaft der technisch-wissenschaftlichen Arbeit," *VDIN* (renamed *RTA Nachrichten)* 13 (1933), No. 26. Although its figurehead Otto Wagener fell into disgrace with Hitler, the RTA did serve as a protective buffer. Cf. Ludwig, *Technik,* pp. 11f, 119f.

47. G. Feder, "Geleitwort," *DT* 1 (1933): 1; "Die Aufgaben der neuen Zeitschrift," *ibid.;* F. Schmidt, "Der Kampfbund der Deutschen Architekten und Ingenieure," *ibid.;* and Feder, "Die Technik und der Techniker im neuen Deutschland," *ibid.*, No. 2.

48. H. Schult, "Aufgaben des VDI," *ZVDI* 77 (1933): 1127f (with the Heß letter and announcement in the *VB* of Sept. 26, 1933); "Der VDI im neuen Staat," *VDIN* 13 (1933), No. 41; "Der VDI im Rahmen der RTA," *ZVDI* 77 (1933): 1247. Cf. Ludwig, *Technik,* p. 118ff; Guse, "Plassenburg," p. 105ff; and Mock, *Technische Intelligenz,* p. 59.

49. "Dem Ziele entgegen . . . 25 Jahre VDDI!" *ZVDDI* (1934): 105ff; F. Romberg, "Die Technik im neuen Staat," *ibid.* 24 (1933): 54ff; and K. F. Steinmetz, "Zur Situation der Zeit," *ibid.*, p. 57ff. Cf. J. Herf, *Reactionary Modernism* (Cambridge, 1984), p. 198ff.

50. "Deutsche Diplom-Ingenieure!" *ZVDDI* 24 (1933): A17; "Vorstand," *ibid.*, p. A21; "Ausschuß und Vorstand," *ibid.*, p. A25; Lynkeus, "Rundblick," p. 112; and F. Romberg, "Quo Vadis, Deutscher Diplom-Ingenieur?" *ibid.*, p. 117f.

51. K. S. von Schweigen, "Die Organisierung der technischen Berufe in einer 'Technik'-Front," *ZVDDI* 24 (1933): 133ff, proposed a tripod with the KDAI forming the political, the RDT the professional, and new sections the scientific legs. F. Romberg, "An alle Fachgenossen im Verband!" *ibid.*, p. 157ff.

52. "Generalinspekteur Dr.-Ing. Todt, Führer der RTA," *ZVDI* 77 (1933): 1344; "Reichskammer der Technik," *ibid.* 78 (1934): 172; and Ludwig, *Technik,* p. 123ff. Feder did not help his case by announcing the end of technology, because Schult could simply point to the success-

ful work of engineers to prove him wrong. G. Feder, "Ende der Technik?" *DT* 2 (1934), No. 1, versus H. Schult, "Aufgaben der Technik im neuen Deutschland," *VDIN* 14 (1934), No. 19.

53. "Zusammenarbeit in der deutschen Technik," *VDIN* 14 (1934), No. 23, as well as *ZVDI* 78 (1934): 760 and *ZVDDI* 25 (1934), No. 6; H. Schult, "Organische Wirtschaftsgestaltung, eine Ingenieuraufgabe," *ZVDI* 78 (1934): 761f. Cf. "Das Amt der Technik der NSDAP," *DT* 2 (1934), No. 11, and E. Schönleben, *Fritz Todt* (Oldenburg, 1943), p. 28ff.

54. "Vom Neuaufbau der Technik," *ZVDI* 78 (1934): 1047 and *VDIN* 14 (1934), No. 35; "Zur organisatorischen Lage," *ZVDDI* 25 (1934): 167f; and "Vom Neuaufbau der Technik," *VDIN* 14 (1934), No. 50 and *ZVDI* 78 (1934): 1464. Another sign of nazification was the appointment of the dubious NS student leader O. Stäbel to the VDI board for the retiring Garbotz. "Bericht über die Vorstandssitzung," *ibid.*, p. 1415f.

55. "Rundschreiben. Betreff: BNSDJ, Fachvereine und Verbände," *DR* 3 (1933): 26; "Organisationsfragen," *Phbl* 41 (1933): 492; "Kommissar Dr. Rust stellt sich den Beamten im Unterrichtsministerium vor," *ADLZ* 62 (1933): 132; DLV, "Kundgebung," *ibid.*, p. 213, and so on.

56. Among primary schoolteachers see "Richtlinien für die Schaffung einer einheitlichen Erzieherorganisation," *ADLZ* 62 (1933): 289; "Die außerordentliche Vertreterversammlung des Preußischen LV," *ibid.*, p. 404ff; and H. Fielitz, "Zum Abschied," *ibid.*, p. 865. Cf. K. Klattenhoff, ed., *Dokumente zur Geschichte der Lehrerschaft in Oldenburg* (Oldenburg, 1979), p. 94ff.

57. H. Schemm, transcript of Magdeburg speech, June 8, 1933, BA, NS 12, No. 967; "Rede des Reichsjustizkommissars Staatminister Dr. Frank," *DR* 3 (1933): 33ff; G. Feder, "Ende der Technik?" *DT* 2 (1934), No. 1. Cf. H. V. Schubert, "Die Anwaltschaft im neuen Staat," *DR* 3 (1933): 6f; K. Jarausch, "Die germanische Religion als Gegenstand des Religionsunterrichts," *SE* 9 (1934): 25ff; and Kater, *Doctors Under Hitler,* p. 19ff.

58. Liebekranz, "Sondertagung des AfT und des NSBDT," quoting G. Feder, *DT* 2 (1934), No. 10; and F. Matthias to G. Scholz-Klink, March 15, 1934, BA, NS 12, No. 861. Cf. P. Hüttenberger, "Interessenvertretung und Lobbyismus im Dritten Reich," in L. Kettenacker, ed., *Der Führerstaat* (Stuttgart, 1981), p. 429ff; G. Schröder, "Die 'Wiedergeburt' der Pharmazie 1933–1934," in H. Mehrtens, ed., *Naturwissenschaft, Technik und NS-Ideologie* (Frankfurt, 1980), p. 166f.

59. Dittenberger, "Aus der Vereinstätigkeit," *Abl* 24 (1933): 51f and 93f; G. Ried, "Vorstandssitzung des Deutschen PhVb am 18. Feb. 1933," *Phbl* 41 (1933): 114ff; "Eine notwendige Liquidation!" *ibid.*, p. 121f; Lynkeus, "Rundblick," *ZVDDI* 24 (1933): 29; Pa, "Arbeitsbeschaffung," *ZVDI* 77 (1933): 757f.

60. Schumann, March 26, 1932, in N. Hammerstein, ed., *Deutsche Bildung?* (Frankfurt, 1988), p. 52; "Rede des Reichsjustizkommissars Staatsminister Dr. Frank," *DR* 3 (1933): 35f. H. Schemm, speech to Gauobmänner, untitled and undated, BS, NS 12, No. 967; G. Feder, "Was ist Wirtschaftstechnik?" *DT* 1 (1933), No. 1.

61. A. Bohlen, "Arbeitsbeschaffung und Arbeitsmarkt," *Phbl* 41 (1933): 97ff; F. Behrend, "Die Vereinbarungen der Länder über die Warnung vor dem Studium," *ibid.*, p. 100ff; Königsberg rector to Ministry of Culture, Jan. 13, 1933; and Reich Ministry of Interior memorandum, Jan. 25, 1933, ZStA Me, Rep. 76, Va, Sekt. 1, Tit. I, No. 7, Vol. II.

62. Berlin rector to Kähler, Jan. 28, 1933; Rust to Verband deutscher Medizinstudenten, April 3, 1933; G. Keiser, "Gutachten über die vermutliche Entwicklung des Hochschulstudiums in den kommenden Jahren," March 3, 1933; and A. Schultz to Rust, April 14, 1933 in ZStA Me, Rep. 76, Va, Sekt. 1, Tit. I, No. 7. Vol. II.

63. "Gesetz gegen die Überfüllung deutscher Schulen und Hochschulen," *Phbl* 41 (1933): 209f, and J. Haupt, *Neuordnung im Schulwesen und Hochschulwesen* (Berlin, 1933). Cf. U. D. Adam, *Judenpolitik im Dritten Reich* (Düsseldorf, 1972), p. 69ff; A. Nath, *Die Studienratskarriere im Dritten Reich* (Frankfurt, 1988), p. 197ff, and K. H. Jarausch, *Deutsche Studenten 1800–1980* (Frankfurt, 1984), p. 176f.

64. Rust orders of June 16, and Sept. 25, 1933, ZStA Me, Rep. 76, Va, Sekt. 1, Tit. 1, No. 7, Vol. II. Although the initial draft "against the *Überfremdung* [foreign control] of German schools and universities" of April 11 was directed only against Jews, the overcrowding provisions were more than window dressing, because they fulfilled long-standing professional desires.

A. Götz von Olenhusen, "Die 'nicht-arischen' Studenten an den deutschen Hochschulen," *VfZG* 14 (1966): 175ff.

65. J. R. Pauwels, *Women and University Studies in the Third Reich, 1933–1945* (New York, 1985). The misogynist aspect of the law is often overlooked. Cf. J. Stephenson, "Girls' Higher Education in Germany of the 1930s," *JCH* 10 (1975): 41ff.

66. Rust, "Übersicht über die Zahl der Abiturienten denen Ostern 1933 vom Hochschulstudium geraten worden ist," Nov. 13, 1933; Frick circular Dec. 28, 1933; and memorandum of Dec. 30, 1933 in ZStA Me, Rep. 76, VA, Sekt. 1, Tit I, No. 7, Vol. II. In effect somewhat more, namely 16,489, were admitted. Cf. Statistisches Landesamt report, April 1935, ZStA Po, Rep. 49.01, 796; and H. Titze, *Das Hochschulstudium in Preußen und Deutschland, 1820–1944* (Göttingen, 1987), pp. 30, 43, 89, 200.

67. Ch. Lorenz, *Zehnjahres-Statistik des Hochschulbesuchs und der Abschlußprüfungen* (Berlin, 1943), Vol. 1, p. 33ff. Cf. C. Quetsch, *Die zahlenmäßige Entwicklung des Hochschulbesuchs in den letzten 50 Jahren* (Berlin, 1960), p. 19ff, and Jarausch, *Deutsche Studenten,* p. 177ff.

68. W. Oberle, "Beschränkung des Zugangs zu den Hochschulen," *Phbl* 42 (1934), No. 1; and Rust decree on "Hochschulreife," Feb. 9, 1935, ZStA Po, Rep. 49.01, 796, substituting continual "selection" and mandatory half-year labor service. See correspondence in ZStA Po, Rep. 49.01, No. 796. The deterrent effect of the law deepened the cyclical contraction. Cf. H. Titze, "Die zyklische Überproduktion," p. 92ff.

69. Material in PrGStA Da, Rep. 84a, No. 35. Cf. Göppinger, *Verfolgung,* p. 21ff; Buchheit, *Richter,* p. 24f; König, *Vom Dienst am Recht,* p. 35ff; Fieberg, *Justiz und Nationalsozialismus,* p. 71; and L. Gruchmann, *Justiz im Dritten Reich, 1933–1940* (Munich, 1988), p. 125f.

70. Rebiztki to Prussian Ministry of Justice, March 17, 1933, PrGStA Da, Rep. 84a, No. 35; *Bericht des Vorstands der Anwaltskammer zu Berlin 1933* and König, *Dienst am Recht,* p. 36f. For estimates of the figure of Jewish lawyers cf. Pr GStA Da, Rep. 84a, No. 75.

71. Schlegelberger to cabinet, March 10, 1933, BA, R 43 II, No. 1534; Kerrl circular, March 31, 1933, PrGStA Da, Rep. 84a, No. 35. Cf. Berlin BNSDJ leader Zarnack's demand for complete disbarment on March 22, *ibid.,* No. 75; König, *Dienst am Recht,* p. 37; Gruchmann, *Justiz,* p. 127f.; and Jarausch, "Jewish Lawyers in Germany," *passim.*

72. Kerrl, April 4, 1933, and other material in PrGStA Da, Rep. 84a, No. 75. Cf. Bohn's memorandum on the need to purge all Jewish attorneys and notaries, April 4, *ibid.,* and König, *Dienst am Recht,* p. 41f.

73. "Auszug aus der Niederschrift über die Ministerbesprechung vom 7. April 1933," BA, Rep. R43 II, No. 1534; *WTB* releases of April 10 and May 12, 1933. Treated as civil servants, 804 Referendare were purged. O. Palandt, "Die große juristische Staatsprüfung in Preußen," *DJ* 96 (1934): 252; M. Hachenburg, *ibid.,* 95 (1933), No. 9.

74. Übersicht über die Zahl der am 1. Mai zugelassenen arischen und nichtarischen Rechtsanwälte und Notare," *ibid.,* p. 950. Cf. *Die Juden in Deutschland* (Munich, 1935), 2nd ed., pp. 33ff, 45ff; Göppinger, *Verfolgung,* p. 34f; S. Neumann, *Nacht über Deutschland* (Munich, 1978), p. 84f; and authoritatively, Gruchmann, *Justiz,* p. 135ff. In the other states, 339 were purged while 1200 Jewish lawyers remained. Fieberg, *Justiz und Nationalsozialismus,* p. 77 gives the Jewish total too low by 3.

75. V. Lutze to Prussian Ministry of Justice, March 11, 1933; and Nachrichtenabteilung des Reichsamt des Innern, Dec. 31, 1931, PrGStA Da, Rep. 84a, No. 75. Cf. König, *Dienst am Recht,* p. 46ff.

76. Gürtner–Freisler correspondence in June 1933 as well as Kunisch to Berlin lawyer chamber, July 1, 1933, PrGStA Da, Rep. 8a, No. 75. Neubert in *JW* 63 (1934): 1763. To keep officials dismissed as Social Democrats from becoming attorneys, a law of July, 20 added "lack of political reliability" to the reasons for nonadmission. König, *Dienst am Recht,* p. 50f.

77. Freisler to Gürtner, May 15, 1933, versus Oelze to Papen, April 4, 1933; Löwenstein to justice minister, April 24, 1933; and "Niederschrift der Besprechung" of July 7 and 11, 1933, in PrGStA Da, Rep. 84a, No. 75. Cf. Göppinger, *Verfolgung,* p. 36f; Gruchmann, *Justiz,* p. 140ff; and Kater, *Doctors under Hitler,* p. 183ff.

78. "Bericht über die Referentenbesprechung im Reichsjustizministerium," June 20, 1933; "2. Durchführungsverordnung" for the April 7 law, Oct. 1, 1933, *Reichsgesetzblatt* 1 (1933): 699; Schraut, *Deutscher Juristentag,* p. 11f. Cf. Gruchmann, *Justiz,* p. 158ff.

79. A. Apfel, *Behind the Scenes of Justice* (London, 1935), p. 172; U. Beer, *Versehrt, Verfolgt, Versöhnt: Horst Berkowitz* (Essen, 1979), p. 55f; F. Grubel, "Martin Drucker," *Festschrift Martin Drucker* (Aalen, 1983), p. xiiff; F. Ostler, "Rechtsanwälte in der NS-Zeit," p. 52ff. By the year 1935, only 2552 of 4500 Jewish attorneys were still allowed to practice. Cf. Grimm, *Mit offenem Visier*, p. 125f, for a troubled Nazi.

80. "Gesetz zur Wiederherstellung des Berufsbeamtentums," *Reichsgesetzblatt*, Pt. I, Nos. 34 and 37. Minutes of the Prussian Ministry of State, April 24, 1933, ZStA Po, Rep. 49.01, No. 152. Cf. H. Mommsen, *Beamtentum im Dritten Reich* (Stuttgart, 1966), p. 39ff. As a result of President Hindenburg's intervention in favor of Jewish veterans, the anti-Semitic provisions contained the same exceptions for pre-1914 appointees and "front-fighters" of the First World War as the law on admission of lawyers.

81. "Durchführungsverordnungen zum Gesetz zur Wiederherstellung des Berufsbeamtentums," *Phbl* 41 (1933): 234f. Rust circular, April 8, 1936, ZStA Po, Rep. 49.01, No. 312. Bölling, *Sozialgeschichte*, p. 142f. For the Nazi beating of seven Hessian pedagogues cf. Grupe memoirs, KA, p. 20ff. For a regional study of the Coblenz district see S. Bittner, "Das 'Gesetz zur Wiederherstellung des Berufsbeamtentums' vom 7. April 1933 und seine Durchführung im Bereich der Höheren Schule," *Bildung und Erziehung* 40 (1987): 167f.

82. Rust order of May 17, 1933, and other material in ZStA Po, Rep. 49.01, No. 152, and personal communication from A. Strauss. For the widespread persecution of leftist teachers cf. H. Schnorbach, ed., *Lehrer und Schule unterm Hakenkreuz* (Königstein, 1983), pp. 76ff, 80ff; and Hochmuth, ed., *Hamburg: Schule unterm Hakenkreuz*, p. 18ff and 106ff.

83. "Durchführung des Berufsbeamtengesetzes im Geschäftsbereich des REM und Preußischen Ministeriums für Wissenschaft, Erziehung und Volksbildung," tabulation of late 1937, ZStA Po, Rep. 49.01, No. 312. A. Ehrentreich, *Pädagogische Odyssee* (Weinheim, 1967), p. 178; V. Wehrmann, ed., *Friedrich Copei 1902–1945* (Detmold, 1982), p. 58ff; O. Geudtner, ed., *"Ich bin katholisch getauft und Arier." Aus der Geschichte eines Kölner Gymnasiums* (Cologne, 1985), p. 39ff; and Schumann, Feb. 20 and April 12, 1934, in Hammerstein, ed., *Deutsche Bildung?*, pp. 65, 80.

84. Figure from *Statistik des Deutschen Reiches 1933*, 451 (1934), No. 5, 26; "Rassische Voraussetzungen für die Mitgliedschaft im VDI," *ZVDI* 79 (1935): 1210. Cf. Ludwig, *Technik*, pp. 113, 156; and Mock, *Technische Intelligenz im Exil*, p. 25ff.

85. Computed from Heuser-König, "Tabellarische Zusammenstellungen zur Geschichte des VDI," Ludwig, ed., *Technik*, p. 559ff. Cf. C. Matschoß, "Der VDI im Jahre 1933," *ZVDI* 78 (1934): 253f; Mock, *Technische Intelligenz*, p. 63ff; and Y. Gelber and W. Goldstern, *Vertreibung und Emigration deutschsprachiger Ingenieure nach Palestina, 1933–1945* (Düsseldorf, 1988), p. 15ff.

86. "Gesetz zur Änderung einiger Vorschriften der Rechtsanwaltsordnung, der Zivilprozeßordnung und des Arbeitsgerichtsgesetzes," with *Begründung;* petition of the "Reichsbund NS Rechtsbeistände" to Adolf Hitler, Aug. 12, 1933; Gürtner to Panse, Oct. 13, 1933; Gürtner to state justice administrations, Oct. 6, 1933; Panse to Gürtner, Oct. 25, 1933, in BA, R 43 II, No. 1534.

87. Raeke to Jonas, Oct. 24, and reply of Oct. 25, 1934 with draft law; Schwartz (for the Reichsstand der deutschen Industrie) to Schlegelberger, Nov. 10, 1934; Raeke to Jonas, Nov. 23; "Begründung" for the law, Nov. 27; "Gesetz zur Änderung der Rechtsanwaltsordnung vom 20. Dezember 1934," *Reichsgesetzblatt*, 1934, Pt. I, in BA, R 22, No. 251. Syndics were readmitted only in 1936. Cf. P. Hüttenberger, "Interessenvertretung," p. 429f.

88. Gürtner circular on admissions requirements, Jan. 25, 1935, BA, R 22, No. 251. "Weiteres Gesetz über die Erstattung von Rechtsanwaltsgebühren in Armensachen," BA, R 43 II, No. 1534. Cf. the self-help program of the BNSDJ in *JW* 63 (1934): 1309f; Ostler, *Rechtsanwälte*, p. 250ff.; and M. Linder, *The Supreme Labor Court in Nazi Germany* (Frankfurt, 1987).

89. "Neuzulassungen von Rechtsanwälten in der Zeit vom 1. 4. 33 bis Ende 1933," and "Übersicht über die zahlenmäßige Entwicklung der Anwaltschaft im Jahre 1934," BA, R 22, No. 251. Dr. Vollmer, "Die Lage der deutschen Anwaltschaft," *DJ* 97 (1935): 1693ff.

90. Figures from Dr. E. Noack, *Hilfe für die Anwaltschaft* (Leipzig, 1935), p. 5f; memorandum for Freisler, Nov. 19, 1935, ZStA Po, Rep. 30.01, 8521; and *Mitteilungen der Reichsrechtsanwaltskammer* 39:107ff. Cf. Jonas' memorandum, "Zur Notlage der Anwalt-

schaft," in June 1935: "The ratio between the work or earning possibilities and the number of professionals has never been as unfavorable as now." BA, R 22, No. 251.

91. W. Bolle, "Neue Bahnen in der preußischen Bildungspolitik," *Phbl* 41 (1933): 187f; "Wiederherstellung der früheren Wochenstundenzahl an den höheren Schulen in Preußen," *ibid.*, p. 209; "Aufhebung der Anstellungssperre für die Lehrer an höheren Schulen," *DHS* 1 (1935): 226f; Nath, "Studienassessor," p. 283ff, and Bölling, "Lehrerarbeitslosigkeit," p. 233. The ministry created room by demoting 430 nonacademic teachers to primary schools. "Hilfsmaßnahmen der preußischen Unterrichtsverwaltung für die Studienassessoren," *RDE* (1934), No. 10. Cf. B. Jarausch, "Geschichte einer schlesisch-märkischen Familie," p. 81f.

92. SOPADE, *Deutschland Berichte,* Vol. 2 (1935), p. 9ff (Frankfurt, repr. 1980); material in ZStA Po, Rep. 49.01, Vols. 119, 121, and 122. Cf. Bölling, *Sozialgeschichte,* p. 153f. Teachers' pay in the Third Reich has yet to be studied in detail.

93. Hellmich to Syrup, Feb. 21, 1933, further correspondence and quarterly reports in ZStA Po, Rep. 39.03, Vols. 184–87. "Arbeit für stellungslose Ingenieure," *VDIN* 13 (1933), June 21; A. Riebe, "Ingenieurdienst," *ibid.,* 14 (1934), Feb. 7; and "Die Ingenieurhilfe des VDI und ihre Entwicklung," *ibid.,* 15 (1935), No. 21.

94. K. F. Steinmetz, "Vom Arbeitsraum der Diplom-Ingenieure," *ZVDDI* 26 (1935): 13ff, 66f, 112f, and 158f. Cf. "Von der Not der akademischen Berufe," *ibid.,* p. 93ff; Vogel, "Memoiren," KA 1384; O. Stäbel, "Zur Frage des Ingenieurnachwuchses," *Der Jungingenieur,* July 17, 1935; "Gibt es keine stellungslosen Ingenieure mehr?" *ibid.,* No. 45.

95. H. Picker, ed., *Hitlers Tischgespräche im Führerhauptquartier* (Stuttgart, 1976), rev. ed., pp. 16, 157, 217, and *passim;* "Rede des Reichsjustizkommissars Staatminister Dr. Frank" *DR* 3 (1933): 33ff; "Die deutsche Rechtsfront proklamiert den deutschen Rechtsstand," *ibid.,* p. 202f; and figures from *Deutsches Führerlexikon 1934/5* (Berlin, 1934).

96. E. Noack, "Die Ehre des Rechtswahrerstandes," *DR* 4 (1934): 105ff; "Die Arbeit der Fachgruppe Rechtsanwälte," *ibid.,* p. 14ff; W. Raeke, "NS Rechtsbetreuung im ersten Jahre ihres Bestehens," *JW* 64 (1935): 81f; J.-A. Reese, "Der Anwalt als Freund und Patronus seiner Klientel," *DJ* 96 (1934): 939f.

97. Hammerstein, ed., *Deutsche Bildung?,* pp. 56, 71, 76, and so on. F. Mehnert, ed., *Partei-Statistik. Stand 1. Januar 1935* (Munich, 1935), p. 70ff; Reiser to Kolb, Nov. 16, 1934, BA, NS 12, No. 978; E. Krieck, "Von der Schule," *Volk im Werden* 3 (1935), No. 4; A. Schröder, "Zur Neuwerdung des Lehrerstandes," *RDE* (1935), No. 1; SOPADE, *Deutschland Berichte,* Vol. 1, June 26, 1934; and Schwedtke, "Betrachtungen zum Jahreswechsel," *Phbl* 42 (1934): 1ff. For NSLB complaints cf. BA, NS 12, No. 1438.

98. G. Feder, "Die Technik und Techniker im neuen Deutschland," *DT* 1 (1933): 66f; "Die Würde der Technik," *ibid.,* p. 381; O. Stäbel, "Die Aufgaben des deutschen Ingenieurs und der Neuaufbau der Technik im NS Staat," *ibid.* 3 (1935): 170f; K. Steinmetz, "Berufsfragen," *ZVDDI* 26 (1935): 156f; H. Schult, "Aufgaben der Technik im neuen Deutschland," *ZVDI* 78 (1934): 705ff; and "Technik ist Dienst am Volke!" *ibid.,* 79 (1935): 819ff.

99. Wienstein memorandum, March 22, 1934; and Neubert to ministry, July 16, 1934, BA R 43 II, No. 1534. RRAK, ed., *Richtlinien für die Ausübung des Anwaltsberufs* (Berlin, 1934); Grimm, *Mit offenem Visier,* p. 130f, and C. Schmitt, "Fünf Leitsätze für die Rechtspraxis," *DR* 3 (1933): 201f. Cf. Ostler, *Rechtsanwälte,* p. 251.

100. G. Ried, "Die höhere Schule im Dritten Reich," *Phbl* 41 (1933): 189ff; "Zu neuen Ufern," *ibid.,* p. 269f; "Reichskultusminister Rust über die Neugestaltung des deutschen Bildungswesens," *ibid.,* 42 (1934): 253f. Cf. Bölling, *Sozialgeschichte,* p. 144ff.

101. SOPADE, *Deutschland Berichte,* Vol. 1, p. 567ff; Vol. 2, pp. 201ff, 687ff, and *passim;* Ehrentreich, *Pädagogische Odyssee,* p. 179f; Wehrmann, *Copei,* p. 66f; Hartig, *Lebenserinnerungen,* p. 52f; and U. Popplow, "Schulalltag im Dritten Reich," *Fünfzig Jahre Schulgebäude des heutigen Felix Klein Gymnasiums* (Göttingen, 1979), p. 25ff. Cf. the reminiscences in M. Reich-Ranicki, ed., *Meine Schulzeit im Dritten Reich* (Cologne, 1982); and M. Klewitz, *Lehrersein im Dritten Reich* (Weinheim, 1987), p. 116ff.

102. "Die Ingenieurtage am Bodensee," *ZVDI* (1933): 725f; "Die Aufgaben des VDI," *ibid.,* p. 1127; C. Matschoß, "Der VDI im Jahre 1933," *ibid.,* 78 (1934): 253f. By 1935, the challenges shifted to "self-sufficiency in food, economic independence and military freedom." Cf. Schult, "1935! Unsere Aufgabe!" *ibid.,* 79 (1935): 1.

103. See the special issue, *ZVDI* 78 (1934): 97ff; W. Blöcker, "Die Reichsautobahnen,"

ibid., 77 (1933): 1021ff, and F. Todt, "Die Reichsautobahnen und ihre Aufgaben," *ibid.*, 78 (1934): 1305ff; F. Münzinger, "Die deutsche Energiewirtschaft," *ibid.*, p. 229ff, and "Rohstoff-Freiheit," *ibid.*, 79 (1935): 81; L. von Bismarck, "Arbeitsbeschaffung durch Siedlung," *ibid.*, 78 (1934): 113f, and C. H. Dencker, "Industrie und Landwirtschaft im neuen Deutschland," *ibid.*, p. 205ff.

104. F. Brommer, "Industrie und Wehrkraft," *ZVDI* 77 (1933): 839ff; and K. Becker, "Wehrtechnik," *ibid.*, 78 (1934): 249ff. Cf. K. Zuse, *Der Computer, mein Lebenswerk* (Munich, 1970), p. 45f; M. von Ardenne, *Ein glückliches Leben für Forschung und Technik* (Berlin, 1973), p. 103f; K. Ludwig, "Vereinsarbeit im Dritten Reich 1933 bis 1945," in *idem*, ed., *Technik*, p. 429ff.

105. Dr. Gülde, "Vom nationalsozialistischen Anwalt," *Abl* 20 (1933): 204; H. Frank, "Der deutsche Rechtsstaat Adolf Hitlers," and "Aufgabe des Rechtslebens nicht die Sicherung der Paragraphenanwendung, sondern vor allem Sicherung des Volkslebens," *DR* 4 (1934): 121ff, 425ff. Cf. Willig, "Theory and Administration of Justice," p. 2ff.

106. W. Raeke, "Anwalt des Rechts—nicht Anwalt der Partei," *JW* 64 (1935): 31f; Dr. Roquette, "Der Anwalt im Verfahren," *DR* 5 (1935): 579ff; F. Gürtner, "Richter und Rechtsanwalt im neuen Staat," *DJ* 96 (1934): 372. Cf. I. Staff, *Justiz im Dritten Reich* (Frankfurt, 1978), p. 124ff; and Fieberg, *Justiz und Nationalsozialismus*, p. 104ff.

107. H. Schulze, "Der Verteidiger," *DR* 5 (1935): 280f; Prof. von Weber, "Aufgaben der Strafrechtvergleichung," *ibid.*, p. 282f; H. Frank, "Die Neugestaltung des deutschen Rechts," *ibid.*, p. 470ff; "Die Zukunft der deutschen Anwaltschaft," *JW* 63 (1934): 668f; and "Zur Tagung des Reichsfachgruppenrats Rechtsanwälte," *ibid.*, 64 (1935): 978f.

108. "Ein Volk—ein Erzieherstand," *Fränkisches Volk*, Jan. 18, 1934; H. Schemm speeches in BA, NS 12, No. 967; and "Reichstagung des NSLB in Leipzig," *Phbl* 41 (1933): 197. R. Eilers, *NS Schulpolitik* (Cologne, 1963), p. 3f.

109. "Erste Arbeitstagung der Reichsfachschaft 2 in Lauenstein," *DHS* 1 (1935): 423f; Schwedtke, "Betrachtungen zur Jahreswende," *Phbl* 42 (1934): 1ff; "Reichskultusminister Rust zu den deutschen Erziehern," *ibid.*, p. 353ff. Cf. essays in Hochmuth and Lorent, eds. *Hamburg: Schule unterm Hakenkreuz*, p. 144ff.

110. "Der neue Geschichtsunterricht," *Phbl* 41 (1933): 229; "Richtlinien für den Geschichtsunterricht," *ibid.*, p. 337; "Vererbungslehre und Rassenkunde im Unterricht," *DHS* 2 (1935): 121f; W. Erxleben, "Zur Berufsvorbildung der Philologen," *ibid.*, p. 842f; and F. Winter, "Der Philologe im Dritten Reich," *ibid.*, p. 313ff. Cf. Klewitz, *Lehrersein*, p. 127ff.

111. R. Heiss, ed., *Die Sendung des Ingenieurs im neuen Staat* (Berlin, 1934), with articles by the editor, H. Hardensett, A. Nägel, E. Heidebroek, F. Syrup, H. Röchling, C. Arnhold, O. Bredt, O. Schwab, W. Hellmich, and others. Cf. the summary in the *VDIN* 15 (1935), No. 3.

112. M. W. "Weltanschauliche Schulung des Ingenieurs," *VDIN* 15 (1935), No. 20; O. Stäbel, "Die politische Erziehung des deutschen Ingenieurs," *ibid.*, No. 23; "Die Feierstunde in der Jahrhunderthalle," *ibid.*, No. 24; and "Mittteilungen des AfT der NSDAP," *DT* 3 (1935): 209. Cf. Hughes, "Technology," in H. Friedlander and S. Milton, eds., *The Holocaust* (New York, 1980).

113. Schlegelberger to chancellery, March 10, 1933, BA, R 43 II, 1534. "Aus der Vereinstätigkeit," *Abl* 20 (1933): 94, 169; "Reich-Rechtsanwalts-Kammer," *ibid.*, 21 (1934): 23ff; "Verordnung des Reichspräsidenten über Maßnahmen auf dem Gebiete der . . . Rechtspflege vom 18. März, 1933," *ibid.*, p. 102ff. Cf. Grimm, *Mit offenem Visier*, p. 137, and Ostler, *Rechtsanwälte*, p. 250f.

114. W. Raeke, "An alle deutschen (arischen) Rechtsanwälte!" *Abl* 20 (1933): 193ff; "Rückblick und Ausblick (Zur Auflösung des DAV)," *ibid.*, 21 (1934): 2f; "Satzungen des BNSDJ," *DR* 3 (1933): 53f.

115. W. Raeke, "Geschlossenes Eintreten des BNSDJ für die deutsche Anwaltschaft," *Abl* 20 (1933): 209ff; "Die Arbeit der Fachgruppe Rechtsanwälte," *DR* 4 (1934): 14f; Jonas, "Vermerk über die Tagung des Reichsfachgruppenrats 'Rechtsanwälte' des BNSDJ," and theses, in BA, R 22, No. 251. Cf. Raeke, "Zur Tagung des Reichsfachgruppenrats Rechtsanwälte," *JW* 64 (1935), No. 13; and "Große Gauführertagung im Hause der Deutschen Rechtsfront," *DR* 5 (1935): 74f.

116. "Der Deutsche PhVb als berufsständische und kulturpolitische Organisation der Lehrer

an höheren Schulen,'' *Phbl* 41 (1933): 443f; ''Organisationsfragen,'' *ibid.*, p. 492f; ''Aus dem NSLB,'' and ''Grundsätzliches zur Trierer Tagung,'' *DHS* 1 (1934), No. 2. Benze criticized the philological meeting as providing ''too much research for its own sake and too little of the völkisch goal.'' Feiten, *NSLB*, 76ff, 87f.

117. Benze to all Gau-leaders, May 7, 1934, and notes of Roder's speech at Lauenstein, BA, NS 12, No. 869. Benze, ''Schulreform und Fachschaftsarbeit,'' *DHS* 2 (1935): 305f; ''Erste Arbeitstagung der Reichsfachschaft 2 in Lauenstein,'' *ibid.*, p. 423f. For the Assessoren agitation see the ''Arbeitsbericht des Gaureferenten für Referendar-und Assessorenfragen'' of Greater Berlin, *DHS* 2 (1935): 626ff.

118. ''Zur Berufsschutz-Frage,'' *ZVDDI* 24 (1933): 61ff; F. Schmidt, ''Der KDAI,'' *Mitteilungen des KDAI*, supplement to Sept. 1933 *DT* issue, p. 47f; ''Reichs-Technik-Kammer,'' *ZVDDI* 25 (1934): 14; G. Feder, ''Von der Wirtschaftsführung, Wirtschaftsorganisation und den Berufen,'' *ibid.*, p. 29ff; ''Reichskammer der Technik,'' *ibid.*, p. 36; W. von Pasinski, ''Ingenik im Dritten Reich,'' *ibid.*, p. 37ff; and G. Feder, ''Die Würde der Technik,'' *DT* 2 (1934): 381ff. Cf. Ludwig, *Technik*, p. 121ff, 138ff; and Guse, ''Plassenburg,'' p. 110ff.

119. ''Generalinspektor Dr.-Ing. Todt auf der Kundgebung in Leipzig,'' *DT* 1 (1934): 428; Gtz, ''Tag der deutschen Technik,'' *VDIN* 14 (1934), No. 11; F. Romberg, ''Reichskammer der Technik,'' *ZVDDI* 25 (1934): 69f; F. Steinmetz, ''Zur Frage der Organisierung im technischen Berufskreis,'' *ibid.*, p. 71ff; and ''Die Lösung der Berufsschutzfrage in Verbindung mit der Reichskammer der Technik,'' *DT* 1 (1934): 604ff. Cf. A. Steinweis ''The Reich Chamber of Culture'' (Diss., Chapel Hill, N.C., 1988).

120. ''Reichskammer der Technik,'' *ZVDDI* 25 (1934): 101; ''Zur organisatorischen Lage,'' *ibid.*, p. 167ff; F. Romberg, ''Der technische Akademiker im neuen Staat,'' *ibid.*, p. 197ff; ''An unsere Mitglieder!'' *ibid.*, 26 (1935): 165; and O. Stäbel, ''Die Aufgaben des deutschen Ingenieurs und der Neuaufbau der Technik im NS Staat,'' *DT* 2 (1935): 170.

121. O. Schumann, March 26, 1932, and M. Havenstein, April 22, 1933, in Hammerstein, ed., *Deutsche Bildung?*, pp. 52, 59, and Dick, *Oppositionelles Lehrerverhalten*, pp. 237, 295. Cf. Kater, *Doctors Under Hitler*, p. 35ff.

122. H. Thenorth, ''Professionen und Professionalisierung,'' in *Lehrer:* 457ff, uses the concept of deprofessionalization. Logically, a reversal of this process ought to be called reprofessionalization. Cf. Burrage *et al.*, ''An Actor-Oriented Framework for the Study of the Professions,'' in *Professions in Theory and History*.

123. Vogel, ''Memoiren,'' KA 1384; M. Havenstein, Aug. 28, 1934, in Hammerstein, ed., *Deutsche Bildung?*, p. 77. Cf. D. Silverman, ''Nazification of the German Bureaucracy,'' *JMH* 60 (1988): 498ff; Mommsen, *Beamtentum*, p. 23; and Jarausch, *Studenten*, p. 176.

124. N. Gürke, ''Völkerbundsaustritt und Abrüstung,'' *DR* 3 (1933): 162f; Bohm, ''In Treue zum Führer!'' *Phbl* 41 (1933): 485; ''Der 12. November ist Entscheidungstag!'' *ibid.*, No. 45; Reichsgemeinschaft der Technisch-wissenschaftlichen Arbeit, ''Entschließung,'' *ZVDI* 77 (1933): 1176.

125. H. Frank, ''Kameraden der Rechtsfront!'' *JW* 64 (1935): 1; H. Röchling, ''Die Saar bleibt deutsch!'' *ZVDI* 78 (1934): 673; ''Die Ingenieurtage in Trier,'' *ibid.*, p. 785; H. Röchling, ''Die Entscheidung über die Saar,'' *ibid.*, 79 (1935): 33f; and ''Die Saar ist heimgekehrt!'' *ibid.*, p. 123.

126. Bohm's appeal in *Phbl* 42 (1934): 353; Schult, ''Hindenburg,'' *ZVDI* 78 (1934): 945; ''Angelegenheiten des Vereins,'' *ibid.*, p. 992; SOPADE, *Deutschland Berichte*, Vol. 1, pp. 115f, 579f; Grimm, *Mit offenem Visier*, p. 138f. Cf. L. Gruchmann, ''Erlebnisbericht Werner Pünders über die Ermordung Klauseners am 30. Juni 1934,'' *VfZG* 19 (1971): 404ff.

127. H. Frank, ''Zum Tag der deutschen Justizeinheit!'' *JW* 64 (1935): 977; G. Ried, ''Zur Schaffung des Reichsministeriums für Wissenschaft, Erziehung und Volksbildung,'' *Phbl* 42 (1934): 217f; and ''Deutschlands Weg zu Arbeit und Frieden,'' *JW* 64 (1935): 312f.

128. C. Schmitt, ''Nationalsozialismus und Rechtsstaat,'' *JW* 63 (1934): 713; H. Frank, ''Der deutsche Rechtsstaat Adolf Hitlers,'' *DR* 4 (1934): 121f; ''Schülerauslese an den höheren Schulen,'' *DHS* 1 (1935): 262f; and W. Rust, ''Ingenieur/Industrie/Landesverteidigung,'' *VDIN* 13 (1933), No. 24. Cf. W. Heintzeler, *Der rote Faden* (Stuttgart, 1983), p. 32ff.

129. Raeke in ''Die große Gauführertagung im Hause der Deutschen Rechtsfront,'' *DR* 5 (1935): 74f; ''Rede des Reichswalters des NSLB und Gauleiters Wächtler,'' *DHS* 2 (1936):

587ff; O. Schumann, May 11, 1933, in Hammerstein, ed., *Deutsche Bildung?*, p. 60; F. Schmidt, "Der KDAI," *DT* 1 (1933): 47ff. According to A. Ehrentreich, *Fünfzig Jahre Erlebte Schulreform* (Frankfurt, 1985), p. 130, "no pedagogue could escape [NSLB] membership in the long run."

130. SOPADE, *Deutschland Berichte,* Vol. 2, pp. 207ff, 246ff; Schumann, April 12, 1934, *Deutsche Bildung?*, p. 79. The Socialist exile conclusion that "90 percent of the teachers are in opposition" was wishful thinking. Schnorbach, ed., *Lehrer,* p. 101f.

131. H. Frank, "Kameraden der Rechtsfront!" *JW* 64 (1935): 1; H. Schult, "1935! unsere Aufgabe!" *ZVDI* 79 (1935): 1.

132. Schröder, "Die 'Wiedergeburt' der Pharmazie," p. 166ff; and Hüttenberger, "Interessenvertretung und Lobbyismus," p. 429f.

133. Hüttenberger, "Nationalsozialistische Polykratie," *GG* 2 (1976): 417ff. Both the intentionalists and functionalists, therefore, turn out to be partially correct.

134. Schoenbaum, *Hitler's Social Revolution,* p. 275ff, versus Kershaw, *Nazi Dictatorship,* p. 130ff. Unfortunately, R. Grunberger, *The 12-Year Reich: A Social History of Nazi Germany* (New York, 1971), pp. 116ff, 285ff, is unreliable and oversimplified.

135. Havenstein, July 22, 1934, Hammerstein, ed., *Deutsche Bildung?,* p. 76; and Kater, *Doctors Under Hitler,* p. 54ff.

CHAPTER 6

1. "Der deutsche Juristentag 1936," *DR* 6 (1936): 218ff; F., "Reichstagung des NSLB im Juli 1936," *DHS* 2 (1936): 563ff; K. Zickler, "Arbeitstagung und Messekundgebung der Technik—Leipzig 1936," *DT* 3 (1936): 213f.

2. R. M. Kempner, *Ankläger einer Epoche* (Berlin, 1986), p. 92ff; "Der Geschichtsunterricht im Dienst des Nationalsozialismus," in H. Schnorbach, ed., *Lehrer und Schule unterm Hakenkreuz* (Königstein, 1983), p. 125f; SOPADE, *Deutschland Berichte,* Vol. 3, p. 1089ff.

3. Cf. P. Kleinewefers, *Jahrgang 1905,* 2nd ed. (Stuttgart, 1977), p. 77 ff, and H. and S. Obenhaus, eds., *"Schreiben wie es wirklich war!"* (Hannover, 1985), p. 34ff.

4. For critical approaches to everyday memories, see H. Focke and U. Reimer, eds., *Alltag unterm Hakenkreuz* (Hamburg, 1979); D. Peukert and J. Reulecke, *Die Reihen fast geschlossen* (Wuppertal, 1981); and U. Herbert, "Good Times, Bad Times: Memories of the Third Reich," in R. Bessel, ed., *Life in the Third Reich* (New York, 1987), p. 97ff.

5. A. J. P. Taylor, *The Origins of the Second World War* (London, 1961); and D. L. Hoggan, *Der erzwungene Krieg* (Tübingen, 1961) versus K. Hildebrand, *The Foreign Policy of the Third Reich* (Berkeley, 1979).

6. M. Stürmer, *Dissonanzen des Fortschritts* (Munich, 1986); and W. Schmidt, "Erbe und Tradition in der Diskussion der DDR-Historiker," (Ms., East Berlin, 1988).

7. A. Hillgruber, *Zweierlei Untergang. Die Zerschlagung des Deutschen Reiches und das Ende des europäischen Judentums* (Cologne, 1986), p. 20ff, the retranslation of a text, published in London in 1985.

8. E. Nolte, "Die Vergangenheit, die nicht vergehen will," *Frankfurter Allgemeine Zeitung,* June 6, 1986; *idem, Das Vergehen der Vergangenheit* (Berlin, 1987), p. 13ff; and *idem, Der Europäische Bürgerkrieg, 1917–1945* (Frankfurt, 1987).

9. J. Habermas, "Eine Art Schadensabwicklung," *Die Zeit,* July 11, 1986; and "Vom öffentlichen Gebrauch der Historie," *ibid.*, Nov. 14, 1986.

10. For the central texts cf. E. R. Piper, ed., *"Historikerstreit"* (Munich 1987), and R. Kühnl, *Vergangenheit die nicht vergeht* (Cologne, 1987), *passim.*

11. Among the many analyses see H.-U. Wehler, *Entsorgung der deutschen Vergangenheit?* (Munich, 1988), G. Erler *et al., Geschichtswende?* (Freiburg, 1987), and D. Diner, ed., *Ist der Nationalsozialismus Geschichte?* (Frankfurt, 1987).

12. G. Craig, "The War of the German Historians," *New York Review of Books* 23 (1987): 16ff; R. Evans, "The New Nationalism and the Old History," *JMH* 59 (1987): 761–97; G. Eley, "Nazism, Politics and Public Memory," *Past and Present* 121 (Nov. 1988): 171–208; and C. S. Maier, *The Unmasterable Past* (Cambridge, Mass., 1988).

13. The term was introduced by M. Broszat in H. Graml, ed., *Nach Hitler* (Munich, 1987),

p. 159ff. Cf. the exchange between S. Friedländer and Broszat, "Historisierung des Nationalsozialismus," *Die Zeit,* April 29, 1988, and K. H. Jarausch, "Removing the Nazi Stain? The Quarrel of the German Historians," *GSR* 11 (1988): 285–301.

14. W. Lepenies, "Vorbemerkung," to the special issue on "Wissenschaften im Nationalsozialismus" of *GG* 12 (1986): 287ff. For students cf. M. S. Steinberg, *Sabres and Brown Shirts* (Chicago, 1977) and G. Giles, *Students and National Socialism in Germany* (Princeton, N.J., 1985). For historians see the papers by H. Schleier and K. Schwabe as well as the comment by K. Jarausch at the 1986 GSA meeting in Albuquerque, New Mexico.

15. "Juden in der deutschen Rechtspflege?" *Hakenkreuzbanner,* July 18, 1935; Gürtner to the KG presidents, Feb. 18, 1935; note on "Beiordnung von nichtarischen RA als Armenanwälten arischer Parteien," Nov. 2, 1935, BA, R 22, No. 263; "Die Auswahl von Armenanwälten, Pflichtverteidigern, Konkursverwaltern und dergleichen," *DJ* 97 (1935), Dec. 20. Cf. *Der gelbe Fleck. Die Ausrottung von 500,000 deutschen Juden* (Paris, 1936), pp. 126–32.

16. W. Stuckart, "Die völkische Grundordnung des deutschen Volkes," *DR* 5 (1935): 557ff; Dr. Vollmer, "Die jüdischen Notare," *DJ* 98 (1936): 28; and W. Mock, *Technische Intelligenz im Exil* (Düsseldorf, 1986), p. 66ff. Cf. R. Hilberg, *The Destruction of European Jews* (New York, 1979 ed.), p. 46ff, and K. Pätzold, *Verfolgung, Vertreibung, Vernichtung* (Leipzig, 1983), pp. 84ff, 108ff.

17. Gürtner circular, Feb., 6, 1935; K. and R. Eder to Gürtner, March 14 and 26; Gürtner to OLG president Breslau, April 7, 1936, all in BA, R 22, No 264; and H. Göppinger, *Die Verfolgung der Juristen jüdischer Abstammung durch den Nationalsozialismus* (Villingen, 1963), p. 72ff. Cf. S. König, *Vom Dienst am Recht* (Berlin, 1986), p. 114ff; G. Fieberg, *Justiz und Nationalsozialismus* (Cologne, 1989), p. 111ff; and L. van Dick, *Oppositionelles Lehrerverhalten 1933–1945* (Weinheim, 1988). p. 88ff.

18. Neubert, "Aufstellung," Feb. 16, 1938, ZStA Po, Rep. 30.01, No. 8518; Jonas, "Vermerk" on negotiations of Schlegelberger with RRAK and NSRB representatives, April 8, 1938; "Ausgangspunkte für die Versorgung der jüdischen Anwälte," April 6, 1938; and Kritzinger, "Vermerk," April 12, 1938, BA, R 22, No. 253. Cf. L. Gruchmann, *Justiz im Dritten Reich, 1933–1940* (Munich, 1988), p. 174ff.

19. Jonas, "Vermerk," May 6, 1938; "Vermerk," June 1, 1938; Gürtner to Frick, June 28, and to Heß the same day; Bormann to Gürtner, July 8, 1938; J. Fließ to Gürtner, June 30, 1938; "Vermerk" on Jewish *Frontkämpfer,* July 28, 1938, in BA R 22, No. 253. Cf. Gruchmann, *Justiz,* p. 176ff.

20. "Entwurf I" of the "fünfte Verordnung zum Reichsbürgergesetz," n.d.; Hueber to Gürtner, July 14, 1938; Mackensen to Gürtner, July 30, 1938; Noack to Pohle, Aug., 5, 1938; Gürtner to Frick, Aug. 27, 1938, BA R 22, No. 253.

21. Note on "Ausscheiden der Juden aus der Rechtsanwaltschaft," Aug. 31, 1938; "Vermerk," Sept. 5, 1938; Gürtner to Heß, Sept. 9, 1938; Bormann to Gürtner, Sept. 29, 1938; "Keine jüdischen Rechtsanwälte mehr!" *Deutsches Nachrichtenbüro,* Oct. 15, 1938, BA R 2, No. 254. Cf. "Vertretung von Juden in Rechtsangelegenheiten," *Mitteilungsblatt des NSRB,* Jan. 15, 1939; "Rechtsanwälte," *DR* 9 (1939): 141; and Dr. Lorenzen, "Das Eindringen der Juden in die Justiz vor 1933," *ibid.,* pp. 731–40, 768–77, 956–66. Cf. Gruchmann, *Justiz,* p. 178ff.

22. E. Noack, "Die Entjudung der deutschen Anwaltschaft," *JW* 67 (1938): 2796f; "Durchführungsbestimmungen zu Paragraphen 5 und 14 der 5. VO zum Reichsbürgergesetz," *ibid.,* p. 2797f; "Angelegenheiten der jüdischen Konsulenten," *ibid.,* p. 2798ff; and "Angelegenheiten der Konsulenten," *DR* 9 (1939): 1427. Cf. U. Beer, *Versehrt, Verfolgt, Versöhnt* (Essen, 1979) p. 55f; Fieberg, *Justiz und Nationalsozialismus,* p. 121ff; I. Hecht, *Als unsichtbare Mauern wuchsen: Eine deutsche Familie unter den Nürnberger Rassengesetzen* (Munich, 1987), p. 23ff.

23. S. Neumann, *Nacht über Deutschland* (Munich, 1978), p. 84ff; R. Kempner, *Ankläger,* p. 119ff; R. Bendix, *Von Berlin nach Berkeley* (Frankfurt, 1985), p. 197ff; and Göppinger, *Verfolgung,* p. 115ff, with many heart-rending individual examples. Cf. W. Benz, ed., *Die Juden in Deutschland, 1933–1945. Leben unter nationalsozialistischer Herrschaft* (Munich, 1989), p. 282ff; and Jarausch, "Jewish Lawyers in Germany," *passim.*

24. Ronge, *Im Namen der Gerechtigkeit* (Munich, 1963), p. 186f; A. Apfel, *Behind the Scenes of Justice* (London, 1935), p. 167f; M. Hachenburg, *Lebenserinnerungen eines Rechts-*

anwalts und Briefe aus der Emigration, reissued by J. Schadt (Stuttgart, 1978), p. 12f; A. von Brünneck, "Ernst Fraenkel (1898–1975)," in Kritische Justiz, ed., *Streitbare Juristen* (Baden-Baden, 1988), 451ff; Göppinger, *Verfolgung,* p. 121ff; Schnorbach, ed., *Lehrer und Schule,* p. 137ff; and Kronstein, *Briefe an einen jungen Deutschen* (Munich, 1967), p. 144ff. Cf. J. Walk, "Jüdische Schule und Erziehung," *IZEBF* 33 (1988): 165ff; L. van Dick, *Oppositionelles Lehrerverhalten,* p. 100ff; and Glen Sharfman's dissertation on the "German Jewish Youth Movement" (Chapel Hill, N.C., 1989). While H. Strauss includes prominent professionals in his *Biographisches Handbuch der deutschsprachigen Emigration nach 1933* (Munich, 1980), there is little information on the fate of average practitioners.

25. C. Riess, *Der Mann in der schwarzen Robe. Das Leben des Strafverteidigers M. Alsberg* (Hamburg, 1965), p. 331f; Bendix, *Von Berlin,* p. 187ff; Göppinger, *Verfolgung,* p. 131ff; and *Der gelbe Fleck,* p. 254ff. The standard histories pay too little attention to this frightful toll. Cf. Ostler, "Rechtsanwälte in der NS-Zeit," p. 54f versus Reifner, "Freie Advokatur," p. 62ff. Other cases in: Fieberg, *Justiz und Nationalsozialismus* p. 123; U. Hochmuth, ed., *Hamburg* (Hamburg, 1985), p. 177ff, 201ff; Mock, *Technische Intelligenz,* p. 67ff; and L. van Dick, *Oppositionelles Lehrerverhalten,* p. 115ff.

26. W. Schwabroth, *Im Ganzen Gut* (Hamburg, 1980); and Vogel, "Memoiren," KA 1384. Cf. M. H. Kater, *Doctors Under Hitler* (Chapel Hill, N.C., 1989), p. 192ff. and Dick, *Oppositionelles Lehrerverhalten,* p. 209.

27. H. Frank, "Die Neugestaltung des deutschen Rechts," *DR* 5 (1935): 470ff; *Im Angesicht des Galgens* (Munich, 1953), p. 174ff; and N. Frank, *Der Vater* (Munich, n.d.), p. 67ff. Cf. Willig, "Theory and Administration of Justice," p. 49ff; and D. Anderson, "The Academy of German Law" (Diss., Ann Arbor, Mich. 1982).

28. H. Frank, "Die Zeit des Rechts," *DR* 6 (1936): 1ff; "Nationalsozialistische Rechtspolitik," *ibid.*, p. 389ff; and "Das Recht im Reich," *ibid.* 7 (1937): 1ff; E. Noack, "Volk, Gesetz und Recht," *ibid.*, p. 3ff; F. W. Adami, "Das Programm der NSDAP und die Rechtssprechung," *ibid.*, p. 486ff. Cf. H. Loebel, ed., *Justiz und Nationalsozialismus* (Hannover, 1985); and H. Salje, ed., *Recht und Unrecht im Nationalsozialismus* (Münster, 1985).

29. H. Schneider, "Drei Jahre NS Rechtspflege," *DR* 6 (1936): 117ff; R. Heydrich, "Die Bekämpfung der Staatsfeinde," *ibid.*, p. 121ff; W. Best, "Die Gestapo," *ibid.*, p. 125ff; H. Tesmer, "Die Schutzhaft und ihre rechtlichen Grundlagen," *ibid.*, p. 135ff; H. Frank, "Die Durchsetzung der NS Ideale auf dem Gebiete des Rechts," *ibid.*, 8 (1938): 348; and "Kampf um deutsches Volksrecht," *ibid.*, 9 (1939): 354ff.

30. H. Schneider, "Der Rechtsanwalt und das Deutsche Recht," *DR* 6 (1936): 375ff; and W. Wienert and M. Esch, *Der Rechtsanwalt,* 3rd ed. (Berlin, 1940), p. 8ff.

31. F. Gürtner, "Richter und Rechtsanwalt im neuen Staat," *DJ* 96 (1934): 369–72; H. Droege, "Wahrheitssuche und Rechtssuche—die wirksamsten Waffen des Rechtsanwalts," *DR* 9 (1939): 548ff; H. Fritzsche, "Die Aufgaben des Strafverteidigers," *ibid.*, p. 1118f; W. Meyer, "Darf der Rechtsanwalt, ohne seine Berufspflichten zu verletzen, eine offenkundig aussichslose Revision begründen?" *ibid.*, p. 208f, and H. Hillrichs response, *ibid.*, p. 753f. Cf. Leupolt, "Der deutsche Rechtsanwalt," *Der deutsche Rechtsstand* (Berlin, 1939), p. 126ff.

32. Text of Frank speech in "Bericht über die Sondertagung der Fachschaft 2," *DHS* (1936): 564ff; and his predecessor Benze's address "Aus der Arbeit der Fachschaft 2," *ibid.*, p. 31f. Cf. H. Scholz, *Erziehung und Unterricht unterm Hakenkreuz* (Göttingen, 1985), p. 56ff; U. Herrmann, ed., *"Die Formung des Volksgenossen"* (Weinheim, 1985); and R. Dithmar, ed., *Schule und Unterricht im Dritten Reich* (Neuwied, 1989).

33. Rust, Jan. 29, 1938, "Neuordnung des höheren Schulwesens," and "Erziehung und Unterricht in der höheren Schule," *DHS* 5 (1938): 160f; Havenstein, May 8, 1936, N. Hammerstein, ed., *Deutsche Bildung?* (Frankfurt, 1988), p. 104f. Cf. B. Zymek, "Die pragmatische Seite der NS Schulpolitik," in Herrmann, *Formung,* p. 269ff.

34. K. Frank, "Reichsfachschaft 2," *RDE* (1936), No. 7; "Rede des kommissarischen Reichsfachschaftsleiters Karl Frank," *DHS* 3 (1936): 564ff; K. Frank, "Aufgaben, Ausbildung und Anstellung der Lehrer an den höheren Schulen im Dritten Reich," *ibid.*, 4 (1937): 185ff; "Die höhere Schule im Dienste der NS Jugenderziehung," *ibid.*, 6 (1939): 113ff; and Akademisches Auskunftsamt, ed., *Der Lehrer an Höheren Schulen* (Berlin, 1939), p. 3ff.

35. Dr. Todt, "Die übergeordneten Aufgaben," *VDIN* 17 (1937), No. 17; G. Nonnemacher,

"Technik—rassisch gesehen," *DT* 4 (1936): 534f; A. Gießler, "Der nordische Mensch und die Technik," *ibid.*, 5 (1937), No. 2; O. Stäbel, "Kulturwert der Technik," *Der Jungingenieur,* March 1937; A. Rosenberg, "Weltanschauung und Technik," *VDIN* 18 (1938), No. 1; and F. Nonnenbruch, "Über Technik und Wirtschaft," *ibid.*, 6 (1938): 8f.

36. "Generalinspektor Dr.-Ing. Fritz Todt zur Eröffnung des neuen Hauses der Technik in Essen," *DT* 4 (1936): 627; "Die deutsche Volkswirtschaft unter NS Führung," *ibid.*, p. 278f; F. Todt, "Kongreßrede auf dem Nürnberger Parteitag 1936," *ibid.*, p. 478f. E. Maier-Dorn, "Technik bestimmt Völkerschicksale," *VDIN* 18 (1938), No. 37.

37. Wesemann, "Technik und Nationalsozialismus," *DT* 5 (1937): 56f; O. Streck, "Ingenieurberuf und Ingenieurerziehung," *ibid.*, p. 365f; F. Todt, "Menschenführung und politisches Soldatentum," *VDIN* 19 (1939), No. 21; Wesemann, "Der soldatische Ingenieur—ein neuer Techniker-Typ," *DT* Suppl. *Betrieb und Wehr* 6 (1938): 149ff; and O. Stäbel, "Jungingenieurarbeit," *DT* 4 (1936): 6f.

38. W. Müller, *Der Bauingenieur,* 4th rev. ed. (Berlin, 1941), and Streck to NSDAP Prüfungskommission July 28, 1938 (draft article on "engineers" for *Meyer's Lexikon*), BA, NS 14, No. 19, Vol. I. Cf. J. Herf, *Reactionary Modernism* (Cambridge, 1984), p. 205ff.

39. R. Freisler, "Neue Grundsätze für die Auslese der Rechtswahrer," *DJ* 97 (1935): 583ff; R. Höhn, "Die neue Studienordnung für Rechtswissenschaft im Rahmen der Universitätsreform," *DR* 5 (1935): 51ff; H. Frank, "Zur Reform des Rechtstudiums," *ibid.*, 3 (1933): 23f; Cf. G. Vollmer, *Rechtsanwalt,* p. 11f; L. Gruchmann, *Justiz im Dritten Reich, 1933–1940* (Munich, 1988), p. 300ff; and Fieberg, *Justiz und Nationalsozialismus,* p. 170ff.

40. O. Palandt, "Der Werdegang des jungen Juristen im NS Staat," *DJ* 97 (1935): 586ff; Frank to Heß, Feb. 8 and July 18, 1935, and Gumpert deposition, Nov. 13, 1936, claiming that instead of listening to a Hitler speech, the inmates watched the movie *"So endet die Liebe,"* BA, NS 16, No. 112. Cf. O. Palandt, "Die Arbeit der Ausbildungsabteilung," *DJ* 100 (1937): 22ff; and the Berlin and Baden reports of July 5, 1938 and July 6, 1939, BA, NS 16, No. 127. Cf. Gruchmann, *Justiz,* p. 303ff.

41. "Wechsel in der Herausgeberschaft der *JW,*" *JW* 65 (1936): 225; and Göppinger, *Verfolgung,* p. 140ff. Cf. W. Raeke, "Deutscher Juristentag einst und jetzt," *DR* 6 (1936): 179f; "Der Deutsche Juristentag 1936," *ibid.*, p. 218ff; R. Freisler, "Gedanken zum Deutschen Rechtswahrertag 1939," with summaries of speeches, *DJ* 101 (1939): 821ff, 888ff; and H. Schraut, ed., *Deutscher Juristentag* (Leipzig, 1936 and 1939).

42. For example, "Die Zukunft der Deutschen Anwaltschaft," *JW* 63 (1934): 668f; "Zur Gauführertagung des BNSDJ," *ibid.*, 64 (1935): 241; "Zur Tagung des Reichsfachgruppenrats Rechtsanwälte," *ibid.*, p. 978ff; "Die große Gauführertagung des BNSDJ," *JW* 65 (1936): 563.

43. H. Frank, "Anordnung 19/36," and Fischer to all Gau legal leaders, Nov. 25, 1936 on "political indoctrination," BA, NS 16, 112. Gau Berlin, *Tätigkeitsbericht für das Jahr 1939* (Berlin, 1940), hardly mentions *Schulung* per se.

44. W. Erxleben, "Zur Berufsvorbildung der Philologen," *DHS* 2 (1935): 842ff; NSLB memorandum, "Vorschläge zu einer Neugestaltung des deutschen Schulwesens"; Kolz, "Richtlinien für die Lehrtätigkeit und das Studium an den HfL," April 19, 1936, BA, NS 12, No. 1338; Krieck, "Lehrerbildung," *RDE* (1934), No. 9; and special *RDE* issue, March 1937.

45. K. Frank, "Aufgaben, Ausbildung und Anstellung der Lehrer an den höheren Schulen im Dritten Reich," *DHS* 3 (1936): 185ff; "Richtlinien für die Ausbildung für das Lehramt an höheren Schulen," *ibid.*, p. 627ff; "Reichsordnung der pädagogischen Prüfung," *ibid.*, p. 549f; L. Müller, "Gedanken zur Neugestaltung der Ausbildung unserer Studienreferendare," *ibid.*, p. 262ff. Cf. H. Scholz and E. Stranz, "NS Einflußnahme auf die Lehrerbildung," in Heinemann, ed., *Erziehung* 2: 110f.

46. E. Michelsen, "Zur Auslese des Lehrernachwuchses in den höheren Schulen," *DHS* 4 (1937): 266f; "Erstes ständiges Studienreferendar-Lager," *ibid.*, p. 792f. Cf. O. Ottweiler, *Die Volksschule im Nationalsozialismus* (Weinheim, 1979), p. 199ff.

47. Rust, Dec. 15, 1933; comment by Ministry of Education on July 7, 1935, and other material in ZStA Po, Rep. 49.01, No. 4605; Rust order, Feb. 22, 1935; Education to Ministry of Finance, Sept. 24, 1935; Schemm to Rust, Feb. 2, 1936 and Rust decree of May 12, 1936, in ZStA Po, Rep. 49.01, No. 4607; "Bericht über die Schulung im NSLB bis August 1934," *RDE* (1934): No. 11 and E. Kolb, "Unser Schulungslager in seinem Leben und seiner Schau,"

ibid. (1935), No. 2. Cf. L. van Dick, *Oppositionelles Lehrerverhalten* (Weinheim, 1988), p. 187f.

48. "Die Führertagung des NSLB in Bayreuth," Jan. 29, 1936, BA, NS 12, No. 690; periodic reports in *DHS* 1 (1935): 423f; 2 (1936): 564ff; 3 (1937): 207f; 5 (1939): 136f and entries under "Schulung" in *RDE*. See the district Section Two reports beginning in the fall of 1935 in BA, NS 12, No. 826. Cf. W. Feiten, *Der NSLB. Entwicklung und Organisation* (Frankfurt, 1981), p. 173ff; and N. Franck, ed., *Heil Hitler, Herr Lehrer* (Berlin, 1983), p. 125ff.

49. G. Garbotz, "Gleichschaltung in der technischen Erziehung," *VDIN* 13 (1933), No. 19; Stäbel, "Die Entwicklungslinien des technischen Schulwesens," *ibid.*, 14 (1934), No. 24; O. Streck, "Gedanken zu einer Neuordnung des akademischen Ingenieurstudiums," *DT* 4 (1936): 4ff; G. Garbotz, "Zum Neuaufbau der technischen Erziehung," *VDIN* (1936), No. 16; Prof. Bacher, "Ausbildung zum technischen Beruf," *DT* 5 (1937): 320f.

50. R. W. "Reichsschulungslager des NSBDT," *DT* 3 (1935): 317; "Weltanschauliche Schulung des Ingenieurs," *VDIN* 15 (1935), No. 20; M. Wend, "Die Schulung des NSBDT," *ibid.*, June 5, 1935; O. Stäbel, "Durch Schulung zur Auslese," *ibid.*, 16 (1936), No. 22; "Einheit der technischen Erziehung," and "Die technischen Erzieher auf der Plassenburg," *ibid.*, 18 (1938), No. 5; W. Arnold, "Fahrt zur Plassenburg," *ibid.*, 18 (1938), No. 45. Cf. J. C. Guse, "The Spirit of the Plassenburg: Technology and Ideology in the Third Reich" (Diss., Lincoln, Neb., 1981), p. 173ff.

51. Ministerial memorandum of June 19, 1936; Frank to Gürtner, July 11, 1936; and note of their Sept. 9 meeting, in ZStA Po, Rep. 30.01, No. 8522. Cf. the material on appointments to the local lawyer chambers, *ibid.*, No. 8523.

52. Raeke in *JW* 63 (1934): 793f. Case citations from the published decisions of the EGH, Vol. 29, p. 71; Vol. 32, p. 30ff; and Vol. 33, p. 8ff. Neubert, "Standesaufsicht und Ehrengerichtsbarkeit der Anwaltschaft," *JW* 67 (1938): 2507f. Cf. König, *Dienst am Recht,* p. 59ff, and I. Müller, *Furchtbare Juristen* (Munich, 1987), p. 74ff.

53. For Nazi prosecution purposes, the topical NSLB records in the BDC were transformed into 148 alphabetic files. The above-mentioned citations stem from an 8 percent sample, taking every twelfth folder. Beurteilung des HA für Erzieher Danzig on H. Abel, May 15, 1938; NSLB Stabsleiter to Reichsleitung, June 6, 1934; NSLB to NS Gauleitung, Jan. 1, 1934, all in Vol. "Abel"; and Kreisamtsleiter to Gauleitung, March 9, 1939, Vol. "Kainz." Cf. Schumann, Aug., 16, 1935, in Hammerstein, ed., *Deutsche Bildung?,* p. 89.

54. Application by H. Abel and letter of Prussian ministry, March 17, 1936, BDC, NSLB Vol. "Abel"; political autobiography G. Kaiser, April 1, 1937, Vol. "Kainz"; Gauamtsleiter to Reichsleitung, June 27, 1934, Vol. "Faas"; "2. Vorschlagsliste über die bevorzugte Beförderung," vol. "Brandau"; Kunstmann to Bavarian Ministry of Education, July 13, 1943, Vol. "Seyfried"; and Gauamtsleiter *Beurteilung,* Sept. 20, 1938, Vol."Zill."

55. Letter by W. Sichting, March 6, 1934, BDC, NSLB, Vol. "Seyfried"; NSDAP Kreisinspektor to E. Ohlhof, Nov. 7, 1934, Vol."Nordmann"; M. Lohnke to K. Skorczyk, June 28, 1934, and other correspondence, vol. "Seyfried." To the protest that double memberships were not prohibited, the NSLB replied: "You don't seriously want to maintain . . . that the Philologenverband is 'National Socialist'?!"

56. Heussler to Stadtschulbehörde Aschaffenburg, Oct. 12, 1937, BDC, NSLB, Vol. "Zill"; Dienstverfahren against Max Abresch, Dec. 13, 1936, Vol. "Abel"; Dienststrafsache Oelmann, March 17, 1936, Vol. "Nordmann"; NSLB Kreiswalter, Feb. 8, 1938 on Sippel case, Vol. "Seyfried"; Dienststrafsache against A. Voigt, April 26, 1937, Vol. "Vogel"; and "Urteil in Privatklagesache H. Otto, Moers," March 12, 1934, Vol. "Abel." Cf. W. Jubelius, "Beamtenpflichten und Disziplinarrecht unter der Herrschaft des Nationalsozialismus," *Recht und Unrecht im NS,* p. 150ff.

57. The NSBDT files in the BDC have similarly been reorganized alphabetically. The cases cited below come from a systematic sample of 11 of the 109 volumes that have survived. "Eignungsbericht über Prof. Dr. Ing. habil. Hermann Alker," Aug. 8, 1939, Vol. "Abcouwer"; "Lebenslauf Ing. Hans Alzinger," *ibid.;* A. Schweizer to Pg. Wissmann, May 12, 1935 with supporting letter, Vol. "Schulze."

58. Saur to VDI Aug. 19, 1938, BDC, NSBDT, Vol. "Burchartz"; Irrek to Zentralkartei VDCh, Nov. 27, 1940, Vol. "Francke"; Reichsberufswart to Heß, July 5, 1937, Vol. "Leitz";

suitability report on Paul Lippert, Vol. "Lichey"; Kreisleiter report on Julius Schwalm, Feb. 9. 1938, Vol. "Schulze"; orange file card, warning against the acceptance of Otto Frerichs with addenda, Vol. "Francke."

59. Schumann, Jan. 21, 1936, in Hammerstein, ed., *Deutsche Bildung?*, p. 98 and April 12, 1935, *ibid.*, p. 80. Cf. Kater, *Doctors Under Hitler*, p. 111ff.

60. Pg. Link, "10 Grundforderungen für den neuen deutschen Ingenieur," BA, NS 14, No. 18, Vol. 12. T. Mason, *Sozialpolitik im Dritten Reich*, 2nd ed. (Opladen, 1978), and M. Prinz, *Vom neuen Mittelstand zum Volksgenossen* (Munich, 1986) dispute the benefits of collaboration. Although the coordination of journals restricted the voices of professionals, the considerable evidence on conflicts within the NS system helps resolve some of the contradictions in the behavior of practitioners.

61. E. Noack, "Praxis, Studium und Prüfung," *DR* 8 (1938): 244ff; K. Lang, "Die Erziehung des Rechtswahrernachwuchses," *ibid.*, 9 (1939): 3ff; A. Scheel, *Die Reichsstudentenführung* (Berlin, 1938), p. 17ff; and K. Zuse, *Der Computer, Mein Lebenswerk* (Munich, 1970), p. 44f. Cf. Giles, *Students*, p. 189ff; M. H. Kater, "The Reich Vocational Contest and Students of Higher Learning in Nazi Germany," *CEH* 7 (1974): 225ff; and M. Klewitz, *Lehrersein im Dritten Reich* (Weinheim, 1987), p. 168ff.

62. G. A. Scheel, "Die Neuordnung des deutschen Studententums," *DR* 7 (1937): 5ff; SOPADE, *Deutschland Berichte*, three reports on "Jugend im III. Reich" of Feb. and Oct. 1936. Cf. K. H. Jarausch, *Deutsche Studenten 1800–1970* (Frankfurt, 1984), pp. 165ff, 188ff.

63. H. Titze, *Das Hochschulstudium in Preußen und Deutschland, 1820–1944* (Göttingen, 1987), tables 1 and 2; Ch. Lorenz, *Zehnjahres-Statistik des Hochschulbesuchs und der Abschlußprüfungen* (Berlin, 1943), Vol. 1, p. 20ff; Jarausch, *Deutsche Studenten*, p. 177ff; and Kater, *Doctors Under Hitler*, p. 150ff.

64. *Deutsche Hochschulstatistik* 14 (1935): 46ff; Lorenz, *Zehnjahres-Statistik*, Vol. 1, p. 85ff; H. Streit, *Aus der Arbeit des Reichsstudentenwerks* (n.p., n.d.). According to W. Pellny, "Die Abhängigkeit des technischen Studiums von Schule und Vaterhaus," *DT* 5 (1937): 69ff, 32 percent of 2000 Darmstadt engineering undergraduates between 1928 and 1934 stemmed from "higher officials, leading employees or academic professionals." Cf. Jarausch, *Deutsche Studenten*, p. 180ff.

65. Ch. Lorenz, *Zehnjahres-Statistik*, Vol. 2 on *Abschlußprüfungen*, pp. 11ff, 27ff, 42ff, 46ff, 56ff, 63ff, 68ff, is a unique source for the years 1932 to 1942 that deserves more systematic study.

66. Hauptabteilung Berufsbetreuung, "Bericht über die Arbeiten des Jahres 1936," *Mitteilungsblatt des NSRB* (appendix to *DR* 7) (1937): 20ff; "Aus dem Jahresbericht der NSRB-Arbeitsvermittlung für 1938," *ibid.*, (1939): 11f; "Die NSRB-Arbeitsvermittlung im 2. Vierteljahr," *DR* 9 (1939): 1628f. Cf. Gruchmann, *Justiz*, p. 312ff.

67. Figures from A. Nath, *Die Studienratskarriere im Dritten Reich* (Frankfurt, 1988), pp. 207ff, 305ff; H. Wefelscheid, "Der Altersaufbau unserer Lehrerschaft," *DHS* 5 (1938): 111ff; "Die Berichte über die Lage der Studienassessoren besagen Folgendes," examples from Bavaria, Berlin, Essen, and so on, *ibid.*, p. 477ff.

68. K. Steinmetz, "Vom Arbeitsraum der Diplom-Ingenieure," *ZVDDI* 27 (1936): 20f, 51f, 110f; M. Wend, "Nachwuchsplanung im Ingenieurberuf," *VDIN* 15 (1935), July 17; and W. Peters, "Unser Ingenieurnachwuchs," *ZVDDI* 30 (1939): 13ff, with figures on graduates.

69. K. Elbel, "Ingenieurbedarf und Berufswerbung," *Der Jungingenieur*, March 31, 1937; E. Simon, "Droht ein Mangel an Philologen?" *Monatsschrift für höhere Schulen* (1938): 191f, and the articles under "Lehrermangel" in *RDE* (1939): 20ff, 256ff; Goens, "Richtermangel—eine Gefahr für die Rechtspflege," *DR* 8 (1938): 72f, and Gürtner, "Pflicht und Aufgabe des Justizbeamten," *DJ* 100 (1938): 363f.

70. C. Barzel, "Die Verkürzung der Schulzeit in Zahlen," *DHS* 4 (1937): 28ff; W. Oberle, "Hundertfünzig Jahre Reifeprüfung," *ibid.*, 5 (1938): 132ff; F. Bacher, "Vorbildung und Berechtigung," *Der Jungingenieur*, June 30, 1937; *idem*, "Gefahren der Hochschulreform," *VDIN* 19 (1939): Feb. 9; and L. Pister, "Hochschule, Wissenschaft und Technik," *DT* 7 (1939): 2ff.

71. W. Best, "Die Nachwuchsfrage," *DR* 9 (1939): 501ff; F. Todt, "Jugend, die Technik ruft Euch!" *DT* 5 (1937): 313 and 347ff; K. Meyer, "Jugend und Technik," *ibid.*, 6 (1938): 427ff. Cf. J. Handrick, "Der Nachwuchs für die technischen Berufe," *RDE* (1937), No. 11.

72. E. Eggener, "Die Frau im öffentlichen Leben," *DR* 8 (1938): 92ff; Frida Holaschke, "Wie ich Maschinen-Ingenieurin wurde," *VDIN* 19 (1939), No. 37; and J. R. Pauwels, *Women and University Studies in the Third Reich, 1933–1945* (New York, 1985), p. 27ff. "Wiedereinstellung von Lehrkräften," *DHS* 3 (1936): 618; and ZStA Po, Rep. 49.01, No. 312.

73. Ch. Lorenz, *Zehnjahres-Statistik,* Vol. 1, p. 28; Titze, *Hochschulstudium,* tables, p. 1ff; "Berufsabsichten der Reifeschüler 1939," *RDE* (1939): 256.

74. Raeke to Steinbrecher, Jan. 10, 1935, BA, R 22, 252; Quandt to Lammers, Nov. 9, 1935, BA, R 34II, 1535; self-help program of the Reichsfachgruppe Rechtsanwälte, BA, NS 16, No. 251; Noack draft, May 30, 1935; memorandum of Oct. 16, and other materials in ZStA Po, Rep. 30.01, 8520. Cf. E. Noack, *Hilfe für die Anwaltschaft!?* (Leipzig, 1935), p. 22ff; Vollmer, "Die Lage der deutschen Anwaltschaft," *DJ* (1935): 1693ff; Gürtner, "Hilfe für die Anwaltschaft," *ibid.,* 1789ff; and ZStA Po, Rep. 30.01, No. 8520ff.

75. Protocol of the Nov. 19, 1935 discussion and supplementary material, ZStA Po, Rep. 30.01, 8521; "Zweites Gesetz zur Änderung der RAO vom 13. Dez., 1935," BA, R 43II, 1534. R. Freisler, "Die neuen Gesetze zur Behebung der Not des Rechtsanwaltstandes," *DJ* (1935): 1790ff; Vollmer explanation, *ibid.,* p. 1820ff; and R. Neubert, "Neujahrsgedanken zum neuen Anwaltsrecht," *ibid.,* (1936): 18f; versus G. Bohne, "Die gefährliche Auswirkung des Anwaltsgesetzentwurfs," BA, R 43II, 1534. Cf. O. Glöckler, *Die Zulassung zur Rechtsanwaltschaft* (Würzburg, 1937), p. 51ff.

76. "Übersicht über die zahlenmäßige Entwicklung der Anwaltschaft im Jahre 1938" and for 1939, BA, R 22, No. 266. Additional figures in E. Noack, "Die Altersversorgung der Rechtsanwälte," *DR* 9 (1939): 833ff.

77. Dr. Meuschel, "Ergebnisse der Einkommenssteuerstatistik für 1936," *Deutsche Steuer Zeitung,* Jan. 21, 1939; "Vermerk über das Ergebnis der Ermittlungen hinsichtlich der Frage welche LG Bezirke als sogenannte 'Notbezirke' anzusehen sind," from 1937, BA, R 22, No. 153; Neubert to Gürtner on "Die Lage der Anwaltschaft," March 31, 1938, *ibid.,* No. 265; and Feb. 14, 1939, *ibid.,* p. 254. Cf. Kater, *Doctors Under Hitler,* p. 31ff.

78. Figures from W. Günther, "Beschäftigung und Anstellung im höheren Schuldienst," in *Der Lehrer an höheren Schulen,* p. 19ff; material in ZStA Po, Rep. 49.01, Nos. 119–22; and remarks in SOPADE, *Deutschland Berichte,* Vols. 3 (Feb. 1936) and 6 (March 1939). Cf. R. Bölling, *Sozialgeschichte der deutschen Lehrer* (Göttingen, 1983), p. 154f.

79. C. Zinnemann, "Die Bedeutung der Arbeit in der Wehrwirtschaft," *ZVDI* 81 (1937): 97ff; C. Welkner, "Der Ingenieurnachwuchs," *ibid.,* 82 (1938): 689ff; H. Schult, "Zum Arbeitseinsatz im Ingenieurberuf," *ZVDI* 81 (1937): 618; "Die Berufsaussichten des Ingenieurs," *VDIN* 18 (1938), No. 4; K. F. S., " 'Fast fürstliche Bezahlung'," *ZVDDI* 29 (1938): 106. Cf. Prinz, *Vom neuen Mittelstand,* p. 174ff.

80. H. Aly, "Hat Deutschland zu wenig Ingenieure?" *DT* 4 (1936): 432; K. F. Steinmetz, "Eine Staatsnotwendigkeit," *ZVDDI* 29 (1938): 69ff. According to D. Müller's figures, *Datenhandbuch,* Vol. 1, p. 209, this propaganda had some effect on Prussian graduates, increasing their willingness to study from 47.9 percent to 57.3 percent between 1935 and 1939.

81. NSRB Baden to Reichsgruppenwalter, March 30, 1939, BA, NS 16, No. 127; "Die Tagung des Reichsfachgruppenrats 'Rechtsanwälte' des BNSDJ," March 29 and 30, 1935, BA, R 22, No. 251; H. Boberach, ed., *Meldungen aus dem Reich* (Herrsching, 1984), Vol. 2, p. 278ff; "Rechtsanwälte," *DJ* 101 (1939): 900; "Rechtswahrer als Judengenossen," *Der Stürmer,* summer 1937, ZStA Po, Rep. 30.01, 8517; R. Höhn, "Der erste großdeutsche Rechtswahrertag," *DR* 9 (1939): 737ff.

82. Lapicida, "Titel im Dritten Reich," *ZVDDI* 28 (1937): 156f; and S. "Titel im Dritten Reich," *ibid.,* 29 (1938): 163. Initially titles were restored on April 7, 1933 and the honorary professor was reintroduced in Jan. 1934.

83. "Flucht aus dem Lehrerberuf," BA, NS 12, No. 1438; H. B, "Jetzt ist's genug!" *RDE* (1939): 20ff; "Abwanderung aus dem Erzieherberuf," *ibid.,* p. 64; and "Wenn das so weitergeht . . . !" *ibid.,* p. 144. Cf. Nath, "Studienassessor," p. 288.

84. "Aus dem NSLB," *DHS* 6 (1939): 60f; Fröhlich, "Zur Vorlage," Dec. 19, 1938 (calling for the collection "of all public press attacks on teachers"), BA, NS 12, No. 1438; Berchtold to NSLB, Oct. 31, 1938, and reply of Nov. 11, BA, NS 12, No. 1447; and Boberach, *Meldungen,* Vol. 2, p. 133ff.

85. H. Kölzow, "Der Weg des VDI als Ausdruck seiner inneren Haltung," *ZVDI* 82 (1938): 785; K. Steinmetz, "Der Mangel an Ingenieur-Nachwuchs," *ZVDDI* 28 (1937): 117ff; and Prof. Streck to Munich TH rector, May 20, 1938, BA, NS 14, No. 19, 2; Himmler, "Reichsschulungskurs der deutschen Technik," and "Die Stellung der Truppeningenieure im Heere, Dec. 1938," *ibid.*, No. 15.

86. "Der rechtliche Schutz der Bezeichnung Ingenieur," *ZVDDI* 28 (1937): 140ff; 29 (1938): 7ff; NSBDT, "Berufsbezeichnung 'Ingenieur'," BA, NS 14, No. 8; "Beratende Ingenieure im NSBDT," *VDIN* 19 (1939), No. 19. Cf. K. Klein, "Das zwingende Erfordernis des reichsgesetzlichen Schutzes der technischen Berufsbezeichnungen sowie der technischen Berufsausübungen" in BA, NS 14, No. 18, II.

87. Greiner to the press, July 22, 1939, circulating "Nur ein Techniker. . . ." and "Nachwuchs, dem der Marschallstab aus dem Tornister gestohlen wurde" in BA, NS 14, No. 78. Streck to Kandler, Jan. 13, 1939, *ibid.*, No. 19, 1; Dr. Flg, "Die Technik, ein wertvoller Teil deutschen Kulturschaffens," *ibid.*, No. 78; "Vier Ingenieure Träger des Nationalpreises 1938," *ZVDI* 82 (1938): 1903.

88. BNSDJ, "Thesen und Grundforderungen," and "Vermerk über die Tagung des Reichsfachgruppenrats," March 29 and 30, and Ministry of Justice to Raeke, May 13, 1935, BA, R 22, No. 251; Raeke to Gürtner, Aug. 5, 1935, and Ministry of Justice to Ministry of Labor, Dec. 24, 1935, *ibid.*, No. 263. When a backlog of applicants raised the divisive issue of *Simultanzulassung,* the ministry ruled that "the LG attorneys will have to live with it." Gürtner to LG president in Landsberg, May 12, 1936, and "Vermerk" of May 10, 1937, *ibid.*, No. 252.

89. Gürtner, "RRAO," Feb. 21, 1936, *Reichsgesetzblatt* 1 (1936): 107ff, and R. Freisler, "Die neuen Gesetze zur Behebung der Not des Rechtsanwaltstandes," *DJ* 97 (1935): 1790ff; Schwartz to Neubert, Oct. 8, 1935, and Neubert to the lawyer chambers, Feb., 28, 1936, BA, R 22, No. 251; Notar Wolpers, "Zur Reichsnotarordnung," *DR* 7 (1937): 291f; and Droege, "Gegenwartsprobleme der Anwaltschaft," *ibid.*, 9 (1939): 1114ff. Cf. the rich material in ZStA Po, Rep. 30.01, 8517–8.

90. "Zulassungs- and Prüfungsordnung für 'Wirtschaftstreuhänder NSRB'," *DR* 7 (1937): 54ff; Pohle, "Betätigung von Rechtsanwälten in Steuersachen," April 14 and "Vermerk," Aug. 6, 1937, BA, R 22, No. 264; "Fachanwälte für Steuerrecht," *DJ* 99 (1937): 1761f; Neubert to Gürtner, March 31, 1938, *ibid.*, No. 265; Schlegelberger note ZStA Po, Rep. 30.01, 8518. Cf. Frische, "Was ist ein Eingriff in die Berufsaufgaben des Rechtsanwalts?" *JW* 66 (1937): 525; and Schoppe, "Wie wehrt sich der Verteidiger . . . ?" *ibid.*, pp. 802, 1051f, and 1053.

91. U. Beer, *Versehrt: Verfolgt, Versöhnt: Horst Berkowitz* (Essen, 1979), p. 69ff; A. Roesen, *Aus dem Leben eines Juristen* (Düsseldorf, 1979), p. 98ff; Ronge, *Gerechtigkeit,* 160ff; and D. Oberndörfer, *Begegnungen mit K. G. Kiesinger* (Stuttgart, 1984), p. 107f. Cf. H. Rüping, "Strafjustiz im Führerstaat," *Justiz und NS,* p. 97ff; Ostler, "Rechtsanwälte in der NS-Zeit," p. 58f; and Gruchmann, *Justiz,* p. 564ff.

92. L. Röhrsheim, "Unsere deutsche höhere Schule. Betrachtungen eines amerikanischen Schulmannes," *DHS* 4 (1937): 688ff, versus "Der Verfall des höheren Schulwesens im Dritten Reich," in Schnorbach, *Lehrer,* p. 130ff. "Erziehung und Unterricht in der höheren Schule," *DHS* 5 (1938): 162ff; "Einheitliche Gestaltung der Lehrpläne an den höheren Schulen in Düsseldorf," *ibid.*, 3 (1936): 470f. The *DHS* started a practical column, "Einführung," 5 (1938): 794f. Cf. O. Geudtner, ed., *"Ich bin katholisch getauft und Arier." Aus der Geschichte eines Kölner Gymnasiums* (Cologne, 1985), p. 107ff; and Francke, *Heil Hitler,* p. 100ff.

93. D. Schäfer, "Grundsätze für die Aufstellung eines Geschichtslehrplans in der NS höheren Schule," *DHS* 3 (1936): 257ff; "Die zweite Geschichtstagung des NSLB," *ibid.*, p. 895; "Schulungslehrgang der Gaufachbearbeiter für Geschichte im NSLB," *ibid.*, 4 (1937): 207; A. Fuchs, "Behandlung der Judenfrage im Geschichtsunterricht der Mittel- und Oberstufe," *ibid.*, p. 416ff; U. Haacke, "Die neuen Lehrpläne für den Geschichtsunterricht," *ibid.*, 5 (1938): 558ff. and K. Jarausch, "Wie steht es heute mit der Methode in unserem Unterricht?" *SE* 13 (1938): 48ff. Cf. Flessau, *Schule der Dikatur* (Munich, 1977), p. 59ff; and R. Dithmar, ed., *Schule und Unterricht im Dritten Reich* (Neuwied, 1989), p. 39ff.

94. SOPADE, *Deutschland Berichte,* Vol. 3 (reports of Feb. and Oct. 36), and Vol. 4 (June 1937). Because the SD reports of 1938, Boberach, ed., *Meldungen,* Vol. 2, p. 138ff, agree, this

critical evaluation is likely to be correct. Cf. *Schule im Dritten Reich—Erziehung zum Tod?* (Munich, 1983), p. 81ff; Hochmuth, ed., *Hamburg*, p. 74f and 90f; and Klewitz, *Lehrersein*, pp. 132, and 212ff.

95. H. Schult, "Die Technik im Dritten Reich," *VDIN* 17 (1937), No. 1; C. Föhl, "Vom Sinn der fachlichen Gemeinschaftsarbeit," *ibid.*, 16 (1936), July 1; "Wir sprechen von Leistungssteigerung," *DT* 5 (1937): 400; Seebauer, "Warum Leistungssteigerung?" *ibid.*, 7 (1939): 116ff; A. Speer, "Neues Gütezeichen für vorbildliche Arbeitsplätze," *VDIN* 18 (1939), No. 18; Hasse, "Lärmminderung—Leistungssteigerung," *ibid.*, No. 47.

96. Fö., "Die Hand am Steuer," *VDIN* 16 (1936), No. 8; A. Liese, "Der KdF-Wagen," *DT* 6 (1938): 604ff; "Amerikanisierung der Autoindustrie?" *VDIN* 19 (1939), No. 7; E. Heinkel, "Wege und Ziele des deutschen Flugzeugbaus," *ibid.*, Nos. 14 and 15; F. Todt, "Bauschaffen im Dritten Reich," *ibid.*, 18 (1939), No. 14; "Neue Werkstoffe auf der Messe," *ibid.*, 17 (1937), No. 10; and "Zur Kunststoff-Tagung in Düsseldorf," *ibid.*, No. 17.

97. "RRAO," *Reichsgesetzblatt* 1 (1936): 107; "Vermerk über die Tagung des Reichsfachgruppenrats 'Rechtsanwälte' des BNSDJ," BA, R 22, No. 251; W. Raeke, "Dienst am Recht," *JW* 65 (1936): 1ff and 67 (1938): 1300ff; Glöckler, *Zulassung*, 46f. "Rede des kommissarischen Reichsfachschaftsleiters Karl Frank," *DHS* 3 (1936): 564ff; "Erziehung und Unterricht in der höheren Schule," *ibid.*, 5 (1938): 162ff; H. Knust, "Von tragischen Lehrerschicksalen," *ibid.*, p. 216ff. "Der Tag der Deutschen Technik," *DT* 3 (1935): 367; H. Schult, "Die Aufgaben des VDI," *ZVDI* 80 (1936): 613ff; and SOPADE, *Deutschland Berichte*, Vol. 5 (June 1938).

98. Quotes from Frank and others in "Der deutsche Juristentag 1936," *DR* 6 (1936): 218ff; H. Gutjahr, "Ziel und Sinn der Wissenschaftsarbeit des NSRB," *ibid.*, 7 (1937): 188ff; W. Heuber, "Erfolge und Ziele des Rechtsstandes," *ibid.*, p. 352ff; H. Frank, "Zehn Jahre NSRB," *ibid.*, 8 (1938): 398f. Cf. P. Sülwald, "Aufbau und Aufgaben des Reichsrechtsamtes der NSDAP," *ibid.*, 7 (1937): 416f.

99. Mimeographed, "Unterlagen für die Arbeitstagung" and "Entschliessungen der Tagung der Mitglieder des Reichsgruppenrats und der Gaugruppenwalter Rechtsanwälte. . . ." BA, R 22, No. 265; E. Noack, "Die Altersversorgung der Rechtsanwälte," *DR* (1939): 833ff. Cf. the typed organization plan of the NSRB, BA, NS 16, No. 112.

100. Clipping, "Erster Großdeutscher Rechtswahrertag in Leipzig," and Gau Berlin, "Tätigkeitsbericht für das Jahr 1939," BA, NS 16, No. 112; "Pflicht . . . zur Teilnahme an der ehrenamtlichen NS-Rechtsbetreuung," *JW* 65 (1936): 244; "Rechtsbetreuung 1938," *DR* 9 (1939), No. 11; Boberach, *Meldungen*, Vol. 2, p. 121ff; and Frank to Reinhardt, Nov. 19, 1937, ZStA Po, Rep. 30.01, 8518. The consulting service handled 304,164 cases without fees in 1938. Cf. M. H. Kater, *The Nazi Party: A Social Profile of Members and Leaders 1919–1945* (Cambridge, 1983), 110ff, and *idem. Doctors Under Hitler*, p. 54ff.

101. "Die Führertagung des NSLB in Bayreuth," Jan. 29, 1939, BA, NS 12, No. 690; F. Wächtler, "Die Aufgaben und der Aufbau des NSLB," *ibid.*, No. 1438. Cf. Wächtler interview, *RDE* (1936), No. 1; Feiten, *NSLB*, p. 148ff.

102. Based on Gau Section Two leader reports, beginning in the fourth quarter of 1935, in BA, NS 12, 826. While the genre has a certain bias toward exaggerating "success," the NSLB demanded "unvarnished reporting" to remedy shortcomings. Quotes from Beyl (Danzig), Jan. 10, 1936; Troß, "Geschichte" (n.d.); Franke (Hesse), July 7, 1937.

103. Gliemann (Essen), Sept. 30, 1937; Beer (Eastern Bavaria), 2nd and 3rd quarter, 1937; K. Dietz (Mainfranken), Oct. 17, 1937; Griep (Berlin), 2nd and 3rd quarter, 1937; Gau Franken report for 2nd and 3rd quarter 1937, and so on, in BA, NS 12, No. 826. Stricker and Frank to the Gau-trainee specialists, Jan. 11, 1937, *ibid.*, No. 690.

104. Feiten, *NSLB*, p. 313f, and *Statistik des Deutschen Reichs*, census of 1939 with Sudeten and Vienna figures subtracted; untitled subscriber list of *Der Deutsche Erzieher*, BA, NS 12, No. 690; "Bericht über die Arbeit der Fachschaft 2 im NSLB, Gau Thüringen," Jan. 15, 1936, *ibid.*, No. 826; "Rede des Reichswalters des NSLB und Gauleiters Wächtler," *DHS* 3 (1936): 587f; and SOPADE, *Deutschland Berichte*, Vol. 3 (Feb. 1936), and Vol. 4 (June 1937). Although about 5 percent had not yet joined the NSLB in Thuringia during late 1935, 35.0 percent were in the NSDAP. Cf. Dick, *Oppositionelles Lehrerverhalten*, p. 207, 332.

105. "Die Grundlage der Neuordnung. Anordnung des Stellvertreters des Führers," Nov.

20, 1936, *VDIN* 17 (1937), No. 17; Dr. Kurz, "Der politische Einsatz der Technik," BA, NS 14, No. 17. Cf. K.-H. Ludwig, *Technik und Ingenieure im Dritten Reich* (Königstein, 1979), p. 130ff.

106. Saur, "Neuordnung der deutschen Technik," *VDIN* 17 (1937), No. 12; Todt, "1. Durchführungsverordnung," March 7, 1937, *ibid.*, 17 (1937), No. 17; Saur, "Neuordnung der Technik," *ibid.*, No. 15. Cf. Ludwig, "Der VDI als Gegenstand," p. 419ff.

107. "Bericht über die Vorstandssitzung am 4. März zu Berlin," *ZVDI* 81 (1937): 468; Fö., "Deutschlands Technik geeint," *VDIN* 17 (1937), No. 17; Todt, "Die übergeordneten Aufgaben," *ibid.;* Schult, "Zum Zusammenschluß der Technik," *ZVDI* 81 (1937): 525; "Die Großkundgebung der deutschen Technik," *ibid.*, p. 526; and "Die Ingenieurtage 1937," *ZVDI* 81 (1937): 897ff. Cf. Guse, "Plassenburg," p. 167ff.

108. "Dr. Todt übernimmt den Vorsitz des VDI," *VDIN* 18 (1938), No. 22; Kölzow, "Dr. Todt, Vorsitzender des VDI," *ibid.*, 19 (1939), No. 1; "Dr.-Ing. Todt, künftiger Vorsitzender des VDI," *ZVDI* 82 (1938): 713; and "Die Ingenieurtage 1938," *ibid.*, p. 761ff; note by Pg. Link, March 4, 1939, BA, NS 14, No. 6, II; Ludwig, *Technik,* p. 140f.

109. Steinmetz, "30. Jahrgang," *ZVDDI* 30 (1939): 1; "40 Jahre 'Diplomgesetz' und der 'VDDI'," *ibid.*, 141ff. Cf. Heuser-König, "Tabellarische Zusammenstellungen," p. 561. Though continued by the DAF for two more years, *Technik und Kultur* effectively ceased publication at the end of 1939.

110. Todt report on a NSBDT membership survey, "Aufgaben der deutschen Techniker," at the 1937 Nuremberg party rally, *VDIN* 17 (1937), No. 39; "Die Berufszählung der technischen Berufe," *ZVDI* 79 (1935): 1342f. Since 21 journals of technical associations had a mandatory circulation of 108,817 (with another 11 accounting for 35,906 optional subscribers), this number seems to be a more appropriate base than the 1933–1939 census figures that contain many semiprofessionals. "Zeitschriften des NSBDT," BA, NS 14, No. 6, II.

111. SOPADE, *Deutschland Berichte,* Vol. 5 ("Das kommende NS Strafverfahren"), Vol. 3 ("Jugend im III. Reich"), Vol. 4 (May and Nov. 1937), and Vol. 3 (Sept. 1936); Havenstein, May 29, 1937, Hammerstein, ed., *Deutsche Bildung?,* p. 118. For recollections of stability cf. L. Niethammer, *Lebensgeschichten und Sozialkultur im Ruhrgebiet 1930 bis 1960* (Berlin, 1983).

112. R. Höhn, "Der erste großdeutsche Rechtswahrertag," *DR* 9 (1939): 737ff; K. Frank, "Zum Geleit ins Neue Jahr," *DHS* 6 (1939): 3; "Reichsminister Dr. Goebbels über die Bedeutung der Technik," *DT* 7 (1939): 105; F. Todt, "Das Ziel des neuen Jahres," *VDIN* 19, No. 1.

113. SOPADE, *Deutschland Berichte,* Vol. 5 (Feb. 1938); Ronge, *Gerechtigkeit,* p. 194ff; Grupe, "Böse Zeit," p. 37ff; M. von Ardenne, *Ein glückliches Leben für Forschung und Technik* (Berlin, 1973), p. 103ff. Cf. Hochmuth, ed., *Hamburg,* pp. 18ff, 144ff.

114. R. Hensen, "Das Recht ist bei Deutschland," *JW* 65 (1936): 769ff; Dr. Zeller, "Der nationalsozialistiche Kampf für Wahrheit, Recht und Ehre dient dem Weltfrieden," *ibid.*, p. 837ff; F. Wächtler, "Deutsche Erzieher und Erzieherinnen," *DHS* 6 (1939): 1f; "Seien wir auf der Hut!" *VDIN* 18 (1938), No. 47; F. Todt, "Dreifach genäht hält besser!" *ibid.*, No. 25.

115. Preuß, "Die nationale Friedenspolitik Adolf Hitlers," *JW* 65 (1936): 771f; W. Raeke, "Anwaltschaft und Reichstagswahl," *ibid.*, p. 834f; Todt, "Zum Abstimmungstage," *ZVDI* 82 (1938): 421; "Zu des Führer's Geburtstag," *ibid.*, 83 (1939): 421.

116. "Politische Prozesse im Kampf gegen Deutschland," *JW* 66 (1937): 526f; Burczek, "Staatsbürgerpflichten bei der Bekämpfung von Staatsfeinden," *ibid.*, 67 (1938): 2377ff; recent history curriculum, *DHS* 4 (1937): 28; H. Bauermeister, "Der Ingenieur in der Waffenentwicklung," *ZVDI* 81 (1937): 1295f; F. Löb, "Gemeinschaftsarbeit im Rahmen des Vierjahresplanes," *ibid.*, p. 1233ff; and F. Todt, "Menschenführung und politisches Soldatentum," *VDIN* 19 (1939), No. 20.

117. R. Freisler, "1938—Großdeutschland," *DJ* 101 (1939): 3ff; F. Wächtler, "Deutsche Erzieher und Erzieherinnen!" *RDE* (1939): 5; "Der Reichsrechtsführer auf der ersten Kundgebung des NSRB im freien Österreich," *DR* 8 (1938): 135ff; H. Stingl, "Anwaltschaft und Notariat in der Ostmark," BA, R 22, No. 254; Oswald, "Die sudetendeutsche Rechtsanwaltschaft," *JW* 68 (1939): 742f. F. Ostler, *Die deutschen Rechtsanwälte, 1871–1971* (Essen, 1971), p. 264f.

118. "Verordnung über Angelegenheiten der Rechtsanwälte . . . in Österreich," *Reichsgesetzblatt* 1 (1938): 353; "Vermerk" on discussions of May 26 and 27, 1938; "Zweite VO über

Angelegenheiten der Rechtsanwälte und Notare im Lande Österreich''; Gürtner to Frick, June 28, 1938; Gürtner to Lammers, Aug. 27, 1938; and ''Dritte VO über Angelegenheiten der Rechtsanwälte . . . in Österreich,'' BA, R 22, No. 253. ''Vermerk,'' Nov. 3, 1938, BA, R 22, No. 254. Cf. Mock, *Technische Intelligenz,* p. 67f.

119. ''VO über die Befähigung zum Richteramt, zur Staatsanwaltschaft, zum Notariat und zur Rechtsanwaltschaft,'' *Reichsgesetzblatt* 1 (1939): 5ff; memorandum Dr. Lippert, Nov. 29, 1938; Gürtner to Lammers, Feb. 6, 1939; Droege, ''Erläuterungen zur Tagesordnung,'' and ''Entschliessungen des Reichsgruppenrats RA,'' Feb. 23; ''Vermerk'' on interministerial negotiations, March 20; Bormann to Gürtner, March 11; and ''VO Zur Einführung der Reichs-Rechtsanwaltsordnung . . . in den sudeten-deutschen Gebieten. Vom 31. März 1939,'' BA, R 22, No. 254.

120. K. H. Dworczak, ''Österreichs Jugend—befreit!'' *DHS* 5 (1938): 300; G. Leberwurst, ''Reichslehrgang der Gaufachschaftsleiter und Gaureferentinnen der Fachschaft 2,'' *ibid.,* 6 (1939): 136ff; and H. Engelbrecht, ''Zur Organisierung der österreichischen Lehrerschaft an höheren Schulen,'' in M. Heinemann, ed., *Der Lehrer und seine Organisation* (Stuttgart, 1977), p. 220ff.

121. Todt, ''Leistungen und Aufgaben der Technik im Lande Österreich,'' *DT* 6 (1938): 209f; B. Gürke, ''Gedanken zum Aufbau in Österreich,'' *VDIN* 18 (1938), No. 14; E. Jung, ''Die Entwicklung der Ingenieurberufsfragen in der Ostmark und im Sudetenland,'' *DT* 6 (1938): 593ff. The Austrian and Sudeten dimension is usually neglected in German accounts.

122. For instance, W. Kempowski, *Tadellöser und Wolff* (Hamburg, 1978); T. Elsaesser, ''Heimat,'' *Monthly Film Bulletin,* 52 (1985): 48ff; versus Hildebrand, *Das Dritte Reich* (Munich, 1980), p. 187ff.

123. Boberach, *Meldungen,* Vol. 2, p. 278ff; and Küngler to NSBDT, Dec. 2, 1938, NS 14, No. 17, II.

CHAPTER 7

1. H. Frank, ''An die Rechtswahrer Großdeutschlands,'' *DR* 9 (1939): 1600; ''Die Wellen im Osten und der Wall im Westen,'' *VDIN* 19 (1939), No. 37; ''Englische oder neue Ordnung in der Welt!'' *ibid.,* No. 36.

2. W. Heuber, ''Rechtswahrer Deutschlands!'' *DR* 9 (1939): 1600; K. Frank, ''Berufskameraden und Berufskameradinnen!'' *DHS* 6 (1939), No. 23 and 24, and ''Zum Geleit ins Neue Jahr,'' *ibid.,* 7 (1940): 2; ''Kameraden der Ost- und der Westfront,'' *VDIN* 19 (1939), No. 38; W. Lammert, ''Der technische Krieg,'' *ibid.,* No. 50.

3. ''Dr. Todt über Krieg und Technik,'' *VDIN* 19 (1939), No. 45; Todt, ''1940,'' *ibid.,* 20 (1940), No. 1; ''Das deutsche Kriegsrecht,'' *DR* 9 (1939), No. 45 and 46; F. Wächtler, ''Deutsche Erzieher! Deutsche Schuljugend,'' *DHS* 7 (1940): 1. Cf. H. Frank, ''Aufruf an den NSRB,'' *DR* 11 (1941): 1f; K. Frank, ''Zum Geleit ins Neue Jahr,'' *DHS* 8 (1941): 1; Schult, ''1941,'' *VDIZ* 85 (1941): 1.

4. K. Frank, ''Zum Geleit ins Neue Jahr,'' *DHS* 9 (1942): 1; Todt, ''Männer der deutschen Technik!'' *ZVDI* 86 (1942): 1; D. Thierack, ''Meine jungen Berufskameraden,'' *DR* 13 (1943): 1f; K. Frank, ''Zum Geleit ins Neue Jahr,'' *DHS* 10 (1943): 1; Todt, ''Männer der deutschen Technik!'' *VDIN* 23 (1943), No. 1 and 24 (1944), No. 1, as well as ''Unser Kampf 1944,'' *ibid.*

5. For examples cf. W. Keber, ''Erinnerungen an das Jahrzehnt 1940–1950,'' in F. Sundergeld, ed., *Land und Leuten Dienen* (Minden, 1980), pp. 235ff; R. Göhmann, ''150 Jahre Advokaten- und Rechtsanwaltsverein Hannover,'' *Festschrift zur 150-Jahr Feier,* p. 16f; and P. Kleinewefers, *Jahrgang 1905* (Stuttgart, 1977) 2nd ed., p. 110ff.

6. See I. Staff, *Justiz im Dritten Reich* (Frankfurt, 1979), p. 9f; Eilers, *Die Nationalsozialistische Schulpolitik* (Cologne, 1963), p. 135ff; and G. Hortleder, *Gesellschaftsbild des Ingenieurs. Zum politischen Verhalten der technischen Intelligenz in Deutschland* (Frankfurt, 1970), 2nd ed., p. 127ff. Cf. M. Kater, ''The Burden of the Past: Problems of a Modern Historiography of Physicians and Medicine in Nazi Germany,'' *GSR* 10 (1987): 31ff.

7. M. H. Kater, ''Medizinische Fakultäten und Medizinstudenten,'' in F. Kudlien, ed., *Ärzte im Nationalsozialismus* (Cologne, 1985), p. 82ff, and *idem, Doctors Under Hitler* (Chapel Hill, N.C., 1989), p. 150ff; D. Light, ''Social Medicine vs. Professional Dominance,'' *American*

Journal of Public Health 76 (1986): 78ff, and *idem,* ed., *Political Values and Health Care: The German Experience* (Cambridge, Mass., 1986).

8. U. Geuter, *Die Professionalisierung der deutschen Psychologie im Nationalsozialismus* (Frankfurt, 1984), p. 23ff; G. Cocks, *Psychotherapy in the Third Reich* (New York, 1985), p. 4ff; and K.-H. Ludwig, "Der VDI als Gegenstand der Parteipolitik," in *Technik und Ingenieure im Dritten Reich* (Königstein, 1979), p. 423ff.

9. R. J. Lifton, *The Nazi Doctors: Medical Killing and the Psychology of Genocide* (New York, 1986), pp. xiif, 3ff, and 489ff, poses the question in moral rather than in professional terms. Cf. K. Jarausch, "The Perils of Professionalism," *GSR* 9 (1986): 122ff; Beyerchen, *Scientists under Hitler* (New Haven, 1979), p. 199ff; and the essays by M. Ash and J. Caplan in G. Cocks and K. H. Jarausch, eds., *German Professions* (New York, 1990), pp. 163ff, 289ff.

10. Most histories of the professions treat the war as a complicating factor without exploring its impact systematically. F. Ostler, *Die deutschen Rechtsanwälte 1871–1971* (Essen, 1971), p. 280ff; R. Bölling, *Sozialgeschichte der deutschen Lehrer* (Göttingen, 1983), p. 136ff; and Ludwig, *Technik,* p. 301ff.

11. Ranz to Gürtner, July 26, 1939, stamped *"Geheim"* (secret) BA, NS 22, No. 255; B. Hoja, "Die Verordnung über die Vertretung von Rechtsanwälten," *DR* 9 (1939): 1842f; Hueber to Bormann, Sept. 27, 1941, BA, NS 22, No. 260; Klemm to justice minister, July 24, 1942, *ibid.,* No. 256; and R. Neubert, "Ein ernstes Wort an meine Berufskameraden," *DR* 12 (1942): 1090f.

12. Neubert to Thierack, Feb. 15, 1943; and Thierack to Gropp, Feb. 16, 1943, BA, R 22, No. 271; Thierack to Reich defense commissars, March 18, 1943, *ibid.,* No. 268; Thierack to Sauckel, April 9 and 15, 1943, *ibid.,* No. 271.

13. Dresden OLG president to Thierack, April 9; Dresden RAK to Rothenberger, April 21 with "Übersicht vom 21. 4. 1943 der berufsfremd eingesetzten Rechtsanwälte"; and RJM request for law office employees, July 21, 1943, all in BA, R 22, No. 271.

14. Among the divergent figures in "Einsatz der Rechtsanwälte und Notare für Aufgaben der Reichsverteidigung" and "Bezirksweise Übersicht," the "Berechnung des Reichsdurchschnitts" (excluding Düsseldorf) was the latest and most complete, Sept. 6, 1943, BA, R 22, No. 271. Cf. "Meldungen zum Arbeitseinsatz der Rechtsanwälte," July 15, 1943, *ibid.;* and Letz to Stuckart, Sept. 18, 1944, *ibid.,* No. 262.

15. OLG president Dresden to Bürkner, Jan. 18, 1945, BA, R 22, No. 272; "Meldungen zum Arbeitseinsatz der Rechtsanwälte," M. H. Boberach, ed., *Meldungen,* Vol. 14, July 15, 1943; T. Dobler, "Wie Tübingen vor der Zerstörung bewahrt wurde," in M. Schmid, ed., *Wiedergeburt des Geistes: Die Universität Tübingen im Jahre 1945* (Tübingen, 1985), p. 15ff. Cf. D. Yelton's dissertation on the *Volkssturm* (Chapel Hill, N.C., 1990). In Dresden 90 percent of those left were 61 or older.

16. K. Frank, "Berufskameraden und Berufskameradinnen!" *DHS* 6 (1939), No. 23 and 24; W. Oberle, "Der Kunze-Kalender," *ibid.,* 7 (1940): 166ff; Thuringian ministry to REM, June 12, 1941, ZStA Po, Rep. 49.01, 4507; "Das höhere Schulwesen des großdeutschen Reiches zu Beginn des Krieges," *ibid.,* p. 285ff; and Arnold to Reichspropagandaleitung, Jan. 12, 1942, T 81, roll 675, RPL 499, frame 5484075ff.

17. "Zur Frage Schule und schulfremde Aufgaben im Kriege," in Boberach, ed., *Meldungen,* Vol. 12, p. 4805ff; and "Sicherstellung der Schulerziehung als kriegswichtige Aufgabe," *DHS* 10 (1943): 228; A. Ehrentreich, *Fünfzig Jahre Erlebte Schulreform* (Frankfurt, 1985), p. 178f; Schumann, April 30, 1944, in N. Hammerstein, ed., *Deutsche Bildung?* (Frankfurt, 1988), pp. 230, 256ff.

18. Martin Vogel, "Memoiren," KA 1384; "Kameraden der Ost- und Westfront!" *VDIN* 19 (1939), No. 38; P. Münch, "Einsatz der Technischen Kommandos in Warschau," *ZVDI* 84 (1940): 125ff; and K. Heinrich, "Die Technischen Truppen im Ostfeldzug," *ibid.,* 87 (1943): 34ff. Ludwig, *Technik,* p. 288f, gives no mobilization figures.

19. "Dr. Todt über Krieg und Technik," *VDIN* 19 (1939), No. 45; Oberstleutnant Klingholz, "Ingenieure—Gestalter der Kriegswirtschaft," *ibid.,* 20 (1940), No. 28; Speer, "Architekten und Ingenieure!" *ibid.,* 22 (1942), No. 7 and 8; "Arbeitssitzung des Vorstandsrats des VDI," *ZVDI* 87 (1943): 303f; "Richtiger Arbeitseinsatz," *VDIN* 23 (1943), No. 21 and 22; and

"Erste Stimmen zum Einsatz von Arbeitseinsatz-Ingenieuren," in Boberach, ed., *Meldungen* Vol. 15, p. 5914ff.

20. Neubert to Schoetensack, Sept. 15, 1939; Volkmar, "Vermerk," Dec. 1; Ministry of Justice to Ministry of Interior, March 8, 1940; and reply, April 29, BA, R 22, No. 266. Cf. G. Maier, "Einkommen und Vermögen bei der Familienunterstützung," *DR* 10 (1940): 11ff, and Stieglitz, "Noch offene Fragen beim Familienunterhalt und der Wirtschaftsbeihilfe," *ibid.*, p. 527f.

21. Merten, "Vermerk," July 29, 1940; Heuber to Gürtner, Oct., 16; Neubert, "Anordnung über die Erhebung eines Sonderbeitrags zur Bildung eines Kriegsausgleichstocks," Nov. 14; Merten, "Vermerk," Feb. 14, 1941, BA, R 22, No. 267. Neubert to Thierack, Feb. 22, 1943; Neubert, "Anordnung über die Beitragsfestsetzung für das Geschäftsjahr 1943/44," Sept. 14; Strohm to Thierack, Feb. 4, 1944; Ministry of Justice to Neubert, July 10, 1944, BA, R 22, No. 268f. Cf. in Boberach, ed., *Meldungen*, Vol. 10, p. 297f.

22. Neubert during the Oct. 1939 board meeting of the RRAK in the published transcript, p. 6ff. Cf. E. Noack, "Die Versorgung der Angehörigen der freien Berufe bei besonderem Einsatz," *DR* 9 (1939): 1877ff.

23. P. Ronge, *Im Namen der Gerechtigkeit* (Munich, 1963), p. 205ff; W. Heintzeler, *Der rote Faden* (Stuttgart, 1983), p. 62ff; E. Loest, *Durch die Erde ein Riß* (Hamburg, 1981), p. 34ff; and C. Schmid, *Erinnerungen* (Bern, 1979), p. 175ff.

24. Citations from Konrad Jarausch's letters to his wife during 1939 to 1942, in Bruno Jarausch's family chronicle (Ms., Berlin, 1962), p. 95ff, and in "Aus den Briefen Dr. Konrad Jarauschs" (Ms., transcript, 1952). Cf. M. Vogel, "Memoiren," KA 1384; "Kriegsbriefe an die deutschen Erzieher im Felde," H. Schnorbach, ed., *Lehrer und Schule unterm Hakenkreuz* (Königstein, 1983), p. 159ff; and "Der Feldpostbrief," *VDIN* 23 (1943), No. 1. Cf. Kater, *Doctors Under Hitler*, p. 43ff.

25. H. Schneider, "Erfahrungen mit dem Kriegsverfahrensrecht," *DR* 10 (1940): 1866ff; Gaedeke, "Die Änderung der Vereinfachungsverordnung," *ibid.*, p. 1761f; "Paragraph 752 ZPO—eine Schutzvorschrift für den Soldaten," *ibid.*, 13 (1943): 25f; H. Seydel, "Bilanz der Vereinfachung," *ibid.*, 12 (1942): 995f; and L. Gruchmann, *Justiz im Dritten Reich, 1933–1940* (Munich, 1988), pp. 974ff and 1068ff.

26. Dr. Lichtenberger, "Das Strafverfahren im Kriege," *DR* 10 (1940): 2132ff; M. Jonas, "Gedanken über die Neugestaltung der Gerichtsorganisation," *ibid.*, 11 (1941): 1329ff and 2024ff; and S. König, *Vom Dienst am Recht. Rechtsanwälte als Strafverteidiger im Nationalsozialismus* (Berlin, 1987), p. 179ff.

27. Thierack, "Der Antrittserlaß der Reichsjustizministers," *DR* 12 (1942): 1202f; H. Schneider, "Die Kriegsmaßnahmenverordnung," *ibid.*, 13 (1943): 778ff; and Ostler, *Rechtsanwälte*, p. 280ff.

28. Rust to Bormann, Jan. 11, 1940, and further material in ZStA Po, Rep. 49.01, 4611. "Die Organisation des Unterrichts an den höheren Schulen im Kriege," *DHS* 7 (1940): 174f; "Arbeitstagung der Gaufachschaftsleiter 2," *DHS* 9 (1942): 285ff Cf. K. Flessau, *Schule der Diktatur* (Munich, 1977), p. 66ff; and N. von Hammerstein, ed., *Deutsche Bildung?* (Frankfurt, 1988), p. 142. Cf. R. Dithmar, ed., *Schule und Unterricht im Dritten Reich* (Neuwied, 1989), p. xvff.

29. "Sonderlehrgänge und Reifeprüfung für Kriegsteilnehmer," *DHS* 8 (1941): 135ff; "Versetzung der Schüler an höheren Schulen," *ibid.*, 9 (1942), No. 7 and 8; "Reifezeugnis für Kriegsteilnehmer," *ibid.*, p. 363; "Lehrpläne für die Oberstufe der Oberschulen für Jungen und der Gymnasien," *ibid.*, 11 (1944): 32f; note on the lack of "war curricula," early 1944, ZStA Po, Rep. 49.01, 4337. Cf. N. Franck, *Heil Hitler, Herr Lehrer* (Berlin, 1983), p. 196f.

30. J. Gr. "Schöpferische Technik im Krieg," and W. Lammert, "Der technische Krieg," *VDIN* 19 (1939), No. 50; "Kämpfer und Streiter," *ibid.*, 20 (1940), No. 1; "Einheitliche Durchführung der Umschulung," *ZVDDI* 31 (1940): 14ff; K. Zuse, *Der Computer, Mein Lebenswerk* (Munich, 1970), p. 92; and Ludwig, *Technik*, p. 344ff.

31. Waffenbaudirektor Bauermeister, "Der Ingenieur in der Waffenentwicklung," *VDIN* 20 (1940), No. 40; Oberstleutnant Klingholz, "Ingenieure—Gestalter der Kriegswirtschaft," *ibid.*, No. 28; "Bauen und Kämpfen," *ibid.*, 22 (1942), No. 1.

32. "Kriegs-Sicherheitsrecht," *DR* 9 (1939): 1697; Frank, "Das deutsche Kriegsrecht," *ibid.*,

No. 45 and 46; "Die Verordnung über außerordentliche Rundfunkmaßnahmen," *ibid.*, p. 1697f; "Die Verordnung gegen Volksschädlinge," *ibid.*, p. 1698f. Cf. Gruchmann, *Justiz*, p. 901ff; and G. Fieberg, *Justiz und Nationalsozialismus* (Cologne, 1989), p. 211ff.

33. Schmidt-Leichner, "Das Gesetz zur Änderung des Reichsstrafgesetzbuchs," *DR* 11 (1941): 2146ff; R. Freisler, "Grundsätzliches zur Ministerratsverordnung über das Strafrecht gegen Polen und Juden," *ibid.*, 11 (1941): 2629ff; Lämmle, "Aus der Rechtsprechung des Volksgerichthofs zum allgemeinen Teil des Strafgesetzbuchs," *ibid.*, 14 (1944): 505ff; and M. Mittelsbach, "Übersicht über die Rechtsprechung zum Kriegsstrafrecht," *ibid.*, 12 (1942): 13f. For cases see Ronge, *Gerechtigkeit*, p. 212ff.

34. E. Holler, "Die Schule im Krieg—Der Krieg in der Schule," *DHS* 7 (1939): 109ff; H. Holtdorf, "Grundlinien wehrgeistiger Erziehung," *ibid.*, 8 (1940): 151ff. Cf. the disappointing G. W. Blackbourn, *Education in the Third Reich* (Albany, N.Y., 1985), p. 126ff.

35. W. Hohmann, "Der 'kriegerische Geist' und die seelische Widerstandskraft des deutschen Soldaten," *DHS* 8 (1940): 3f; K. Schmidt, "Zum Geschichtsunterricht in Klasse 8," *ibid.*, 10 (1942): 102ff; and Rust to Bormann, Nov. 11, 1940, ZStA Po, Rep. 49.01, 4335. Cf. Franck, *Heil Hitler*, p. 185ff.

36. F. Todt, "1940," *ZVDI* 84 (1940): 1; Bauermeister, "Der Ingenieur in der Waffenentwicklung," *VDIN* 20 (1940): 40; H. Kölzow, "Technische Forschung im Kriege," *ZVDI* 83 (1939): 1083; K. Bringmann, "Die technischen Hilfsmittel des Heeres-Sanitätswesens," *ibid.*, 86 (1942): 256ff; and O. Engelke, "Ingenieur und orthopädische Technik," *ibid.*, 84 (1940): 737ff.

37. H. Benkert, "Echte Leistungssteigerung im Industriebetrieb," *ZVDI* 86 (1942): 585ff; "Arbeitssitzung des Vorstandsrats des VDI," *ibid.*, 87 (1943): 303f; "Großaufgaben," *VDIN* 23 (1943), no. 7 and 8; B. Jansen, "Mehr Arbeitsteilung!" *ibid.*, 24 (1944), No. 1; and Ludwig, "Vereinsarbeit im Dritten Reich," in *Technik*, p. 446ff.

38. H. Frank, "Die Rechtsarbeit der Partei im Kriege," *DR* 9 (1939), No. 45 and 46; and countless references in Boberach, ed., *Meldungen*, Vol. 2, Oct. 20, 1939; Vol. 9, p. 247; Vol. 15, Nov. 29 and Dec. 12, 1943. Cf. Ronge, *Gerechtigkeit*, p. 208ff; U. Beer, *Versehnt, Verfolgt, Versöhnt: Horst Berkowitz* (Essen, 1979), p. 77ff.

39. Boberach, ed., *Meldungen*, Vol. 7, p. 190; Vol. 13, p. 374; "Vermeidet Rechtsstreit! Haltet Rechtsfrieden!" *DR* 13 (1943), No. 9; J. von Medeazza, "Die deutsche Rechtsvertretung im Generalgouvernement," *ibid.*, 10 (1940): 929ff; and L. Wolfgramm, "Deutsche Rechtsanwälte und Notare im Generalgouvernement," *ibid.*, 12 (1942): 1428f. Cf. H. Focke and M. Strocka, *Alltag der Gleichgeschalteten* (Hamburg, 1985), p. 226ff; and G. Fieberg, *Justiz und Nationalsozialismus* (Cologne, 1989), p. 206.

40. Memorandum on "Aufgaben und Leistungen des NSLB im Kriege," BA, NS 12, No. 1338; Holler, "Die Schule im Krieg," p. 109ff; Hohmann, "Der 'kriegerische Geist'," *ibid.*, p. 3ff; J. von Leers, "Die Umerziehungspläne gegen das deutsche Volk," *ibid.*, 11 (1944), final issue.

41. K. Frank, "Rückschau und Ausblick zum 30. Jan. 1943," *DHS* 10 (1943): 39ff; H. Wendt, "Höhere Schule des Ostens als politische Funktion," *ibid.*, 8 (1941): 385ff. Membership figures from NSLB sample, Appendix I. Cf. Franck, *Heil Hitler*, p. 196f.

42. "Dr. Todt wurde Reichsminister für Bewaffnung und Munition," *VDIN* 20 (1940), No. 13; F. Todt, "Bewegliche Rüstungswirtschaft," *Betrieb und Wehr*, 2nd Series, Feb. 1941; VDI, "Bericht über die Arbeiten des VDI," Nov. 5, 1942, BA, NS 14, No. 10; H. Ude, "Die Fachverbände des NSBDT: Der VDI," *VDIN* 22 (1942), No. 21 and 22; and Ludwig, *Technik*, p. 344ff.

43. "Reichsminister Speer an die deutsche Technik," *VDIN* 22 (1942), No. 5 and 6; H. Benkert, "Sofort mehr Leistung!" *DT* 10 (1942): 328ff; figures from Ludwig, "Vereinsarbeit im Dritten Reich," p. 447ff. Cf. A. Speer, *Inside the Third Reich* (New York, 1970), p. 189ff.

44. M. Reich-Ranicki, "Geliehene Jahre," in *idem*, ed., *Schulzeit im Dritten Reich* (Munich, 1984), p. 52ff; J. Lifton, *The Nazi Doctors* (New York, 1986), p. 489ff; G. Boehnert, "The Jurists in the SS-Führerkorps, 1925–1939," p. 361ff; and H. F. Ziegler, *Nazi Germany's New Aristocracy: The SS Leadership, 1925–1939* (Princeton, 1989), p. 111ff. Cf. I. Kershaw, *Popular Opinion and Political Dissent in the Third Reich* (Oxford, 1983).

45. For example, D. Güstrow, *Tödlicher Alltag* (Berlin, 1986), *passim;* Reich-Ranicki, "Ge-

liehene Jahre,'' p. 52ff; and ''Dem Ingenieur Lautrich wurde Unrecht getan,'' in L. Poliakov and J. Wolf, *Das Dritte Reich und seine Diener* (Berlin, 1956), p. 317f. Cf. M. Schreiber, ''F. J. Perels. Rechtsberater der Bekennenden Kirche,'' in Kritische Justiz, ed., *Streitbare Juristen* (Baden-Baden, 1988), p. 355ff; and ''Walter Bacher,'' in *Hamburg,* p. 159ff and 312ff.

46. Gruchmann, *Justiz,* 1884ff; W. Angress, *Between Fear and Hope: Jewish Youth in the Third Reich* (New York, 1987) and K. Friedrich memoirs in KA 508/1.

47. Though broadly conceived and critically argued, the collaborative histories of the Second World War edited by W. Deist of Das Militärgeschichtliche Forschungsamt and of the collective of the German Democratic Republic, *Deutschland im Zweiten Weltkrieg* (Berlin, 1974) slight domestic social history. Cf. E. Kogon, *Der SS-Staat* (Frankfurt, 1946).

48. Reichsarbeitsführer survey of 259,000 labor service participants, Jan. 31, 1939, BA, NS 14, No. 178; Boberach, ed., *Meldungen,* Vol. 2, No. 13; Vol. 4, p. 958, Vol. 11, p. 4151; Vol. 12, p. 4603; Reutter to Rust, April 23; OKH to Rust, Aug. 26; Ulrich to Rust, Sept. 25, 1940; and various draft answers that were never sent, ZStA Po, Rep. 49.01, 4335. Cf. Francke, *Heil Hitler,* p. 197f.

49. E. Schwarzinger, ''Leistungssteigerung in der Höheren Schule,'' *DHS* 8 (1941): 342f; address by Kerst at the ''Arbeitstagung der Gaufachschaftsleiter 2,'' *DHS* 9 (1942): 295ff; rescript of Reich education minister, April 12, 1943, and further materials in ZStA Po, Rep. 49.01, 4340.

50. F. Klausing, ''Zum Rechtsstudium von Kriegsteilnehmern,'' *DR* 11 (1941): 2549ff; VDI memorandum on ''Leistungsrückgang des Ingenieurnachwuchses,'' Dec. 13, 1940, BA, NS 14, No. 18, II; and documents in H. Seier, ''Niveaukritik und partielle Opposition,'' *Archiv für Kulturgeschichte* 58 (1976): 231ff.

51. Rust to Göring, July 18, 1941, ZStA Po, Rep. 49.01, 4335. Quote from Oskar von Niedermayer (OKW) in Seier, ''Niveaukritik,'' p. 235ff. Cf. Boberach, ed., *Meldungen,* Vol. 4, p. 1312 and Vol. 11, p. 4281f, and G. Giles, *Students and National Socialism in Germany* (Princeton, N.J., 1985), p. 266ff. Professors blamed the decline on the high school.

52. Protocol of rector conference, Jan. 4, 1941, ZStA Po, Rep. 49.01, 4336; Freysoldt memorandum, March 1, 1943, and debate on Röver's training reports, ZStA Po, Rep. 49.01, 4340; Rothenberger, ''Nahziele der Ausbildungsreform,'' *DR* 13 (1943): 2ff; and ''Ursachen, Werden und Zwecke der Praktiker AG an den Universitäten,'' *DR* 14 (1944): 385ff. G. Hopp, ''Neuordnung der Hochschulpraktikanten-Ausbildung,'' *DT* 8 (1940): 429f; and G. Himmler, ''Studium und Fortbildung des Ingenieurs,'' *VDIN* 23 (1943): 1.

53. Ch. Lorenz, *Zehnjahres-Statistik des Hochschulbesuchs und der Abschlußprüfungen* (Berlin, 1943), stops in 1941, but her supplement on *Die Entwicklung des Fachstudiums während des Krieges* (Berlin, 1944) continues to the winter of 1943–1944. The authoritative H. Titze, *Das Hochschulstudium in Preußen und Deutschland, 1820–1944* (Göttingen, 1987), pp. 33, 110f, 124f, and 142f, ends with the first trimester of 1941. Rust decree, Sept. 1, 1944, ZStA Po, Rep. 49.01, 4337. Cf. Boberach, ed., *Meldungen,* Vol. 3, pp. 433, 646; Vol. 5, p. 141; Vol. 6, p. 173; Vol. 7, p. 201; Vol. 10, p. 300; W. Förster, ''Nachwuchs für die Wissenschaft,'' *Münchener Neueste Nachrichten,* May 29, 1943; and Giles, *Students,* p. 329f.

54. Figures from Lorenz (note 53). Quotes from Boberach, ed., *Meldungen,* Vol. 10, No. 300; Vol. 15, Sept. 20, 1943. Prof. Streck, ''Fräulein Ingenieur,'' *VDIN* 19 (1939), No. 1, and Frida Holaschke, ''Wie ich Maschinen-Ingenieurin wurde,'' *ibid.,* No. 37, versus ''Frauen als Ingenieure,'' *Der Führer,* Sept. 13, 1938. Cf. J. R. Pauwels, *Women and University Studies in the Third Reich, 1933–1945* (New York, 1985), p. 119ff. The philology enrollments include students of the humanities and sciences preparing for teaching.

55. The separately documented share of students from parents with higher education increased from 22.6 percent to 26.9 percent between 1932 and 1941. Cf. Lorenz, *Zehnjahres-Statistik,* p. 371; K. H. Jarausch, *Deutsche Studenten 1800–1980* (Frankfurt, 1984), p. 181ff; and Kater, *Doctors Under Hitler,* p. 150ff, for more detail.

56. Lorenz, *Abschlußprüfungen,* p. 68ff. Even if graduations might have recovered somewhat in 1941, the trend during the rest of the war is likely to have been downward. Boberach, ed., *Meldungen,* Vol. 11, No. 311.

57. Liebenberg, ''Großer Mangel an Rechtswahrern,'' *DR* 10 (1940): 965 and ''Um den Berufsnachwuchs,'' *ibid.,* p. 1488f. W. Oberle, ''Zur Frage des Lehrernachwuchses an den

höheren Schulen Preußens," *DHS* 7 (1940): 88ff, and Röm, "Zur Frage des philosophischen Nachwuchs," ZStA Po, Rep. 49.01, 4340. J. Greiner, "Technischer Nachwuchs im Kriege" *DT* 8 (1940): 138; and G. Himmler, "Die Ingenieurschule und die Anforderungen an den Nachwuchs," *ibid.*, 10 (1942): 496ff. Cf. Boberach, ed., *Meldungen,* Vol. 11, p. 4123ff, and Vol. 12, p. 4673ff.

58. Thierack, "Meine jungen Berufskameraden!" *DR* 13 (1943): 1f; appeals by Speer, Saur, and Axmann, "Jugend und Technik," *VDIN* 24 (1944), No. 11 and 12. F. Klausing, "Zum Rechtsstudium von Kriegsteilnehmern," *DR* 11 (1941): 2549ff; "Sonderlehrgänge und Reifeprüfung für Kriegsteilnehmer," *DHS* 8 (1941): 135ff.

59. Rust, "Studium für das wissenschaftliche und das künstlerische Lehramt an höheren Schulen," *DHS* 7 (1940): 27 and 102; D. Scheid, "Die vereinfachte große juristische Staatsprüfung," *DR* 10 (1940): 271f; "Ordnung des Vorbereitungsdienstes für das Lehramt an höheren Schulen," *DHS* 8 (1941): 56ff; Frank letter, Oct. 28, 1940, and Volkmar reply of March 6, 1941, BA, R 22, No. 256; "VO zur weiteren Ergänzung der RRAO," *Reichsgesetzblatt,* (1941): 333; and "Zulassung als Rechtsanwalt," *DR* 11 (1941): 1653f. Cf. H.-G. Merz, "Von den NS-HfL zu den NS-Lehrerbildunganstalten," *IZEBF* 33 (1988): 189ff.

60. Schlegelberger to Lammers, Feb. 20, 1942, and reply of March 13, BA, R 22, No. 259; Letz to Bormann, June 21, 1943, *ibid.*, No. 261; Johannes, "Jahresstatistik über die Personalbewegung bei den Rechtsanwälten" for 1940–1942, *ibid.*, Nos. 261 and 267. Rust–Bormann negotiations and REM decree, Aug. 10, 1940, ZStA Po, Rep. 49.01, 312; Oberle, "Das höhere Schulwesen des Deutschen Reiches," *DHS* 9 (1942): 401ff; and A. Nath, *Studienratskarriere im Dritten Reich* (Frankfurt, 1988), pp. 211ff, 305ff. G. Himmler, "Die Ingenieurschule und ihre Anforderungen an den Nachwuchs," *DT* 9 (1941): 499f. Boberach, ed., *Meldungen,* Vol. 15, p. 5781ff.

61. Boberach, ed., *Meldungen,* Vol. 5, p. 1420ff; Neubert to Thierack, June 6, 1943, with "Übersicht der Berufseinkommen der Rechtsanwälte für das Kalenderjahr 1941," note of July 14, 1943, "Liste aller Rechtsanwälte über 70" of April 1, 1942, BA, R 22, No. 268; Kruse, "Aufstellung," Nov. 25, 1942, BA, NS 16, No. 61. "Einnahmen und Ausgaben der Rechtsanwälte und Notare," *ibid.*, No. 260; Rothenberger to cabinet, July 27, Thierack to minister of interior, Aug. 31, and Neubert to Thierack, Oct. 13, 1943, BA, R 43II, 1536c.

62. Boberach, ed., *Meldungen,* Vol. 3, p. 867ff; Vol. 5, p. 1464ff; Vol. 10, p. 3843; and Vol. 12, p. 4675. Cf. Arnold to Reichspropagandaleitung, Jan. 12, 1942, and "Abschrift eines Feldpostbriefs," RPL, No. 499, T 81, roll 675, frame 548, 4075ff and 4154f.

63. K. Rummel, "Mobilisierung von Leistungsreserven durch zweckmäßige Entlohnung," *VDIN* 24 (1944), No. 15; Boberach, ed., *Meldungen,* Vol. 6, pp. 2085ff and 2099ff; Vol. 12, p. 4494f. Himmler circular, Jan. 18, 1944, BA, NS 14, No. 8.

64. G. d'Alquen to Neubert, Oct. 21, 1940 and reply, Nov. 20, BA, R 22, No. 260. For the Gröpke case cf. König, *Dienst am Recht,* p. 199ff.

65. Neubert to chambers, Feb. 12, 1941, BA, R 22, No. 257; "Das muß aufhören!" *Schwarzes Korps,* June 18, 1942; "Sie könnten viel helfen," *ibid.*, July 2, and "Gesundung von innen her," *ibid.*, Dec. 17, versus Schlegelberger to Bormann, June 27 and July 6, 1942, BA, R 22, No. 260. Cf. König, *Dienst am Recht,* p. 213ff.

66. H. Ehlers to Lammers, Sept. 3, 1942 with a long memorandum, "Über den Sinn des Anwaltsberufs," forwarded by Lammers to Bormann, Oct. 3, BA, R 22, No. 1536c. W. Weber, "Rechtswahrer von Morgen," *Leipziger Neueste Nachrichten,* Feb. 2, 1944.

67. "Abschrift eines Feldpostbriefs," RPL 499, T 81, roll 675, frame 548, p. 4154; Winkler to Brehm and reply, Dec. 4 and 6, 1940, BA, NS 12, No. 1447; and B. Brehm, "Eingriff in die Geschichte," *VB,* Jan. 3, 1942.

68. "Wirbt man so für den Erzieherberuf?" and numerous clippings such as "Bis hierher und nicht weiter," in *RDE,* June 15, 1939 and 1940, No. 9 and 10, in RPL 499, frames 4120, 4137, and 4172f; Arnold to *FZ* and reply, Sept. 29 and Oct. 14, 1940, BA, NS 12, No. 1447. Teachers even complained about a short story based on Chekhov! Altenmüller letter, Sept. 20, 1940, *ibid.* Cf. W. Fischer, ed., *Erzieher. Zeugnisse bedeutender Deutscher über ihre Lehrer* (Leipzig, 1942), p. 287ff.

69. Arnold to Reichspropagandaleitung, Jan. 12, 1942, and Kreisamtsleiter of eastern Bavaria to NSLB Selb, n.d., in RPL, 499, frames 548,4063f and 4075–82. Cf. Arnold to Atzrott,

March 18, 1942 and to KdF Reichsamtsleitung, Nov. 9, BA, NS 12, No. 1447 and 1438; "Knallke Greift Ein!" *Essener National-Zeitung,* Sept. 20, 1942; and Boberach, ed., *Meldungen,* Vol. 9, p. 3180ff.

70. "Die Stellung der Truppeningenieure im Heere," Dec. 1938, BA NS 14, No. 15; and "Der Mensch der Technik. Die Herrschaft des Technikers," *Kölnische Zeitung,* Feb. 15, 1942.

71. Himmler letter, Nov. 19, 1941; Himmler to Streck, Feb. 12, 1940; and Kraus to Weinmar, Sept. 24, 1941 in BA, NS 14, No. 15, I; Kraus to Herbst, June 6 and Sept. 21, 1940, *ibid.,* No. 15, II; *NSBDT Merkblatt,* edition June 1943, *ibid.,* No. 10; and Himmler circular, June 26, 1942, *ibid.,* No. 8.

72. Annual NSBDT section report on "Berufsfragen" for 1940, BA NS 14, No. 20, I, and for 1942, *ibid.,* No. 8. Himmler circular, Jan. 18, *ibid.,* and Jan. 20, 1944, *ibid.,* No. 14. Himmler to *Schwarzes Korps,* June 17, 1941, *ibid.;* Karl to NSBDT, May 3, 1940, *ibid.,* No. 18, II; "Der Ingenieur im Kriege," *VDIN,* 23 (1943), No. 7 and 8; and W. Ostwald, "Die ersten 10 Jahre NS Technik," *DT* 11 (1943): 48ff.

73. Hueber to Bormann, Sept. 27, 1941, in BA, Rep. 22, No. 260; Freisler to Heß, Dec. 7, 1939, *ibid.,* No. 259; *idem* to OLG presidents, Jan. 22, 1941; Hueber to Todt, Nov. 14, 1941, *ibid.,* No. 261; ministry to Wadsack, Oct. 2, 1941, *ibid.,* No. 259; and Boberach, ed., *Meldungen,* Vol. 3, p. 662ff. Cf. H. Reuß, "Der Anwalt als Rechtswahrer im Raum der Verwaltung," *DR* 10 (1940): 2209ff.

74. "Fachanwälte für Steuerrecht," *DJ* 1941, No. 2; Neubert to Gürtner, Oct. 14, 1940; Ministry of Justice and Ministry of Finance announcement, Feb. 25, 1941, in BA, R 22, No. 258; Neubert to Gürtner, Aug. 21, 1941, *ibid.,* No. 259; Hueber to Bormann, Sept. 27, 1941; Neubert to Schlegelberger, Jan. 30, 1942; Klucki to Ministry of Justice, April 24, *ibid.,* No. 260; Neubert to Thierack, March 6, 1944, *ibid.,* No. 262. Cf. Delbrück, "Der Rechtsanwalt als Steuerberater," *DR* 12 (1942): 1358f.

75. Bormann to Thierack, June 30, 1943; Neubert to Thierack, Sept. 10; Thierack to Bormann, March 3, 1944; Friedrich to Klemm, March 31, with reply of June 2; Friedrich to Klemm, Aug. 29, 1944, in BA, R 22, No. 268; and Klemm to Neubert, Nov. 8, *ibid.,* No. 269. Cf. Ministry of Justice to Ministry of Nutrition, Feb. 2, 1942; and Woestendieck to Neubert, Oct. 2, 1941, *ibid.,* No. 259, for complaints about the war economy bureaucracy.

76. Ranz to Gürtner, July 26, 1939; "Verordnung über die Vertretung von Rechtsanwälten," Sept. 18; Hueber to court presidents, Nov. 7, in BA, R 22, No. 255; Klemm to Thierack, July 24, 1942; Hornig memorandum "Ergänzung der RRAO," June 8, *ibid.,* No. 256. Substitution required bending other rules such as admission to more than one court at a time.

77. Zeilemann to RAK, March 27, 1936, ZStA Po, Rep. 30.01, 8517; RJM to Neubert, Jan. 26, 1943; ministry to chief of Sipo, June 22; Thierack to Neubert, June 6, 1944, in BA, R 22, No. 262; Wurmstrich to Thierack, Jan. 25, 1944, BA, NS 16, No. 111. Cf. Güstrow, *Tödlicher Alltag,* p. 15ff; Ronge, *Gerechtigkeit,* p. 212ff; Beer, *Berkowitz,* p. 77f; Gruchmann, *Justiz,* pp. 694ff and 738ff; and Fieberg, *Justiz und Nationalsozialismus,* p. 246ff.

78. Speech by Baldur von Schirach, Jan. 13, 1936, BA, NS 12, No. 1134. Gnade to Gutterer, Dec. 15, 1939, reprinted in Popplow, "Schulalltag im Dritten Reich," p. 79. Rust and Axmann, "Schule und Hitlerjugend," Jan. 31, 1941, ZStA Po, Rep 49.01, 4335, and implementation instructions in *DHS* 8 (1941): 138ff; "Stimmen zum Abkommen . . . ," Boberach, ed., *Meldungen,* 7, p. 2290ff and Vol. 19, p. 3843ff. Cf. Kater, "HJ und Schule," p. 578f.

79. Draft article on "Der Klassenführer" and Arnold note with Wächtler marginalia, May 14, 1942; press release on "HJ in der Schule," May 27; Arnold memorandum, May 28; Arnold to Krüger, May 30, and various draft statements on "Verhältnis HJ—NSLB," in BA, NS 12, No. 1438; Hohlfelder to Schrewe, July 7, 1944, in ZStA Po, Rep. 49.01, 3919; Klamroth note, Feb. 26, 1943, *ibid.,* 4337. Cf. Hochmuth, ed., *Hamburg,* p. 40ff and 75f.

80. Kürer to REM, Dec. 2, 1940, ZStA Po, Rep. 49.01, 4335; E. Holler, "Schule im Krieg," *DHS* 7 (1940): 111; "Amtszeit und Pflichtstundenzahl der Lehrkräfte," *ibid.,* 9 (1942): 363f; quotes from the first "NLSB Kriegsbrief an die deutschen Erzieher im Felde," in Schnorbach, ed., *Lehrer,* p. 159ff; Boberach, ed., *Meldungen,* Vol. 5, p. 1508; Vol. 8, p. 2715ff; Vol. 11, p. 4149f; and Vol. 12, p. 4805ff; Röver report, Dec. 14, 1942, ZStA Po, Rep. 49.01, 4340; Schumann, Nov. 22, 1941, in Hammerstein, ed., *Deutsche Bildung?,* pp. 141 and 242; and M. Klewitz, *Lehrersein im Dritten Reich* (Weinheim 1987), p. 149.

81. Rust decree on school opening, Sept. 23, 1940, and KLV order, Oct. 2, 1940, ZStA Po, Rep. 49.01, 4335; instruction on teaching Luftwaffenhelfer, Nov. 10, 1943; REM decree against disruption of teaching, July 25, 1944; and KLV figures March 1 and April 3, 1944, *ibid.*, No. 4337. Cf. Boberach, ed., *Meldungen,* Vol. 15, p. 5917ff; and Vol. 16, p. 6270; Popplow, "Schulalltag," p. 80ff; Ehrentreich, *Fünfzig Jahre,* p. 148ff; Franck, *Heil Hitler,* p. 192ff; Schumann, June 20, 1943, in Hammerstein, ed., *Deutsche Bildung?,* pp. 188, 231.

82. B. Jansen, "Mehr Arbeitsteilung!" *VDIN* 24 (1944), Nos. 1 and 2; W. Taubmann, "Leistungssteigerung und Leistungserhebung," *ibid.;* Todt, "An die deutschen Ingenieure!" *ibid.*, 20 (1940): 14; "Der Generatorenantrieb im Vormarsch," *ibid.*, 21 (1941): 36; and F. Stumpf, "Der Arbeitseinsatz von Kriegsgefangenen," *ibid.*, 20 (1940): 36.

83. J. Greiner, "Führungsaufgaben von einmaliger Größe," *VDIN* 20 (1940), No. 52; R. Ley, "Der Frontarbeiter," *ibid.*, 21 (1941): 18; "Chronik der Rüstung," *ibid.*, 23 (1943), No. 13 and 14; and Boberach, ed., *Meldungen,* Vol. 8, p. 2768ff; and Vol. 14, p. 5312ff. Cf. Kleinewefers, *Jahrgang 1905,* p. 128ff and Zuse, *Computer,* pp. 93 and 105ff.

84. Neubert to RAK presidents, in printed protocol (Berlin, 1939), p. 17ff; RJM memorandum on "Kriegsnovelle zur RAO," Jan. 16, 1940, BA, R 22, No. 255; Freisler to Lammers, May 30, 1940, *ibid.*, No. 256; note of June 13, BA, R 43 II, No. 1535; Merten, "Vermerk," Sept. 14, 1940; RJM to Heß, Oct. 8; NSRB to Gürtner, Oct. 29, in BA, R 22, No. 256; Boberach, ed., *Meldungen,* Vol. 3, p. 751f; and König, *Dienst am Recht,* p. 203ff. For the closer "guidance" of judges cf. Fieberg, *Justiz und Nationalsozialismus,* p. 280ff.

85. RJM to Neubert, Dec. 20, 1940, BA, R 22, No. 258; Sipo chief to Ministry of Justice, Jan. 24, 1941, *ibid.*, No. 259; Neubert to chamber presidents, Feb. 12, 1941, *ibid.*, No. 258; Volkmar to Heß, March 3, 1941, *ibid.*, No. 256; and "VO zur weiteren Ergänzung der RRAO," *Reichsgesetzblatt* 1 (June 27, 1941): 333. Hueber to Himmler, July 29, and 31, 1941, BA, R 22, No. 259; Staege, "Anwaltliche Ehrengerichtsbarkeit," *DR* 11 (1941): 517ff; and "Kritisches Tagebuch," *ibid.*, pp. 39f and 557f.

86. Schlegelberger to Neubert, July 10, 1942, BA, R 22, No. 259; "Meldungen über Auswirkungen der Plädoyers und des Auftretens einzelner Strafverteidiger," in Boberach, ed., *Meldungen,* Vol. 11, p. 3997ff; "Ein ernstes Wort an meine Berufskameraden," *DR* 12 (1942): 1090f, and *Mitteilungen der RRAK,* Sept. 10, 1942. Cf. König, *Dienst am Recht,* p. 210ff. In a column called "critical diary," the *DR* provided guidance for appropriate behavior.

87. Letz memorandum, Oct. 6, 1942; Neubert, "Bemerkungen zur VO zur Änderung und Ergänzung der RRAO," Nov. 24; Letz, "Entwurf zur Änderung der RRAO," Nov. 27, 1942, BA, R 22, No. 256. H. Seydel, "Zur Lage der Anwaltschaft," *DR* 12 (1942): 1572ff, asserted that "at present the legal profession is in a crisis." Cf. König, *Dienst am Recht,* p. 212ff.

88. Droege to Rothenberger, Nov. 16, 1942, BA, R 22, No. 256; Ehlers to Lammers, Sept. 3, 1942; with his long memorandum of 1940, "Über den Sinn des Anwaltsberufs"; Lammers to Bormann, Oct. 3; and Thierack to Lammers, Nov. 17, 1942, BA, R 43 II, No. 1536c. Cf. Fieberg, *Justiz und Nationalsozialismus,* p. 267.

89. Bormann to Thierack, Dec. 27, 1942; Thierack to Lammers, Dec. 22, and note of March 1, 1943, BA, R 22, No. 256; "Vermerk" of Feb. 5, 1943, BA, R 43 II, No. 1536c; "VO zur Änderung und Ergänzung der RRAO," *Reichsgesetzblatt* 1 (March 6, 1943): 123f; Rothenberger to OLG presidents, March 25, BA, R 22, No. 261; Thierack to Ley, May 4, *ibid.*, No. 256. Cf. "Beiratstagung der RRAK," *DR* 13 (1943): 478; Neubert, "Die neuen Maßnahmen auf dem Gebiete des Anwaltsrechts," *ibid.*, p. 593ff; and Hornig, "Neue Vorschriften für den Rechtsanwaltsberuf," *DJ,* May 14, 1943.

90. Engel to Rothenberger, Feb. 22, 1944, and March 7, 1943, BA, R 22, No. 274. Neubert, "Anwaltliche Ehrenrechtsprechung in der Spruchpraxis des Dienststrafsenats," *DR* 14 (1944), No. 25 and 26. Sattelmacher to Thierack, April 14, 1944, discussing 15 problem cases, BA, R 22, No. 262. Cf. König, *Dienst am Recht,* p. 223.

91. Bredenkamp, "Die Unentbehrlichkeit der Rechtsanwaltschaft," *DR* 13 (1943): 282f; Hanssen, "Die Stellung des Rechtsanwalts als Organ einer starken NS Rechtspflege," *ibid.*, 14 (1944): 353ff. Speeches by Bogenrieder and Pickel, "Stellung des Rechtsanwalts in der NS Rechtspflege," April 27–May 5, 1944, in BA, R 22, No. 262; and draft on "Die Neuordnung der Rechtsanwaltschaft durch die neue Justizführung als Voraussetzung für eine künftige freie und starke Rechtsanwaltschaft," *ibid.*, No. 257.

92. Ministry of Justice to Neubert, June 1, 1944, BA, R 22, No. 275; and to OLG president Vienna, Sept. 4, 1944, *ibid.*, No. 262. Thierack, ed., *Rechtsanwaltsbriefe. Mitteilungen des Reichsministers der Justiz,* 1 (1944): 1ff. "Verteidigung von Staatsfeinden und Volksschädlingen," *DR* 14 (1944): 327. Cf. König, *Dienst am Recht,* p. 235ff.

93. O. Nehring, "Der Krieg und das Berufsethos," *DHS* 11 (1944): 6f; Göttingen principal to Oberpräsident, June 27, 1942, in Popplow, "Schulalltag," p. 39; material in BA, R 21, Nos. 16ff; and W. Kircher, "Schule im Krieg," RPL, No. 499, T 81, roll 675, frames 548,4177ff.

94. Ernst Behm, "Zur Umgestaltung des Erziehungswesens," in the 1944 exile Socialist program reprinted by Schnorbach, ed., *Lehrer,* p. 177ff. Documents on Ernst Faust, including Kreisamtsleiter to Gestapo, Feb. 7, 1944, and Buschman to Faust, Nov. 17, 1943, in BDC, NSLB, "Faas." Cf. the case of Franziska Faupel, March 6, 1942, and Israel Oppenheim, Kreisleiter to Gestapo Giessen, Jan. 25, 1941, *ibid.* Ulrich to Rust, Sept. 25, 1940, ZStA Po, Rep. 49.01, 4335. See also countless cases of dissent in Hochmuth, *Hamburg,* 152, 159, 214, 259, 267 and so on.

95. Boberach, ed., *Meldungen,* Vol. 14, pp. 5314f and 5428f; Vol. 12, p. 4612ff; Vol. 10, pp. 3566 and 3862. Kraus to Vogt, Jan. 7, 1942, and to Dortmund NSBDT, June 6, as well as warning card on Otto Frerichs versus Welkner to NSBDT Munich, April 2, BDC, NSBDT, "Niemann," and "Francke." Cf. "Fritz Graebe's helping hand," *Daily Tar Heel,* April 26, 1986.

96. Summaries of "Arbeitstagung des NSRB," *DR* 12 (1942): 164ff, and "Arbeitstagung des Reichsgruppenrats der Rechtsanwälte," *ibid.,* p. 1090; Heuber to Schlegelberger, March 20, 1941; Neubert to Schlegelberger, March 27, Schlegelberger to Heuber, April 7, and Heuber reply, April 19, BA, R 22, No. 272.

97. Unsigned memo on "Arbeitsbesprechung am 30. 9. 1942," BA, NS 16, No. 113; press release, "Reichsminister Dr. Thierack über die Aufgaben des NSRB," n. d. *ibid.,* No. 115; Thierack, "Die Aufgaben des NSRB," *DR* 12 (1942): 1473f; Droege to Rothenberger, Nov. 16, 1942, BA, R 22, No. 256; Klemm to Thierack, March 18, 1943, BA, NS 16, No. 116; and Reichsrechtsamt, "Aufgaben des NSRB," *ibid.,* No. 112.

98. Thierack to Ley, March 27, BA, NS 16, No. 116; Thierack to Bormann, June 16, and organization schema, *ibid.,* No. 109; Hännsgen, "Aktenvermerk," March 4, *ibid.,* No. 112; and "Die Aufgaben des NSRB im Kriege," in *Mitteilungsblatt des NSRB,* No. 2, June 1943.

99. Schneidenbach, "Rechtspolitik des NSRB," Oct. 20, 1943, BA, NS 16, No. 2; Thierack to Neubert, Aug. 11, *ibid.,* No. 117; memorandum on "Die Schulungsarbeit des NSRB," *ibid.,* No. 114 and Dageförde, "Tätigkeitsbericht des Schulungsamts im NSRB," *ibid.,* No. 110; Klemm to Klopfer, April 1944; "Veranstaltungsfolge für die Reichsarbeitstagung der Gauschulungsbeauftragten . . . Juni 1944"; "Tätigkeitsbericht des Schulungsamtes im NSRB für den Monat Juli 1944"; Thierack to Reichsleiter, Sept. 27, 1944, *ibid.,* No. 110; Jünger, "Die Schulungsarbeit des NSRB," *DR* 14 (1944): 593f.

100. "Vergleichsaufstellung der Gaue der NSDAP nach Fläche und Einwohnerzahlen mit dem Mitgliederstand des NSRB nach dem Stand vom 1. 1. 41"; and "Mitgliederstand vom 1. 10. 44," BA, NS 16, No. 44.

101. Anonymous, "Aufgaben und Leistungen des NSLB im Kriege," likely to have been written in 1942, BA, NS 12, 1438. Cf. "Arbeitstagung der Gaufachschaftsleiter 2," *DHS* 9 (1942): 285ff, and K. Frank, "Gauleiter Fritz Wächtler . . . 50 Jahre alt," *ibid.,* 8 (1941): 3f.

102. Arnold to Bormann, Jan. 30, 1943, BA, NS 12, No. 1438; Bormann to Wächtler, Jan. 26, and the latter's protest, March 17, BA, NS 12, Nos. 567 and 637; Rust to Bormann, April 12, 1943, ZStA Po, Rep. 49.01, 4340. Even Karl Frank's self-congratulations in "Rückschau," *DHS* 10 (1943): 39ff, did not help. Cf. W. Feiten, *Der NSLB. Entwicklung und Organisation* (Frankfurt, 1981), p. 186ff.

103. J. Greiner, "Arbeitstagung des Hauptamts für Technik," *DT* 8 (1940): 138; Saur, "Der NSBDT," *VDIN* 21 (1941), No. 31 and 32; and "Ingenieur-Fortbildung des NSBDT," *ibid.,* No. 36. Cf. W. Greiling, "Die Rolle der Juden in der Chemie," *DT* 7 (1940): 322ff; W. Ostwald, "NS-Technik," *ibid.,* 9 (1942): 48ff; K. Nonn, "Judentum und Technik," *VDIN* 23 (1943), No. 13 and 14; "Abteilung Berufsfragen," BA, NS 14, No. 17; "Leistungsbericht 1942," *ibid.,* No. 8; and Guse, "Plassenburg," 215–75.

104. Todt to Gauwalter, Oct. 26, 1941, BA, NS 14, No. 10; "Der NSBDT im Kriege,"

DT 10 (1942), No. 5; Himmler memorandum, "Behandlung wirtschaftlicher Fragen für NSBDT-Mitglieder," April 17, 1942, BA, NS 14, No. 20, II; report on "Berufsfragen" for 1940, *ibid.,* II; H. Uhde, "Der VDI," *VDIN* 22 (1942), No. 21 and 22; VDI, "Bericht über die Arbeiten des VDI," Nov. 5, 1942, BA, NS 14, No. 10; and Heuser-König, "Tabellarische Zusammenstellungen," p. 561. In contrast to Ludwig, "Der VDI als Gegenstand," p. 424ff, and "Vereinsarbeit im Dritten Reich," p. 446ff.

105. Kater, *Doctors Under Hitler,* p. 222ff.

106. "Bericht aus Akten der Geschäftsführenden Reichsregierung Dönitz vom Ende März 1945," Boberach, ed., *Meldungen,* Vol. 17, p. 6734ff. Cf. *idem, Meldungen,* Vol. 17, pp. 6663f and 6711ff, and Giles, *Students,* p. 310ff. During the chaos of the last months of the war, many documents were destroyed by bombing or burning.

107. H. Schroer to Thierack, July 8, 1943, describing a severe air raid, BA, NS 16, No. 117; Thierack circular, March 11, 1944, BA, R 22, No. 262; REM Decree, Sept. 28, 1944, ZStA Po, Rep. 490.01, 4337; Lietzmann to Bindig, Sept. 10, 1944 in Popplow, "Schulalltag," p. 85ff; Francke, *Heil Hitler,* p. 226ff; Boberach, ed., *Meldungen,* Vol. 16, pp. 6270ff, 6315ff, 6322ff, and 6354ff; and Kleinewefers, *Jahrgang 1905,* p. 158ff.

108. Dageförde, "Tätigkeitsbericht des Schulungsamtes im NSRB für . . . November 1944," BA, NS 16, No. 32; NSRB to Reichsleiter, *ibid.,* No. 118; Letz, "Vermerk," and letter to Friedrich, Jan. 4, 1945, *ibid.,* No. 111. Cf. Vogel, "Memoiren," KA 1384, and Güstrow, *Tödlicher Alltag,* p. 187ff.

109. G. Buchheit, *Richter in roter Robe* (Munich, 1968), *passim;* Feiten, *NSLB,* p. 40ff; and J. Herf, *Reactionary Modernism* (Cambridge, England, 1984), p. 189ff. For the full range of reactions in one school faculty, cf. W. Pflughaupt, "Lebenserinnerungen," KA 733. Cf. Jarausch, "Perils of Professionalism," p. 132f.

110. K. Schwedtke, "Besinnung," *Phbl* 43 (1935): 1ff; Ludwig, *Technik,* p. 114ff; and R. Neubert, "Standesaufsicht und Ehrengerichtsbarkeit der Anwaltschaft," *JW* 67 (1938): 2507f. Cf. Heintzeler, *Der rote Faden,* p. 40ff., for portraits of F. Gürtner and F. Schlegelberger versus R. Freisler.

111. A. Speer, *Inside the Third Reich,* pp. 15ff and 22f. The older ministerial bureaucrats and professional leaders largely fit into the nationalist group. Cf. Lutz Schwerin von Krosigk, *Memoiren* (Stuttgart, 1977); and Gruchmann, *Justiz,* p. 63ff.

112. Schumann, Sept. 27, 1942, in Hammerstein, ed., *Deutsche Bildung?,* p. 177; SOPADE, *Deutschland Berichte,* Jan. 1940. A foreign visitor observed that 20 percent would defend the regime "with all means," 60 percent seemed indifferent, and another 20 percent were sharply opposed. Cf. M. Hachenburg, *Lebenserinnerungen eines Rechtsanwalts und Briefe aus der Emigration,* reissued by J. Schadt (Stuttgart, 1978), pp. 213f, 227f: Grupe, "Die böse Zeit," KA 121; Zuse, *Computer,* p. 93; as well as Hochmuth, ed., *Hamburg,* p. 244ff; and Klewitz, *Lehrersein,* p. 208, 227.

113. Güstrow, *Tödlicher Alltag,* p. 170ff; Schumann, June 21, 1942, in Hammerstein, ed., *Deutsche Bildung?,* pp. 158, 185f, 235; "Anklageschrift," Feb. 16, 1945, ZStA Po, Rep. 31.01, No. 8568. Cf. P. Hoffmann, *The History of the German Resistance, 1933–1945* (Cambridge, England, 1977) versus, *Zeugnis für ein anderes Deutschland* (Tübingen, 1984), p. 56f.

114. Ger van Roon, ed., *Helmut James Graf von Moltke* (Berlin, 1986), p. 105ff; Hochmuth, ed., *Hamburg,* p. 152ff; and L. van Dick, *Oppositionelles Lehrerverhalten* (Weinheim, 1988), p. 179ff; R. Stover, "Spurensuche," KA 71. Cf. Ronge, *Gerechtigkeit,* p. 303ff; R. Rürup, ed., *Topographie des Terrors* (Berlin, 1987), p. 167–76; W. H. Schroeder, "Die Reichstagsabgeordneten der Weimarer Republik als Opfer des Nationalsozialismus," *HSR* 36 (1985): 55ff; and R. Mann, *Protest und Kontrolle im Dritten Reich* (Frankfurt, 1987). The resistance literature has yet to address the role of professionals. For a first effort see K. Jarausch, "Between Conformity and Compliance," paper delivered at the symposium on "Forms of Resistance under the Nazi Regime," SUNY Buffalo, October 1989.

115. Ludwig, *Technik,* p. 382ff; H. Frank, *Im Angesicht des Galgens* (Munich, 1953), p. 468ff. Interestingly enough, both Todt (until his mysterious death) and Frank (as governor general of Poland) continued to work for Hitler in spite of their scruples.

116. Kleinewefers, *Jahrgang 1905,* p. 141f; Schumann–Havenstein correspondence, 1940–1944, in Hammerstein, ed., *Deutsche Bildung?,* pp. 160, 178, 182, 199, 244, 267 and *passim.*

Popplow, "Schulalltag," 82ff; "Klare Luft," *VDIN* 24 (1944), Nos. 15 and 16; Boberach, ed., *Meldungen,* Vol. 17, p. 6732f; and H. Oelert, "Memoiren eines Rechtsanwalts," KA 728.

117. Geuter, *Die Professionalisierung,* p. 448ff; Light, "Social Medicine," p. 78ff; Cocks, *Psychotherapy in the Third Reich,* p. 248f; and Ludwig, "Der VDI als Gegenstand," in *Technik,* p. 423ff.

118. Schumann, Nov. 12 and 26, 1944, in Hammerstein, ed., *Deutsche Bildung?,* pp. 262, 271. Lifton, *Nazi Doctors,* p. 489ff, and M. H. Kater, "The Burden of the Past: Problems of a Modern Historiography of Physicians and Medicine in Nazi Germany," *GSR* 10 (1987): 31ff.

119. Jarausch, "Perils of Professionalism," p. 134ff and Burrage *et al.*, "An Actor-Oriented Framework for the Study of the Professions," p. 208f. Cf. Kater, *Doctors Under Hitler,* p. 222ff.; R. Ericksen, *Theologians under Hitler* (New Haven, Conn., 1985), p. 198ff; Jill Stephenson, "Women and the Professions in Germany, 1900–1945," and G. Cocks, "The Professionalization of Psychotherapy in Germany, 1928–1949," in *idem* and K. Jarausch, eds., *German Professions* (New York, 1990), pp. 270ff, 308ff.

CHAPTER 8

1. H. Oehlert, "Memoiren," KA 728, 74. P. Ronge, *Im Namen der Gerechtigkeit* (Munich, 1963), p. 330f; Friedrich, "Memoiren," KA 508/1, 54.

2. H. Dittenberger, "Die Anwaltschaft um die Jahrhundertmitte," *Abl* 1 (1950): 2ff; and K. Bader, "Geleitwort," *DRZ* 1 (1946): 1.

3. H. Frank, *Im Angesichts des Galgens* (Munich, 1953), p. 23f; B. von Schirach, *Ich glaubte an Hitler* (Hamburg, 1967); and A. Speer, *Inside the Third Reich* (New York, 1970), p. 1. Cf. N. Frank, *Der Vater* (Munich, n.d.), p. 253ff.

4. *LG-Direktor* Schürholz, "Eine Entgegnung," *DRZ* 1 (1946): 175f; K. S. Bader, "Die deutschen Juristen, *ibid.*, p. 33ff; A. Bohlen, "Wilhelm Bolle—70 Jahre alt," *HS* 2 (1949), No. 2; W. Hellmich, "Der geistige Aufbruch der deutschen Ingenieure," *ZVDI* 90 (1948): 2f.

5. G. Ried, "Schulreform in der Lauge der 'Aspekte'," *HS* 2 (1949), No. 5; Dr. Rotberg, "Entpolitisierung der Rechtspflege," *DRZ* 1 (1946): 107ff; "Grundgedanken zur Kasseler Tagung," *HS* 2 (1949), No. 8; Kurt Oppler, "Justiz und Politik," *DRZ* 1 (1946): 323ff; and O. Geudtner, ed., *"Ich bin katholisch getauft und Arier." Aus der Geschichte eines Kölner Gymnasiums* (Cologne, 1985), p. 147.

6. J. Kocka, "1945: Neubeginn oder Restauration?" in C. Stern and A. Winkler, eds., *Wendepunkte deutscher Geschichte 1848–1945* (Frankfurt, 1979), p. 141ff. Cf. A. Kleßmann, *Doppelte Staatsgründung. Deutsche Geschichte 1945–1955* (Göttingen, 1982) and G. Kraiker, ed., *1945—Die Stunde Null?* (Oldenburg, 1986).

7. F. Ostler, *Die deutschen Rechtsanwälte 1871–1971* (Essen, 1971), p. 307ff; R. Bölling, *Sozialgeschichte der deutschen Lehrer* (Göttingen, 1983), p. 156ff; Kurt Mauel, "Die technisch-wissenschaftlichen Arbeiten des VDI 1946 bis 1981," in K.-H. Ludwig, ed., *Technik* (Düsseldorf, 1981), p. 455ff; and M. H. Kater, "Medizin und Mediziner im Dritten Reich," *HZ* 244 (1987): 299ff. Cf. B. Eberan, *Wer war an Hitler schuld?* 2nd ed. (Munich, 1985). Relying on professional journals, memoirs, and printed evidence, this postwar sketch intends to round out earlier themes rather than fully investigating new departures.

8. "Geleitwort," *NJW* 1 (1947): 1; R. Monje, "Grundgedanken zur Kasseler Tagung," *HS* 2 (1949), No. 8; W. E. Ewers, "Ingenieurarbeit und Ausfuhr," *ZVDI* 90 (1948): 97f.

9. E. von Sauer, "Aufbau und Entwicklung der Anwaltschaft nach dem Kriege," *Juristisches Jahrbuch* 1 (1960): 150ff; U. Beer, *Versehrt, Verfolgt, Versöhnt: Horst Berkowitz* (Essen, 1979), p. 98. Cf. J. Tent, *Mission on the Rhine: Reeducation and Denazification in American-Occupied Germany* (Chicago, 1982); and J. Vaillant, "La Rééducation du personnel enseignant allemand en zone d'occupation française en Allemagne," *Lez Valenciennes* 20 (1984): 173ff.

10. W. Fischer, "Die Rechtsanwaltschaft in der britischen Zone," *DRZ* 1 (1946): 124f; H. Fechner, "Schulreform unter dem geteilten Recht?" *HS* 2 (1949): No. 2; Agatz, "Ingenieuraufgaben beim Wiederaufbau unserer Städte und Verkehrswege," *ZVDI* 90 (1848): 27ff. Cf. W. Abelshauser, *Die Wirtschaft der Bundesrepublik* (Frankfurt, 1985); and G. Fieberg, *Justiz und Nationalsozialismus* (Cologne, 1989), p. 315ff.

11. E. Kern, "Ausbildungsfragen," *DRZ* 1 (1946): 14ff; K. Duden, "Bildung und Stand

der Juristen," *Abl* 5 (1955): 149ff; "Vom Abiturienten . . . zum Studienassessor," *HS* 1 (1948), No. 2; "Arbeitsplan für den Philologenverein," *ibid.*, No. 1; C. Pfleiderer, "Vergleichende Behandlung der Strömungsmaschinen im Hochschulunterricht," *ZVDI* 90 (1948): 45ff; R. Vieweg, "Über einige Fragen der Hochschulreform," *ibid.*, 92 (1950): 729ff. Cf. Hochmuth, ed., *Hamburg* (Hamburg, 1985), p. 283.

12. Friedrich, "Memoiren," p. 54. C. Quetsch, *Die zahlenmäßige Entwicklung des Hochschulbesuchs* (Berlin, 1960); and G. Kath, *Das soziale Bild der Studentenschaft in Westdeutschland und Berlin* (Frankfurt, 1952ff), Vols. 1–3. Cf. K. H. Jarausch, *Deutsche Studenten 1800–1980* (Frankfurt, 1984), p. 215ff.

13. "Stand der Zulassung zur Rechtsanwaltschaft 1950/1," *Abl* 1 (1950): 94; "Rechtsanwälte und Nachwuchs," *ibid.*, p. 84; W. Kimmig, "Der Wiederaufbau der Rechtsanwaltschaft," *DRZ* 1 (1946): 170f; W. Ranz, "Lösung des Überfüllungsproblems durch einen Numerus Clausus?" *NJW* 2 (1949): 935f; and F. Ostler, "Auslese zur Eindämmung des juristischen Nachwuchses," *Abl* 1 (1950): 75ff.

14. A. Becking, "Die höheren Schulen Nordrhein-Westfalens und ihre Lehrer," *HS* 2 (1949), No. 9; R. Hoffmann, "Die Lage der Flüchtlingslehrer im Bundesgebiet," *ADLZ* 2 (1950): 236f; "Um Grundsatzfragen der höheren Schule und ihrer Lehrerschaft," *HS*, No. 12; E. Kardel, "Zum 'Frauenparagraphen' im neuen deutschen Beamtengesetz," *ibid.*, 3 (1950), No. 4; M. Roething response, *ibid.*, No. 5; and "Doppelverdienertum oder soziale Regelung?" *ibid.*, No. 6.

15. Br., "Statistische Angaben über die berufsfremde Betätigung von Ingenieuren in der Nachkriegszeit," *VDIN* 2 (1948), No. 1; "Der Ingenieur als Flüchtling," *ibid.*, No. 5; "Notschrei eines erwerbslosen Ingenieurs," *ibid.*, No. 22; "Alte Ingenieure—altes Eisen?" *ibid.*, 3 (1949), No. 4. Figures in table 8.1 are from *Statistisches Jahrbuch des Deutschen Reichs and Statistisches Jahrbuch für die Bundesrepublik Deutschland* in the appropriate years.

16. Vogel, "Memoiren," KA 1384; H. Jungbluth, "Zuviel Technik-Studenten?" *VIDN* 2 (1948), No. 4; Data from Quetsch, *Zahlenmäßige Entwicklung, passim;* Jarausch, *Deutsche Studenten,* p. 215f; and Appendix A, Tables A.5–A.7.

17. H. Dittenberger, "Die Anwaltschaft um die Jahrhundertmitte," *Abl* 1 (1950): 1f; "Resolution des Deutschen Anwaltstages 1951 zur Gebührenerhöhung," *ibid.*, No. 7; "Gebührenreform," *ibid.*, p. 112; W. Kimmig, "Zur Gebührenfestsetzung gemäß Paragraph 63 RAGebo," *ibid.*, 4 (1954): 206ff; and D. Rueschemeyer, *Lawyers and Their Society: A Comparative Study of the Legal Profession in Germany and the United States* (Cambridge, Mass. 1973), p. 64.

18. "Mitteilungen aus den Verbänden," *HS* 1 (1947), No. 1; "Im Dickicht der Besoldungskämpfe," *ADLZ* 3 (1951): 89ff; G. Ried, "Wann endlich Wiederherstellung eines gerechten Realwertes der Gehälter?" *HS* 5 (1952): 221ff; "Philologen, Richter, Staatsanwälte," *ibid.*, 6 (1953): 141ff; O. Scheunemann, "Wie hoch war tatsächlich mein Gehalt?" *ibid.*, 7 (1954): 114f; H. Pieper, "Beamtenrechtliche und besoldungspolitische Umschau," *ibid.*, 8 (1955): Cf. K. Walter, "Entwicklung der Philologenbesoldung," *Bildung aktuell* (1974): 84ff.

19. Vogel, "Memoiren," KA 1384; Friedrich, "Memoiren," p. 66; "Geschäftsbericht des VDI für das Jahr 1949," *VDIN* 4 (1950), No. 1, and for 1950, *ibid.*, 5 (1951), No. 5; N. Zimmer, "Europäische Gehälter und Lebenshaltungskosten für Ingenieure und Techniker," *ibid.*, 9 (1955), No. 22. Figures in Table 8.2 calculated from VDI, ed., *Der deutsche Ingenieur in Beruf und Gesellschaft* (Düsseldorf, 1959), a 1956 membership survey with 23,905 valid responses.

20. K. Bader, "Die deutschen Juristen," *DRZ* 1 (1946): 33; Schürholz, "Eine Entgegnung," *ibid.*, p. 175; Prof. Duden, "Bildung und Stand der Juristen," *Abl* 5 (1955): 149ff; Dr. A. Sträter at the "deutsche Anwaltstag in Coburg" 1949, *NJW* 2 (1949): 458; H. Dahs, "Das Recht der Anwaltschaft auf ihren Namen," *ibid.*, p. 253.

21. W. Dederich, "Vom äußeren Ansehen der höheren Schule," *HS* 2 (1949), No. 11; H. Fechner, "Von der Würde unseres Berufs," *ibid.*, 6 (1953):41ff; Dederich, "Die soziale Stellung der Lehrerschaft," *ibid.*, p. 127f; G. Ried, "Sinngehalt und Einheit der höheren Schule," *ibid.*, 7 (1954): 230. Cf. M. Schwonke, "Das Gesellschaftsbild des Lehrers," *Die deutsche Schule* 58 (1966): 73ff.

22. VDI, ed., *Der deutsche Ingenieur in Beruf und Gesellschaft* (Düsseldorf, 1959), p. 23ff; E. Kothe, "Der Ingenieur in Politik und Verwaltung," *VDIN* 4 (1950), No. 9; "Die Bezeichnung VDI hinter dem Namen," *ibid.*, 2 (1948), No. 7 and 8; and K. Klein, "Aufgaben der

Technik und ihrer Berufsträger," *ibid.*, 4 (1950), No. 23. Cf. M. Bolte, *Deutsche Gesellschaft im Wandel* (Opladen, 1966), p. 326ff.

23. Ronge, *Gerechtigkeit,* 359ff; Heintzeler, *Der rote Faden* (Stuttgart, 1983), p. 78ff; Beer, *Berkowitz,* p. 102ff. Cf. J. R. Wenzlau, *Der Wiederaufbau der Justiz in Nordwestdeutschland 1945 bis 1949* (Königstein, 1979); and Kritische Justiz, ed., *Streitbare Juristen,* p. 166.

24. Dr. Lange, "Maßnahmen gegen die weitere Einengung der anwaltlichen Aufgabengebiete," *Abl* 1 (1950): 43ff; "Wieder 'Fachanwälte für Steuerrecht' in Bayern," *NJW* 2 (1949): 59f; O. Toepfer, "Gutachtliche Stellungnahme des Verfassungsrechtsausschusses des DAV zu Paragraph 11 Arbeitsgerichtsgesetz," *Abl* 1 (1950): 137ff; E. von Sauer, "Rechtsanwälte zur Vertretung vor den Arbeitsgerichten zugelassen," *ibid.*, 2 (1952): 210.

25. Quote from a resolution of the PhVb, *HS* 1 (1947), No. 1; "Um Grundsatzfragen der höheren Schule und ihrer Lehrerschaft," *ibid.*, 2 (1949), No. 12; Dr. von Jungenfeld, "Der Beamte und das Streikrecht," *ibid.*, 3 (1950), No. 2; M. Roething, "DGB oder DBB?" *ibid.*, 1 (1948), No. 10; and J. Barfaut, "Wo stehen wir?" *ADLZ* 1 (1949), No. 2.

26. W. Dederich, "Die Verwaltung des höheren Schulwesens als demokratische Aufgabe," *HS* 1 (1948), No. 11; Dr. Bohlen, "Revolution der Schulverwaltung?" *ibid.*, 3 (1950), No. 7; PhVb, "Grundsätze und Voraussetzungen für eine Neugestaltung des höheren Schulwesens," *ibid.*, 7 (1954): 64f; and G. Ried, "Ein leistungsfähiges deutsches Schulwesen unentbehrlich für den deutschen Wiederaufstieg," *ibid.*, p. 124.

27. A. Agatz, "Ingenieuraufgaben beim Wiederaufbau unserer Städte und Verkehrswege," *ZVDI* 90 (1948): 27ff; Vogel, "Memoiren," KA 1384; W. E. Ewers, "Ingenieurarbeit und Ausfuhr," *ZVDI* 90 (1948): 97ff; "Für und wider die Rationalisierung," special issue of *ZVDI* 92 (1950): 361ff; K. Zuse, *Der Computer, mein Lebenswerk* (Munich, 1970), p. 156ff; and E. Hartrich, *The Fourth and Richest Reich* (New York, 1980).

28. W. Lewald, "Deutscher Anwaltstag in Coburg," *NJW* 2 (1949): 458ff; V. Heins, "Die Bundesrechtsanwaltsordnung," *ibid.*, 3 (1950): 617ff; E. Sauer, "Aufbau und Entwicklung," p. 150ff; H. Dix, "Bundesrechtsanwaltskammer und Ehrengerichtsbarkeit," *NJW* 5 (1952): 121ff; W. Haussmann, "Rechtspflege und freier Beruf," *Abl* 5 (1955): 201ff. Cf. F. Scholz, *Berlin und seine Justiz* (Berlin, 1982), p. 173ff; Fieberg, *Justiz und Nationalsozialismus,* p. 331ff; and B. Diestelkamp and M. Stolleis, eds., *Justizalltag im Dritten Reich* (Frankfurt, 1988), p. 121f.

29. "Vorwort des Herausgebers," *HS* 1 (1947): 1; program of the Deutsche Philologenverband, *ibid.*, No. 2; Knoll, "Die rechtliche und wirtschaftliche Stellung des Lehrers," *ADLZ* 1 (1949): 129f; K. Bunghardt, *Die Odyssee der Lehrerschaft,* 2nd ed., (Hanover, 1952), p. 120ff.

30. R. Monje, "Der deutsche PhVb und seine Aufgaben," *HS* 5 (1953): 126; K. Bosl, "Bildungsidee und Bildungsaufgabe der höheren Schule," *ibid.*, 2 (1949), No. 8; Monje, "Mission, Bedeutung und Gestaltung der höheren Schule," *ibid.*, 4 (1951), No. 3; Dederich, "Die Lehrer an den Gymnasien," *ibid.*, No. 4. Cf. W. Sprondel, "Bildung, Ungleichheit und die professionalisierte Lehrerschaft," *Soziale Welt* 21 (1970): 73ff.

31. W. Hellmich, "Der geistige Aufbruch der deutschen Ingenieure," *ZVDI* 90 (1948): 2–7; O. Jacobi, "Die Technik in Abhängigkeit vom bewertenden Menschen," *ibid.*, p. 227ff; "Der Ingenieur und die heutige Zeit," *VDIN* 2 (1948), No. 1; "Eine Union der Technik," *ibid.*, No. 4; and "Die neuen Aufgaben der europäischen Technik," *ibid.*, No. 6.

32. "Bekenntnis des Ingenieurs," *VDIN* 4 (1950), No. 11, developed out of W. Hellmich, "Die kulturelle Sendung des deutschen Ingenieurs," *ibid.*, 3 (1949), No. 8. Cf. the surrounding speeches by R. Planck and others "Über die Verantwortung des Ingenieurs," *ZVDI* 92 (1950): 589–628.

33. For example, "Mensch und Arbeit im technischen Zeitalter," *VDIN* 5 (1951), No. 7; "Die Wandlung des Menschen durch die Technik," *ZVDI* 96 (1954): 113ff; "Der Mensch im Kraftfeld der Technik," *ibid.*, 97 (1955): 897–926; and "Berufung und Verantwortung des Ingenieurs," *VDIN* 9 (1955), No. 18. Cf. F. Platzer, "Der Ingenieur, seine Ausbildung, Aufgabe und Eingliederung und seine Tragik," *Festschrift für J. F. Schütz* (Graz, 1954), p. 208ff.

34. E. von Sauer, "Aufbau und Entwicklung," p. 150ff; "DAV," *NJW* 1 (1948): 619f; H. Dittenberger, "Die Aufgaben des DAV," *ibid.*, 2 (1949): 321ff; "Deutscher Anwaltstag in Coburg," *ibid.*, p. 458f; "Tätigkeitsbericht des DAV," *ibid.*, 3 (1950): 257f; "Der Deutsche Anwaltstag 1951," *ibid.*, 3 (1951): 433.

35. "Geleitwort," *DRZ* 1 (1946): 1; "Geleitwort," *NJW* 1 (1947): 1; and E. von Sauer,

"Zum Geleit," *Abl* 1 (1950): 1. Cf. Ostler, *Rechtsanwälte,* p. 330ff and Scholz, *Berlin,* p. 179ff.

36. H. K., "Wir Lehrer und der 1. Mai," *ADLZ* 1 (1949): 75; R. Morell, "Die Anfänge der westdeutschen Lehrerbewegung nach 1945," *Das Argument* 80 (1973): 208ff; W. Brinkmann, "Die Berufsorganisationen der Lehrer und die 'pädagogische Selbstrolle.' Zur Professionalisierungs- und Deutungsfunktion der GEW and des Deutschen PhVb 1949–1974," Heinemann, ed., *Lehrer,* (Stuttgart 1972), p. 393ff; and Bunghardt, *Odyssee,* p. 125ff.

37. Dr. Erdmann, "Zum Geleit," *HS* 1 (1947): 1; Deutscher PhVb, "Gemeinsame Programmpunkte," *ibid.,* No. 2; "Die höhere Schule als geprägte Form, die lebend sich entwickelt," *ibid.,* 2 (1949), No. 12; "Zur Begrüßung," *ibid.,* 4 (1951), No. 11; G. Ried, "Bildung und Ethos als Voraussetzung des politischen Handelns," *ibid.,* 5 (1952): 1ff; PhVb, *Achtzig Jahre Deutscher Philologen-Verband 1904–1984* (Düsseldorf, 1984), p. 29ff.

38. Monje, "Proklamation," *HS* 5 (1952): 112; W. Padberg, "Schule und Gewerkschaft," *ibid.,* p. 133ff; and H. Böckler, "Gewerkschaft und Kulturpolitik," *ADLZ* 2 (1950): 169ff. According to J. Koch, "Untersuchungen zum Gesellschaftsbild des Gymnasiallehrers," *ZfP* 16 (1970): 445, about 70 percent of a Hessian sample belonged to the PhVb, while only 6 percent were active in the GEW.

39. "Wieder am Werk!" *VDIN* 1 (1947), No. 1 and 2; "Aus der Tätigkeit des VDI," *ibid.,* No. 3 and 4; "WSI und 'Ingenieurkammer'," *ibid.,* No. 5 and 6; "Ein Jahr Aufbauarbeit am VDI," *ibid.,* No. 11 and 12; "Antwort an die Kammer der Technik der SBZ," *ibid.;* and K. Mauel, "Die technisch-wissenschaftliche Arbeit des VDI 1946 bis 1981," in Ludwig, ed., *Technik,* p. 445ff.

40. *ZVDI* 90 (1948): 1; "Ingenieurwissenschaftliche Tagung des VDI in Hamburg," *VDIN* 1 (1947), No. 13 and 14; "Deutscher Verband technisch-wissenschaftlicher Vereine," *ibid.,* 2 (1948), No. 9; "Rückblick auf die VDI-Tagung München 1948," *ibid.,* No. 10; "Der VDI baut auf," *ibid.,* No. 15; "Geschäftsbericht des VDI für das Jahr 1949," *ibid.* 4 (1950), No. 1; and VDI, ed., *Der deutsche Ingenieur,* pp. 15 and 27.

41. O. Brandt, "Das Studium Generale," *HS* 2 (1949), No. 2; R. Planck, "Der naturwissenschaftliche Humanismus als philosophische Grundhaltung des Ingenieurs," *ZVDI* 93 (1954): 145ff.

42. Friedrich, "Memoiren," p. 55ff; B. Heck, *Die Lage der Studenten nach dem Kriege* (Stuttgart, 1947); A. Flitner, "Studentisches Gemeinschaftsleben und Hochschulreform," *Die Sammlung* 7 (1952): 116ff; and F. Bollenrathe, "Die Rheinisch-Westfälische TH Aachen," *ZVDI* 91 (1949): 414ff. Cf. Jarausch, *Deutsche Studenten,* p. 213ff.

43. M., "Der Juristentag in Konstanz," *DRZ* 2 (1947): 232f; G. Strucksberg, "Zur Anwendung des Kontrollratsgesetzes Nummer 10," *ibid.,* p. 277f; H. Thiele-Fredersdorf, "Das Urteil des Militärgerichtshofes Nummer III im Nürnberger Juristen-Prozeß," *NJW* 2 (1947–1948): 122ff; Speer, *Inside the Third Reich,* p. 507ff. R. E. Conot, *Justice at Nuremberg* (New York, 1983), p. 77ff; and Fieberg, *Justiz und Nationalsozialismus,* p. 333ff.

44. Oelert, "Memoiren," p. 109ff; Herrmann, "Wüstenprediger," p. 22; Beer, *Berkowitz,* p. 106f; A. Ehrentereich, *Fünfzig Jahre Erlebte Schulreform* (Frankfurt, 1985), p. 180f; W. Fischer, "Die Rechtsanwaltschaft in der britischen Zone," *DRZ* 1 (1946): 124ff; L. Niethammer, *Entnazifizierung in Bayern* (Frankfurt, 1972); Vaillant, "Rééducation," p. 173ff. Cf. T. Bower, *Blind Eye to Murder* (London, 1981), p. 189ff; and Fieberg, *Justiz und Nationalsozialismus,* p. 314ff.

45. E. Natter, "Der Wiederaufbau der Rechtsanwaltschaft," *DRZ* 1 (1946): 46f; J. Cüppers, "Das neue Zulassungsverfahren für Rechtsanwälte in der britischen Zone," *NJW* 2 (1949): 363ff; L. Niethammer, "Zum Verhältnis von Reform und Rekonstruktion in der US-Zone am Beispiel der Neuordnung des öffentlichen Dienstes," *VfZG* 21 (1973): 177ff; "Rückblick auf die VDI-Tagung München 1948," *VDIN* 2 (1948), No. 10; and Fieberg, *Justiz und Nationalsozialismus,* p. 361ff.

46. H. Grabert, "Friedrich Grimm," *Veröffentlichungen des Instituts für deutsche Nachkriegsgeschichte* 1 (1961): 1ff; W. Hartnacke, "Das unterschiedliche Maß der Geister und seine Bedeutung für Bildungswesen und Sozialgefüge," *HS* 2 (1949), No. 6; H. Roser and H. Schult, "Der Beitrag Deutschlands zur Sicherstellung der westeuropäischen Stromversorgung," *ZVDI*

93 (1951): 305ff. Cf. A. Kahn, ed., *Hitlers Blutjustiz* (Frankfurt, 1980), p. 57ff, for three former people's court jurists who became attorneys after 1945; and Hochmuth, ed., *Hamburg*, p. 203ff. 285ff for left-wing teachers with postwar difficulties.

47. E. J. Freese, "Immanenter Nazismus," *HS* 2 (1949), No. 11 versus N. Wilsing, "Verkappter Nazismus?" *ibid.*, No. 12. Cf. W. Lewald, "Carl Schmitt redivivus?" *NJW* 3 (1950): 377 and R. Ericksen, *Theologians under Hitler* (New Haven, Conn., 1985), pp. 77ff, 190ff, and 191ff.

48. E. von Sauer, "Zum Entwurf der Bundesrechtsanwaltsordnung," *Abl* 1 (1950): 4ff; V. Heinz, "Die Bundesrechtsanwaltsordnung," *NJW* 3 (1950): 617ff; H. Dix, "Bundesrechtsanwaltskammer und Ehrengerichtsbarkeit," *ibid.*, 5 (1952): 121ff; W. Ranz, *Das Anwaltsrecht in den Ländern des Bundesgebietes* (Stuttgart, 1950).

49. E. von Sauer, "Zur neuen Bundesrechtsanwaltsordnung," *Abl* 4 (1954): 185f; V. Heins, "Betrachtungen zum Entwurf einer Bundesrechtsanwaltsordnung," *NJW* 8 (1955): 281ff; and W. Kalsbach, *Bundesrechtsanwaltsordnung und Richtlinien für die Ausübung des Rechtsanwaltsberufs* (Cologne, 1960).

50. Dr. Erdmann, "Das Schlagwort im Kampf um die höhere Schule," *HS* 1 (1948), No. 2; "Autorität und Demokratie," *ibid.*, No. 9; G. Torges, "Probleme des gegenwärtigen Geschichtsunterrichts," *ibid.*, No. 1; W. Dederich, "Schulreform und Schulpolitik," *ibid.*, No. 2; G. Ried, "Schulreform in der Lauge der 'Aspekte'," *ibid.*, 2 (1949), No. 5. Cf. Vaillant, "Rééducation," p. 179ff, and G. Schefer, *Das Gesellschaftsbild des Gymnasiallehrers* (Frankfurt, 1969).

51. W. Ehmer, "Demontage der höheren Schule," *HS* 1 (1948), No. 3; "Der Deutsche PhVb in Berlin," *ADLZ* 5 (1953): 151f; PhVb memorandum, "Die Zersplitterung des höheren Schulwesens in der westdeutschen Bundesrepublik," *HS* 4 (1951), No. 4; "Grundsätze und Voraussetzungen für eine Neugestaltung des höheren Schulwesens," *ibid.*, 7 (1954): 66ff; G. Ried, "Das Düsseldorfer Schulabkommen vom 17. Feb. 1955," *ibid.*, 8 (1955): 61f.

52. Heintzeler, *Der rote Faden*, p. 109ff. Special issue of *ZVDI* on the Arbeitsgemeinschaft Deutscher Betriebsingenieure 92 (1950): 239ff; "Zum Gesetz über die Berufsbezeichnung 'Ingenieur'," *VDIN* 5 (1951), No. 13 and *ibid.*, 8 (1954), No. 21; "Wie steht es um das Gesetz zum Schutze der Berufsbezeichnung 'Ingenieur'?" *ibid.*, 9 (1955), No. 14. When declared unconstitutional in 1969, the law was adopted by the individual states.

53. F. Koelsch, "Berufskrankheiten als Begleiterscheinungen technischer und chemischer Prozesse," *ZVDI* 96 (1954): 189ff; O. Graf, "Erster Arbeitswissenschaftlicher Kongreß Nürnberg," *ibid.*, p. 688ff; and lectures on "Der Mensch im Kraftfeld der Technik," *ibid.*, 97 (1955): 897ff. Cf. W. Neef, *Ingenieure* (Cologne, 1982), p. 126ff.

54. F. Hartung, "Einführung des englisch-amerikanischen Strafverfahrensrechtes in Deutschland," *NJW* 5 (1952): 205ff; Ried, "Schulreform in der Lauge der 'Aspekte'," *HS* 2 (1949), No. 5; "Zum Demontageplan," *VDIN* 1 (1947), No. 15 and 16.

55. G. Ried, "Die höhere Schule im gesamtdeutschen Raum," *HS* 4 (1951), No. 7; E. List, "Organisation der Anwaltschaft in der sowjetischen Besatzungszone Deutschlands," *Abl* 1 (1950): 48ff; G. Ried, "Bericht über die HV des Deutschen PhVb am 15/6. Mai in Berlin," *HS* 6 (1953): 121f; and "Der VDI wirbt für Berlin," *VDIN* 4 (1950), No. 12.

56. C. F. Ophüls, "Juristische Grundgedanken des Schumanplans," *NJW* 4 (1951): 289ff; F. Etzel, "Die Europäische Gemeinschaft für Kohle und Stahl," *ZVDI* 95 (1953): 1021ff; F. Graap, "Holzauge sei wachsam!" *ADLZ* 4 (1952): 57f. Cf. W. Lipgens, *Die Anfänge der europäischen Einigungspolitik 1945–1950* (Stuttgart, 1950), Vol. 1.

57. Dr. Bu., "Von der 'inneren' Schulreform," *ADLZ* 2 (1950): 269; "Wir stehen noch ganz am Anfang," *ibid.*, 3 (1951): 157ff; W. Apelt, "Bemerkungen zum Bonner Grundgesetz," *NJW* 2 (1949): 481; H. Schneider, "Fünf Jahre Grundgesetz," *ibid.*, 7 (1954): 940f.

58. Schuman, Sept. 6, 1945, in N. Hammerstein, ed., *Deutsche Bildung?* (Frankfurt, 1988), p. 275ff; R. Muziol, "Die Bedeutung der Marshallplanhilfe für Deutschland," *ZVDI* 95 (1953): 136ff; H. Hellmich, "Die wirtschaftliche Entwicklung seit dem Jahre 1945," *ibid.*, p. 146ff; L. Erhard, "Geleitwort," *ibid.*, p. 529ff; and Dr. Nordhoff, "Der Klassenkampf ist tot," *VDIN* 8 (1954), No. 1.

59. W. Lewald, "Das Vermächtnis der Paulskirche," *NJW* 1 (1947), No. 8; G. A. Stolting,

''An alle deutschen Juristen!'' April 15, 1952; B. Plewe, ''Ein Wort deutscher Erzieher zur Wiederaufrüstung,'' *ADLZ* 7 (1955): 38; and H. Scholtissek, ''Innere Grenzen der Freiheitsrechte,'' *ibid.*, 5 (1952): 561ff; Heintzeler, *Der rote Faden*, p. 242ff.

60. E. von Sauer, ''Der Bundesverband der freien Berufe,'' *Abl* 1 (1950), No. 2; ''Ansprache des Herrn Bundesjustizministers auf dem Deutschen Anwaltstag,'' *ibid.*, No. 7; ''Frau Kultusminister Teusch,'' *HS* 5 (1952): 6f; C. Seebohm, ''Mißverhältnis zwischen Straßenkapazität und Straßenverkehr,'' *ZVDI* 96 (1954): 903. Cf. the ministerial curricula vitae in *Deutscher Justizkalender* for 1953, p. 59ff and 1956, p. xviff.

61. K. Blanke, ''Der Beruf des Anwalts in unserer Zeit,'' *Abl* 4 (1954): 134ff. Cf. Ostler, *Rechtsanwälte*, p. 330ff; Schefer, *Gesellschaftsbild*, p. 60ff; F.-J. Schlösser, ''Der VDI in der Demokratie, 1947–1981,'' in Ludwig, *Technik*, p. 513ff.

62. G. Mosse, *The Crisis of German Ideology* (London, 1966); F. Stern, *The Politics of Cultural Despair* (Berkeley, Calif., 1963); and H. Schulte, *The Tragedy of German Inwardness?* (Hamilton, Ont., 1990).

63. F. K. Ringer, *The Decline of the German Mandarins* (Cambridge, Mass., 1969), p. 367ff; M. H. Kater, *Studentenschaft und Rechtsradikalismus in Deutschland 1918–1933* (Hamburg, 1975), p. 197ff; G. Giles, *Students and National Socialism in Germany* (Princeton, N.J., 1985), p. 314ff; and K. H. Jarausch, *Students, Society and Politics in Imperial Germany: The Rise of Academic Illiberalism* (Princeton, N.J., 1983), p. 416ff.

64. H.-U. Wehler, *The German Empire* (Leamington Spa, England, 1985) versus D. Blackbourn and G. Eley, *The Peculiarities of German History* (New York, 1984). Cf. R. Fletcher, ''Recent Developments,'' *GSR* 7 (1984): 451ff; and J. Retallack, ''Social History,'' *ibid.*, p. 423ff.

65. W. Conze and J. Kocka, eds., *Das Bildungsbürgertum im 19. Jahrhundert* (Stuttgart, 1985), Vol. 1, p. 9ff; J. Kocka, ed., *Bürger und Bürgerlichkeit im 19. Jahrhundert* (Göttingen, 1987), especially the essays by H.-U. Wehler, R. Lepsius, and H. Mommsen. Cf. K. Jarausch, ''Die Krise des Bildungsbürgertums, 1900–1930,'' in J. Kocka, ed., *Bildungsbürgertum im 19. Jahrhundert*, part IV (Stuttgart, 1989), p. 180ff.

66. M. H. Kater, ''Medizin und Mediziner im Dritten Reich. Eine Bestandsaufnahme,'' *HZ* 244 (1987): 299ff; Jarausch, ''Academic Life in the Third Reich: Students, Professors and Professionals'' (lecture, Madison, Wisc., Feb. 1987), and M. Klewitz, *Lehrersein im Dritten Reich* (Weinheim, 1987), p. 277ff.

67. In contrast to the professional preoccupations of German lawyers, teachers, and engineers, Mannheim's notion of ''intellectuals'' addresses the radical politics of literati. Cf. Lepsius, ''Kritik als Beruf,'' pp. 75–91.

68. C. E. McClelland, ''Zur Professionalisierung der akademischen Berufe in Deutschland,'' in Conze and Kocka, eds., *Bildungsbürgertum*, Vol. 1, pp. 233ff; H. Siegrist, ''Bürgerliche Berufe. Professionen und das Bürgertum,'' in *idem*, ed., *Bürgerliche Berufe* (Göttingen, 1988), pp. 11–48; L. Karpik, ''La Morale comme catégorie de l'action collective: Les Avocats'' and Burrage *et al.*, ''An Actor-Oriented Framework for the Study of the Professions,'' in M. Burrage, ed., *Professions in Theory and History* (London, 1990).

69. H. Siegrist, ''Public Office or Free Profession? German Attorneys in the Nineteenth and Early Twentieth Centuries,'' in G. Cocks and K. H. Jarausch, eds., *German Professions* (New York, 1990), p. 45ff. Cf. H. Rottleuthner, ''Die gebrochene Bürgerlichkeit einer Scheinprofession. Zur Situation der deutschen Richterschaft zu Beginn des 20. Jahrhunderts,'' in Siegrist, ed., *Bürgerliche Berufe*, p. 145ff.

70. A. La Vopa, ''Specialists against Specialization: Hellenism as Professional Ideology in German Classical Studies,'' in Cocks and Jarausch, eds., *German Professions*, p. 27ff; H.-E. Thenorth, ''Professionen und Professionalisierung,'' in Heinemann, ed. *Lehrer*, p. 457ff; and J. Herbst, ''Professionalism in Public Teaching, 1890–1920: The American High-School Teacher,'' in Conze and Kocka, eds. *Bildungsbürgertum*, 1, p. 495ff. By the 1960s, philologues themselves began to talk about *Professionalisierung*, such as Schefer, *Gesellschaftsbild*, p. 32ff.

71. H.-J. Dreßen, ''Die Hierarchisierung der Ingenieurberufe,'' in U. Beck, ed., *Die soziale Konstitution der Berufe* (Frankfurt, 1971), p. 63ff; Gispen, ''Engineers in Wilhelmian Germany,'' in Cocks and Jarausch, eds., *German Professions*, p. 104ff.; and W. König, ''Science

and Practice: Key Categories for the Professionalization of German Engineers,'' in M. Kranzberg, ed., *Technological Education, Technological Style* (San Francisco, 1986), p. 41ff.

72. To a considerable degree, this ideal type of Central European profession can be found in other academic occupations such as doctors and pastors. Cf. K. Jarausch, ''The German Professions in History and Theory,'' in *idem* and G. Cocks, eds., *German Professions* (New York, 1990), p. 9ff.

73. For a critique of closure theories and other approaches see R. Torstendahl, ''Essentialist, Strategic and Temporal Analysis of Professionalism'' as well as S. Selander's paper on strategies, forthcoming in M. Burrage, ed., *Professions in Theory and History.*

74. M. Ramsey, ''The Politics of Professional Monopoly in 19th Century Medicine: The French Model and its Rivals,'' in G. Geison, ed., *Professions and the French State 1700–1900* (Philadelphia, 1985), and Burrage *et al.,* ''Framework,'' in M. Burrage, ed., *Professions in Theory and History,* p. 203ff.

75. For example cf. C. Huerkamp, *Der Aufstieg der Ärzte im 19. Jahrhundert* (Göttingen, 1985).

76. See C. McClelland's forthcoming book on the rise of the German professions, and Cocks and Jarausch, eds., *German Professions,* pp. 27–160.

77. H. A. Winkler, *Von der Revolution zur Stabilisierung* (Berlin, 1984) and G. D. Feldman, *Industrie und Gewerkschaften 1918–1924* (Stuttgart, 1985), p. 128ff, stress Weimar's *Verbände* struggles.

78. Jarausch, ''The Decline of Liberal Professionalism,'' in *idem* and L. E. Jones, eds., *In Search of a Liberal Germany* (Oxford, 1990), pp. 261–286.

79. G. Cocks, *Psychotherapy in the Third Reich* (New York, 1985), p. 3ff; and W. Kirchhoff, ed., *Zahnmedizin und Faschismus* (Marburg, 1987).

80. Jarausch, ''The Perils of Professionalism,'' *GSR* 9 (1986): 107ff; and Kater, ''Medizin und Mediziner im Dritten Reich,'' p. 352.

81. Research on the postwar reemergence of the professions is barely beginning. Cf. M. H. Kater's critical comments, ''Problems of Political Reeducation in West Germany, 1945–1960,'' *Simon Wiesenthal Center Annual* 4 (1987): 99ff.

82. By the mid-1960s, this reprofessionalization led to the reintroduction of the concept of *Professionalisierung* into the German discussion through sociologists such as H.-J. Daheim, *Der Beruf in der modernen Gesellschaft* (Cologne, 1967) and A. H. Hesse, *Berufe im Wandel. Ein Beitrag zum Problem der Professionalisierung* (Stuttgart, 1969).

83. A. J. Heidenheimer, ''Comparing Status Professions: The Evolution of State–Profession Relationships of Lawyers and Physicians in Britain, Germany and the US,'' forthcoming in his volume on the professions and the state.

84. For the classification of generations in the various periods of the empire, cf. Jarausch, *Deutsche Studenten,* pp. 59–103. For a conception of professionalism as ''liberation of the human spirit from the bonds of nature'' see S. Feuchtwanger, *Die freien Berufe* (Munich, 1922), p. 604f.

85. C. E. Timberlake, ''Higher Learning, the State, and the Professions in Russia,'' in K. Jarausch, ed., *The Transformation of Higher Learning* (Chicago, 1983), p. 321ff; M. Burrage, ''Revolution as a Starting Point for the Comparative Analysis of the Legal Profession,'' in R. Abel *et al.,* eds., *Lawyers in Society* (Berkeley, 1989), Vol. 3, p. 322ff.

86. M. Barbagli, *Education for Unemployment: Politics, Labor Markets and the School System—Italy, 1859–1973* (New York, 1982). Cf. the papers of the conference ''Ideologie, professioni e techniche nel periodo fascista,'' Milan, 1985; and W. Tousijn, *Le Libere Professioni in Italia* (Il Malino, 1987).

87. W. Kotschnig, *Unemployment in the Learned Professions* (London, 1937), p. 105ff. Cf. H. Engelbrecht, ''Zur Organisierung der österreichischen Lehrerschaft an höheren Schulen,'' in Heinemann, ed., *Lehrer,* p. 201ff; and M. M. Kovacs, ''Luttes professionelles et antisémitisme,'' *Actes de la Recherche en Sciences Sociales* 56 (1985): 31ff, as well as *idem,* ''The Ideology of Illiberalism in the Professions: Leftist and Rightist Radicalism among Hungarian Doctors, Lawyers and Engineers, 1918–1945'' (Ms., Washington, D.C., 1988).

88. Kotschnig, *Unemployment,* p. 179ff. There has been little research on the crisis of the

professions in Western Europe. Cf. M. König, "Bürgerlichkeit und Professionalisierung kaufmännischer und technischer Angestellter. Deutschland und die Schweiz, 1880–1930" (Ms., Bielefeld, 1987); C. Charle, "Des 'Capacités' aux 'Intellectuels': Les professions libérales en France au XIXème siècle entre la politique et l'économie"; and M. Burrage, "Unternehmer, Beamte und freie Berufe. Schlüsselgruppen der bürgerlichen Mittelschichten in England, Frankreich und den Vereinigten Staaten," all in H. Siegrist, ed., *Bürgerliche Berufe,* pp. 51ff, 127ff.

89. J. Kocka, "Bürgertum und Bürgerlichkeit als Probleme der deutschen Geschichte vom späten 18. zum frühen 20. Jahrhundert," in his *Bürger und Bürgerlichkeit im 19 Jahrhundert;* and H. Siegrist, introductory remarks to his *Bürgerliche Berufe,* p. 11ff.

90. Cf. K. Jarausch, "The Decline of Liberal Professionalism: Reflections on the Social Erosion of German Liberalism, 1867–1933," in *idem* and L. E. Jones, eds., *In Search of a Liberal Germany* (Oxford, 1990), pp. 261–286.

91. Kater, *Doctors Under Hitler* (Chapel Hill, N.C., 1989), p. 54ff.

92. W. Loest, "Zur 75-Jahr-Feier des Patentamtes," *ZVDI* 94 (1952): 497ff. From 1926 to 1933, there were 20,888 new patents annually, but from 1934 to 1943 their number fell to 15,500.

93. W. Lewald, "Freiheit der Advokatur—die wir meinen," *NJW* 1 (1947): 2ff; H. Fechner, "Der Erzieher—Untertan oder Staatsbürger?" *HS* 2 (1950), No. 9; W. Hellmich, "Der geistige Aufbruch der deutschen Ingenieure," *VDIZ* 90 (1948): 2–7.

94. Feuchtwanger, *Die freien Berufe,* p. 604f; and T. Haskell, "Introduction" to his volume, *The Authority of Experts* (New York, 1984), pp. ix–xxxix.

INDEX

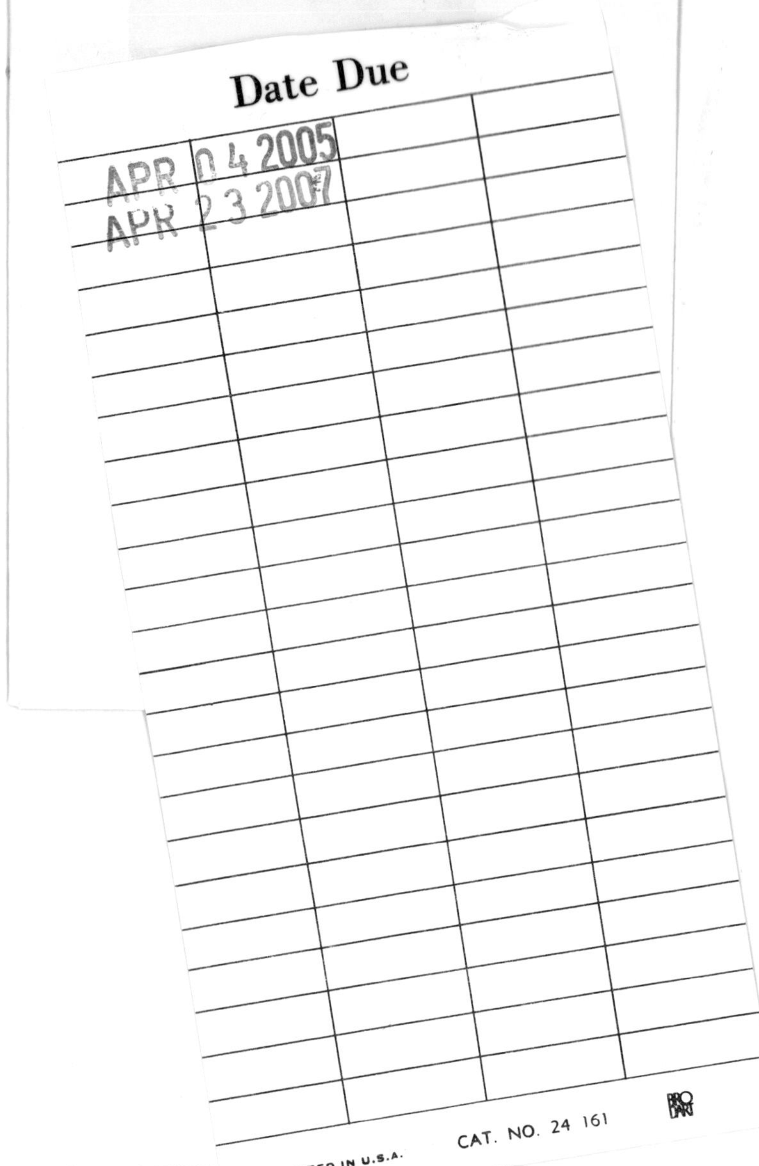
Date Due
APR 0 4 2005
APR 2 3 2007
PRINTED IN U.S.A.
CAT. NO. 24 161
BRODART